The Music of
Charlie Chaplin

The Music of Charlie Chaplin

JIM LOCHNER

McFarland & Company, Inc., Publishers
Jefferson, North Carolina

3064516124502

Library of Congress Cataloguing-in-Publication Data

Names: Lochner, Jim, 1962– author.
Title: The music of Charlie Chaplin / Jim Lochner.
Description: Jefferson, North Carolina : McFarland & Company, 2018. |
Includes bibliographical references and index.
Identifiers: LCCN 2018036806 | ISBN 9780786496112
(softcover : acid free paper) ∞
Subjects: LCSH: Chaplin, Charlie, 1889–1977. Motion picture music. |
Motion picture music—United States—20th century—History and criticism.
Classification: LCC ML410.C4176 L63 2018 | DDC 780.92—dc23
LC record available at https://lccn.loc.gov/2018036806

British Library cataloguing data are available

ISBN (print) 978-0-7864-9611-2
ISBN (ebook) 978-1-4766-3351-0

Front cover images © 2018 iStock

Printed in the United States of America

McFarland & Company, Inc., Publishers
Box 611, Jefferson, North Carolina 28640
www.mcfarlandpub.com

For Justin

Table of Contents

The Kid (1921 Compilation Score)   378 • *A Woman of Paris* (1923 Original Compilation Score)   378 • *A Woman of Paris* (1923 Revised Compilation Score Cue Sheet)   379 • *The Gold Rush* (1925 Compilation Score)   380 • *The Gold Rush* (1925 Cue Sheet)   380 • *The Circus* (1928 Compilation Score)   382 • *The Circus* (1928 Cue Sheet)   383 • *City Lights* (Original Cue Sheet, 1931)   384 • *City Lights* (Revised Cue Sheet, July 1972)   385 • *Modern Times*   387 • *The Great Dictator*   388 • *The Gold Rush* (1942 Score)   389 • *Monsieur Verdoux*   390 • *Limelight* (Handwritten Cue

Copyright Notices

Preface

MORE THAN SIX DEGREES separate the Satanic Black Mass of Jerry Goldsmith's score to *The Omen* from the English music hall homages of Charlie Chaplin's music. Or do they?

Goldsmith's score, the first soundtrack album I ever bought, made a deep impression on this impressionable 13-year-old. When it won the Oscar I began using the annual list of Academy Award nominees as my personal course in Film Music 101. I learned all the legendary names and many far less famous. Nestled among the giants of film music like Max Steiner, Alfred Newman, Bernard Herrmann, Miklós Rózsa, Franz Waxman, Erich Wolfgang Korngold, and John Williams was another legend I was not expecting—Charles Chaplin. Chaplin's Best Original Score win for *Limelight* in 1972 has been one of the great mysteries—and controversies—in Academy Awards history. Part of the controversy stems from Chaplin being unable to read or write music and having to hire other musicians to transcribe the notes and flesh out his musical vision. The mystery surrounds the name Larry Russell, one of the co-winners of the Oscar with Chaplin and his arranger Raymond Rasch. For decades I hoped someone would solve the mystery. There were online clues over the years but nothing concrete. Then one night during a home viewing of the 1942 sound version of *The Gold Rush*, the idea for this book was born.

Toward the end of the film, with the cabin teetering perilously on the edge of the cliff, Big Jim jumps to safety, but Charlie slides dangerously close to plummeting to his death, cabin and all. He hikes himself up onto his elbows, looks in Big Jim's direction through the doorway, and crooks his right index finger as if to say, "Hey, you … throw me a rope!" The movement goes by so fast, and Chaplin's movements are so subtle if you blink you will miss them. I certainly had in my previous viewings. This time, I burst out laughing. Not a smirk or a chuckle, but a full-throated, seal-like belly laugh. It exploded with such force and volume that I scared my dog. The *Gold Rush* score had also been nominated for an Oscar, as had *The Great Dictator*, so these were Chaplin films I already semi-knew. I am sure I had seen *City Lights* and *Modern Times* at some point, but that was as far as my knowledge of Chaplin's canon went. With that seemingly inconsequential *Gold Rush* moment, not only did I laugh out loud for the first time at a Chaplin film, but the six-degree gulf vanished and I tentatively began digging into Charlie Chaplin the man.

As a classically trained musician, I had paid my dues in practice rooms, music theory classes, and analyses of Bach four-part chorales. So Chaplin's lack of formal musical training had always perplexed me. How do you "compose" music if you are missing even the basic elements of musical theory? The more I investigated, the more I became intrigued

1

by the many dramatic events in Chaplin's long, storied life, a life authors had dissected from nearly every major angle except music. But was there enough of a musical story to fill a book? Indeed, there was.

Because of its musical focus, this is not a conventional Chaplin biography. Though the book adheres to Chaplin's life chronologically, the story follows Chaplin as a composer, deviating at times from the expected chronology of a particular film's original release date. I dispense with an in-depth discussion of much of Chaplin's early film work—his days with Mack Sennett, and the Essanay and Mutual comedies. Major life events that have little to do with music are condensed just enough to continue the story.

After establishing some historical backstory of Chaplin's early years, the music time-line officially begins with his purchase of a violin and cello and his first compositions published by the eponymous Charlie Chaplin Music Publishing Co. in 1916. This is fol-lowed by his supervision of the compilation scores for many of his last silent features and his first original score for *City Lights* in 1931. Silent shorts and feature films for which he later went back and composed original music appear in their proper place in the time-line. For instance, *The Gold Rush* is discussed twice—once in an early chapter for its 1925 compilation score and later sandwiched between *The Great Dictator* (1940) and *Monsieur Verdoux* (1947) for the 1942 reissue in which Chaplin eliminated the title cards and added his own voiceover and original score. *A Dog's Life*, *Shoulder Arms* (both 1918), and *The Pilgrim* (1922) are included as part of Chaplin's 1959 compilation, *The Chaplin Revue*. And *The Idle Class* (1921), *Pay Day* (1922), and other silent films show up in the final chapters as part of the last group of shorts and features Chaplin scored at the end of his life. Along the way, Chaplin worked with well-known musicians such as Alfred Newman, David Raksin, and Meredith Willson, and a host of lesser-known and often-forgotten names. It is my hope that this book will provide a new way to approach Chaplin's films—through his music—as well as shine a light on these unsung musicians and give them their proper due.

The book dissects the music of Chaplin (and others) in the contexts of his films. While it was written for the general reader, it is next to impossible to discuss music with-out using musical terms. Hopefully, I have adequately explained them and non-musicians will find something of interest in these discussions. I have also included copious musical examples for those who can read music, finally bringing much of Chaplin's music to light for the first time beyond the recording stage.

With so little written about Chaplin's relationship to music, I was unable to rely on much of the research done by generations of Chaplin scholars. Their writings certainly provided confirmation for many of the biographical details and the chronological frame-work. But, understandably, the story of Chaplin the composer had to be constructed from scratch. The bulk of the research relies on primary sources taken from papers and music manuscripts in the Chaplin Archive located at the Cineteca di Bologna in Italy, the Archives de Montreux in Switzerland, and the Association Chaplin/Roy Export SAS offices in Paris.

Much as Chaplin needed help to realize his vision, a host of generous folks scattered around the globe helped me realize mine. First and foremost I have to thank Kate Guy-onvarch of Association Chaplin/Roy Export SAS. Kate was my first point of contact—and provided the first glimmer of encouragement—when I began to research whether or not the subject of Chaplin's music was a viable project. With her colleague Arnold

Lozano, she has answered years' worth of emails and questions, no matter how small, how constant, or how irritating—sometimes all three. Along the way, she has championed the book, welcomed me into her home, and given me open-ended access to the Chaplin Archive, without which this book could not have been written.

When I first arrived at the Cineteca di Bologna in June 2014 to begin my research into Chaplin's papers, Cecilia Cenciarelli and Andrea Dresseno took care of my every need and have continued to do so with their own set of small/constant/irritating emails from me over the years.

Nicole Meystre-Schaeren, Julien Tieche, and the entire team at the Archives de Montreux put up with my numerous music manuscript demands, all the while suffering through my occasional sad, Texas-twanged, unsuccessful attempts at communicating in French.

Throughout the process, my research has been aided and abetted by four of the top Chaplin scholars—Kevin Brownlow, Lisa Stein Haven, Hooman Mehran, and David Robinson. They have shared not only private documents and their vast wealth of Chaplin knowledge to help correct errors, but their friendship as well. Their efforts have enriched the depth of the book beyond measure.

Angels at libraries around the country provided access and copies of hard-to-find primary documents and pieces of music—in particular, Ned Comstock and Michaela Ulmann at the University of Southern California, Richard Forster and Jackie Willoughby of The New York Public Library, Mark Horowitz and Loras Schissel at the Library of Congress, Kristine Krueger and Robert Reneau from the Academy of Motion Picture Arts and Sciences, Lisa Lobdell and Taylor Scott at the Great American Songbook Foundation, and Carlos Peña in the Theodore M. Finney Music Library at the University of Pittsburgh. Eileen Fitches of PRS for Music helped locate descendants of the European musicians who worked with Chaplin, and Marco Berrocal and Keith Rudolph of Bourne Co. spent months digging into every music example included in this book. Special thanks to the descendants and family members of the musicians—Mae Findlay, R. Craig Findlay, Gina Garcia, Phyllis James, Lance Kozlowski, Shelby Ticsay, Kelly Jo Williams Ticsay, and Laverne Williams—who gave so freely of their time and memories to lend a more personal slant to the stories within. Thank you to Claude Wolff and Petula Clark for her reminiscences, and to Paul Rasch for helping clear up much of the mystery surrounding the controversial *Limelight* Oscar.

Shunichi Ohkubo shared parts of his Chaplin collection, Alyce Mott and Peter Hilliard helped identify themes from Victor Herbert's opera *Natoma* in the 1925 compilation score to *The Gold Rush*, and Tim Rose Price generously provided the story and his unpublished lyrics for Chaplin's last song. Thanks to Gillian Anderson, Andrew Greene of the Peacherine Ragtime Orchestra, and Rodney Sauer of the Mont Alto Motion Picture Orchestra for their help in identifying many of the missing pieces in Chaplin's compilation scores. Then there's Timothy Brock, whose knowledge of Chaplin's music far outstrips mine (and anyone else for that matter, probably even Chaplin himself). Along with his reconstruction of Chaplin's scores, his help and encouragement provided new musical insights I might have missed otherwise, and I treasure the friendship that has evolved from this most esoteric of connections.

Thanks to my parents Stewart and Sally, who instilled my lifelong love of music and books simply by having them in the house, and my brother Jeff. Though they may never read this book, I'm grateful for their love and support even if they may have often wondered what I was doing or why. Then there are the friends and film music colleagues who have provided immeasurable help along the way, both personally and professionally, and whose assistance has meant the world to me—Tim Burden, Jon Burlingame, Tim Curran, Jon Kaplan, Amy Imhoff, and Shana O'Donnell. Last but not least, special, heartfelt thanks to the touchstones who keep me afloat on a daily basis—Doug Adams, Justin Craig, Jonathan Duchock, and Eric Rockwell.

Some authors come to their subject after a lifetime of study. Others find a gem hidden in the sands of time. This book is the result of the latter. Alan Jay Lerner said it best in the finale of *Camelot*—"We are all less than a drop in the great blue motion of the sunlit sea. But it seems that some of the drops sparkle ... some of them *do* sparkle." If certain drops of this book do indeed sparkle, I am but the humble jeweler hunched over his work desk, trying to polish a diamond in the rough.

Charlie Chaplin remains the jewel.

Introduction—And the Winners Are...

T HE NIGHT OF CHARLIE CHAPLIN'S greatest musical triumph, he stayed home, nearly six thousand miles away.

Nineteen seventy-two was the year of Chaplin's renaissance. He had recently entered into an agreement to officially repackage many of his old films for re-release after decades of shoddy bootleg copies. But there was bigger news—Chaplin was returning to the U.S. for the first time after twenty years of self-imposed exile to receive an inaugural award from the Film Society of Lincoln Center and an honorary Academy Award from the Academy of Motion Picture Arts and Sciences (AMPAS). After that well-publicized (and emotional) trip, Chaplin was in Oscar news once again. Now the twenty-year-old *Limelight*, no longer under the cloud of pressure from the American Legion that halted its original 1952 Los Angeles release, finally opened in December 1972 for a qualifying run. There was even talk Chaplin might be recognized finally for his work as a composer. But not if the co-chairman of the Academy's Music Branch subcommittee had anything to say about it.

The subcommittee was still feeling the sting from the previous year's Academy Awards when Isaac Hayes was nominated for the score and hit title song from *Shaft*. The song's scandalous production number on the telecast created a stir as Hayes, his naked upper torso draped in gold chains, led the funky tune surrounded by scantily clad dancers. The controversial song won, but months later there were still lingering questions about whether or not Hayes had written the entire score to the film and if that nomination was legitimate. *Shaft* musical director Tom McIntosh claimed he "put the whole thing together" along with J. J. Johnson but, not surprisingly given Hayes's marquee value in the music industry, "Isaac got all the credit." For the 1972 eligibility year, the Music Branch wanted to showcase "integrity" and "authenticity" in the music nominees, a plan that quickly went awry.[1]

In the Best Song category, the Academy pulled Curtis Mayfield's "Freddie's Dead" (from *Superfly*) from the list when they discovered the lyrics were not part of the instrumental in the film. Nino Rota's love theme from *The Godfather* was also ruled out because the melody first appeared in the 1958 Italian film *Fortunella*. At the Oscar nominations on February 12, 1973, the Song category was missing, pushed back three weeks to March 5 while the Music Branch re-balloted its members. But there was trouble brewing in the Original Score category as well.

Academy rules defined a composer as "a person who can compose music and commit to paper in a form more detailed than a simple lead sheet and proof may be required from any composer that he is capable of doing this." That is where Chaplin ran into trouble. He had never hidden the fact that he could not read or write music and had relied on other musicians to transcribe, arrange, and orchestrate his notes. Chaplin's eligibility as a composer for a twenty-year-old film rankled John Green, co-chair of the subcommittee, who snidely commented that Chaplin was "a considerably arrogant gentleman and a world-famed hummer—although he considers himself a nonhummer."[2] Green's meaning was clear—how dare an amateur musician submit himself for Oscar consideration as an actual composer.

Though there had been a campaign to nominate *Limelight* for Best Picture and Chaplin for Best Actor, neither made the cut. But the members of the Music Branch had cast their votes, and Chaplin (along with Raymond Rasch and Larry Russell) was among the nominees for Best Original Dramatic Score, his first competitive Oscar nomination since his *Monsieur Verdoux* original screenplay twenty-five years earlier. The other score nominees included John Williams for Robert Altman's *Images* and the disaster flick *The Poseidon Adventure* (the first of many double nominations in his long, illustrious career), Disney stalwart Buddy Baker for the kid-friendly lion movie *Napoleon and Samantha*, and Nino Rota for his iconic score to *The Godfather*.

Francis Ford Coppola's gangster epic led the Oscar pack with twelve nominations and Rota was a shoo-in to win. But Rota had also recycled portions of the score from *Fortunella* (the fourth of his *15 Preludes* for piano from 1964 provides the basis for another theme) and, in an "unprecedented action," the Academy re-balloted members of the Music Branch to choose the fifth slot.[3] The list included the remaining five scores on the shortlist—*Ben* (Walter Scharf), *The Life and Times of Judge Roy Bean* (Maurice Jarre), *The Other* (Jerry Goldsmith), *Sleuth* (John Addison), and Rota for *Fellini's Roma*, plus *The Godfather* again. At the end of voting, Addison was in, and Rota was out. (Two years later Rota shared the Oscar with Carmine Coppola for *The Godfather Part II*, naturally recycling many of the same *Godfather* themes that were ineligible the first time around. Such are the incomprehensible vagaries that muddy the waters of Academy Awards history.)

At the awards ceremony on March 27, as is often the case at the Oscars (or any awards show), the presenters seemed to be an odd pair that had no connection with the category they were presenting. Burt Reynolds, riding high with his recent dramatic performance in *Deliverance*, nominated that year for Best Picture, teamed with Dyan Cannon (*Bob & Carol & Ted & Alice*), who seemed positively giddy at sharing the stage with her *Shamus* co-star, giggling at his sexual innuendo about presenting "scoring" awards. "I can't even carry a tune," Reynolds quipped. "Really?" Cannon replied. "But that's not really important, is it? I mean, you can be here to present the award and not have to carry a tune." The line in the telecast script seems like a verbal slap on the wrist regarding Chaplin's compositional skills. But voters did not care about such things. After reading the list of nominees, with an exclamation of "Wow!" Cannon proclaimed Chaplin, Raymond Rasch, and Larry Russell the winners.[4]

*　　*　　*

Chaplin's musical legacy primarily rests with the 1954 classic song "Smile," which began life as a simple instrumental love theme in *Modern Times* nearly twenty years earlier, and Petula Clark's rendition of "This Is My Song," based on a melody from 1967's *A*

Countess from Hong Kong. But Chaplin's compositional efforts began with his first published pieces in 1916. He helped compile the scores for his last feature films of the silent era. And starting with *City Lights* in 1931, he took the unprecedented step of composing the scores for all his films for the rest of his life, including new scores for the remainder of the earlier silent shorts and features for which he still retained copyright.

Chaplin usually refused to discuss his working methods, which included his music. Even as late as 1973, Rachel Ford, Chaplin's business manager, told David Raksin, who worked on the score for *Modern Times*, "it would not be possible to induce Charlie to talk about his music 'on tape.' He has refused similar requests.... Charlie continues to compose the most delightful music and will shortly be recording again. I therefore went on wishfully hoping he might end in writing down/or put something on tape about it."[5] Perhaps as an amateur musician, Chaplin felt awkward discussing the technicalities of music outside of short quotes in newspaper interviews. Or maybe he felt that, like his films, "if people know how it's done, all the magic goes."[6] On those rare occasions he discussed his music, Chaplin vacillated between dismissing his contributions as mere "la-la'ing" or boasting that he loved everything he ever wrote. In interviews he would often praise his musical collaborators, giving credit where credit was due, while in their contracts they signed away all rights to their work.

As someone who could not read or write music, Chaplin relied on those collaborators to translate his humming, singing, and amateur violin and piano playing into a cohesive score. Chaplin wanted his amanuenses, arrangers, and orchestrators, like his actors, to be malleable, and he often hired musicians with little or no experience when it came to the nuts and bolts of film music. No matter how good it looked on a resume, working with Chaplin was not easy and most of his music associates did not last for more than one film. "As a matter of record, few musicians have found it possible to work with Chaplin who tolerates no contradiction," said Associated Press journalist Henry Gris, who filed a lengthy report from the set of *Limelight*. "He plays by ear in one key, that of 'F,' even if he doesn't know it, but goes into a tantrum when corrected or told his tune is wrongly constructed."[7]

Throughout his life, Chaplin never did learn to read or write music. "It's a pity, too," said Raymond Rasch, "because he feels music so deeply. I've tried to teach him. I'd suggest he use the full keyboard, pointing to the simplicity of the scale. I'd say, he for one could master it. There are just four triads, major, minor, diminished and augmented, and these four are the basis of however many voice chords. And I'd show it to him on the piano. He would listen. Chaplin goes along for a while on anything because he is willing to pick up more knowledge from anyone. Then he would say, 'Ray, I cannot do it. You want me to mechanize my thoughts. This is quite impossible!'"[8] Composer and conductor Timothy Brock, who has restored the majority of Chaplin's scores for live performance, notes that for Chaplin "the tune came first, meter second. As an avid non-conventional composer he freed himself of metronomic servitude, and composed just as he heard in his head."[9] And that may have been part of John Green's problem.

When he won his only competitive Oscar, the whole world knew Charlie Chaplin, but who were the other two gentlemen named alongside him? The story of Chaplin the composer is by extension the stories of those mostly forgotten musicians (both credited and uncredited) who collaborated with him, often under stressful and unpleasant circumstances. It also examines Chaplin's films through the lens of his music. Chaplin is seldom mentioned in histories of film music with anything kinder than elitism and more often derision. "As a writer and as composer of music for his films, Chaplin remains an amateur," critic Gilbert Seldes said in 1952. But, Seldes also grudgingly pointed out, "he gains because his movies (and his alone) are the product of a single individual, as a novel is or a poem."[10]

And therein lies the tale...

CHAPTER 1

Music First Entered My Soul

CHARLIE CHAPLIN WAS FOND of telling the story of when "music first entered my soul." The place was Kennington Cross in London. The moment, which he first wrote about in *My Trip Abroad* in 1922, was tinged with the warm sepia tone of memory.

> It was here that I first discovered music, or where I first learned its rare beauty, a beauty that has gladdened and haunted me from that moment. It all happened one night while I was there, about midnight. I recall the whole thing so distinctly.
>
> I was just a boy, and its beauty was like some sweet mystery. I did not understand. I only knew I loved it and I became reverent as the sounds carried themselves through my brain *via* my heart.
>
> I suddenly became aware of a harmonica and a clarinet playing a weird, harmonious message. I learned later that it was "The Honeysuckle and the Bee." It was played with such feeling that I became conscious for the first time of what melody really was. My first awakening to music.
>
> I remembered how thrilled I was as the sweet sounds pealed into the night. I learned the words the next day. How I would love to hear it now, that same tune, that same way!
>
> Conscious of it, yet defiant, I find myself singing the refrain softly to myself:
>
> > "You are the honey, honeysuckle. I am the bee;
> > I'd like to sip the honey, dear, from those red lips. You see
> > I love you dearie, dearie, and I want you to love me—
> > You are my honey, honeysuckle. I am your bee."
>
> Kennington Cross, where music first entered my soul. Trivial, perhaps, but it was the first time.[1]

Even decades later, writing in his 1964 autobiography, Chaplin still felt nostalgic about the encounter:

> It was approaching midnight and Kennington Cross was deserted but for one or two stragglers. All the lights of the shops began going out except those of the chemist and the public houses, then I felt wretched.
>
> Suddenly, there was music. Rapturous! It came from the vestibule of the White Hart corner pub, and resounded brilliantly in the empty square. The tune was "The Honeysuckle and the Bee," played with radiant virtuosity on a harmonium and clarinet. I had never been conscious of melody before, but this one was beautiful and lyrical, so blithe and gay, so warm and reassuring. I forgot my despair and crossed the road to where the musicians were. The harmonium player was blind, with scarred sockets where the eyes had been; and a besotted, embittered face played the clarinet.
>
> It was all over too soon and their exit left the night even sadder.[2]

But on April 16, 1889, in East Lane, Walworth, a subsection of London, years before it entered his soul, Chaplin was born with music in his DNA.

⋆ ⋆ ⋆

Home "was still the London of Dickens."[3] Queen Victoria was in the forty-first year of her sixty-three-year reign. Gilbert and Sullivan had a song to sing with *The Yeomen of the Guard* at the Savoy Theatre. Over at the Lyceum, operagoers thrilled to Verdi's green-eyed monster with Italian tenor Francesco Tamagno reprising his role as *Otello* in its London premiere. The pillars of the English music halls—the Empire and Alhambra—ruled over Leicester Square. The major stars of the music halls lived in style in nearby Clapham and Brixton. But many "lesser lights" lived in and around Chaplin's neighborhood at Kennington Road, including "Gentlemen Acrobats" the Crags, "America's Greatest Double Somersault Flying Trapeze Artists" Lauck and Dunbar, and sketch artist (and Chaplin's future employer) Fred Karno.[4] Chaplin's parents, Charles Chaplin, Sr., and Hannah Harriet Pedlingham Hill, were also music hall performers, as was Hannah's sister, Kate Hill.

Charles Sr. was born March 18, 1863, and began his stage career as a mimic and later/achieved some level of success as a comedian and "dramatic and descriptive singer." His first recorded performance was during the week of Queen Victoria's Golden Jubilee, June 20, 1887, at the Poly Variety Theatre. His stage persona was often the character of, what David Robinson describes, "a masher, a man about town, or an ordinary husband and father, bedevilled by problems all too familiar to his audiences such as mothers-in-laws, landladies who wanted to be paid, nagging wives and crying babies."[5] Chaplin remembered, "He had a light baritone voice and was considered a very fine artist. Even in those days he earned the considerable sum of forty pounds a week."[6] Charles wrote the music to many of his songs, and he achieved enough success between 1890 and 1897 that Francis, Day & Hunter published many of them with his face on the cover, a practice that was awarded only to stars whose image would help sell sheet music.

Charles's dashing portrait on the covers of "Eh! Boys?," "Oui! Tray Bong!," and "Every-Day Life" bears little resemblance to that of his famous son. He was "a quiet, brooding man with dark eyes," Chaplin remembered. "Mother said he looked like Napoleon."[7] Usually donned in a waistcoat and topcoat, bow tie or cravat, and straw or top hat, Charles sang lyrics that were at odds with his elegant attire but resonated with his mostly working-class audience:

> *In every-day life many marvels around*
> *Fill us with a feeling of wonder profound.*
> *Often the heart aches, and tears dim the eye,*
> *As sad scenes in passing through life we espy*
> *Poor wretches huddled on bridges at night,*
> *Beggars who plaintively beg just a mite,*
> *These make us wonder,*
> *"How can such things be,*
> *In our Christian England,*
> *So great and so free?"*
>
> REFRAIN
> *Then see the swell in his carriage dash by,*
> *Little cares he for the poverty night;*
> *He gives them nothing to save them from strife*
> *These are characters taken from Every-Day Life.*[8]

Harry Boden's lyrics provide some examples of the old-fashioned style of lyric writing from the period. Adjectives ("wonder profound"), verbs ("As sad scenes in passing through life we espy"), and pronouns ("Little cares he") are moved, all for the sake of end rhymes. Chaplin would use this style in his lyrics (e.g., "I care not what the world may say" from "This Is My Song"), much to the annoyance of his critics and even some of the artists who recorded his songs.

*   *   *

Chaplin's favorite memory of his mother, Hannah Harriet Pedlingham Hill (b. August 6, 1865), was as "a *mignonne* in her late twenties, with fair complexion, violet-blue eyes and long light-brown hair that she could sit upon." Chaplin and his half-brother Sydney "adored" her. "Though she was not an exceptional beauty, we thought her divine-looking. Those who knew her told me in later years that she was dainty and attractive and had compelling charm."[9] Using the stage name Lily Harley, Hannah was a serio-comic who, as author Barry Anthony describes her, stood barely five feet tall with "delicately moulded features" and "sometimes wore short, schoolgirl dresses, assuming an air of juvenile ingenuousness as she sang songs laced with double meaning."[10] *The Stage* commented she was "a clever and graceful little lady."[11] "Miss Lily

Charles Chaplin Senior, Chaplin's father, was a comedian and "dramatic and descriptive singer" on the English music hall stage, c. 1885 (from the archives of Roy Export Co. Ltd.).

Harley's songs are rendered with great taste and her dancing is both graceful and refined," wrote a reviewer for the weekly British newspaper *The Era*.[12] "We must not forget to mention the appearance of Miss Lily Harley," the paper later claimed, "a young lady who sings coquettish ballads with much grace and archness of manner, and is extremely well received."[13]

Hannah never matched her husband's level of success, but, like Charles, she was also a capable songwriter, writing songs such as "My Lady Friend" and "The Lady Judge" for her younger sister Kate, who went by the stage name Kitty Fairdale. Kate was born January 18, 1870, almost five years after her sister. Hannah's songwriting skills were noted when Kate, "in long golden wig, a velvet gown, and a mortar-board, sang 'The Lady Judge' which is a fairly good specimen of its kind."[14] "Miss Kitty Fairdale is very merry and dances in splendid style," said a review of her performance of the 1891–1892 pantomime *Aladdin and His Wonderful Lamp*.[15] She was "an artiste who gives much pleasure."[16]

In an interview published posthumously in *Pearson's Weekly*, Kate waxed eloquent on the musical childhood of her now-famous nephew:

> As a baby, [Charlie] would stop playing with his toys the instant he heard music of any description, and would beat time with his tiny hand and nod his head until the music ceased. In later years I have seen him sit for hours at the piano, composing as he went along.
>
> The 'cello was the instrument I think he loved best, "because it was so plaintive," he said. I took a delight in watching his changing expression and his small hand quivering as he touched the cords. It was almost a caress.

It was only when he caught my eyes glistening that he would laugh, and suddenly do some funny little movement or dash off a gay air. This would immediately change my sad mood to one scream of laughter.[17]

The reminiscence is full of sweet images which, given the despair of much of Chaplin's childhood, are all too rare. But this calls into question the details attributed to Kate, especially since the interview was printed five years after her death. Besides, Chaplin said she "wove in and out of our lives sporadically. She was pretty and temperamental and never got along very well with Mother. Her occasional visits usually ended abruptly with acrimony at something Mother had said or done."[18] Kate died of cancer in 1916 at age forty-six.

*   *   *

Chaplin's mother, Hannah Harriet Pedlingham Hill, was also a music hall performer under the stage name Lily Harley, c. 1885 (from the archives of Roy Export Co. Ltd.).

Hannah met Charles in approximately 1882 when they were appearing in the Irish melodrama *Shamus O'Brien*. Two years later, at age eighteen, she eloped with a middle-aged man to Africa. On March 16, 1885, nineteen-year-old Hannah gave birth to Sydney (registered as Sidney) John Hill. She claimed Sydney's father was a man named Sydney Hawkes. "I was told [Sydney] was the son of a lord," Chaplin said, "and that when he reached the age of twenty-one he would inherit a fortune of two thousand pounds, which information both pleased and annoyed me."[19] Within a few weeks of the birth, Hannah traveled to northern France for a month-long engagement at the Royal Music Hall, Le Havre. Soon after she returned to London, she married Charles on June 22, 1885.

"I was hardly aware of a father and do not remember him living with us," Chaplin said. The trouble was Charles's drinking. Every theater sold alcohol and performers were expected to go to the bar following their act and drink with the patrons. "Thus many an artist was ruined by drink—my father was one of them."[20] Charles's touring (including one trip to the U.S.) put further strains on the marriage. By April 1891, Charles and Hannah separated, and she, Sydney, and Charlie moved in with Hannah's mother.

The following year, Hannah met singer Leo Dryden. Known as the "Kipling of the Halls," Dryden had become famous for his patriotic song "The Miner's Dream of Home." Dryden said Hannah "was one of the smartest vaudeville artists of her day. She was wonderfully versatile, and had a sweet voice. She was a great mimic." He later hired her to sing in the chorus. And, if his memories are correct, Dryden apparently fulfilled the role of surrogate father figure. While teaching Charlie to walk, "his mother sat on one chair, and I on another and the future King of Mirth toddled backwards and forwards, looking comically rueful when he fell."[21]

Chaplin attributes the following memories to Charles, but it is more likely Leo that he remembered:

> He would set me upon the table in my nightgown, with the bright light hurting my eyes and every one would laugh and tell me to sing for the drops of wine in their glasses. I always did, and the party applauded and laughed and called for more. I could mimic every one I had seen and sing all the songs I had heard. They would keep me doing it for hours until I got so sleepy I could not stand up and fell over among the dishes. Then mother picked me up and carried me to bed again. I remember just how her hair fell down over the pillow as she tucked me in. It was brown hair, very soft and perfumed, and her face was so full of fun it seemed to sparkle. That was in the early days of course.[22]

On August 31, 1892, Hannah gave birth to Leo George (later known as Wheeler) Dryden. Six months later, Leo abruptly removed Wheeler from Hannah's custody and stopped giving her money. Wheeler later arrived in the U.S. as an adult and presented himself to Chaplin as his half-brother. Chaplin provided him with an allowance while he pursued his career as a stage actor and briefly in films. By 1939, Wheeler was a regular member of Chaplin's staff, working on *The Great Dictator* as an assistant director and as the voice of the translator, Heinrich Schtick; as an uncredited salesman in *Monsieur Verdoux*; and as the doctor and Pantaloon the clown in *Limelight*.

Hannah liked to bring Charlie to the theater at night, rather than leave him alone in a rented room. "So Charlie spent most of his evenings running in and out of the various dressing-rooms," remembered Nellie Richards, a major star of the 1890s.

> He was a regular little demon at times, though. He would stop *there* in the wings, singing my choruses half a line ahead of me, and so vigorously that I'm sure people in front must have heard him. The harder I frowned at him, the wider he grinned, and went right on with it. I was always threatening to spank him, so usually he ran like a hare when the last lines of my songs were on my lips…. He had a wonderful ear for music even then, and picked up almost everything I sang.[23]

Hannah's voice, never particularly strong, began to plague her more and more. At one point she had laryngitis that lasted for weeks. But her financial situation would not allow her to stop working, which in turn made her voice progressively worse. "The worry of it impaired her health and made her a nervous wreck," Chaplin said. "As a consequence, her theatrical engagements fell off until they were practically nil."[24] Hannah's misfortune, however, gave Charlie his first taste of fame at age five.

One evening at the Aldershot Canteen, performing before a tough audience made up mostly of soldiers, Hannah lost her voice and rushed off stage. Charlie took her place and began to sing the cockney song "'E Dunno Where 'E Are," a recent hit for comedian Gus Elen. "Half-way through, a shower of money poured on to the stage," Chaplin remembered.

> Immediately I stopped and announced that I would pick up the money first and sing afterwards. This caused much laughter. The stage manager came on with a handkerchief and helped me to gather it up. I thought he was going to keep it. This thought was conveyed to the audience and increased their laughter, especially when he walked off with it with me anxiously following him. Not until he handed it to Mother did I return and continue to sing. I was quite at home. I talked to the audience, danced, and did several imitations including one of Mother singing her Irish march song…. And in repeating the chorus, in all innocence I imitated Mother's voice cracking and was surprised at the impact it had on the audience. There was laughter and cheers, then more money-throwing; and when Mother came on the stage to carry me off, her presence evoked tremendous applause.[25]

Director Richard Attenborough opened his 1992 Chaplin biopic with this scene, though he employed dramatic license with young Charlie singing "The Honeysuckle and the Bee," no doubt a nod to the moment years later outside the White Hart pub when "music first entered my soul."

Hannah's bookings eventually dried up, and circumstances went from bad to worse. Once she depleted her meager savings, she pawned her jewelry and other small possessions. "From three comfortable rooms we moved into two," Chaplin said, "then into one, our belongings dwindling and the neighbourhoods into which we moved growing progressively drabber."[26] He later told a reporter, "My boyhood ended at the age of seven."[27]

*   *   *

"My childhood was sad," Chaplin said *My Life In Pictures*, "but now I remember it with nostalgia, like a dream."[28] At the time, it must have seemed closer to a nightmare. In June 1895, Hannah was admitted (as "Lillian Chaplin") to the Lambeth Infirmary, beginning an on-again-off-again period of illness that would eventually result in being committed, like her mother, to an asylum. Over the next eighteen months, Charlie and Sydney were in and out of the forbidding Lambeth Workhouse and Hanwell School for Orphans and Destitute Children. In November 1896, Sydney transferred to the Training Ship *Exmouth* because, as Chaplin wrote, "At the age of eleven a workhouse boy had the choice of joining the Army or the Navy."[29]

Hannah did not seek alimony from Charles. "Being a star in her own right, earning twenty-five pounds a week," said Chaplin, "she was well able to support herself and her children. Only when ill-fortune befell her did she seek relief; otherwise she would never have taken legal steps."[30] According to Barry Anthony, Charles had earned a reputation as a "morose drunkard and womanizer," but he could not forgive his wife's infidelity and refused to pay for her maintenance.[31] Chaplin said, "To gauge the morals of our family by commonplace standards would be as erroneous as putting a thermometer in boiling water."[32] On January 18, 1898, two days before Sydney was discharged from the *Exmouth*, Charles was arrested for non-payment of support for his sons. Charlie and Sydney eventually went to live with Charles, his mistress Louise, and her young son. Not surprisingly, Louise did not want to share her lodgings with two children that were not hers. She tolerated Charlie's presence, but she took an instant dislike to Sydney, who eventually left again for the sea rather than endure the indignities of living there.

Charlie got his first professional job at age nine as a member of the Eight Lancashire Lads, a troupe of young clog dancers. Charles knew William Jackson, the leader of the troupe (whose daughter Rose, with her hair cut like a boy's, was the eighth "lad"), and persuaded him to take on his son. As David Robinson describes:

> Even to a ten-year-old in a troupe of clog dancers, the music halls of those times must have provided an incomparable schooling in method, technique and discipline. A music hall act had to seize and hold its audience and to make its mark within a very limited time—between six and sixteen minutes. The audience was not indulgent, and the competition was relentless. The performer in the music hall could not rely on a sympathetic context or build-up: Sarah Bernhardt might find herself following Lockhart's Elephants on the bill. So every performer had to learn the secrets of attack and structure, the need to give the act a crescendo—a beginning, middle and a smashing exit—to grab the applause. He had to learn to command every sort of audience, from a lethargic Monday first-house to the Saturday rowdies.[33]

Charlie received board and lodging on tour, and Hannah received half a crown a week. For three weeks the Lads even appeared on the same bill with Chaplin's father. Charlie left the Lads in 1901.

Charles Sr.'s last recorded stage appearance was in September 1900 at the Granville Theatre of Varieties in Walham Green. On April 29, 1901, he was admitted to St. Thomas's Hospital, where he died on May 9. Though "an Uncle Albert from Africa" paid for the funeral, Charles was buried in a pauper's grave in Tooting Cemetery. Chaplin carried with him a distant memory of "sitting in a red plush seat" watching Charles perform.[34] "I'm very proud of my father," he said, "and a little disappointed. He was a fine artist but he drank too much."[35] For the rest of Hannah's life, Chaplin's said, "Mother would tell stories about him with humour and sadness."[36]

*   *   *

Hannah's mental health continued to worsen, and on May 5, 1903, she was admitted to Lambeth Infirmary. Four days later Hannah was committed as a lunatic and on May 11, she transferred to the Cane Hill Asylum, where she remained for the next eight months. In the meantime, Charlie began his stage career in the part of Sam in *Jim, A Romance of Cockayne* at the Royal County Theatre, Kingston. At the end of July, he played Billy in *Sherlock Holmes* for the first time and within a couple of weeks was touring throughout the provinces in the part. Sydney joined the cast on tour and when Hannah was discharged from Cane Hill in January 1904, she accompanied her sons on tour. In October 1904, Charlie joined the second tour of *Sherlock Holmes* while Sydney embarked on his last voyage, as assistant steward and bugler on the *Dover Castle* to Natal.

While Charlie was on tour, Hannah was once again admitted to Lambeth Infirmary and committed as a lunatic at Cane Hill Asylum, spending many years there and at Peckham House Asylum, a private nursing home. With Hannah again indisposed, Charlie went out on the third *Sherlock Holmes* tour before returning to play the part of Billy in *The Painful Predicament of Sherlock Holmes* with William Gillette, the creator of Holmes on stage, at the Duke of York Theatre. Charlie was also part of the fourth *Holmes* tour before joining Wal Pink's *Repairs* and the *Casey's Court Circus* company.

Meanwhile, Sydney signed on with the Fred Karno troupe on July 9, 1906. Karno (1866–1941), a former gymnast and acrobat, conceived of silent burlesque sketches that were fast and furious, involving various mimes and acrobats. Another trait of Karno's sketches was the use of romantic ballet music as an ironic accompaniment; a feature Chaplin later incorporated into his own music.

In the autumn of 1907, Charlie attempted a single act at Foresters' Music Hall, a small theater situated off Mile End Road in the center of London's Jewish quarter. He had played there with *Casey's Court Circus* "and the management thought I was good enough to be given a chance. My future hopes and dreams depended on that trial week.... Although I was innocent of it, my comedy was most anti–Semitic, and my jokes were not only old ones but very poor, like my Jewish accent. Moreover, I was not funny." After the first couple of jokes, the audiences started booing, throwing coins and orange peels. "When I came off the stage, I did not wait to hear the verdict from the management; I went straight to the dressing-room, took off my make-up, left the theatre and never returned, not even to collect my music books."[37]

Charlie was now unemployed and Sydney tried to persuade Karno to hire his brother, but the impresario showed no interest. In February 1908, Karno finally gave Charlie a two-week trial with the possibility of a contract if he proved to be up to snuff. He was "a pale, puny, sullen-looking youngster," Karno said. "I must say that when I first saw him, I thought he looked much too shy to do any good in the theatre, particularly in the knockabout comedies that were my specialty."[38] But Chaplin proved his worth and, within three weeks, signed a contract. The agreement provided for one year at a weekly salary of £3 10s, the second year at £4, and a third year's option at the same rate. Over the next five years, he perfected his comedic pantomime craft in a variety of sketches. Chaplin later paid tribute to his old boss by adapting one of Karno's biggest hits, *Mumming Birds* (also known as *A Night in an English Music Hall*), as *A Night in the Show* (1915). Being on tour, while exhausting, consists of much downtime. Chaplin filled his off hours with the first confirmed seeds of his musical aspirations.

*   *   *

"Because of some obligations," Chaplin kept "very little more than half" of his Karno salary "to start afresh every week."[39] At age sixteen, "as soon as he was able to afford instruments," David Robinson says, Chaplin taught himself to play the violin and cello.[40] A discarded note from the original script for *Limelight* has Calvero relating to Terry the struggles of learning to play the violin, no doubt based on Chaplin's personal experience:

> Have you ever tried playing a violin for the first time? Well, first you twist your wrist until it's paralysed; then you hold the instrument tight under your chin until you get a comfortable [*illegible*] then you bow in a little space between the bridge and the kneck [*sic*]; the first time, you usually bow up the kneck—if you bow down too far, then you fall off the bridge; and you're lucky if the end of the bow doesn't dig into your nostril—poke out your eye or dig into your ear … and if you get a sound out of it, it's like the moaning of a sick cat with [*illegible*]. It takes time to play a violin if you want to be good at it; eight hours a day for five years.[41]

Chaplin felt he had greater dexterity in the fingers of the right hand and had a special violin made that reversed the fingerboard. He carted the instrument along on the Karno tour of the U.S. in 1912. Stanley Jefferson, better known as Stan Laurel, Chaplin's roommate on the tour, later recalled Chaplin carried his violin "wher-

Chaplin had a special violin made, reversing the fingerboard, because he felt he had greater dexterity in the fingers of the right hand, c. 1925 (from the archives of Roy Export Co. Ltd.).

ever he could…. And he would practise for hours."[42] One night, while Laurel and Chaplin were frying some chops in their room, which was strictly forbidden, they heard the landlady coming down the hallway. "With characteristic resourcefulness," Laurel said, "Charlie promptly snatched up his violin and played a lively air to drown out the sound of the sizzling, whilst I snatched the chops from the gas jet and held the pan out the window to get rid of the smell!"[13] Chaplin only "plays" the violin on screen twice. In *The Vagabond* (1916), the Tramp uses his violin to seduce a gypsy prisoner (Edna Purviance). Chaplin played the instrument on the set, including "The Honeysuckle and the Bee." And there is the classic teaming with Buster Keaton for the violin-piano duet at the Empire benefit in *Limelight* (1952), with Chaplin mimicking the strains of the offstage musician. "I wouldn't call him a good violinist," Laurel said, "but he sure as hell wasn't a bad one."[44]

Once Chaplin became famous, many of the newspaper articles in the late 'teens and '20s played up his left-handed abilities and unique instrument. The verbiage was nearly always the same, taken from press releases that rehashed the same language for years. "If you were to drop into Chaplin's home in Los Angeles some evening, you might be surprised to find him playing a selection from *Carmen* or *La Bohème* on his violin," read an unsigned article from Chaplin's time with the Mutual Film Corporation, probably written by studio's press chief Terry Ramsaye. It praised Chaplin as "an exceptionally good violinist…. Every spare moment away from the studio is devoted to this instrument. He

In *The Vagabond*, one of the few times Chaplin is seen "playing" a musical instrument on screen, the Tramp uses his violin to seduce a gypsy prisoner (Edna Purviance), c. 1916 (from the archives of Roy Export Co. Ltd.).

does not play from notes excepting in a very few instances. He can run through selections of popular operas by ear and if in the humor, can rattle off the famous Irish jig or some negro [*sic*] selection with the ease of a vaudeville entertainer."[45]

A headline in a 1921 edition of *Musical America*, "Roderick White, Right-Handed; Chaplin Still the Sole Left-Handed Violinist," was meant as an apology to White.

> By reason of error in the engraving department a cut was used in a recent issue of MUSICAL AMERICA, showing Roderick White, well-known American violinist, in the act of playing a violin and holding the bow in his left hand. So far as is known, the only well-known personage who has yet attempted to play the violin using the left hand for the bow is "Charlie" Chaplin and his affectation of such a peculiar mannerism has been limited to his appearances on the screen, where he is seen but not heard. Incidentally, Mr. Chaplin, in private life, is reputed to be a very good violinist.[46]

Journalist Charles Lapworth noted on a visit to the Chaplin studio, "[Chaplin] will permit you to sit in his dressing room, and let you do the talking while he affixes the horsehair to make up his moustache. You will notice a violin near at hand, also a cello. And it will be unusual if Charlie does not pick up the fiddle and the bow, and accompany your remarks with an obbligato [*sic*] from the classics, what time he will fix you with a far-away stare and keep you going with monosyllabic responses."[47] While that makes for descriptive reading, it is doubtful Chaplin ignored a visiting journalist like that. Given the lengthy breaks Chaplin would take during filming that halted production for weeks and months at a time, it is not surprising that while he was working on *The Gold Rush*, reported *The New York Times*, Chaplin "became so fascinated with playing the violin that he neglected his brain-child for the instrument."[48]

As *The Music Trade Review* reported in 1918:

> Charlie Chaplin received a letter from a certain manufacturer of musical instruments, proposing to present him with a saxophone providing he would be photographed with it, and permit the maker to use the indorsement [*sic*] for advertising purposes. Not being particularly interested in the saxophone but appreciating the gentleman's courtesy, Mr. Chaplin in part replied:
> "If you happen to have a spare 'Strad' violin knocking about that you don't want, well, you might send it on. I will have my picture taken with it, and I will give you a letter to the effect that I can thoroughly recommend it."[49]

"I used to play my violin a great deal up to a couple of years ago," Chaplin said in a 1921 interview, "but since then I've hardly touched it. I seem to have lost interest in such things."

As Lapworth mentioned, Chaplin later kept a cello in his office. And if the remarks attributed to his Aunt Kate are to believed, it is no surprise he always longed to own one. While on tour with Karno, he saw one in the window of a store in Los Angeles for twelve dollars.

> With that sum in my hand, I rushed to the store, plunked down the money on the table and said breathlessly: "Give me that," pointing to the window. They gave me the 'cello. Only the price did not include a bow. That was an extra few dollars which I did not happen to have. I remember carrying the 'cello in my hand naked, as it were, for it had no case, and boarding a car for home. So anxious was I to hear its sound that I plucked its strings while in the car. I wonder what people thought of the bleary-eyed boy plucking the strings of that instrument! …
> I had to wait another week before I had money to buy a bow and a piece of rosin.[50]

Like the violin, Chaplin carried the cello around with him. "At these times," Stan Laurel said, "he would always dress like a musician, a long fawn coloured overcoat with

Chaplin and his cello on the set of *The Gold Rush*, c. 1925 (© Roy Export Co. Ltd.).

green velvet cuffs and collar and a slouch hat. And he'd let his hair grow long at the back. We never knew what he was going to do next."[51] Chaplin took lessons from the musical directors of the various theaters on tour and claimed he practiced four to six hours a day.

The Boston Globe reported in 1925 that Chaplin would be the guest cello soloist with Leopold Stokowski and the Philadelphia Orchestra at a children's concert, stating, "Mr. Chaplin is said to be a very good cellist."[52] But there is no record of his appearance and Chaplin certainly had no illusions about his abilities on the instrument—"I could pose well with it but that's about all."[53] During the filming of *The Gold Rush*, Chaplin had photos taken of him in his Tramp costume posing with the cello. "Because it is like a symbol of my poverty, although I am still passionately fond of the cello, I seldom play it," he said in an interview at the time. "My heart sinks when I touch it."[54]

Chaplin turned instead to the instruments he installed in his home. And, not surprisingly, music companies wanted it known when he bought one of their products. *The Music Trade Review* reported in 1918 that "Charley" Chaplin bought a Brambach baby grand player-piano, "which he says he will be able to play even with his face interred in pies."[55] Four years later, Chaplin purchased a Bilhorn Telescope Organ from Richardson's, Inc, perhaps for use in *The Pilgrim*. "This convenient little instrument will be used by Mr. Chaplin, who is exceedingly musical when away on camping and outing trips, as well as by his company when out 'on location,' where it is desirable to create the desired atmosphere and temperament which music alone inspire[s]."[56]

"Movie fans in the country seldom realize the true character of their screen stars," said an item in *PRESTO*. "Screen action, plot, and the vehicle representing our favorite doesn't always fully interpret the temperament of the actor."

> It may be news to many readers that Charlie Chaplin is a clever musician, playing violin, piano and organ with unusual skill. The first intimation that many of Chaplin's friends and followers knew of this musical talent was the placing of an order for a Robert-Morton organ to be installed in his new Beverley [*sic*] Hills home in the course of construction. This is one of the finest residences in the Hollywood district. In the music room provision was also made for an echo organ and a special roll device will also be installed on the instrument.
>
> It is expected Charlie will "shoulder arms" over the console of the new instrument when the Pipes of Pan are playing in the springtime.[57]

"Chaplin is not dependent on mechanical devices to play his new instrument," *The Music Trade Review* reported. "He plays the piano, organ and violin and is an unusually good amateur. The American Photo Player men, who installed the organ, were surprised to discover that the versatile Charlie is a musical performer."[58] "One of the ways in which Charlie charms his visitors," said *Screenland*, "is by improvising soft music to the mood of the occasion on his lovely organ, built into the walls of his library. One time Charlie was cross with a newspaper woman for marrying a second time. (Now, Charlie!) He cut her off his visiting list for a few months but then relented and invited her and her husband to dinner. The new and wrathy spouse felt like socking Charlie and went to the party very reluctantly—prepared to hate the little comedian. But Charlie sat down at the organ and played so magnificently that the guy who came to fight remained to praise."[59] In 1926, Chaplin purchased an Ampico player piano and joined a list of "many of the crowned heads of filmdom" who owned one, including Douglas Fairbanks, John Barrymore, Billie Burke, Norma Talmadge, Pearl White, Peggy Wood, Gloria Swanson, Peggy Hopkins Joyce, Mary Pickford, Jackie Coogan, and Harold Lloyd.[60]

Upton Sinclair visited the *City Lights* set with journalist Egon Erwin Kisch for the *Frankfurter Zeitung* in tow and Kisch was invited to Chaplin's house to hear him play the organ. "The boys assure us that the boss has a huge organ at home on which he knows how to play loud and long, whether the visitor likes it or not. 'I play awfully well,' laughs Charlie, 'only you don't understand a damn bit of my music.'"[61] Journalist Mayme Ober Peak also described a visit to Chaplin's home in 1929—"There was music in his voice,

Chaplin carts his violin and cello around on one of the Karno tours, Sacramento, California, June 5, 1911 (© Roy Export Co. Ltd.).

and in his finger tips too as I discovered to my surprise when he climbed the high seat of his pipe organ and flooded the room with the sweetest chords ear ever heard. For an hour the pipes wailed out the longings and discontent of this far-famed comedian—the world's playfellow and the loneliest man in it."[62] Later, Chaplin's official publicity blurb about his music waxed eloquent about the instrument—"If at home the comedian may read, play tennis, have a circle of friends or turn to music. It is then that he enjoys his seat at the console of his massive pipe organ. Here he will sit for hours, not knowing of the passing time. All the while he is turning ideas of this picture work over in his mind."[63]

Charles Chaplin, Jr., said his mother, Lita Grey Chaplin, "told of my father's moodiness, his periods of abstracted silence, his intense need to be alone, his long, lonely walks at night, the weird, sad music he used to improvise by the hour."[64] Charles said the organ room, which opened onto the master bedroom, was "the most mysterious one in the whole house—for so my father made it appear to us."

> Every now and then Dad, [Chaplin's son Sydney] and I would make a solemn pilgrimage upstairs to this room. Dad would stand in front of the double doors which sealed it off and open one, causing a suction that would make the other fly out with a swish, as though released by an invisible hand. Then all three of us would go reverently into the big oblong room that housed the organ pipes. A shadowy stairstep army, they marched from the very small slender trebles at one end to the massive, dignified basses at the other.
>
> "It took a lot of work to get them all in there. A lot of work!" Dad would say proudly. And he would lay his hands on the pipes in a caress, as though they were old friends.[65]

Chaplin's Aunt Kate reminisced that he loved to sit for hours at the piano as a child, "composing as he went along."[66] Whether the memory is accurate or not, the adult Chaplin spent many hours at the piano composing. When he stayed at the Savoy in London, he had a small grand piano moved into the drawing room of his suite. As with the violin and cello, piano mastery "was always to elude him," said Eric James, Chaplin's music associate for the last twenty years of life.[67]

> Charlie really loved that piano and he would spend many hours each week attempting to play it. I found it deeply distressing watching and listening to his efforts to do so. Even when he managed to get some sort of melody with his first three fingers of the right hand—the only ones he ever succeeded in using, in the key of F, his favorite key—the minute he started to try and use the left hand frequent discords resulted and he would curse vehemently in his frustration. Although it was his limited ability to play that resulted in my working with him, I did feel deeply sorry that he had not been able to find time to develop a talent that would have meant so much to him.[68]

But twenty hours' worth of tape recordings with Chaplin composing at the piano, located in the Chaplin Archive, tell a different story. The tapes encompass musical ideas spanning nearly twenty years, with fragments of melodies and lyrics from *Limelight*, *The Pilgrim*, *A Countess from Hong Kong*, and *The Circus*. Chaplin's working method, when by himself, consisted of a series of chord progressions and pianistic flourishes, while his reed-thin voice worked out the melody on top. The tapes demonstrate Chaplin possessed far more skill than mere three-finger piano playing. He was a competent amateur pianist who knew what he was doing at the keyboard with both hands and hunted and pecked, like many composers before and after him, until he found what he wanted. If the tapes are any indication, Chaplin certainly never would have had the pianistic chops for a concert career. But there was more to his musical abilities than his music associates have given him credit for over the years. "What a grand piano player has the motion picture lost," the legendary pianist Ignacy Jan Paderewski remarked. "What a great pie thrower has the music world gained in the fine Mr. Chaplin."[69]

*   *   *

On the second Karno U.S. tour in 1913, someone from Mack Sennett's Keystone Film Company saw Chaplin perform *A Night in an English Music Hall* in New York. Reports vary as to who saw him. Sennett says he did; other accounts allege that Adam Kessel, who owned Keystone with Charles Baumann, or his brother Charles did. A 1973 letter to Kevin Brownlow suggests that it was Harry Aitken, the studio's major stock owner. On May 12, 1913, Kessel and Baumann sent Alfred Reeves, the Karno tour manager, a telegram which allegedly read, "IS THERE A MAN NAMED CHAFFIN IN YOUR COMPANY OR SOMETHING LIKE THAT IF SO WILL HE COMMUNICATE WITH KESSEL AND BAUMANN, 24 LONGACRE BUILDING BROADWAY NEW YORK."[70]

Chaplin went to visit what he assumed were lawyers, thinking that possibly his great-aunt, Mrs. Wiggins, had died in New York and left him a fortune. Instead, Kessel and Baumann asked Chaplin if he would join Sennett's company to replace Fred Mace, the star of the earliest Keystone comedies, who had left the company at the end of April. By July a contract was drawn up to engage Chaplin "as a moving picture actor to enact roles in the moving picture productions of the party of the first part" for $150 a week, tripling his current salary.[71] Chaplin played his last Karno performance on November 28, 1913, at the Empress Theatre in Kansas City.

"Fred Karno didn't teach Charlie and me all we know about comedy," Stan Laurel later said. "He just taught us most of it. If I had to pick an adjective to fit Karno, it would be supple…. He was flexible in just about everything, and above all he taught us to be supple. Just as importantly he taught us to be precise. Out of all that endless rehearsal and performance came Charlie, the most supple and precise comedian of our time."[72]

CHAPTER 2

Chaplinitis

CHAPLIN REACHED LOS ANGELES in early December 1913. On his first night in the city, he accidentally ran into Mack Sennett and Mabel Normand. Chaplin realized Sennett had the same reaction as Karno did to his youth and he reassured his new employer, "I can make up as old as you like."[1] When he showed up for work at the Keystone Studios, he got a quick lesson in the Sennett style—"We get an idea, then follow the natural sequence of events until it leads up to a chase which is the essence of our comedy."[2] In his first film, *Making a Living*, attired in a long coat, top hat, monocle, and a leering gaze, there is no evidence of the Chaplin the world would soon grow to know and love. Critics immediately singled him out—"The clever player who takes the part of a sharper … is a comedian of the first water."[3] For Chaplin's entrance in *Mabel's Strange Predicament*, his second film, he was simply supposed to enter a hotel lobby and provide some comic business. "Put on some comedy makeup," Sennett said. "Anything will do." "I had no idea what makeup to put on," Chaplin wrote in his autobiography.

> However, on the way to the wardrobe I thought I would dress in baggy pants, big shoes, a cane and a derby hat. I wanted everything to be a contradiction: the pants baggy, the coat tight, the hat small and the shoes large. I was undecided whether to look old or young, but remembering Sennett had expected me to be a much older man, I added a small mustache, which, I reasoned, would add age without hiding my expression.
>
> I had no idea of the character. But the moment I was dressed, the clothes and the make-up made me feel the person he was. I began to know him, and by the time I walked on to the stage he was fully born.[4]

Chaplin described the character as "many-sided, a tramp, a gentleman, a poet, a dreamer, a lonely fellow, always hopeful of romance and adventure. He would have you believe he is a scientist, a musician, a duke, and a polo-player. However, he is not above picking up cigarette-butts or robbing a baby of its candy. And, of course, if the occasion warrants it, he will kick a lady in the rear—but only in extreme anger!"[5] In Chaplin's third film, *Kid Auto Races at Venice, California*, shot one Saturday at a soapbox derby race in the seaside resort, cameras rolled on the birth of a legend.

Kid Auto Races was released two days before *Mabel's Strange Predicament* and gave audiences their first taste of Chaplin's soon-to-be-iconic character. The film is little more than a series of shots with the Tramp mugging in front of the camera, getting in the way of the director, and being a general nuisance. But, as Walter Kerr later pointed out, "he is elbowing his way into immortality, both as a 'character' in the film and as a professional comedian to be remembered. And he is doing it by calling to the camera as camera."[6]

Chaplin released six knockabout comedies over the next two months, all the while continuing to learn his craft. On his eleventh picture, *Mabel at the Wheel*, Chaplin clashed with director Mabel Normand. Sennett almost released him from his contract, but exhibitors were clamoring for more of the funny-looking funny man. Chaplin convinced Sennett to let him direct his next picture after agreeing to pay $1,500 if the film was unsuccessful. In 1924, Chaplin said his debut as a director was *Twenty Minutes of Love*, while in his autobiography he stated it was *Caught in the Rain*, his thirteenth picture. Whichever it is, from that point on, Chaplin directed nearly every film he appeared in through the remainder of his Keystone contract. With control came a newfound enjoyment in his work. "It was this charming alfresco spirit that was a delight—a challenge to one's creativeness," Chaplin said. "It was so free and easy—no literature, no writers, we just had a notion around which we built gags, then made up the story as we went along."[7] He often said, "All I need to make comedy is a park, a policeman and a pretty girl."[8]

Over the course of the year at Keystone, Chaplin made thirty-five films—split reels, one- and two-reelers—averaging one a week, including playing a supporting role in the first feature film comedy, *Tillie's Punctured Romance*, starring Marie Dressler. With such a hectic schedule, Chaplin was too busy learning his craft and adjusting to his new fame to pursue the violin and cello lessons that had occupied his spare time on the Karno tours. But even in his early comedies, Chaplin used music to create a mood. "Simple little tunes gave me the image for [certain] comedies." In *Twenty Minutes of Love*, "full of rough stuff and nonsense in parks, with policemen and nursemaids," he "weaved in and out of situations" to the tune of the 1914 two-step *Too Much Mustard*.[9] For *His Musical Career*, Chaplin used an upright piano as a silent catalyst frustrating the Tramp and Mack Swain as a pair of bumbling piano movers.

When Chaplin's contract was up at the end of a year, Sennett tried to hold his most valuable asset with an offer of $400 a week. Chaplin countered with $750, but Sennett foolishly turned it down, and his star went looking elsewhere.

*   *   *

The Essanay Film Manufacturing Company offered Chaplin an unprecedented $1,250 a week, plus a signing bonus of $10,000. The name Essanay came from the letters S and A of founders George K. Spoor, who managed the company and provided the financing, and G. M. Anderson, better known as "Broncho Billy" Anderson, the first cowboy film star. Essanay began in 1907, headquartered in Chicago, with a second studio in Niles, California.

Chaplin began work at the Chicago studio during the frigid winter of 1915 but quickly moved to the warmer climate of California, far away from Spoor's prying eyes. Over the course of the year, Chaplin made fourteen films for the studio, each distinctly marked with the "Essanay-Chaplin Brand." In these films, Chaplin paid homage to his past and sewed the seeds for future films. He reproduced Karno's classic *Mumming Birds* sketch as *A Night in the Show*, which gave audiences two Chaplins for the price of one, a gimmick he would reprise in *The Idle Class* (1921). He refined the boxing sequences from *The Champion* (1915) in *City Lights* (1931), and the Tramp's problems with the *Police* (1916) found even greater hilarity in *Easy Street* (1917), *A Dog's Life* (1918), and *The Kid* (1921). Within months of starting his work at Essanay, Chaplin's popularity exploded. Audiences could not get enough of the Tramp. Often, all it took was a poster of the character with the words "I'm here today" outside the theater to reel in audiences.

"The world has Chaplinitis," *Motion Picture Magazine* reported. "Any form of expressing Chaplin is what the public wants."[10] A barrage of newspaper articles detailed Chaplin's every move. The Tramp started appearing in comic strips, animated cartoons, and books. Tramp dolls and toys lined shelves. But it was not only the public who wanted a piece of Chaplin; celebrities did too, and Chaplin made it a point over the course of his career to meet the leading lights in music. Even in 1909, while the Karno troupe was playing at the Folies Bergère in Paris, Claude Debussy, who would debut his *Prélude à l'après-midi d'un faune* later that year in England, asked to meet the 20-year-old Chaplin. "The gentleman said that he had enjoyed my performance and was surprised to see how young I was," Chaplin remembered in his autobiography. "'You are instinctively a musician and a dancer,' said he." Not knowing how else to reply, Chaplin stood up and bowed. Debussy stood as well and extended his hand saying, "Yes ... you are a true artist."[11] "My father has always considered those moments with Debussy one of the highlights of his career," Charles Chaplin, Jr., said. "He spoke of it often to me when I was a boy."[12]

Prominent musicians such as pianists Ignacy Jan Paderewski and Leopold Godowsky later visited Chaplin at his studio. Chaplin claimed to have played "a bit of Bach" for virtuoso violinist Jascha Heifetz over dinner at the Chaplin home.[13] Fourteen-year-old violin prodigy Yehudi Menuhin visited the set of *City Lights* in 1930. David Raksin brought his composition teacher Arnold Schoenberg and his wife, Gertrude, on the set of *Modern Times.* Chaplin called the father of the tone row "a frank and abrupt little man whose music I much admired, and whom I had seen regularly at the Los Angeles tennis tournaments sitting alone in the bleachers wearing a white cap and a T-shirt." After seeing *Modern Times,* Schoenberg said he "enjoyed the comedy but my music was very bad," Chaplin said, "and I had to partly agree with him. In discussing music one remark of his was indelible: 'I like sounds, beautiful sounds.'"[14]

Artur Rubinstein and Igor Stravinsky later visited Chaplin at his home. "Rachmaninoff came once," Charles Chaplin, Jr., remembered, "but I missed seeing [him] because he visited my father on a week end when I wasn't there. Dad told me about it the next time I came up and I was almost inconsolable. Imagine it! Rachmaninoff at my father's house! Rachmaninoff, who was brilliant not just in one but in three fields, composer, pianist and conductor, and who had studied under Tschaikovsky [*sic*], my first guide in to the beautiful world of classical music!"[15] Once Chaplin moved to Switzerland in 1952, he continued to entertain a host of celebrated musicians, including Isaac Stern, Rudolf Serkin, Pablo Casals, and Clara Haskil.

It is also not surprising that Chaplin met the legendary Enrico Caruso, an unhappy meeting of two superstars. In 1920, Chaplin recounted the backstage event:

> Opera singers make me tired ... and I did not consider it complimentary at all when Mr. Guard of the Metropolitan Opera House once told me that Caruso had called me the "Caruso of the Movies."
>
> Some time later Mr. Guard made great preparations to present me to the famous tenor. I was taken to the opera house with a delegation of publicity promoters.
>
> Caruso was in his dressing room making up for the evening...
>
> When all was ready I was taken in the presence of the great Enrico, who not only did not receive me in state, but stood with his back toward me gluing something on his face in a mirror.
>
> The humor of the assumed superiority of a tenor over a comedian struck my funnybone

instantly. The questionable compliment for being called the "Caruso of the Movies" again rankled in my risibilities. So when, after several minutes had elapsed and my feet were getting cold and Caruso's back grew less and less inviting, I bawled out, looking over his shoulder into his face in the mirror:

"Greetings from the Caruso of the Movies to the Charlie Chaplin of the Operatic Stage!"
Enrico whirled around and I got a close-up of two angry eyes.
I did a quick fade.[16]

*　*　*

Chaplin's early fame extended to popular song as well. In the 1914 revue *Watch Your Step*, Lupino Lane sang "That Charlie Chaplin Walk." The *Charlie Chaplin Glide, Charlie Chaplin—March Grotesque*, "Those Charlie Chaplin Feet," "Charlie Chaplin, the Funniest of Them All," and "The Funniest Man in Pictures" also capitalized on the funnyman's fame. The French, who revere Chaplin to this day, had their own popular "Charlot One-Step." As late as 1925, the year of *The Gold Rush*, Chaplin was still being immortalized in song, albeit offensively, with W. G. Vance's "Why Can't Coons Have a Charlie (Chaplin) of Their Own?"

But for all the worldwide popularity his Essanay films brought him, Chaplin's experience at the studio was not a pleasant one. At the end of 1915, he got into a legal dispute with the studio over failing to complete five of the ten films he had promised. Essanay was asking half a million dollars in remuneration and postponed the release of *Burlesque on Carmen*, Chaplin's final film with the studio, a witty parody of Cecil B. DeMille's 1915 take on the Bizet opera. The studio eventually released it in an unauthorized version expanded with scenes filmed after Chaplin left. While Chaplin and Sydney were negotiating the new contract, the brothers entered into two unsuccessful business ventures.

The Charlie Chaplin Advertising Service Company, while short-lived, was the forerunner of Bubbles, Inc., S.A., which protects Chaplin's image from unauthorized reproduction. The second business venture may have been trying to cash in on some of Chaplin's popularity in music. Chaplin went into business with his old friend Bert Clark, a vaudevillian and former Keystone co-worker, and co-founded the Charlie Chaplin Music Publishing Company, the purpose of which was to "popularize the music written by the well known comedian."[17] The office was a room on the third floor of Blanchard Hall, a now-demolished downtown Los Angeles office building "devoted exclusively to music, art and science" at 233 South Broadway across from City Hall.[18] On the Broadway side, the building honored Frederick W. Blanchard, an influential force in the city's music scene and later the first president of the Hollywood Bowl. "H. Newmark," one of Los Angeles's leading citizens, was chiseled into the façade of the Hill Street side of the building on the site of Newmark's former residence. Bartlett Music Company was located on the ground floor, while the second floor was devoted to an 800-seat music hall for chamber music concerts and other programs, as well as studio space for 150 musicians and an art gallery.

Chaplin's publishing company printed two thousand copies of what he called "two very bad songs and musical compositions of mine—then we waited for customers."[19] Actually, Chaplin published *three* of his compositions—"Oh! That Cello," "There's Always Someone You Can't Forget," and *The Peace Patrol*. An envelope from the company stored at the Academy of Motion Picture Arts and Sciences' Margaret Herrick Library lists two other songs in which the authorship is unclear—"Little Madam Butterfly" and "The Return of the Troops." No evidence has surfaced to substantiate these two pieces, in authorship or as a product of Chaplin's company.

Popular music of the time was not surprisingly affected by the overwhelming shadow of the war in Europe. Recordings of "It's a Long Way to Tipperary," "I Didn't Raise My Boy to Be a Soldier," "The Star-Spangled Banner," and "America" (or "My Country, 'Tis of Thee") all topped the charts in 1915 and 1916. Irving Berlin and Jerome Kern penned their latest hits, while sentimental immigrant ballads such as "Ireland Must be Heaven, for My Mother Came from There" and "A Little Bit of Heaven (Sure, They Call It Ireland)" struck a deep chord. Chaplin's early songs may seem quaint given his overwhelming talent in so many other areas, but his musical output in 1916 was right in line with current trends.

"This Number Should Be On Every Piano," read the ad for "Oh! That Cello," which appeared on the back of the piano sheet music for Chaplin's instrumental, *The Peace Patrol*.

Cover image for the sheet music of "Oh! That Cello" (1916), one of three Chaplin compositions published by the short-lived Charlie Chaplin Music Publishing Co. "This Number Should Be on Every Piano," read the publicity ads (© Roy Export Co. Ltd.).

VERSE
The autumn leaves were swaying
A music man was playing,
I heard a girlie saying,
I love that fellow,
Who plays the Cello.
His music so apealing [sic]
Into my heart comes stealing.
I get a wond'rous feeling
From that melody.

CHORUS
Oh! that Cello!
It sounds so sweet and mellow,
When I hear you play that Cello
I get dreaming
I get a sentimental mood
A loving feeling
Play that music once again.
That fascinating mating
Love refrain.
Oh! memories that burn and pain,
Play that Cello for me once again.

VERSE
That fellow heard her saying
Oh! how she loved his playing.
So there was no delaying,
They never tarried,
Until they married.
There's not a little fellow,
Who's voice is not so mellow,
For when he starts to bellow
To that melody.

(Repeat CHORUS)[20]

The lyrics demonstrate the first instance of Chaplin using the antiquated rhyming style of the music halls. The prosaic "His appealing music came stealing into my heart" would not have scanned properly with the melody but has a much more subtle internal rhyme. Instead, "His music so apealing [sic] / Into my heart comes stealing" scans correctly but does not sit as well on the ear with its reordering of adjectives and verbs, all for the sake of the end rhyme. The overall mood of the music is indeed "sweet and

"Oh! That Cello" (1916, music and lyrics by Charles Chaplin)—The complete vocal line and lyrics for one of Chaplin's earliest published compositions (© Roy Export Co. Ltd.).

mellow." Arpeggiated eighth notes mimic a cello bow gently navigating the strings, while the descending stepwise half notes sigh as if autumn leaves were indeed swaying. Cellists Thomas Beckman and Gregory Hamilton have featured versions of the song for cello and piano on recent recordings, but the vocal version never gained a foothold.

Scholars usually ascribe the inspiration behind "There's Always One You Can't Forget" to Chaplin's lingering love for Henrietta (Hetty) Kelly, whom he had met in the summer of 1908 when she was a dancer with Bert Courts's Yankee Doodle Girls. Chaplin never indicated he wrote the song with Kelly, who later died in the flu epidemic of 1918, in mind, but it is easy to equate the words to the feelings he had for her.

Cover image for the sheet music of "There's Always One You Can't Forget" (1916), the inspiration for which is usually ascribed to Chaplin's lingering love for Henrietta (Hetty) Kelly, whom he had met in the summer of 1908 (© Roy Export Co. Ltd.).

VERSE
I sit alone at twilight gazing in the firelight glow,
And my mem'ry takes me back again to days of long ago;
Those happy days when you and I would share the sun and rain.
Ah! What would I give if I could live those happy days again.

CHORUS
There's always one you can't forget;
There's always one, one vain regret.
Tho' grief is dead, mem'ry survives;
Fate linked us two, mated our lives.
Why did we meet only to part?
Love comes but once into the heart.
Tho' it may cause pain and regret,
There's always one you can't forget.

VERSE
Tho' destiny decreed that we should live our lives apart,
Yet your mem'ry dear will ever be engraven in my heart.
The pain and anguish we endured, unspoken and unseen,
Why it nearly breaks my heart to think of that which might have been.

(Repeat CHORUS)[21]

There's al - ways one, you can't for - get, There's al - ways one, one vain re - gret,

The opening measures of the chorus from "There's Always One You Can't Forget" (1916), another early Chaplin composition published by the Charlie Chaplin Music Publishing Co.

Another indication that Chaplin may have written the song with Hetty in mind is a note at the top of the sheet music—"In this song the notes should be sustained: Legato—played as organ music." The instructions to play the slow waltz like an organ raises funeral images of lost love. Accidentals play a significant role in the melody, with the half notes bearing the brunt of the lover's pain on the downbeat before resolving to a passing tone above or below. The chorus is laid out primarily in a descending stepwise motion that circles back upon itself every two bars, as if trying to contain the "vain regret" and "grief." Only on "Fate linked us two / mated our lives" in the chorus does the melody open up beyond the stepwise motion to a C7 arpeggio.

The press did not believe it was *the* Charlie Chaplin behind the compositions, much less the owner of a music publishing business. "We are not sufficiently acquainted with the arcana of music publishing," said *Music Trade Review*, "to know whether the 'Charlie Chaplin' heralded in the September Autograph bulletin as the composer of a masterpiece entitled 'O! that Cello' [*sic*] (played by Lee S. Roberts), is actually the eminent artist whose ability to run down an ascending escalator or tap another gentleman on the coco with a billet of stove wood is the admiration of countless millions. We do not know, we say, but we certainly do care. Won't Mr. Roberts withdraw the veil and let us into the secret?"[22] Two weeks later, the riddle was solved. After "considerable anxiety [had] been expressed in various quarters" as to the identity of the composer, "the Q R S Co. aver that it is the simon pure Charles. He is doing quite a bit of composing nowadays between acts, so to speak, and moreover is publishing his own compositions. 'Oh that 'Cello' [*sic*] is quite pleasing even to the ear of one who does not revel in the popular music of the day. Lee Roberts made a hand played roll of it and has a nice letter from the real Charles written from Los Angeles giving his permission for its inclusion in the Q R S catalog."[23]

The "vague and impractical" Bert Clark put his dresser and handyman, Tom Harrington, in charge of the Chaplin publishing office. Once word got out, other publishers such as The Orpheus Music Publishing Co. and the British Music Company wanted a piece of the potentially lucrative pie. But "the enterprise was collegiate and quite mad," Chaplin later wrote. "I think we sold three copies, one to Charles Cadman, the American composer, and two to pedestrians who happened to pass our office on their way downstairs."[24] Chaplin's name alone should have been enough to ensure success, but he did not have the time to devote to a side business and certainly not while he was in the middle of negotiating a new film contract.

The office shuttered after a month and Clark went back to New York. Harrington stayed behind to become Chaplin's handyman, valet, and secretary—"the *sine qua non* of my existence," Chaplin said.[25] The company letterhead boasted of satellite offices in New York, Chicago, London, Paris, Johannesburg, and Sydney, though, given Chaplin's description of the company's poor sales record, the list seems little more than hyperbole. "Yes, I've composed my own music, I'm ashamed to confess," Chaplin said in 1921. "Were

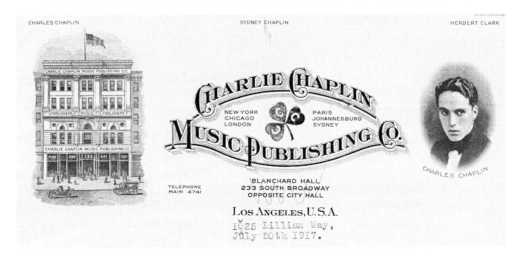

The letterhead for Chaplin's music publishing company boasted of unlikely satellite offices in New York, Chicago, London, Paris, Johannesburg, and Sydney (July 20, 1917). The address, 1025 Lillian Way, was the site of Chaplin's studio for his Mutual shorts and later Buster Keaton's studio (© Roy Export Co. Ltd.).

they bright, gay tunes? Not at all—very sentimental ballads. Almost weepy."[26] Today, all that remains of the Charles Chaplin Music Publishing Company are a few letters on the company masthead (which Chaplin used for years after the company had folded), some priceless, yellowed copies of sheet music, and a few unanswered questions.

*   *   *

On February 20, 1916, Chaplin appeared for one performance—"in the flesh—as he really is"—at a benefit concert starring John Philip Sousa's band at the Hippodrome in New York.[27] Sousa had a standing engagement at the 5,200-seat theater from September 1915 through June 1916 in a show called *Hip! Hip! Hooray!* He also conducted Sunday evening concerts, which included appearances by guest artists such as opera singers, dancers, and comedians.

Chaplin and Sousa met at the Hippodrome during one of the Sunday concerts, at which he told the bandleader, "I

Charlie Chaplin and John Philip Sousa, probably backstage at the Hippodrome in New York City, c. 1916 (Music Division, Library of Congress, https//www.loc.gov/item/sousa.200031365).

want to lead your band!" When Sousa asked him which number he wanted to conduct, Chaplin said Franz von Suppé's *Poet and Peasant* Overture. At an invitation from Hippodrome general manager Charles B. Dillingham, Chaplin agreed to appear at the benefit on two conditions—Sousa's band would play one of his own compositions ("The Peace Patrol"), and his fee would go to charity. Reports of Chaplin's fee were as high as $7,700, but he was actually paid $2,595.12, with the check divided between the Actors' Fund and the Variety Artists' Fund of England.[28]

The Peace Patrol, the third known composition published by Chaplin's music publishing company, is a lively 2/4 march that shows early evidence of rhythmic and melodic figures Chaplin would incorporate later in his film music. Though the march is ostensibly in the key of F major, the flatted third, sixth, and seventh notes of the scale (A, D, E) move much of the first and second strains into minor key territory. Chaplin inserts a brief repeated scalar melody where the trio should be, and the breakstrain's A-flat key signature becomes unstable with naturalized flats. Finally, the delayed trio gives us a bright F-major melody to finish the march in its home key. The Metropolitan Military Band later recorded the piece on Emerson Records, with a replica of Chaplin's signature embedded in the runout of the record.

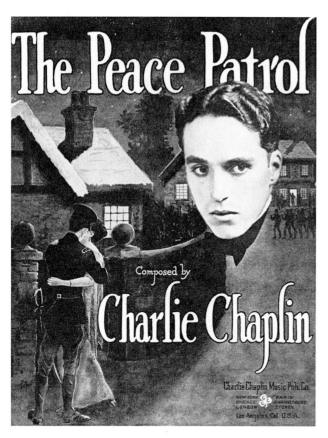

At the Hippodrome, Chaplin conducted Sousa's band in performances of von Suppé's *Poet and Peasant* Overture and his own *The Peace Patrol*, 1916 (© Roy Export Co. Ltd.).

A march, with its steady beat, would have been relatively easy for Chaplin to conduct, even as an amateur. But when it came time to rehearse *Poet and Peasant*, Sousa remembered in his autobiography, Chaplin "mounted the podium, took my baton and as the band started the stately measures of the opening, he proceeded to beat time fully four times too fast! That well-known blank expression came over his face but this time it was involuntary. 'That isn't it!' he exclaimed. I smiled. 'But I've played it many years,' I reminded him. Suddenly I realized that he remembered only the *allegro* and had forgotten all about the *moderato*, so I told the band to begin again, this time with the *allegro*, and we were off!"[29]

Opposite: The first strain (above) and trio (below) of *The Peace Patrol* (1916), the last of Chaplin's compositions published by his music publishing company.

FIRST STRAIN

TRIO

The benefit program also included ballerina Xenia Maclezova, formerly of Sergei Diaghilev's Ballets Russes, soprano Bettina Freeman, and pianist Leo Ornstein, who played "some real and some futurist music."[30] But the real guest star, of course, was Chaplin. Backstage, Chaplin ran a silver-topped baton, a gift from a female admirer, through his hair, chatting and walking around "as nervously as a schoolboy valedictorian before his ordeal." "Oh, God," he kept saying in mock anguish, "if it only was over!" Actor Tom Wise introduced Chaplin, thanking him on behalf of the Actors' Fund, who then strode onto the stage, said the *New York Tribune*, "look[ing] pleased and withal seemed to have a bad case of stage fright."[31]

"On the night of the performance," remembered Sousa, "the audience, reading his name on the program and never having seen him in the flesh, suspected a trick—some clever impersonator of Chaplin—but, as he came from the wings, he did his inimitably funny little step and slowly proceeded to the band-platform. The house, convinced, rang with applause."[32] As *The New York Times* reported,

> Charles Chaplin … broke all records when he appeared on the regular concert program at the Hippodrame [sic] last night. More than 600 persons occupied chairs on the stage, the orchestra pit was filled, and hundreds were turned away because there was no place to put them…
>
> The audience greeted him with prolonged applause when he walked out and shook hands with Mr. Sousa. He relieved the latter of his baton and conducted the band with apparent knowledge of how to do it and with a great variety of gestures. Then he turned and acknowledged the applause with a toss of his black hair and the familiar Chaplin smile, with its generous dental display. After he had led the band while it played his own composition, *The Peace Patrol*, Mr. Chaplin tried to bow himself off the stage, but the applause brought him back several times. Once he traversed a few steps to the wings with the walk that did more than anything else to make him famous. That brought a chorus of shouts and yells for more, but he only shook his head and in a bit of pantomime explained that he could only do his trick before the camera.[33]

The St. Louis Post-Dispatch reported, "On a curtain call he shook hands toward the audience, thanked it for the applause and told how pleased he was to be there. Still polite applause. Then, on the third curtain call, he shuffled off the stage with that funny little walk of his, known to movie fans all over the country. If there ever was pandemonium in a New York theatre it broke loose then and there. Handclapping, shrill whistles, the stamping of feet, cries of 'Do it again, Charlie!' from the gallery and all sorts of enthusiastic noises came from the largest crowd ever in the Hippodrome."[34]

Chaplin and Sousa remained friends. While the war still raged overseas, he conducted and performed with Sousa's 300-piece Great Lakes Naval Training Center Band to help raise money at Liberty Loan Rallies throughout the U.S., but his conducting career was short-lived.[35] "Some time ago I used to think it would be fine to be the leader of an orchestra," Chaplin said in 1921. "The grace as he waved his baton attracted me, the sense of command. I felt that way when I conducted the Hippodrome orchestra. But somehow I don't seem to care so much about it any more."[36]

Less than a week after his appearance with Sousa, Chaplin made history. On February 26, 1916, at age twenty-six, Chaplin signed with the Mutual Film Corporation. His new contract called for twelve two-reel comedies at a salary of $10,000 per week with a signing bonus of $150,000, totaling $670,000 a year. "Next to the war in Europe Chaplin is the most expensive item in contemporaneous history," proclaimed Mutual's publicist. The money and support from the company gave Chaplin the freedom he had been seeking. "It means that I am left free to be just as funny as I dare, to do the best work that is in me…. There is inspiration in it. I am like an author with a big publisher to give him circulation."[37]

Without Chaplin on their roster, Essanay struggled before shuttering in 1918, likely to be forgotten today if not for Chaplin's involvement. Like the Essanay films, the freedom Chaplin experienced in making the Mutual films also resulted in aspects that would color his films going forward. *The Rink* (1916) foreshadows the skating scene in *Modern Times* (1936), Chaplin used the "T" set from *Easy Street* (1917) in numerous films, and the mixture of comedy and pathos in *The Immigrant* (1917) became a Chaplin hallmark. "How the hell could he make ten thousand dollars a week after just two years in this country?" Mack Sennett asked rhetorically. "Because he was a genius, that's how. That little English boy was a pretty bright boy."[38]

Toward the end of his Mutual contract, Chaplin was offered a million dollars for another series of twelve films, and Mutual would bear all the production costs. But the contract came to an amicable end and Chaplin went in search of a new distributor, one that would grant him even more freedom. "Charlie [must] be allowed all the time he needs and all the money for producing [films] the way he wants," Sydney told the press. "It is quality, not quantity that we are after."[39] In June 1917, Chaplin signed with the First National Exhibitor's Circuit for eight films in eighteen months in return for $1 million, plus a $75,000 signing bonus. Chaplin was now his own producer and would shoulder the costs. First National paid for the prints and advertising, and received thirty percent of the total rents for their distribution fees, splitting the remaining net profits equally with Chaplin. Even more importantly, after five years, the rights to his films reverted to Chaplin. Those rights gave Chaplin control over their presentation and allowed him to repackage them—whether as a compilation (*The Chaplin Revue*), separately, or paired—and compose new scores later in his career.

Since First National did not have a studio, Chaplin paid $35,000 for four acres of land at the southeast corner of La Brea and Sunset Boulevard to build his own. The site had "a very fine ten-room house and five acres of lemon, orange and peach trees," he said. "We built a perfect unit, complete with developing plant, cutting room, and offices."[40] Chaplin designed the studio "to give the effect of a picturesque English village street"[41] and broke ground in October. He also made sure that music stayed close, with his small office consisting of "one small window, three straight-back wooden chairs, an old table, about half a dozen books with peeling spines, and an ancient upright piano hideously out of tune," said Alistair Cooke.[42] From that little office came comedic ideas for some of Chaplin's most enduring classics and his first attempts at marrying music with film.

CHAPTER 3

The Sound of Silents

THE LIST OF SILENT FILMS that had original scores written for them is relatively small. Scholars usually credit Camille Saint-Säens with the first original score for the 1908 French film *L'assassinat du duc de Guise*. A few major American productions like *The Birth of a Nation* (1915) received original (or mostly original) scores, at least for the premiere, but the music for most films was either left up to the theater's music director or in-house musicians. Chaplin films in a hundred different theaters had a hundred different accompaniments. In 1915, *Music Trade Review* commented on the "Need for Intelligent Film Players"—"The next picture portrayed the adventures of one Chaplin, who went through innumerable divagations, which no doubt were most amusing, for we laughed till our sides shook. So it was not until the end of this film that it suddenly dawned on us that the player was still playing the *Rienzi* overture. We are not, we trust, unduly fussy, but it distinctly annoys us to have to associate Wagner with Chaplin. In the words of Archer avenue, 'It can't be did.'"[1]

The nickelodeon houses consisted of an orchestra "pit" of three players—violin, piano, and drums, occasionally augmented by a cornetist and trombone player, which performed during the presentation of the vaudeville segment. Arranger and conductor Carli Elinor, who worked with Chaplin on *The Gold Rush*, gave a colorful account of his days in silent film music:

> The grinding of the projection machine, the crying of an infant, or the deep breathing of a tired businessman, became very disturbing. So a decrepit piano player began to tinkle waltz music during death scenes and a drummer would shake a sandbox whenever he saw a lake on the screen, to let the audience know that the lake was made entirely of water. Smaller theaters had an electrical piano which was going all the time, playing the *Merry Widow* waltz to a prize-fighting scene or the *Unfinished Symphony* to a comedy scene. When the instrument stopped, an usherette would walk down the aisle and you would see her putting on a new roll, maybe her favorite tune, disregarding the mood of the scene on the film; or if there were not many rolls to choose from, the same one would be played over and over again. In those days music to pictures was an incidental matter regarded by the house manager as so much necessary noise to be obtained as cheaply as possible."[2]

The "necessary noise" eventually transformed into combinations that allowed greater flexibility, which cost anywhere from $10,000 to $100,000. As the orchestras grew, so too did the reputation of the man in charge—the music director—whose name would be noted in programs, on the screen, in newspapers and billboard ads, and even in marquee lights on the front of the theater. The music budget in the larger theaters far exceeded the cost of the film rental, with some paying $2,000–$5,000 weekly for their music.[3]

Fredrick Stahlberg, director of the Rivoli Theatre orchestra who would later revise and adapt Louis F. Gottschalk's already revised score to *A Woman from Paris*, gave a detailed description of the life of theater musicians:

> I wonder if the average person appreciates the knowledge, both technical and theoretical, a musician must possess to be a first rate member of a "movie" orchestra. I am inclined to think they don't realize it. For every man in our orchestra here has had a great deal of ensemble experience before he came to us. That is necessary. And every man must not only be able to read anything at sight—that means the most difficult music, but he must play it well. He must not only be able to play whatever is put before him correctly, but he must always be on the job. He can't go to sleep for one moment. These are the prime prerequisites, but there are others, too.
>
> If you attend the movies here or anywhere, possibly you know what it means for the orchestra to interpret films, but you may not realize the mental effort constantly required. Of course, you know that instead of being able to play a composition in its entirety that often, in the very middle of an intensely difficult selection, the scene depicted on the screen shifts suddenly and the music must be made to interpret a totally different atmosphere. But do you appreciate the mental activity each man of the orchestra must possess to still hold your interest in that film? At any rate, it is only by watching his conductor as a cat watches a mouse that he is ready on the instant to shift from, let us say, Wagner's "Ring" music to a dainty French gavotte, written in different time—and shift not as an individual but as a member of the orchestra, always together. That is difficult, very difficult indeed...
>
> Every performance goes like clock-work and to this day, I cannot get over the fact that although the orchestra plays the same music four times every day for one week—in all, twenty-eight times—they play it each time just as conscientiously as at the first performance when it is fresh and interesting to them. On Sundays, we rehearse from nine-thirty till twelve or after, and with this one rehearsal the men play the afternoon and evening performances, and are pretty well fagged out when the day is over. This is the only rehearsal we have each week. I think it is remarkable the way they do it, and I have nothing but the greatest praise for them.[4]

Every theater hired its own musicians, from lone piano player to multi-piece symphony orchestras, and the quality of the accompanying music depended on their whims and skill level. In an attempt to bring uniformity to the live performance, American Vitagraph was the first to suggest "cue lists" for its films in the *Vitagraph Bulletin*. Music publishers quickly recognized it as an opportunity to plug their product. In 1913, Carl Fischer was the first publisher to start printing cue sheets, compiled by employee Max Winkler, which consisted of a list of works from classical masters, popular ballads and dance tunes, and short pieces explicitly composed for various emotions and actions. The following year J. Bodewalt Lampe published *Remick Folio of Moving Picture Music*, which contained over a hundred "dramatic, descriptive and characteristic numbers suitable for any theatrical performance or exhibition requiring incidental music."[5] Prolific composer J. S. Zamecnik released his tunes in a series of volumes for Sam Fox Publishing—*Sam Fox Moving Picture Music* and later the *Sam Fox Photoplay Edition*. Soon after, magazines and trade journals added regular columns to their publications for the silent film musician, like "Playing the Pictures" (*Film Index*) and "Music for the Pictures" (*The Moving Picture World*).

Ernö Rapée, the conductor at the Rialto, Rivoli, and Capitol Theatres in New York, compiled two of the most comprehensive publications. In 1924, Rapée published *Motion Picture Moods*, an exhaustive 658-page "rapid-reference collection" that categorized the musical entries into fifty-two "moods and situations," everything from Aeroplane, Battle, and Birds to Misterioso, Monotony, Wedding, and Western. The following year he published the 510-page instruction manual *Encyclopedia of Music for Moving Pictures*, which proclaimed itself on the cover "As Essential as the Picture." The book listed suggestions and publisher information for nearly every conceivable scene (from Cannibal Music to the Zoo), emotion (Happy, Neutral), and musical form (Agitato, Andante), plus extensive instructions on orchestra make-up and information on maintaining a proper theater music library.[6]

In 1925, Ernst Luz, musical director of the Loews theater chain, developed his system called *Motion Picture Synchrony* in which the various emotions and actions were color-coded to make it easier for musicians to synchronize the music in performance. Luz broke his system down into a dozen colors, each representing a separate action, mood, or emotion. Some colors were obvious—red for actions or characters "which wield an influence of evil or threaten danger" or white for love themes.[7] There were light shades of blue and green. Yellow served as a transition between pieces marked by primary colors like dark blue and red. Gray was labeled "the Player's Color."[8] Luz encouraged musicians to "THINK IN COLORS! SEE IN COLORS!! DO IN COLORS!!! WIN WITH COLORS!!!!"[9]

Cue sheets of the period were laid out textually with numbered cues followed by an (A) or (D) to describe the action on screen or a (T) and the first few words of text from the title card. The name of the piece, the composer, and timing for the cue followed. In July 1922, "a new idea in music cue sheets" was conceived and patented by M. J. Mintz and James C. Bradford called the "Thematic Music Cue Sheet" and published by Cameo Music Publishing Company in New York. The "new idea" was to include a few bars of manuscript, plus the publisher for each piece of music. "The new cue sheet does away with the error," said an announcement in the *Exhibitors Herald*, "because of the fact that on it, the musician not only gets the correct tempo, but the correct mood, and actual melody, so that when he is compelled to use a different number, he can make the substitution without injuring the presentation."[10]

While cue sheets provided inspiration for small-town theater musicians, major films featured specially compiled orchestral scores using the same process of combining classical, popular, and library pieces. Occasionally, larger theaters outside of New York and Los Angeles received the "roadshow" version, which incorporated the compiled score, but only theaters with the requisite orchestra and music budget featured this luxury. Cue sheets might have been fine for the smaller theaters, but Chaplin had bigger plans for his premieres.

In November 1920, the short-lived Synchronized Scenario Music Company was formed to provide musical scores "for every motion picture feature of merit.... The music scenarios are so arranged that they may be used by piano or organ alone or by a ten-piece orchestra. It is declared that all can be used in perfect accordance with any speed of projection."[11] With the promise of "no more trouble cueing pictures according to the various conflicting 'cue sheets'"[12] and the tagline "Better Music Draws Better Crowds," an ad for the new company explained the new rental service:

> The pulling power of good musical programs has been proved by the most successful theatre managers everywhere. But no matter how big your orchestra, no matter how large the salaries you pay to your musicians, your music is not good unless every bar and line of it is expressly arranged and adapted to each foot of every film as it is run.
>
> No matter how beautiful it is played, neither "The Star Spangled Banner" [*sic*] nor the "Memphis Blues" is a suitable and fitting musical accompaniment for a "sad parting" on the screen. Yet just such "bulls" are made every day in theaters everywhere, while audiences laugh in derision.
>
> Synchronized Scenario Music Service makes all such mistakes impossible by supplying with each day's new film a specially prepared and arranged music score to meet the needs of the largest orchestra or a single pianist.[13]

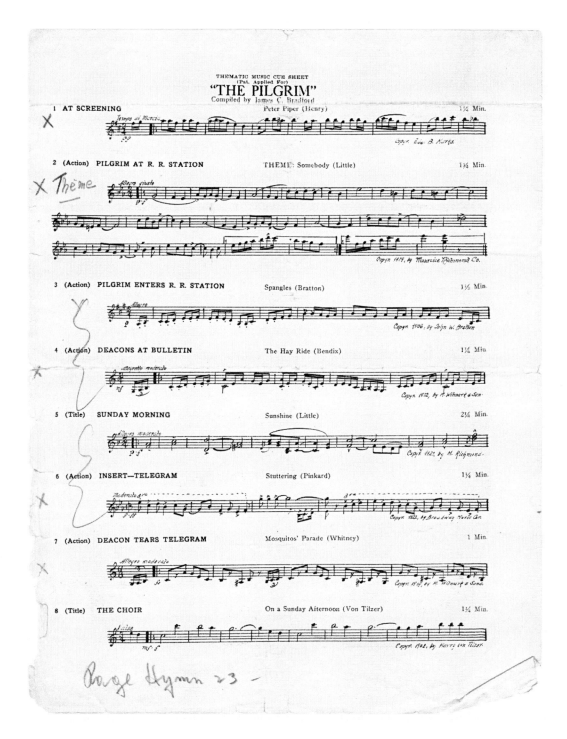

The cue sheet for *The Pilgrim* (1922), compiled by James C. Bradford, shows the "new idea" of including snippets of actual music to assist theater musicians and help the publisher sell music (courtesy Theodore Huff Collection, George Eastman House, International Museum of Photography and Film).

Composers began to vary different familiar melodies to fit the actors' changes of mood, so that "the entire emotional gamut of the story was vividly presented to the audience. The key of one tune was in perfect relation to the one that followed, and blending was done with such artistry that through the entire picture there was no sharp break."[14] In the beginning, the company produced scores written for a twelve-piece orchestra— piano, organ, and ten other pieces—and "a central theme will run through all scores," said *Exhibitors Herald*. "The music will be simplified so that all musicians can readily play it. The scores are timed. On the margins appear notations of the change of scenes and all of the subtitles, so that a leader can follow the film closely. This is expected to be of special value to cities where a film has been censored, as notations on the margin will make it a simple matter to bring the orchestra up to the film when an elimination is noted. Black arrows on the margin call attention to an approaching subtitle. Other warning notations serve similar purposes."[15]

Three of the top names in film music personally supervised the music—Joseph Carl Breil, James C. Bradford, and Carl Edouarde, the musical director at the Strand Theatre in New York, where Chaplin's *The Kid* began its theatrical run in 1921. Within six months, prominent theater conductors Hugo Riesenfeld and Ernö Rapée also joined the staff. *The Kid* was the first score prepared and issued by the new company, with Edouarde no doubt having a great deal to do with the preparation.

*   *   *

Chaplin and Jackie Coogan on the set of *The Kid*, c. 1920 (© Roy Export SAS. Courtesy Cineteca di Bologna).

In February 1921, with the release of *The Kid*, Chaplin's eighteen-month First National contract was entering its fourth year. His output so far included two bona fide classics (*A Dog's Life* and *Shoulder Arms*), a couple of pleasant shorts (*Sunnyside* and *A Day's Pleasure*), and *The Bond*, a propaganda film for the Liberty Loan Committee to help sell Liberty Bonds during the war. *The Kid* represents a major leap forward for Chaplin as a filmmaker, in length and story. "Before that my pictures were expanded gags," he said. "Funny situations run into one another. They were pretty rough around the edges."[16] Originally called *The Waif*, the tale of the Tramp caring for a baby he finds in an alley and rearing as his own is one of Chaplin's most famous films. The Tramp's garret bears a striking similarity to Chaplin's description of his childhood home and the scenes of separation when the authorities cart off the Kid in tears to the orphanage no doubt owe their poignant verisimilitude to similar scenes of separation and reconciliation with Hannah when Chaplin was a boy. Chaplin spent $500,000 and eventually devoted eighteen months to *The Kid*, except for a two-week break during which he quickly finished work on *A Day's Pleasure* to appease his distributors, who were not accustomed to waiting such a long time for a Chaplin picture. However, it was a period plagued with drama and heartbreak.

Much of the drama stemmed from to Chaplin's marriage to Mildred Harris, the first in a string of disastrous relationships that would plague his career. Chaplin met the sixteen-year-old actress in 1917 at a party held at Samuel Goldwyn's beach house. Mildred asked him to drive her home and what followed were "dinners, dances, moonlit nights and ocean drives," Chaplin said, "and the inevitable happened—Mildred began to worry."[17] Shortly after Chaplin finished filming *Shoulder Arms*, Mildred announced she was pregnant. Fearing scandal, Chaplin arranged for a quiet marriage ceremony on September 23, 1918. The pregnancy was a false alarm, and Chaplin quickly became bored with his child bride, complaining to Douglas Fairbanks she was "no mental heavyweight."[18] Mildred finally became pregnant, but on July 17, 1919, she gave birth to a malformed son, Norman Spencer Chaplin. The child lived only three days and was buried in Inglewood Cemetery in a grave marked "The Little Mouse," Mildred's pet name for the boy.

Suppressing his grief, Chaplin went back to work and began auditioning children for *The Waif* ten days after his son's death. He discovered Jackie Coogan in a Sid Grauman Prologue, "The 1920 Bathing Girl Revue," at Grauman's Million Dollar Theatre in August of 1919.[19] In addition to twenty-four bathing girls in beach attire who represented different Los Angeles motion picture studios, the Prologue featured ten children from two to five years of age, also in bathing costumes. "Little Jackie Coogan, the four-year-old boy," said *Motion Picture News,* "gave a burlesque version of the 'shimmy' in his bathing suit and brought down the house."[20] Chaplin hired the talented boy at $75 a week. "All children in some form or another have genius; the trick is to bring it out in them," Chaplin said. "With Jackie it was easy. There were a few basic rules to learn in pantomime and Jackie very soon mastered them. He could apply emotion to the action and action to the emotion, and could repeat it time and time again without losing the effect of spontaneity."[21] The musicians, Coogan recalled, "helped a lot. We had music on the set. And Chaplin used to talk, as every director did, while the shot was in process, being silent pictures. He'd say, 'Now you really love this man, and he's gone, and they're going to take you.' … It works on you."[22]

While work proceeded quickly, Chaplin's marriage was crumbling. "Although I had grown fond of Mildred, we were irreconcilably mismated. Her character was not mean, but exasperatingly feline. I could not reach her mind. It was cluttered with pink-ribboned foolishness. She seemed in a ditch, looking always for other horizons."[23] The two separated and Mildred eventually filed for divorce, originally accusing Chaplin of desertion, which her attorneys later changed to cruelty. Chaplin halted the filming of *The Kid* on March 15, 1920, and in August he was forced to flee California with the negative of the film to keep Mildred from attaching it in her divorce settlement. In the early morning hours, Chaplin ordered cinematographer Rollie Totheroh and his second cameraman Jack Wilson to pack the 400,000 feet of uncut negative into coffee tins and travel by train to Utah, where California community property laws did not apply.

"There had been satire, farce, realism, naturalism, melodrama and fantasy, but raw slapstick and sentiment, the premise of *The Kid*, was something of an innovation," Chaplin said.[24] He asked for more money, but First National offered instead to pay him as if the film were three two-reelers. Chaplin took the film to New York, traveling incognito for fear Mildred's lawyers might subpoena him, and completed the editing and lab work in a rented vacant studio in Bayonne, New Jersey. Chaplin eventually received his advance of $1,500,000 and fifty percent of the net profits after the company recouped the advance. First National's "ruthless attitude had so embittered me that it impeded the progress of my work."[25] They continued to edit the film in a hotel room in Salt Lake City, where they later previewed a rough cut. The divorce went through on November 19, 1920. Mildred was awarded $100,000 and a share of community property.

Patrons of Carnegie Hall saw the world premiere of *The Kid* on January 21, 1921, in a pre-public subscription showing as part of a benefit for the National Board of Review's Children's Fund. Tickets ranged from seventy-five cents to $2.50 and the announcement "started a demand for boxes among producers and stars of motion picture companies

Program listing for *The Kid* premiere on January 21, 1921, in a pre-public subscription showing at Carnegie Hall as part of a benefit for the National Board of Review's Children's Fund (courtesy Carnegie Hall Archives).

which indicates that the house will be sold out before the doors are opened for the show-ing."[26] The evening began with a screening of Ernst Lubitsch's *Passion* (1919), starring a future Chaplin paramour, Pola Negri. A musical program followed, supervised by the powerful film impresario Samuel "Foxy" Rothapfel, including a set of three dances by Michio Ito—Tchaikovsky's *Nutcracker*, Delibes's *Sylvia*, and Debussy's "Golliwog's Cake-Walk" from *Children's Corner*. *The Kid's* regular public engagement began on February 6 at Rothapfel's Strand Theatre in New York.

When it opened in 1914, the Strand, which stood at the corner of Broadway and 47th Street, cost over $1 million and became the largest theater in the country devoted exclusively to motion pictures. It seated 3,500 people and accommodated an onstage orchestra of twenty-five musicians. The screen was built especially for the theater and set on a double stage—"a stage built upon a stage." The theater installed two organs and hired two separate organists. Ferns and flowers surrounded the orchestra, with a large fountain directly in front of them. The theater boasted eighty-five employees and Rothapfel staged every picture produced at the theater.[27]

Conductor Carl Edouarde's long tenure at the Strand, as was the case with his col-leagues at other theaters, yielded "one of the best musical organizations in the country."[28] Cleveland-born Edouarde (1875–1932) received his musical education at the Royal Con-servatory in Leipzig, where he graduated in 1889, receiving a violin from Kaiser Wilhelm II. He returned to the U.S. as a solo violinist with Allessandro Liberati's band and taught

New York's Strand Theatre during a presentation of the opera *Carmen* in tabloid form. The orchestra sits in its usual spot on the stage, while four principals from the opera sing the chief arias in the back where the movie screen is normally located. *Motion Picture News*, January 26, 1918, 554 (courtesy Media History Digital Library).

violin in Cleveland before giving up teaching to move to New York. Edouarde was music director at a series of hotels before meeting Rothapfel in 1912 and joining him at the Regent Theatre.

Rothapfel and Edouarde went to the Strand when it opened in 1914, where its thirteen-piece orchestra was the largest at the time. "There is no 'bunk' about the Strand orchestra," said *Variety*, "no blatant brass, all the music being rendered legitimately from the proper instruments required for their proper interpretation. Edouarde doesn't prance about like a jumping-jack when directing, employing only such gestures as are essential to a proper emphasizing of such passages in the score as require it." And in perhaps a dagger aimed at certain other conductors, "Edouarde gets his hair cut regularly and otherwise comports himself like a human being."[29] "All my colleagues predicted failure, holding that Broadway was not ready for it," Edouarde later said of employing large orchestras. "That 60,000,000 paid admissions prove the contrary. Our musical library has grown from a dress-suit case full of music for the opening performance to a collection costing $50,000 in the care of two librarians."[30]

For *The Kid*, Edouarde conducted a program that began with Victor Herbert's overture from his 1915 operetta *The Princess Pat*. The *Strand Topical Review*, a newsreel made up of extracts from the Pathé and International weeklies, preceded the Paramount-Bray Pictographs and "Topics of the Day," selected and compiled by the Strand's Managing Director, Joseph Plunkett. An educational travelogue, *Hide and Go Seek*, led into the musical prologue to the film featuring the Strand Male Quartette. After the screening, soprano Eldora Stanford sang "The Barefoot Trail," followed by the Kineto educational film *Thrills*, which showed "thrills experienced in sports and everyday life."[31] Organists Frederick M. Smith and Herbert Sisson closed out the program with Eugène Gigot's majestic *Grand Choeur Dialogué*.[32]

The New York Times said *The Kid* was "about the best" of all Chaplin's films. The review

Joseph Plunkett, Managing Director of the Strand Theatre in New York, and Music Director Carl Edouarde. Edouarde was also a staff member of the Synchronized Scenario Music Company and helped compile the score for the premiere of *The Kid*. *Moving Picture World*, April 18, 1925, 661 (courtesy Media History Digital Library).

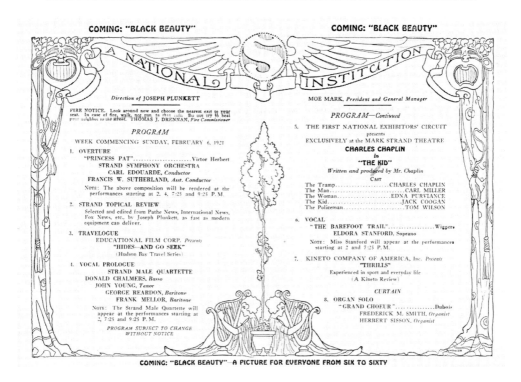

The souvenir program for the regular run of *The Kid* at the Strand Theatre, c. 1921, details a typical mixture of live music, newsreels, and other shorts that accompanied the feature film (Billy Rose Theatre Division, The New York Public Library for the Performing Arts).

remarked on the "spots of the vulgarity and witless horseplay that seem ineradicable from the Chaplin comedies," a comment that critics had hurled at nearly every Chaplin film for the past seven years, but "it is a real cinematographic work in the universal language of moving pictures."[33] The National Board of Review said, "There is … more feeling, and more understanding of childhood, than in a hundred Little Lord Fauntleroys…. An astonishing picture, true to the common stuff of human attributes. A picture that makes a very deep scratch in the possibilities of the screen."[34]

Chaplin said film resembled music more than any other medium. "Like music, it always starts—for me at least—not from an idea, but from an emotion, and of that emotion the idea is born."[35] Even before he began composing his own scores, Chaplin had distinct ideas of how music should function within a film. "You cannot emphasize too much the importance of orchestral scores for pictures," he said in a 1925 interview. "I believe that the score should be made as the picture is made, and not that people should spend a year making a film and then have a score written in a week. It is just as though Pavlova were to say, 'I shall dance—and, oh, yes, we will have some music, too,' at the last minute. The picture of to-day is the dance, the swing and the movement, the orchestral arrangement being just as important."[36]

At *The Kid* premiere in Los Angeles at the Kinema Theatre, First National's first-run movie house, the playbill contained a list of musical pieces "synchronized by Rene Williams from the score selected by Charles Chaplin."[37] There is no information whether the Kinema score was the same that premiered in New York. And unlike all the other scores Chaplin

The playbill for *The Kid* at the Kinema Theatre in Los Angeles included a page listing pieces "from the score selected by Charlie Chaplin." It is unclear whether these compositions were part of the compilation score that premiered with the film earlier in New York (© Roy Export Co. Ltd.).

worked on from this point forward, no conductor's score, instrumental parts, or cue sheet for *The Kid* exist in the Chaplin Archive. Unless one of these elements surfaces at some later date, "selected by" is the extent of Chaplin's attributable musical involvement.

     This list provides a welcome window into Chaplin's original musical ideas for the film, even taking into account the playbill editor's sloppiness with titles and composer spellings. Assuming that the musical selections for the Kinema and Strand matched, the list is a typical example of compilation scores of the period—dated parlor songs, popular stage selections, instrumental works by the best in opera and operetta, and library pieces written by some of the most popular silent film music composers of the period.

Without a score or cue sheet to reference, and taking the program list in film order, some numbers are relatively easy to place within the context of the story. Gounod's arrangement of *Ave Maria* fits easily over the early scenes of Edna Purviance's saintly Woman released from the imposing charity ward with her newborn in her arms. "Rock-a-Bye Baby" is an obvious choice to underscore Charlie's first scenes with his young charge on the curb. The tender lullaby provides humorous musical irony to the Tramp's consideration of dropping the baby down the sewer grate. Walter E. Miles's *Cupid's Frolic* undoubtedly scored the Tramp's dream sequence, which Chaplin took "bodily" from J. M. Barrie's *A Kiss for Cinderella*—"I told him so when I came back to London a year later."[38] Chaplin cast twelve-year-old Lillita MacMurray as the flirting angel, three years before he signed her as his leading lady in *The Gold Rush*, where he gave her the professional name Lita Grey. The inclusion of Sol P. Levy's *Flirty-Flirts* seems a sly wink to Chaplin and MacMurray's budding relationship on set.

The Kid was so popular that it broke the Strand Theatre's one-week policy for the first time and played a second week. As David Robinson points out, over the next three years, Chaplin distributed the film in some fifty countries across the world. By 1924 the only places that had not seen it were the Soviet Union, Yugoslavia, and Colombia.[39] First National President Robert Lieber later visited Chaplin on the set of *The Idle Class* to commend him personally on the world's record set by *The Kid*—an astonishing 56,700,000 people in the U.S. had seen the film in its first twelve weeks. "I want to congratulate you," Lieber said, "for the joy, the sunshine and the laughter you have brought to countless millions."[40]

Lieber may have been happy with *The Kid*'s box office performance, but Chaplin was still smarting at First National's poor treatment of him when he had asked for more money. He wanted nothing more than to be done with the contract, but he still had three more films to deliver. Over the next year and a half, Chaplin completed work on *The Idle Class*, *Pay Day*, and *The Pilgrim* before his contract with First National was finally at an end, and he could release films under his new distribution company.

The idea for United Artists was born during the 1918 Liberty Bonds tour with Douglas Fairbanks and Mary Pickford. Chaplin was unhappy with First National's refusal to better his contract and Paramount was not interested in renewing Fairbanks and Pickford's contracts. While on tour, the trio met Oscar Price, press agent for Secretary of the Treasury William Gibbs McAdoo. Price suggested that the three friends band together and distribute their own films. In late 1918, amid rumors of the film companies collaborating on a plan to put a stop to the astronomical star salaries, they met with director D. W. Griffith and Western star William S. Hart to discuss the prospect. Fairbanks and Chaplin hired a private detective to infiltrate the meeting of industry heads held in January 1919 at the Alexandria Hotel in Los Angeles. As a result of the detective's discreet reports, a press conference was called on January 15 to announce the formation of a new distribution company called United Artists. Hart pulled out of the deal by the time Chaplin, Fairbanks, Pickford, and Griffith signed the articles of incorporation on February 5. It would be four long years before Chaplin could contribute a film as part of the new company. And as a symbol of his newfound freedom and control, he decided to film something incredibly risky.

* * *

In 1923, Chaplin was at a turning point in his filmmaking. "My future production activities will be largely guided by the manner in which the public receives my latest picture *A Woman of Paris*," he told *Exhibitors Trade Review*. Edna Purviance stars as Marie St. Clair, a French country girl who tries to elope with her lover, artist Jean Millet (Carl Miller). When Jean's father dies the evening of their elopement, leaving Marie stranded at the train depot, she takes the train to Paris, not knowing what has transpired, eventually becoming the mistress of wealthy playboy Pierre Revel (Adolphe Menjou). Marie later accidentally meets Jean and rekindles their affair. Hearing the news that Pierre is engaged, she breaks it off, though she reneges when she thinks Jean proposed in a moment of weakness. Jean confronts Pierre and Marie in a restaurant and shoots himself in despair. Distraught, Marie leaves Pierre and does penance by helping Jean's mother care for orphaned children in the country. Chaplin appears only in shadow (and uncredited) as a porter at the train station.

The film was the result of relationships with three women in Chaplin's life. Edna Purviance had been Chaplin's leading lady for eight years in over thirty-five films, and he wanted to give her a proper dramatic starring role. Though the two were "emotionally estranged, I was still interested in her career," Chaplin said. "But, looking objectively at Edna, I realized she was growing rather matronly, which would not be suitable for the feminine confection necessary for my future pictures." Chaplin had toyed with the idea of adapting *The Trojan Women* for her as well as starring as Napoleon opposite her Josephine. "But the further we delved into the life of Josephine," Chaplin remembered, "the more Napoleon got in the way. So fascinated was I with this flamboyant genius that a film about Josephine ended in a pale cast of thought, and Napoleon loomed up as a part I might play myself."[41]

Chaplin had had a "bizarre, though brief, relationship" with Peggy Hopkins Joyce (1893–1957), a barber's daughter who became an actress, artist model, and Ziegfeld girl. He remembered her as "bedecked in jewels and with a collected bank-roll of three million dollars" from her five millionaire ex-husbands. "She came direct from Paris, attractively gowned in black," Chaplin said, "for a young man had recently committed suicide over her. In this funereal chic, she invaded Hollywood."[42] One of Joyce's anecdotes about her affair with Henri Letellier, the well-known French publisher of *Le Journal*, inspired the tragedy in the film.

The third woman was the glamorous yet temperamental Polish-born actress Pola Negri. For the first time, Chaplin's private life became a public spectacle and the ups and downs of his tempestuous affair and engagement with Negri, whom he had met in October 1922 at the Actors' Fund Pageant, were reported and read with delicious glee. The break-up three days after filming wrapped on *A Woman of Paris* lends credence to the theory that Chaplin based much of Marie St. Clair's sophistication on Negri's cosmopolitanism.

Chaplin filmed *A Woman of Paris* like he did his comedies—without a formal script—highly unusual for a dramatic production. Journalist Monta Bell, who had helped document Chaplin's 1921 European trip in *My Trip Abroad*, and had become an assistant and gag man on *Pay Day* and *The Pilgrim* (even acting a small role as a policeman), served as assistant director and scenario consultant on the new film. Chaplin considered nearly two-dozen titles, including *Public Opinion* and *Destiny*. He also stuck to his habit of filming in narrative order, which was as rare then as it is today. But Chaplin's most striking innovation was his attempt "to convey psychology by subtle action."[43]

The public has long been saying that it wants something new in the way of pictures. It has been saying that directors are too frank in the handling of details in a picture. People have been complaining that directors did not give them credit for having any intelligence. Well, I have taken them at their word in my picture and I have left the greater part of it for solution to their intelligence.

I have tried to create something human and something natural. There are subtleties in the picture, numbers of them, which will require rapt intelligence to catch or many of them will be overlooked. I have tried to keep my principals from acting. I have tried with delicate little natural touches to make my pathos, humor and drama clear, and at the same time I have tried to keep the members of the cast from "mugging."

One of the most difficult tasks I had when I started this picture eight months ago was to make my cast forget that they had ever appeared before a camera before. It required great energy and patience to keep them from registering joy, gloom and the other stock elements of pictures that are invariably registered in the same way. I think I have gotten my points over better by the naturalness of the action and the lack of facial expression than it could otherwise have been accomplished...

I have every confidence that the public will get the meaning of the action in the picture and will grasp most of the points. Out in Vernon, California, I had a showing to which I invited quite a number of factory workers in order to get their reaction. At some of the more subtle points over which I had some doubts there were such ejaculations as "Oh, boy," and "Hot dawg," so I figured the stuff must be pretty good...

I only hope *A Woman of Paris* is received in the way in which I expect it to be. If it is you will find a different art and quite a change in future productions generally.[44]

But audiences—then and now—are not known for their appreciation of cinematic subtlety. "Does the public want truth in motion pictures?" Chaplin wondered. "Does the public feel willing to accept an unhappy ending? Would the public like to see a problem presented to them entertainingly and let them solve it themselves? ... [*A Woman of Paris*] is rather intimate, simple and human, putting forth a problem that is as old as the ages, handling it with as much truth as I can put into it and giving it a treatment as near realism as I have been able to devise."[45]

A Woman of Paris premiered on September 26, 1923, the opening attraction of the Criterion Theatre (formerly the Kinema) on Grand Avenue and 7th Street in Hollywood. The Criterion's renovation, redecoration, and rebranding for the film's premiere made news. "Only the walls of the old structure remain," reported the *Los Angeles Times*, "the inside having been rebuilt into one of the most luxurious of Los Angeles theaters. The style of architecture is Byzantine. So are the decorations and furnishings. The ceiling has been transformed into a great dome of massive squares, brilliantly illuminated. From these squares hang brilliant clusters, flashing colors of the rainbow. Rich tapestries adorn the walls, while the stage is framed in flowing colors. The walls of antique stone in colors of gray and silver are touched with bolder hues, letting in here and there the mellow shades of sunlight." The premiere program described the new Criterion as "a Byzantine jewel box.... Treasure chests overflowing, in spirit a promise of glorious days of entertainment. Graceful and luxurious leather chairs—chairs that insinuate days when men and women gazing forward will sit spellbound and read the color poems of the motion picture art."[46]

Though many of the critics pointed out that *A Woman of Paris* was primarily an "old story," they appreciated Chaplin's attempts at realism.[47] The reviewer for the preview section of the *Los Angeles Times* called it the "caviar of picture entertainment.... It is the sophisticated film drama of the year. It is so full of novelty and subtlety that it will perhaps open a new epoch for the photoplay technician, and intrigue and mayhap delight the taste jaded by too much routine."[48] "Now comes something different; now comes a photoplay which smashes the old conventions and—what is more important—gives something better in place of what is smashed," said *Motion Picture News*. "Simple? Yes, but not too simple to hold one breathless with interest. And that is because of the way the story is told. And it is treatment, not material, which makes it a classic."[49] The trade journal later declared, "Chaplin, the Pied Piper, the magician, the guide, has taken us out of the wilderness."[50]

The New York Times called Chaplin the "O. Henry of the silent drama."[51] *Motion Picture Magazine* proclaimed he "has taken everything that anybody ever learned about motion pictures and rolled it all up in a ball and tossed it gaily into the garbage-can.... The method of acting is so new and revolutionary that he had to take one scene eighty-six times before he could persuade the actors to let go their old traditions."[52] The cast had to learn their dialogue and say it "exactly as it was written," said Adolphe Menjou, "something that none of us had ever done before in pictures. This was because [Chaplin] felt that certain words registered on the face and could be easily grasped by the audience."[53] "[Chaplin] assumes that his audience is made up of people with at least one lobe in the brain," said Burton Rascoe of the *New York Tribune*. "Is that an unwarranted assumption? If *A Woman of Paris* is a failure I shall begin to believe so."[54] *Motion Picture Magazine* accurately predicated, "Charlie Chaplin may never reap the full benefit of the great things he has done."

"They broke down the lobby trying to get in to see *A Woman of Paris*," said the congratulatory message to Chaplin from Criterion manager H. B. Wright. "It would have done your heart good to have heard the complimentary remarks on every hand of your picture. The music is perfect. I predict *A Woman of Paris* will be this year's sensation." "Congratulate you most sincerely on great artistic success," said Ernst Lubitsch. "Feel your picture marks epoch in history of motion pictures."[55] The reviewer for the *Los Angeles Times* quoted "one of the screen's greatest stars, who, for obvious reasons, must not be named here, said to me, 'Chaplin's picture is the greatest ever made. He shows 'em all up, and now Griffith and Lubitsch can join hands and jump into the ocean without being missed.'"[56]

"That music should play an important part in the programs of the Criterion Theater is not to be wondered," said a blurb in the premiere program, "for as the pipes of Pan lure one beyond the everyday cares past mystic gates of fancy and bear one away on the wings of enchantment, so music becomes the soul of the eye."

> At the Criterion Theater [*sic*] the divinest of the arts will be welded to the universal language of the silver sheet in a new harmony. Not the blatant blare of the trumpet, but a musical counterpart molded to and paralleling the dramatic theme. Music is the voice that will creep beyond the shadows and speak with the understanding tongue of all—a symphony of sight and sound which, with its subtle alchemy, sways the soul in perfect rhythm…
>
> So music is mooded to the shadows and the empty husks of men and women that flash on the Criterion screen are made to throb with the breath of life. With changing tempo the moods are transformed while crash of cymbal may emphasize some primitive impulse or the unity of strings and wood wind [*sic*] vivify life in its divinest phases.[57]

The Criterion orchestra pit could accommodate up to fifty musicians, and it hired Adolf Tandler, former director of the Los Angeles Symphony Orchestra, to lead the new orchestra. "I am so glad to be back in my home town," Tandler was quoted in the program,

"Europe and the East are nice—but Los Angeles for me. Realizing that a house of refinement like the Criterion gives me a wonderful chance to bring the message of good music to the people as a whole, I thank you." The program supplied the names of every member of the twenty-piece orchestra hired for *A Woman of Paris*, which was called the Criterion Symphony Artists and consisted of five violins, one viola, two cellos, one bass, flute, clarinet, two French horns, a trumpet, trombone, percussion, harp, and Tandler's brother, H. J., on piano.[58]

The premiere of *A Woman of Paris* included a seven-unit program of entertainment *à la française* that honored the film's French storyline. Assistant Director and Concert Master Jaime Overton opened with Louis Ganne's *La marche Lorraine*. Ganne was born in the Auvergne countryside of France (shades of Marie St. Clair) and his 1917 march was popular during World War I. Ganne had died in July and perhaps the inclusion of the piece on the program served as a tribute. *Around the World with Criterion Cameramen* ("a compilation of the world's most interesting pictorial news events") preceded a dramatic reading of "The Criterion Creed"[59] and a screening of Louis H. Tolhurst's education film *The Ant*.[60]

Adolf Tandler, conductor of the Los Angeles premiere of *A Woman of Paris* (1923), as he appeared in the premiere program (courtesy of a private collection).

Tandler was introduced in grand style to bring the proceedings back on a Parisian foot, conducting the "Concert De Luxe"—a performance of Offenbach's overture to *Orpheus in the Underworld* (with a special cadenza written by Overton and dedicated to Tandler) and its famous can-can. But beyond the film, the refurbished theater, and Tandler's appointment, what gave the premiere its cache was a special live mimed prologue titled "Nocturne," conceived and supervised by Chaplin.

> I had no script or story but I remembered a sentimental coloured print captioned "Beethoven's Sonata," depicting an artistic studio and a group of bohemians sitting moodily about in half-light, listening to a violinist. So I reproduced the scene on the stage, having only two days to prepare it.
>
> I engaged a pianist, a violinist, apache dancers and a singer, then utilized every theatrical trick I knew. Guests sat around on settees or on the floor with their backs to the audience, ignoring them and drinking Scotch, while the violinist poured out his sonata, and in a musical pause a drunk snored. After the violinist had played, the apache dancers had danced, and the singer had sung "Auprès de ma blonde," two lines were spoken. Said a guest: "It's three o'clock, I must be going." Said another: "Yes, we must all be going," ad libbing as they exited. When the last had gone, the host lit a cigarette and began turning out the lights of the studio as voices were heard singing down the street, "Auprès de ma blonde." When the stage had darkened, except for the moonlight streaming in through the centre window, the host exited and, as the singing grew fainter, the curtain slowly descended.
>
> During this nonsense you could have heard a pin drop from the audience. For half an hour nothing had been said, nothing but a few ordinary vaudeville acts had taken place on the stage. Yet on the opening night the cast took nine curtain calls.[61]

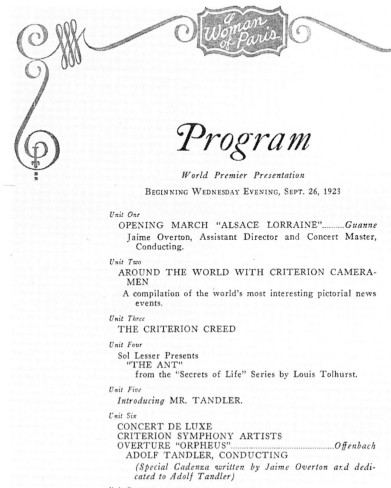

Program

World Premier Presentation

BEGINNING WEDNESDAY EVENING, SEPT. 26, 1923

Unit One
OPENING MARCH "ALSACE LORRAINE"..........*Guanne*
Jaime Overton, Assistant Director and Concert Master, Conducting.

Unit Two
AROUND THE WORLD WITH CRITERION CAMERA-MEN
A compilation of the world's most interesting pictorial news events.

Unit Three
THE CRITERION CREED

Unit Four
Sol Lesser Presents
"THE ANT"
from the "Secrets of Life" Series by Louis Tolhurst.

Unit Five
Introducing MR. TANDLER.

Unit Six
CONCERT DE LUXE
CRITERION SYMPHONY ARTISTS
OVERTURE "ORPHEUS"...*Offenbach*
ADOLF TANDLER, CONDUCTING
(*Special Cadenza written by Jaime Overton and dedicated to Adolf Tandler*)

Unit Seven
ATMSPHERE PRELUDE
"NOCTURNE"
Conceived and Supervised by CHARLES CHAPLIN

The Artists:

RENE HEMERY - - - - - -	*Violin Virtuoso*
HENRY GOODMAN - - - - -	*Cello Soloist*
JACK BERESFORD - - - -	*Concert Pianist*
GINETTE VALLON - - - - -	
CARLOS ROMERO - - - - - - -	*Apaches*
OTTO PLOETZ - - - - - -	*Tenor Robusto*
VALENTINA ZELMINA - -	*French Character Singer*

Program for *A Woman of Paris* premiere on September 26, 1923, including Chaplin's prologue, "Nocturne" (courtesy of a private collection).

"The atmospheric prologue," said the *Los Angeles Times*, "is a distinct novelty, introducing a clever company of singers, dancers and instrumentalists."[62] After the opening at the Criterion, Chaplin immediately traveled to New York to join Arthur Kelly, his representative at United Artists, who had gone ahead to prepare for the east coast premiere at the Lyric Theatre. An interviewer with *The New York Times* described the chaos surrounding the New York premiere, where Chaplin was directing rehearsals for a new pro-

Louis F. Gottschalk, compiler of the two scores for *A Woman of Paris*, lending his celebrity name in an ad for Wright DeCoster speakers. *Exhibitors Herald-World*, April 13, 1929, 49 (courtesy Media History Digital Library).

logue written by playwright and journalist Jack Lait and staged by Allan K. Foster for $1,500.[63] Chaplin "was all over the room, acting the parts of the prologue actors, making them live the parts as he showed them."[64] The paper reported it was "a beautiful musical prologue … the songs being sung by singers garbed as Latin Quarter students, in a setting representing an artist's studio. The lighting effects are especially well done."[65] The *Evening Telegram* said it was "at once the most novel and most real seen in these parts."[66] Burton Rascoe of the *New York Tribune*, however, said the prologue was "strikingly unnecessary … it could be dispensed with to the film's benefit."[67]

Of all the scores composed or compiled for Chaplin's films, none has had the checkered history of *A Woman of Paris*. The film had four different scores at various stages. Composer Louis F. Gottschalk compiled the first score for the Los Angeles premiere. He followed that with a second, completely different compiled score that took the form of a "musical synopsis" cue sheet that was handed out to smaller theaters and may have been performed at the New York premiere. The printed score, "revised and arranged" by Frederick Stahlberg, follows the basic layout of Gottschalk's cue sheet with different cue numbers and a few different pieces. Lastly, Chaplin composed a new score in 1976 score, his final musical work.

Gottschalk (1864–1934) first gained fame as the conductor of Franz Lehár's *The Merry Widow* and later, as an associate of Victor Herbert's, directing nine of Herbert's operettas beginning with *The Wizard of the Nile*. He produced the *Wizard of Oz* plays for L. Frank Baum and collaborated in writing the music for *The Tik-Tok Man of Oz*. After the Oz company dissolved, Gottschalk arranged scores for all of D. W. Griffith's productions for three years, including *Broken Blossoms* (1919). He also scored Douglas Fairbanks's *The Gaucho* after Mortimer Wilson's scores for *The Thief of Bagdad* and *The Black Pirate* failed to meet Fairbanks's expectations. Oddly enough, Fairbanks later replaced Gottschalk's *Gaucho* score with a new one compiled by Arthur Kay, which may have helped Kay get a job with Chaplin in 1927 compiling the score for *The Circus*.

Harry Carr of *Motion Picture Magazine* attended a preview of *A Woman of Paris* and gave a glimpse into Chaplin's backstage musical workings:

> Charlie has the worst-looking projection-room in Hollywood. There is one sad-looking leather chair upon which I imagine the fair Pola [Negri] has sat many a time and oft.
> In one corner, stands an old-fashioned cottage organ. For the rest, the room is a collection of old camp stools and dubious-looking kitchen chairs.
> Several times during the performance Charlie felt the need of music to adorn the action and tried to whistle it; that didn't seem to supply the emotional need, so he tried to sing an obligato by the do-de-da-da process. But as this seemed to fall short, he finally groped his way thru [*sic*] the dark to the organ.
> Charlie plays exceedingly well and so he stuck there for the rest of the picture. I imagine that not many persons have had the chance to see a picture with Charlie Chaplin as the orchestra.[68]

At the west coast premiere, "one of the most unusual demonstrations of the ability of an orchestra conductor is being given patrons of the Criterion Theater," reported the *Los Angeles Times*.

> Adolf Tandler, conductor, directing the body of symphony artists comprising the orchestra, does not use a single sheet of music during any performance. He conducts the entire intrinsic score from memory, and the minutest cues necessary toward a detailed synchronization are perfect in his memory.
> The overture of Offenbach's opera *Orpheus* is also being conducted by Tandler without notes.

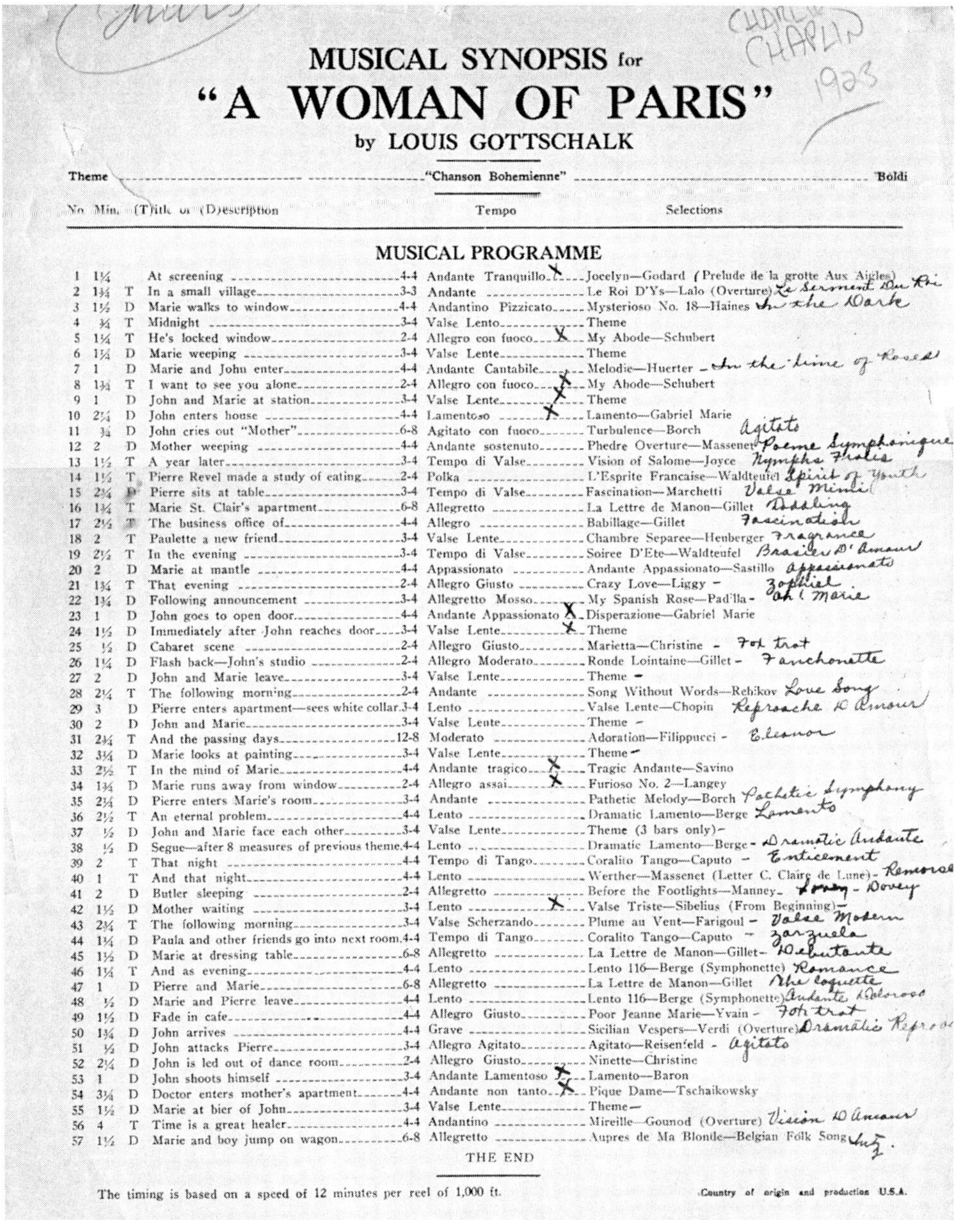

MUSICAL SYNOPSIS for
"A WOMAN OF PARIS"
by LOUIS GOTTSCHALK

Theme ———————————— "Chanson Bohemienne" ———————————— Boldi

No. Min. (Title or (D)escription) Tempo Selections

MUSICAL PROGRAMME

No.	Min.	T/D	Title or Description	Tempo	Selections	Handwritten
1	1¼		At screening	4-4 Andante Tranquillo	Jocelyn—Godard (Prelude de la grotte Aux Aigles)	
2	1½	T	In a small village	3-3 Andante	Le Roi D'Ys—Lalo (Overture)	Le Serment Du Roi
3	1½	D	Marie walks to window	4-4 Andantino Pizzicato	Mysterioso No. 18—Haines	In the Dark
4	¾	T	Midnight	3-4 Valse Lento	Theme	
5	1¼	T	He's locked window	2-4 Allegro con fuoco	My Abode—Schubert	
6	1¼	D	Marie weeping	3-4 Valse Lente	Theme	In the time of Roses
7	1	D	Marie and John enter	4-4 Andante Cantabile	Melodie—Huerter	
8	1¾	T	I want to see you alone	2-4 Allegro con fuoco	My Abode—Schubert	
9	1	D	John and Marie at station	3-4 Valse Lente	Theme	
10	2½	D	John enters house	4-4 Lamentoso	Lamento—Gabriel Marie	
11	¾	D	John cries out "Mother"	6-8 Agitato con fuoco	Turbulence—Borch	Agitato
12	2	D	Mother weeping	4-4 Andante sostenuto	Phedre Overture—Massenet	Poeme Symphonique
13	1½	T	A year later	3-4 Tempo di Valse	Vision of Salome—Joyce	Nymphs Frolic
14	1½	T	Pierre Revel made a study of eating	2-4 Polka	L'Esprit Francaise—Waldteufel	Spirit of Youth
15	2¾	D	Pierre sits at table	3-4 Tempo di Valse	Fascination—Marchetti	Valse Minuet
16	1¾	T	Marie St. Clair's apartment	6-8 Allegretto	La Lettre de Manon—Gillet	Babbling
17	2½	T	The business office of	4-4 Allegro	Babillage—Gillet	Fascination
18	2	T	Paulette a new friend	3-4 Valse Lente	Chambre Separee—Heuberger	Fragrance
19	2½	T	In the evening	3-4 Tempo di Valse	Soiree D'Ete—Waldteufel	Brasier D'Amour
20	2	D	Marie at mantle	4-4 Appassionato	Andante Appassionato—Sastillo	Appassionato
21	1¾	T	That evening	2-4 Allegro Giusto	Crazy Love—Liggy	Zophiel
22	1½	D	Following announcement	3-4 Allegretto Mosso	My Spanish Rose—Pad'lla	Ah! Marie
23	1	D	John goes to open door	4-4 Andante Appassionato	Disperazione—Gabriel Marie	
24	1½	D	Immediately after John reaches door	3-4 Valse Lente	Theme	
25	½	D	Cabaret scene	2-4 Allegro Giusto	Marietta—Christine	Fox trot
26	1¼	D	Flash back—John's studio	2-4 Allegro Moderato	Ronde Lointaine—Gillet	Fanchonette
27	2	D	John and Marie leave	3-4 Valse Lente	Theme	
28	2¼	T	The following morning	2-4 Andante	Song Without Words—Rebikov	Love Song
29	3	D	Pierre enters apartment—sees white collar	3-4 Lento	Valse Lente—Chopin	Reproache D'Amour
30	2	D	John and Marie	3-4 Valse Lente	Theme	
31	2½	D	And the passing days	12-8 Moderato	Adoration—Filippucci	Eleanor
32	3½	D	Marie looks at painting	3-4 Valse Lente	Theme	
33	2½	T	In the mind of Marie	4-4 Andante tragico	Tragic Andante—Savino	
34	1½	D	Marie runs away from window	2-4 Allegro assai	Furioso No. 2—Langey	
35	2¾	D	Pierre enters Marie's room	3-4 Andante	Pathetic Melody—Borch	Pathetic Symphony
36	2½	T	An eternal problem	4-4 Lento	Dramatic Lamento—Berge	Lamento
37	½	D	John and Marie face each other	3-4 Valse Lente	Theme (3 bars only)	
38	½	D	Segue—after 8 measures of previous theme	4-4 Lento	Dramatic Lamento—Berge	Dramatic Andante
39	2	T	That night	4-4 Tempo di Tango	Coralito Tango—Caputo	Enticement
40	1	T	And that night	4-4 Lento	Werther—Massenet (Letter C. Claire de Lune)	Remorse
41	2	D	Butler sleeping	2-4 Allegretto	Before the Footlights—Manney	Lovey-Dovey
42	1½	D	Mother waiting	3-4 Lento	Valse Triste—Sibelius (From Beginning)	
43	2¾	T	The following morning	3-4 Valse Scherzando	Plume au Vent—Farigoul	Valse Modern
44	1¼	D	Paula and other friends go into next room	4-4 Tempo di Tango	Coralito Tango—Caputo	Zarzuela
45	1½	D	Marie at dressing table	6-8 Allegretto	La Lettre de Manon—Gillet	Debutante
46	1½	T	And as evening	4-4 Lento	Lento 116—Berge (Symphonette)	Romance
47	1	D	Pierre and Marie	6-8 Allegretto	La Lettre de Manon—Gillet	The coquette
48	½	D	Marie and Pierre leave	4-4 Lento	Lento 116—Berge (Symphonette)	Andante Doloroso
49	1½	D	Fade in cafe	4-4 Allegro Giusto	Poor Jeanne Marie—Yvain	Fox trot
50	1¾	D	John arrives	4-4 Grave	Sicilian Vespers—Verdi (Overture)	Dramatic Repr...
51	½	D	John attacks Pierre	3-4 Allegro Agitato	Agitato—Reisenfeld	Agitato
52	2¼	D	John is led out of dance room	2-4 Allegro Giusto	Ninette—Christine	
53	1	D	John shoots himself	3-4 Andante Lamentoso	Lamento—Baron	
54	3¾	D	Doctor enters mother's apartment	4-4 Andante non tanto	Pique Dame—Tschaikowsky	
55	1½	D	Marie at bier of John	3-4 Valse Lente	Theme	
56	4	T	Time is a great healer	4-4 Andantino	Mireille—Gounod (Overture)	Vision D'Amour
57	1½	D	Marie and boy jump on wagon	6-8 Allegretto	Aupres de Ma Blonde—Belgian Folk Song	

THE END

The timing is based on a speed of 12 minutes per reel of 1,000 ft.   Country of origin and production U.S.A.

Gottschalk's compilation score for *A Woman of Paris* (1923) went through a number of revisions. Yet theatre musicians would still substitute whatever pieces of music they had in their own libraries, as evidenced by the handwritten selections on this published cue sheet (courtesy David Robinson).

This fact has become a revelation even to his own men, who know better than the average layman just what manuscripts are included in the score for *A Woman of Paris*, and the fact that Tandler has memorized such compositions as the entire last movement from the *Pathetique* symphony by Tschaikowsky, or the Prelude of *Manon Lescaut* or the entire book of compositions by Borch and Offenbach seems almost impossible…

Mr. Tandler is receiving an ovation at practically every performance.[69]

"Adolf Tandler, conducting the Criterion Symphony artists promises to eclipse in popularity even his most successful career as conductor of the Los Angeles Symphony," said the *Los Angeles Times*.[70] Tandler's return "was an event, and the excellence of his musicianship was plentifully evident in the rendition of a very well-judged accompaniment to the picture."[71]

The original compilation score consists of thirty-four cues, a stack of sheet music from various publishers, which opens with the finale of Tchaikovsky's Symphony No. 6, the *Adagio lamentoso* of B minor foreshadowing the film's tragic ending. The cues are numbered but have no indication of where in the film they were to be played. Blue pencil markings on each instrumental part indicate exactly which sections in each piece to cut.

Chaplin loved waltzes, using them in every score from the compilation scores for *A Woman of Paris* right up to his final original score for the same film in 1976. Johann Strauss's *Thousand and One Nights* (1891) makes an appearance as does Al B. Coney's more recent and evocatively titled *The Vampire* (1921). But it is the waltzes of French composer Émile Waldteufel that give the score much of its Gallic flavor. His 1890 *Tout Paris* is labeled as a "prelude." As with the cue numbers, there is no indication exactly where the waltz's repeated thirty-two bars occur, but it was most likely meant to be played somewhere during Chaplin's mimed prologue. Waldteufel's *Les sirènes* (1878) and *Je t'aime* ("*I Love Thee*") (1882) also figure as cue numbers 22 and 27. In the revised score, the lively *L'Esprit français* polka (1882) accompanies Pierre back to the kitchen in a delicious comedic scene as he chooses his own game bird. When Pierre later arrives at Marie's apartment after she nonchalantly sloughs off the news she has read of him getting married, the flowing dotted half notes of the *Soirée d'été* waltz (1883) convey a relaxed atmosphere captured in the bored kiss exchanged between the two.

Newspaper reports indicated that Chaplin reworked the score for the New York premiere. An interviewer with *The New York Times* described Chaplin "mapping out the music plot so that it fitted in with all the varying moods of the film, and whenever necessary humming over snatches of old French songs for the musical director to orchestrate."[72] Gone was most of the music from the original score, including Gottschalk's own love theme from *The Girl I Loved*, which United Artists had released in February. On the afternoon prior to the New York premiere, Mordaunt Hall later remembered, "the picture was being screened and Chaplin, in the gloom of the theater, told me that he did not like the music. He is very partial to a suitable orchestral score to a picture."[73] Still, Chaplin must have worked through whatever misgivings he had. The score was later "compiled and revised" by Frederick Stahlberg and printed (albeit with a number of sloppy mistakes in the various instrumental parts, not least in the misspelling of "John" instead of "Jean," an unfortunate holdover from Gottschalk's official cue sheet).

In the sound era, Chaplin obviously wanted to showcase his own music and used pre-existing tunes judiciously, primarily for comedic effect (e.g., "How Dry I Am" for the drunk millionaire in *City Lights*, snippets of "London Bridge Is Falling Down" buried in the swirling accompaniment of *Modern Times*' feeding machine sequence). For his first drama, particularly in the revised score, Chaplin stays away from melodies that would conjure pre-existing images in the audience's mind. The second score, also compiled by Gottschalk, is also a mixture of lesser-known works by heavyweight classical composers, library cues from the usual suspects, lesser tunes by little-known composers, and more Waldteufel waltzes. Chaplin also peppers the revised score with more French composers, perhaps feeling that the original score was not Gallic enough.

The revised score for *A Woman of Paris* provides the first clear indication of how Chaplin is beginning to view music in film with the use of a central theme—in this case, J. B. Boldi's 1907 *Chanson bohémienne*, which represents the doomed love between Marie and Jean. Sometimes scored uptempo, at other times at a more funereal speed, the tune is orchestrated mostly for full orchestra, though a plaintive solo cello voices certain cues. The theme comes to a head in a furious declamation as Jean attacks Pierre in the nightclub before one last mournful statement with Marie at Jean's deathbed. The piece was recorded twice in 1924, with the Jean Goldkette Orchestra and the Victor Salon Orchestra. Whether the sudden interest in the piece was due to its use in accompanying the film or not is unclear.

Gottschalk retained certain pieces of music for the revised score. Archibald Joyce's *Vision of Salome* waltz (1910) underscores the lavish scene of wealthy patrons dancing and dining at the restaurant. The minor key, dotted half notes, and low range of the melodic line provides a discreet accompaniment to the bejeweled dowagers, their boy toys, and other patrons who are there to see and be seen "in the magic city of Paris, where fortune is fickle and a woman gambles with life." Chopin's *Valse Lente* (1838), also in a minor key, underscores the tragic scene when Marie discovers the belated news of Jean's father death and Pierre realizes that she has been seeing Jean behind his back.

After leaving Marie at the train station to wait for him, Jean returns home to pack his bags. Jean Gabriel-Marie's *Lamento* (1916) has a plodding certainty as Jean's mother pleads with her husband to reconcile with his son. The music changes to a major key when the father gives in and peels off a stack of bills to give to Jean. The solo violin (or cello) line plays in lonely isolation, much as the two stubborn men who refuse to give in to their true unspoken feelings. With its gentle syncopated accompaniment, another plodding tune, Irénée Bergé's *Dramatic Lamento* (1922), later signals "an eternal problem—Mother and son." Jean consoles his grieving Mother. Maries walks in unannounced and hears Jean admit he proposed "in a moment of weakness," while a solo cello sobs out the main theme before Bergé's music returns at a slightly faster tempo as she walks out on him.

Chaplin and Gottschalk make subtle use of Schubert's "My Abode" ("Aufenthalt") from *Schwanengesang* ("Swan Song"), D. 957, a collection of songs written in 1828 at the end of Schubert's life and published posthumously in 1829. The triplets in the second violins and violas, which normally accompany words by German poet Ludwig Rellstab— "Dull murm'ring stream, wild rustling wood / Cold senseless rock, my lone abode"—

A Woman of Paris (1923 compilation score)—J. B. Boldi's *Chanson bohémienne* (1907) served as the primary theme in the revised and printed versions of the score.

indicate Marie and Jean's restless need to escape. The tune accompanies the two scenes of Jean and Marie's fathers banishing them from their respective houses. Even though the song is purely instrumental in the score, the song, usually sung by a baritone, represents the "cold senseless" paternal actions. Jean Sibelius' *Valse triste* (1903) is the somber theme for Jean's waiting mother. And the 17th-century French folk song "Auprès de ma blonde" serves as a unifying melodic figure between Chaplin's prologue and the end of the film. Not only did Chaplin remember using the tune when he was describing the prologue in his autobiography thirty years later, it is also one of the few pieces of music that he held over for the second compilation score.

Another French composer used numerous times in the revised score is cellist Ernest Gillet. *La lettre de Manon* (1896) becomes the theme for Marie's elegant lifestyle, heard in three separate cues within the confines of her apartment, where a carefree melody flows in a leisurely 6/8 time over a bubbling brook of sixteenth notes in thirds in the second violins and violas. *Babillage* (1886), scored for strings only, underscores Pierre's business office. Once again, bubbling thirds in the second violins and violas indicate activity from the ticker tape and Pierre's assistant wheeling and dealing on the phone, while the fluid melody in the first violins embodies Pierre's nonchalant attitude as he lounges on the chaise in his pajamas. Gillet's delightful salon piece *Ronde Lointaine* (1902) provides pointed irony to the awkward scene at tea with the elegant Marie, the struggling artist Jean, and his disapproving mother. Joseph Farigoul's impromptu *Plume au vent* (1898) adds a lively musical backdrop to the massage scene. Scored only for strings with a lyrical cello countermelody, staccato eighth notes in the melody and accompaniment pointedly underscore Fifi's (Betty Morrissey) pick-a-little, talk-a-little gossiping as well as the kneading and pounding movements of Nelly Bly Baker's disapproving, scene-stealing masseuse.

Chaplin's fondness for opera appears time and again in his scores. Verdi's *Rigoletto* and Victor Herbert's notorious 1911 flop *Natoma* weave throughout the compilation score for *The Gold Rush*, while Ruggero Leoncavallo's *Pagliacci* (1892) forms the musical backbone of *The Circus*. And, of course, Richard Wagner's *Lohengrin* (1850) underscores *The Great Dictator*'s dance with the balloon globe and the film's moving finale, while the "Evening Star" melody from *Tannhäuser* (1845) serves as the "Hunger Theme" from the 1942 revised version of *The Gold Rush*.

Rimsky-Korsakov's exotic *Sadko* (1898) seems out of place in Gottschalk's original score for *A Woman of Paris* and Chaplin turned more to French opera for the revision. The foreboding "Prélude de la grotte aux Aigles" ("Prelude to the Cave of the Eagles")

A Woman of Paris (1923 compilation score)—The traditional French folk song "Auprès de ma blonde" was one of the few pieces that survived all three iterations of the compilation score.

A Woman of Paris (1923 compilation score)—The constantly moving eighth notes in Joseph Farigoul's impromptu for strings, *Plume au vent* (1898), underscored the memorable massage scene.

from Act II of Benjamin Godard's 1888 opera *Jocelyn* plays out over the main titles. Though scored in A major, chromatic passing tones and a narrow melodic range keep the tonal center off-kilter, while the brass and winds tap out a funeral motif. Édouard Lalo's overture to his 1875 opera *Le roi d'Ys* begins the story in "a small village, somewhere in France." Marie's confined loneliness and her threatening stepfather are embodied by tremolo strings and in Lalo's theme, a call-and-answer session between a plaintive solo oboe and a foreboding, accidental-filled line in the lower winds and strings. Massenet's tender "Clair de lune" from his 1887 opera *Werther* consoles Marie in bed after overhearing Jean take back his proposal, while her despondent former lover watches from under a street lamp. Verdi's ominous overture to *Les vêpres siciliennes* (1855) accompanies

In *A Woman of Paris*, Fifi (Betty Morrissey) gossips with Marie (Edna Purviance, on the massage table), while Nelly Bly Baker's masseuse looks on disapprovingly, c. 1923 (© Roy Export SAS).

Jean into the restaurant to confront Pierre. Pauline's mournful Act I aria from Tchaikovsky's *Pique Dame* (1890) provides somber underscore to the scenes of the doctor delivering the news of Jean's death to his mother. "Time is a great healer" in the shimmering strings, French horn hunting call, and rollicking 6/8 theme of Gounod's *Mireille* overture (1864) as the dawn awakens for Marie following Jean's suicide.

　　　Gottschalk's "musical synopsis" cue sheet was provided to most theaters. But for the printed score, Frederick Stahlberg "revised and adapted" Gottschalk's cues. Stahlberg (1877–1937) emigrated from Germany to the U.S. at age twenty-two as a protégé of Victor Herbert, who appointed him first violinist of the Pittsburgh Symphony Orchestra. Stahlberg conducted many of Herbert's operettas and the friendship between the two men lasted until Herbert's death in 1924. He became conductor of the Rivoli Theatre orchestra in New York and joined the staff of Samuel Rothapfel's Roxy Theatre, and was "affectionately known" as "The Musicians' Friend" in New York musical circles.[74]

　　　Though Stahlberg sticks to Gottschalk's cues for the most part for the printed version of the score, his "adaptation" changes six cues, often substituting less well-known tunes. For the scene where a waiter (Henry Bergman) prepares truffles for Pierre, the cue sheet lists Fermo Dante Marchetti's popular 1904 song "Fascination," which was discarded for the printed score, perhaps due to copyright issues. The same fate met Richard Heuberger's moving "Im chambre séparée" from his 1898 opera *Der Opernball*, a lovely melody that was too sincere for the backstabbing Paulette (Malvina Polo). When Jean attacks Pierre in the restaurant, Gottschalk chose Hugo Riesenfeld's innocuous *Agitato*, while Stahlberg went with a more evocative choice—an agitato rendering of the main theme, *Chanson bohémienne*. The New *York Times* said the musical accompaniment was "most interesting and satisfying."[75]

The film was banned in Pennsylvania and Ohio. "Everything is wrong with this picture," said Vernon M. Riegel, head of the Ohio Department of Censorship. "I don't think it is possible to change it so it can be passed by the board and I don't think it has one commending feature."[76] Chaplin made changes to the subtitles and, within the month, the board passed the film for exhibition. The big question was how Chaplin's fans would react to a Chaplin film without their onscreen hero. "The film was a great success with discriminating audiences," Chaplin wryly noted. "It was the first of the silent pictures to articulate irony and psychology."[77] Though *Variety* predicted *A Woman of Paris* would be "a money picture,"[78] by the end of the Criterion's seven-week run, the management was "disappointed at the film's showing."[79] With a gross of $634,000, approximately the same amount as the least successful pictures of the other UA partners,

Conductor Frederick Stahlberg further "revised and adapted" Louis F. Gottschalk's already revised *Woman of Paris* score. Photograph: *Encyclopedia of American Biography*, ed. Winfield Scott Downs, New York: The American Historical Society, Inc., 1938.

A Woman of Paris was not the hit Chaplin or United Artists had hoped for.[80] Chaplin pulled the film from distribution and it would be another fifty-four years before the public laid their eyes on his dramatic experiment, this time featuring the filmmaker's final score.

⋆   ⋆   ⋆

Chaplin said in a publicity statement he wanted to be remembered for *The Gold Rush*, though he later admitted to director Peter Bogdanovich that *City Lights* was his favorite film. The inspiration for *The Gold Rush* came at a Sunday morning breakfast with Douglas Fairbanks and Mary Pickford in September or October 1923. Now that *A Woman of Paris* was finished, as two of the partners in United Artists, Fairbanks and Pickford were anxious for Chaplin to get to work on a new film. Looking at stereograms after breakfast, he found an image of the 1896 Klondike gold rush showing a line of prospectors snaking up Chilkoot Pass that he later recreated in the film. Chaplin was inspired further after reading a book on the disastrous journey of the infamous Donner Party, a group of immigrants traveling to California who became snowbound in the Sierra Nevada and had to eat their moccasins and the corpses of their dead to survive. The third inspiration came from theater impresario Sid Grauman. Chaplin met Grauman in San Francisco in 1911 when he was touring with the Karno troupe in *Wow-Wows*. "If you ever decide to leave Karno," Grauman said, "I can always find ample backing at my own theaters for any kind of show you might want to create and stage. Just say the word, Charlie, and we're in business together."[81] While a stage collaboration never materialized, Grauman shared his experiences living in the Yukon and eventually became an integral part in the premiere of Chaplin's new film.

By the end of November 1923, Chaplin had copyrighted a scenario titled *The Lucky Strike*. He began shooting on February 8, 1924, and cast as his leading lady Lillita MacMurray, the flirting angel in *The Kid*. He put the teenager, who the studio said was nineteen years old but was not yet sixteen, under contract and changed her name to Lita Grey. "I have held firm to my ambition to go into pictures," Grey said at the time of signing her contract, "but I felt that I didn't want to work with anyone except Mr. Chaplin. Patience has its reward."[82] The two began a secret affair and six months into shooting Lita found out she was pregnant. Chaplin was again forced into marriage and shut down the production for three months. When it resumed in January 1925, 24-year-old Georgia Hale came on board as Grey's replacement. Rumors of marital disharmony began in April

Publicity photograph of Chaplin reportedly leading Abe Lyman's (standing on chair in the rear) band for the recordings of "Sing a Song" and "With You, Dear, in Bombay," though there is no evidence he actually conducted on the disc, c. 1925 (© Roy Export Co. Ltd.).

US and UK sheet music covers for "Sing a Song," c. 1925 (US edition © Margaret Herrick Library, Academy of Motion Picture Arts and Sciences, UK edition © Roy Export Co. Ltd.).

and Lita gave birth to Charles Spencer Chaplin, Jr., on May 5, while Chaplin was still cutting the film.

To help publicize the film, Chaplin composed two fox-trots as musical tie-ins that were published as sheet music and recorded on Brunswick Records with the Abe Lyman Orchestra. According to *Variety*, Lyman urged Chaplin to elaborate on "one of his many extempore themes for commercial purposes."[83] And as a publicity stunt, Lyman broadcast the melody regularly with his band from the Cocoanut Grove in The Ambassador Hotel, offering a $50 prize for "a suitable title."[84] Out of the two eventual titles— "Sing a Song" and "With You, Dear, In Bombay"—it is unclear which of the two tunes Lyman broadcast. But the stories behind the songs are not as simple as their melodies would suggest.

On May 15, 1925, popular Tin Pan Alley lyricist Gus Kahn (1886–1941) copyrighted a lyric titled "I Like That Little One" to a melody composed by Chaplin and Lyman that would eventually become "Sing a Song." Kahn had already penned a string of hits—"On the Sunny Side of the Street," "Yesterdays," "Ain't We Got Fun," "My Buddy," "I'll See You In My Dreams," "It Had To Be You," to name a few.

It is doubtful "I Like That Little One" was one of the titles submitted based on Lyman's broadcast; Kahn was too well known for that. The "little one" in the title suggests the Tramp, but the song has nothing to do Chaplin's iconic character or *The Gold Rush* and, like "Sing a Song" and "With You, Dear, In Bombay," was only intended for publicity purposes.

I have a pal named Bertie
Who's just a trifle flirty.
He loves to roam the beaches
Admiring all the peaches.
He doesn't flirt directly.
He tries to act correctly.
But as the girls go passing by
You'll hear him softly sigh.

CHORUS
I like that little one
That pretty little one
I mean the middle one with roguish eyes.
When she came passing by
It spelled romance.
She seemed to catch my eye
With just a glance (a little glance).
You take the other one
And give your brother one.
But there's another one I wish I knew.
I mean that little one.
I like that little one.
I wish that little one
Liked me a little bit too.

VERSE
Now Bertie's brother Harold
Goes round the town apparelled (sic)
(In) very latest fashion
For clothes he has a passion.
He too is quite flirtatious
And when they meet, good gracious,
They sally forth to capture hearts
And this is how it starts.

REPEAT CHORUS[85]

While the song is pure fluff, Kahn displays his trademark linguistic ease and lyric craftsmanship, with rhymes like "Bertie"/"flirty" and "beaches"/"peaches" providing winking sexual nods. With the downbeat occurring on the first syllable of "little one" in the chorus, each successive phrase—"I like that little one"/"That pretty little one"/"I mean the middle one with roguish eyes"—increases in tension as Bertie explains his desires. The internal rhymes go one step further as Bertie generously instructs Harold, "You take the other one"/"And give your brother one," until the story takes a poignant turn ("But there's another one I wish I knew") as we learn "that little one" is not interested in Bertie.

No record exists of Chaplin's reaction to Kahn's contribution. But a month later, on June 17, Chaplin copyrighted a new song with the same melody, "Sing a Song," co-written with Lyman and Lyman's pianist Gus Arnheim, though only Chaplin's name is recorded in the copyright notice.

Most all our worldly troubles
Are only drifting bubbles;
Most all our cares and sorrows
Are gone with our tomorrows.
So don't you let them fret you,
Or some day they will get you.
When skies are grey, stop work and play.
And laugh your cares away.

"Sing a Song" (1925, music and lyrics by Charles Chaplin, Abe Lyman, and Gus Arnheim)— **The opening measures of the chorus.**

CHORUS
Just smile and swing along,
The while you sing a song.
Your troubles fade away
When you are gay;
If all your cares appear
As dark as night,
You'll find it won't be long
With just a song
They'll be all right.
And when you're feeling blue
And so unhappy too,
When all the skies are grey
And shadows fall;
Things are not what they seem,
You'll find them just a dream,
If you will sing a song,
Swing along too.

VERSE
Just turn your tears to laughter
And joy will follow after;
If May days you'll remember,
You'll soon forget December.
Instead of asking pity,
Just say you're sitting pretty;
Then you will see that life will be
A wondrous melody.

REPEAT CHORUS[86]

Neither of the verses of "Sing a Song" was sung on Lyman's recording, and it is easy to see why. Though they are in keeping with the song's sunny G-major key signature, the lyric borders on trite, even for the mid–1920s. It is also missing Gus Kahn's clever wordplay and lyric craft. On the recording, Charles Kaley, who was also a violinist and tenor "whose vocal interludes have heretofore been a feature of the band's recordings," only sings the first rendition of the chorus, while Lyman's band renders the repeat instrumentally.[87] A tenor saxophone and pizzicato strings play the first half before the full orchestra joins to finish off the record, squaring off the slight syncopation.

No paperwork for "Sing a Song" survives. But the contract for "With You, Dear, In Bombay" stated music publisher M. Witmark & Sons would pay "⅔ Cents royalty on each copy sold, and for all mechanical reproducing rights 8⅓ Cents for every [piano] role [*sic*]." All proceeds and royalties were to be split three ways, "by private agreement" between Chaplin, Lyman, and Arnheim. (Again, neither Lyman nor Arnheim appear on the copyright notice; only Chaplin.) The three also had a verbal agreement to pay uncredited lyricist Mort Nathan ten percent of their joint royalties. A handwritten note on the contract, dated June 15, detailed a phone conversation with Nathan, who stated "the 10% for him was abrogated and not included as far as Mr. C. was concerned."[88]

"With You, Dear, In Bombay" boasts a slightly more interesting musical construction. The 24-bar verses in C minor and 32-bar chorus in its parallel C major might seem monotonous in the synchronicity of the key signatures, but the accidentals hint at Indian flavor without choking the melody in a perfume of incense and jasmine.

Publicity photograph of Gus Arnheim, Chaplin, and Abe Lyman, c. 1925 (© Roy Export Co. Ltd.).

Where golden palms are swaying,
'Mid perfumed breezes playing,
My thoughts are straying night and day.
Where mystic waters gleaming
Beneath the starlight beaming,
I'm always dreaming of Bombay.
Temple bells are ringing in the air,
Wonderland, your love commands me there.

CHORUS
Soon I'll sail away, sail to old Bombay.
Where your arms and your charms will hold me.
Skies of fairest blue
Eyes of rarest hue
Haunt me, taunt me endlessly.
Tantalizing lights I'm heeding your call.
Oriental nights I love most of all.
When I'm there I'll pray
I can always stay
With you near in my dear Bombay.

Where nightly shades are falling,
And birds their mates are calling,
Comes then the hour I dream of you.
With love my heart is filling
And all the world is thrilling;
I know 'tis then you're dreaming too.
Fragrant roses silvered in the dew,
Tell her that my love will e'er be true.

REPEAT CHORUS[89]

Nathan's lyrics try to supply the proper feeling of the Orient—"golden palms," "perfumed breezes," "fragrant roses silvered in the dew." And some of the internal rhymes—"haunt me"/"taunt me," "near"/"dear"—flow effortlessly like water down the Ganges. But odd lyric placements on the downbeat ("*your* arms"/"*your* charms") disrupt that flow and contractions like *'tis* and *e'er* probably sounded outdated even back in 1925. Not surprisingly, none of Nathan's lyrics made it onto the recording, which served as the "B" side to "Sing a Song." "With You, Dear, In Bombay" plays better as an instrumental where Lyman can summon the Orient through bent notes in the saxophones or an eerie violin duet.

For the recording, publicity reports trumpeted Chaplin playing the violin and conducting Lyman's orchestra, though there is no evidence of either outside of some surviving staged photos. "Chaplin has been accused of being a violinist," said *The Billboard*.[90] "Chaplin is an accomplished musician," reported *Variety*, "this violin being his hobby."[91] "Chaplin himself conducts the orchestra on this record," said the *Gravesend Report,* "and, therefore, we get a true interpretation of his fine melody."[92]

In mid–July, *The Music Trade Review* reported, "Brunswick Co. has inaugurated a special publicity department and will feature ("Sing a Song").... It is a lively fox-trot with an appealing swing and very tuneful melody. The Witmark Co. will exploit the number on a wide scale."[93] *Variety* said, "Brunswick is counting on a heavy scale [*sic*] of the Charlie Chaplin records."[94] Within a week, the trade journal published an update—"Brunswick dealers have been showing considerable interest during the past ten days in the Charlie Chaplin record, and special efforts are being made to bring this record before the attention

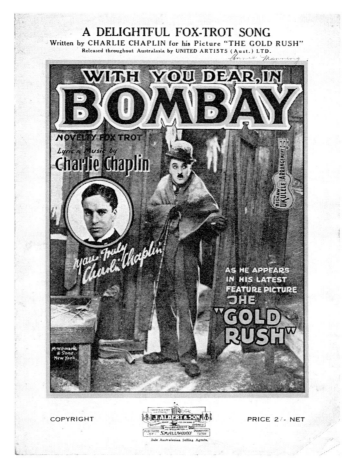

Australian sheet music for "With You, Dear, in Bombay," c. 1925. Though Chaplin is the only writer listed, the contract also mentioned Abe Lyman and Gus Arnheim as co-writers. Payment to lyricist Mort Nathan (also uncredited) was handled by verbal agreement (© Roy Export Co. Ltd.).

of the public.... Dealers feel that the record will be a very popular number when the public becomes familiar with it."[95] By October, the records were "in great demand."[96]

Women's Wear Daily said the songs were "an exploitation tie-up that probably will prove of incalculable value to exhibitors."[97] An ad for British music publisher B. Feldman & Co. in *The Stage* called "With You, Dear, In Bombay" "a delightful song.... Apart from the fact that the number will achieve great popularity through its association with Chaplin's latest and greatest film, *The Gold Rush* ... we place it before our professional friends with the assurance that it is a first-class song. Vocally, [it] is especially suitable for double singing acts, while the fox-trot arrangement should prove to be highly popular with every band in the British Isles."[98] *Variety* thought otherwise:

> With a stellar attraction like Charlie Chaplin ... it would be the nicest thing to say complimentary things about everything concerned. But in view of the shortcomings of the basic compositions, both in lyric and melody, everything else suffers, despite the Lyman instrumental treatment.
>
> "Sing a Song" ... is monotonous in its construction. "Bombay" is somewhat better, but both are mediocre and if not because of the "name" angle would never see light under ordinary circumstances. Both lack distinction, but will probably sell in view of the Chaplin connection.[99]

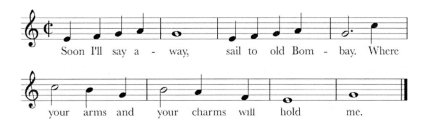

Soon I'll say a - way, sail to old Bom - bay. Where
your arms and your charms will hold me.

"With You, Dear, in Bombay" (1925, music by Chaplin and uncredited Abe Lyman and Gus Arnheim, lyrics by Mort Nathan, also uncredited)—The opening measures of the chorus.

No doubt the images from the film on the covers of the sheet music and in ads mistakenly stating "the two pieces are included in the Musical Score of New Stupendous Film—THE GOLD RUSH" helped to generate sales.[100] But that language probably caused confusion for moviegoers who expected to hear those tunes played somewhere in the film. There is no evidence that the songs were ever meant for use in the compilation score, though smaller orchestras and theater musicians may have utilized them. "Sing a Song" was performed daily at the Tivoli Theatre in London "with great success at each performance of *The Gold Rush*," but it is unclear whether it ever served as part of the film's musical accompaniment or as a separate performance.[101] At the East Coast premiere of the film at New York's Strand Theatre, a Brunswick representative presented Chaplin with a gold "mother record" of "With You, Dear, In Bombay."[102]

The world premiere of *The Gold Rush* on June 26, 1925, at Grauman's Egyptian Theater was a lavish, star-studded event, where *Women's Wear Daily* mistakenly reported that Chaplin would serve as "guest of honor, leading man, soloist and conductor."[103] "Sid Grauman," said the *Los Angeles Times*, "always attaches great importance to the musical accompaniment of his spectacular prologues and the big productions featured in the theater, and has given his personal attention to this portion of

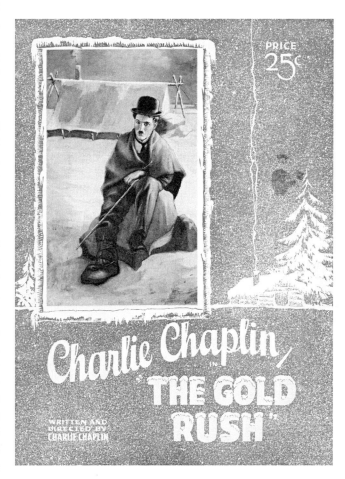

Program for *The Gold Rush* premiere at Grauman's Egyptian Theatre, Jun 26, 1925 (© Roy Export Co. Ltd.).

the entertainment."[104] Grauman "has spared no pains or expense in preparing a scintillating spectacle. Alaska in the days of the Klondike gold rush will be presented in an elaborate ten-act prologue to introduce the master comedian's most pretentious production. Those who have had a peep at Grauman's spectacle pronounce it an epoch-making exhibition."[105]

The prologue, "Charlie Chaplin's Dream," featured over a hundred people on stage and lasted over seventy minutes. It opened with a film tribute to *The Gold Rush* by "leading lights of the film world appear[ing] before the camera in seriocomic poses with Fred Niblo, master of ceremonies, in various whimsical attitudes, introducing the stars." For

A Sid Grauman Presentation

Mr. Grauman presents
the colorful prologue

"CHARLIE CHAPLIN'S DREAM"

A—Tribute to "The Gold Rush" by the
    prominent stars of the Moving Picture
    Industry which was made especially for
    the Premiere Performance.

B—Overture — Grauman's Egyptian
    Orchestra. Gino Severi, Conducting.
    Julius K. Johnson at the Mighty
    Egyptian Organ.

C—Land of the Midnight Sun
        1—Entry of the Lonely Prospector
        2—Meeting with the Eskimos
        3—Eskimo dance
        4—Pastimes of the Eskimos
        5—Charlie's dream

D—The Spirit of the Frozen North
    As Beauty Depicts the Moods of the
    Northland

E—Ballooon Dance by Lillian Powell

F—Festival of Dancing Ice Skaters

G—The Monte Carlo Dance Hall

H—Charlie's Awakening

                Curtain

Prologue Staged and Presented by
            SID GRAUMAN
Ralph P. Borst, Assistant to Mr. Grauman

*Costumes for "The Spirit of the Far North" designed and
supervised by Adrian, executed by Rosa Rehn.
Ice skating ballet executed by Fanchon.*

The inside of *The Gold Rush* premiere program, detailing Sid Grauman's elaborate prologue (© Roy Export Co. Ltd.).

instance, Rudolph Valentino appeared in a bathing suit and bathrobe, an oceanside victim of car thieves. At the premiere, Valentino ran down the aisle in a bathrobe. When Niblo chastised the Sheik for wearing such an outfit, Valentino peeled off the bathrobe to reveal a tuxedo.[106] The "novel idea" of the film tribute was so popular that Grauman continued it during the film's regular engagement.[107] Gino Severi, a former member of the San Francisco Symphony and the conductor of the city's Imperial, Granada, and California theaters, was "especially engaged" for the premiere.[108] He conducted a medley of "semi-classical numbers for a brief and snappy overture" followed by Tyrone Power's recital of Robert W. Service's poem "Spell of the Yukon." Grauman's "Scenic Alaskan Spectacle," said *Variety*, "lived up to its title."

> The lay out covered the entire stage, with a back and two side scenic drops depicting receding hills of snow. A steep trail through the hills was set backstage, with an Eskimo hut nearby. Blue flood-lights and falling snow were used effectively to portray the Artic [*sic*] setting.
>
> A character in the make-up of Chaplin entered from the left, and aroused the Eskimos in their hut, who came out to step through an eccentric dance. While the dance was on, the tramp character fell asleep on the trail, which served to present "Charlie Chaplin's Dream." This opened with the presentation of six girls attired in sparkling silver mesh costumes. The sextet formed a background for the individual presentations of six other girls gorgeously gowned in white fur and silk creations. The introductions were made through traps in centre stage.
>
> A balloon dance by Lillian Powell was next, followed by the Festival of Dancing Ice Skaters, a brilliant and effective dance ensemble consisting of six men and twelve girls, all attired in white skating costumes.
>
> The next scene, the Monte Carlo Dance Hall, brought forth rounds of applause. The stage was darkened, and the two side drops flied. On each side of the stage a half of the dance hall interior slowly moved toward the centre until they completely joined. The set was an exact replica of the dance hall shown in the picture, with bar, faro layout, tin-pan piano, tables and narrow balcony, and with about thirty characters in their places for the spectacle.[109]

The transformation to the Monte Carlo Dance Hall, reported the *Los Angeles Times*, was done in full view of the audience utilizing the "lap-dissolve" technique from film.

> Sid has produced the same effect for his audience achieved by the motion-picture cameraman in taking dream or illusion episodes in which the costumes of the characters must be changed. In making the "lap-dissolve" in the films the action is carried to the point desired, the camera stopped, the character in the new costume introduced in the same position or attitude as before, the film reeled back a few feet and the action continued.
>
> On the stage Grauman introduces a replica of the dance hall in two sections, simultaneously from opposite sides of the stage into a panoramic special of the Northland, before the eyes of the audience. The players of the scene are in their respective places, ready to start the instant the scene transformation is complete.
>
> The great set, weighing tons, and bearing its load of human freight, moves into the Arctic setting so mysteriously that it appears to be the work of some monster genii. The only artifice employed to enhance the illusion is a slight lowering of the intensity of the stage lighting during the process.[110]

"This setting provided Sid Grauman with a sure-fire opportunity," *Variety* continued, "and he put it over effectively. Three old time ballads and a clog dance were staged, with everything moving at a fast pace. The two halves of the dance hall were then moved back to their original positions, and the side drops lowered again. An Arctic storm was then depicted and a file of sourdoughs clambering up the steep trail. One of the number awakened Chaplin, who took his place in line as the scene faded out. On opening night, this presentation ran for about 70 minutes, with a smoothness and zip that held everyone's attention. It is undoubtedly the most spectacular stage presentation ever conceived by Sid Grauman."[111]

On September 26 at 7:30 p.m., the BBC broadcast to every station on the British Isles an "interlude of laughter"—"Ten minutes with Charlie Chaplin and his audience," heard at the Tivoli Theatre in London." In "what so far has been the most original experiment in radio work," reported Scotland's *Dunfermline Journal*, "Uncle Rex," the announcer, stated the BBC was trying "a unique experiment—that of broadcasting 'a storm of uncontrolled laughter, inspired by the only man in the world who could make the people laugh continuously for the space of five minutes, viz., Charlie Chaplin.'" The scene—Charlie and Big Jim awake to find the cabin resting perilously on the edge of the cliff—reported one listener, "proved highly successful."[112]

As part of the publicity for the film, Chaplin and Grauman scheduled a "gold rush" for Sunday, September 27. Chaplin had left for New York in July and sent a wire to Georgia Hale instructing her to plant five hundred dollars worth of cash in twenty small bags in the beach sands of Santa Monica. In addition to the money, each bag would contain a free pass to that evening's showing of the film. Following tips provided daily at screenings and in the columns of the *Los Angeles Examiner*, thousands of "prospectors" planned visits to the beach to find the twenty small bags.

Women's Wear was one of the few outlets that mentioned Chaplin "took time to arrange the musical score for the picture."

> Mortimer Wilson, who wrote the score for Douglas Fairbanks' new film, *Don Q. Son of Zorro*, speaks highly of the musical setting prepared for *The Gold Rush*, and believes the only successful way to write music which actually describes a motion picture is to conceive them simultaneously, declaring the best scores are always composed while the picture is "in the shooting."
>
> And that is exactly what Chaplin has done in the case of *The Gold Rush*. While he was being filmed as a pathetic tenderfoot, struggling along with thousands of others in search for Klondike gold, he was humming certain refrains that suggested themselves to him as typical of the spirit of blended pathos and whimsical comedy. Throughout the picture Chaplin has tried to make his music symbolic of the story—man's eternal hunt for happiness. Gladness and sorrow alternate.[113]

Chaplin worked with Carli D. Elinor for two weeks to compile a suitable musical accompaniment to the film. Elinor (née Carol Einhorn) (1890–1958) studied at the Bucharest Conservatory of Music and emigrated to New York City in 1910, where he worked as an interpreter for a bank before joining *The Great Wilhelm* as a vaudeville performer on the violin within the year. When the production reached Los Angeles, he stayed, worked as a violinist in Clune's Theatre and later served as the theater's music director. In 1915, Elinor became the general music director for D. W. Griffith Productions, compiling scores for the West Coast

Carli Elinor, compiler of *The Gold Rush* compilation score, during his tenure at the California Theatre, c. 1918–1926 (photograph by Albert Witzel, courtesy SilentHollywood.com).

premiere of *The Birth of a Nation* (1915), as well as *Hearts of the World* (1918) and *Broken Blossoms* (1919).

The *Los Angeles Times* called *The Gold Rush* an "elaborate musical score."[114] But "Carli couldn't write his name, frankly," said one-time Elinor staff member and future Oscar-winner Hugo Friedhofer (*The Best Years of Our Lives*). "And I know that he had on his staff a pianist, and a couple of arrangers, and a copyist. Reginald Bassett, or Rex, as he was known, used to do the writing. He used to compose the incidental music that was required that they couldn't find in the library, and used to orchestrate."[115] It is unclear if anyone other than Elinor did actual writing as only Elinor's name is attached to the manuscript.

The Gold Rush represents a significant leap forward in Chaplin's musical thought processes. While *A Woman of Paris* used one primary theme (*Chanson bohémienne*), *The Gold Rush* weaves in a number of them throughout the score. Chaplin's penchant for opera is on display from the start. Victor Herbert's notorious operatic flop *Natoma* sets the musical stage. The opera, with a libretto by lawyer Joseph D. Redding and produced by the Chicago Opera Company, premiered in Philadelphia on February 25, 1911, starring John McCormack and Mary Garden in the title role. Three days later, it opened at the Metropolitan Opera in New York, becoming only the second American opera produced at the Met. The story was set in the early mission days of California and tells of the tragic love of the Indian princess Natoma for a naval lieutenant. Herbert "tried to get the effect of Indian music without using the thing itself," and Chaplin and Elinor make use of Herbert's dark, Indian-flavored tunes.[116]

The main titles open with a sweeping rendition of Don Francisco's aria, "Oh, Child of Love." The theme represents Big Jim's discovery of gold and is reprised towards the end of the film when Jim embraces Charlie after the shack falls off the cliff and plummets to the ground. Originally, the film was shown with an intermission after Charlie bests Jack (Malcolm Waite) and walks out of the dance hall, to the tune of Elgar's *Pomp and Circumstance No. 1*. The following scene, as Charlie looks in the window of Hank's (Henry Bergman) cabin, Natoma's love theme underscores the cabin's internal warmth while Charlie stands in the frozen snow outside. One of Victor Herbert's lighter, and lesser known, melodies accompanies Charlie's transition into a millionaire. After having his photo taken on the ship (to the tune of Fred Gilbert's "The Man Who Broke the Bank at Monte Carlo"), Charlie and Jim enter their stateroom to the tune of Herbert's "There Once Was An Owl" from his 1903 operetta *Babette*. The melody provides a carefree bounce to the fortunes of the newly minted prospectors and gives the transition scene a musical lift.

Evil Black Larsen (Tom Murray) does not deserve a melody much less a full-fledged theme. His oily four-bar motif comes from Giuseppe Verdi's *Rigoletto*. In the opera, the motif mirrors the blackness in the heart of court jester Rigoletto ("Quel vecchio malevidami"—"The old man cursed me!") in his meeting with the assassin swordsman Sparafucile. An accented chord in D minor and sneaky three-note figures in the violas, cellos, and basses convey the characters'—Rigoletto's and Black Larsen's—wicked intentions. Chaplin uses the theme every time the camera lingers on Black Larsen's grizzled, scowling face. With his demise on the crumbling cliff at the end of the first third of the film, the motif quite literally disappears with him.

Chaplin and Elinor also use Verdi to give Mother Nature her own theme. *Rigoletto*'s

The Gold Rush (1925 compilation score)—Victor Herbert's 1911 opera *Natoma* provided numerous themes for the score, including the aria "Oh, Child of Love," which represented Big Jim's discovery of gold.

Act III storm music stands in for the furiously blowing snow in *The Gold Rush*. In the opera, the music serves as the underlying tension surrounding Scarafucile and the pending murder. In the film, the music returns any time the camera focuses on the blustery weather outdoors or when Charlie, Big Jim, or Black Larsen let nature's violent forces into the cabin. Chromatically moving fourths moan in the bitter cold while swirling violin figures and a wind machine blow across the frozen wasteland. Woodwinds make a jagged run

The Gold Rush (1925 compilation score)—Natoma's love theme underscores the warmth in Hank's cabin.

of staccato diminished chord arpeggios, harp and piccolo fly through D-minor arpeggios as if nothing can be battened down, and muted brass signal a desperate S.O.S.

For a film set primarily in the Yukon, the music of Norwegian composer Edvard Grieg must have seemed like a perfect fit. The "Intermezzo" ("Borghild's Dream") from Grieg's incidental music for the 1872 play *Sigurd Jorsalfar* provides a somber accompaniment to Big Jim's cry for "Food! Food!" A sequence of slow-moving rising and falling eighth notes in the cellos and basses articulate Charlie and Jim's precarious situation. The allegro section of the "Intermezzo" is heard later as the door bar falls on Charlie's head and he swings his gun around inside the shack, thinking someone is attacking him. Famous melodies from Grieg's *Peer Gynt* incidental music (1876) also appear in the score. Big Jim lights the stove and makes himself king in his own castle to the tune of the menacing "In the Hall of the Mountain King." The dulcet oboe strains of "Morning Mood"

The Gold Rush (1925 compilation score)—A number of themes from Giuseppe Verdi's 1851 opera *Rigoletto* weave throughout the score, including this oily four-bar motif that links two villains across the decades—Verdi's hunchback court jester and Black Larsen.

The Gold Rush (1925 compilation score)—Percy Gaunt and Charles H. Hoyt's "The Bowery"
(1891) serves as the Tramp's theme.

provide an ironic counterpoint to the audience's first shot of the cabin hanging precari-
ously off the cliff.

Chaplin chose Percy Gaunt and Charles H. Hoyt's classic "The Bowery" as the theme
for the Tramp. The song, written for the 1891 musical *A Trip to Chinatown*, pertained to
a particularly seedy part of New York City's Lower East Side around the turn of the century. But the waltz tune's major key helped the song become a big hit. The musical ran
on Broadway for 650 performances, a record that would stand for twenty years, and the
song sold over a million copies of sheet music. Audiences in 1925 would have instantly
recognized the tune, and the use of staccato gives the orchestration of the melody an
ironic elegance to the Tramp's shabby attire.

Hugo Riesenfeld wrote *American Festival March* in 1917 for the first anniversary of

The Gold Rush (1925 compilation score)—Hugo Riesenfeld's *American Festival March* (1917), written for the first anniversary of New York's Rialto Theatre, where Riesenfeld was conductor, was used as Big Jim's theme.

New York's Rialto Theatre, where he was the conductor. Unlike the rousing contemporary marches of John Philip Sousa, Riesenfeld's piece is a more somber affair, at least in the *molto cantabile* section of the piece used in Chaplin's score. Set against a steady quarter-note beat, the yearning tune propels the snaking line of prospectors to the top of Chilkoot Pass at the beginning of the film. At other times, set against block half-note chorale chords or in a plaintive solo line, it becomes the theme for Big Jim, "another lone prospector."

Chaplin had selected Léonard Gautier's 1916 piano piece *Le Secret* for *The Kid*'s compilation score. In *The Gold Rush*, the piece again takes center stage accompanying the classic Thanksgiving scene in which Charlie and Big Jim dine on boot leather, laces, and nails. The flexible *rubato* of *accelerandos* and *ritardandos* are like musical grumblings from their starving stomachs. Fermatas over caesuras break up the piece into bite-sized chunks to match the humor on screen.

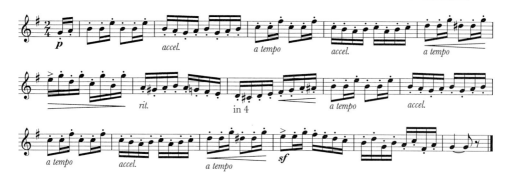

The Gold Rush (1925 compilation score)—Léonard Gautier's *Le Secret* (1916) was used in the 1921 compilation score for *The Kid* in Los Angeles. Carli Elinor repeated the practice for *The Gold Rush,* this time accompanying the memorable Thanksgiving scene with the Tramp and Big Jim.

The other major comedic set piece is the famous dance of the rolls. According to French journalist Robert Florey (who later served as associate director on *Monsieur Verdoux*), "Long before he immortalized his 'dance of the rolls' on the screen, on many occasions when we lunched at Musso & Frank restaurant, Chaplin provided us with endless fun by draping a napkin round his neck like a curtain, spearing two rolls with forks and making them dance to the accompaniment of songs in the style of the [Eight] Lancashire Lads," the British clog group that Chaplin had appeared with as a young boy.[117] From where does such inspiration come? Roscoe "Fatty" Arbuckle, who had worked with Chaplin in a number of shorts at Keystone, earlier performed a roll dance in 1917's *The Rough House*, though the sequence is played strictly for laughs and is missing the grace and pathos that Chaplin creates in his scene. Did he learn it from Chaplin or the other way around? Or was this a dance Chaplin picked up in the Lancashire Lads?

Chaplin filmed his dance in only three takes, refining it and completing the sequence in another eight retakes the following day. "There was music played for it, and not only was there music played for it, but he sang (hummed)," Georgia Hale remembered. "He made his own little noise, not actually a song but like little beats, so it would have a perfect tempo. It was a surprise to everyone. The actors, the electricians, everybody— and I still don't know whether Charlie did it inspirationally, spontaneously, or whether he had worked it out. All any of us knew was that he just sat down there and out of the air came this beautiful little dance. When he'd finished, everyone in the studio applauded."[118]

It was customary at most studios during the silent period to have a group of musicians, and even occasionally a small orchestra, playing offscreen to provide mood music for the actors. Jackie Coogan remarked that musicians were on the set of *The Kid,* but that was a rarity for Chaplin. When the *Gold Rush* crew moved back to the studio from location shooting in January 1925, Chaplin regularly employed musicians over the next nine weeks. During the first two weeks, scenes shot in the dance hall included two days with the dog (provided by director Hal Roach for thirty-five dollars a day) that gets caught up in Charlie's rope belt during his dance with Georgia. Off screen, Abe Lyman and two members of his band provided music for $37.50 a day ($12.50 each) and the onscreen violinist, "Mr. Meyers" (sometimes spelled "Myers" in the production report), was paid ten dollars a day. Three days were devoted to the big New Year's Eve party, which necessitated a raise in Lyman's salary to fifty dollars a day. Lyman went solo for the day Chaplin filmed Georgia's "I guess I'm bored" closeup. Lyman and his musicians, as well as Mr. Meyers, returned for three days in March as Chaplin filmed the scenes in the dance hall when Big Jim returns and recognizes Charlie.

In February, shooting moved into the cabin, with the Hollywood String Quartet being paid fifty dollars a day (again, at $12.50 per musician) to play offscreen for six days. Filming included the tender scene where Georgia finds her photo and the rose under Charlie's pillow, as well as the mule (hired from Hal Roach for twenty-five dollars) stealing the New Year's Eve gift from the table. The mule scene was tough to film and went into two hours of overtime, providing each member of the quartet with an extra six dollars in their pockets.

The production report for February 12 lists that Chaplin was the only person in the scenes that date, with the dance of the rolls the most likely scene on tap for the day. Over the next three days, Chaplin filmed the dream sequence and the scene where Georgia remembers she has forgotten her promise to Charlie for New Year's and visits the empty cabin. A new trio of musicians—Betty Schirmerhorn, Norman Mathews, and F. James Houseley—was employed for this period. Though the reports do not detail the instrumentation, most likely it was piano, violin, and drums. Abe Lyman and his musicians were brought back for the last two days of shooting at the cabin and they even provided music as the crew prepared the street set.

Over the two days of filming the dance of the rolls, Lyman and a trio of musicians performed off camera so that all eleven takes were the same length. Chaplin surely used

Chaplin filmed the classic "Dance of the Rolls" from *The Gold Rush* over three days in February 1925 (screen capture—© Roy Export SAS).

the same music in each take but there is no record of what music was played to accompany the filming. Max Terr, who would help Chaplin on the music for the 1942 reissue of *The Gold Rush*, claimed he was one of the offscreen musicians, though there is no record of any of the names of Lyman's trio. Oscar-winning film historian Kevin Brownlow related an anecdote that Terr recalled playing Irving Berlin's "All Alone" during the sequence.[119]

In a later interview, Terr remembered his experience working as an offscreen musician on the film. "Every time they finished—any kind of scene—Chaplin usually looked to the top to the electricians and they had been with him for quite a long time … he used to asked them, 'What do you think?' And if they laughed and they liked it, the scene was in…. And that's the way usually he used to establish in his mind that the scene was acceptable—if that could be acceptable to the electricians at the top, it certainly would be acceptable very much for the audience in the theatre." Chaplin and Terr talked "quite a bit about music … we played lots of things for the mood of the scene…. In between the people were sitting around, we played popular music at that time…. We usually talked about classical music … and he was telling me about his composition."[120]

Chaplin's title card for the sequence has the Tramp saying, "I'll dance the Oceana Roll." Lucien Denni's popular 1911 song would have been instantly recognizable to audiences in 1925 and the tune would have fit into a story set in the late 1800s when ragtime was at its peak. So what kept Chaplin from using the tune (or at least changing the title card)?[121] Perhaps it was too recognizable or he was unwilling to pay the necessary fees for a song still in copyright.

Instead the cue uses the traditional 18th-century English folk song "The Keel Row." Chaplin's dance certainly has a clog-like rhythm to it that fits the song's circular, jaunty melody and even beat. But the music as heard in the compilation score comes across as monotonous and not nearly as charming as Chaplin's own melody for the 1942 sound version of the film. The sequence was a big hit when the film premiered in Berlin. When the Tramp finished the dance, the audience went wild. The manager of the theater rushed up to the projectionist and instructed him to roll the film back and play the scene again.

The Gold Rush (1925 compilation score)—Carli Elinor used the traditional 18th-century English folk song "The Keel Row" to accompany Chaplin's famous "Dance of the Rolls."

The reprise, with orchestra, was greeted with even more thunderous applause. Whether the dance of the rolls began with the Eight Lancashire Lads, Roscoe Arbuckle, or elsewhere, it is Chaplin's version that endures and the dance has been recreated numerous times on screen in homage. In Richard Attenborough's 1992 Chaplin biopic, Robert Downey, Jr., recreated the dance on a table in a restaurant, perhaps as a reference to Robert Florey's memories of his experiences with Chaplin. The next year, Johnny Depp provided his own version in *Benny & Joon* (1993). Amy Adams does a bit brief in *The Muppets* (2011), and even Grampa Simpson gets into the act using potatoes in a 1994 episode of *The Simpsons*.

Chaplin gives Georgia three themes, all of them using pre-existing tunes that would have struck a chord with audiences of the day. Her first feisty appearance in the film is underscored with the appropriately titled "My Wild Irish Rose," though there is nothing particularly wild about Irish-born Chauncey Olcott's 1899 turn-of-century waltz tune. It is Georgia as seen through Charlie's loving eyes. Florence Methven's "When You Look in the Heart of a Rose" serves as Georgia's second theme. Written in 1918, John McCormack had a hit with the song the following year. The lyrics—"Dear little rose, with your heart of gold / Dear little rose, may your petals unfold, / My secret sweet I will trust you to keep, / Deep in your heart 'twill repose"—though not heard in the score, would have been familiar to audiences of the day and would have evoked the appropriate emotional response from the tune alone.[122] The tune becomes the love theme, heard any time Charlie looks at Georgia's photo and again at the end of the film when the two finally reunite.

Not surprisingly, Fermo Dante Marchetti's "Fascination," which Louis F. Gottschalk had used in his revised compilation score for *A Woman of Paris*, accompanies Charlie's obsession with the mysterious, dark-haired beauty. The song began life as an instrumental piece in 1904 titled "Valse Tzigane," or "Gypsy Waltz." Maurice de Féraudy added lyrics the following year to become the more popular song version. Chaplin was fascinated with gypsy music, incorporating ethnic musical flourishes in various scores, including *The Great Dictator*, *A King in New York*, and *A Countess from Hong Kong*. In a 1925 interview with Konrad Bercovici for *Collier's*, Chaplin said he "found out from my mother a few days ago that I had gypsy blood in my veins. And that has thrilled me more than I have ever been thrilled by anything else. At once a good many things … have become clear to me. I now remember little allusions my grandmother made when gypsies passed by our home during the fruit season in England. And I remember many other things that have new meaning for me, now. In those days it was a great blotch on the escutcheon of a family to have gypsy blood." Chaplin's "great love for music, his great gift of improvisation and his instinctive familiarity with musical instruments pointed to gypsy origin," said Bercovici. "There is hardly an instrument Charlie cannot play more or less well. His gift of improvisation is such that he can sing or play any melody in any mood. Not only that but he can take any melody and give it a Russian, a Hungarian, or a Jewish twist. He can make it into a French chanson or a jazz tune."[123] Even without its famous lyrics—"It was fascination I know / And it might have ended right there at the start, / Just a passing glance, just a brief romance / And I might have gone on my way empty-hearted"—the tune was (and still is) familiar enough to evoke the Tramp's obsession with only the first eight notes of the melody.

In 1991, following the death of Chaplin's widow Oona, his daughter Victoria inherited a bureau that had belonged to her father, containing a locked drawer. Inside was a friendly letter from an octogenarian Jack Hill, who wrote from his home in Tamworth that Chaplin might have been one of South London's most celebrated sons but he had been born "in a caravan [that] belonged to the Gypsy Queen, who was my auntie. You were born on the Black Patch in Smethwick near Birmingham."[124] Though Chaplin's son Michael took up the banner for his father's supposed Gypsy heritage, the veracity of the letter is still in doubt.

Lady Dufferin's "Terence's Farewell to Kathleen," also known as "Pretty Girl Milking a Cow," underscores Charlie's sad plight as an outsider. In 1827, Helen Sheridan Blackwood (1807–1867), the granddaughter of Irish playwright and poet Richard Brinsley Sheridan, married Price Blackwood, heir to the Marquess of Dufferin and Ava. As Lady Dufferin she published plays and a number of songs. The melancholy melody of "Terence's Farewell" accompanies the Tramp's New Year's Eve preparations as he's waiting for Georgia and her friends to arrive. As usual, the lyrics were not heard in theater. But the words that accompany the popular song's melody—"So, my Kathleen, you're going to leave me, / All alone by myself in this place! / But I'm sure that you'll never deceive me, / Oh, no! If there's truth in that face!"—provide clues to the melancholy atmosphere Chaplin wanted for the scene.[125]

Chaplin said "Auld Lang Syne" "set the mood" during filming.[126] The song is heard most obviously during the sing-along in the dance hall, followed by a rousing rendition of "Turkey in the Straw" for the first celebratory dance in the new year. Chaplin sandwiches an elongated version in between renditions of "When You Look in the Heart of the Rose" at the end of the film as the authorities discover that Charlie is not a stowaway and he tells his butler to make room for Georgia in his suite. Joseph M. Daly's 1910 "Chicken Reel" was an obvious choice for Big Jim's starvation hallucinations of Charlie as poultry, though Chaplin and Elinor break up the familiar melody to match Charlie's pecking and scratching on screen. Only when Big Jim threatens to shoot the bird does the music speed up to a furious pace to match Charlie running out of the shack.

Library cues play a big part in the early third of the film with Charlie, Big Jim, and Black Larsen, especially in a series of misterioso's from Leo Kempinski, Ernö Rapée and William Axt, Gaston Borch, and Paul Fauchey. Gilbert and Sullivan's "A Wand'ring Minstrel I" from *The Mikado* provides humorous accompaniment for the dance hall fiddler, "Mr. Meyers." Louis F. Gottschalk had used Richard Heuberger's "Im chambre séparée" from his 1898 opera *Der Opernball* in the second compilation score for *A Woman of Paris*. Chaplin and Elinor once again make good use of the beautiful melody as Charlie begins his New Year's vision. One of the most humorous uses of popular tunes is the cabin rocking sequence set to the tune of John Walter Bratton's "The Teddy Bear's Picnic" (1907) coupled later with Offenbach's overture to *Orfée aux enfers* (1858).[127]

According to the studio's daily production report, work began on a "new musical score" for the film from July 3 through July 17, nine days before the New York premiere.[128] No record exists of exactly how much changed in the music between Los Angeles and New York. Before the New York opening, Chaplin was still mulling over changes to the score. Mordaunt Hall in *The New York Times* reported Chaplin "felt that a few more old-fashioned airs such as 'After the Ball Is Over' would be effective in the musical score."[129] Among Chaplin's papers is sheet music for the classic waltz marked "OK" in red pencil next to it and a handwritten note indicating "Georgia & Charlie Dance," though it never

The Gold Rush (1925 compilation score)—Louis F. Gottschalk incorporated the melody for "Im chambre séparée" from Richard Heuberger's 1898 operetta *Der Opernball* in the revised version of the compilation score for *A Woman of Paris,* though it was deleted from the print version, possibly because of copyright restrictions. Carli Elinor also incorporated the lovely melody in *The Gold Rush* for the opening of the Tramp's New Year's Eve vision.

made it into the finished score. Other tunes earmarked for the score but ultimately discarded included Grieg's *Erotik*, which had the handwritten direction "Hank leaving with partner"; "The Bluebells of Scotland"; and other Victorian music hall and turn-of-the-century songs like "Little Annie Rooney" and Felix McGlennon's "Comrades." With the direction to "Cut to Dance Hall," Chaplin's idea to possibly use James Thornton's "She May Have Seen Better Days" (1894) provides some indication of how he viewed Georgia—"She may have seen better days, / Once upon a time. / Tho' by the wayside she fell, / She may yet mend her ways. / Some poor old mother is waiting for her / Who has seen better days."[130]

The Gold Rush made over $4 million worldwide. Chaplin's profit was a cool $2 million. "What I have done in *The Gold Rush*," Chaplin said in *The New York Times*, "is exactly what I wanted to do. I have no excuses, no alibis. I have done just as I liked with this picture. If people do not like it, you see I haven't a word to say…. I was after the feeling of Alaska, with a sweet, poetic, yet comic, love story…. I haven't forgotten, either, those early squalid surroundings in which I struggled. You will find something of me in *The Gold Rush*."[131]

* * *

By the time Chaplin's next film, *The Circus*, opened on January 6, 1928, *The Jazz Singer* had rocked the industry and the long, expensive process of converting studios and

Charlie finds himself in a tight spot atop the tightrope in *The Circus,* **c. 1927 (© Roy Export SAS).**

theaters to accommodate sound in film had begun. It would be a few years before sound was fully integrated—and even longer before it happened at the Chaplin studio—but the writing was on the wall. Silent film and its attendant live music were on the way out.

The new era in film was challenging enough. *The Circus* was a troubled production from the start—on set and off, from natural and personal sources—making it even worse. From the birth of his second son, Sydney, to Lita Grey's crippling divorce suit, Chaplin faced highs and lows in his personal life. Mother Nature's mighty wind destroyed the tent before shooting even began and a fire ravaged the set in the ninth month of shooting, destroying props. The whole experience proved to be so unpleasant that Chaplin did not even mention the film in his autobiography.

According to a press release, the idea for *The Circus* stems from a fairy tale in *Arabian Nights*: "A poor devil becomes a circus artist against his will, and this new life impresses him." Chaplin said the tightrope scene with the monkeys was the impetus. He began working on the story, originally called *The Traveller*, in November 1925. Early daily production reports show that Chaplin intended Georgia Hale to continue as his leading lady, but he did not renew her contract when it ran out at the end of December. Instead, he cast Lita Grey's childhood friend Merna Kennedy, who was only seventeen at the time. Kennedy had accompanied Grey to the studio on the day she tested for *The Gold Rush*. Harry Crocker, who also served as assistant director *The Circus*, was cast as Rex the tightrope walker and Allan Garcia as Merna's cruel stepfather, the circus Ring Master. Chaplin originally wanted Henry Bergman for the role but Bergman, who taught Chaplin how to tightrope walk for the film, told him, "'No, Charlie, I'm a roly-poly kind-faced man, not the dirty heavy who would beat a girl.' So I was cast as the fat old clown."[132]

Shooting for *The Circus* began on January 11, 1926. In February, Chaplin discovered that all the *Circus* rushes so far were scratched and a month's worth of work—which included Chaplin's tightrope scenes and eighteen costly takes with the 377 extras inside the tent—had to be scrapped. In March, Lita gave birth to Chaplin's second son, Sydney Earle Chaplin, but home life was deteriorating and she walked out on Chaplin at the end of November, taking her two sons with her.

Remembering the situation he had faced with Mildred Harris and *The Kid* during their divorce, at the beginning of December Chaplin packed twenty-two reels of *Circus* footage into two boxes and temporarily suspended studio operations. He cut the staff to a minimum and, except for Kennedy, Bergman, Crocker, and Garcia, all the actors were laid off. At the same time, the Internal Revenue Service came after Chaplin for underpayment of income tax to the tune of $1,113,000. Chaplin smuggled the film on a train and left for the east coast, where he ended up cutting the film in a hotel suite in New Jersey and a studio in New York.

On January 10, 1927, Lita filed for divorce. The 52-page complaint listed Chaplin as co-defendant along with his studio, his company, his valet Kono, manager Alfred Reeves, the National Bank of Los Angeles, the Bank of Italy, and various other corporations and banks. The complaint not only charged infidelity with "a certain prominent film actress," it also listed in lurid detail certain sexual practices from the privacy of the bedroom. A paperback of the document called *The Complaint of Lita* became a salacious bestseller. On August 22, the court awarded Lita $625,000 and a $200,000 trust fund was set up for her sons Charles Jr., and Sydney. It was the largest divorce settlement in American history. When filming on *The Circus* resumed, it proceeded quickly and the world premiere was held at midnight on January 6, 1928, at the Strand Theatre in New York.

Variety reported that the Strand's managing director Joseph Plunkett was going away for a rest, "the kid's first chance since he commenced to lose sleep but not weight shaping up a weekly stage bill for the Strand."[133] In the week before the premiere, Plunkett "spiked a report along Broadway" that he was resigning due to the rumor that the theater was raising its prices to 50 cents and "cutting presentations to the bone or out altogether," no doubt in reaction to the success of *The Jazz Singer*. Plunkett told *The Billboard* "he had no such intention, and if a new policy were to be instituted at the Strand, he does not know about it." But the theater was cleaning house and Henry Dreyfuss, designer of scenes and costumes, and Jack Greenberg, who was in charge of music, both turned in their resignations.[134] The Strand's assistant conductor, Alois Reiser, assumed the position of conductor of the orchestra just in time for Chaplin's premiere.

The decorations on the outside of the theater must have stopped traffic at the busy corner of 47th Street and Broadway. "The Strand was dressed up in canvas," reported *The Billboard*, "the marquee simulating the main entrance to a big top." Inside, "Joseph Plunkett's prolog, introducing animal effects by Messier and Damon, doing stunts to the enlivening strains of von Suppé's *Light Cavalry*, played by Alois Reiser's Strand Symphony Orchestra, got the film away to a notable showing."[135] *The Film Daily* said the brief prologue "nicely set the atmosphere for the picture. The curtains parted on a circus flash which had been announced by a 'barker' through a phonograph. The set showed a circus ring with master of ceremonies in his red coat and long whip directing the aggregation of trained wild animals. These were immense papier-mâché constructions which were ingeniously animated, and performed antics as the leader snapped the whip. It was just sufficient to set the audience nicely for the circus atmosphere of the picture."[136]

The New York Times called *The Circus* "Chaplin's latest cure for melancholy…. As soon as the swinging cane, the old bowler and the feet were seen at the opening show the spectators were thrown into a high state of glee."[137] The *Daily News* called it a "howling success. Charlie once again proves a revelation. A screaming delight. A howling, hearty, happy, slightly slapstick cinema production…. It is, in fact, Broadway's perfect film comedy, and we doubt whether the future months of 1928 will render anything as appreciable. One should see Chaplin; one owes it to oneself." "The hardest-boiled crowd in town went to the midnight opening on Friday," said the *New York Daily Mirror*, "and laughed off all its mascara."[138]

Three weeks later, on January 27, the film opened in Los Angeles at Grauman's Chi-

Program cover for *The Circus* premiere at Grauman's Chinese Theatre, Hollywood, January 27, 1928 (University of Washington Libraries, Special Collections, Rene Irene Grage Photograph and Ephemera Collection, UW 37427).

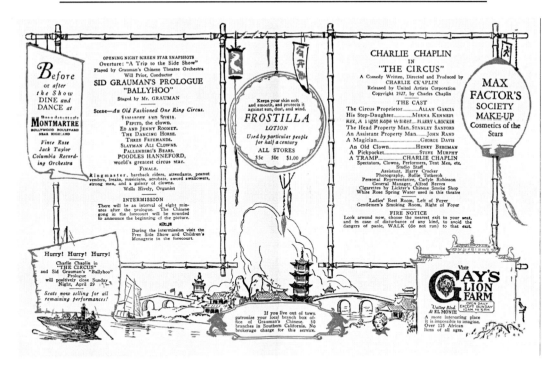

Inside program spread for *The Circus* (1928), including Sid Grauman's "Ballyhoo" Prologue (University of Washington Libraries, Special Collections, Rene Irene Grage Photograph and Ephemera Collection, UW 38049).

nese Theatre, where Sid Grauman made sure his prologue out-topped Plunkett's. The evening began with Arthur Kay conducting the orchestra (though the program listed Will Prior) in the overture, *A Trip to the Side Show*.[139] Grauman's prologue, "Ballyhoo," was set inside "an old-fashioned one ring circus." The bill included acrobats The Three Freehands; Samaroff and Sonia's Russian national dancing and acrobatic dogs; "The Famous Cloudburst"; Pepito the clown; Pallenberg's Bears dancing, roller skating, riding bicycles, walking on stilts, and playing musical instruments; double trapeze artists Ed and Jenny Rooney; and Poodles Hanneford, "ace of clowns, star equestrian and one of the highest-salaried performers in the country." Hanneford arrived in style—once his engagement at the Hippodrome in New York ended, a special train car carried his players and equipment across country.[140]

In between numbers, "Ringmaster, bareback riders, attendants, cowboys, peanut venders [*sic*], freaks, musicians, acrobats, sword swallowers, strong men, and a galaxy of clowns" filled the stage, while Wells Lively played the organ. After the gala premiere, the prologue for the regular run replaced "The Famous Cloudburst" with The Dancing Horse and added the Slayman Ali Clowns. During the eight-minute intermission between the prologue and the film, Grauman encouraged audience members to "visit the Sideshow and the Children's Menagerie in the Forecourt! Free as the air you breathe! Pink lemonade, hot dogs, and other surprises!"[141] Grauman "transferred the foyer of the theatre into a carnival grounds," reported *Moving Picture World*, "with striped awnings, booths and cages of 'wild' animals and the curious crowd which always gather for these openings stood around from five o'clock in the afternoon until well past midnight."[142]

The Circus pulled in $313,136 in box office receipts at the Chinese for the length of its run and eventually grossed over $1 million.[143] Stock themes chosen by the theaters' musical arrangers accompanied the preview screenings. For the premiere performances in New York and Los Angeles, Chaplin worked closely with conductor Arthur Kay to compile a new score.

Kay (1881–1969) attended the Royal Conservatory in Berlin, studying cello under Robert Housman, composition with Max Bruch, and orchestration from Engelbert Humperdinck. After graduation, he sat at the second cello desk in the pit of the Royal Opera and served as assistant conductor under Karl Muck. Muck brought Kay to the U.S. in 1906 as second solo cellist of the Boston Symphony Orchestra, where Kay also acted as assistant conductor, leading out-of-town concerts. For twelve years, Kay was part of Victor Herbert's musical staff, conducting many of Herbert's works, including *The Duchess, Sweethearts, The Only Girl,* and *Eileen.* Kay began his association with Sid Grauman in 1917 as the Musical-Director-General of the Grauman Theatres and the conductor of the Grauman Sunday Morning Concerts until he resigned in 1920 due to "incompatibility of his artistic ideals" with his boss.[144] Kay took charge of the music for the Jensen & Von Herberg theaters in the Northwest, conducting the 65-piece Coliseum Theatre orchestra in Seattle, and was hired to compose his first film score for Maurice Tourneur's *The Last of the Mohicans* in 1920.

The *Los Angeles Times* described Kay as "a dynamic individuality, a mind bristling with ideas and a body almost 'bursting through it[s] shirtsleeves' with energy." "My ideas in synchronization are just a little different from those of many motion-picture conductors," he said. "I do not especially try to imitate an effect in the orchestra because of something which happens on the screen, or not more than two or three times during a performance, and, for the most part, only when the effect is humorous."

> I do not believe that because in the screen picture a man slides down a drain pipe and comes to a stop with a most natural suddenness that everyone in the audience wants to hear the drum rumble while he slides and the cymbals gong when he bumps.

Arthur Kay in the orchestra pit at Grauman's Chinese Theatre. *Motion Picture News,* **February 4, 1928, 333 (courtesy Media History Digital Library).**

Instead, I follow out the picture with well-defined themes. I make one piece which stands for either a person or an idea interpret the changes and development to express almost every emotion. Of course it must be played differently for each individual mood, not cheaply parodied. It must speak in the way that only music can speak.

Then I do not try to rush a theme to get it through in the number of seconds that a certain scene is being shown. Instead, I try to play in the same tempo of the picture. If there is a fade-out then the music, too, fades out; if the scene changes without completing an idea, thus holding the element of suspense, then the music, too, fades out, without finishing the phrase, and goes on with the picture, following for a few seconds some new idea.

The music is sort of a mood background. It is not the trying to imitate the noises which might occur could we hear the actual sounds of that which is being portrayed. In fact the absence of these often grating noises is one thing which makes the silent drama so restful a form of entertainment. It is mirroring in tone the dramatic values which one sees on the screen.[145]

Kay began working with Chaplin on October 25, 1927, and was eventually paid $2,006.75. Chaplin once again turned to the world of opera to set the stage for his latest comedy. In *The Gold Rush*, he conjured Verdian tragedy as counterpoint and unearthed Victor Herbert's 1911 flop *Natoma* to add operatic weight. For *The Circus* he turned to Ruggero Leoncavallo's 1892 tragic opera *Pagliacci*. It was the first opera to be recorded in its entirety and Enrico Caruso's 1907 impassioned rendition of the famous Act I closer, "Vesti la giubba," became the first million-selling recording in history. Later, the Prelude to Act III of Wagner's *Lohengrin* brings Rex and Charlie into the ring in grand style for their tightrope acts.

Rather than open the film with the expected *Thunder and Blazes* march (though it appears in later transition segments), *Pagliacci*'s trumpet fanfares and energetic Act I chorus music underscore the main titles. In the opera, the villagers welcome the arrival of the ragtag band of actors, much as Chaplin welcomes the audience under his cinematic big top. A succession of dotted rhythms and swirling sixteenth notes in the opera Prelude's opening bars open into "a world of sawdust" (a title card removed for the 1969 reissue), ending with a cymbal crash as Merna bursts through the star. Crippled Tonio's revenge music from the opera accompanies the Ring Master's cruelty as he berates Merna ("So you've missed the hoop again"), shoves her to the ground, and denies her food.

Chaplin makes poignant use of "Vesti la giubba" in the Tramp's dream sequence. In the opera, Canio's pain after finding his wife Nedda in the arms of the handsome peasant Silvio exemplifies the time-honored notion of the tragic clown who is smiling on the outside but crying on the inside. In the film, the Tramp sits backstage after yet another failed attempt to get the audience to laugh. Unable to bear Rex's attentions towards Merna any longer, Charlie leaves his body in a clever bit of special effects and gives the smooth talker a swift kick in the pants.

In the compilation score for *A Woman of Paris*, Louis F. Gottschalk had worked in a brief quote of his love theme from *The Girl I Loved*, a film that had opened a couple of months earlier, no doubt in the hopes of generating sheet music sales. Arthur Kay went one step better—he used one of his own instrumental compositions, *A Funny Story* (1926), as Charlie's primary theme. From the moment the Tramp enters "around the side shows," Kay's jaunty bassoon melody, pizzicato strings, and muted brass capture the character's insouciance. Throughout the film, Chaplin and Kay dissect, reformat, and tamper with the theme's tempo to suit the scene's purposes, often with the tune's accompanying grace notes to imitate braying and musical laughter.

Three other Kay compositions, all published in 1925, also make their way into the

The Circus (1928 compilation score)—Ruggero Leoncavallo's 1892 opera *Pagliacci* served as the film's musical sawdust. The opera's introduction and opening chorus underscored the main titles.

score. The *misterioso Mysterious Stranger* cleverly accompanies Charlie's adventures in the lion cage. Dotted rhythms underscore the danger lurking in the cage as the Tramp waves his handkerchief in distress, tries to quiet a barking dog that threatens to wake the sleeping lion, and contends with Merna fainting in fear. Trills and staccato sixteenth notes in the B section of the piece flutter like musical butterflies in Charlie's stomach

***The Circus* (1928 compilation score)—Tonio's revenge in *Pagliacci* provides sinister accompaniment to the Ring Master's cruelty towards Merna.**

when he comes face to face with the tiger before displaying fake courage in front of Merna to a muted trumpet rendition of the "Toreador Song" from Bizet's *Carmen*. Kay's *Gossip* is a light agitato in 6/8 with staccato triplets that underscore Charlie's jerking motions after he accidentally electrocutes himself. *The Accuser* properly underscores the Ring Master's final scene as he points at all the miseries in his life—Merna, Rex, and Charlie. Irving Berlin's mournful "Blue Skies" (1927) ironically comments on the Tramp crumpling up the paper circus star and kicking it into the dust of the departing circus caravan that has left him behind.

The Berlin tune may have been the newest song Chaplin used in the score, but it was by no means the only one familiar to 1928 audiences. A spirited rendition of Chris Smith's 1916 "Down in Honky Tonk Town" (1916) accompanies Charlie being pursued by the mule. "Just a Memory" (1927), by Buddy De Sylva, Lew Brown, and Ray Henderson underscores Charlie's first meeting with Merna, whose life at the hands of her cruel step-father fades in the face of the Tramp's generosity. Charlie mistakenly jumps for joy when he overhears Merna saying she has fallen in love accompanied by De Sylvia-Brown-

The Circus (1928 compilation score)—The humorous bassoon solo of Arthur Kay's *A Funny Story* (1926) provides the perfect musical accompaniment to Charlie's antics.

Henderson's "Lucky Day" (1926), while another De Sylva tune, "When Day Is Done" (1926), inhabits the nighttime quiet with Charlie and Merna around the campfire. Nacio Herb Brown was the bandleader at a club in Hollywood that Chaplin frequented and his popular "The Sneak" (1922), described as "the greatest novelty foxtrot [*sic*] song in a decade," accompanies the pickpocket (Steve Murphy) being nabbed by the policeman.[146] Charlie is an unlikely hit with the circus audience to the tune of Scott Joplin's popular *Maple Leaf Rag* (1899), while he shows off his dance moves on the tightrope to James P. Johnson's "The Charleston" (1923), all the while being attacked by monkeys.

Chaplin also showcases his fondness for operetta. Rudolf Friml's "L'amour, Toujours, L'amour," from his 1922 musical *Bibi of the Boulevards*, is used as Merna's theme, while Victor Herbert's "I'm Falling In Love With Someone" from *Naughty Marietta* (1910) underscores her attraction to Rex. Herbert's "Someday" from his 1917 operetta *Her Regiment* accompanies her admission to the fortuneteller that she has fallen in love, and the maestro's 1900 instrumental *Punchinello* lends musical comedy to the classic William Tell routine. George J. Trinkaus' *Marceline* (1906) accompanies the clowns in performance, while behind the scenes they have a more somber musical identity—Charles Gounod's *Funeral March of the Marionette* (1872).

The Circus (1928 compilation score)—Charlie and the cops chase each around the revolving wheel under the big top to the frenetic accompaniment of Paul Biese's *Speed* (1920).

The Circus (1928 compilation score)—R. Vollstedt's *Jolly Fellows Waltz* (1891) is one of numerous waltzes in the score, this time accompanying scenes with Rex and Charlie shimmying up to the tightrope high above.

Pieces from the silent music folios of the day accompany most of the chases. A series of *agitatos* and *hurrys* by Will L. Becker, Otto Langey, and Carl Kiefert underscore the frenetic pace. Of particular note is Paul Biese's delightful *Speed* (1920), with its circus-like air, chirping woodwind accompaniment, and "speed" propelling Charlie and the chasing cops onto the revolving wheel in the circus tent, much to the delight of the bored audience. And lest Chaplin forget including a waltz, R. Vollstedt's *Jolly Fellows Waltz* (1891) serves as the tightrope music for Rex and Charlie shimmying up the rope.

Most audiences in 1928 would not have heard Chaplin and Kay's efforts. The compiled score was only used at the premiere and perhaps in a few other large theaters that had the requisite orchestra. Musicians at most theaters compiled their own selections or took ideas from the *Circus* cue sheet published by Cameo Music and compiled by Ernst Luz, the musical director of the Loews theater chain and the author of the color-coded *Motion Picture Synchrony*. Many of the pieces suggested in Luz's cue sheet have disappeared into the sands of time, but there are some interesting comparisons to make with Chaplin and Kay's compilation score. Luz foregoes *Pagliacci* and suggests using the expected *Thunder and Blazes* and P. Fahrbach's chaotic *Skaters Galop* to convey a circus atmosphere at the beginning. Oddly, Herman Finck's *Jocoso* is listed to underscore the Ring Master throwing Merna to the ground, whether as irony or as source music playing under the big top is open to interpretation. Victor Herbert's "I'm Falling In Love With Someone" is once again in the mix, though this time as the unrequited love Charlie has for Merna. Another holdover from the compilation score is Herman Finck's delicate *Pirouette* (1911), which underscores Charlie's tryout with the clowns.

At the first Academy Awards banquet on May 16, 1929, at the Roosevelt Hotel, two special awards were given out. One went to Warner Bros. "for producing *The Jazz Singer*, the pioneer outstanding talking picture, which has revolutionized the industry," the second to Chaplin for *The Circus*. A letter from the Academy to Chaplin stated, "The Academy Board of Judges on merit awards for individual achievements in motion picture arts during the year ending August 1, 1928, unanimously decided that your name should be removed from the competitive classes, and that a special first award be conferred upon you for writing, acting, directing and producing *The Circus*. The collective accomplishments thus displayed place you in a class by yourself."[147]

*   *   *

The compilation scores for Chaplin's films, like most scores of this type, are a mixed bag. Because of the tight timeline between the end of production and distribution date,

The Circus (1928 compilation score)—Herman Finck's stately *Pirouette* (1911) gavotte underscores Charlie's clown tryout.

the scores were compiled at a breakneck pace. (This practice, unfortunately, continues today with modern film composers.) The chance to see a Chaplin film and hear what premiere audiences in the 1920s heard is slim at best. Since Chaplin went back later in life and composed new scores for each of these four films, it is understandable that the Chaplin estate wants to keep the filmmaker's final musical vision, both on video and in live performance. But the compilation scores represent Chaplin's musical vision during the making of these films and that reason alone renders them historically valid, not only for study but to hear them in the context of the films themselves.

In a series of concerts in the 1990s, Gillian Anderson, a musical specialist with the Library of Congress, conducted live performances of the compilation scores to *The Gold Rush* and *The Circus*. "The juxtaposition of the music with the action in the film is brilliant," said *The Washington Post* about the National Symphony Orchestra's performance of *The Circus* in 1993. "For example, early in *The Circus*, as Chaplin is seen sprinting from a pursuing policeman, the music keeps a pulse matching the movement exquisitely. Various percussive accents highlight abrupt maneuvers, and touching musical satire is implied at choice moments."[148] The following year, at a performance at the Metropolitan Museum of Art, *The New York Times* said, "The result was extraordinary. *The Circus* is funny and moving. It also gently toys with the fast-fading traditions and genres of silent cinema: a Keystone Kops–like chase intrudes on a circus performance and becomes its star attraction; Charlie Chaplin, the world-famous clown, gets lessons in comedy from failing circus performers. The score is a remarkable companion to the playful plot, a commentator as well as an accompanist."[149]

Once film entered the sound era, Chaplin and the Tramp would go through an identity crisis. How would the world accept an actor whose primary stock in trade was pantomime, much less a character, no matter how beloved, whose only means of communication was silent? While certain doors closed with the advent of synchronized sound, new ones opened.

CHAPTER 4

Who'll Buy My Violets?

W HEN *THE JAZZ SINGER* USHERED in the Sound Era in 1927, Hollywood experienced a seismic shift. Audiences wanted more, and theaters and studios had to scramble—and invest heavily—to rig themselves with new equipment. The number of silent films in production dropped dramatically and actors who had once ruled the box office, but whose voices should have remained silent, quickly found themselves out of work. Chaplin, who had made his fame and fortune without uttering a word on screen, refused to bow to the new technology for his next film, *City Lights*. "I loathe them," he said of sound films. "They are spoiling the oldest art in the world—the art of pantomime. They are ruining the great beauty of silence."[1] By the end of 1929, he had tempered his remarks.

> They fascinate me, anger me and frighten me. Of course, they are here to stay, but not, I think, in their present expression. It's so new that few people know what it's all about and so far most of the results are artistic failures. They are trying to marry the conventions of the theater with the realism of the screen and the result is an illegitimate child…
>
> Don't think I am avoiding dialog because of personal fear. I was on the legitimate stage for years, but I don't wish to give up the eloquence and beauty of pantomime for a spoken title. The printed title is still a legitimate tool. It is optical, the same as the picture, but it has its proper mental effect. I shall still use it when necessary.[2]

Besides, he said, "the Chinese children, the Japanese children, the Hindu, the Hottentot, all understand me. I doubt whether they would understand my Chinese or my Hindustani.[3]

One benefit of the new format, especially for a film composer-in-waiting like Chaplin, was the ability to "absolutely control" the music.[4] "That is something else again," he said. "Quite different and of inestimable value and importance. It is the thing we have most needed. It will prove to be invaluable. It will bring music to people who have never had a real opportunity of hearing it. It will tell its own story, for music, like pictures, is a universal language, everywhere understandable. And it will raise up a whole new school of people, writing scores and librettos just for individual pictures."[5] Sound also offered a chance for audiences around the world to have the same experience at the cinema, and that included music. The technology offered new opportunities for musicians in Los Angeles, but it also put hundreds of amateur and professional musicians around the country out of work. The day of the live theater orchestra was at an end. By the end of 1929, even with studios promising they would still produce silent films, 9,000 cinemas were wired for sound and attendance increased by 15 million for a total of 110 million.[6]

The audience had spoken.

⋆   ⋆   ⋆

Chaplin began working on the story for *City Lights* on December 31, 1927, shortly after *The Circus* had finished shooting. "I began," he said, "with a hazy idea of a blind flower girl sitting on the sidewalk. She is going to be the heroine. And this is the first time the little fellow meets her. She must sell him a flower, and she must mistake him for a rich man. That's what I started with."[7] Chaplin fully embraced synchronized music, but he wanted only minimal sound effects (primarily for comic effect) to tell this simple love story. Only a star of Chaplin's stature—and one with complete control of his own studio—would have dared to buck the trend and have his characters remain silent. By the time he released *City Lights* four years later in 1931, the longest period he had ever devoted to a film, audiences had moved on from silent film and Chaplin's latest cinematic venture seemed riskier than ever.

Many factors resulted in the delay in finishing the film. The first was the death of Chaplin's mother in the summer of 1928. Hannah had been transferred from Cane Hill Asylum to the Peckham House Asylum in September 1912. Sydney and Charlie were not always punctual with their payments for her care but Aunt Kate kept an eye on her sister. When Kate died in 1916, Aubrey Chaplin, Charlie's cousin, took over her duties. Sydney had wanted to bring Hannah to the U.S. in 1917 when Alfred Reeves was traveling from England to become the manager of the Chaplin studio. When the necessary permits were not forthcoming, Hannah was forced to remain in Peckham House. In mid–March 1919, Aubrey cabled Charlie that he hoped he could complete the necessary arrangements by May. But Chaplin was in the middle of his disastrous marriage to Mildred Harris and did not want to take on the extra burden of his sick mother. He sent Tom Harrington to England in 1921, shortly after the release of *The Kid*, to finally bring Hannah to the U.S., setting her up in a rented house with a married couple to look after her. Chaplin still found it painful to witness his mother's mental state and did not visit her often. Hannah died on August 28, 1928, after being admitted to Glendale Hospital with an infected gall bladder. "It is perhaps no coincidence," said author Jeffrey Vance, "that in [*City Lights*] his character rescued a disabled woman and caused her to be cured of her affliction."[8] It is also perhaps no coincidence that Chaplin later named Paulette Goddard's determined heroine in *The Great Dictator* after his mother.

The dilemma of what to do with sound was another reason for the delay in finishing *City Lights*. "I think [Charlie] fully intends to make one version with sound," Reeves wrote to Sydney in January 1929, "but of course he will have a universal picture for those countries where they have not facilities for the new inventions."[9] No doubt the expense of creating two versions of the film was enough to scrap the idea.

Perhaps the greatest frustration and delay came from the film's female lead. "To be a leading lady for me," Charlie told *Photoplay*, "a girl must have appeal, but not necessarily sex appeal."

> She must have youth, but not necessarily screen experience. In fact, I prefer that she have no picture experience. Without it, she has fewer faults to correct. She must be adaptable, too, in order to take direction. She should have some appreciation of music in order to be susceptible to vibrations. When one becomes absorbed in a part one is only a sounding board reflecting the play of emotions.
>
> Also, a girl must be ambitious. Otherwise, she will not take her work seriously. And to succeed, one must be intensely serious, particularly in pictures.[10]

Chaplin's *Circus* co-star Merna Kennedy "preferred not to act the part of the blind girl," so Chaplin went searching for a fresh new face.[11] At 5 foot 5 inches tall and weighing 117 pounds, 20-year-old newcomer Virginia Cherrill was "rumored to be the last natural blonde in Hollywood," said *Variety*. "But who wants figures when the figure is so attractive?"[12] *Photoplay* quipped, "She probably didn't know a Kleig light from an assistant property man, but, P.S., she got the job."[13] Though stories circulated that Chaplin saw Cherrill at a boxing match, in an interview with author Kevin Brownlow years later, she said that Henri d'Abbadie d'Arrast, an assistant on *A Woman of Paris* and assistant director on *The Gold Rush*, had seen her at The Ambassador Hotel in Los Angeles, claiming she was blind. "I'm so short sighted," Cherrill told Brownlow. "I really can't see at all."[14] Chaplin picked Cherrill "because she was the only one who could look blind without being offensive."[15]

It proved to be a difficult casting choice. In one legendary story from the set, it took 342 takes over five days to film the opening scene of Cherrill simply handing the Tramp a flower. Chaplin reasoned the numerous takes were justified—"Has to be perfect. It took a long time. She was an amateur."[16] Chaplin "didn't care how many takes he took," Cherrill said. "In fact, I often thought that if he couldn't think what he was going to do next, he simply went on doing the same shot over again until he thought of it. But he was a perfectionist, and to us it often seemed to be exactly the same, but to him it was not. I think he must have shot enough film to sink the Queen Mary, but he'd take it over and over

It took 342 takes for Chaplin to finally get what he wanted from Virginia Cherrill in *City Lights*'s first scene of the Blind Girl handing a flower to the Tramp, c. 1930 (© Roy Export SAS).

again and when he'd finally say 'It's a take,' we'd breathe a sigh of relief and he'd say, 'Well, perhaps just once more.' ... I'm afraid I wasn't very dedicated."[17] The strain of working with an amateur finally took its toll and Chaplin fired Cherrill in the middle of filming. He cast his *Gold Rush* co-star Georgia Hale in the part, but quickly realized he could not afford to go back and reshoot all the scenes he had already filmed and rehired Cherrill. "I don't think Charlie really liked me very much," Cherrill admitted later. "I don't know why. I liked him. I was very impressed with him. But we had almost no social contact of any kind. I was never invited to his house because he didn't entertain very much, but when he did entertain, I wasn't invited.... Perhaps he saw me as the blind girl, and not as me, and for this reason didn't like me."[18] In later interviews, she was more forthright— "I didn't like Charlie. And Charlie didn't like me."

As the months and years dragged on, and the public eagerly awaited Chaplin's latest picture, journalists kept tabs on the delays. In January 1930, *The New York Times* stated Chaplin had already spent $1 million. In July, the paper of record reported, "It is not often that one is lucky enough to discover Charlie Chaplin actually at work before the camera. In the last eighteen months he has often been lured away from his studio by either tennis, swimming or a desire to play the violin."[19] Nine months later, "It is fairly safe to predict that Chaplin's forthcoming voiceless comedy, *City Lights*, on which he has been working only when the spirit moved him during the last two years, will not only be as great a financial success as any of his previous productions, but may lead to the making of quite a number of other voiceless productions."[20]

Chaplin hoped so too. "Because the silent or non-dialogue picture has been temporarily pushed aside in the hysteria attending the introduction of speech," he said, "by no means indicates that it is extinct or that the motion picture screen has seen the last of it."

> Why did I continue to make non-dialogue films? The silent picture, first of all, is a universal means of expression. Talking pictures necessarily have a limited field, they are held down to the particular tongues of particular races. I am confident that the future will see a return of interest in non-talking productions because there is a constant demand for a medium that is universal in its utility.... Understand. I consider the talking picture a valuable addition to the dramatic art regardless of its limitations, but I regard it only as an addition, not as a substitute.... There is nothing in *City Lights* that a child won't follow easily and understand."[21]

Though he did not like to portray it to the press, Chaplin was nervous about the film's reception. Even with a glitzy reception in Los Angeles (where he attended the premiere with Albert Einstein and his wife), Chaplin rented the George M. Cohan Theatre in New York and, unhappy with United Artists' publicity campaign, spent $60,000 of his own money. "They were running tiny ads which referred to me as 'our old friend,'" he said. "Never mind telling them about 'our old friend,' I said. You're not selling chewing gum. Talk about the picture. We've got to let them know we're in town."[22] The film ran at the Cohan for twelve weeks with as many as nine showings daily.

"*City Lights* won't change the talkies back to silent pictures (incidentally, no one in these talkative times could get away with a silent picture except Mr. Chaplin)," said the *New York Sun*. "But what *City Lights* will do will be to put Chaplin among the welcoming shades of immortal comedians."[23] The "master of screen mirth and pathos ... proved so far as he is concerned the eloquence of silence," said Mordaunt Hall in *The New York Times*. "Many of the spectators either rocking in their seats with mirth, mumbling as their sides ached, 'Oh, dear, oh, dear,' or they were stilled with sighs and furtive tears.... It was a joyous evening. Mr. Chaplin's shadow has grown no less."[24]

City Lights grossed $2 million in the U.S. alone but studio executives were quick to point out that the success of Chaplin's film did not signal a return to silent films. "Regardless of the success of *City Lights*," said Paramount's Adolph Zukor, "there will be no change in the production policy of our company as regards the making of talking pictures. Talking pictures are here to stay and it is unthinkable that any definite movement will be made toward the return of silent pictures. Talking pictures not only gave the screen greater scope by giving it a voice, but they have proved that they are much more popular with the public than silent pictures." Winfield Sheehan, general production manager of Fox Film, said, "The presentation of Mr. Chaplin's film, great though it is, will not affect the proportion for talking pictures to be made by the Fox Film Corporation. Talking pictures are firmly implanted, and so far as silent films are concerned there will be only occasional exceptions, such as those made by the world's finest pantomimist, Chaplin. But remember, there is at present only one Chaplin." Samuel Goldwyn admitted, "Chaplin is a great artist, but because his picture is a huge success—and I believe it will gross more than any other picture—there is no reason to think that a person who is not a Chaplin can accomplish the same thing.... I might say, so far as Chaplin is concerned, that I would give Charlie a million dollars to appear in a dialogue film." Joseph M. Schenck, president of United Artists, no doubt sticking up for his company's own product, said, "*City Lights* is truly a great picture.... Chaplin proves the value of pantomime on the screen. I am sure in future a minimum of dialogue will be employed in the making of motion pictures."[25]

* * *

"By far the finest screen marriage is that of pantomime and music," Chaplin said. "It always has been, but heretofore all we could do was to have some one score a picture to well-known themes and then hope that the organist would play them. You know what happened in the small towns—the high-school girl played anything she wishes and usually out of all harmony with the action."

> Now, however, we can absolutely determine the music and as it is part of the mechanical projection, nobody can change it and the smallest theater will hear it just as completely as the Roxy.
> This is a wonderful thing for me, and even though I'm using no dialog in my picture I think you'll find that the musical accompaniment will satisfy all expectations for "sound."
> Furthermore, I am using no popular airs; my music will be just as original as the picture, for *I am writing every bit of it myself!* [Italics original] I am having it scored and orchestrated as I go along and every movement and gesture is accompanied by its own musical theme.[26]

In many versions of the film's story, the blind girl refers to the Tramp as "the Duke," taken from her opening scene in which she mistakes him for a man of wealth. Early story continuity documents detail Chaplin's original idea for the use of a song:

> The blind girl shall own a phonograph which she operates at her flower stand. Her favorite record shall be "Bright Eyes" or some other semi-jazzy number. The Duke becomes haunted by the melody and whistles the tune as he strolls. In a penny arcade he seeks the number and listens to it through the old-fashioned ear receivers and his mannerisms attract attention by onlookers. This means is also suggested for a love-making scene between the Duke and the girl through his answering her song with another of significance. The Duke also buys or gets in some manner new records for the girl.[27]

The entertainment magazines and trade journals often offered conflicting stories on Chaplin's musical plans for the film. In 1928, *Exhibitors Herald* reported the film would feature an Irving Berlin tune. "Hold everything!" trumpeted *Motion Picture News*. "Charlie Chaplin is reported to be capitulating to talkers. Not that it's to be any grand plunge from pantomime to talk, but he's reported planning to have three songs in his *City Lights*, which he had planned on absolutely voiceless. Charlie is reported practicing, which means that he is considering singing at least one of the songs himself."[28] Even the film's program book mentions other numbers "created by Chaplin to be heard while *City Lights* glides across the screen"—"Tomorrow the Sun Will Shine," "Happy Romance," "Promenade," "Orientale" and the title piece, a one-step which "will undoubtedly find favor with those terpsichorean in desire."[29] There is no evidence in Chaplin's papers of the Berlin tune, much less any of the other titles, not as songs or score cues.

Instead, on September 27, 1929, Chaplin sent a copy of his new song, "Beautiful, Wonderful Eyes," to the Copyright Office at the Library of Congress. He neglected to send the dollar fee to officially copyright the song, but quickly remedied the situation and as of October 9, Chaplin's proposed theme for *City Lights* was legally protected. "Yes, I have a 'theme song,'" he told *Screenland*, "but it is not registered in the usual way. No principal sings. I, in my character of *Charlie*, first hear it as a phonograph record. You get the title from the disc itself—*Wondrous Eyes* [*sic*], by Charles Chaplin. The song is strongly impressed upon me so that later, when I fall in love with the little blind girl, whenever *Wondrous Eyes* is played by street musicians or in saloons it has a very dramatic significance. In fact, all through the picture music and song become a background for the action almost as important as the pantomime itself."[30]

The gentle tango has a narrow vocal range, no more than a sixth in each section and no higher than an octave, which perhaps lends credence to the report that Chaplin, with his limited vocals, had plans to sing the song himself. Chaplin likes to repeat rhythmic figures in the melody, a feature of his compositions that at times turns monotonous.

"Beautiful, Wonderful Eyes" (1929, music and lyrics by Charles Chaplin)—Chaplin's original theme for the Blind Girl in *City Lights*.

The triteness of the unimaginative lyrics also, unfortunately, mar whatever pleasure can be found in the chorus' repeated word structure.

> *I can't forget when first we met beneath the starry skies.*
> *But most of all I would recall the magic of your eyes.*
>
> *CHORUS*
> *Beautiful eyes, what have they seen to make them so beautiful?*
> *Wonderful eyes, what have they dreamed to make them so wonderful?*
> *Sorrowful eyes, what have they lost to make them so sorrowful?*
> *Beautiful wonderful eyes*
>
> *Through all the tears, through all the years, the vision never dies.*
> *Again I see in memory, the magic of your eyes.*
>
> REPEAT CHORUS[31]

Even the film's program book notes that "Beautiful, Wonderful Eyes" was to be "one of the outstanding numbers to be offered with his latest picture." It mentions Irving Berlin as its publisher and that "only the music accompanies the film."[32] (It does not.) Without its inclusion in the picture, that "outstanding number" probably did not sell many copies of sheet music. But Chaplin's name was reason enough for the Original American Orchestra to record the song in London on March 3, 1931. In 1957, Chaplin refused to sign the song's copyright renewal form "as he does not wish for the publication of this song to be continued."[33] The song was finally published in the 1992 compilation *The Songs of Charlie Chaplin*, and The Fureys recorded it on their 2001 *Charlie Chaplin & The Fureys* album.

*   *   *

The day Chaplin completed work on *City Lights* was one of "extreme relief," he said. "After fretting and stewing for almost two years, to see the end in sight was like the finish of a marathon. Usually after each picture I go to bed for a day or two to replenish my nerves, but this time there was another task ahead—the composing of music and synchronizing it to the picture."[34] He worked for almost four months and spent nearly $40,000 on the music.[35]

In a 1952 radio interview, Chaplin said, "I use music as a counterpoint and I learned that from the Fred Karno Company. For instance if they had squalid surroundings with a lot of comedy tramps working in it, they would have very beautiful, boudoir music, something of the 18th century, very lush and grandiose, and it would be satirical, a counterpoint."[36] He admitted, "I don't write music, so I have to have another man there."[37] That other man was Arthur Johnston of the Irving Berlin Company. The similarities between Chaplin and Johnston were many. Johnston (1898–1954) was "a self-made man of music," proclaimed *Billboard*. And like Chaplin, "he made the grade in Tin Pan Alley under his own power without taking the trouble to acquaint himself with the techniques of old world composers and spending years and money in acquiring a classical education." Johnston "was born with sharps and flats in his blood" and "mastered the piano in 'six easy lessons.'"[38] He could play in any key and, after working as a staff pianist for music publisher Fred Fisher, became Irving Berlin's "personal music secretary."[39] He arranged and conducted the first *Music Box Revue* at Berlin's new Music Box Theatre in 1921, and he continued to serve those roles on subsequent Berlin musicals.

"A young man well known to all Broadwayites will go down in history as the originator of all those funny sounds like, 'Doo doodle doo,' 'Vo-de-o-do' or what have you," wrote Sam Coslow, Johnston's frequent writing partner.

> His name is Arthur Johnston, and he is noted for being the man who puts all of Irving Berlin's melodies on paper—in fact Berlin never goes anywhere without having Arthur along, as he may think of something at any moment and if Arthur isn't there with a piece of manuscript paper, the world might lose another masterpiece.... Arthur suddenly blossomed forth one day with a harmony arrangement of "Sittin' in a Corner," in which every line ended with "that's all I do—doodle-oo-do" if you get what I mean. That was the germ that started it all. From then on, every sister act, harmony team, etc. on the stage commenced putting "Doodles," "Vo-de-o's," "How-de-ows" and various noises and sounds of all descriptions between the lines of their ditties. The rest is history.[40]

When Berlin went west to Hollywood in 1929, he took Johnston with him, where he orchestrated the scores for *Putting on the Ritz, Mammy*, and *Reaching for the Moon*. Johnston was Berlin's pianist for twenty years but when Berlin went back east, Johnston stayed out west.

As Eric James, Chaplin's music associate the last twenty years of life, related in his autobiography, Chaplin would convey his musical wishes "by singing, humming, or three-fingered playing on the piano."[41] Chaplin admitted of his piano playing, "I can play ... I have no technique, but I know myself what I want—what to do. I'm not very good." Chaplin would often tell his music associates, "I want it just crude—I want it like me.... Play the tune—I want the tune first, then you can go into the violins and all that afterwards, but I want to hear the tune clean." He loved music in general, but "I find that when I do this business with the composing, my fingers get more alive and more flexible.... Everything I see is in design.... And partly feeling the moves.... The mood you're in and the situation."[42]

"It was amazing how, from this, music would emerge that was both acceptable and correct, fitting to the mood of the pictures," said James. Chaplin often carried around a cassette recorder to log his musical thoughts. "His other method of committing to memory some melody that might suddenly come to him was extremely bizarre."

> He would jot down on paper the names of established pieces of music that contained the notes he required. For instance he might put down "first two notes of Grieg's 'Morning,'" [*sic*] "next four notes, those in the opening bars of Liszt's 'Liebestrmaume,'" [*sic*] another three bars from something else and so on and so on. Later he would give me the list and I would notate them on sheet music and begin to create the melody I felt he had in mind. It was the most arduous and difficult way I've ever heard of in music composition. I always felt quite amazed that Charlie, with all his talents, had never taken the trouble to acquire the elementary knowledge of music that would have saved the agony of the foregoing, and made life a good deal easier, and maybe done away with the need to employ a musician like me!

City Lights **arranger Arthur Johnston, c. 1934 (Photofest).**

Charlie would always voice his opinion as to which instrument in the orchestra should be given the various passages of the music. "This phrase," he would say, "must be given to the violins, and we must have a cello obbligato with it," or "Let us give this phrase to the woodwind and then throw it to the brass," and so on, until every phrase had been allocated.

Charlie was not a lover of the brass section but preferred the strings, and in particular the cellos. He would have used them in every conceivable passage of the music had I not taken a firm stand and pointed out that their repetitious use would destroy the validity of all that we had done.[43]

According to Jerry Epstein, who would later serve as Chaplin's assistant on *Limelight* and *The Chaplin Revue*, and as producer on *A Countess from Hong Kong*, "Charlie went along with Irving Berlin's theory: 'All that any composer has in him … is one song. Every song he writes after that is a variation on the original.'"[44]

Chaplin making music was big news. "In making his picture silent, for subsequent synchronization," said *The New York Times*, "Mr. Chaplin has not been unmindful of music that is to come. Thus, in a cabaret sequence he devotes a considerable part of a reel to photographing a negro orchestra as it plays for dancers. But the skill of the craftsman is so marked that one is not conscious of a need for sound as a saxophone player or a trombone player attacks his blaring with much visual gusto; the rhythm of the music is there already."[45]

Thank the studio's publicity department for much of the discrepancies—and hyperbole—passed down over the years regarding Chaplin's musical talents.

Charlie Chaplin is an accomplished musician. In this art he is self-taught and he is known to be the master of numerous instruments. His talent in this regard includes the violin, chello [*sic*], piano, organ, concertino and several of the brasses…

There is not a human voice used at anytime throughout the picture but the unique manner employed through instrumental music is declared to be a revolutionary step in synchronization…

With the presentation of *City Lights* Chaplin makes his debut as a musician…. Many months were devoted to this phase by the producer, who is, although not generally known, an accomplished pianist, organist, violinist, cellist and harpist.[46]

In his review of *City Lights*, critic George Jean Nathan incorrectly stated the score consisted of "nothing more than a cheap paraphrase of … past popular tunes."[47] Because Chaplin's career had blossomed during the silent era when compilation scores of past (and present) popular tunes were the norm, it is no surprise that he chose to continue the practice to a certain extent, albeit judiciously placed primarily for comic effect.

The first recognizable tune occurs in the opening scene where the Tramp is discovered sleeping underneath a tarp at the dedication of a new statue. Chaplin made fun of the cinema's new sound technology and the pomposity of elected officials using his own voice "with an instrument in my mouth," not a kazoo as has been historically assumed but most likely a saxophone or brass mouthpiece.[48] When he wakes up and gracefully tries to get down, he impales himself on the sword of a statue. The band strikes up "The Star-Spangled Banner," and he struggles to remain erect and properly patriotic, all the while still impaled on the sword. The cue is only twenty-one seconds long but Chaplin mines further humor from the situation by contrasting the Tramp's silliness against a typically solemn tune. A novelist who had viewed the rushes of the first reel said it would be "a good touch if Chaplin were to beat time to the national anthem while the spear caused his position to be ridiculous." Chaplin, who did not like to receive suggestions from even his closest friends and advisors unless asked, would have none of it—"He wants me to tell everybody what a funny man I am."[49]

Music notes in the Chaplin Archive paint a different musical portrait (and actions)

City Lights (1931)—A boozy take on the melody from Charles Marshall and Harold Lake's 1908 British hit "I Hear You Calling Me" serves as humorous underscore to Charlie's hiccupping from swallowing the whistle.

for this scene. "On the unveiling of statue when figure is fully revealed, get ready for intro-duction of Chaplin. On insert start call in low register. On insert of Henry [Bergman], begin hurry music. When policeman stops saluting, go right into elephant theme. As C.C. stands erect and touches trousers—play 'Hail, hail, the gang's all here.' As C.C. folds trousers, start, 'I wish I was in Dixie.'"[50] Chaplin had secured the copyrights for these tunes, as well as "Home, Sweet Home," but eventually discarded them.

The next popular melody may be unfamiliar to many of today's audiences, but it underscores one of Chaplin's cleverest uses of music. In the party scene at the millionaire's mansion, the Tramp accidentally swallows a whistle that chirps as he hiccups. The situ-ation gives Chaplin one of his best audio gags, one that would not have been nearly as successful without synchronized sound. "The whistle was very difficult to synchronize," Chaplin said. "We took the scene some eighteen times. Either the whistle was a little too soon or too late."[51] When a singer stands up to perform, the melody he "sings" is only heard in the solo violin introduction that accompanies him. The humor comes from the song title—"I Hear You Calling Me," a British ballad by Charles Marshall and Harold Lake from 1908 that became a hit for Irish tenor John McCormack. When the Tramp moves to the patio, a duet of the tune for boozy trombone and violin subtly heightens the comedy as the whistle "calls" a cab from around the corner. Chaplin's audiences prob-ably would have understood the musical reference, especially since McCormack had recently sung the song in the 1930 film *Song o' My Heart*. Today, the laughs result from a combination of the whistle and Chaplin's peerless facial expressions. But his sly musical take on the song title gives the moment an extra level of clever musical wit.

Somewhere between October 1929 and the film's release in February 1931, Chaplin discarded his own "Beautiful, Wonderful Eyes" and replaced it with "La Violetera," written by José Padilla in 1914 and also known as "Who'll Buy My Violets?" No doubt Chaplin chose to incorporate the tune as a tribute to Spanish singer Raquel Meller, who had pop-ularized the song. Meller had visited Chaplin on the set of *The Circus* and he originally tried to secure her for the lead role in *City Lights*. Charles Chaplin, Jr., said the song "was a favorite" of his father.[52] While the Spanish flavor of the melody does not match the del-icate quality of Virginia Cherrill's performance, the habanera rhythm in the accompani-ment stands in for the Tramp's courtship dance. "Everything I do is dance," Chaplin admitted in a later interview. "I think in terms of dance. I think more so in *City Lights*. The blind girl—beautiful dance there. I call it a dance."[53] The weight on the downbeat followed by a lift up to the first quarter note and back paints a subliminal impression of his shy reticence in pursuing her. In other words, there is hesitation in the musical rests, followed by a slight "step" forward, then back. This understated rhythm underscores the Tramp's actual back-and-forth movements in his first meeting with the flower girl. At this stage, it also provides a more interesting musical clue to their budding relationship than the overt sentimentality of the main melody.

In an interview with the *San Francisco Call-Bulletin*, Spanish-American bandleader Xavier Cugat said he played the violin on "La Violetera" for the score. "Chaplin chose me to do it, I suppose, because I know Miss Meller, because I am Spanish, and because he felt I had the 'feel' of it. Any other musician could have done it, but Chaplin is that way."[54] Further corroboration has yet to surface regarding Cugat's participation and there is no record in the daily production reports or other studio records to indicate that he had anything to do with the film. It makes a nice story though.

City Lights (1931)—José Padilla 1914 song "La Violetera" ("Who'll Buy My Violets?"), the primary theme for the score.

Chaplin had "strange work habits," director Luis Buñuel later reminisced, "which included composing the music for his films while sleeping. He'd set up a complicated recording device at his bedside and used to wake up partway, hum a few bars, and go back to sleep. He composed the entire score of 'La Violetera' that way, a plagiarism that earned him a very costly trial."[55] Even though Padilla had been given credit on the original cue sheet and properly been paid his royalties over the years, he sued Chaplin in French court for the use of the song to the tune of 500,000 francs. But the court ruled that Padilla and the music publisher would only receive 15,000 francs, about $990.[56] The song was not given onscreen credit until Padilla's heirs protested and title cards were finally reconstructed for later reissues.

Chaplin quotes other popular tunes such as Stephen Foster's "Old Folks at Home," W. C. Handy's "St. Louis Blues," and some clever uses of "How Dry I Am" for the drunk millionaire. Though Chaplin reportedly composed some original themes for *The Idle Class* and *The Kid* in 1921, if he did, they are now lost. But the task of writing eighty-two minutes of music for *City Lights* was a daunting prospect for even the most seasoned composer. And since he could not read or write music, Chaplin was forced to convey his musical vision by whatever means necessary.

*   *   *

Chaplin described his musical style as "simple," in keeping with the character of the Tramp.[57] "It was evident that Chaplin had constantly sought to simplify, to get rid of arrangements that were too complicated," said composer Carl Davis, who rearranged *City Lights* for live performance in 1989 for the Chaplin centennial and has conducted numerous Chaplin's scores live to picture. "In this way he was making the score stronger and also less distracting. It was a process of intense simplification."[58] This "simple music," combined with Chaplin's natural melodic gifts, produced hummable tunes that often harkened back to his days in the English music halls. On the original cue sheet, all of Chaplin's newly composed music was simply listed as "Original," with the occasional distinction of a "Valse" or "Fox-trot." In 1972, Eric James compiled a revised cue sheet to conform to requirements from collection societies like ASCAP and PRS for royalty collections. The new cue sheet had cue titles like a silent film—"Fade in to crowd (fanfare)," "Title: 'To the people of this city, etc.,'" "Speaker beckons," "Statue unveiled."

In *City Lights*, Chaplin laid the groundwork for certain musical styles that he would continue to use through the rest of his career. The two "Promenade" themes embody the Tramp's carefree walk through life. The first is an ascending melody that accompanies the Tramp on his first leisurely sidewalk stroll. The triplets and dotted rhythms give the theme an easygoing bounce that offsets the cruelty of the taunting newspaper boys on the corner. Chaplin, in turn, uses this "Promenade" music as a springboard for other themes, which also incorporate bright major key signatures and dotted rhythms, and provide further musical confirmation of the Tramp's innocence and essential good nature.

The second half of the promenade music is a waltz, one of several Chaplin composed for the film and a musical genre he used in nearly every score. The "Valse Promenade" immediately follows the earlier "Promenade" theme as the Tramp eyes a naked bronze statue through a store window. The melody line mimics the Tramp's back-and-forth steps as he comes perilously close to falling into the elevator shaft in the sidewalk. Caesuras, musical markings that indicate a complete pause, give the theme a halting quality as if the Tramp is thinking during these musical rests.

These two "Promenade" themes are associated with the Tramp's elegant view of himself, at least as seen through the eyes of his creator. An outsider's view of the Tramp is decidedly different. Chaplin neatly presents the more obvious bumbling side of the Tramp's personality with a loping, staccato theme in the bassoon. Though it is not a strict

City Lights (1931)—**Charlie walks around the city streets to a graceful "Promenade."**

City Lights (1931)—Charlie dances a halting "Valse Promenade" with a naked bronze statue in a store window.

City Lights (1931)—The opening jazz clarinet melody.

interpolation of the first "Promenade" theme, the dotted rhythms and triplets relate this theme to its predecessor.

Chaplin began work on the film in the waning years of the Jazz Age. By the time the film opened in 1931, the Great Depression had the country in its grips, and the jazz elements incorporated into the score harken back to a simpler time and provide an ironic counterpoint to a population that was closer to the Tramp's baggy clothing than the millionaire's hedonistic lifestyle. The jazz clarinet that opens the score pays more than a passing nod to Gershwin's *Rhapsody in Blue* and serves as an introduction to major set pieces, from the main titles to the unveiling of the statues and the Tramp's boxing preparations. A swaggering three-note syncopated figure brashly spells out the film's title ("cit-y lights"), which recurs later in the boxing scene with the equally swaggering pugilists.

Chaplin employs a number of other dance rhythms. The trumpets and violins play a flamenco theme that swirls along with harp glissandi and chattering castanets. First heard in the main title, like the "city lights" motif, the theme conveys the energy of the city and later the boxing match being slugged out off screen. The triplets and dotted rhythms of a quickstep fox-trot unveil Charlie asleep on the statue and his hilarious attempts to climb down gracefully, as if the two subdivisions of the beat were the two characters struggling with each other. Later, the theme comes back as the Tramp and the suicidal millionaire grapple to pull each other out of the river. The restaurant scene features a pair of lively fox-trots in delightful dance band arrangements of muted trumpet and saxophones.

If "La Violetera" is the *pas de deux* for Charlie and the blind girl, then the delicate F major theme for solo violin is hers alone. Like the "Valse Promenade," the theme is a

City Lights (1931)—**Chaplin captures the bustling city streets in swirling flamenco music.**

halting melody that conveys her essential kindness as well as loneliness, and the challenges of going through life disabled. Later as the Tramp walks with her, solo becomes duet. The Tramp's bumbling bassoon theme uses a triplet pickup note feature that can be found in numerous Chaplin themes throughout his career as a composer.

While Chaplin liked to write elegant music to frame his comedies, he often set the music on autopilot and got out of the way. For instance, the violins and violas play a furious series of eighth notes in thirds, chugging along at a fast clip and descending the scale every four bars. Brass punctuate the rhythm with staccato notes that arpeggiate up the

City Lights (1931)—A solo violin theme conveys the Blind Girl's loneliness.

chord. By itself, the music is not particularly memorable. But it serves as straight man to the onscreen comedy in scenes such as the dignitary speeches at the statue unveiling, Charlie and the millionaire careening through the city streets, and the one-two punch of the boxing sequence, giving them all a sense of implacable forward momentum.

Chaplin's most affecting theme bookends the Tramp's expression of love and is heard only twice within the body of the film, at moments of maximum emotional impact. The first instance occurs after the Tramp drives the blind girl home in the millionaire's car. On the steps to her flat, he seals his affections with a kiss of her hand. In the finale, she touches the Tramp's hand, a sweet reversal of fortune, finally realizing that he provided the money for the operation to restore her sight. In both cases, the glacial pace of the melody hovering over sustained chords gives the theme an ethereal quality and adds greatly to the poignancy of the scenes. In its earlier incarnation, the theme is scored softly for nearly the entire orchestra, with gentle, syncopated afterbeats in the accompaniment. For the emotional final scene, Chaplin and Johnston orchestrated the tender melody for violin quartet.

Chaplin's immortal final shot to *City Lights,* c. 1930 (© Roy Export SAS).

As Chaplin fades the film to black, he scores the music against expectations with the theme morphing into a full-bodied rendition in the full orchestra. After such a delicate and heartbreaking visual and musical finale, why did Chaplin choose to close the score so forcefully? Was it to cap off the film on a grand, dramatic scale? Or does it add even further to the ambiguity of what happens to the two characters after the final shot? The final A-minor chord does not lean toward a happy res-

City Lights **(1931)—The ethereal musical finale.**

olution for them. But in the nearly eighty years since its release, this classic ending is still open to interpretation and discussion, which has as much to do with Chaplin's music as his memorable visuals.

The *New York Sun* commented that the score's "*Pagliacci* strains, coupled with Chaplin's few moments of affectation, induced the fear that he was deliberately projecting himself as the quaint clown, the Grockish literary pantomimist, but after the swallowing of the whistle we knew that he had kept his head."[59] *The New York Times* said, "The synchronized music score helps the movement of this comedy.... There are times when the notes serve almost for words."[60] Chaplin himself took a rare humble view of his accomplishment. "I really didn't write it down," he told the *New York Telegram*. "I la-laed and Arthur Johnston wrote it down, and I wish you would give him credit, because he did a very good job. It is all simple music, you know, in keeping with my character."[61]

George Jean Nathan took Chaplin at his word and trashed him as "a sometimes moderately imaginative scenarist and a very shabby musician."[62] But documents in the Chaplin Archive prove otherwise. A look at the music notes for the Tramp's first scene with the flower girl illustrate the amount of detail that went into the timings for Chaplin's cues:

Reel 1, No. 7 Fade in on flowers
   1. On verse, sustain note as girl is offering flowers to passers-by. No note sustain on second passage as C.C. comes in until insert of girl and then sustain note again.
   2. On first big insert of girl offering flowers to C.C.—start phrase of note and sustain to C.C. looking at her.
   3. As girl kneels, start chorus.
   4. On title "Did you pick it up, sir?" play second strain on second chorus
   5. As C.C. moves, start phrase and sustain note as C.C. looks around corner. Last note of first phrase as C.C. peeks around corner.
   6. After cameras move, start second phrase.
   7. Hold phrase as C.C. starts tip-toeing toward her to sit down.
   8. Start next phrase as C.C. moves to sit down and sustain note after he sits down and cameras move.
   9. As girl gets up to get water, start next phrase.
   10. Play the last strain as C.C. is on corner of picture making exit.
   11. When title "afternoon" is fully in, play Promenade. Leave out introduction.
   12. As C.C. starts up to window first time, start first note of waltz.
   13. As C.C. goes back stop and pause on second half of chorus.
   14. As elevator goes down with C.C. on it, run down the scale.[63]

After filming on *City Lights* ended on October 4, 1930, the daily production reports listed that Chaplin was "in conference" on the musical synchronization. Arthur Johnston worked with Chaplin beginning November 14 for the next ten weeks. Conductor Alfred Newman, the musical director at United Artists, arrived the week of Christmas and began to look over the score in preparation for orchestra rehearsals the following week. Newman (1900–1970) had already had a rich, full career on the vaudeville circuit as the "The Marvelous Boy Pianist" before eventually picking up the baton and becoming the youngest musical director in the country. In 1919, he was hired by Victor Herbert to conduct *The Dream Girl*. The following year he began a decade-long stint on Broadway conducting musicals for the likes of George Gershwin and Rodgers & Hart. Newman moved to California in 1930 to work with Johnston on Berlin's *Reaching for the Moon*.

The Chaplin Studios did not have a music department of its own and never would, which is odd considering how important music was to the studio boss. Chaplin and his staff attended the first rehearsal of the 36-piece orchestra at United Artists on December 29. Chaplin wrote for an Abe Lyman-size "dance orchestra," a group that had recorded two of his previous compositions. The *City Lights* ensemble consisted of a small group of strings and winds, three trumpets, two trombones, tuba, banjo, harp, piano, and drums.[64]

Chaplin described his synchronization process in a section that's was edited out of "A Comedian Sees the World," his series of articles about his world tour in *Woman's Home Companion*:

> There is a large room about 100' × 60'. At one end is a screen and the other a padded projection room. The orchestra sits in front of the screen. There are "fishing rods" on wheels but instead of a fish at the end of the line, there is a microphone. These are placed meticulously about the orchestra. On one side there is a small sound-proof room on wheels big enough for a man to sit on. Here the occupant controls the sound which is transmitted to the main recording room where it is actually produced on film and disc. Before recording, the picture is run and music and sound effects are rehearsed. The man in the box tells if you are playing too loud, or whether your noise effects are properly timed with the action of the picture. When everything is perfected, the sound operator signals to the Recording Room and then to the Projection Room: The Projection machine[s] are inter-locked so that they synchronize: then the sound effects are played to suit the action. One reel at a time is completed which is immediately played back for your approval. Something may be out of time. Then you must do it over again."[65]

Though stories from recording sessions on later films tell a different tale, Chaplin usually had high praise for the musicians—"There is nothing so warm and moving as the sight of a symphony orchestra. The romantic lights of their music stands, the tuning up and the sudden silence as the conductor makes his entrance, affirms the social, cooperative feeling."[66]

The first recording session took place on New Year's Eve 1930, two sessions totaling nearly eight hours of recording. Recording resumed on January 2, 1931, with the orchestra breaking at 7:45 p.m. and Chaplin, Johnston, and Newman working until two o'clock the following morning. The session on January 3 lasted from 2:00 p.m. to 1:30 a.m., with a three-hour break for dinner. The most brutal sessions came on the final two days—January 5, which lasted from 9:00 a.m. to 8:15 p.m., with only an hour break in the middle of the afternoon, and January 6, recording from 3:00 p.m. to 2:00 a.m. Chaplin, Johnston, and Newman spent the next couple of weeks going over the recordings and making notes of changes. Following the preview screening on January 20, they tinkered further with the score to match newly edited scenes. The orchestra went back into the recording studio for two days beginning January 23 to resynchronize the revised music. Henry Bergman was deeply disappointed in the final musical results. "The terrible deficiencies of the medium are too apparent," he said. "I don't think they will ever overcome them. Thirty-five [*sic*] of the very finest artists played the score for *City Lights* so beautifully on the set. Through the mechanics of the microphone it became something else."[67]

Chaplin paid Alfred Newman and the Sound Department staff $800 per week for seven weeks, totaling $5,600. The musicians' payroll amounted to $19,232.26, and Arthur Johnston and bandleader Jimmie Grier (who was a friend of Johnston's and may have helped in the arranging of the score) received a total of $5,880.94. Other fees brought the total cost of music and synchronization to $38,997.77.

On July 24, 1931, Sydney signed an agreement on behalf of his brother granting Editions Campbell Connelly "the rights in all the musical numbers owned and controlled by him" in *City Lights* for all the countries in Europe, including Great Britain and Ireland. Chaplin would receive a ten percent royalty on all sheet music sales—"the Edition to be of high class and in keeping with his name and prestige"—and sixty-five percent of the gross amount from performing rights "throughout all territories."[68] One of the pieces attributed to the publishing company was a bizarre piano-vocal version of the score with lyrics by Gene Silver. The 132-page score has a vocalist singing the entire film with choice lyrics such as "In the spell of city li-ghts, li-ghts, li-ghts / City lights are beaming now, / City lights are streaming now, / Covering the joys and the sorrows of all" for the jazz clarinet and opening syncopation.[69] The lyrics throughout make no attempt to tell the story of the film. How, when, where, or what was the purpose of this version is hard to imagine.

Chaplin re-released *City Lights* in 1950 and *Life* magazine named it the best film of the year, besting contemporary classics such as *All About Eve* and *Sunset Boulevard* (which contains Gloria Swanson's delightful Tramp impersonation). When Chaplin decided to re-release a number of his feature films for extended runs at New York's Plaza Theater in late 1963 and 1964, *City Lights* was the first film that played and, with *Monsieur Verdoux*, enjoyed the longest run (nine weeks each).

With *City Lights*, Chaplin was definitely bitten by the composing bug. "Charlie had a flair for watching the action on screen, singing to a pianist or into a tape recorder, and composing melodies to accompany each scene," Jerry Epstein later said. "He always found writing music 'a cinch,' and never understood the difficulties other composers experienced."[70] But composing the score for his next film was anything but "a cinch."

CHAPTER 5

Charlie + The Machine

CHAPLIN WROTE IN HIS AUTOBIOGRAPHY, "Although *City Lights* was a great triumph, I felt that to make another silent film would be giving myself a handicap—also I was obsessed by a depressing fear of being old-fashioned.... Occasionally I mused over the possibility of making a sound film, but the thought sickened me, for I realized I could never achieve the excellence of my silent pictures."[1] When Chaplin decided to release another silent film in 1936, nearly a decade into the sound era, "everyone in Hollywood thought my father was crazy," said Charles Chaplin, Jr. "While other producers like Jesse Lasky, David O. Selznick and Cecil B. DeMille were studying new ways of improving talkies, Dad was stubbornly clinging to the passé era of silent film. People began to think of him somewhat patronizingly as a former Hollywood great who was now a has-been, unable to adjust himself to the new techniques. He was finished in pictures—you heard that all over town."[2] Only an artist of Chaplin's stature, popularity, and chutzpah would have dared such a risky proposition.

For his new film, *Modern Times*, Chaplin still employed limited title cards, but he expanded the use of sound effects and included brief snippets of dialogue, though none for the Tramp. Chaplin still felt it was "unthinkable" to have the character speak, "for the first word he ever uttered would transform him into another person. Besides, the matrix out of which he was born was as mute as the rags he wore."[3] The Blaine-Thompson advertising agency offered Chaplin $650,000 for a series of six radio broadcasts following the release of *City Lights*, but he was "not interested." Carlyle Robinson, Chaplin's personal representative, said the comedian intended "at all costs" to preserve the "mystery" and "illusion" of the character he had created on the screen. "Mr. Chaplin has rarely been heard in public for that reason, and at public appearances it is his habit to bow and smile." In *Modern Times*, Chaplin allowed the mystery and illusion to slip slightly, and test the waters for himself as an actor in sound films. Audiences were about to hear the Tramp's voice on film. *Modern Times* was Chaplin's most ambitious and expensive film to date. But by the time the film was released, Chaplin had closed the book on his iconic Tramp and the silent era, at least for a while.

The genesis for *Modern Times* was the result of Chaplin's 1931–32 world tour, which he later described in "A Comedian Sees the World," a series of magazine articles for *Woman's Home Companion*. On the trip, Chaplin took along books with weighty titles like *Behind the Scenes of International Finance* and *The Economic Consequence of Peace* by British economist John Maynard Keynes, and throughout the journey, he witnessed scenes of indigence and the quandaries faced by workers. At a meeting with Albert Einstein in Berlin, Chaplin discussed "past economic depressions" and "inventions and new enterprises." He was of the opinion that "since those days the necessity of man power has been rapidly decreasing because of modern machinery … whatever new enterprises crop up in the future, they will not require the man power that was necessary in the past…. The business world has acquiesced and welcomed the fundamental industrial change from man power to machine power."[4] Chaplin espoused his views further at his meeting in England with Gandhi, asking the Mahatma why he was "opposed to machinery. After all, it's the natural outcome of man's genius and is part of his evolutionary progress. It is here to free him from the bondage of slavery, to help him to leisure and a higher culture. I grant that machinery with only the consideration of profit has thrown men out of work and created a great deal of misery, but to use it as a service to humanity, that consideration transcending everything else, should be a help and benefit to mankind."[5]

By the time production began on *Modern Times*, Chaplin's opinions on the benefits of mechanization had flipped. "I was riding in my car one day and saw a mass of people coming out of a factory, punching time-clocks, and was overwhelmed with the knowledge that the theme note of modern times is mass production," he said. "I wondered what would happen to the progress of the mechanical age if one person decided to act like a bull in a china shop—for instance to say 'nuts' to a red light and drive on—or scream at a concert that was boring. I decided it would make a good story to take a little man and make him thumb his nose at all recognized rules and conventions."[6]

The original title for the film—*The Masses*—neatly countered Chaplin's new viewpoint—"If machinery is used in the altruistic sense, it should help to release man from the bondage of slavery, and give him shorter hours of labor and time to improve his mind and enjoy life."[7] These themes no doubt resonated with a country still recovering from the Great Depression. The opening title card sums up the film—"a story of industry, of individual enterprise—humanity crusading in the pursuit of happiness." The film explores thorny issues such as unemployment, poverty, and contemporary politics, while the Tramp makes his final appearance, this time as a factory assembly line worker caught in the day-to-day monotony of the Electro Steel Corporation. Dwarfed by oversized levers, tools, and turbines, Charlie and his coworkers are mere cogs in a machine, repeating the same tasks over and over.

Chaplin began preparations on *Modern Times* in September 1933, but it would not go before the cameras until October 11, 1934. He showed a rough cut of the film in the summer of 1935 to the head of the Soviet film industry, Boris Shumyatsky, who promptly told *The Daily Worker* that *Modern Times* was to be "a sharp satire on the capitalist systemic in which [Chaplin] derides capitalist rationalization, crisis, the decrepit morality of bourgeois society, prison and war."[8] But Chaplin did not need this kind of publicity. Studio manager Alfred Reeves was obliged to issue a statement that Shumyatsky "reads deep, terrible social meanings to sequences that Mr. Chaplin considers funny."[9]

The New York premiere of *Modern Times* on February 5, 1936, was a raucous affair. Outside the Rivoli Theater on Broadway, a "near riot" of two thousand "curiosity seekers crowded and pushed for a chance to view those arriving," said the *New York Herald Tribune*.[10] Among the attending celebrities were Lillian Hellman, Edward G. Robinson, Eddie Cantor, George Burns and Gracie Allen, Douglas Fairbanks and Douglas Fairbanks, Jr., Ginger Rogers, Kitty Carlisle, and Gloria Swanson. An emergency call brought nearly a hundred patrolmen to the scene to disperse the mob, which impeded traffic on Broadway for more than fifteen minutes.

If Chaplin and skeptics wondered about audience interest for a silent film this far into the sound era, they had nothing to worry about. "This morning there's good news: Chaplin is back again," said Frank S. Nugent in *The New York Times*.[11] *Variety* called *Modern Times* "box office with a capital B.... Not only does he not falter but Chaplin perhaps scales new heights in maintaining a barrage of guffaws that is the more remarkable considering the advanced comedy efforts that have hit the screen since the advent of sound."[12] But Otis Ferguson in *The New Republic* had a valid point when he remarked, "*Modern Times* is about the last thing they should have called the Chaplin picture."[13] Brooks Atkinson was even blunter—"If he is offering *Modern Times* as social philosophy it is plain that [Chaplin] has hardly passed his entrance examinations, his comment is so trivial."[14]

Modern Times was not the financial hit Chaplin was expecting. Its $1.4 million domestic gross did not cover the $1.5 million production cost. But the film's overseas distribution eventually put the picture in the black.

*   *   *

Modern Times is Chaplin's most accomplished score, thanks in no small part to the extraordinary musical talent he employed on the film. Alfred Newman, head of United Artists's music department, took to the podium again after conducting *City Lights* to his boss's great satisfaction, while Edward Powell handled the orchestrations along with a brash twenty-three-year-old outsider named David Raksin, who was also responsible for the arrangements.

Edward Powell (1909–1984) got his start as a performer on Broadway in the 1929 play *Zeppelin*. He began to orchestrate for the *Earl Carroll Vanities of 1932* and went on to orchestrate musicals for Irving Berlin (*As Thousands Cheer*) and George Gershwin (*Let 'Em Eat Cake*). After moving to Los Angeles in 1934, he became Alfred Newman's primary orchestrator for nearly three decades.

Powell knew David Raksin from his days at Tin Pan Alley music publisher T.B. Harms & Francis, Day, & Hunter, Inc. Raksin (1912–2004) was largely a self-taught musician, though he later studied with Arnold Schoenberg. He became part of Benny Goodman's band and arranged for Fred Allen's radio show. Raksin got his big break when Broadway conductor Al Goodman bought his arrangement of Gershwin's "I Got Rhythm." Oscar Levant, who played piano with Goodman, introduced the young arranger to his close friend Gershwin, who hired Raksin to work at Harms.

On August 8, 1935, four days after his twenty-third birthday, Raksin was in Boston arranging and orchestrating the pre–Broadway tryout for the Arthur Schwartz-Howard Dietz musical *At Home Abroad* when he received a telegram from Powell:

> HAVE WONDERFUL OPPORTUNITY FOR YOU IF INTERESTED IN HAVING SHOT AT HOLLYWOOD STOP
>
> CHAPLIN COMPOSES ALMOST ALL HIS OWN SCORE BUT CANT WRITE DOWN A NOTE
>
> YOUR JOB TO WORK WITH HIM TAKE DOWN MUSIC STRAIGHTEN IT OUT HARMONICALLY DEVELOP HERE AND THERE IN CHARACTER OF HIS THEME PLAY IT OVER WITH PICTURE FOR CUES
>
> WE WILL ORCHESTRATE TOGETHER NEWMAN CONDUCT STOP
>
> BEST CHANCE YOU COULD EVER HAVE TO BREAK IN HERE CHAPLIN FASCINATING PERSON

ALTHOUGH MUSIC VERY SIMPLE AM SURE NEWMAN WILL LIKE YOU AND KEEP YOU
HERE
   YOU [orchestrator Herbert] SPENCER AND I CAN HAVE GRAND TIME WORKING
TOGETHER STOP THIS OFFER TWO HUNDRED PER WEEK MINIMUM OF SIX TRANS-
PORTATION BOTH WAYS STOP
   YOU CAN STUDY WITH SCHOENBERG WHILE HERE
   I HAVE SOLD YOU TO NEWMAN BECAUSE I FEEL HOLLYWOOD PROVIDES BEST
OPPORTUNITY FOR YOUR DEVELOPMENT AS COMPOSER AND ORCHESTRATOR
   CAN ALSO GET YOU IN WITH MAX STEINER AT END OF THIS JOB IF YOU WISH
   ANSWER IMMEDIATELY BY WESTERN UNION REGARDS.[15]

"There are some situations that transcend the professional's creed of playing it cool," Raksin later said, "so I was allowed some leeway in my demeanor, some youthful elation as the telegrams and telephone calls flew thick and fast."[16] Raksin's fee of $200 per week for "taking down Charlie's music" also included an additional five dollars per page of orchestrations, "which is the customary price for a man of his musical calibre [sic]," Newman later wrote to Alfred Reeves.[17] The prospect of working with Chaplin and the monetary incentive—small though it may seem by today's standards—sealed the deal and Raksin boarded the Broadway Limited, "bound for glory and enjoying my first experience as a member of the expense-account aristocracy."[18]

Newman, whom Raksin described as "a small, intense, and dapper man who exuded power and strong cologne,"[19] was "offended" by his first meeting with the young orchestrator "because I was so enthusiastic, that he thought it was gauche," Raksin said. "It would be surprising to think of anyone who would not have been aroused in great ridiculous thrills by the prospect of working with Charlie.... Al apparently thought this beneath the dignity of a musician."[20]

Powell had promised Chaplin Raksin was "brilliant, experienced, a composer, orchestrator and arranger with several big shows in his arranging cap." But the legendary star was somewhat disconcerted when "this infant turn[ed] up." "For some reason, it often seems to surprise me that great artists are indeed people," Raksin remembered. "The man who stood before me was certainly exotic enough—from his abundant white hair to his anachronistic shoes with their high suede tops and mother-of-pearl buttons— and equally urbane. However, he was neither multidimensional nor ten feet tall, yet so charming and gracious that I was immediately captivated."[21] The two men "got along well" and Raksin "nearly fell apart" when Chaplin showed him the latest cut of *Modern Times*. "When we got to the feeding machine sequence, I laughed so hard I nearly fell off the seat. [Charlie] said later he was wondering, before he really got to know me and how independent I was, whether I wasn't putting it on. Of course I wasn't."[22]

Chaplin "knew a good deal about music," Raksin said. "And what he didn't know, he would pick up from everybody."[23] His head "would be full of music which he'd been thinking about.... Sometimes I'd talk to him about whether or not I considered that the idea was appropriate for that place in the film.... I wanted to make sure that the music for that film was just about as good as it could possibly have been. As far as I was concerned, the best composer in the world would not have been too good for Charlie and the film."[24]

Raksin described Chaplin as "a total autocrat. He had his own studio and was the one hundred percent complete boss of it.... He was absolutely unused to having anybody dare to differ with him."[25] He seemed "unable, or unwilling, to understand the paradox that this imposition of will over his organization had been achieved in a manner akin to that which he professed to deplore in *Modern Times*. I, on the other hand, have never accepted the notion that it is my job merely to echo the ideas of those who employ me; and I had no fear of opposing him when necessary, because I believed he would recognize the value of an independent mind close at hand."[26] Raksin later found it "appallingly arrogant to have argued with a man like Chaplin about the appropriateness of the thematic material he proposed to use in his own picture. But the problem was real.... In the area of music, the influence of his years in the English music halls was very strong, and since I felt that nothing except the very best would do for this remarkable film, when I thought his approach was a bit ordinary I would say, 'I think we can do better than that.' To Charlie this was insubordination—and the culprit had to go."[27]

Chaplin fired Raksin after only a week and a half. "That about broke my heart," Raksin said. "I mean, it's impossible to describe what that does to you. And I was not uninfluenced by the fact that I would be going back to New York in disgrace.... I was really hurt because I thought Charlie and I had really arrived at something."[28] Raksin later admitted, "I was having hi-falutin' ideas but Chaplin was unconsciously realizing the communicative, linking power of simple, lyrical music to coat or strengthen a given dramatic situation."[29] Powell delivered the blow to his friend, who was living in Powell's home studio. The studio's daily production report, which had not even listed Raksin by name up to this point, merely reported on September 21, "New arranger reported this A.M.," though there is no record of who this new arranger was. The next night, Raksin accompanied the Powells and Herb Spencer to the popular restaurant Don the Beachcomber's, when Newman came over and told Raksin, "I've been looking at your sketches and they're marvelous—what you're doing with Charlie's little tunes. He'd be crazy to fire you."[30]

As Raksin was packing to leave, Reeves called him in and said they wanted to rehire him. Raksin replied that he would "like nothing more, but that before I could give him an answer I wanted to talk to Charlie—alone—otherwise the same thing would happen again. So Charlie and I met in his projection room and had it out." In his meeting with Chaplin, Raksin explained that "if it was a musical secretary he wanted he could hire one for peanuts; if he wanted more 'yes' men, well, he was already up to his ears in them. But if he needed someone who loved his picture and was prepared to risk getting fired every day to make sure that the music was as good as it could possibly be, then I would love to work with him again. We shook hands, and he gave me a sharp tap on the shoulder— and that was it, the beginning of four and a half months of work and some of the happiest days of my life."[31] On September 23, the daily production report finally listed Raksin by name—"Original arranger [Raksin] back on job today."[32]

Chaplin's projection room consisted of a small grand piano, a phonograph, a portable tape recorder, a large screen for 35mm projectors, and a smaller screen for the "Goldberg," a movieola that runs forwards or backwards to help sync the film. Chaplin and Raksin spent day after day hunched over the machine, running sequences over and over, discussing the scenes and the music. "Charlie always had ideas. He would come in, [having] given them some thought, and would play them with one finger."[33] Chaplin enjoyed telling Raksin that he got some of his best ideas "while meditating [raising of an eyebrow]—on the throne, you know."[34] Even so, Raksin usually liked his boss's ideas.

> I would say, "Charlie, look, if we did this to it, we could make it work this way." Sometimes I'd actually say, "Why don't you play those four notes?" Like, for instance, the first scene where you see Charlie working there's a little piece of thematic material there which consists of three notes

repeated. Now, when you're going to have eight minutes of that, something's got to happen to the music. So we would go through it and various things would happen. And Charlie, contrary to what people think, was not doing the whole thing by any means, nor was he not participating, because he would actually talk about what should happen. What we should do, what curlicues, where we should get away from the tune and go to another tune…. That was the way we worked. We would play the scene back and forth, and since I'm a very limited pianist, I believe, I would be able to play only parts of it. We would sing it and I would play the accompaniment on the piano too. And we would get it so it was exactly right and the bars were exactly right.[35]

Chaplin "also had a very large share" in determining the orchestrations, Raksin said.

I remember we got into a kind of a funny conversation about who should play a certain melody…. And I said, well, I don't know exactly what you're thinking, Charlie, originally we talked about doing this on a bassoon. He said, no, it sounds too sissified. So I said, well it doesn't sound right on the trombone, it sounds too heavy and I don't think the French horn should play this and it certainly is not for strings according to what you're doing on the screen. We finally agreed a tenor saxophone to play it and that's what plays it in the picture. But the very fact that he was able to do that and visualize the sound, I mean to hear it in his ear, is marvelous and something few people understand—when you're orchestrating, you're hearing what the instrument sounds like."[36]

Raksin described his shorthand sketches as "exceptionally rudimentary, because you don't keep God himself or one of his chief disciples waiting while you make a complete sketch, which takes lots and lots of time."[37] The sketches would contain the melody and any other ideas the two men came up with, plus suggestions for scoring and orchestral color, which Raksin would later refine that night or on the weekend into a cleaner sketch that would serve as the basis for his and Powell's orchestrations.

Chaplin and Raksin worked hand in hand, with work sessions often lasting until one o'clock in the morning. "No informed person has claimed that Charlie had any of the essential techniques," said Raksin. "But neither did he feed me a little tune and say, 'You take it from there.' On the contrary; we spent hours, days, months in that projection room, running scenes and bits of action over and over, and we had a marvelous time shaping the music until it was exactly the way he wanted it."[38] When they got "stir crazy from concentrating, we would often let off steam by doing acting improvisations—the crazier the better."[39]

Charles Chaplin, Jr., said, "If the people in his own studio had suffered from Dad's perfectionist drive, the musicians who now began working with him endured pure torture."

Dad wore them all out. Edward Powell concentrated so hard writing the music down that he almost lost his eyesight and had to go to a specialist to save it. David Raksin, working an average of twenty hours a day, lost twenty-five pounds and sometimes was so exhausted that he couldn't find strength to go home but would sleep on the studio floor. Al Newman saw him one day in the studio street walking along with tears running down his cheeks.[40]

On October 30, Chaplin began conferring with Newman for an orchestra of sixty-one players—two piccolos, two flutes, oboe, English horn, five clarinets, bass clarinet, contrabass clarinet, soprano saxophone, two alto saxophones, tenor saxophone, bassoon, two horns, three trumpets (with nine different mutes each), tenor trombone, bass trombone, tuba, four percussionists (snare drum, bass drum, large cymbals, suspended cymbal, choke cymbal, Turkish and Greek finger cymbals, gong, drum kit, two xylophones, vibraphone, marimba, glockenspiel, chimes, three sets of tuned anvils, temple blocks, woodblocks, castanets, triangle, and timpani), harp, piano, celesta, eight first violins, eight second

At the United Artists recording sessions for *Modern Times*—Charles Dunworth, inventor of the system of visual cues for synchronization; conductor Alfred Newman; Chaplin; arranger and co-orchestrator David Raksin; recording engineer Paul Neal; and co-orchestrator Edward Powell. Photograph by Max Autrey, c. November 1935 (© Roy Export Co. Ltd.).

violins, six violas, four cellos, and two contrabasses—plus male vocal quartet.[41] Recording sessions began at United Artists on November 18.

"*Modern Times* is the most important scoring task in Hollywood," Sidney Skolsky correctly stated in *The Washington Post*, "for the Chaplin flicker is silent, and it is through the musical arrangements and sound effects that it will talk."

Chaplin sits in a camp chair on a large recording set at the United Artists' studio, supervising the scoring. His hair is gray. He has stubble gray beard. He wears black patent leather shoes with white suede tops, and his right arm is carried in a sling. A blue silk muffler serves as the sling. Chaplin broke his right thumb in the door of his auto.

Al Newman stands on a small platform, waving a baton at sixty-five musicians [*sic*]. David Raksin, who made the music arrangements for Chaplin, is also present to supervise.

There is a screen hanging in mid-air in back of the orchestra…. Chaplin is chewing gum in time with the orchestra…

The orchestra starts rehearsing the music for the factory sequence in which Chaplin revolts against being a slave of the machinery. He throws the place into confusion and does a wild dance. The music is as difficult as the scene. Every note must be timed exactly with the film, and the music is not loud and brazen as expected of factory sounds. The orchestra rehearses these few bars again … again … again. An hour later, they're still doing those few bars. The orchestra stops playing. The men leave their chairs. There's time out for five minutes, like a football team. It is strenuous work. The musicians work only three, four hours at the most, at a stretch. Then they have an hour for relaxation. Yesterday, they worked from 9 in the morning until 4 o'clock the next morning, and about half a reel was completely scored. It costs Chaplin on the average of $1,000 an hour to score this flicker.

Now, after several hours of rehearsing, Al Newman and Chaplin agree they will try to record this scene. The signal is given. The picture is ready to be flashed on the screen…

The flicker is on. Chaplin is performing. The first impression is very strange. I see Chaplin moving, his mouth opens—but no sounds, no words are heard. For a moment I believe something is wrong. Then I remember it is a silent flicker. The orchestra plays the same few bars again and again, and the picture is started over and over. By now I am becoming accustomed to silent pictures. Chaplin watches the picture and listens to the music. He jumps up to stop the music. He okays a take. He asks Newman or Raksin or [recording engineer Paul] Neal how it sounded…

Hours later they are still rehearsing, recording.[42]

The orchestra "included the best virtuosi in Hollywood," said Raksin, "which is saying the best virtuosi in the *world*." Among those virtuosi was noted violinist Louis Kaufman, who was later featured on such legendary Hollywood film scores as Newman's *Wuthering Heights* (1939) and Raksin's immortal *Laura* (1944). In his autobiography *A Fiddler's Tale*, Kaufman, who recorded the first recording of Vivaldi's *The Four Seasons* and would play again on Chaplin's scores to *The Great Dictator* and *Monsieur Verdoux*, talked about his experience playing for *Modern Times*:

Newman usually agreed with Chaplin's suggestions; however, for one sequence where Chaplin described to the girl, Paulette Goddard, what their future dream house would be, he wanted the music "Mickey Moused" for laughs.

Alfred insisted this would destroy the mood of the dream and convinced Chaplin to accept a lyric passage. Alfred placed me with muted violin very close to a microphone, separated from the orchestra by a large screen for greater clarity, which permitted the muted violin to soar over the orchestral texture. He used this device for many solo passages in this score. Chaplin, who knew how to play violin backwards, fingering with the right hand, was delighted with the results. I greatly enjoyed my rare encounters with that unique film genius.[43]

"The sound [Newman] got from his hand-picked ensemble was nothing less than gorgeous," Raksin said, "and his ability to elicit beautiful and impeccable playing at extremely slow tempi was a revelation to me. For some reason, I had failed to anticipate what this style of conducting would do for the notes I had set down during the long night, so that when he turned his attention to one of those sequences I did not immediately relate the glowing sounds that emerged from the orchestra with the monochromatic symbols I had written on the score pages."[44]

Recording sessions continued through November 22, with further work on the score November 25–27. Recording resumed on November 29–30 and December 2–6. At the sessions, "Charlie was always there, always dressed, with his spats," Raksin said. "Sometimes it was more informal. But he dressed elegantly and would sit around and would kid around a lot with the musicians. He admired them and understood what it took to be about to do what they were doing."[45] Raksin remembered these sessions as "a unique combination of working concentration and social event. Charlie was at his best … sitting near the podium, listening and carrying on a bit, sometimes 'conducting,' and generally charming everyone with his antics. He was delighted with the way the score was turning out, and his euphoria was contagious."[46]

Newman liked to work in the small hours of the night. When the sessions were over for the day, Powell and Raksin had to keep "one jump ahead of the copyists and the orchestra, to provide the music for the next recordings," Raksin said, "so we would usually resume work on the orchestrations when everyone else had gone home." After a while "we were both ready to be carted away from sheer exhaustion." One day Newman noticed that Raksin looked sick and gave him the night off from attending the recording session. "I must have been pretty well worn out to agree to miss the session, but it was either that or collapse."[47]

Chaplin had already postponed the original premiere date (October 11, 1935) because he was dissatisfied with the ending and particularly the music, threatening to record an entirely new score to replace it. Trouble had been brewing for months and on December 4, Raksin's night off, Chaplin and the explosive Newman had a vicious argument. "It was Al Newman who finally broke under the pressure," Charles Chaplin, Jr., said.

> With only two hundred feet more of sound track to go, and after endless changes and grueling work night and day for weeks, his nerves were as taut as though they had been subjected to the Chinese water torture. He just exploded one day and called my father every name he could think of, throwing his baton all the way across the stage to emphasize what he was saying. Then he stalked out, went to his suite in the building across from the stage, tossed down a half pint of whiskey to calm his nerves and phoned [Samuel] Goldwyn to tell him he was through. Nor would he go back, despite pleas and pressure."[48]

The New York Times recorded their impressions:

> Chaplin's interest in everything was intense. He required that he be present at both the writing and the recording of the score. He criticized the orchestration and the way the musicians played. He demanded rewrites of much of it and many parts were recorded twenty or thirty times.
>
> When all but 200 feet had been recorded, an explosion occurred that furnished the town with a gay morsel of conversation. Newman had slept at the studio for five nights trying to complete the recording in time for the picture's scheduled release date. With his men he had been working sixteen hours a day. Chaplin returned one evening from a dinner given to H. G. Wells and, seating himself beside Newman, he said, "I'm tired of this stalling."
>
> It was too much for the distraught conductor. He hurled his baton across the stage and unburdened himself of all the opinions he had kept smothered during the weeks of recording. Chaplin, who, in his younger days, had a reputation for pugnacity, sat there without moving. He hadn't been talked to that way in twenty years. Newman reviewed every incident that had occurred during the scoring, to the delight of the orchestra, and then walked off the stage. Attempts were made to bring him back to complete the picture, but he refused.[49]

Newman had allowed Raksin to conduct some of the rehearsals. So when Raksin found out about the altercation the next morning, Goldwyn executives told him he was expected to take over and conduct the remaining sessions. "I realized later that they would have enjoyed watching me struggle with the temptation offered by such an opportunity," Raksin said, "believing that ambition was certain to supersede whatever loyalty I might feel toward Newman. But I replied that if what they had told me about the circumstances was true, then Charlie had been at fault and owed Al and the orchestra an apology; also that I would not consent to anything that would hurt Al or weaken his position."[50] Instead the studio invoked Powell's contract and he was forced to complete the sessions. Raksin's loyalty to Newman resulted in an estrangement from Chaplin that lasted for years. "Chaplin remained cordial," Raksin said, "but he was offended that, having been caught in the cross fire between him and Newman, I had sided with Al. I guess he did not understand how hard that was for me to do. We parted without formalities."[51] Though Raksin contributed a couple of klezmer pieces to *The Great Dictator* that never made it into the final film, it would be years before his former cordiality with Chaplin resumed.

With Powell now on the podium, Raksin claimed he finished most of the remaining orchestrations, "and the recordings tapered off in a rather sad spirit."[52] But the daily pro-

Happier times with Chaplin and conductor Alfred Newman on the *Modern Times* recording stage, c. November 1935 (© Roy Export Co. Ltd.).

duction reports tell a different story. The report for December 10 states, "Engaged Ross," with no mention of who exactly Ross is. The mysterious "Ross" worked until four o'clock the morning of December 12, 5:30 the following morning, and until 4:30 the morning of Saturday, December 14. "Ross and arrangers" worked Saturday night and Sunday while Chaplin went to Cecil B. DeMille's ranch for the weekend.

"Ross" and his arrangers rescored only a handful of cues. Most notably different is the unused main title sequence with sixteenth notes substituted for triplets in the fanfare and a flurry of scalar runs and trills in the woodwinds and strings. Chaplin did not like what he called a "drowned sound" in the orchestra. "It's like a piece of film out of focus."[53] And no doubt the texture of Ross's revision was too thick for Chaplin's taste. Sections of the opening sheep montage were also rescored, in particular, the two bars of syncopation, as was nearly all of the first prison scene and the delightful theme that underscores Charlie and the Gamin in their dilapidated shack. Recording sessions resumed on December 16 and lasted until 6:00 a.m. the following morning. One brief session was held on December 17 from 7:00 to 11:00 p.m., and the tense recording of *Modern Times* finally came to an end.

Raksin was employed from September 11 to December 7, 1935, at a salary of $200 a week plus $5 per sheet of orchestration. It later came to Newman's attention that Raksin had been overpaid, collecting an extra two weeks salary, which "he had no right … to accept." "In view of the unfortunate circumstances which severed Charlie's and my relations," Newman wrote in a letter to Alfred Reeves, "it was difficult to present this, when the bills were due, to Charlie personally, who, as far I knew, understood this arrangement from the beginning." Newman suggested a settlement "deducting moneys collected as salary during the time Raksin was orchestrating." He added the caveat that Raksin "is inclined to talk a great deal and might cause publicity which would be distasteful and unnecessary."[54]

Reeves wrote to Loyd Wright, a lawyer for United Artists, questioning the matter, specifically two bills—one for $1,000 and another for $1,225. "When I saw these I could not understand it," wrote Reeves, "as [Raksin] was getting regular weekly salary from us, and I looked upon him as a weekly employee." Reeves intimated in the letter that Raksin had applied for the money "on several occasions" and "suggested he would have to take some proceedings" if the money was not forthcoming. Neither of the parties wanted to go to court and Reeves suggested that Wright hear both Newman and Raksin's sides of the story on his next visit to the studio. There is no documentation as to whether Raksin collected the additional fees or not.[55]

Some years later, Raksin saw Chaplin at the ballet. Raksin did not want "to risk being snubbed … but Paulette was also looking around, and when she saw me she nudged Charlie and waved, indicating that I was to come over during intermission … [Charlie] was so charming and affectionate that our differences seemed to have evaporated. [Chaplin's guest Konrad] Bercovici later told me that when we returned to our seats Charlie said, laughing, 'There goes the only man who ever defied me and lived to talk about it!'"[56] Raksin made his final visit to the studio the day before Chaplin's departure from America in 1952.

"Thinking about my time with Charlie," he said, "I realize that at some time or other in my young life I must have done something right to have been blessed with such good fortune. I cannot imagine a more auspicious and inspiring way of beginning a career in film music than working with an artist—and man—of his caliber. Not only were we doing something worthwhile, and in style, but the experience itself was unique."[57] Raksin called it "the greatest thing that could ever have happened to me. Imagine spending four and a half months with the greatest figure, I believe, in the history of films."[58]

⋆   ⋆   ⋆

The score for *Modern Times* is rich in thematic material with spacious orchestrations that belie the intricacy of the arrangements. In fact, the music is such a challenge in live performance that Roy Export instructs Bourne Co., the current rights holder of most of Chaplin's music, to only license the score to conductors who have the ability to do it justice. The official cue sheet lists 110 cues, ranging from a few seconds of fanfare to longer musical sequences, such as the feeding machine. Cue titles correspond to points of action within the script, locations, title card verbiage, or sometimes a simple metronome marking, such as "fast," "presto" or "agitato."

Over the main title, Chaplin musically sets up the dark, dramatic aspects of the film with a minor-key trumpet fanfare that represents the hovering omnipresence of the factory, followed by rolling chromaticism and a melodramatic string melody for the plight of the unemployed. The film opens with a barbed montage of stampeding sheep contrasting with crowds of men and women emerging from an underground subway and

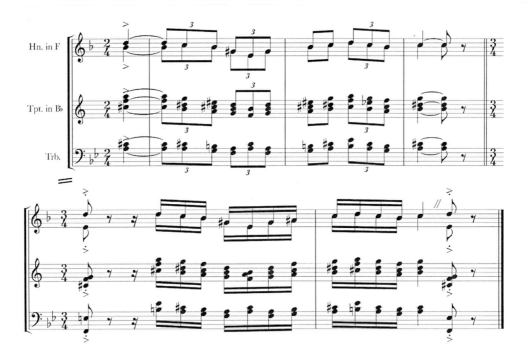

Modern Times (1936)—The opening fanfare.

rushing to work. The galloping rhythmic figures and syncopated brass propel the workers to the factory while a nervous melody on the staccato trumpet hurries them to the day's drudgery. Inside, a metallic scherzo of xylophone, pizzicato strings, staccato piccolo, and muted trumpet captures the endless, tedious, repetitive tightening of nuts and bolts on the assembly line, and underscoring the constant, monotonous movement of limbs and tools. Meanwhile, chromatic sixteenth-note runs in the violins buzz around the constantly moving worker bees.

The factory floor provided ample opportunity for Chaplin to experiment further with sound and dialogue than he had in the past. "Natural sounds part of composition, i.e., auto horns, sirens, and cowbells worked into the music," noted a production memo for the film.[59] In addition to the factory whistle, oversized machines are given a prominent role—humming, ratcheting, and squealing in exaggerated, but carefully controlled, cacophony—while the omnipresent president of the factory (Allan Garcia), the only character in the film that speaks directly on camera, spies on his workers and barks orders from Orwellian video screens in his office. In the same manner of the "speeches" at the beginning of *City Lights*, Chaplin again uses musical instruments to substitute for voices. The nameless workers in overalls and grease-stained wife beaters "speak" by way of trombone, saxophone, and oboe solos. Chaplin also employs this instrumental speech later when the Tramp meets his old co-worker Big Bill (Stanley "Tiny" Sandford) as a down-and-out thief in the basement of the department store and during his conversation with the owner of the café (Henry Bergman).

As far back as his earliest published musical compositions in 1916, Chaplin was fond of waltzes in his music, a practice that remained throughout his career. Even in the midst of his mechanized maelstrom, Chaplin finds a comedic use of three-quarter time in the

Modern Times (1936)—**Chromatic passing tones moan the plight of the unemployed.**

most unlikely of places. When the Tramp goes to the bathroom for a cigarette break, a lackadaisical "Valse" in the violins provides a brief respite to the musical cacophony out on the factory floor. Chaplin scores the classic sequence of the Tramp caught in the internal gears of the assembly line with a delicate music box waltz, and he later channels his inner Johann Strauss to underscore the Tramp and the Gamin's oom-pah-pah visit to the department store's fifth-floor bedroom display and their imagined life of luxury.

One of Chaplin's most famous visual gags involves the feeding machine. A "mechanical salesman" touts the advances of a new, "practical device that automatically feeds your men while they are at work" and will "increase your production and decrease your overhead." The machine fits around the Tramp's neck like a metallic collar, effectively chaining him to his post on the assembly line. When the machine is turned on, a plate spins and the machine's arms slide bits of food into Charlie's mouth and lift a bowl of soup for him to sip, while a half-moon-shaped block of wood pivots on a hinge to forcibly "wipe" his mouth. Chaplin maneuvered the levers himself underneath the contraption and off camera. The sound effects become more chaotic as the machine shorts and runs out of con-

Modern Times (1936)—Sixteenth notes tumble over one another as the workers (i.e., "sheep") hurry to their factory stations.

Modern Times (1936)—This gentle "Valse" accompanies Charlie's softer side.

trol—hissing, fizzing, and spitting in a maelstrom of electrical malfunction. In most of the sound effects-laden sequences throughout the film, Chaplin dials out the music so that the sounds can produce their intended comedic effect on their own. In this sequence, like the boxing scene in *City Lights*, the music quietly and subtly underscores the frenzy onscreen as the strings move through the circle of fifths in a series of repeated melodic and rhythmic figures. The cue, based on the galloping sheep music, yearns upwards as if Charlie finally has a handle on the machine and then descends harmonically when he realizes he does not.

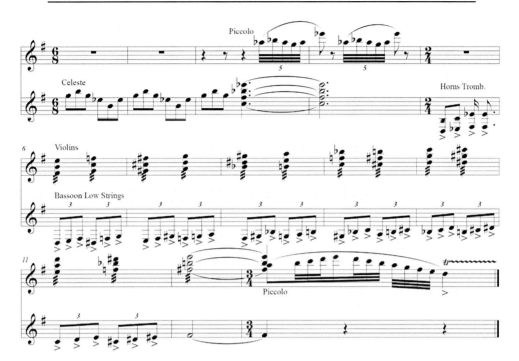

Modern Times (1936)—**Charlie gets caught in the gears to the tune of this tinkling music box waltz.**

Modern Times (1936)—**The sheep music rolls around and around sequentially as Charlie is pummeled by the feeding machine.**

Chaplin often used the bassoon as the Tramp's musical personification. In these early scenes, the assembly line music captures every spasm and convulsion while the bassoon adds further comedic commentary. When Charlie finally goes crazy from the monotony, the resulting dance is a delightful whirling dervish of a scherzo. The music moves at a breakneck pace as he leers at passing women and prances around the factory floor. Though Chaplin hated Mickey Mousing in his scores, he could not resist the comic visual and audio gag of a heehawing muted trumpet mimicking Charlie's wrench donkey ears, and staccato xylophone hits and piccolo chirps as he uses those wrenches to musically tweak noses, fire hydrants, and the buttons on the ample bosom and bustle of a woman passing by. Timothy Brock, who reconstructed the score for live performance, translated the musical sequence into prose. This section contains fourteen tempo changes, nine meter changes, and twenty-seven synch points, where the music precisely mimics the movement of the actors or their actions, all within the span of sixty-eight seconds.

Measures 743–744: Leggiero 6/8 in 2 at 52 bpm (beats per minute): "CC in machine"

Measures 745–746: "CC tightens nuts 1–2"

Measure 747: Andante con moto 2/4 in 2 at 72 bpm: "foreman reverses gears"

Measures 748–749: "CC in reverse"

Measures 750–751: "feet at 9:00"

Measures 752–753: "CC out"

Measure 754: "Big Bill shocked"

Measure 755: "CC sits up, turns"

Measures 756–757: Tempo rubato in 2: "CC tightens B. Bill 1–2" (stop)

Measures 758–761: Allegro 2/4 at 152 beats per minute: "tightens nuts 1–2–3–4–5"

Measure 762: in 3/4: "tightens foreman's nose"

Measures 763–766: Tempo di Waltz 3/8 in 1 at 60 bpm: "tightens worker's nose" (stop)

Measures 767–771: "B[ig] Bill's nose"

Measure 772: "CC sees girl, donkey ears rise"

Measures 773–780: "CC pursues girl, around corner, corridor"

Measure 781: "stops, runs again"

Measures 782–783: "exterior of factory"

Measures 784–787: "stops, sees hydrant"

Measures 788–789: Allegro 4/4 in 4 at 144 bpm: "tightens bolts 1–2–3–4"[60]

Back inside the factory, the music is marked "presto" as the Tramp continues to wreak havoc with the machines, pulling levers, squirting coworkers with oil, and disrupting the orderly regimentation, until he is finally taken away in an ambulance accompanied by the trumpet fanfare. "It is one of the most extraordinary examples of conducting to something which is actually a comic ballet on the screen that you will ever see," praised David Raksin. "It's a feat for which any conductor would be remembered, and Al Newman did that."[61]

One of the tunes that would have been recognizable to audiences in 1936 but may be unfamiliar today is the American folk song "Hallelujah, I'm a Bum," which Chaplin weaves into the fabric of the score as pointed commentary on the Tramp's on-again/off-again employment status. But the song's origin and subsequent history give no hint of its later protest fervor. The seeds of the tune can be found as far back as 1813 in a waltz for *The Miller and His Men*, a Romantic-era melodrama composed by Sir Henry Bishop (1786–1855), composer of "Home, Sweet Home." In 1815, British-born John J. Husband (1760–1825), who had emigrated to Philadelphia in 1809 and combined his church post with teaching music, interpolated the melody into the chorus of a hymn originally titled "Thine the Glory." The melody also made an appearance in an 1858 hymnal as "Rejoice and Be Glad," with words by Horatius Bonar. In 1863, at the height of the Civil War, William P. Mackay (1839–1855), a Scottish-born doctor and later Presbyterian minister, used Husband's tune for his hymn "Revive Us Again"—"Hallelujah! Thine the glory. / Hallelujah! Amen. / Hallelujah! Thine the glory. / Revive us again."[62]

The authorship of "Hallelujah, I'm a Bum" offers a more rural set of stories. One tale tells of a Kansas City hobo known as "One-Finger Ellis" writing some verses, reportedly scribbling them on the wall of his prison cell in 1897. Around the same time, fifteen-

Charlie goes crazy on the factory floor in *Modern Times*, c. 1935 (© Roy Export SAS).

***Modern Times* (1936)—Every time Charlie heads back to jail, Chaplin interpolates Harry McClintock's classic 1928 hobo song "Hallelujah, I'm a Bum."**

year-old singer Harry McClintock (1882–1957), who later became well known for "Big Rock Candy Mountain," was hoboing on the open road, bumming his meals and singing for his supper, after having run away to join the circus. McClintock took the old Presbyterian hymn and called his version "Hallelulia on the Bum." "There were only two or three verses at first but new ones practically wrote themselves," McClintock said. "The jungle stiffs liked the song and so did the saloon audiences, most of whom had hit the road at one time or another, and the rollicking, devil-may-care lilt of the thing appealed to them."[63] During the Spanish-American War, McClintock reportedly sang the song in Army training camps in Tennessee. The soldiers added new verses and helped spread the song around the country. By the late 1920s, when more than a dozen publishers had turned out sheet music of the song, McClintock charged them all with copyright infringement and managed to establish his authorship claim legally.

McClintock was a lifelong member of the Industrial Workers of the World (IWW), a labor organization dedicated to the overthrow of capitalism. The IWW used parodies of songs (sung by a leader known as a Wobbly) to compete for the attention of crowds, inspire militancy and solidarity in its ranks, and to help enlist new members. Cards bearing the lyrics to familiar tunes were printed and sold to the audience. The organization printed "Hallelujah, I'm a Bum" in 1908, and IWW's Spokane, Washington, branch adopted the song as their anthem that year. It found widespread popularity during the IWW's Free Speech fights of 1909. The song gained further traction with McClintock's 1928 recording and another one that same year by Al Jolson. But it is Chaplin's musical treatment in *Modern Times* that has stood the test of time, primarily because of the main scene it accompanies.

Released from jail after his nervous breakdown, Charlie walks the city streets as one of the many unemployed from the now-shuttered factory. When a flag drops off the back of a delivery truck, he picks it up and waves it to get the driver's attention. As a crowd of protesters rounds the corner, he is mistakenly accused of leading the protest and hauled off to jail. As he shuffles along the city streets, the "Hallelujah" melody starts in a muted trumpet with a gentle rocking motion in the accompaniment. Strings take up the tune and a snare drum foreshadows the marchers off screen. A full-throttled statement of the melody brings the revolutionaries around the corner until the police break up the rally with an interruption of fanfare snippets and sheep music from the beginning of the film. A succession of brass paraphrases of the seven-note "Hallelujah, I'm a Bum" melody underscore the policemen throwing Charlie into the back of the police van, and the gentle strings suggest that his return to jail is almost like returning home. The lyric, though not heard in the film, fits in with the philosophical points Chaplin is trying to make, asking questions such as "How the hell can I work when there's no work to do?" and "Oh, why don't you save all the money you earn? If I didn't eat, I'd have money to burn." The refrain not only provides the musical quote used in the score but captures the Tramp's carefree attitude towards his unemployment—"Hallelujah, I'm a bum, / Hallelujah, bum again, / Hallelujah, give us a handout / To revive us again."[64]

The scene states Chaplin's support of the American worker in pantomime, but he has the genius to turn a potential political diatribe into a visual moment of pointed comic levity. When *Modern Times* was set to premiere in Vienna, government censors cut the scene.[65] The revolutionary implications of this particular sequence would come back to haunt Chaplin in later years, adding to the numerous accusations about his political affiliations. Elsewhere in the film, Chaplin deliberately uses the tune to underline his political points—when the Tramp foils the jailbreak and hands back the cell block keys, and when he unwittingly sabotages a succession of new jobs (the ship, the department store, and with fellow mechanic Chester Conklin at the reopened factory) and is once again "on the bum." Most of the cues using the tune are less than fifteen seconds long, just enough time for the ear to register the melody and get the joke, without detracting from the visuals on screen. If the use of "Hallelujah, I'm a Bum" was "revolutionary," so was Chaplin's choice for his leading lady.

Chaplin's numerous problems with Virginia Cherrill on *City Lights* ensured she was passed over for the lead. Paulette Goddard had been working for the Hal Roach Studios when she met Chaplin in 1932. Though he was forty-three at the time, he was smitten with the twenty-two-year-old actress and the two started dating. Goddard later moved in with him, though they both remained circumspect when reporters questioned them about their relationship. Chaplin maintained in public that they married in China in 1936, but privately to associates and family, he claimed they had a common law marriage.

As for her acting ability, unlike Virginia Cherrill, Georgia Hale, or even Chaplin's longtime silent film partner Edna Purviance, Goddard was a vibrant screen presence and her raw, fiery, youthful energy proved to be the perfect complement to Chaplin's beloved Tramp.

Goddard portrays the Gamin, "a child of the waterfront." Like the factory workers and other characters in the film, the Gamin represents something broader, and to give her a name would have diminished the universal political points Chaplin wanted to make. Stealing food to support her sisters and unemployed father, the Gamin is usually accompanied by a four-note clarion call on the soprano saxophone while furious sixteenth notes in the strings and syncopated, staccato woodwinds capture her desperate, vibrant spirit as she claws her way through life. The plaintive, sentimental string melody from the main title serves as her father's theme and accompanies scenes of her downtrodden family life.

Back in the Big House, under the eerily prophetic title card "Held as a communist leader, our innocent victim languishes in jail," Chaplin briefly quotes Vernon Dalhart's

Modern Times (1936)—**The Gamin's scrappy personality is represented by a four-note soprano saxophone motif and furious sixteenth notes.**

"The Prisoner's Song" in the brass. The song was a huge hit in the 1920s, selling a staggering seven million-plus copies worldwide. The Dalhart recording charted for thirty-two weeks during 1925 and 1926, with twelve of those weeks spent at number one. A brief bassoon and violin theme in a minor key marches the Tramp to his cell. The theme extends in the violins and woodwind solos while he annoys his gruff cellmate's (Dick Alexander) needlepoint. When the two later fight over who gets first dibs on the lunch food, the theme is passed back and forth between the strings, muted trumpets, and solo woodwinds. A two-note brass motif and sliding, chromatic lines announce the warden and other prison officials searching for cocaine. The offending substance, transferred to a saltshaker, provides comic genius for Charlie as a jaunty string theme accompanies his wild-eyed reaction to the "nose-powder." The minor-key bassoon theme again marches the prisoners back to their cells while a drugged-up Charlie goes twirling out of line and eventually gets involved in an attempted jailbreak. He foils the escape attempt and shakes the warden's hand underscored by an ironic statement of "Hallelujah, I'm a Bum."

The Tramp reads the headlines of the outside riots back "in his comfortable cell," while the radio announces his pardon for his role in thwarting the jailbreak. The waltz from his earlier cigarette break in the factory ushers him into the Warden's office, while a loping, Laurel and Hardy-like theme in the clarinet and oboe announce the arrival of the minister and his prune-faced, disapproving wife. The chromatic triplets and chirping grace notes underscore Chaplin's dim view of religion, a topic he also explored in his 1923 short *The Pilgrim*. Chaplin wisely allows the extended audio sequences of his bubbling gastric juices to play uninterrupted by music. The opening fanfare in the bassoon offers pointed ironic comment to the Warden's statement that the Tramp is now "a free man."

"Sometimes the ideas [Charlie] would propose were based on various similarities to other pieces," David Raksin said. "Sometimes they were very far from the original piece … but he had a great memory for all kinds of stuff. At one time, there was this place where he said, 'A little Gershwin would be very nice here.' What he meant was he was not going to steal any of George Gershwin's music, but there is a place where there's a secondary theme, which clearly would never have happened without *Rhapsody in Blue*. It's not *Rhapsody in Blue*, because otherwise there would have been a [law]suit. But it was clearly based on that kind of thing. It's fairly common among musicians to do this."[66]

Gershwinesque violins, clarinets, saxophones, and muted trumpets give the syncopated "Allegro" cue underscoring Charlie's brief stint at the shipbuilder's the timbre of period jazz bands. Chaplin had no qualms about repeatedly using themes and entire

Modern Times (1936)—A Gershwinesque "Allegro" underscores Charlie's many short-lived jobs.

musical sequences in a score, usually with no changes in orchestration, tempo or key, and this particular music appears anytime the Tramp takes on a new job, such as his position as a night watchman at the department store. As that sequence moves to the toy department and the classic skating scene, rather than transitioning smoothly from one cue to the next—a common practice in film scoring, even in 1936—the cue is abruptly dialed out and a graceful new string theme takes its place. The dialing out happens at the end of a musical phrase, making the transition less noticeable than it could have been. But the abruptness of the musical treatment, unfortunately, would become a common feature of later Chaplin scores where cues are suddenly dialed in or dialed out, seemingly indiscriminately.

Back on the mean streets, the Gamin, "alone and hungry," steals bread from a baker's truck. When a nosy passerby reports her, the Tramp comes to the rescue, taking the fall for her actions and trying to get himself arrested in her stead. A poignant, yearning new string theme is introduced, conveying the growing relationship between the two down-at-heel urchins. Dance band saxophones and the lilting waltz from the prison cell accompany the many meals he eats, cigars he smokes, and candies he shares with the homeless children—all of which he refuses to pay for—until he is finally arrested for his petty crimes. The loping bassoon theme from the earlier jail scene mixes with the Gamin's music and their sentimental theme as the Gamin fights her way out of the van and the two escape.

Chaplin's most famous melody appears smack dab in the middle of the film, bookending the scene of Charlie and the Gamin sharing their dreams for a better life. For that particular moment, Chaplin told Raksin, "A little Puccini would go well here." "Of course, the tune we came up with was not Puccini by any means," Raksin said, "but you can certainly see what he meant. It had that kind of melodic, all-out expressiveness."[67] In 1936,

Modern Times (1936)—The love theme, today better known as the melody from the song "Smile."

this lovely string theme must have seemed nothing more than a pretty tune. Today, that memorable melody is better known as the song "Smile." The now-famous tune is only featured four times in the score, including later recurrences of the Gamin waiting for the Tramp outside the jail and the famous finale. The "Dream House" sequence features shimmering strings, harp glissandi, and flitting woodwind solos that represent the pastoral sounds of birds and nature as the Tramp and the Gamin imagine their home life together, including a particularly amusing sequence with a cow expressing milk on command. The same music will later provide ironic counterpoint during the scene with the two lovebirds setting up hearth and home in a dilapidated shack. The theme's final appearance is one of cinema's most famous moments. Having fled the authorities one last time, the Gamin and the Tramp sit by the side of the road. Despondent, she wonders, "What's the use of trying" (later interpolated in the lyrics to "Smile"). With exhortations of "Buck up…. We'll get along!" and one last moving rendition of the love theme, Charlie finally gets the girl and they waddle off down the dusty road into a hopeful, bright new future.

The most famous musical moment, at least in 1936, came from the Tramp's performance number in the café. Much like M-G-M's well-publicized "Garbo laughs!" for *Ninotchka* a few years later, hearing his voice on screen was a major cultural milestone in cinema. Chaplin used this occasion to gauge the audience's reaction to his voice for later sound films by only "speaking" for a few minutes and in context of a humorous situation. "Titine" was based on Léo Daniderff's 1917 novelty song, "Je cherche après Titine." Rather than risk potentially offending his audience with hearing the Tramp's voice in

At the end of *Modern Times*, Charlie and the Gamin waddle off, hand in hand, into a new dawn, c. 1935 (© Roy Export SAS).

English for the first time, Chaplin wrote a set of lyrics composed of a grab bag of French, Italian, and gibberish. But filming the number proved to be a challenge.

The "Titine" sequence was the only scene in *Modern Times* that was filmed with sound and because of the traffic on La Brea during the day, Chaplin decided to shoot the scene at night. Several hundred extras were called for nine o'clock, as were Alfred Newman and the orchestra. After several rehearsals to gauge mic levels with Chaplin's voice, "quiet" was called and Chaplin began. *The Evening Review* reported on the shoot:

> The opening bars of the song had no sooner been recorded, however, than the recorder rushed out of his sound booth calling, "Cut!"
>
> "What's wrong?" asked Chaplin.
>
> "Crickets!" came the alarmed reply.
>
> Absolute silence was ordered. Grips, carpenters, sound men, property boys and even the extras set about locating the offenders. It was a maddening search. They chirped here. They chirped there. Spray guns were brought into play. Carpenters began prying between sets. But the insects proved marvelously elusive.
>
> The game went on for hours. The midnight dinner turned cold. Finally, the search was given up in despair and the company was dismissed, which, of course, was far from the worst fate that could have befallen the several hundred extras at work on the scene who, thanks to a handful of pesky crickets, were assured of another day's pay.
>
> Bright and early next morning, a horde of workers went to work with a vengeance, located and routed the crickets, and that night the number was recorded without difficulty.
>
> So while you howl at this scene … remember that a few lone crickets came even closer to wrecking one of the most novel and hilarious scenes any Chaplin flm has ever featured.[68]

Concerned that non–English-speaking audiences might be confused, the post-production film dialogue continuity for foreign distribution stated: "<u>NOTE! VERY IMPORTANT</u>. Mr. Chaplin sings a song in a 'Bogus' language (no translation needed)."[69] Nicknamed "The Nonsense Song," the lyrics anticipate the comical lingual mash-up of Hynkel's speeches in *The Great Dictator*. It is easy to underestimate the impact that the song had on audiences in 1936. At the preview of *Modern Times* in San Francisco, the audience encored Chaplin's performance on screen "as if it were the actual personage appearing."[70] When Chaplin rereleased the film in 1954, he cut the final verse of "Titine" and so it remains to this day.[71]

Chaplin ran into trouble with the copyright for "Titine" and some of the other source songs used in the film. Originally, Chaplin paid Harms, Inc., $1,250 for the world rights to "Titine." But when the publisher neglected to clear the French copyright with Daniderff, United Artists and Harms each had to put up half of 27,500 francs ($1,650 USD) needed to settle the matter. Also, Harms forgot to clear the song for Holland, Spain, Portugal, Denmark, Sweden, Norway, Finland, Lithuania, Russia, German Switzerland, Asia, Africa, Oceania, and the Balkan States. As with the situation in France, United Artists and Harms equally split the 50,000-franc settlement (approximately $3,000). (Daniderff originally asked for 100,000 francs.)[72] The situation in Italy was even worse. Producer Vittorio Vassarotti owned the rights and unless they were cleared, *Modern Times* would not be shown in Italy. Vassarotti originally wanted 100,000 lire but settled for 40,000, split three ways between UA's Italian agent Mario Luporini (10,000), and 15,000 each for Chaplin's lawyers and Warner Bros.

In March, shortly after the film opened, attorneys for Hitchcock Publishing Co. submitted a claim for "In the Evening by the Moonlight," the song performed by the barbershop quartet in the café. UA paid $150 for worldwide rights to Harry Von Tilzer Music

Publishing Co., but Tilzer had nothing to do with the song. United Artists had to negotiate a new deal with Hitchcock Publishing, who agreed to $500. The studio got back the original $150 and had to make an additional payment of $350.[73]

Chaplin assigned the performing rights to the *Modern Times* music to Irving Berlin Inc., the forerunner of Bourne Co. Berlin, who, like Chaplin, also could not read or write music, had formed the company in 1919 with Max Winslow and Saul Bornstein (who later shortened and changed his last name to Bourne). Unlike most film composers, who gave up all rights to their music to the studio that hired them, Chaplin *was* his studio. Berlin's company had "complete and absolute ownership" of the music and was "granted all rights with respect to said music and specifically the exclusive right to collect all performing fees with respect to such music throughout the world."[74] However, Chaplin still retained his rights in the U.S. and Canada and received fifty percent collected from Berlin's performing fees. One bone of contention, however, in the matter of rights and royalties was the name Raphael Penso.

Penso (1918–1981) was a staff writer at Columbia Pictures, composing stock music on several titles and co-composing *The Fredric March*, which frequently appeared *in Three Stooges* shorts. The official cue sheet for *Modern Times* lists Chaplin and Penso as co-composers on each and every cue. A letter in June 1936 from United Artists' lawyers to Irving Berlin Publishing Co. enclosed a slip for Chaplin to sign "in reference to designating a co-composer of the music in *Modern Times*." Later inquiries made by Association Chaplin into Penso's involvement questioned whether Penso might be a pseudonym for David Raksin, though "that would be surprising as Chaplin never gave away shares of his music rights," says Association head, Kate Guyonvarch. Indeed, the prospect of Chaplin doing so, even at this early stage and considering the tumultuous relationship with Raksin, seemed unlikely.

When Chaplin re-released the film in 1954, there was still some question about Penso's attribution, especially about "Smile." Arthur Kelly at United Artists cabled Chaplin:

> CLARIFY PENSO AS COWRITER BEFORE WE PRINT AND FOR RECORD COMPANIES UNQUOTE
> IF PENSO IS COAUTHOR THEN THERE WILL BE A ROYALTY TO BE PAID TO HIM
> CAN YOU CLARIFY HIS POSITION STOP
> ADVISE QUICKLY SO WE CAN RECEIVE THE MUSIC AND RECORDS[75]

But a telegram a few days later from Kelly to Saul Bourne emphatically states: "PLEASE ADVISE YOUR NEW YORK OFFICE THAT CHARLIE IS THE ONLY PERSON TO COLLECT ROYALTIES ON MUSIC AND RECORDS OF MODERN TIMES."[76] Kelly instructed Bourne "to remove Penso's name from everything, even to the extent of copying the original cuesheets of the score, without the name of Penso. In presenting these cuesheets which we claim are the originals, if any of the actual originals show up in any of the Societies with the name of Penso, it may present a problem, we hope not, but if it does, it may involve loss of revenue not only the publisher's share but also for Charlie who is a Composer Member of all Performing Rights Societies. It is my opinion that nothing will happen, of course, I cannot be definitely positive but I thought it best for you to know about this."[77]

Association Chaplin later made inquiries with ASCAP and the UK's Performing Right Society (PRS) to confirm whether or not Penso was indeed credited, but neither organization listed an account in his name. "From your own revised cue sheet we [the

PRS] observe that the music is stated to have been composed by Charles Chaplin and Raphael Penso. There is a composer member of the French society of this name, but in view of the fact that the music is of American origin, it may be that this is a question of duplication of names and that Charles Chaplin's collaborator is not the French Society's member referred to."[78]

In 1983, Raksin wrote a lengthy reminiscence for *The Quarterly Journal of the Library of Congress* about his experience working with Chaplin. Though he discussed Alfred Newman and Edward Powell, there is no mention of Penso. Over the years, in countless interviews, Raksin was asked to relay the tale of *Modern Times*. He was remarkably consistent in his story but never once mentioned Penso's involvement in the film. Author Clifford McCarty, in his authoritative *Film Composers In America: A Filmography, 1911–1970*, states that Penso (who also went by the first name Raffaelo) was a "European composer whose name was put on many American cue sheets of the 1930s in order to collect European royalties."[79] Indeed, Alfred Newman listed Penso on the cue sheets for later Samuel Goldwyn productions *These Three, Woman Chases Man*, and *You Only Live Once*. McCarty appears to be is correct in his statement and Penso's name on the *Modern Times* cue sheets was likely included strictly to assist with collecting royalties from Europe.

Otis Ferguson in *The New Republic* wrote of the score, "The 'dance' music is a cross between Vienna and a small-town brass band, twenty years old at least."[80] But Mollie Merrick of *The Detroit Free Press* said, "Without the musical score ... the film itself would have been decidedly antiquated and you may understand what a big part music plays in the motion pictures, whether they be silent, or of talkie variety."[81]

While Chaplin's later scores often contain a string of pretty—and even more outdated—string-heavy tunes, the score for *Modern Times* remains an intricate element to the success of the film. Edward Powell and David Raksin brought their musical talents to orchestrations that crackle with wit and invention, while Alfred Newman conducted with his customary (and later legendary) energy and skill on the podium. With all the backstage drama, it is a tribute to Chaplin and his musical team that the score sounds cohesive and complete. Many of his future collaborators were fine musicians in their own right, but Chaplin would never again employ such a celebrated group. Together, their collective skills turned Chaplin's inspired—though fractured—vision into something musically memorable.

At the end of the film, with one final iris wipe and the heart-wrenching strings of the "Smile" theme swelling on the soundtrack, Chaplin closed the window on the Tramp. "So now the film ends on a beautiful note of hope, with conquerable worlds on the horizon," Raksin wrote in his journal following the recording of the music for the finale during the last session, "and we spent much time deliberating [as to] how the music should soar—but Charlie is a bit cynical about the future of his ... hero and his gamine [*sic*]. 'They'll probably get kicked in the pants again,' [Charlie] says (as we watch them trudging hopefully away into the dawn). And they probably will, and it will probably happen in his next film."[82]

As he waddled off into a new dawn, hand in hand with the Gamin, little did Chaplin realize the challenges—or the kicks in the pants—that lay ahead. Without the mask of his iconic character, he would later face a devastating paternity case, exile from his adopted country, and a world that no longer wanted him or his art. On the cinematic front, Chaplin faced a changing landscape and he could no longer rely on his tried and true recipe of pantomime. The full use of dialogue and sound effects would require changes in the way Chaplin wrote and filmed his stories, as well as scored the music.

Storm clouds were also forming in the real world. In Germany, the Nazis banned *Modern Times* amid reports of the film's "Communist tendency" and doubts of Chaplin's Aryan ancestry.[83] Events were heating up politically and Chaplin was disturbed at the news coming out of Europe. By the time his next film was released much of the world would again be at war. Safe for the time being in an isolationist country still at peace, Chaplin took a brave (and what many considered a foolish) step, defying the advice of the Hollywood community and the U.S. government by ridiculing the most infamous man in modern times—Adolf Hitler.

CHAPTER 6

Hope Springs Eternal

AFTER *MODERN TIMES*, Chaplin searched for a new project for Paulette Goddard. One was an adaptation of D. L. Murray's period costume romance *Regency* about a high-spirited young girl in Regency England. But that project was shelved for a story that Chaplin had been working on inspired by a trip to a dance hall in Shanghai with Paulette and Jean Cocteau. The story of a Russian Countess forced to earn her living as a taxi-girl, who stows away to America in the cabin of a U.S. diplomat, *Stowaway* was written with Paulette and Gary Cooper in mind and eventually filmed thirty years later as *A Countess from Hong Kong*.

"I don't know how many ideas my father mulled over in his long search for a story for Paulette," Charles Chaplin, Jr., said, "but I do recall some interesting details about one of them. It came to him by way of a curious little item which someone clipped from a newspaper and mailed him. The item concerned an edict by Adolf Hitler banning Chaplin films from Germany because Dad looked so much like him."[1] The similarities were more than physical. Chaplin and Hitler were born in the same year, the same month, four days apart, and both came from a background of extreme poverty. Hitler also had musical aspirations, at one point wanting to write an opera, as did Chaplin. But "one was to make millions weep, while the other was to set the whole world laughing. Dad could never think of Hitler without a shudder, half of horror, half of fascination. 'Just think,' he would say uneasily, 'he's the madman, I'm just the comic. But it could have been the other way around.' And he couldn't resist concluding with the quote, 'There but for the grace of God go I.'"[2]

Chaplin's new film was labeled simply "Production No. 6" to keep secret the story details of a Jewish barber mistaken for a famous dictator. As this was to be his first talking film, Chaplin had to work for the first time from a completed script, which he began to write in October 1938, a few weeks before the *Kristallnacht* anti–Jewish pogrom in Germany and Austria on November 9 and 10. Production work commenced on the film in January 1939, mere days after *Time* magazine named Hitler "Man of the Year." He completed the final stenciled copies of the script on Sunday, September 3, the day Britain declared war on Germany. Three days later Chaplin began to rehearse, and shooting began on September 9. Filming continued nearly every day, except most Sundays, until the end of March 1940.

Chaplin considered other titles—*The Two Dictators*, *Dictatomania*, and *Dictator of Ptomania*—though the original title was *The Dictator*. But this was also a title of a 1922 Paramount film starring Richard Harding Davis, and the studio wanted Chaplin to pay $25,000 to use it. "I can't spend $25,000 for two words," he told *The New York Times*. "So I said, 'All right, I'll call mine *The Great Dictator*—three words and all for free.'"[3]

During the weeks of preparation, Chaplin ran films for the staff in the studio projection room, among them his 1918 wartime comedy *Shoulder Arms*, plus all the newsreels
of Hitler he could find. He later returned often to a particular sequence showing Hitler
at the signing of the French surrender. As the Fuehrer left the railway carriage, he seemed
to do a little dance. Chaplin would watch the scene with fascination, exclaiming, "Oh,
you bastard, you son-of-a-bitch, you swine. I know what's in your mind."[4] Assistant director Dan James commented forty-five years later, "Of course [Chaplin] had in himself
some of the qualities that Hitler had. He dominated his world. He created his world. And
Chaplin's world was not a democracy either. Charlie was the dictator of all those things."[5]
Nobody knew this better than Paulette.

Relations between Chaplin and Paulette were strained by the time *The Great Dictator*
rolled around. Paulette's contract had expired on March 31, 1938, and she signed with the
Myron Selznick agency. Chaplin hired her at $2,500 a week and was furious when she
brought her agent to demand bigger billing. Though they were "somewhat estranged we
were friends and still married," said Chaplin.[6] But the tension bled into their working
relationship. "There was some anger on both sides," said Dan James. "But he worked very
hard with her. Sometimes he would make 25 or 30 takes. He would stand in her place
on the set and try and give her the tone and the gestures. It was a method he had been
able to use in silent films; it could not work so well with a talking picture." Goddard put
on a good face when speaking to the press. "[Charlie] thinks in rhyme and tempo," she
said. "To the people who are to play a scene, he will describe it as though they were
dancers. If they find themselves doing a bit of business awkwardly he will say, 'That's
because you started on the wrong foot.' Doing a scene with him is so exactly like working
to music that you can't help falling into it."[7]

Even though the sound era had been in effect for over a decade, Chaplin finally
making a dialogue film was still news. "Whether I would or wouldn't talk has been a very
great mystery hasn't it?" he said. "You see, I haven't a very large studio, just one sound
stage and not a very big one; not much extra space about, and I just couldn't figure out
how to have a lot of big bulky sound machinery in such a small place. Also, I always like
to understand things I work with and the first sound mechanics were so complicated I
didn't know what it was all about. Now the equipment is simplified … and I'm delighted.…
That's the extent of the mystery."[8]

Critics complained of Chaplin's outdated film techniques. For instance, instead of
filming at the standard rate of 24 frames per second, Chaplin filmed most of the sequences
with the barber at 22 frames, a procedure he had been using since 1914, to give the character the Tramp's signature walk.[9] "Now that the waiting is over and the shivers of suspense
at an end," Bosley Crowther said in *The New York Times*, "let the trumpets be sounded
and the banners flung against the sky. For the little tramp, Charlie Chaplin, finally
emerged last night from behind the close-guarded curtains which have concealed his
activities these past two years and presented himself in triumphal splendor as *The Great
Dictator*—or you know who.… *The Great Dictator* may not be the finest picture ever
made—in fact, it possesses several disappointing shortcomings. But, despite them, it
turns out to be a truly superb accomplishment by a truly great artist—and, from one
point of view, perhaps the most significant film ever produced." Crowther was one of
many critics who felt the barber's final five-minute speech at the end of the film was
"completely out of joint with that which has gone before.… But the sincerity with which

Chaplin voices his appeal and the expression of tragedy which is clear in his face are strangely overpowering. Suddenly one perceives in bald relief the things which make *The Great Dictator* great—the courage and faith and surpassing love for mankind which are in the heart of Charlie Chaplin."[10]

The National Legion of Decency took Chaplin to task for allegedly making a remark "suggesting his disbelief in God" and placed the film in its "Class A—Section Two—Unobjectionable for Adults" category. "In view of the star's following," said the Legion's statement, "this utterance in its possible harmful effect on audiences is deplored."[11] The critical consensus was "the subject-matter was ill advised and would do the industry little good."[12] "We, too, regarded [*The Great Dictator*] with certain reservations," Crowther admitted. "It *is* too long and repetitious, it shamefully shows the cutters' seams and it lacks an artistic conclusion like September Morn lacks clothes."

> But the complaint muttered 'round and about that it adds up to disappointment finds no support from us. We have frankly declared that *The Great Dictator*, in our opinion, is a superlative accomplishment by a great and true artist, that it is unquestionably the most significant—if not the most entertaining—film that Chaplin has ever made. And, with dead cats flying all around us, we confidently stick to that belief...
>
> Chaplin's intention is not just to ridicule Hitler and his system, to make it all appear very funny. He is seriously applying the talents at his command—keen and withering mimicry and a genius for comic distortion—to reveal the monstrous abnormality of the most dangerous man in the world. He is actually making a most profound and tragic comment upon a truly evil state of affairs...
>
> If *The Great Dictator* seems less funny to some than anything Chaplin has done before it is because the evil which he is exposing seems more immediate and threatening. It is the fearful preconceptions in the mind of the auditor, not the artistic execution of Chaplin, which prohibits a full enjoyment of this magnificent creation...
>
> And now, more in sadness than in anger, we must deservedly agree with the general objection to the ending...
>
> Yes, it is bad construction—confusing, banal and embarrassing. For it is just as though Chaplin were revealing, in an unguarded moment, the details of his most intimate grief. But for that very reason ... we found it one of the most poignant and affecting things we have ever beheld on a screen. During that tragic outburst, we weren't listening so much to the words, which really do not add up. We were listening rather to a voice which was coming from the soul of Charlie Chaplin, the little fellow we have known and loved for many years, finally speaking out bravely and defiantly against the brutal forces loose in this sad world.[13]

"*The Great Dictator* on the screen is pretty much what I meant it to be," Chaplin explained.

> I had a story to tell and something I wanted very much to say. I said it. I enjoyed saying it. I think it is funny when it should be funny. And, more than I can tell you, I enjoy the laughter of audiences at the story. I am grateful and proud that it is liked by many of the critics and is so popular with the public. To me, it does "come off." ...
>
> As to Hitler being funny, I can only say that if we can't sometimes laugh at Hitler then we are further gone than we think.... Laughter is the tonic, the relief, the surcease from pain...
>
> People have said that [the barber] steps out of character. What of it? The picture is two hours and seven minutes in length. If two hours and three minutes of it is comedy, may I not be excused for ending my comedy on a note that reflects, honestly and realistically, the world in which we live, and I not be excused in pleading for a better world? Mind you, it is addressed to the soldiers, the very victims of a dictatorship...
>
> There is no promised land for the oppressed people of the world. There is no place over the horizon to which they can go for sanctuary. They must stand, and we must stand."[14]

The Great Dictator was Chaplin's greatest financial success. The film ran for fifteen weeks in New York and grossed nearly $5 million worldwide, netting him $1.5 million in profit.[15] The New York Film Critics named Chaplin Best Actor but he refused the award based on his belief that the only aim of actors is to please the public and not to compete with one another. If he accepted the award, he said, he would be acknowledging this competition, "and such an approach to one's work is not very inspiring."[16] The film received five Academy Award nominations, including Best Picture, Actor, Supporting Actor (Jack Oakie), Original Screenplay, and one for Original Score, credited to Meredith Willson. But Willson was a late consideration for the job.

"Every composer in pictures was angling" for the *Dictator* gig, said *The Austin American*.[17] And at a party at the home of Clifford Odets in the late 1930s, Chaplin met German émigré composer Hanns Eisler, who had been a member of the Communist Party of Germany and whose music was decidedly political in tone. The Nazi Party had banned Eisler's music in 1933 and he was now one of many musicians living in exile in Los Angeles. Robert Lewis, who later starred in *Monsieur Verdoux*, said the meeting with Eisler was "an example of the hopelessness of artistic collaboration with Chaplin."

> Charlie remarked how wonderfully ironic it would be if the German composer would contribute the music for *The Great Dictator*, which Chaplin was preparing, the leading character of which, Adolph Hitler, was responsible for Eisler's exile from his homeland. Hanns bowed and said it would be an honor to work with such a film master.
>
> Charlie moved to the piano. "For instance, here's a tune I've been working on," he said, and with one finger he picked out a simple, pleasant melody. "What would you do with that?" Rushing to the piano stool, Eisler went to work. "We might arrange something like this," said Hanns. He then built the tune into a charming little piece with marvelously original harmonies.
>
> "That's fine, Hanns," said Charlie, reclaiming the piano seat, "but what I meant was more in this vein." He then repeated his original few simple bars, exactly as he had played them the fist time.
>
> "Ah, I see what you mean," said Hanns with all the ingratiation he could summon. "Let me give you another approach." This time he improvised a completely unadorned, but still enchanting, version of the tune.
>
> "That's beautiful," Charlie assured Hanns. "But actually what I need is something like this." Again he picked out his same original notes. It was clear that even Bach, Beethoven, or Mozart couldn't shake Charlie from what he heard in his head.[18]

Nicolas Slonimsky, in *Music Since 1900*, claimed that Eisler was part of the team who "set on paper, organized and harmonized" Chaplin's score, though there is no evidence to support this.[19]

David Raksin, apparently not completely ousted after the *Modern Times* backstage musical drama, wrote two klezmer pieces—"Kazatchok" and "Doina." Raksin scored both numbers for four instruments—violin, cello, accordion, and clarinet. "Kazatchok," named for a Ukrainian and Russian folk dance, was most likely composed for the film's original ending, which was shot but not used. The half-step grace notes and swirling sixteenth notes give the piece a hora-like feel and the modulation to the parallel minor (C major-C minor) darkens the tune in order to provide ironic counterpoint to the images of happy stormtroopers dancing at the rally.

"Doina" is marked *Andante con tristezza* ("moderately slow with sadness"). The mournful C-minor piece is written in 6/8 and only lasts sixteen bars. It was probably written for a scene in the ghetto, though there is no note in the music or in any of Chaplin's papers indicating which scene he had in mind. The original manuscript parts for both pieces have notes and measures marked up and crossed out, meaning both "Kazatchok"

The Great Dictator (1940)—The unused "Kazatchok" klezmer piece composed by David Raksin, presumably for the film's original ending.

and "Doina" were probably recorded to fit the timings of their respective scenes, though there is no record of this on the recording schedule. "I would have loved to do that picture," Raksin said. "That's one of the cases where I said to Charlie, 'Charlie, when you get around to it, I'd love to work with you again.' I would have done the entire film, I would have stopped work wherever I was. But Charlie wanted another guy, Meredith Willson."[20]

Willson (1902–1984), Mason City, Iowa's most famous son, studied composition with Mortimer Wilson and conducting with Henry Hadley at the Institute of Musical Art in New York, known today as the Juilliard School of Music. To help meet expenses, he played

The Great Dictator (1940)—"Doina," David Raksin's second unused cue for the film, was probably written for a scene in the ghetto.

in the orchestras of the Rivoli and Rialto theaters under the direction of Hugo Riesenfeld. At age nineteen, Willson became only the second player ever to be hired by John Philip Sousa without an audition. After three seasons, he joined the New York Philharmonic in 1925, playing under Arturo Toscanini.

In 1923, Willson played flute scales for Dr. Lee De Forrest's early attempts at synchronizing music to film. While he was at the Philharmonic, Willson was part of on the first Vitaphone synchronized film, John Barrymore's *Don Juan* (1926). Abe Meyer, Riesenfeld's secretary back at the Rialto, got Willson a job scoring two B films at Tiffany-Stahl Productions—*Peacock Alley* and "a horrible thing" titled *The Lost Zeppelin*. "Didn't know much about picture scoring—in fact, didn't know *anything* about picture scoring," Willson said, "but my cigar gave out the proper smoke screen."[21] He was more interested in radio and in 1932 Willson became the music director for NBC's Western Division. Over the next ten years, he directed as many as seventeen radio programs a week. Chaplin contacted Willson after hearing his second symphony, *Missions of California*, which premiered in April 1940 with Albert Coates and the Los Angeles Philharmonic.[22]

Willson began work on *The Great Dictator* on July 3, though he did not sign his twenty-page contract (the longest of any musician contract on record in the Chaplin Archive) until July 24. The gap was standard practice with Chaplin and his musicians, most of whom took the job with a verbal agreement, a process that would cause numerous problems over the years. Willson was hired as musical director at $833.33 per week for six weeks "to write, compose, orchestrate, arrange, prepare, rehearse, direct and record, and to supervise the writing, composition, orchestration, arrangement, preparation, rehearsal, direction, recordation and dubbing of, the complete musical score, musical sound track and cue sheet." He would act as Chaplin's agent "in employing all musicians, composers, and other necessary personnel, and in securing musical material, all salaries of persons so employed" to be paid by Chaplin. Though he was to "render his services exclusively" to the film throughout the term of the contract, Chaplin allowed Willson to take Tuesdays and Thursdays off to continue conducting the Maxwell House Coffee and Johnson Floor Wax radio broadcasts. And in a rare show of generosity, Willson was provided with a separate title card in the credits. As with all Chaplin music contracts, Willson agreed that "any and all musical material which he may write or compose" would "automatically become [Chaplin's] property as the author thereof."[23]

*   *   *

"Things did relax for Paulette and the rest of the cast when the shooting came to an end in the spring of 1940, but not for Dad," said Charles Chaplin, Jr. "Still the human dynamo, he turned his attention to composing the music for *The Great Dictator*. And because many of his sessions with the musicians were held at the house, I had the opportunity of watching first-hand a man who couldn't read a note and knew nothing of the mechanics of the art, work at being a composer—and drive men mad as he had Al Newman in earlier years."

> The musicians were actually musical secretaries taking Dad's dictation. The music was always his. He would hum or play his tune and the musicians would take it down and then play it back for him. Dad would listen carefully. He has a wonderful ear.
>
> "That part's good," he'd say. "But there's something wrong here. Wait a minute."
>
> He would concentrate and hum the phrase again, and the musicians would get back to their dictation. It might take a number of tries before Dad had the tune to his satisfaction.
>
> He and the musicians not only worked long hours at home, but more long hours at the studio, where they used a Movieola so that a scene could be played, reversed and played again until the music to match it popped into Dad's head. Once he had it in its entirety he would give the musicians a description of how he wanted it scored for each scene—the tempo, the rhythm, the style. Though he knew some of the various musical forms and could correctly use a great deal of terminology such as pizzicato, rubato, allegro and the like, he preferred to describe what he wanted by referring to a composer's name or an instrumental label by way of illustration.
>
> "We should make this Wagnerian," he would say, or, "This part should be more Chopin. Let's make this light and airy, a lot of violins. I think we could use an oboe effect in this passage."
>
> Sometimes when Dad described what he wanted the musicians would shake their heads, because Dad's timing of a musical phrase to suit a bit of action was sometimes so unorthodox it threw them off. They would try to explain the technical reasons for not being able to give him what he asked for.
>
> "Well, I'm not concerned about that," Dad would say. "Just put it down here the way I want it."
>
> It was only after they'd done so that they could see that, though unorthodox, Dad's dramatic instinct as it related to music was brilliant. So phrase after phrase, literally note by note, Dad and his valiant musicians worked their way through *The Great Dictator*. The musicians turned gray and were on the verge of nervous breakdowns by the time it was over, but whatever they suffered they couldn't say that working with Dad was ever dull. He gave them a free performance at every session, because he didn't just hum or sing, or knock out a tune on the piano. He couldn't stay quiet

that long. He would start gesturing with the music, acting out the parts of the various people in the scene he was working on, but caricaturing their movements to evoke a tonal response in himself. At those times his acting was closer than ever to ballet.[24]

"I have never met a man who devoted himself so completely to the ideal of perfection as Charlie Chaplin," Willson said. "During the two months I was associated with him … I was constantly amazed at his attention to detail, his feeling for the exact musical phrase or tempo to express the mood he wanted, and his ability to inspire the same fanatical zeal in those who work for him."

When Chaplin is making a picture, it becomes his life during the time it is in production. I remember the day he phoned me to inquire whether I could collaborate on the music for the film. I was immensely flattered, for though I had never met Chaplin, I had seen every picture since his earlier two-reel days.

I went to his house at once and we were hardly seated before he began talking about *The Great Dictator*. Throughout the afternoon he described it, acting out scene after scene with his marvelous pantomime, switching from his cultured English accent to Charlie, the tramp's curious dialect.

It was a strange feeling, being the first outsider to hear Charlie's film voice—the one he uses in *The Great Dictator*. Then Charlie told me: "Now I'm going to show you the picture. You'll be the only person out of the studio to see it. I want your frank opinion."

And that was the way I grew to know Chaplin during the weeks of composing, orchestrating and recording the music for the film. Always he is seeking to ferret out every false note, however minor, from film or music. And Chaplin, though he professes to be only a layman in the matter of music, has a remarkably keen musical sense. His selective judgment is extraordinarily fine. If he had studied music instead of entering the theater he would have been a great musician.

The Great Dictator (1940)—Chaplin and Meredith Willson take time out of their busy schedule writing the score for *The Great Dictator* to sit for publicity photographs with photographer Max Autrey, c. July 19, 1940 (© Roy Export Co. Ltd.).

The Great Dictator (1940)—**The main title music, based on the first movement of Meredith Willson's Symphony No. 1 in F Minor ("A Symphony of San Francisco").**

The creation of music for a picture such as *The Great Dictator* presents unique difficulties. Most picture scores are used purely as background for the action. Chaplin makes his music almost as much a part of the picture as the story itself. The music conveys humor, satire, the ageless sorrow of a people oppressed by tyrants.

Throughout the long weeks of fitting music sequences to the film, Chaplin sat with me constantly, suggesting, advising, listening to improved melodies or offering his own. Most of the melodic themes you will hear in the film are his own.[25]

By 1959, Willson had apparently changed his tune. "Mine was the actual scoring and the original music," he said in an interview with Columbia University's Oral History project. "But wherever you heard a recognizable tune, that was all Chaplin."[26]

Chaplin worked differently with Willson than he had with David Raksin and most likely Arthur Johnston. "[Charlie] would come into the studio they had given me to work in, and he would have ideas to suggest—melodies. After that, he would leave me alone," Willson said. The daily production reports bear this out. On *Modern Times*, for example, the reports would list "C.C. with arranger all day."[27] On *The Great Dictator*, the reports note Chaplin was at the studio primarily cutting and dubbing, leaving Willson on his own. "When he came in to see me again I would show him what I was doing, and often he would have very good suggestions to make. He liked to act as though he knew more music than he actually did, but his ideas were very good."[28] On July 19, both men took time out of their schedules to sit for publicity stills for photographer Max Autrey.

The Austin American-Statesmen reported the two sometimes worked "18 hours a day together, but Willson found his association with Charlie more stimulating than fatiguing."[29] *The Daily Republican* in Belvidere, Illinois, reported that Chaplin pleaded with Willson to "take it easy." "How can I?" asked Willson. "After 10 years in radio doing two to five shows a week?"[30] "These melodies came to me as I studied the film, I sing them or scribble them down, just the melody line," Chaplin told film music critic Bruno David Ussher. "Willson or one of the boys then work them out."[31] "The boys" included M-G-M staff orchestrator Leo Arnaud, who worked on a number of musicals including *Born to Dance*, *Broadway Melody of 1938*, and *Babes in Arms*, orchestrating Max Steiner's massive score for *Gone with the Wind*, the classic Munchkinland sequence from *The Wizard of Oz*, and *Pinocchio*'s harrowing Monstro scenes. Willson also brought along his assistant,

Arranger and conductor Meredith Willson (on the podium) confers with Chaplin on a break during the recording sessions for *The Great Dictator,* c. August 1940 (© Roy Export Co. Ltd.).

Max Terr, who conducted the chorus on Willson's radio broadcasts and would later work with Chaplin on the sound version of *The Gold Rush*, as well as a trio of his arrangers—Roy Chamberlain, Carmen Dragon, Romo Falk—and John Hicks, most likely the trombonist in Willson's *Blue Monday Jamboree* orchestra on KFRC Radio in San Francisco.

The Great Dictator score was broken down into seventy cues, many of them with multiple revisions and substantial rewrites, of which only forty-seven made it into the finished film. "The themes we used," Willson said, "excepting for a bit of Wagner and Brahms interpolation, are about half Mr. Chaplin's and half mine, with my development and orchestration. And it's uncanny how right he always is when technically he isn't a musician and can't read a note of music. In scoring the picture we'd run it through, then in this place or that one he'd sing a few notes; something he'd call a 'twiddeldy bit,' and it would unerringly work out to be exactly what the sequence needed."[32] Though Willson claimed that "every note of music in the picture," except for Brahms and Wagner "is original and composed expressly for *The Great Dictator*," that is not entirely true.[33]

An early draft of the script begins with "Open with music playing the Jewish good luck song, 'Muzzletoff' during Credit Titles. The orchestra runs through a series of themes from songs of the Great War, including 'Over There,' 'Tipperary,' 'Marseillaise,' etc. The effect should be stirring and reminiscent of pre-war days."[34] Originally, Chaplin had an elaborate vision of the titles with them imprinted on the screen by rolling tanks. "Frightful idea, wasn't it?" he told *The New York Times*. "I have many garish ideas and am very enthusiastic about them. I spring them on the people here and…. I'm hurt and angry when they disapprove—and stubborn. But always before the picture is released, something saves me. I return to simplicity just in time."[35] While Chaplin didn't use that medley of war-time tunes he mentioned in the script, most of the music for the main titles is not his either. It consists primarily of themes taken from the first movement of Willson's first symphony, *A Symphony of San Francisco*, which had premiered in April 1936 to commemorate the thirtieth anniversary of the San Francisco earthquake. In the program notes, Willson said the symphony "was inspired by the incomparable traditions of San Francisco and a delineation of the spiritual personality that is San Francisco…. Generally speaking, the first movement is intended to convey pioneer courage, loyalty, strength of purpose and freedom."[36] The chromatic runs, brass fanfares, and the primary theme of the main title were lifted directly from Willson's symphony.

On July 29, Chaplin heard portions of the score played on two grand pianos. The following day he began working with Max Terr in editing the music that had already been composed and scored. Beginning August 3, Chaplin took a few days off aboard his yacht, while the "Music Department continued its work of Composing and Arranging Musical Score."[37] Rehearsals finally got under way on Stage 2 at RCA on August 12 with Willson and the orchestra. Once the musicians were dismissed at 5:00 that day, Chaplin joined Paulette in the projection room and listened to Max Terr play some of the score on the piano.

At the recording sessions, "Chaplin was really in his element," said Willson. "A music lover, he spent every moment in the recording studio, listening intently to the rehearsals, suggesting that a passage be quickened here, retarded there or expanded into greater significance."[38] Robert Van Gelder of *The New York Times* described his experience visiting the sound stage:

> To the fanfare of a seventy-five-piece orchestra [*sic*], the rather dim screen at the south end of a Charles Chaplin Studio sound stage [*sic*] showed "Charles Chaplin Presents…. *The Great Dictator*…. Written and Produced by Charles Chaplin…. The Cast…. Charles Chaplin, Jack Oakie, Paulette Goddard…." Charles Chaplin rubbed his stomach enthusiastically and purred. He swayed to the music. "That lilt, that swing. Beautiful. It always gets me." …
>
>   He had come onto the sound stage at 10 o'clock in the morning and it was perhaps significant that at that hour his aides had been decidedly hard to please in respect to the sound dubbing. In every take the brass was too loud, or the fiddles came in too late, or the pause before the bugles was not sufficiently pronounced. "But I like it," Chaplin had argued over and over again. "Aren't you being academic? I liked it. It was stirring." Along about noon all this had changed. His aides were much better satisfied and Chaplin much less so. "Not enough emotion. You'd better do it again," Chaplin would say. "There wasn't enough wail in the brasses when those newspaper headlines came up." "About 5 in the afternoon, when the others are exhausted," whispered one of his employees, "he'll be right up beside Meredith Willson … swinging a baton."[39]

Herb Caen from the *San Francisco Chronicle*, though he was talking about radio, said, "It's a treat, indeed, to watch Willson in action."

> He's the symphony conductor, Hollywood style, come to life. He brings at least a dozen batons to the studio for each broadcast, and their mortality rate is high, so high, in fact that he keeps a stock of 25 extras always on hand. His dark hair, usually neatly parted, becomes a waving mass as he leans from the podium and implores his musicians to "Give! Give!" Each wave of his baton, each gesture with his left hand means something as he seeks to draw the utmost from the orchestra. And if he doesn't like someone's performance, he isn't hesitant in expressing his views.
>
>   Musicians like Willson. We mean all types of musicians, from the most finished symphony soloist to the hottest "jam" trumpeter. And where music is concerned, Willson is broad-minded…. But no matter what style Meredith Willson is called on to direct, he insists upon accuracy, brilliance, finish. Perfection is not enough. He seeks something even higher. And someday he'll find it.[40]

Because of the many types of music in the score, the recording sessions split into one of three instrumental combinations—Grand Orchestra (sixty-three musicians), Semi-

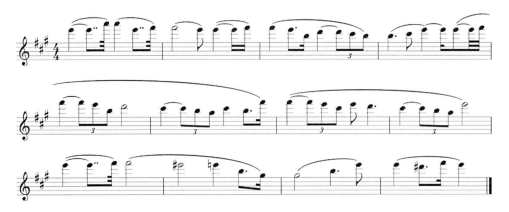

The Great Dictator (1940)—The ethereal strings of Wagner's *Lohengrin* form the ironic musical counterpoint to Hynkel's dance with the globe balloon (marked "Bubble Dance" in the score). The choice to use the music of Wagner, Chaplin and Hitler's favorite composer, was surely no accident.

Grand Orchestra (forty musicians), and Band (forty-two musicians). The Grand Orchestra was on tap for the first day, August 15. Director King Vidor and his wife visited the set and spent an hour listening to the first recording session. First up was Wagner's *Lohengrin* music that Chaplin used for the globe balloon sequence (labeled "Bubble Dance" on the cue sheet) and the finale.

Chaplin called it a "Dance Routine" in the script and laid out the four-page description in ten movements, with directions that Hynkel was supposed to pick up the globe to the "soft strains of *Peer Gynt*."[41] Chaplin had used Grieg's incidental music effectively in his compilation scores for *The Gold Rush* and *The Circus*, but Wagner was Chaplin's— and Hitler's—favorite composer. Eric James later stated he believed that Chaplin's choice to use Wagner was coincidental, but it is doubtful the choice was arbitrary. "Just listen to this, just listen to it," he said of Wagner's music to Charles Chaplin, Jr. "How could such a bastard write this beautiful music? Why, it's not mortal, it's heavenly, and he was such a son of a bitch in his personal life!"[42] Chaplin spent three days (December 21–23, 1939) filming the memorable sequence, and then retakes on six other days in January and February 1940. Chaplin felt the scene contained the film's "main message"—"By his movements, the dictator expresses all his contempt for the world."[43] Wagner's anti–Semitic reputation and the lofty pedestal his music sat upon during the years of the Third Reich make a choice to use his music a clear expression of that contempt. But here, the Prelude to Act III of *Lohengrin* represents something deeper.

On one level Wagner's ethereal string writing for his 1850 fantasy romance is another example of Chaplin using elegant music to frame his comedy, as in the dance with the globe. When the music appears at the end of the film following the barber's speech, however, Chaplin seems to be thumbing his nose at Wagner, reframing the music as inspiration for not only the Jews but all mankind—"We are coming into a new world, a kindlier world."

For the barber shop shaving sequence, the script calls for "MUSIC—A FAST OVERTURE…. Charlie speeds up—keeping time to the racing music, Almost in a single movement, the customer is lathered, shaved and washed. The job is finished at the same time as the final chord of the overture. Tada!"[44] Chaplin rehearsed the scene on October 2, 1939, from a wax record of Brahms' *Hungarian Dance No. 5*. "One of our toughest problems," said Willson, "was synchronizing the Brahms music to the picture."

> For the full orchestral recording we locked ourselves in a glassed inclosure [*sic*], with headphones leading to the orchestra. Then we played the phonograph record, watched the picture on the screen and I directed the orchestra through the glass partition. The difficult job here was in keeping the beat always a fraction of time ahead of the phonograph so that the inevitable time lag for the orchestra to pick up the direction would be counteracted.
>
> To Chaplin's intense delight, we were able to do a perfect recording in two "takes." When such good breaks came he bubbled over like a small boy.
>
> "Marvelous!" he'd shout. "Everybody relax while I send out for sandwiches and coffee. We'll celebrate!"
>
> And then he'd hop over to the piano and begin pounding out old English music hall tunes—for Chaplin is first and always the irrepressible Charlie of the derby hat, the baggy trousers and the funny mustache, and no success ever will make him different.[45]

Willson later claimed in his autobiography *And There I Stood With My Piccolo* that the sequence took only one take. Neither number is correct—it was actually four.[46]

According to the script, Hynkel's famous dance with the globe balloon was originally supposed to be accompanied by the "soft strains" of Grieg's *Peer Gynt*, c. 1940 (© Roy Export SAS).

Chaplin composed three separate pieces of music to accompany the barber's many escapes from the storm troopers. The first, "Barber Shop Fight," underscores a storm trooper hauling the barber away for trying to wipe the word "JEW" off his shop window. The piece had gone through two major revisions before Chaplin settled on the version heard in the film. The original cue had no key signature. The harmony was kept in con-

The Great Dictator (1940)—**It took three tries for Chaplin to settle on a proper cue for the "Barber Shop Fight."**

stant flux, though always in minor, dotted rhythms muddied the music and accidentals kept the tonal center off balance. By the time Chaplin and Willson revised the cue a second time, it consisted of sequences of chugging staccato quarter notes in the violins swirling themselves around a major third, mimicking the barber turning and twirling on the ghetto street, trying to escape the clutches of evil. The sequences ascend chromatically, with octave hiccups and unison fanfares punctuating the cue. Chaplin obviously felt the original music was too dark and the upbeat tone of the revised cue not only plays up the comedy, but it also serves as a call to arms for the ghetto neighborhood. It took cuts from three separate takes to splice together the cue. The same music is used a few scenes later ("Charlie's Last Escape") as the barber tries to flee after dousing a storm trooper with paint. Later, when Schultz and the barber attempt to escape over the rooftops, the cue, now called "The Escape," replaces the appropriately named "Roof Top Hurry." The original cue for the scene alternated between 6/8 and 2/4, with a lighthearted tone that matched what Chaplin was looking for. But he obviously felt it made more sense to have all the escape scenes scored with the same basic music.

The music of Willson's first symphony used in the main title also serves as the backbone for war-related montages in the film. The first, "The Old Order Changeth," occurs at the end of World War I as the barber lies in a coma and, quoting a newspaper headline,

The Great Dictator **(1940)—The "Osterlich Bridge" theme, which later served as the chorus for the song "Falling Star."**

"Hynkel Party Takes Power." Willson's dramatic brass theme is interpolated in Ivesian fashion with quotes from the Civil War staple "When Johnny Comes Marching Home" and Beethoven's "Ode to Joy." Later, the maniacal trumpet fanfares trample over each other and Willson's theme takes on even more evil connotations as Hynkel's storm troopers invade Osterlich.

    One of the final cues recorded the first day was the moving "Osterlich Bridge" as Hannah and the Jaekels cross over into what hopefully will be (but is not) freedom—Osterlich. The cue took seven takes, with earlier takes ruined by "Solo Violin too forced" or a "Bum Horn Note."[47] "The music which [Chaplin] composed," said columnist Louella Parsons, who was at the final recording session, "is a haunting melody that lingers and I found myself humming it long after we left the projection room."[48] Chaplin and Willson later converted the theme into a song, "Falling Star," with lyrics by Eddie DeLange ("Moonglow," "Solitude").

> *All my life I've been a lonely lover*
> *I couldn't discover romance.*
> *Somewhere love is hiding undercover,*
> *And to find it I'll take almost any chance.*
>
> CHORUS
> *FALLING STAR you heavenly messenger from above.*
> *Find me the one to love, FALLING STAR.*
> *Near or far I gladly would follow your welcome beams into a land of dreams, my star.*
>
> *I find this earth so sad and dreary without some love.*
> *And for help I turn to you above to*
> *FALLING STAR while searching for someone who's lonely too*
> *I'll ride along with you, FALLING STAR.*
>
> REPEAT CHORUS[49]

Written in Chaplin's favorite key—F major (as opposed to E major in the film)—the song is an entirely different composition than the "Osterlich Bridge" theme as heard in the film. Only the first phrase of the chorus, with the words "Falling Star you heavenly messenger from above," uses the "Osterlich Bridge" music. The remainder of the chorus and the bridge ("I find this earth") are new, while the verse uses the melody from a little heard cue later in the film ("They've Gone"). "I did the music for that," Willson claimed. "Kind of a popular song in the Rachmaninoff harmony period style."[50]

Chaplin and Willson signed the agreement for "Falling Star" with Irving Berlin, Inc. on December 11, 1940. Apparently, the publisher had little faith in the song as the two men surprisingly agreed to lower terms than the standard Berlin contract— two cents (instead of three) for every piano copy and 1⅓ cents (instead of two) for every complete orchestration or band copy. "In the event that

Sheet music for "Falling Star" (1941) (courtesy The Great American Songbook Foundation).

not more than fifty (50) regular copies … shall be sold within any six months royalty period," said the contract, "the PUBLISHER shall have the right to sell any and all copies on hand at any price obtainable and free from the payment of any royalties."[51] Willson conducted the vocal on his *Maxwell House Coffee Time* show in 1942, and various instrumentalists recorded the song, but there is no evidence of any vocal recordings in ASCAP's repertory listing and it is doubtful sheet music sales were high. New lyrics were attached to the song at some later date, still credited to the three songwriters, under the title "Now I Know" (not to be confused with another Willson song with the same title written in the 1960s). The melody had to be altered to accommodate the new lyrics.

All my life I've been a lonely lover
I couldn't discover romance
Love was always hiding under cover
But at last my heart has given me the answer
CHORUS
NOW I KNOW
I know what it means to be born again
I have been born again
I'm in love
NOW I KNOW

I know why a song is a wondrous thing
My heart has learned to sing
I'm in love
My skies are bluer than the never were before
Friends just seem to appear in front of every front door—for
NOW I KNOW
I know that the loveliest dreams come true
Since I confessed to you
I'm in love.[52]

The second day of recording (August 16) was a full one, with the smaller orchestra of forty musicians recording twelve cues, many of which never made it into the final film. The manuscripts for all of Chaplin's scores, including the compilation scores during the silent era, contain instances of cuts and changes that were made for performance or on the sound stage during recording. Chaplin always wrote more music than was necessary and then scaled back, but no Chaplin score before or since left as much rejected music as *The Great Dictator*. Notably, Chaplin originally scored most of the opening ten minutes of the film.

The music for "Grease Her Up" was written to accompany the barber greasing up the oversized Big Bertha cannon. Marked "Very Cute—Nice" in the notes next to the approved take, the music is a delightful scherzo interpolating motifs from "How Much Is That Doggie in the Window" and "Three Blind Mice." Chaplin obviously rethought the opening of the film and unfortunately jettisoned this cue, though this music later underscores the shop opening when the barber returns to the ghetto after waking from his coma. "Grenade Humoresque," the barber's jittery dance when the grenade falls in his sleeve, written in part by Max Terr, and the spinning of the dud bomb are two other significant musical sequences that did not make it into the film. The cues are a mélange of musical styles—from skittering sixteenth notes and furious chromatic runs to cartoon musical flights of fancy that mimic Chaplin and the bomb's every move.

In an interview with the *New York Herald Tribune*, Willson pointed out, "Almost all of [the score] is in the symphonic field. There are no saxophones, no popular music, no excerpts from present-days tunes. In one brief boulevard scene we developed a bit of light, semi-danceable music."[53] The latest in a line of Chaplin's promenade cues—"Ze Boulevardier"—accompanies the barber and Hannah as they stroll down the ghetto street. Willson incorrectly predicted it would be a hit, though the music is most effective when it dials out at Hannah's exclamation, "Do you know, that Hynkel isn't such a bad fella after all!"

The beginning of the chorus of "Falling Star" (1941), music by Charles Chaplin and Meredith Willson, lyrics by Eddie DeLange.

The Great Dictator (1940)—The unused "Grease Her Up" cue for the Big Bertha cannon interpolates motifs from "How Much Is That Doggie in the Window" and "Three Blind Mice," and was later reused to underscore the barber shop opening.

The session also included two delightful musical sequences—the "Three Blind Mice" interpolations of the barber shop opening and Chaplin's classic "stagger dance" after Hannah accidentally bonks the barber on the head with a frying pan (which was tuned to D natural). The cue is a charming music box interpolation of the 19th-century German folk song "Du, du liegst mir im herzen." The melody, which would later be featured memorably in *Judgment at Nuremberg*, *The Producers*, and *Blazing Saddles*, circles itself as the barber staggers on and off the curb in a daze. Two other cues—"Dissolve to Palace" and "Jaeckel's Exit"—were only two bars in length and served as scene transitions, neither of which are missed musically in the film.

The Great Dictator (1940)—The Parisian-flavored "Ze Boulevardier" lightly strolls the ghetto streets alongside the Jewish barber and Hannah.

The lovely violin melody that accompanies the barber and Hannah's relief at the departure of the storm troopers ("They've Gone") is unfortunately barely noticeable in the film. Rolled chords in the harp and celeste signal relief, though a "Celeste too loud" note in red on the recording schedule may indicate why the music is dialed down so low in the audio mix. Willson made up for the oversight by repurposing the theme for the verse section of "Falling Star."

Day three was devoted to the many pastiche marches composed for the film, fanfares, and trumpet calls. As the daily production record noted, "Some of the Recording was done on the Lot to get 'open air' playing effects."[54] The lumbering pompous brass of the "Horse's A--manship (Assmanship) March" serves as Hynkel's theme, a musical middle finger to Hitler. Willson wanted "an exaggerated German march, with the tuba and all the scales coming down, and I invented instruments that would go lower and lower—real Horst Wessel Teutonic everything."[55] The "Pretzelberger March," with its drunken optimism of a German beer hall, underscores the meeting between "our Phooey" and Napaloni (Jack Oakie), the dictator of Bacteria. Napaloni's music, the "Napoli March," forgoes the squared cut time of the German marches, opting instead for a more Italian 6/8 time signature as the two dictators view Tomania's armed forces marching by in review. Two other marches were written for the sequence but not used. "Schweine Knocken March" (short for "pig bones") owes much to John Philip Sousa with its active woodwind countermelody, while the pedestrian "Spaghetti March" was orchestrated but never recorded.

The fourth day of recording was the busiest yet, with two sessions—one for the Semi-Grand Orchestra, and another for strings and woodwinds only. By the end of the day, Willson recorded eighteen cues. Many of these were retakes from earlier sessions

The Great Dictator (1940)—Chaplin's classic "Stagger Dance" on the ghetto sidewalk was accompanied by a tinkling music box waltz based on the 19th-century German folk song "Du, du liegst mir im herzen."

The Great Dictator (1940)—The cue "They've Gone," barely noticeable in the film, was repurposed for the verse section of "Falling Star."

The Great Dictator (1940)—Hynkel's theme, titled "Horse's A--manship (Assmanship) March."

The Great Dictator (1940)—Napaloni's "Napoli March."

("They've Gone," "Charlie's Capture") as well as a number of cues that never made it into the final film. Particularly grand was the sweeping "Ball Room Appassionato," a source cue that is unfortunately barely audible in the film. This session also brought the music into the ghetto, with the hora-like dance rhythms of the brief "Ghetto Sign" transition cue, and the yearning Hebraic harmonies and plaintive violin solos of Hannah's theme.

Brief cues like the snaking flute solo that underscores Hynkel's snarling "rape" of his secretary Leeda and the cuckoo clarinet that scampers Hynkel up the curtain of the short "Scene de Ballet" before his globe dance were dispatched quickly in two or three takes. Other short cues such as the four-bar entrance for Schultz and the significantly rewritten "Empty Street Montage" for the ghetto were recorded but ultimately discarded. The "Concentration Camp" cue, though recorded in one "perfect" take, was unsatisfactory and was also rewritten.

Following the afternoon lunch break, the orchestra shrunk to just strings and woodwinds. The arpeggiated harp and celeste chords that accompany "Schultz's Dream" also underscore Schultz's recognition of Hynkel on the ghetto street, though Chaplin discarded the cue in the latter sequence. "Hannah's Soliloquy" in the barber chair is underscored for a lovely violin solo atop the strings and harp arpeggios. Willson inserted a novachord in the "Barber Shop Opening," and a mandolin borrowed the hora ghetto music for a discarded "Fade Into Ghetto" cue. The most significant cue recorded that afternoon was the somber "Zigeuner" ("gypsy") cue for mandolin and guitar that accompanies three scenes with Hannah and her neighbors wondering what life would be like outside of the ghetto.

The music department had a couple of days away from the soundstage to focus on the changes Chaplin wanted. The session on August 21 featured an Army bugler doing bugle calls, which the orchestral trumpet soloist had played "Too good & Polite," plus "typical Army Bugle Calls, recorded for the Charles Chaplin Library, [which] will not be used in the picture *The Great Dictator*."[56]

The Grand Orchestra was back in session on August 23, the final day, recording the remainder of the cues of the score, including a few retakes and, again, some rejected cues. Willson finally recorded the main titles and unused "Exit Music," which reprised the Osterlich theme one last time. The brutal "Invasion of Osterlich" sequence, with its warring trumpet fanfares and Willson's symphony theme, took three takes. Ominous

The Great Dictator (1940)—The sweeping "Ball Room Appassionato" source cue.

The Great Dictator (1940)—The somber "Ziegeuner" cue for mandolin and guitar contemplates life outside the ghetto.

brass chords were inserted to the end of the globe dance. There was another retake of "They've Gone," and an insert of the shaving sequence "hair combing to end" was labeled "perfect."[57] Two cues from the opening scenes—"Trench Sequence" and "Lost in the Fog"—were recorded but never used.

Film music critic Bruno David Ussher, who attended the final session, recalled, "Willson rehearses and records with the bright energy of the radio veteran who knows that seconds are part of eternity." Chaplin "feels music actually and gives his reactions with a minimum of words."—"Too much orchestra under the solo trumpet. That sounds too symphonic." One of the chief problems of background music, Chaplin told Ussher, "is that the entry and exit of music must neither hurry nor hamper the flow of action. I want simple, unpretentious, not symphonic music. It is not our function to provide concert music.... Music must form a counterpoint to the actor or actors. Every actor is an 'instrument,' so to speak, which must not be 'drowned' by the background music. Even during the silent scenes, during pantomime, when music is indispensable, there must be maintained a 'counterpoint' between the visual and auditory."[58]

A prime example of Chaplin's use of musical counterpoint is the "Pudding Mysterioso." In the scene, the barber and his neighbors are lined up at the dinner table *a la* The Last Supper. The men pool their coins into the barber's pudding, which he swallows and burps with an amusing jangly sound effect reminiscent of the whistle swallowing sequence in *City Lights*. Ussher called the sequence "musically not important, but typically Chaplinesque." Sneaky grace notes, tremolos, and portamentos in the strings provide trademark stealth music that would have been right at home in the silent era. The staccato and accented notes give the music weight, while the rests provide space and turn the cue into something more sinister as the "winner" of the coin contemplates having to give up his life for the liberation of his people. The rewritten "Concentration Camp" cue also incorporates the "Pudding Mysterioso" music. The final pieces to be recorded were the somber "Valse Triste," which owes more than a passing nod to Grieg's piece of the same name as it twirls Hynkel and Napaloni's wife around the dance floor, plus retakes, cut cues ("Transformation Scene" and "Our Only Hope"), and the Wagner-inspired "Hope Springs Eternal."

✳   ✳   ✳

Journalist Dixie Willson, Meredith's sister, described her visit to the recording session that final day—"Seventy-five musicians in typical Hollywood dress; sweaters, flannel shirts and bright neckerchiefs, the usually immaculate Mr. Willson on the podium now

***The Great Dictator* (1940)—The "Pudding Mysterioso" cue serves as sneaky musical counter-point to the Jewish barber trying to hide the coins he has swallowed and burps.**

in wilted shirt and galluses, his hair looking very much like that of a gentleman just out of a shower. Facing the orchestra, he also faced a picture screen above them. At a long rough-wood table, a keenly observant Mr. Chaplin watched it all." At one point, Chaplin suggested, "We could do some very funny music where my clothes slide to the floor." "Something chromatic?" suggested Willson. "Something like this…" When Willson came down from the podium, Chaplin demonstrated what he meant with "a bit of vocal illustration accompanied by a bit of illustrative wriggling."[59]

Meredith Willson called the scoring process "long" and "arduous," but it paid off.[60] "No one but Chaplin's staff has heard the full score of *The Great Dictator*," said *Time* magazine. "They think it is terrific."[61] Columnist Hedda Hopper later proclaimed, "Meredith Willson's score was something to shout about."[62] "Music is important in *The Great Dictator*," said the *New York Herald Tribune*. "Meredith Willson, young composer-conductor, worked with Chaplin in creating burlesqued but majestic military marches, ghetto dances, swinging waltzes, tavern ditties and a score as varied as Chaplin's moods in the picture."[63]

Bruno David Ussher correctly surmised that Chaplin "has done a good deal of pruning of the music background for *The Great Dictator* since I heard certain sequences in the making on the recording stage."

> All in all *The Great Dictator* score may be called a filmically useful score, unpretentious musically.
> Neither Charlie Chaplin, who contributed several melodic ideas, nor composers Meredith Willson and Max Ter [*sic*] have gone beyond the above quoted dictum of the producer-director-actor who has such a keen sense of screen values.
> I liked the title fanfares, some genuinely deserving that description, others bizarre as facial grimaces and sneering like Bronx cheers. There are a couple of tender themes, born of that upwelling sympathy for persecuted people for whom Chaplin professes a human oneness attested by the very production of this film play.
> On some occasions Willson has woven quite innocent material into brightly dramatic bits of counterpoint, the successive instrumental voices stepping up action…
> Chaplin, in short, did what he set out to do."[64]

Critic Paul Goodman disagreed, calling it "calamitous music."[65] "It is to be presumed," said future Pulitzer Prize-winner Virgil Thomson, "that the opening fanfares and such occasional bits as occur throughout the film that are not recognizably quotations are of [Chaplin's] composition. They are not very good; they are musically uninteresting." But Thomson offered the most cogent analysis of the score.

What is good and extremely interesting is Mr. Chaplin's way of using music in films. This concept has been clear since his first sound film, *City Lights*. His way of integrating music with animated photography is to admit auditive elements to the rank of co-star with the poetic and visual elements in the final unified effect.

He does not try to use music as mere accompaniment, as neutral background. He knows that a well-cut film can get along without that. Nor does he try to drag in tonal appeal by making one of his characters a music student who can go into a song if necessary. Unless he can coordinate music with the action in such a way that the two play a duet, each commenting upon and heightening the other, he leaves it out altogether. For the same reason, he has hitherto omitted the speaking voice from his own characterizations, because there was no need of it. It would have introduced a jarring naturalistic element into his far from naturalistic acting-style.

The Mayor's wordless speech, sounded on a trombone, in *City Lights*, is one of Chaplin's procedures. The dictator's speeches in semi-nonsense German are the same trick done with his own voice. His bubble dance (to the *Lohengrin Prelude*) and the shaving scene (to a Brahms *Hungarian Dance*) are a different form of musical integration. The first procedure is a substitution of stylized sound for naturalistic speech. (Note then when he is acting naturalistically he speaks naturalistically.) The second procedure is not a substitution; it is an adding of stylized sound to stylized movement without speech, to pantomime. He has here introduced the straight music-hall turn he was brought up to, as artificially a thing as the classical ballet, into movies, the most naturalistic form of theatre that has ever existed. The result is artistically successful.

Mr. Chaplin has not made a complete musical film. He has made a silent film with interpolated musical numbers. But he has obviously reflected about the auditive problem, and so far as he uses music at all, his use of it is unfailingly advantageous. He uses all the auditive effects correctly. He employs very little naturalistic noise, for instance. He takes as his basic esthetic principle the fact that movies are pantomime. Anything expressible by pantomime is not expressed otherwise. He introduces speech, music and sound-effects only when they are needed to do something pantomime can't do. There is a little bombing in the war scenes, a strict minimum. When he belches after having swallowed three coins, he lets the coins jingle. But nowhere does he overlay the film with speech that says nothing, with music that just accompanies, with noises that merely express hubbub…

Chaplin has not included in *The Great Dictator* every device known to film art of incorporated auditive effect. That was not his aim. But in no other film that I have seen are speech and music and sound incorporated into a photographed pantomimic narrative with such unvarying and deadly accuracy, nor omitted from the spectacle so rigorously when no way seems to present itself for using them to advantage.[66]

The Great Dictator cost a little over $1.4 million, though press reports rounded it up to $2 million, with the music budget occupying $35,779.74, by far the largest amount of any Chaplin film. Certain theaters used specially selected tracks for an overture, intermission, and exit music.

The five-minute overture consisted of the "Horses A--manship March" and the "Pretzelberger March." Certain theaters played the film with an intermission, using "Ball Room Appasionato" as accompaniment, though there is no indication in the script or studio documents exactly where that break was supposed to occur. Four tracks made up the exit music—"Osterlich Bridge," "Ze Boulevardier," "Ghetto Sign," and the unused "End Title."[67]

*   *   *

On August 27, which was Meredith Willson Day at the San Francisco World's Fair, Willson conducted the San Francisco Symphony in the *Prelude to The Great Dictator*.

Chaplin is, of course, listed as composer with the piece "transcribed for orchestra" by Willson. With a series of cues strung together with connective musical tissue, the piece is closer to an overture to a musical than a cohesive concert work. The *Prelude* begins with the raucous opening fanfare from the "Invasion of Osterlich," which leads directly into the "Barber Shop Opening," with its humorous interpolations of "How Much Is That Doggie in the Window?" and "Three Blind Mice." The yearning "Hannah at the Doorstep" pairs with the Osterlich theme ("Falling Star"), followed by the unused "Exit Music" cue reprising the Osterlich theme for a grandiose finish. *Time* magazine, which did not have a high opinion of the piece, wanted to make sure it quoted other critics in its review—"Obvious as most satirical attempts.... Interesting.... A pleasant trifle.... It cannot claim to be concert music."[68] Donald Martin in *The Etude* disagreed—"The Chaplin score can stand by itself, without accompanying pictures." NBC broadcast the premiere across the country and "the response from the listening public amply proved that the music from *The Great Dictator* can take its place on an orchestral program."[69] There is no evidence the piece was performed beyond its premiere in 1940.

"I can't say I see eye to eye with Mr. Chaplin about a lot of things, including his politics," Willson said, "and I think he is a very selfish and in many ways an inconsiderate man, but I also think he is a great artist and I will certainly say that it was a real pleasure to watch him day after day and see him tick."[70]

> He kept us laughing through every lunch, day after day, and never told a single joke—only true experiences or things he had observed during the morning. He is a real genius, I guess, though he does some awfully strange things for a genius, like not becoming a citizen. I read his explanation of that in the paper. He said he was an international citizen. Didn't belong to any one country. And that remark hit me like a nightmare. Imagine standing in the middle of the world like in a Dali painting as an international citizen. Suddenly this made me remember one of those things we used to rattle off in grammar school: "Breathes there a man with soul so dead, who never to himself hath said..." And right then those old lines practically drowned me in goose-pimples, and pride, and purpose, and obligation, and gratitude. The goose-pimples quieted down, but those other things will never leave me from here on out. So thank you very much, Mr. Chaplin, for a real lesson in patriotism.[71]

Chaplin was entering a decade in which his patriotism was constantly called into question. Legal hassles surrounding *The Great Dictator* also hounded him. Writer Konrad Bercovici, who had known Chaplin for years, visiting him on the sets of *The Gold Rush* and *City Lights*, brought suit against the filmmaker in April 1941, claiming he provided Chaplin with the idea for the film. The case revolved around five counts, including $5 million in damages. Three of the five counts were dismissed as repetitious, which still left $3,067,500 in damages for plagiarism. Tim Durant, who testified for his friend, told Charles Chaplin, Jr., he thought Bercovici "would have had a hard time winning the case if [Chaplin] had fought it through to the end." By the time the suit came to trial in 1947, "Dad had had enough of trials."[72] Because of "my unpopularity in the States at that moment and being under such court pressure," Chaplin said, "I was terrified, not knowing what to expect next."[73] Chaplin paid Bercovici $95,000 with the stipulation that he dropped all claim to coauthorship of the film.[74]

"Had I known of the actual horrors of the German concentration camps," Chaplin said, "I could not have made *The Great Dictator*, I could not have made fun of the homicidal insanity of the Nazis."[75] After such a controversial subject, Chaplin understandably took a step back to the comedy he knew so well. Perhaps he wanted to try something revolutionary in the sound era. Or maybe with the war raging on nearly all continents, Chaplin realized he was right when he justified his reasons for making *The Great Dictator*—"More than ever now the world needs to laugh. At a time like this, laughter is a safety valve for our sanity."[76] For laughter, he added music and words to one of his most famous silent films and released it with sound.

CHAPTER 7

Valse Mange

CHAPLIN HAD AT ONE TIME or another discussed synchronizing *A Woman of Paris*, *The Gold Rush*, and *The Circus* with music. In February 1934, he decided to "discontinue offerings" of all three. "The returns were quite unimportant," Alfred Reeves wrote to Sydney. Reeves had tried to convince Chaplin to start with *The Gold Rush*, "but Charlie did not go on with it, and of course he will not do so now—at any rate, until the new picture [*Modern Times*] is off his hands."[1] The subject was brought up again six years later shortly after *The Great Dictator* was released. Chaplin told *The New York Times* "he was considering reissuing some of his old silent features" and mentioned *The Gold Rush*. "Nothing will be done, however, until after *The Great Dictator* has its day."[2]

Chaplin began work on the reissue of *The Gold Rush* "with music and words" on June 18, 1941. For this new version, Chaplin hired editor Harold McGhean and trimmed eighteen-and-a-half minutes from the film. They removed the title cards, Chaplin wrote and recorded the voiceover narration, and changed the ending to remove the original's lingering kiss between the Tramp and Georgia, leaving the fate of their relationship, much like the end of *City Lights*, open to interpretation. *The New York Times* reported the retooling of the film cost $125,000. Even before *The Gold Rush* opened and Chaplin had a chance to see whether or not the public would welcome a reissue like this, he had already started talking about streamlining *The Circus*.[3]

If critics were any indication, audiences were going to be charmed once again. The *Motion Picture Herald* wrote, "The reviewer who wrote of *The Gold Rush* in the August 8th, 1925 edition of this publication, 'it is at once a classic and a certain money maker,' can say that again…. It is the new and oral Chaplin who speaks a running commentary, written by himself, which supplies something more effective than dialogue to the refurbished version of the silent success, a music score scored by himself and Max Terr supplementing the narration as if a part of it…. The film was a hit in every type of theatre in 1925. There are in evidence no reasons for doubting that it may duplicate that success this year 1942."[4] "Although *The Gold Rush* is seventeen years old," said *Showmen's Trade Review*, "the re-issue … is as delightful as the original silent version…. Chaplin's style of narration, and the musical score are masterful strokes of showmanship…. The original version grossed millions and the new one should equal that take."[5] *The Film Daily* called *The Gold Rush* a "great institutional comedy enhanced by fine narration and music. Will be ace b.o. draw."[6]

* * *

In October 1941, Georgia Hale signed a new contract with Chaplin, which "was to last until he was forced to close his studio in the United States" in 1952. During his work on the reissue of *The Gold Rush*, Hale claimed she helped him with the score. "[Charlie] would hum the melodies and I'd pick them out on the piano and write them down."[7] Chaplin would often play his organ "into the small hours. He would improvise and find lovely melodies, while I would read and enjoy the Bible and other great books."[8]

> On his seven-acres estate he felt free to play the organ as late as he pleased, knowing for certain that he could not disturb his far away neighbors. He said one night, "I'm going to work late to-night. I feel so inspired. Thank goodness, nobody can hear me. That's the joy of having a large estate … the marvelous privacy."
>
> The following day I didn't see him until noon, for I knew he must have worked far into the night on his music. I came bounding in, eager to hear his new numbers. But something seemed to be troubling him. All the inspiration of the night before was gone."[9]

When Chaplin had gone down to the garden that morning, he heard a voice calling "Charlie, Charlie." He looked up saw Georgie Jessel across the road on his estate, waving his hand and shouting, "Thank you for the concert last night. I can't tell you how much I enjoyed it." "I could see there was no talking him out of this or getting him to laugh it off," Hale said. "This left a deep impression on Charlie. I begged him to play the organ but he wouldn't go near it."

> However soon this void was filled. We were out shopping for a pretty set of dishes for my sister's wedding one day, when quite accidentally his eyes fell on a sparkling new accordion. He had missed playing his organ. He just could not resist this instrument. It was like a toy and he was like a boy. He bought it there and then. When he returned to my house, he walked around my place trying to play it, while I changed my clothes for the evening. He had never touched an accordion before. By the time I was ready, he was playing that instrument like a trouper.[10]

Whether or not Hale helped Chaplin get his melodies down on paper, Max Terr did the bulk of the work assisting him with the new score. Odessa-born Terr (1890–1951) became a U.S. citizen in 1918, led a popular dance band beginning in the early 1920s, and began his film career in 1930 at Paramount Pictures, working on early sound musicals like *The Love Parade* and *The Vagabond King*. Terr provided choral arrangements for *Snow White and the Seven Dwarfs* (1937) and *The Great Victor Herbert* (1939), and conducted a 110-person chorus for Max Fleischer's animated version of *Gulliver's Travels* (1939).

For the new *Gold Rush*, Terr, who had served as Willson's assistant on *The Great Dictator*, "was engaged at a moment's notice and went to work at once" without a contract, at a salary of $200 per week. He started working with Chaplin on Saturday, August 23, 1941, and worked for sixteen weeks, during which "he [gave] his whole time and services—has hired all the musicians and arrangers, and conducted the orchestra at the recordings," said Alfred Reeves.[11] Terr shared co-composing credit on nearly every cue of the score and onscreen credit as the film's music director. But, as always, the contract specifically stipulated that the score "was entirely written, composed and/or arranged by Charles Chaplin, and you agree not to make or issue, or authorize the making or issuance of, any statement or claim in contraction thereof."[12] Still, had the music been published, Chaplin magnanimously agreed to split the royalties equally.[13]

Terr began recording the score on Monday, October 27, at RCA Studios. The 41-piece orchestra had a 5:00 p.m. call and recorded until 3:30 a.m. Tuesday morning. Calls

Lyricist Leo Robin, future *Gold Rush* arranger/conductor Max Terr, and director Edmund Goulding on the set of *The Devil's Holiday*, c. 1930 (Photofest).

for the rest of the week were between 5:00 and 5:30, with the sessions ending between midnight and 12:30 a.m. The longest session was a call for 6:00 p.m. Sunday, November 22, which lasted until 5:00 a.m. Monday morning. Terr and the musicians later went back into the studio to record re-takes, as well as a 26-piece chorus for "Auld Lang Syne."[14]

A four-page color press packet explained Chaplin's method of scoring the new film.

> In remaking *The Gold Rush* with music and words, Charlie Chaplin and Max Terr devoted four and a half months to what is probably one of the most distinguished musical scores ever composed for a motion picture.
>
> Fully ninety-five percent of the music is original, composed at the Steinway grand piano in the studio projection room by Chaplin and Terr, while *The Gold Rush* was run and re-run hundreds of times on the screen before them...
>
> Chaplin's idea was to make the music interpret and complement the action in the film, instead of serving only as an unobstrusive [*sic*] background in the usual manner. He feels that as it now stands, the score is as important as the film scenes themselves.[15]

Variety reported, "A corps of arrangers has been following the comedian about for weeks. As Chaplin hums, the arrangers get the music down on paper."[16] Other than Terr, the only other member of the "corps" listed in studio documents was Terr's colleague over at Paramount, Gerard Carbonara, who co-composed certain cues and even wrote a few of his own. Carbonara (1886–1959) studied at the National Conservatory of Music under Antonin Dvořák and continued his musical training in Italy at the Conservatory of Naples. In 1939, he composed several cues for John Ford's *Stagecoach*, a score that

***The Gold Rush* (1942 reissue)—The love theme was based on Brahms's *Romance,* Op. 118.**

included a number of composers adapting several Americana tunes. The score won an Oscar for Music (Scoring) but since Carbonara was under contract at Paramount, he could not receive onscreen credit for a film at another studio (in this case, Universal Pictures), and his name was not among the four composers who received the award.

As he did in the 1920s, Chaplin once again followed a standard template for a silent film score, mixing classical music with original tunes. The love theme is an adaptation of the fifth of Johannes Brahms's six *Klavierstücke,* Op. 118, *Romance.* The *Klavierstücke,* completed in 1893 and dedicated to Clara Schumann, was the second to last work composed for solo piano and the second to last work published during Brahms's lifetime. The *Romance* is in Chaplin's favorite key—F major—in 6/4 (converted to 3/4 and D-flat major in the film score) and Chaplin adapts the two sections of the piece into three separate themes. The beginning *Andante* melody is buried in the left hand, giving it a darker quality, which suits the unrequited love between Charlie and Georgia. The *Allegretto gracioso* section becomes the seed for the lighthearted cues out in the snow. The final six bars of the *Romance* form the basis of the other half of the love theme, which is usually scored high in the strings.

In *The Great Dictator,* the use of Wagner's ethereal *Lohengrin* music provided an ironic counterpoint to Hynkel's globe dance and a sincere ray of hope to Hannah and the Jews from the ghetto. Chaplin borrows the beautiful "Evening Star" melody from Wagner's *Tannhäuser* for one of the primary themes in *The Gold Rush.* In the opera, Wolfram's Act III aria hints at Elizabeth's approaching death—*Wie Todesahnung Dämmrung deckt die Lande.... O du mein holder Abendstern* ("Like a premonition of death the twilight shrouds the earth.... O thou my fair evening star"). For Chaplin, the "premonition of death" is hunger. The melody line's chromatic passing tones provide a melodic counterpoint to Big Jim's melodramatic cry for food, while the wide trombone vibratos heighten the comedy.

Tchaikovsky's *Sleeping Beauty* waltz serves as the dance for Georgia and Charlie, with the dog tied to the rope holding up his pants. The piece was in the public domain except in France and its colonies, Portugal, Syria, Lebanon, Luxembourg, and Morocco, and Chaplin had to pay $110 to license it.[17] He also licensed the use of Rimsky-Korsakov's

The Gold Rush (**1942 reissue**)—**The "Hunger Theme" was based on Wagner's "Evening Star"** from *Tannhäuser.*

The Flight of the Bumblebee to replicate the storm howling outside the cabin, an expected substitution that was probably funnier for general audiences but not nearly as elegant as Verdi's *Rigoletto* storm music that had accompanied the same scenes in the original compilation score. The oboe solo from Rossini's *William Tell* naturally signals the dawn.

Chaplin obviously wanted to portray the Little Fellow as a member of the upper British Isles. A "Chaplin Medley" of Scottish tunes, including "The Bluebells of Scotland," "Coming Thru the Rye," and "Loch Lomond" accompanies his first appearance on the mountain ledge. Revelers in the dance hall, many of whom may have been migrants seeking their fortune, begin the New Year with rousing renditions of Ireland's "Speed the Plow" reel and Scotland's "Liverpool Hornpipe."

Archibald Joyce's 1913 waltz *A Thousand Kisses* is a holdover from the 1925 compilation score. The tune is given prominent placement in the earlier score as the accompaniment to Charlie and Georgia's dance. In the reissue, Chaplin uses only the primary melody in two brief cues as source music in the dance hall. Charlie puts Jim to bed with a boozy trombone rendition of "Good Night, Ladies" and "For He's a Jolly Good Fellow" welcomes the newly minted millionaires onto the ship. Terr's arrangement of Louis Bourgeois's "Doxology" rings in the New Year, leading into the 26-piece chorus singing "Auld Lang Syne." The *Pacific Coast Musician* called the sequence "in questionable [musical] taste…. I doubt if even drunken miners would do that."[18]

Chaplin and Terr's "On the Trail" is the most prominent original theme in the score, beginning with the opening shot of the line of prospectors snaking up Chilkoot Pass. The dramatic melody represents the harsh conditions in the frozen north and the natural obstacles faced by the characters. The melancholy "Pagliapin" begins with Charlie's entrance into the mining town and conveys the character's pathetic predicament and loneliness. Chaplin had used "Pretty Girl Milking a Cow" for the same purpose in the 1925 compilation score, and he retains the traditional Irish ballad (replacing another rendition of "Pagliapin") in the same spot—as a solo accordion accompanying a lonely Charlie mournfully looking through the dance hall window at the New Year's festivities inside.

As usual, Chaplin composed a series of waltzes for the score. "Valse Mange," using the French definition of "mange"—"eat"—accompanies the classic boot-eating sequence. The lush waltz underscores Chaplin's dainty picking apart of the boot, twisting the laces like spaghetti, and holding a wishbone aloft with his pinky for Big Jim to tug. There is a handwritten note at the top of the short score that says "get effect of nails on plate," accomplished through a series of delicately accented, rolled piano chords. The theme returns as Jim wanders into the frontier town to record his claim for gold, and later ironically juxtaposed against the newly wealthy Charlie and Big Jim entering their stateroom on the ship, hungry no more.

"Valse Charmante" is reminiscent of Chaplin's waltz for the *pas de deux* in *City Lights* with the bronze statue in the shop window. Like that earlier waltz, the first appearance of "Valse Charmante" is broken up into bite-sized chunks with elongated rests, a halting dance of indecision underscoring Georgia's attraction to and resentment of Jack. In the New Year's Eve dream sequence, as the scene dissolves to Georgia and her friends at Charlie's table, the music again conveys a faltering hesitation. Charlie is at odds with his beloved, even in his dream.

"Valse Elegante," which required fifteen takes at the recording session, underscores the tentative bond between Georgia and Charlie, especially as he prepares the table for New Year's Eve. In the final scene as Georgia tries to convince the sailors aboard the ship that Charlie is not a stowaway, the theme's orchestra-

A famous publicity still from *The Gold Rush*, c. 1925 (© Roy Export SAS).

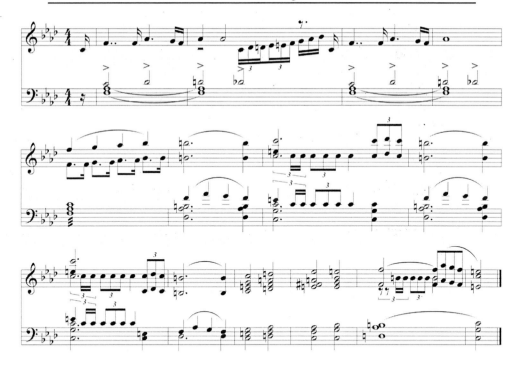

The Gold Rush (1942 reissue)—Prospectors snake up Chilkoot Pass to the accompaniment of Chaplin and Max Terr's "On the Trail," the most prominent theme in the score.

The Gold Rush (1942 reissue)—The loneliness of Charlie's character is conveyed in Chaplin's melancholy "Pagliapin" melody.

tions are richer and deeper, with the melody in the lower strings, indicating a much stronger bond between the two characters.

The soaring "Farewell" theme represents the friendships Charlie makes with Big Jim and Hank. The melody displays warmth as Charlie says goodbye to Jim and they go their separate ways. It also conveys the internal warmth of Hank's cabin as Charlie finally

The Gold Rush (1942 reissue)—"Valse Mange" underscores the classic boot-eating sequence.

The Gold Rush (1942 reissue)— Chaplin's "Valse Charmante" accompanies the hesitant attraction between Georgia and Jack, and Charlie and his unrequited beloved.

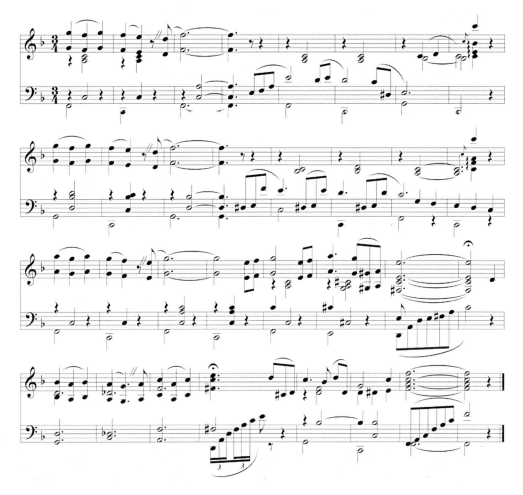

The Gold Rush (1942 reissue)—"Valse Elegante" accompanies Charlie's New Year's Eve party preparations for Georgia.

makes a new friend. The "Easy" theme is a signature Chaplin promenade tune on the ship, displaying a carefree quality that matches Charlie and Big Jim's new life of ease.

But perhaps Chaplin's finest musical moment, no doubt due to the famous scene it accompanies, is the dance of the rolls. The "Oceana Roll" cue (as marked on the piano score) originally used the melody for "The Keel Row" in the 1925 compilation score. But a handwritten note at the top of the piano score for the new cue indicates that other preexisting tunes were considered for the sound version, including "Tea for Two or City Lites" [*sic*], and Felix Arndt's popular 1915 hit, "Nola." Both "Tea for Two" and "Nola" certainly would have been recognizable to 1942 audiences, but anachronistic with a story set in the late 1800s. It is doubtful Chaplin seriously considered using any of his *City Lights* music in *The Gold Rush* and whatever theme he had in mind remains a mystery. Instead, Chaplin and Terr composed delightful music that perfectly captures the magical moment.

The original piano score of the cue shows the melody with a combination of boxy dotted rhythms (perhaps left over from "The Keel Row") and triplets. But pencil markings

The Gold Rush (1942 reissue)—Charlie and Big Jim's friendship is underscored by the soaring "Farewell."

on the score converted the dotted rhythms into triplets, which give the melody a skittering grace that matches Chaplin's elegant movements on screen and propels the music forward. The new cue title—"Mother's Dance"—also raises questions. If the dance was, as Robert Florey mentioned, "in the style of the Lancashire Lads," was this something Chaplin learned during his tenure with the clog group? If so, is "mother" the "loyal and dutiful wife" of Lads co-founder William Jackson, who, "although still nursing her son at her breast," Chaplin later wrote, "worked hard at the management of the troupe" while they were on tour?[19] Is it instead a dance Hannah performed to entertain Charlie and Sydney? Chaplin, as usual, provides no answers and lets the screen—and the music—speak for themselves.

The Gold Rush (1942 reissue)—**Chaplin and Max Terr wrote the delightful "Mother's Dance" to accompany the classic "Dance of the Rolls."**

The Gold Rush (1942 reissue)—**The skittering "Work Theme," one of three cues composed solely by Max Terr, accompanies Charlie's many scenes of employment.**

Chaplin retains sole authorship of the "Leaps" cue (listed as "Leaps & Creeps" and "Leaps Around" in various editions of the cue sheet). The staccato theme, which also includes the "Pudding Mysterioso" music from *The Great Dictator*, does what the title suggests—leaps—anytime Charlie is being chased. Of the three cues on which Terr is credited alone as composer (which includes "Papillons" and "Carnival"), the "Work Theme" (credited as co-composer with Chaplin on two of the cues bearing its name) is by far the most delightful. The skittering melody provides an active underscore to Charlie's many scenes of work, especially as "the Little Fellow hustled and shoveled in order to buy that New Year's dinner."

Terr and Carbonara co-composed "Snowbound," "The Fight," and "Larsen & the Law." The pair also collaborated on two cues musically painting animals. The famous "Chicken Sequence" uses pizzicato strings and staccato woodwinds to mimic Charlie's hunting and pecking, while a loping 6/8 time signature and grace notes bray in the woodwinds during the "Donkey Serenade," hinting at Ferde Grofé's similar musical treatment of the packhorse in his *Grand Canyon Suite*. Carbonara was also responsible for "Larsen's Escape" and the furious "Blizzard" cues at the cabin.

✶   ✶   ✶

Max Terr received an Academy Award nomination for Music Score of a Dramatic or Comedy Picture, though he lost to Max Steiner's *Now, Voyager*. Surprisingly, for a beloved silent film that proclaimed "with music and words" in every ad, reviewers paid little attention to the score other than a simple statement of Chaplin and Terr's collaboration. The *Pacific Coast Musician* bucked that trend and devoted four of the five paragraphs of its review to the music:

> Musically, there is varying interest in the score. A light-hearted, care-free theme is used for Chaplin. A quite musical bit is a theme for Georgia, the dance hall girl. These two constitute the major part of the original score. For the rest, a long parade of old favorites finds its way through the background. Wether [sic] intentionally or not, the compiled part of the score is much like the sort of thing we used to hear when an expert organist would "cue" a picture from established material. Well-known compositions are used for "hurries," "agitatos," "chases" and the like. Indeed, this is one of the delightful features of the production. It takes one back to the early days of pictures and requires little imagination to "see" the organist or the pit pianist doing his manful best to supplement action with music...
>
> The score is well recorded. String effects are particularly nice and where the identifying themes appear as atmospheric scoring, they are adeptly used.
>
> *The Gold Rush*, because of the narrative and the musical score, is even better entertainment than it was originally. Surely, one can say no more.[20]

There would be, however, plenty to say about Chaplin's public and private life over the next five years. On June 4, 1942, Paulette Goddard and Chaplin divorced, but he would not be single for long. On October 30, he met 17-year-old Oona O'Neill, daughter of Pulitzer Prize-winning playwright Eugene O'Neill, at a dinner party hosted by Oona's agent Minna Wallace. Wallace knew that Chaplin was looking for an actress to play the role of Brigid in his adaptation of Paul Vincent Carroll's 1934 play *Shadow and Substance*. Chaplin began working on the story of a young Irish girl who sees visions of her namesake, St. Brigid, at the same time he was working on *The Gold Rush*. Oona's youth, beauty, and intelligence enraptured Chaplin. And though he felt she did not have the experience to play the role, he offered her a contract. Within two months, Chaplin shelved the project and plans were underway for his fourth and final marriage, which took place on June 16, 1943.

With Oona, Chaplin finally attained a stable home life. But that stability did not spill over into his public and work lives. The next five years would see Chaplin continually in and out of the courtroom, and crucified in the press. His next film not only shattered all traces of the Tramp's screen persona, it closed the lid on any remaining good feelings that remained with his once-adoring public.

CHAPTER 8

Tango Bitterness

A N ANTAGONISTIC TAGLINE FOR Chaplin's new film, *Monsieur Verdoux*, reads "*Chaplin Changes! Can You?*" Unfortunately, audiences could not. The world was not ready for Chaplin as a serial killer. The consensus has been that in early 1941 Orson Welles first discussed the idea of directing Chaplin in a film based on the notorious French bluebeard Henri Landru. But author Lisa Stein Haven raises questions about *Verdoux*'s origin.

Chaplin was a fan of "true crime" stories. Charlie Chaplin, Jr., remembers "pulp detective magazines that were always stacked by the bed. My father might read Spengler and Schopenhauer and Kant for edification, but for sheer relaxation he chose murder mysteries."[1] Chaplin also enjoyed visiting prisons and spent a stint sitting in an electric chair, both of which incidents he recounted in *My Trip Abroad*. On his homecoming tour in 1921, Landru—"the Charlie Chaplin of the cinema of crime"—was on trial in Paris. Chaplin insisted on speaking to crime reporters covering the trial to get various details. Twenty years later, he paid Welles $5,000 for the idea that would eventually become *Monsieur Verdoux*. Perhaps he had filed away information from Landru's trial, or maybe he simply realized the dramatic possibilities in the story.[2] If the controversial subject matter of a man who serially marries and murders women for their money was not enough to raise eyebrows, Chaplin's personal life over the next six years made scandalous headlines, setting the stage for a public flogging.

Chaplin started working on the script for *Monsieur Verdoux* in November 1942 and continued throughout most of 1943. The film went by many names, including *Landru* and "Production No. 7: *Bluebeard*." Chaplin wanted to call it *The Lady Killer* but Eric Johnston, the Chairman of the Motion Picture Association of America, "nixed" the title.[3] Chaplin finally started prep work on the film in April 1946 and shooting ran from June 3 to September 5 with no retakes, a rarity for a Chaplin film.[4] It took another six months to finish cutting, dubbing, and composing and recording the score, at a total cost of $1.5 million.

"To M. Verdoux," Chaplin explained to the press, "murder is the continuation of business—with different methods. He leads, not a double life, but even a fifth or sixth life! And he does it to make a living for his family, whom he loves."

> Upon this basis I derive my humor and my humorous considerations. Verdoux has the same instincts as any other man. He is no monster to give people goose pimples, but a madman, a crazy faun, who verges on genius. His is the tragedy of the petite bourgeoisie in France during the depression—any depression.
>
> The story is told from Verdoux's viewpoint; psychologically, and with what I would call a healthy bitterness. His victims are not simps; some of them are tough, but Verdoux is tougher. At the end, he makes a couple of slips and time catches up with him…

I was fascinated by the idea of man having several wives—and trying to get rid of them. It is not as easy as people think.[5]

Nor was the idea an easy sell in the midst of Chaplin's political and private upheaval.

*   *   *

Politically, the "moment my troubles began," Chaplin said, was a speech on May 18, 1942, in San Francisco on behalf of Russian War Relief.[6] He spoke extemporaneously for forty minutes, finishing with a rousing, yet controversial, "Stalin wants it, Roosevelt has called for it, so let's all call for it—let's open a Second Front now!"[7] A July 22 speech via telephone to Madison Square Garden advocating "the fate of the Allied nations is in the hands of the Communists" was printed in pamphlet form.[8] He also spoke at a "Salute Our Russian Ally" meeting in Chicago and an "Arts for Russia" dinner in New York that fall. It was all fodder for Chaplin's FBI file, which had been opened twenty years earlier in 1922. It was also good news for the House Un-American Activities Committee, which began investigating Chaplin in August 1939 and became a thorn in his side for the next decade. But Chaplin's private troubles were about to take a severe turn for the worse.

In the early summer of 1941, Chaplin met twenty-two-year-old actress Joan Barry (Berry), who was a guest at one of his weekly tennis parties. Barry had limited acting experience, but Chaplin felt she would make a good candidate to play Brigid in *Shadow and Substance*. He put her under a six-month contract on June 23, 1941, and sent her to study acting at Max Reinhardt's drama school. Joan pursued Chaplin, and the two began an affair. She got a two-month extension on her contract, but by May 1942 she was pregnant. Chaplin and friend Tim Durant pressured her into an abortion, but Barry resisted. Chaplin eventually relented, saying he would support the child. Barry terminated her contract, but Durant finally convinced her to get the procedure. She became pregnant again, and during her altercations with Durant over getting another abortion, he physically abused her, at one point leaving her with a badly bruised face, until she meekly agreed to have it done.[9]

Signs of Barry's mental instability appeared prior to the first pregnancy. She would drive up to Chaplin's house in the wee hours of the morning, drunk, at one point crashing her Cadillac in the driveway, and later breaking windows when Chaplin would not open the front door. To get rid of her, he paid $500 to cover her debts and bought one-way tickets for Barry and her mother, Gertrude Berry, to go to New York in October 1942. Joan made her way back to California and on December 23 used a ladder to break into Chaplin's home, brandishing a gun and threatening to kill herself. Chaplin let her stay the night, with a locked door between them, and gave her money the next morning to leave. A week later she was back, and Chaplin was forced to call the police. Barry was given a 90-day suspended sentence and told to leave town. An employee of the Chaplin studios gave her $100 and a train ticket. In May 1943, Barry called Chaplin's house and informed the butler that she was pregnant. On June 4, she made the same announcement to the press, naming Chaplin as the father. The press had a field day and readers who had gobbled up salacious reports of past relationships with Mildred Harris, Lita Grey, Pola Negri, Paulette Goddard, and others, eagerly followed Chaplin's latest personal drama—a two-year legal hell that Los Angeles attorney Eugene L. Triope called "a landmark in the miscarriage of justice."[10]

On the date of the press announcement, Gertrude, as guardian of the unborn child, filed a paternity suit against Chaplin, asking for $10,000 in pre-natal care, $2,500 a month in child support, and $5,000 court costs. Chaplin countered with a statement saying that Joan had asked for $150,000—$75,000 for the child and $75,000 for Gertrude, with nothing for herself—when she contacted him in May. He agreed to pay $2,500 in cash and $100 a week for Barry's support, as well as $500 thirty days before the birth, $1,000 at the birth, and $500 a month for the following four months, a total of $4,600. Joan agreed to permit blood tests on the infant to determine the child's paternity at age four months. "If at least two of the doctors say 'no,' the suit would be dropped," said her lawyers, "if they said 'maybe' (a positive 'yes' is impossible from blood tests) the girl will be free to press her claims."[11]

On August 17, the FBI began investigations to collect evidence on charges that Chaplin had violated the Mann Act, a 1910 piece of legislation that made it illegal to transport a woman across state lines for immoral purposes, and the U.S. Code on the Violation of Civil Liberties. They bugged telephones and hotel rooms, and posted stops on border posts in case Chaplin tried to leave the country. The Bureau questioned Chaplin's entire staff, his sons, and Oona, who had never met Barry, with columnist Hedda Hopper proving to be a reliable—and willing—informant. The subsequent report ran to four hundred pages.

On October 2, Joan gave birth to a daughter, Carol Ann. Blood tests five months later proved Chaplin was not the girl's father. On April 4, 1944, he was acquitted of charges regarding the Mann Act, and the violation of civil rights charges was dropped on May 15. Author Lion Feuchtwanger told his friend, "You are the one artist of the theatre who will go down in American history as having aroused the political antagonism of a whole nation."[12] While that should have closed the book on Chaplin's legal troubles, they were just beginning.

Joan had agreed that the doctors' decision in the paternity test would be binding. Chaplin's lawyer Loyd Wright had filed for a dismissal of the paternity suit, but Superior Court Judge Stanley Mosk overruled the motion. Now the Court of Los Angeles was suing Chaplin on Carol Ann's behalf. The trial began December 13, and prosecuting attorney Joseph Scott pulled out the emotional stops in his presentation, portraying Chaplin as a "grey-headed old buzzard," a "little runt of a Svengali," a "lecherous hound," and "a cheap Cockney cad."[13] In his final summation before the jury, he told the seven women and five men:

> There has been no one to stop Chaplin in his lecherous conduct all these years—except you. Wives and mothers all over the country are watching to see you stop him dead in his tracks. You'll sleep well the night you give this baby a name—the night you show him the law means him as well as the bums on Skid Row.[14]

After four hours and forty-five minutes of deliberation, the jury came back seven to five for acquittal. Judge Clarence L. Kincaid offered to arbitrate, but Chaplin wanted complete exoneration and foolishly refused. The retrial lasted from April 4 to April 17, 1945, with a one-day interruption on April 12 for the death of President Roosevelt. The blood tests were disregarded since it was not legal in California to allow them as evidence in paternity cases. A jury of eleven women and one man voted eleven to one for a "guilty" verdict. The one hold-out was a housewife named Mary James, who said, "I'm not upholding Mr. Chaplin at all…. Only I don't think he was the father of the child."[15] Chaplin had to pay $75 a week to Carol Ann, who could now legally take his name, with increases to $100, until she reached the age of twenty-one. The judge dismissed Chaplin's motion for a new trial. The public nightmare was finally over, and Joan Barry and her mother quickly disappeared from Chaplin's life. But the damage was done.

*   *   *

Chaplin's only refuge during these turbulent years was his work on *Monsieur Verdoux* and the support of Oona, who gave birth to their first child, Geraldine Leigh Chaplin, on August 1, 1944, with Michael John Chaplin following on March 7, 1946. Chaplin began working on the music in mid–September 1946 and continued over the next four months. Though Rudy Schrager received arranging and musical direction credit on the film, his name does not appear in the daily production reports until mid–November. It is possible Chaplin worked with Hanns Eisler in the two months prior to Schrager's participation.

Eisler (1898–1962) had studied with Arnold Schoenberg and Anton Webern, and in 1923 composed the first twelve-tone work by a Schoenberg disciple, *Palmström*, Op. 5. In 1926, Eisler suffered a painful rift with his mentor, who denounced his former student as a coffeehouse radical. That same year he applied for membership in the Communist Party of Germany (KPD), though he allowed the application to lapse. The following year Eisler worked with the Agitprop choral ensemble "Das rote Sprachrohr" ("The Red Megaphone") and became the music critic for the KPD daily *Die Rote Fahne* (*The Red Banner*).

Eisler started teaching at the Marxist Workers' School in Berlin in 1928, and continued to write protest songs and *kampflieder* ("songs for the struggle"). His 27-year friendship and creative partnership with Bertolt Brecht began in 1930. Two years later, he became a committee member of the International Music Bureau in Moscow and later served as its chair. When Hitler came to power in January 1933, Eisler quickly went into exile, living in Vienna, London, Paris, and Copenhagen. In 1938, he became a professor of composition and counterpoint at the New School for Social Research in New York, but because of visa difficulties, he left to be a guest professor at the Mexico City Conservatory. Once he was finally ensconced in Los Angeles in 1942, he reconciled with Schoenberg and continued his partnership with Brecht, who had also moved there.

"I helped [Charlie] out with *Verdoux*," Eisler said in a later interview, "it was painful in that he composed everything himself. [He] is a highly gifted composer. I must say, he is much more gifted than some of my colleagues, especially in America. Although, of course,

Monsieur Verdoux **arranger Rudy Schrager, c. 1955 (Photofest).**

he cannot read notes, but he plays a nice violin like an amateur and also plays on the piano…. When I was with him he would have some fabulous inspiration and I was supposed to take it down immediately. And I orchestrated some of it, and a cancan for *Verdoux*. That was just a matter of friendship."[16] Chaplin had already been working on the score for two months before Rudy Schrager's name appeared in studio documents. Schrager (1900–1983) began his film career in 1939 contributing uncredited music to the score of *Stanley and Livingstone*, along with Robert Russell Bennett, David Buttolph, Cyril J. Mockridge, Reginald Bassett, David Raksin, Edward Powell, and Louis Silvers. Silvers was the conductor of the popular *Lux Radio Theatre*, which provided hour-long adaptations of Broadway plays and films. He hired Schrager as the rehearsal and orchestra pianist, and to serve as his assistant. When the four radio networks rebelled against ASCAP's licensing rate increase in 1941, Silvers, who was an ASCAP composer, was not allowed to play his music on the *Lux* program, though he could continue conducting. Schrager stepped up for the duration of the ASCAP ban, composing and arranging the music for every episode. He continued to provide original themes even after the ban. Silvers used Schrager's music in his own incidental music for the next nine years until he handed over the baton to Schrager permanently.

It is unknown through which channels Schrager came to work for Chaplin. As a freelance composer, he was able to move between radio and film, and among the movie studios without being tied to a long-term contract, working at major studios like Columbia, Paramount, and 20th Century Fox, as well as smaller studios. In 1940, Alfred Newman began his twenty-year powerful reign as the music director for Fox, where he would have assigned Schrager to compose the scores for *Deadline for Murder* and *Strange Journey* in 1946. Schrager surely would have heard about Chaplin's working conditions from Newman, Raksin, and Powell, if not elsewhere, though the estrangement the trio suffered during *Modern Times* makes it unlikely they would have had any bearing on Chaplin hiring him for *Monsieur Verdoux*.

Chaplin and Schrager began work on the score on November 18 for the next seven weeks. Recording sessions took place over five days beginning January 9, 1947, once again at RCA Studios. At the sessions, "the 57-year-old comedian arrived in an expansive mood and began humming and singing bits of the score," said *The New York Times*. "As isolated scenes flashed on the screen," reported the *Los Angeles Times*, "Charlie would cry … 'More percussion!' or 'Top it with violins!' Then, with a boy's springy step, he would dash to the piano and illustrate."[17]

No doubt finding the right musical tone for such a risky story and an unlikeable lead character was a challenge. Eisler's angular, dissonant style would have made a vibrant musical commentary on the film, but he apparently did not enjoy the process of working with Chaplin. There are no reports of dissent from Schrager's corner. "Schrager is tolerant of all my whimsies," said Chaplin, who stood behind the conductor during the recording session, occasionally pantomiming the playing of a violin or a piano. "He never patronizes me."[18] The same probably could not be said of the prickly Eisler, friend or not.

As *Monsieur Verdoux* introduced a new Chaplin on screen, he switches musical gears with the score, favoring primarily a collection of short motifs rather than themes. For Verdoux's first entrance in the garden, with wisps of smoke caused by his latest victim rising from the incinerator, "Chaplin adjured the orchestra to keep the music gay as 'counterpoint' to the cinematic action," *The New York Times* reported. The *Los Angeles*

Chaplin as Monsieur Varnay, one of Henri Verdoux's many aliases, c. 1947 (© Roy Export SAS).

Times compared Chaplin's "pixie" theme to the music for Richard Strauss' titular hero in *Till Eulenspiegels lustige Streiche*.[19]

The historical basis for Strauss's tone poem was a lowborn German peasant, a character completely at odds with the debonair Verdoux. But the comparison is apt when comparing the brutality of Verdoux's murders and his bitter condescension of the world with the serious themes behind Eulenspiegel's practical jokes in which "the individual gets back at society; the stupid yet cunning peasant demonstrates his superiority to the narrow, dishonest, condescending townsman, as well as to the clergy and nobility."[20]

Verdoux's theme can be broken down into three distinct sections. The first is "a frivolous little phrase" for the piccolo and oboe followed by a bassoon solo that continues the descent until settling into a lush, five-bar melody in a series of changing meters—2/4, common time, 3/4, back to 2/4.[21] The Strauss influence is particularly evident in the use of accidentals, half-step appoggiaturas and suspensions, and a tonal center that is constantly in motion (also traits of Eisler's music). During the recording sessions, when Verdoux stooped to pick up a caterpillar, Chaplin halted the orchestra and said, "I think we need a cliché here. After all, it is a comedy." He and Schrager developed a "cliché then and there," a set of quick sixteenth-note triplet motifs heard in the flute and bassoon.[22]

If any musical figure in the score is a "cliché," it is the train motif. This furious four-bar motif chugs along with Verdoux as he hurriedly travels back and forth across the

Monsieur Verdoux (1947)—With its mixed meters, Verdoux's theme has as many personalities as he does.

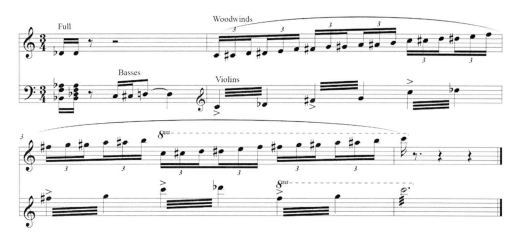

Monsieur Verdoux (1947)—**The brief, four-second "Train" cue is heard twelve times in the score as Verdoux dashes back and forth between engagements.**

French countryside between women. Clarinets, oboes, flute, and piccolo rush chromatically up the scale in quick-moving sixteenth note triplets, while the harp plucks out a series of C-F# tritones and the strings incorporate jittery half-step tremolos. The motif, which lasts a mere four seconds, becomes more and more comical (or annoying, depending on your viewpoint) over the twelve instances it occurs in the film.

The other frequent theme is the can-can "A Paris Boulevard." Paris is Verdoux's hiding place, where he can wheel and deal away from prying eyes and lose himself in the anonymity of a big city far from his family responsibilities and money problems. As such, the music is a delightful Parisian musical *bon mot* in Chaplin's favorite key—F major—one of the few cues in the score that uses a key signature. With its hints of the Moulin Rouge, the theme primarily serves as upbeat accompaniment to Verdoux's interactions with other Parisians or simply strolling down, as the cue titles say, a Paris boulevard. Hanns Eisler claimed to have written the theme, though it hardly sounds like his work. Whatever the veracity of the claim, the orchestration was a late entry by Leo Arnaud, dated Friday, January 3, 1947, only a few days before the recording sessions were due to begin the following week.

The other primary theme represents Mona (Mady Corell), Verdoux's disabled wife, the charity reason behind Verdoux's desperate, murderous moneymaking schemes. In his performance, Chaplin keeps Verdoux's love for Mona reigned in tightly, but not in the music. The lush melody soars with emotion in the high winds and strings above a constant ripple of arpeggiated triplets that convey Verdoux's internal struggle as he continually lies to his wife about his work and whereabouts. The theme also underscores the scene in which Verdoux suffers a change of heart at poisoning the girl (Marilyn Nash) he picked up on the street. She breaks down at what she perceives as his kindness and Mona's theme indicates the empathetic heart still beating behind the killer's façade.

The pair of dance numbers Chaplin includes at the climax of the film denote the "healthy dose of bitterness" he was aiming for in the film. At the nightclub, the relatives of Verdoux's first murderous conquest discover him sitting with the girl at a nearby table. The "Tango Bitterness" source cue accompanies an emotional turning of the tables as Verdoux's penniless despair over the death of his wife and son contrasts with the girl's

Monsieur Verdoux (1947)—"A Paris Boulevard" can-can accompanies Verdoux's carefree strolls along the city streets.

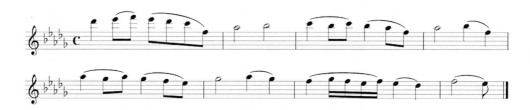

Monsieur Verdoux (1947)—The lush love theme for Verdoux and his crippled wife, Mona.

Monsieur Verdoux (1947)—The halting "A Paris Apartment" waltz for Monsieur Varnay and Madame Grosnay.

newfound wealth as the rich mistress of an arms manufacturer. The "Rhumba Hysteria" that follows serves as a raucous accompaniment to Verdoux's desperate attempts to circumvent the relatives, who have identified him as the killer and called the cops.

Of course, no Chaplin score would be complete without a waltz. Titled "A Paris Apartment," the elegant theme in three-quarter time is the embodiment of the equally elegant Madame Grosnay (Isobel Elsom). Verdoux is in over his head with the rich dowager but the music says otherwise. Verdoux's "frivolous little phrase" is elongated as an introduction before launching into the waltz. Though his passions run wild on the screen, Chaplin holds them in check musically in the theme's hummable melody, primarily contained in the first octave of the violins. The halting rubato of the tune, marked by caesuras in nearly every bar, is reminiscent of the Tramp's *pas de deux* with the bronze statue in the store window in *City Lights*.

Chaplin breaks the "Prelude to Murder" theme into two sequences, both of which cause confusion when trying to reconstruct the score using the cue sheet. The first occurrence of "Prelude to Murder" is the "Stairway Mysterioso" that accompanies the continually suspicious, nagging Lydia (Margaret Hoffman) up the stairs prior to her murder offscreen. The piccolo and oboe begin the cue with Verdoux's "pixie" motif while shimmering chords in the violins, harp, and celeste evoke the moonlit night. Bassoon and flute solos trade Verdoux's lush main theme with the strings overtaking it in ever-increasing intensity until shrill trills and tremolos signal Lydia's demise. The mysterioso later accompanies another potential death walk, foreshadowing Verdoux's thoughts about killing the girl as he escorts her to his apartment in Paris.

The dawn following Lydia's murder is marked "Prelude to Murder (2nd Sequence)." As Verdoux counts Lydia's money, the cue is made up of a series of short motifs. Quick staccato eighth notes in the bassoon and cellos, stinging muted brass, chirping woodwind grace notes, and F-minor arpeggiated runs that split, moving in opposite directions, one indicating Verdoux's pride in his accomplishment, the other sinking to the lower depths of his soul in the cello. Whether he knows it or not, for Verdoux there is no turning back. This cue was later extended for the scenes in Verdoux's Paris apartment and at Annabella's (Martha Raye) as he mixes poison into the wine bottles.

At a preview screening of the film for two hundred Hollywood celebrities, Hanns Eisler and Bertolt Brecht laughed in all the wrong places, including the stock market crash scene with bankers jumping out of windows. The chaotic cue for the scene alternates triplets and quadruplets, changing time signatures nearly every bar while a shrill version of Verdoux's theme in the trumpets screams in horror over the musical turmoil. The theme is also the focus for the montage immediately following with the world caught in the grips of the Depression. Desperate high violins are punctuated by the brass with

***Monsieur Verdoux* (1947)—A "Stairway Mysterioso" that accompanies Lydia up the stairs to her off-camera death.**

rough versions of the shimmering chords from the "Stairway Mysterioso." Brand new music is introduced for Verdoux's walk to the guillotine, an odd decision at first glance. But the old Verdoux is gone and new music is necessary. The cellos and basses voice a plodding funereal chorale interrupted by muted brass sneering at Verdoux's (or is it Chaplin's?) cynical view of the world. More instruments join the march of death before a final flourish to hollow tremolos and a series of three short motifs in the brass pointing the finger in judgment.

Monsieur Verdoux (1947)—The quick staccato eighth notes in the skittering "Prelude to Murder" match Chaplin's physical comedy with Verdoux quick counting his bounty left behind by the recently murdered Lydia.

In an interview years later with *Music Journal*, David Raksin said, "*Monsieur Verdoux*, the most 'intellectual' of Chaplin's films, used music of an uncomplicated nature with deft touches of emotion and irony to point up a scene or a whole philosophy expressed with a mere gesticulation."[23] But by the time the film was in its final stages, Chaplin's politics came to a head, creating a new set of problems that eventually derailed the project.

*   *   *

Things heated up in March when Senator William Langer (R) of North Dakota asked why some people are deported when "a man like Charlie Chaplin, with his communistic leanings, with his unsavory record of lawbreaking, of rape, or the debauching of American girls 16 and 17 years of age, remains?"[24] With the political cards stacked against him, Chaplin premiered *Monsieur Verdoux* at the Broadway Theatre in New York on April 11, the day after Hanns Eisler appeared before the House Un-American Activities Committee. The Production Code Administration refused to give the film a seal and the National Legion of Decency slapped the film with a B classification, "objectionable in part" because it "reflects erroneous moral philosophy and moral skepticism."[25] Chaplin believed "the

American public, as well as the public of the world, should expect and demand something new and different in motion pictures—at least every 25 years. I know that in *Monsieur Verdoux* they will not be disappointed."[26] He was wrong.

Robert Lewis, one of the original members of the Group Theatre in the 1930s and co-founder of the Actors Studio in 1947, played Verdoux's friend Maurice and attended the film's premiere with his sister. "The response of the movie audience, and the party afterward at '21,'" he said, "made a sickening evening for us both. Chaplin's awareness of his atrocious publicity resulting from a paternity case he was involved in, as well as from his much misunderstood political statements, prepared him somewhat for the frosty and, at times, frightening reception of some organized, hostile members of the audience. Worried about the possibility of demonstrations, Charlie had flanked himself with his wife, Oona, on one side, and Mary Pickford, America's old-time sweetheart, on the other, when he entered the theater."[27]

As the film unfolded, "insane booing" and "agonized groans" greeted various lines of dialogue.[28] At the party at "21," Chaplin was "surrounded by ill-wishers." Though Oscar-winning screenwriter Donald Ogden Stewart (*The Philadelphia Story*), who was also president of the Hollywood Anti-Nazi League, complimented him on the film, "the other celebrities didn't even mention the picture. They simply took over the party," Lewis said. "I watched Louella Parsons, dressed in black, sitting in a corner, her disapproving eyes glued on Chaplin. She looked like some predator waiting for him to do or say something that might be used against him in her column." Chaplin, "in a desperate attempt to recapture his own party," leaped to his feet to perform his bullfight act, pantomiming both the matador and the bull. "It was an exquisite pantomime, executed brilliant, but apparently it was not enough to get much response from that crowd." Stewart suggested that Lewis get Chaplin out of there. "It was easy to see that Charlie ... was genuinely shaken," Lewis said, "not only by the awful party, but by the antagonism of the movie audience to what he felt was a truthful, as a well as entertaining, expression of the times." "They couldn't take it, could they?" Chaplin asked Lewis back at the hotel. "I kicked them in the balls, didn't I? I hit them where it hurt."[29]

A few critics saw promise. "The film is a daring individual gesture," said *Time*, "daring in an era when such acts are rare. [Chaplin] has replaced his beloved sure-fire tramp with an equally original character." The *New York Post* said *Verdoux* was "most emphatically not a picture to be shunted off among the common run of American pictures, serious or comic.... It is great in intention, big in theme and thoroughly original." James Agee's legendary review in *The Nation* ran five thousand words, requiring three installments. "A magnificent and terrifying song," he wrote. "The richness and quality of the film is a work of art, in fact, of genius.... Verdoux embodies much of the best that can be said of modern civilization."[30] Most reviewers were not so kind.

"Chaplin will have to carry this one. And how," said *Variety*. "Its very premise is a false note. Comedy ... treads danger shoals indeed ... Chaplin generates little sympathy."[31] The *Herald Tribune* lamented "a woeful lack of humor, melodrama or dramatic taste.... Chaplin is enmeshed in a world of his own personal confusion." The *Daily News* said Chaplin "has tried to make the business of wholesale killing a joke, but the joke, I'm afraid, is on him."[32] No joking matter was the lack of onscreen credit for Orson Welles, an important element of the 1941 agreement with Chaplin. Ten days after the film's premiere, the studio finally added Welles's name and sent five new main title sequences to New York.

The Monday following the premiere, Chaplin faced a hundred journalists in a private dining room at the Hotel Gotham. They had no intention of discussing Chaplin's latest film. This was a political lynching—they were out for blood. Ed Sullivan, who was not at the interview, had thrown down the gauntlet earlier in the week in his *New York Daily Mirror* column, asking three questions that set the tone for the afternoon—"1. Why didn't Chaplin entertain U. S. troops or visit our wounded in military hospitals during the war? 2. Does Chaplin prefer democracy as defined by Russian Communism to democracy as defined in the United States? 3. For 30 years, Chaplin has earned a lush living in the U. S. Why hasn't Chaplin become an American citizen?"[33]

Chaplin knew what he was in for and was willing "to answer any and all queries which the working press fraternity may wish to have answered." "If there's any questions anyone wants to ask," he said, "fire away at this gray head." James W. Fay, the editor of *The Catholic War Veteran*, hammered away at Chaplin's war record and citizenship, asking questions that bore a striking resemblance to Sullivan's. Chaplin, answering "calmly and unruffled,"[34] said he had not become an American citizen "because I am not a nationalist.... I am a very good paying guest." When asked about his political views, Chaplin said, "I'm for the progress of the human race. I'm for the little man. I won't enter into any political discussions. I'll leave that to the men in Washington."[35]

The press conference was recorded and broadcast that evening on WNEW-AM radio. WNEW's correspondent said, "It was interesting for me—a radio man—to watch newspapermen at work. But I must admit that if the working press gave a representative performance yesterday then I'm just a little disappointed in them."

> Several of the so-called gentlemen of the press behaved exactly unlike gentlemen and pounced upon Mr. Chaplin with a series of questions which would have been perfectly suitable for a nazi spy but hardly appropriate for the worlds [*sic*] greatest living actor. However, Mr. Chaplin's performance was magnificent! He answered every question without evasion, with honesty and with clarity. This in spite of the fact that many of the questions directed to him were so poorly phrased, so inexpertly formulated that at times it was almost impossible to determine the nature of the question."[36]

Two days later, United Artists withdrew the block of 250 seats that were reserved for every showing and cut the admission price, which sold from $1.80 to $2.40, to $1.50. On May 7, the Independent Theatre Owners of Ohio issued a lengthy diatribe against Chaplin because "[he] is again attempting to reach into the pockets of the American moviegoers." His "personal conduct during the past several years ... has been the cause of bringing much criticism and condemnation of the motion picture industry.... Chaplin did little or nothing during the war years to help maintain the morale of our service men and women, either at home or overseas, and.... Chaplin, who has been a resident of this country for many years and has built up a tremendous fortune through the generosity of the citizens of this country in patronizing his pictures, has nevertheless refused to become a citizen of the United States." The organization encouraged their 325 theaters to boycott the film "until [Chaplin] proves that he is worthy of the support of American moviegoers."[37] "*Monsieur Verdoux* need not be boycotted by exhibitors on the basis of Chaplin's personal conduct," said Mo Wax in his op-ed in *Film Bulletin*, "it will be a box-office flop because it is a poor film lacking popular appeal."[38]

The Memphis Board of Censors also slapped a ban on the film. "We don't have to give our reasons," said Lloyd T. Binford, chairman of the three-member board.[39] Over in

Washington, Rep. John Rankin (D) of Mississippi, founder of the House Un-American Activities Committee, paid "tribute" to Binford for "banning a rotten picture made by Charlie Chaplin. If every other city in America had a man like Binford at the head of its censorship bureau we would get rid of a lot of this filth that is being spread before the eyes of our children through the moving picture shows."[40] "If [Chaplin] wants to preach his ideals by means of the screen," *Harrison's Reports* snidely suggested, "why doesn't he offer *Monsieur Verdoux* to the exhibitors free? Under such circumstances no one could accuse him of imposing upon an unwary public—the blame would then be placed on the exhibitors. But, no, he will do no such thing—he wants to eat his cake and still have it."[41]

Chaplin's political troubles were also far from over. Rankin demanded that Attorney General Tom Clark "institute proceedings to deport Charlie Chaplin. He has refused to become an American citizen, his very life in Hollywood is detrimental to the moral fabric of America. In that way he can be kept off the American screen, and his loathsome pictures can be kept from before the eyes of the American youth. He should be deported and got rid of at once."[42] Rep. Chet Holifield (D) of California took exception to the remark, not to defend Chaplin, but to object to "using a few individuals to smear an entire great industry." Holifield said this was what "the Un-American Committee" was attempting to do. Holifield was "grounded" for the day and Rankin asked that his remark be stricken from the record, even though Holifield admitted he had inadvertently omitted the word "activities" from the name of the committee.[43]

After its six-week run in New York, UA pulled the film, planning to release it in other markets later in the year with a new ad campaign. "Withdrawal of *Verdoux* is an 'I-told-you-so' victory for UA's sales and pub-ad departments," said *Variety*, "which strongly objected to Chaplin's insistence on opening … without adequate time for a promotional buildup."[44] "Master publicist" Russell Birdwell came on board to mount a new campaign, which included full-page ads in *Daily Variety*, *The Hollywood Reporter*, and other trade journals with quotes of praise for the film. He also instigated the memorable tagline "Chaplin Changes! Can You?"[45] The exhibitors' manual contained a number of scripted warnings for audience members, as well as a letter from UA's distribution head Gradwell Sears. "Now that the volcanic blasts, both of praise and attack, are simmering in the pool of controversy," said Sears's note, "we can with some sobriety take a cold look at Charles Chaplin's *Monsieur Verdoux*."

> Without going any farther away than shouting distance the deafest of us know there are, or will be, two camps in respect to *Verdoux*, the most controversial figure that has ever talked from the screen. One camp will hate and deplore the charming and diabolical figure which has, at least temporarily, replaced the baggy-panted tramp of another day. But there is, and will be, another camp of followers who enthusiastically welcome the revolutionary comedy-drama, believing the screen too, has the right to explore and entertain as well as has the free-speech media of press and literature.[46]

Chaplin was subpoenaed to appear before HUAC in September. "I understand I am to be your 'guest' at the expense of the taxpayer," Chaplin wired committee chairman J. Parnell Thomas. "Forgive me for this premature acceptance of your headlined newspaper invitation."

> You have been quoted as saying you wish to ask me if I am a Communist. You sojourned for ten days in Hollywood not long ago, and could have asked me the question at that time, effecting something of an economy, or, you could telephone me now—collect. In order that you are com-

pletely up-to-date on my thinking, I suggest you view carefully my latest production, *Monsieur Verdoux*. It is against war and the futile slaughter of our youth. I trust you will not find its humane message distasteful.

While you are preparing your engraved subpoena I will give you a hint on where I stand. I am not a Communist. I am a peace-monger.[47]

The film was due to open in Washington, D.C., on September 26, the day after HUAC resumed its hearings on alleged communistic inroads in Hollywood. "Sensing that the coincidence of the film's opening and the start of the hearings would appear to be a desire to capitalize the probe for publicity purposes,"[48] Carter Barron, the district manager for the Loew's theater chain, withdrew the film "to avoid any appearance of linking the opening of the picture with the possible appearance of Chaplin before the House Committee."[49] Mo Wax, in his op-ed in *Film Bulletin*, called the move "a display of intelligence and tact for which Mr. Barron and the company are to be commended." But, in what Wax said was a "booby prize" for "sheer stupidity in public relations," United Artists instead opened the film in five other theaters in the city. *Variety* reported HUAC postponed the hearings until late October, cheating UA of "its golden opportunity to use the United States Congress as a publicity device. The damage has been done."[50]

By the end of its meager run, *Monsieur Verdoux* grossed only $325,000, though it pulled in $1.5 million internationally. Despite the protests and the film's lukewarm critical reception, the National Board of Review named it the year's Best Picture, calling it the "greatest of all Chaplin films."[51] Nevertheless, Chaplin ordered the film withdrawn from distribution two years later. What got lost in the political machinations and Red-baiting was a score that *Motion Picture Herald* called "especially effective"[52] and *Variety* claimed was "above par, fortifying the progression in no small measure."[53]

*   *   *

In February 1946, Irving Berlin, Inc. was dissolved. Saul Bourne (nee Saul Bornstein), the manager for the publishing house, formed his own company, assuming Berlin's accounts and changing the name to Bourne, Inc. While Chaplin's earlier scores stayed with Bourne, *Monsieur Verdoux* went to Chappell & Co. The contract stipulated that Chappel would publish "a collection of the principal melodic themes … and offer the same for sale in sufficient quantities to satisfy the public demand therefor." Chappel released *Music from Monsieur Verdoux*, piano arrangements of three numbers from the score—"A Paris Boulevard," "Tango Bitterness" and "Rumba." Chaplin was entitled to ten percent "of the retail selling price of each piano, vocal or instrumental copy" in the U.S. and Canada, ten percent for "orchestrations in any form," and fifty percent of "any and all net sums actually received by you in respect of any licenses issued authorizing the manufacture of parts of instruments services to reproduce the Work or any part thereof, mechanically or upon so-called electrical transcriptions for broadcasting purposes in the United States and Canada."[54] With the film's poor reception and Chaplin's subsequent political troubles, he probably made little money from the collection. The agreement was in effect for nearly forty years until the contract was terminated on December 31, 1983, and the music became the property of Roy Export.

RCA Victor also planned to release a soundtrack album. Studio documents note that on January 5, 1947, George Marsh, most likely an RCA employee, worked on music cues. Two months later, Marsh lined up the musical compositions that Chaplin had selected for the album. Chaplin's political brouhaha and the film's poor box office receipts eventually helped kill the project. In 1963, Bourne, Inc., was interested in making some new recordings of Chaplin's score. Frank Chacksfield, an RCA recording artist and who had topped the charts a decade earlier with his instrumental "Terry's Theme" from *Limelight*, was responsible for the new arrangements. But Chappell still owned the worldwide rights to the music and that project too never materialized.

Chaplin's music for *Monsieur Verdoux* is a reflection of his state of mind following the years with the Joan Barry trials and the pressures from HUAC. The shrill quality of the train theme, a spry "pixie" theme that is less than fairy-like in its use of accidentals, and the cacophonous layering of themes as the world dives into the Depression are all composed in service of the story. But they also easily reflect a justifiable sour bitterness and would have made a good fit for Hanns Eisler's particular musical talents.

There is no indication on the music manuscript which cues were done by Eisler (if any) and those by Rudy Schrager. "Since working with you on *Monsieur Verdeux* [*sic*], which to me will always be one of the loveliest experiences," Schrager later wrote to Chaplin, "I have looked forward to that time when I may again have such a privilege."

> That desire was almost gratified, when your office called to arrange for an appointment with you, an appointment which was made and subsequently postponed. Some time has now elapsed, and I am wondering if you are still entertaining the idea of using me in your forthcoming production.
>
> I am not applying for the job as such, because being music director of the Lux Radio Theater [*sic*], and composing and conducting the scores for about three pictures per year, more than meets my financial needs. The reason for my desire to work with you again stems from the fact that I have a very deep respect for you as an artist, and also because of your expressed satisfaction for me personally and my work.[55]

The job for which Schrager was (or was not) applying? Chaplin's most personal musical statement.

CHAPTER 9

Awakening

After the poor box office showing of *Monsieur Verdoux*, Chaplin began working on "something completely opposite to the cynical pessimism" of the previous film.[1] *Limelight*, the love story between a young ballerina and an older vaudeville clown down on his luck, paid homage to the English music halls of Chaplin's youth. The inspiration came from an encounter with Frank Tinney, a blackface comedian who had been popular in vaudeville and on Broadway in the early 20th century. "I saw him again on the stage a few years later," Chaplin said in his autobiography, "and was shocked, for the comic Muse had left him. He was so self-conscious that I could not believe it was the same man. It was this change in him that gave me the idea years later for my film *Limelight*. I wanted to know why he had lost his spirit and his assurance. In *Limelight* the case was age; Calvero grew old and introspective and acquired a feeling of dignity, and this divorced him from all intimacy with the audience."[2] Many authors and critics over the years have commented on the autobiographical nature of the film and the resemblances to Chaplin's history. "Everything is autobiographical," Chaplin told *The New York Times*, "but don't make too much of that."[3]

At the beginning of 1948, Chaplin began writing a novel called *Footlights*. He never intended to publish it, but the process helped him work out the backstory of the *Limelight* characters before dictating the script. In 1949, a blind item reported that while working on his new film, "a musical with Charlie doing some of the singing," Chaplin was involved in "another Hollywood row…. This time it is a purely local quarrel. His neighbours complain that he is doing too much singing and that it is disturbing the peace and quiet."[4] On September 11, 1950, he registered the name *Limelight* and copyrighted the script.

The production took nearly four years of continuous work, longer than any other Chaplin production. Filming began in November 1951, by which time he had welcomed daughter Josephine (b. May 28, 1949) to the familial fold, and shooting wrapped on January 25, 1952. "We whipped through that picture in 54 days," Jerry Epstein, Chaplin's assistant on the film, said, "which was nothing for a big picture. Because [Chaplin] never moved the camera, every long shot [on a given set] for every scene in the picture was the same, and it worked! It worked! [Assistant director Robert] Aldrich would tear his hair. 'Don't you want a tracking shot here? Don't you want to move sometime?' Charlie said, 'The camera should not be noticed. Just keep me in the middle as you pan. They're here to see Charlie Chaplin, not fancy lighting.'"[5]

To find the young woman for the part of the ballerina, Chaplin reportedly placed an advertisement in the press—"Wanted: young girl to play leading lady to a comedian generally recognised as the world's greatest."[6] Barbara Bates, best known for her role as

Phoebe in the final scene of *All About Eve*, was the "chief candidate" for the part. But Chaplin also wanted to test the young English actress Claire Bloom, who was appearing in *Ring Around the Moon* in London, if she could come to Hollywood immediately for the test.[7] Playwright Arthur Laurents recommended the twenty-year-old Bloom to his friend Chaplin, who praised her as "very intelligent, charming, alive and has a wealth of talent."[8] "Both had little enough experience," Associated Press journalist Henry Gris said of Bates and Bloom, "for a man who doesn't want to take on talent already mishandled by others. It seemed that Bates would get it. Chaplin having taken such a liking to her that he was working with her every afternoon for a week, going over the actual role with her. One evening, he suddenly said, 'Send for Bloom.' That was how he made the choice: Following a sudden impulse."[9]

The film was also a family affair. In addition to Chaplin's son

Arranger Ray Rasch seated at the piano, Chaplin in makeup, and assistant producer Jerry Epstein leaning over the piano, backstage during the filming of the *Limelight* ballet, c. January 1952 (© Roy Export Co. Ltd.).

Sydney's starring role as the composer and Charles Jr., in a minor role, youngsters Geraldine, Michael, and Josephine appeared in the opening scene. Wheeler Dryden, Chaplin's other half-brother, played the doctor and the part of a clown in the ballet, and even Oona was on board, doubling as Terry in two brief shots. But long before the cameras started to roll, Chaplin began work on the music.

*   *   *

When newspapers reported Chaplin's next film was to be a musical, musicians in Hollywood made every effort to get their names in front of the filmmaker. Arthur Johnston, the arranger on *City Lights*, wrote Chaplin in May 1950 "to let you know that I am available should you have some musical ideas to put on paper."[10] Johnston received a dismissive reply—"Mr. Chaplin is working on the story for his next picture—however, the starting date is quite indefinite."[11] The following year, Claude Lapham offered his services. Lapham (1890–1957) worked as a pianist-conductor in a number of New York theaters and as an arranger for various music publishers, including Irving Berlin. "Dear Friend,"

Lapham wrote to Chaplin, "I am wondering if you will recall my name as one of your former music arrangers and music editors. I remember that you liked my pianistic ability. Also, it might be interesting to note that I wrote an opera on the Ringling Brothers Circus in 1944. I would be happy to be of musical service to you at any time."[12] If Lapham worked on any Chaplin films, and there is no reason to doubt his word, the information is lost. In January 1952, lyricist Harry Tobias, who had written hits for Rudy Vallee and Bing Crosby, also pitched his services "regarding new song material." But the musical cast was set long before.[13]

In November 1950, Bernard Katz wrote to introduce himself. In the 1930s, Katz (1909–1992) became a pianist with the NBC Orchestra in San Francisco and later a featured pianist on Los Angeles radio station KHJ's *Katz on the Keys*. Throughout the 1940s, he served as a composer, arranger, and conductor in radio for the *Union Oil Program*, *Mayor of the Town*, *Hollywood Star Theatre*, and *This Is My Best*, produced by Orson Welles. Chaplin hired Katz sometime in November, but by the end of the month NBC had lured him away to become the network's general music director. Katz did not "want to hold up musical production" on the film and sent Chaplin all of the scores that he had worked on for his one week of employment, which included the short cues for the street musicians. "There is to be no charge for this work," Katz said, "and I sincerely hope I have not inconvenienced Mr. Chaplin in any way."[14] Apparently not—Chaplin asked Katz to return to conduct the first recording of the ballet music in August 1951.

Raymond Rasch took the job "on a temporary basis," Henry Gris reported, "having been tricked into it by other arrangers who assured him they would take over later."[15] Rasch (1917–1964) began his music career in radio before heading to the west coast. He worked with Donald O'Connor and the vocal group The Smoothies, and also played piano for Tommy Dorsey, Freddy Martin, Horace Heidt, and Ina Ray Hutton. Rasch's sister, Mae Findlay said, "I do remember a pianist asking me, 'Do you realize your brother is a genius at the piano?' I didn't realize that."[16]

Chaplin gave Rasch a choice—he could receive a cut of the profits from the film or five hundred dollars a week. "Five hundred dollars a week was a lot of money back in those days," said Ray's son, Paul. "My dad was hungry and had my mother and myself to take care of. Chaplin also told him he had no intention of ever publishing the music. So my dad took the [money]."[17] Working with Chaplin was always an ordeal for the musicians he hired, even more so for Rasch, who previously had never attempted to transcribe melodies into notes. The two men no doubt found common ground as Rasch later described to Chaplin his upbringing in a poor Polish family in Toledo, Ohio, with a mother boiling potatoes to feed six children and a father "who fiddled around the saloons."[18] Rasch began work on December 15, 1950, meeting with Chaplin sometimes as many as six days a week. "Tricked by his colleagues," Henry Gris reported, "the former bar room pianist, however, got so fascinated by the Chaplin personality that he stayed on" for a year, becoming "a Chaplin human Guinea-pig, the source of stories."[19]

When a melody satisfied Chaplin, Rasch said, "he would go over it and over it. He didn't seem to care that I was just playing on a piano. He would ask for French horns in one spot: then violins and cellos and woodwinds. I just kept pounding away until he was satisfied."[20] Chaplin would stride about the room at his home humming as Rasch struggled to keep up on the piano, occasionally varying the routine by bellowing the melodies while lying stretched out on a couch. "I hear plucking," Chaplin would say. "I want something 'nasty-nice' but not disgusting."[21] "At first," Rasch said, "I was sure that I had met up with a madman. I couldn't believe that this was genius at work. He would bellow for hours at a time and all that I could hear was a senseless jumble. But suddenly he would strike a note or sometimes a whole phrase and would scream at me to play it and jot down the notes."[22]

One day, writing the music for one of the key scenes, Rasch was transcribing Chaplin's humming, and, according to the report by Gris, Chaplin was "expressing as best he could the melody that sung inside him. Before long Rasch was going through the most complicated calisthenics, trying to reproduce on the piano the instruments Chaplin had in mind. 'Now the French horns,' he ordered, 'where are the French horns?' A moment later, 'Where is the counter melody?' When he stomped, 'Where is the harp?,' Rasch stopped abruptly, and looked up. 'There is no harp here,' he said, 'this is only a piano.' Chaplin shuddered and his eyes winked as though he had just been slapped. It was as if he had been mistreated by crude reality that wouldn't let a piano be anything else."

Chaplin tolerated no interruptions during his working sessions. "It didn't matter how important the caller was," a member of his household observed, "he would see no one." "It would scare me," Rasch said, "the way he would brush off these famous people. He would have the same answer for Darryl Zanuck, Selznick and even an important visitor from New York who had been given a set appointment. Yet all he was doing at the time was arguing with himself if the melody would go di-da-da-da or di-da-di-di. The melody was all that mattered to him at the time, and that was that."[23] After one "hectic session," Rasch emerged from the sunroom "so shaken up he couldn't start his automobile."[24]

One evening, Chaplin was awakened by the sound of music. "The music was within him and he thought he would never give birth to anything more beautiful," Gris reported. "The missing melody for the finale! But the horrible possibility it would leave him before he reached the recording machine in the sunroom made him break out in cold sweat."

> He slipped into his robe, all the time humming frantically, and stole downstairs to the machine by the side of the Steinway. He turned it on. The reels of magnetic tape spinning, he sang the melody into the microphone. "La-Di-Di-Di-Di..." His fingers groping across the keyboard recaptured the tune too, and held it. This went on for a quarter hour, or so. Finally, satisfied he had saved the melody for posterity, he stole back to the bedroom, making sure he would not wake up the household...
>
> The next day Rasch arrived and Chaplin could at last play to his "interpreter" the music he had caught in the dead of night, and recorded on his player so that it is not lost. He told Rasch the story, and eagerly approaching the recording machine, he began fumbling with its switches. He was talking about the melody and how wonderful it would be for the finale, and his face was growing perplexed as he couldn't find the switch that would make the darn thing run.
>
> The excited speech was now changing to growling and a furious look was coming into his eyes.... Suddenly sound came and it was the wild twitter of reverse. Chaplin was ready to chuck it out the window, melody and all. And then, the machine played.
>
> He found the spot and they listened. There came a cacophony of noise, wild shrieking of a man, stomping of feet, but behind all that and the rumble on the piano in the key of "F" there was harmony. Rasch picked it out and played it, first simply, then coming up with rich chords.
>
> "Beautiful," said Chaplin, "beautiful. He gulped happily, the battle with the tape recorder forgotten. "Now let's try to go on from here."[25]

Chaplin paid Rasch an extra ten dollars a sheet for the orchestrations, which Rasch had also never done before. "You have got to do it somehow," Chaplin said.[26] No contracts for any of the *Limelight* musicians survive. But according to notes made in 1973, studio financial ledgers indicated that Rasch was paid a total of $16,000.[27]

Rasch felt "Chaplin's musical genius is that of organized revolt against conventions combined with perfect feeling for the real thing," Henry Gris reported. "[It] is closely connected with his inner hearing, the way he hears the world, his eyes closed." Rasch remarked, "You think first, it's musically wrong, but he insists it can be done, and eventually you find a way of doing it, only to agree with him. What he hears without knowing is what a Stravinsky has introduced into modern music, for effect with knowledge, things like any number of tempos intermixed, for instance. He doesn't know, just feels, but it's fabulous!"[28]

Rasch said working with Chaplin was "a wonderful experience and I learned a good deal I didn't know before about music."[29]

*   *   *

Composing the ballet, *The Death of Columbine*, was one of the biggest challenges for Chaplin—and by extension Rasch. It was the musical centerpiece of the film and the first piece of music recorded. Originally Chaplin envisioned a twenty-five-minute ballet, which no doubt would have stretched the patience of audiences. Chaplin eventually shaved it to twelve minutes but still found composing the music "an almost insuperable task because I had to imagine the action of the ballet. In the past I had composed music only when my film was completed and I could see its action. Nevertheless, by imagining the dancing I composed all the music. But when it was completed I wondered whether it was suitable for ballet, for the choreography would more or less have to be invented by the dancers themselves."[30]

In February 1950, long before Chaplin began work on the music or even shot a frame of *Limelight*, *Variety* reported that he had written a ballet for Alicia Markova and Anton Dolin, who had been a principal dancer with Diaghilev. Chaplin discussed the idea with them on more than one occasion, including an afternoon at the New York apartment of Constance Collier, "drinking good English tea with nice fresh potted meat sandwiches," Dolin remembered. "As Mr. Chaplin told it it was an enchanting comedy mixed with that tragic muse that is so much part of his great genius."[31] In March 1950, *Variety* reported Chaplin was "completing the music," and the "English dance team expects to include it in their repertoire when they return to England next month."[32] When it came time to cast the ballet in *Limelight*, Chaplin replaced the famous duo, giving no reason. "I admit that I had hoped to dance the ballet episodes myself with Markova," Dolin said. "Alas, the privilege was not ours."[33] Chaplin instead cast another dancer he much admired, André Eglevsky. The Russian-born 33-year-old Eglevsky was a member of the Ballet Russe de Monte Carlo before becoming a U.S. citizen in the late 1930s, dancing with American Ballet Theatre (ABT) and New York City Ballet. Chaplin tailored one of the ballet sequences so Eglevsky could recreate his "Bluebird" dance from Tchaikovsky's *The Sleeping Beauty*, composing forty-five seconds worth of music specifically to match Eglevsky's moves. Indeed, Eglevsky's contract specified that the choreography "for the particular numbers you dance will be a routine you have hitherto done in former ballets."[34] Eglevsky sent pictures of dancers who could convincingly double for Claire Bloom during the dancing sequences, and Chaplin picked twenty-seven-year-old Melissa Hayden, part of the *corps de ballet* at Radio City Music Hall and, like Eglevsky, a member of ABT and New York City Ballet.

Bernard Katz, who had taken time off from his NBC gig, recorded the ballet music on August 3, 1951, at Glen Glenn Sound Studio. A week later, Chaplin spent a day cutting the music. Over the next month, he apparently became unhappy with Katz's efforts and wanted to re-record it. According to Gris, "[Chaplin] seriously intended to take over the job of conducting the orchestra after an unfortunate experience with a conductor who left [Katz]." Chaplin "demanded if it were at all necessary to know all those basic signs conductors use and each of which is a signal for members of an orchestra. He could, he said, do a good job without them, and proceeded to prove it by assuming the conductor's position." Rasch said Chaplin "waved his hands with perfect timing and translated the music into rhythmical gyrations that made sense but still would remain meaningless to an orchestra. When I told him he would still have to learn the signs first, he sulked for a while refusing to accept it. Later as another conductor stepped in he forgot about his intention."[35]

That other conductor was Keith Williams. Williams (1924–2008) served in the Air Force during World War II and organized a 14-piece dance band following his tour of duty. He later became a staff orchestrator for Walter Lantz cartoons and staff composer for Gene Autry Range Writer Productions in television, as well as a producer and writer for KTTV's *Melody Time* and an executive producer for TV Unlimited Productions.

Conductor Keith Williams, arranger Ray Rasch, and Chaplin during the *Limelight* recording sessions, c. June 1952 (© Roy Export Co. Ltd.).

Williams re-recorded the ballet music at Glen Glenn on September 19 and 20, and Chaplin came into the studio a week later, spending two days cutting the new recording. Three days later, Hayden and Eglevsky arrived and spent three days in rehearsals. Chaplin was "anxious" to get their reaction to the music. "I was extremely nervous and self-conscious as they sat and listened, but, thank God, both approved and said it was balle-tique," Chaplin said. "It was one of the thrilling moments of my film career to see them dance to it. Their interpretation was most flattering and gave the music a classic signifi-cance."[36] Hayden "loved the music, I thought it was inspirational."[37] She was not, however, pleased by what she felt was Chaplin's attitude—or lack thereof—towards her. She later recalled that she and Eglevsky only did an hour of improvisation over the three days.

The choreography seems to have been put together much like a Chaplin score. "When you're not prepared for anything," Hayden said, "you use the experience you already have as a performer."

> Since I had danced with André in a number of pieces, he said, "Do this step from a Balanchine, then this step from *Sylphide* and Fokine." And we put together a *pas de deux* by talking to each other.
>   And Chaplin would say, "Good, good, good. This is wonderful."
>   So we did this for an hour. I said to André, "He likes what we're doing, but I don't think he likes me. I'm stopping, I'm tired. You speak to him and ask him if he likes me. If he likes me, that's okay, I'll do it. If he doesn't, it's *finis*, right now."
>   I was softer in my tone than I am now, but he hadn't looked at me; I felt like anybody could have been doing this. Somebody had to show an interest in me personally. You see, André and he had met before. André had the job; I was the one that was auditioning.
>   André said, "Don't worry, just get dressed."
>   From what I gathered, he spoke to Mr. Chaplin and he translated what I had been saying, but we never had a yea or a nay. We left the following morning."[38]

Chaplin may have taken choreography screen credit for himself, but "he didn't chore-ograph a thing," Hayden said, "he didn't know anything about ballet."

> Maybe he took credit for what he was suggesting. All of our dances derived from the two of us, André and myself. And in the montage [of Terry's world tour], I did all that myself. The montage took two or three hours. He just kept saying, "Do it again!"
>   I'm sure Chaplin knew about dance—he loved ballet, although he never spoke about other dancers—but we're talking about classic ballet. I don't know if he was ever in a ballet studio, but he could use the vocabulary of classic ballet, *pliés* and so forth, although he would mispronounce the words.
>   I danced with Balanchine and Ashton. That is a kind of vocabulary, a kind of choreography and inventiveness that belongs only to the world of ballet. I don't think he had that particular experi-ence. He was a vaudevillian, and a lot of vaudevillians know a little or a lot about dance, but not in a classical form; he wasn't trained in that.[39]

Despite this early preparation, Chaplin filmed the ballet late in the schedule, at the end of the R.K.O.-Pathé Studio shoot in Culver City, where he had shot all the music hall sequences. Hayden arrived at the studio on December 27, three days before Eglevsky. On her third day, she filmed the scene in which Terry auditions on the Empire stage accom-panied by Neville on the piano. Like Terry did in the scene, Hayden once again had to improvise. Later she realized that "what [Chaplin] wanted was an improvisational qual-ity—the nerves, the anxiety, the tentativeness, and I think the scene has that."[40] Eglevsky came to the studio the following morning, though he and Hayden did not go before the camera that day. The pair also may have helped to devise the *Scheherezade* ballet seen at

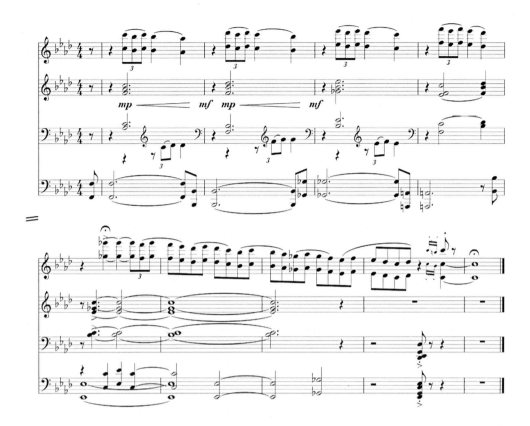

Limelight (1952)—**The dramatic introduction for the ballet.**

the Empire in the film, which was completed that morning. Chaplin filmed his "Spring Song" that afternoon and continued with Calvero's other songs on the following Monday. The ballet was filmed over three days, January 4–6, 1952, and Eglevsky and Hayden departed the next day.

Except for the orchestral background and vocal parts to Calvero's songs, and a few other scattered musical fragments, the two-act ballet music, which is made up of a series of separate cues rather than one long piece, is the only part of the *Limelight* score that still exists in the Chaplin Archive today. The music begins, as does the main titles, with a heavy, grounded low F pedal tone (marked, appropriately enough, "Introduction" on the cue sheet). A five-note motif revolves around three notes and ascends sequentially up the F minor scale. The score's most famous melody, "Terry's Theme," follows. Eighth-note rests give the theme a halting quality, a sign of insecurity in Terry herself and the frailty of Columbine dying in bed. The theme also serves as Terry's audition music with Neville playing on the piano.

Staccato eighth notes convey "Perpetual Slow Motion" underneath Calvero's comic business with the cop. The bridge section of this cue borrows the melody and harmonic progressions from Calvero's "Animal Trainer" song as if his onstage character of a clown is musically thumbing his nose at authority. Mournful cellos voice Calvero's "Anxiety" as he shakes out the smashed egg from inside his pantaloon. Ethereal strings and harp arpeggios belie the fussiness of the G-flat major key signature. Chaplin cut the next cue,

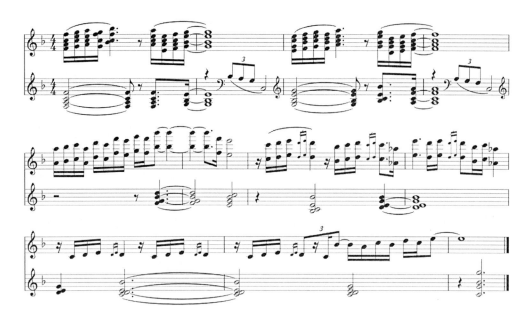

Limelight (1952)—**"Terry's Theme" became a popular instrumental on records.**

"Clown's Emotion," no doubt realizing that to focus too much on Calvero during the ballet, a part that was given to him out of a begrudging sense of duty for his former glory, did not make dramatic sense. The cue was tonally ambivalent, with a multitude of accidentals and short motifs reminiscent of Chaplin's cut cues from the opening scenes of *The Great Dictator*. Violin trills lead to churning eighth notes in the strings underneath a delicate melody in the woodwinds as the *corps de ballet* wordlessly entreat the frail figure in the bed to "Dance Columbine." Harlequin flings himself in despair over Columbine's lifeless body and the "Transition" cue covers the scene change to Act II with a mournful cello theme reminiscent of the "Awakening" music.

Act II begins with "Harlequin's Moon Dance," featuring Eglevsky's *Sleeping Beauty* "Bluebird" solo. With bird chirps in the piccolo and muted French horn hunting calls, Chaplin channels his inner Tchaikovsky with a rousing oom-pah-pah in the lower instruments and a delicate flute waltz. Harlequin's "Emotion" implores Columbine at her grave to dance one last time. A three-note motif plays a call-and-answer session between the strings and woodwinds as if Harlequin and Columbine are having a conversation. Accented unison notes in the low strings punctuate the cue and mimic Harlequin's motions on stage. Following the waltz for the *corps de ballet*, the three-note motif from "Emotion" underscores the scene in the wings when Terry tells Calvero she cannot move her legs ("Regrets"). "Terry's Theme" plays for Columbine's solo, while Calvero prays backstage for her to get through the number. Columbine and Harlequin's "Pas de Deux" begins ethereally for strings and harp before the woodwinds join, combining the three-note motif and the harmonies of "Terry's Theme" for a lovely musical mélange. Earlier versions of the cue sheet indicate that the main titles of the film originally ended with this cue. Chaplin cut "Terpsichore," a dainty waltz in F major, feeling perhaps that the staccato woodwinds and pizzicato strings brightened the mood too much or maybe it disrupted the dramatic flow into "Columbine's Solo Waltz." The ballet ends there though

Limelight (1952)—Calvero's comic business with the cop in the ballet is underscored with a staccato "Perpetual Slow Motion."

Limelight (1952)—In the ballet, Chaplin channels his inner Tchaikovsky for "Harlequin's Moon Dance."

two more cues, "Ballet Final Curtain" and "Final Dance Scene," which also bookended the introduction, and a reprise of "Terry's Theme" were cut from the film. Apparently, Chaplin felt once Columbine had danced her final dance, it was time to move on.

Anton Dolin wrote about the ballet for *Dance and Dancers* magazine in a review that occasionally reads like sour grapes:

Limelight (1952)—The opening notes of "Terry's Theme" form the basis for the "Pas de Deux" for Columbine and Harlequin.

With what high anticipation I went, as soon as my busy life would let me, to see Mr. Charles Chaplin in his film, *Limelight*…

What dire disappointment, for me at least, was the ultimate choreographic film result. The Empire Ballet of those years during the first world war formed an important chapter in the history of English ballet and I am only sorry that I never saw it myself. But a great deal of first-hand information and knowledge has been imparted to me by that great ballerina of the period—Adeline Genée.

The travesty of a period as one sees it in *Limelight* is but another failure of ballet in films. That of all people Mr. Chaplin, who knew this aspect and period of ballet better than anyone else, should have failed, was unbelievably sad. I had had such faith that with the coming of *Limelight* we should at least see a real film ballet.

Instead, what do we see? A Balanchine cum Roland Petit affair with its everlasting *pirouettes* and a quite out-of-period costume for André Eglevsky. We see Melissa Hayden "improvising her solo dance" for an audition. We are told this by the ballet master. Yet when we see the dance proper, the same steps and the same solo is danced again. It looked just like anything we have seen in any Balanchine or Lichine ballet of the past ten years.

A dozen *corps de ballet* girls, who should have known better but probably did not, were all that was allowed of the famed Empire girls. Where in all this was the style and the atmosphere of the musical hall in its hey-day. A period often referred to as glorious and breath-taking with its splendour of scenery and costumes. The utility setting we see in the film surely belongs to Les Ballets des Champs-Elysées of today.

Please, Mr. Chaplin, I feel sure that my few words will not lose us a friendship. I very much doubt if you read or even care one jot what my opinion offers. Yet I cannot help but feel that you have let us down. Mr. Chaplin, Mr. Eglevsky and Miss Hayden, especially the first, all know their job, but choreography does not seem to be a part of it. At least not in recreating a ballet depicting a little of those palmy days at the Empire.

Why not dress those lovely ladies, who adorned the foyer and bars of the early 'twenties, in dresses by Dior, Schiaperelli, Balmain or Fath? The result would have been no more stupid than the incongruous spectacle we saw on the stage.[41]

* * *

Limelight (1952)—The quarter-note rests of "Columbine's Solo Waltz" pause in mid-air along with Terry's hesitation.

The other major onscreen musical performances include Calvero's onstage songs and the duet with Buster Keaton at the Empire benefit. The songs, co-written by Chaplin and Ray Rasch, are loving, if occasionally and perhaps deliberately uninspired, pastiches of the English music hall that are lifted up through Chaplin's performances. Chaplin, as ever, was protective of his material and in the crew's copies of the shooting script, the

Limelight (1952)—The opening of Calvero's "Animal Trainer" chorus.

songs, both lyrics and patter, were obliterated, as David Robinson notes, "for no very good reason unless from paranoia that they might be pirated."[42]

The most elaborate (and lengthy) of the three—"Animal Trainer"—is a flea circus routine Chaplin had been trying to work into one of his films for decades, as far back as a never-completed film from 1919 called *The Professor*. Chaplin borrowed one gag from the 1915 Essanay short *By the Sea*. He tried to work the routine into *The Circus* and *The Great Dictator*, though it is hard to imagine this particular musical version in either of those films. The song occurs in *Limelight* during Calvero's first dream sequence, as he remembers loftier days in the music halls, and Chaplin inserts a brief excerpt during the Empire benefit in Calvero's honor at the end of the film.

I'm an animal trainer,
A circus entertainer.
I've trained animals by the score—
Lions, tigers and wild boar.
I've made and lost a fortune
In my wild career.
Some say the cause was women;
While some say it was beer.

Then I went through bankruptcy
And lost my whole menagerie.
But I did not despair,
I got a bright idea,
While searching through my underwear
A thought occurred to me,
I'm tired of training elephants,
So why not train a flea?
Why should I hunt for animals
And through the jungle roam
When there's local talent
To be found right here at home?

I found one but I won't say where
And educated him with care,
And taught him all the facts of life,
And then he found himself a wife.
I give them board and lodgings free
And every night they dine off me;
They don't eat caviar or cake.
But they enjoy a good rump steak
Off my anatomy,

Off my anatomy.
It is an odd sensation
When after meals they take a stroll
Around the old plantation.

Now I'm as happy as can be,
I've bought them lots of tricks you see
And now they're both supporting me;
They're both supporting me.

Walk up! Walk up,
It's the greatest show on earth.
Walk up! Walk up,
And get your money's worth.
See Phyllis and Henry,
Those educated fleas
Twisting and twirling [later changed
    to *Cavorting and sporting*]
On the flying trapeze.
So any time you itch
Don't scratch or make a fuss
You never can tell you might destroy
Some budding genius.[43]

Chaplin employs the music hall style of "Thespian formal" diction, a heightened, elevated speech that is deliberately incongruous to the material, thereby heightening the

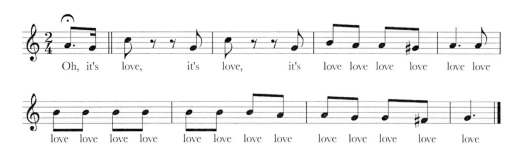

Oh, it's love, it's love, it's love love love love love love
love love love love love love love love love love love love love

Limelight (1952)—The opening of Calvero's "Spring Song" chorus.

Calvero (Chaplin) and Terry (Claire Bloom) during the patter portion of *Limelight*'s "Spring Song," c. 1952 (© Roy Export SAS).

humor. The song is given much more screen time than the other two songs, no doubt because Chaplin was finally able to realize his dream of including the routine in a film. As such, a separate "Animal Trainer Background" orchestral cue was written to underscore Calvero's patter as he performs the routine with Phyllis and Henry, "those educated fleas." A brief four-second excerpt of the background music later introduces the "Sardine Song" during the Empire benefit and underscores the set up for Chaplin and Keaton's routine.

Chaplin naturally uses nature in his lyrics for "Spring Song," which was titled "It's Spring" and "It's Love" in earlier drafts.

> *Spring is here*
> *Birds are calling*
> *Skunks are crawling*
> *Wagging their tails for love.*
>
> *Spring is here*
> *Worms are squirming*
> *Whales are churning* [the *worms/whales* lines are swapped in the film]
> *Wagging their tales for love.*
>
> *What is this thing,*
> *Of which I sing,*
> *That makes us all bewitched?*
> *What is this thing,*
> *That comes in spring,*
> *That gives us all the itch?*
>
> *Oh, it's love,*
> *It's love,*
> *It's love love love love love*
> *Love love love love love love love love love love love love love love*
> *Love love love love love love love love love love love love love love*
> *Love love love love love love love love love love love love love love*
> *Love love love love love love love love love love love love love love*
> *Love love love love love love love love love love love love love.*[44]

Unlike the other two songs, Chaplin knew exactly where he wanted the "Spring Song" to occur in the film—during Calvero's second dream sequence, this time as an introduction to his patter duet with Terry. Woodwind solos signal the beginning of spring and lugubrious oscillating chords convey the welcome end of winter by traveling down the dreaded tritone from G-flat to C. The nonsensical repetition of the word *love*, with its rapid-fire patter, was an easy way to generate humor and set up the wooing of Terry on stage immediately following. The song is later excerpted with Calvero on the banjo busking out on the street. An earlier draft of the song contained this beginning:

> *Spring is here!*
> *The birds are calling;*
> *Wagging their tails for love;*
> *Flyes* [*sic*] *are flying;*
> *Skunks are sighing*
> *Wagging their tales for love.*
> *It's in the air;*
> *It's everywhere,*
> *The sea, below, and above.*
> *Fish are swimming*
> *Stingrays stinging*
> *Wagging their tales* [*sic*] *for love....*[45]

Chaplin had bigger plans for the "Sardine Song," at least if the lyrics included in the vocal manuscript are any indication. The song was originally slotted into the first dream sequence, where "Animal Trainer" eventually ended up. During editing, Chaplin excerpted a small bit from the end of the chorus for the disastrous Middlesex show and later reprised the first half of the song during the Empire benefit.

When I was three, my nurse told me
About reincarnation.
And ever since, I've been convinced,
Thrilled with anticipation
That when I leave this earth
It makes my heart feel warm
To know that I'll return
In some other form.

But I don't want to be a tree,
Sticking in the ground, I'd rather be a flea.
I don't want to be a flower, waiting by the hour,
Hoping for a pollen to alight on me;
So when I cease to be,
I want to go back, I want to go back,
I want to go back to the sea.

CHORUS
Oh for the life of a sardine,
That is the life for me.
Cavorting and spawning every morning
Under the deep blue sea.
To have no fear for storm or gale
Oh to chase the tail of a whale.
Oh for the life of a sardine.
That is the life for me.[46]

The song begins in cut time, and caesuras pockmark the vocal manuscript, halting the music so that Chaplin (and Calvero) could clearly render the patter in the verses for an audience. With "But I don't want to be a tree," the music switches to a carefree 4/4 full of dotted rhythms. Calvero's exhortation "I want to go back to the sea" is rendered in a lively 6/8 before returning to the opening cut time and its churning half-step figures. Earlier drafts included an extended version of the song:

When I'm a fish, it is my wish
For lots of recreation.
To drink my fill up to the gill
With no intoxication.
I want fun in the sea
Not in this world of strife,
With it's morality.

Give me the animal life.
But I don't want to be a carrot;
Sticking in the ground. I'd sooner be a maggot.
Life without a will, would surely make me ill;
To get a little action, I'd even be a pill.
So when I cease to be,
I want to go back, I want to go back,
I want to go back to the sea.

CHORUS
Oh for the life of a sardine,
That is the life for me.
Cavorting and spawning every morning
Under the deep blue sea.
To have no fear of a fisherman's net,
Oh what fun to be gay and all wet.
Oh for the life of a sardine.
That is the life for me.[47]

On October 18, 1951, before shooting of the film had even begun, Chaplin recorded the songs (and the two piano "concertos") at Glen Glenn with Rasch accompanying on piano. On November 6, Keith Williams recorded the background music for the songs,

Oh, for the life of a sar-dine, that is the life for me,— Ca-
vort-ing and spawn-ing ev-er-y morn-ing un-der the dep blue sea.—

Limelight (1952)—**The opening of Calvero's "Sardine Song" chorus.**

to which Chaplin later lip-synced during playback on set. Like the ballet, Chaplin shot the songs at R.K.O.-Pathé, not at his studio. "He was very demanding with himself, shooting the vaudeville songs," said production designer Eugène Lourié. "He'd say, 'We'll do it again. I can do it better than that.' Sometimes we would shoot fifteen times."[48]

Chaplin originally had the songs in a different order with all three performed during dream sequences. The copyrighted script and the shooting script listed them in the following order—"Sardine Song," "Spring Song" introducing the double act with Terry, and "Animal Trainer." "Sardine Song" was later reprised for the Middlesex show, with the patter heavily cut. During the editing process, the order changed to "Animal Trainer," "Spring Song," and "Sardine Song" was eliminated as a dream sequence, substituted instead for the Middlesex show. HMV later released "Animal Trainer" and "The Sardine Song" [*sic*] on a 78-rpm record in, of all places, Denmark.

WQXR featured the *Limelight* songs on their *Music Magazine* program in New York on October 9, 1952, in a program titled *Charlie Chaplin, the Tramp Who Makes Music*. *Variety* called it "a first-rate airer." The program included the radio premiere of Chaplin's score, as well as segments of the prizefight music and "Who'll Buy My Violets?" from *City Lights*, and "Titine" from *Modern Times*. "Although cinema music frequently fails to stand up on its own, divorced from the screen," *Variety* continued, "most of the pieces that Chaplin cleared (and in some cases also performed) came over with an impact that would have been strong even if they were not identified with the well-known Chaplin tag. Some of it is worthy of release in record form. One or two instrumental pieces could also be reworked, given lyrics and published as pop tunes; they've got a good melody line and emotional appeal." The program highlighted the three "sly and witty" songs and the "schmaltzy and lyrical" ballet—"it's listenable, but actually is a takeoff on the genre rather than a serious work on its own. A piano theme, in the Chopin manner, has a potent nostalgic effect. The concerto, which in the pic is the musical subject of a riotously funny act by Chaplin and Buster Keaton, stands up as a bright opus with its alternating virtuoso and sentimental passages." Ray Rasch was also interviewed, saying that Chaplin deals "more in phrases, themes and moods rather than in tunes and melodies," that "he feels a few instruments can convey an effect, at times, better than a full orchestra." Fred Grunfeld, the host of the program, commented on the Mendelssohn character of the shadow-boxing motif from *City Lights* and that the *Limelight* ballet "out-Delibes Delibes." He labeled Chaplin a "gifted amateur."[49]

"It is quite possible in the future," said Saul Bourne, "that the score of LIMELIGHT might be used on radio or television and in that case there would be some revenue coming from these mediums as well as the royalty from foreign parts."[50] So in August 1952, Chaplin set about joining the American Society of Composers, Authors and Publishers (ASCAP), one of two organizations (along with BMI) in the U.S. that provide royalties to songwriters. Oscar Hammerstein agreed to propose Chaplin's admission into the organization, but first Chaplin had to prove he actually was a songwriter. He supplied Bourne with copies of the three *Limelight* songs as well as "With You, Dear, In Bombay," for which Chaplin had recently renewed the copyright, no doubt to assist with the ASCAP application. William Starr of Music Publishers Holding Corporation, who instituted the copyright renewal, wrote to Arthur Kelly, "I wonder if Mr. Chaplin remembers writing the song."[51] Bourne, however, was not too enthused about the new *Limelight* material.

I think one of the qualifications for ASCAP membership requires publication of one, or more, songs and, of course, publication requires the making of plates and printing.

   Two of our best men, and myself, went over these songs carefully. We are not sure that the cost of plates and printing, and publication, will be justified by the possible sale of copies. We do not think these songs are the type of songs that are regularly plugged and demanded in the sheet music market. However, we could be wrong, and would like to give the matter some further thought.

   As an illustration of what we are trying to explain, we are looking at the "SARDINE SONG"; it is a very, very long composition, and appears as special material rather than a popular song. However, on the whole, the musical content of all three compositions could easily be ideal background atmospheric film music; but I would not want to see Mr. Chaplin's application for membership in ASCAP made on the basis of atmospheric background film music, but rather on the basis of songs that can be performed and demanded by interpretive artists over radio and TV stations, which are licensed by ASCAP.[52]

ASCAP dragged its feet in granting Chaplin membership. Bourne later recommended that he join the British Performing Right Society, the "so-called English ASCAP," since he was still a British citizen, which would, in turn, grant him automatic membership in the U.S. organization.[53] Chaplin was eventually granted membership in both organizations, securing royalties on nearly every piece of music he wrote, published, and recorded.

*   *   *

Several cue sheets exist for *Limelight*, from handwritten and typewritten versions made during filming to a version sent to Bourne, Inc., before the film's release, and yet another version compiled by Eric James and John Guthridge twenty years later. "Charlie told me that no royalties or performing right fees had ever been paid," James said, "and it was necessary to have a detailed cue sheet prepared in order that the money owing to him would be paid."[54] The earliest versions demonstrate Chaplin's choices and original ordering of cues, especially in the songs, while later versions demonstrate his rethinking of certain cues, especially in eliminating sentimentality. The final film version is an amalgamation of all of these cue sheets.

   The first section of the *Footlights* novella was labeled "Symphony," indicating Chaplin envisioned something on a grander musical scale than he had attempted before. At times the music fires the flames of nostalgia, at others it surges with emotion. The songs provide the most obvious examples of harkening back to the days of the English music halls, but Chaplin also included period flavor in a number of other cues.

   The opening scene is special for the glimpse of Chaplin's children and their onscreen interaction with their father in character as a drunkard stumbling home, accompanied by a barrel organ playing a nostalgic waltz. In *Footlights*, Chaplin originally drew upon his memory of when "music first entered my soul" back in his youth—"As he began taking off his shoes, music came from off the street, rendered by a trio of depressing-looking men, playing 'The Honeysuckle and The Bee,' in the vestibule of the corner pub. One musician, who played a portable harmonium, was blind, with horribly scarred eye sockets; another, a bleary-eyed alcoholic with a walrus moustache, played a clarinet, and a forlorn Paganini played a violin. Although they made a ghastly caricature, their music was sweet."[55] (Chaplin makes another reference to the song and the derelict trio playing it later in the script.) According to Wheeler Dryden, Chaplin originally wanted to use the old Cockney song, "Down At the Old Bull and Bush," for the sequence.[56] Most versions of the screenplay indicate a different Cockney song, "Why Did I Leave My Little Back Room in Bloomsbury?" The cue, simply marked "Hurdy-Gurdy" in the cue sheet, was re-recorded on the last day with Chaplin "waving ecstatically" over a small piano with Rasch at the keyboard, creating the sound of the organ with the help of sheets of paper tacked inside the sound board. "Ray, the organ is not lazy enough," Chaplin commented after the first take. "It was, on the second take," reported Henry Gris. "But however happy over the result, Chaplin went on wondering if he shouldn't come up with a new musical twist, if the organ was 'sad enough.'"[57] Surely, this was a reflection of his childhood.

The three street musicians provide more nostalgia. The "Derelicts" included Snub Pollard (harmonium), who had begun his career in films at Essanay at the time Chaplin was working at the studio. Loyal Underwood (clarinet) joined the Chaplin studio in 1916 with *The Count* and acted in nearly every Chaplin Mutual and First National film from that point forward. *Limelight* was his only credited sound film. Julian Ludwig (violin) was a late addition to the group. Ludwig was a member of Jerry Epstein's Circle Theatre and friends with Chaplin's son Sydney. Chaplin permitted him to attend the shooting and cast him on the spur of the moment for the one-take filming of the musicians' drunken jam in Mrs. Alsop's (Marjorie Bennett) house. "Mr. Chaplin looks at me," Ludwig

"The Derelicts"—Julian Ludwig (violin), Snub Pollard (harmonium), and Loyal Underwood (clarinet)—join Calvero (Chaplin) in his apartment for a drunken jam session, c. 1952 (© Roy Export SAS).

later said, "and he says, 'Julian thinks acting is easy. *He's* going to play that part!' So that's how I got hired.... To do my scenes, they made me up to look older, because I was not exactly as old as everybody there—I was in my twenties, and they were silent film veterans (but come to think of it, so was I). So they made me up with the beard and everything. And the first time I walked on the stage for his approval, Geraldine said, 'Uncle Julian!' and ran up and hugged me. And Mr. Chaplin said, 'Get him back into makeup,' so my progression into an older man depended on whether Geraldine recognized me."[58]

Chaplin filmed the street scenes with the musicians on the Paramount lot. Since there was no music playing to guide them, Ludwig took his cue from Chaplin, who stood off-camera, giving him the tempo. "If you look [at the scene in the film]," Ludwig said, "nobody is looking at him except me, because he's directing me on the tempo."

> And I can see fear in my face because I'm not a musician, but he knew that—he didn't ask me if I knew how to play the violin, he didn't ask me if I knew anything about music—he just gave me the tempo. And when the picture was dubbed and the music was laid in, we were watching it in the dubbing room ... and he's screaming at me on the screen, "God damn it, play faster, play faster!" And I'm sitting right next to him and he's *yelling* at the screen. It's because the tempo of the music that he'd written didn't match the tempo I was playing. I've never forgotten that: he was sitting right next to me and was shouting at me on the screen![59]

The music for the apartment scene, "Nocturne," is a sad, languorous piece for the quartet (including an added viola) that captures the musicians' difficult lot in life.

The other bit of nostalgia, at least for film fans, is the celebrated pairing of Chaplin and Buster Keaton. Originally, Chaplin thought of Sydney's stand-in, who had "a long lugubrious face," for the part. But when someone mentioned that Keaton was available, broke, and needed money, Chaplin hired him. Keaton arrived on the set in his old Buster outfit with his trademark pancake hat. Chaplin pulled him aside and told him gently, "We're not playing our old characters now. I'm not playing the Tramp; you're not playing Buster." "Yes, Charlie, of course," Keaton replied. He removed his hat and went to wardrobe to get fitted for his costume.[60]

Chaplin had explicit notes about how he wanted the music and sound to work in the scene:

> Rounds of applause and laughter at Calvero's and Keaton's entrance. Heard chord of music o.s. [off stage]. Then it becomes quiet.
> Sound: collar ripping—violin music—string snaps—sounding one note on piano—wire pulling sounds—snipping of wire—audience laughter—good run on piano—crash of cymbals, drum noise, triangle knocked over as Calvero falls in drum. Tremendous applause as Calvero carried to wings. Use "more" track.
> After Calvero kisses violin and says, "You darling" first time, cut to actors laughing at side of stage. Then cut to second crying take (quicker music). Use wild track line of "You darling." Audience starts stamping feet when Calvero asks to be carried back on stage.[61]

Offstage musicians played the music during rehearsal while Chaplin's finger and bow movements "perfectly synchronized with the music," said one newspaper report. "Rehearsal over, Chaplin suggests to the violinist and pianist that perhaps the piece should be changed slightly. He hums the change. The musicians agree respectfully. Then Chaplin, the composer, sits at the piano and makes a few more changes in the score."[62] The violin "concerto" is typically Chaplinesque. Calvero, with a crazed look in his eye, plays a series of furious phrases made up of nervous sixteenth-note tics and staccato eighth notes descending chromatically every two bars. Keaton's piano part keeps time but stays out

Calvero (Chaplin) and his partner (Buster Keaton) perform their demented violin "concerto" at the Empire Benefit, c. 1952 (© Roy Export SAS).

of the way while the violin swings through its devilish dance. The lyrical middle section is a lachrymose melody that matches the carefree rubato elements of many other Chaplin tunes.

Chaplin and Keaton "were very conscious about timing," said Eugène Lourié, "and each time we went through rehearsal, it was to make the gags shorter. The same thing with filmed takes, and those takes with Buster Keaton took a very, very long time. They were shooting that routine for many days. I think there was a certain jealousy between them, because each of them wanted to have the better piece of the pie!"[63]

*   *   *

C. Sharpless Hickman in *Music Journal* said Chaplin's use of music in the early scenes "is extremely sparing, and then occurs only momentarily to buoy a scene, a mood, or a simply physical movement. There are long stretches of silence, or of talk without background music, for Chaplin feels that music obtrudes on words when words are the important thing."[64] The first Chaplin theme heard in the body of the film proper is entitled "Awakening." Though "Terry's Theme" became the more famous melody, Chaplin's uses "Awakening" more than any other cue in the score. The plaintive tune, voiced in the cellos and basses, represents Calvero's "awakening" that his day has passed. It underscores scenes of simple poignancy such as the dejected walk along the Thames after his disastrous Middlesex performance and the final blow—when he accidentally finds out he is being replaced in the ballet. One last rendition substitutes for Calvero's ghost in the empty apartment when Terry comes home to find a note saying he has gone.

As with all Chaplin scores, *Limelight* features a number of waltzes, most prominently the "Criterion Waltz," which underscores the glamorous ballet after-party. The theme also plays as a source cue out in the Empire Theatre as Chaplin and Keaton apply their makeup in their dressing room, and serves as the film's exit music. The other primary waltz is the love theme for Terry and Neville during their reunion at the restaurant and later on Terry's stoop as Neville declares his love for her. The "Satire Waltz" follows Calvero's performance of the "Spring Song," underscoring the end of Calvero and Terry's patter as they kick up their heels and waltz off stage to applause. An odd inclusion is the "Shack Waltz" from *Modern Times* (though it is not actually in 3/4 time), which originally played as the Tramp and the Gamin set up home in a dilapidated shack. Chaplin inserts the bright and breezy piece first at the same restaurant as a source cue heard from perhaps some unseen offscreen cafe orchestra. The piece later serves as another source cue faintly heard backstage at the Empire Theatre in Calvero's dressing room.

Limelight originally opened with an extended sequence of Terry's childhood, which Chaplin rewrote and condensed into one of Terry's monologues. But the scenes remained in the script long enough for him to compose what he called a "Child's Theme," yet another waltz. Terry's dream of being a ballet dancer, which she had had since she was a child, is thwarted by her psychosomatic illness that affects the use of her legs. Chaplin uses the "Child's Theme" to underscore Calvero's attempts to get Terry to walk. As he waltzes her around the room, he hums the theme, the only time Chaplin is heard humming one of his pieces of music in any of his films. The gypsy air of the waltz also serves as the musical backdrop for Terry's montage as she dances her way across Europe. Chaplin captures the fashionable hustle and bustle of the Empire Theatre with a brief introduction consisting of a series of five-note figures followed by swirling music that underscores the famous Empire Promenade and serves as the pit orchestra music for the *Scheherezade* ballet on stage.

Limelight (1952)—Ignoring the time signature, Chaplin reused the inappropriately named "Shack Waltz" from *Modern Times* as a faint source cue in the restaurant and at the Empire Theatre.

Chaplin working with the *Limelight* studio orchestra, c. June 1952 (Francis O'Neill, LOOK Magazine Photograph Collection, Library of Congress, Prints & Photographs Division [LC-DIG-ds-05361]).

The piano plays a significant role in the film and the score. When Terry tells Calvero of her past meetings with a young composer, she describes walking by his home and hearing him practicing the instrument, "repeating music passages over and over again," shades of how Chaplin composed at the piano when by himself. The left hand plays the melody of Neville's piano concerto, while the right hand flies over the keys in a flurry of Rachmaninoff-like runs. The theme will later appear in full orchestral glory underscoring Terry's joyful exclamation "I'm walking! I'm walking! Calvero, I'm walking!" The piano reconnects Terry and Neville in a cue called "Twilight" in which Calvero tells Terry his dream of her meeting Neville again one day. And, of course, Neville accompanies Terry's audition on piano with the ballet introduction and "Terry's Theme."

The remainder of the instrumental score was recorded on June 10 and 17, 1952. A photographer from *Look* magazine was on hand to capture the musicians on what must have been an intense couple of days. On June 10 alone, thirty-two cues were scheduled over two sessions totaling six and a half hours. The single session a week later was devoted to miscellanies such as the piano background for the "Child's Theme" and "Twilight" cues, a viola sweetener for Calvero's drunken street musician jam in his apartment, and various percussion fixes. Two cues from *Monsieur Verdoux*—the waltz ("A Paris Apartment") and "Paris Boulevard" can-can—were also recorded but neither appear in the finished film.

"The essentially Tchaikovsky character of the music," David Raksin later said, "adds tremendously to the emotional power of a moving tale. Anything more complicated—thematically speaking—would be a distraction. But this is Chaplin's mark—a fantastic ability to realize just how far sentiment may be pushed toward sentimentality before it becomes too banal as to be disturbingly humorous."[65] "Chaplin's own music," predicted journalist Ivy Wilson Cable, "will be an outstanding feature of the film."[66] *Boxoffice* called it "a haunting musical score" and "a striking ballet,"[67] with the *Chicago Tribune* agreeing—"The music is appealing and well suited to the theme, and so is the ballet."[68] Virginia Graham in *The Spectator* said it was "not strikingly original music perhaps, but plucking effectively at the heartstrings at the appropriate times."[69] "Not the least of the film's assets is the melodic musical score," said *Harrison's Reports*.[70] The *New York Herald Tribune* said, "Its music seems to ache right along with the sensibilities of the characters."[71] The Toronto *Globe and Mail* called it "a rich, melodic score."[72] *Women's Wear Daily* said it was "a thematic obbligato to the action. While the basic motif of the music is reiterated with varied emphasis, it is continuously entrancing."[73]

"*Limelight* is a great tear-jerker," said C. Sharpless Hickman in *Music Journal*, "and its music pulls out all the old stops."

> This is the miracle of Chaplin…. He can produce a modern film masterpiece using a technique rusted by three decades of disuse, and he can wrap that product with ear-caressing loveliness in a musical tissue which would crumble in colder hands.
>
> For, just as the directorial technique of *Limelight* dates from the days of Chaplin's globe-girdling glory of the twenties, so does his music perfectly mirror the music which little ensembles used to grind out on the sets in silent days to set the mood for the actors in each dramatic sequence. It's that kind of music—a compendium of Tchaikovsky and Chopin and Debussy and Gershwin and the deep nocturnal blues…
>
> This is not a great score, but it is a great *film* score in the sense that it is peculiarly right for this great film. And this is, after all, the purpose of any motion picture music. To discuss it apart from the picture as a whole and at much greater length is really unfair. One might, with some justice, say

that the film could be discussed without reference to the music. And yet, recalling it, I cannot help but think that, had this been a silent picture, with all of Chaplin's spiritual homilies capsuled in titles as in the old days, one might logically have created in one's mind and heart music quite similar to this as an unconscious accompaniment.[74]

On August 4, Chaplin held a private preview of *Limelight* for two hundred people, including David Selznick, Humphrey Bogart, and Ronald Colman. "Dad was on edge with excitement, as he always was before previewing one of his pictures," said Charles Chaplin, Jr.

When the film ended he got up to make a short speech. He went only as far as the phrase, "I do want to say thank you…"

"No! No!" a woman in the audience suddenly cried out. "Thank you!"

"Thank you! Thank you!" the cry was taken up by everyone until the room rang. It was the last accolade my father was to hear in Hollywood. And it was such an electric demonstration that columnist Sidney Skolsky described it as "the most exciting night I had ever spent in a projection room."[75]

On September 17, Chaplin and his family left New York on the *Queen Elizabeth* for the London premiere of *Limelight*, to be attended by Noël Coward, Douglas Fairbanks, Jr., John Mills, and Princess Margaret as a charity benefit at the Odeon in Leicester Square.

Two days out at sea, Chaplin received word that U.S. Attorney General James P. McGranery had rescinded his re-entry permit, citing the U.S. Code of Laws on Aliens and Citizenship, Section 136, Paragraph (C), which permits the barring of aliens on grounds of "morals, health or insanity, or for advocating Communism or associating with Communist or pro–Communist organizations."[76] McGranery called Chaplin "an unsavory character"[77] with "an utter, contemptible disregard for the highest state of womanhood." Chaplin was charged with being a member of the Communist party "and with grave moral charges, and with making statements that would indicate a leering and sneering attitude towards a country whose hospitality has enriched him."[78] If he attempted to re-enter the U.S., McGranery ordered the Immigration and Naturalization Services to hold him for hearings, which "will determine whether he

On Chaplin's last day in Hollywood, David Raksin (right) visits his old employer and reminiscences about scoring *Modern Times* in that same projection room, c. September 5, 1952 (photograph by Francis O'Neill) (Photofest).

is admissible under the laws of the United States."[79] Bosley Crowther of *The New York Times* had lunch with Chaplin the day before he left and later reported, "He was under no evident strain."[80] David Raksin visited Chaplin at his studio that day as well. "How odd to think that I met Charlie on my first day in Hollywood," Raksin later remembered, "and I said goodbye to him on his last day there."[81]

*   *   *

"Chaplin has captured [a] quality of longing in *Limelight* and nothing else matters," said the *New York Herald Tribune*. "It whispers through the music; it passes across Chaplin's face in an emotional spectrum of variations; it creeps into the ballets and the tramp comedy routines, and it flows from the screen in the bittersweet contact between the audience and the drama. Chaplin was responsible for all this, and for plenty of things that are wrong with his film. But the sense of longing that he has established throughout *Limelight* hangs over the flaws like a luminous cloud of sympathetic genius, in a haunting movie experience."[82] The *Chicago Daily Tribune* found the film "deftly timed, warmly human, and engrossing, full of people as they are—weak and frightened, frantic or funny, desperate or delightful…. There are some weak spots, probably due to the fact that … such a one-man enterprise is highly subject to a lack of perspective. However, for the most part, it is intriguing entertainment."[83] "As a sheer revelation of the development of a great artist," said Bosley Crowther in *The New York Times*, "it deserves to be seen."[84]

Chaplin's issues with the Attorney General wreaked havoc with the film's distribution in the U.S. "There are hundreds of people in Hollywood, perhaps thousands" Hedda Hopper gloated in her column the day after McGranery's announcement, "stars, directors, producers, and all those wonderful people we call little people, workers behind the camera, electricians, cameramen, props—who are dancing in the street for joy…. I've known [Chaplin] for many years. I abhor what he stands for, while I admire his talents as an actor. I would like to say, 'Good riddance to bad company.'"[85] Popular radio commentator John Cameron Swayze was none too pleased to see Chaplin "blinking from a movie marquee" in the heart of Times Square. "Though it may be un–Christian, I do hope his limelight dims. He is perhaps my most 'unfavorite' person."[86]

Chaplin also was the focus of a resolution from the American Legion urging theater owners not to show any Chaplin films and for Legion members not to attend them until the matter of what author Charles Maland calls "Chaplin's political and moral fitness to return to the country" was cleared up.[87] The Legion was a powerful force in the country, numbering 2.5 million members and another million auxiliary members. The organization picketed *Limelight* in New York. On the West Coast, pressure from the Legion and the Motion Picture Alliance for the Preservation of American Ideals (and its president Ward Bond) prompted the film's cancellation at three Fox theaters in Los Angeles (Grauman's Chinese, the Downtown, and the El Rey). Howard Hughes, head of R.K.O.-Radio Pictures, wrote a letter to the Legion—"I have been making a most concerted effort to persuade the management of the theatre corporation to take the necessary legal measures to cancel all bookings of *Limelight*. It is my strongest hope and sincere belief that this will be done."[88] But not everyone bowed to the censorship.

D. M. Marshman Jr., Oscar-winning screenwriter of *Sunset Boulevard*, writing as "a lifelong Republican and a conservative Republican at that," expressed concern in a letter to the *Los Angeles Times* over "the pressure group activities of the American Legion." Though he found Chaplin "a pretty objectionable character all around," "what I find far more objectionable—and worrisome—is the fact that extra-legal threats by a private organization can now apparently determine what movies the pubic shall and shall not be allowed to see…. When it comes to movies—just as in the case of books or cars or soap or opinions—I prefer to do my own choosing in a free market, without interference from the American Legion or anyone else. And I think that most people feel as I do."[89] One of those people was Al Kvool, manager of the Warner Brothers Theatre in Milwaukee. Kvool refused the local Legion chapter's request to the delay the film, saying he did not believe "any one group had the right to act as a censor for the American people."[90] When Chaplin arrived in Rome for the Italian premiere, most of the people lining the street "cheered and applauded as the gray haired actor stepped from his car in front of the brilliantly lighted theater. But as he waved and smiled, apples, oranges, broccoli, and cabbages flew out of the crowd."[91]

Chaplin announced he wanted to have "six months of peace and quietness" in London. "We will not go in for big parties and large receptions, but keep to ourselves."[92] When it looked more certain that he would not return to the U.S., Chaplin was forced to move his fortune to Europe. As early as January 1951, Syd saw the writing on the wall and foreshadowed his brother's troubles with the re-entry permit. He also suggested Monte Carlo and Montreux, Switzerland, as possible locations to relocate, and provided information on Swiss bank accounts and how to keep the studio from being attached to any legal difficulties if Chaplin was not able to return to the U.S. When he was eventually locked out, Chaplin left the country with his affairs understandably not in order. Oona flew to New York on November 17 and then to Los Angeles on the 20th in the company of Arthur Kelly, spending two days to wrap up Chaplin's personal assets. She arrived back in London in November and the family traveled to Switzerland in the hopes of finding a new home and taking advantage of the country's generous tax laws.

In January 1953, Chaplin and his family moved into the Manoir de Ban in Corsier-sur-Vevey, an elegant villa on thirty-seven acres looking out over Lake Geneva. "I have been the object of vicious propaganda by powerful reactionary groups who, by their influence and by aid of America's yellow press, have created an unhealthy atmosphere in which liberal minded individuals can be singled out and persecuted," he explained. "Under these conditions I find it virtually impossible to continue my motion picture work, and I have therefore given up my residency in the United States."[93] On April 15, 1953, one day before his 64th birthday, Chaplin surrendered his re-entry permit. He lived out the rest of his life in his peaceful corner of the world, watched over by the majestic Swiss Alps, only returning to the U.S. once.

"I shall be glad when I can cut all my ties with the U.S.," Chaplin wrote Syd. "While I still have interests over there I am not completely relaxed—they are like the sinews of a cancer that eat into my concentration and until I can say goodbye and God damn them, I shall not completely enjoy the tranquility of Switzerland." In the fall of 1953, Chaplin put Syd and Wheeler Dryden in charge of shutting down and selling the studio and Chaplin's former home. "It is difficult, being so far away, to manage my affairs," Charlie wrote, "but it is nice that you are on the job. Thanks a lot, Syd."[94] There were letters and files dating back to the opening of the studio in 1918. "I opened one & the first letter I looked at was one from Professor Albert Einstein," Sydney wrote to Charlie. "So, I am having

Wheeler take out all the *personal* letter folders & put them together. I hope he will find nothing of an embarrassing nature in them, or anything bordering on the Kinsey report?" Syd was also appalled at the handling by the studio personnel. "The girls in the office were surprised when I told them your press clipping books were to be retained. If I had not mentioned it, I think they would have been thrown out. Good God! What do they think so much time was spent on these books for?"[95] Eventually Lois Runser, a legal secretary, took over the remainder of the sale of the studio and the close of the house, much to Syd's dismay.

Alistair Cooke explained that the situation surrounding Chaplin at the time was due to the common view he was "a vague nuisance, and a tiresome talking point among the noisy patriots who never felt that the government's 'loyalty' procedures proceeded far enough. Chaplin was all the more offensive in that he could never, after endless investigating, be pinned down as a criminal. He was turned in—by, we should remember, the Truman administration—as a useful sacrifice to the witches who were then supposed to be riding high exclusively on the broomstick of Senator Joseph McCarthy. The Chaplin expulsion was a squalid episode in a shabby period."[96]

But history has a way of smoothing out the political ruffles. As Andrew Sarris later said in *The Village Voice*, "The late Elmer Davis remarked at the time that the resourceful Attorney General would go way down in history as the man who kept Chaplin out of America. Davis was wrong. No one remembers J. P. McGranery, whose name I had to look up in a World Almanac."[97]

CHAPTER 10

Chaplin Charts

"**S**ome enterprising record company should be quick off the mark to record the theme of Chaplin's *Limelight*," *Melody Maker* pointed out shortly after the film's release. "This work ... possesses a haunting quality perfectly matched to the moving story content of the picture."[1] But months passed before anyone took notice.

In January 1952, Chaplin showed rough scenes of *Limelight* to Columbia Records president Goddard Lieberson. That was enough for Lieberson to pursue making an album with selections from the score, though, typically, the process was not a smooth one. Chaplin would not allow the use of the songs from the film's original soundtrack on the album (though he later recanted) and Lieberson did not think the record would sell without them. So he decided to fill the B-side with newly recorded cues from *City Lights*. Columbia would pay $84 per man to the American Federation of Musicians (AFM) based on the number of *Limelight* musicians used in the original recording, but the fee, approximately $5,000, would come from Chaplin's nine percent royalties. Columbia agreed to absorb the $2,000 for the *City Lights* cues. "It seems to me," Arthur Kelly wrote Chaplin, "you have to view this from the standpoint that it might help the picture publicity-wise, as I see little or no money from the royalties because it would take a sale of nearly 20,000 records to wipe off the production cost before you start to tap for your share."[2] Chaplin agreed to the fees, but he pointed out that he did not have the rights to use "La Violetera," the central theme of *City Lights*, so Columbia would be responsible for securing the proper permission to use the tune.

In the meantime, an illegal recording of *Limelight* appeared on the Durium label in Italy. On January 18, 1953, Italian pianist Luciano Sangiorgi played a piece entitled "Arlequinade," based on Chaplin's music, as part of his concert on Radio Audizioni Italiane (R.A.I.). The success of *Limelight* in Italian theaters "was considerably great." Sangiorgi was a Durium recording artist and the label received "many requests" for a record of the tune. "The fact that the music was already played in the radio broadcast gave us the feeling that the rights and everything connected with it was already granted," said a Durium rep, "which as a rule is so, with the exception of rare cases." Durium contacted the Edizioni Curci Milano, the major representative in Italy of American Editors, which was waiting for the *Limelight* music to arrive from New York. Because the original score was on its way Italy, Durium felt "the relative right had been granted for the Italian territory." The label gave notice to the B.I.E.M. (Bureau International de l'Edition Mécanique) to pay royalties, but Chaplin was not a member. Durium still felt they were "legally on the right side."[3]

The situation occasioned a flurry of letters back and forth between Italy and Chaplin's offices in the U.S. "Unless you have someone we can trust looking after the collection of these royalties," Arthur Kelly wrote to Chaplin, "there is a lot of gyping that goes on and Saul Bourne knows all the ropes and 'where the body is buried.'"

> He makes a definite statement that England is where he gets the most honest accounting, but in France and Italy and some other countries he is highly suspicious of the societies. Therefore he makes periodical trips and greases the palms of the right people to get a correct accounting. So I think probably the way we have engineered this we should leave well enough alone and let Bourne handle it and I will keep in touch with him from time to time.
>   In Italy it is important to be dealing with a publisher whom Bourne knows and who acts as Bourne's agent, as your music was never copyrighted and we will use the Italian publisher's sheet music and thus effect a copyright…
>   Curci Edizion [*sic*] has already been sent the score so they can start printing immediately.[4]

Louis Lober, vice president for United Artists, wrote to Kelly, "In view of the fact that Sig. Nicola di Pirro has requested us to help in this matter and he, as head of the entertainment and motion picture division of the Italian government was mainly responsible for the honors bestowed upon Charles Chaplin in Italy, I strongly recommend that this matter be settled immediately."[5] Kelly told Bourne to instruct his Italian agent to "deal very leniently" with Durium. "I am quite sure all the difficulties will be straightened out."[6]

Meanwhile, Columbia dragged their feet on the soundtrack album, due perhaps to Chaplin's political troubles, which also made it difficult to use American musicians while he was still in exile. By February 1953 the label had pulled out of the deal and it took another month before it even notified Chaplin of its decision. "It was with great regret that we had to give up the idea of releasing a sound track album of LIMELIGHT," wrote David Oppenheim, head of Columbia's Masterworks division. "Charming as the music is, it was impossible to make a convincing record from this material. We worked almost a whole day trying to find some way of doing the job, but were unsuccessful."[7]

Columbia brokered the original deal without the participation of Saul Bourne, who would have received none of the mechanical royalties as publisher had the soundtrack come to fruition. When that deal fell through, Bourne made sure he was involved in the new discussions with Arthur Kelly to make the album in the UK with Decca or the London Gramophone Company. "Mr. Chaplin is most anxious to get these recordings made quickly," Kelly wrote Bourne. "Therefore I would appreciate some quick action on this subject, unless you wish us to do the job."[8] But London Gramophone's U.S. arm was "rather scared that the American Legion will go after them," Kelly wrote to Chaplin, "or the retail stores selling the records, and if trouble was experienced from this quarter it would materially cut down the distribution of the records and might not warrant the re-recording fees payable to the A. F. of M. [American Federation of Musicians], etc., so they would want to eliminate U.S.A."[9]

Kelly instead sent to Decca London a tape Columbia made (but did not use) based on a print of the music Chaplin had in New York. "As far as we know here," Kelly said, "the tape is an actual re-recording from the print of the music track."[10] But there was trouble clearing the tapes through customs and Decca went ahead with a recording of "Terry's Theme" based on a musical arrangement that Kelly had already sent to London. As Kelly remarked, "A lot of money was wasted in making these re-recordings."[11]

On April 10, 1953, Chaplin registered the copyright for *Limelight*'s instrumental score and the three songs, plus "The Terry Theme" and the generically titled "The Theme from *Limelight*," alternate titles for "Terry's Theme." He also copyrighted "Eternally," the vocal version, and in January 1954 registered a piano solo version of the film's "Incidental Music." Given that few audiences even had the opportunity to see *Limelight*, there is no reason the score's primary theme should have registered as more than a blip on the radar of the record-buying public. But never deny the appeal of a good tune.

Cover arrangements have always been popular in the record industry. While one artist may "own" a particular rendition, the more recordings of a particular tune, the more royalties streaming in to the writers involved. Decca London was first out of the gate with its recording of "Terry's Theme," performed by Frank Chacksfield and his orchestra, a 40-piece ensemble that featured a large string section known as the "Singing Strings." *The Billboard* called Chacksfield's disc "a lovely instrumental put to a slick arrangement. At times subtle and with great sweep elsewhere, this stacks up as another instrumental that could happen."[12] The trade journal selected it as a "Best Buy" and it "got off to a very fast start." Within a week, interest in the tune was "running high," and, for the week ending May 23, it began to chart as a best-selling single at number nineteen.[13] The following week, it topped the charts in New York, while stations in Seattle and Philadelphia picked it up. Over the coming weeks, the disk registered in St. Louis, the Washington-Baltimore area, Detroit, Chicago, Denver, New Orleans, and Atlanta. The single finally charted on "Most Played by Disk Jockeys" for the week ending June 6 and on the jukebox chart the week after. It stayed strong in the top three throughout the summer in New York, but by the beginning of September it fell off the other major radio markets. Chacksfield's single moved up and down both the jukebox and disc jockeys charts, and it lasted a total of eleven weeks on the retail sales chart, topping at number six. Chacksfield was awarded a gold disc in the U.S. and in the UK, where it won him "Record of the Year" from the *New Musical Express*. "I am glad to say that Charlie liked it," Rachel Ford, Chaplin's business manager, later wrote to Bonnie Bourne of Chacksfield's recording, "incidentally, so did I."[14]

Word got out quickly and within one week of Chacksfield's recording, three different orchestral versions of "The Terry Theme" were released. Richard Hayman, best known as the principal arranger of the Boston Pops Orchestra, a position he held for over thirty years, had an arrangement on Mercury Records, which did "full justice to the beautiful melody," said *The Billboard*, which reviewed nearly every recording. "The strings bow it lushly in this dramatic reading. If tune builds as big as expected, there could be loot left over for this one, too." At the time, Hugo Winterhalter's rendition was "probably the most different in concept. There are plenty of strings as in the others, but on this a piano leads as if it were a concerto. Tempo is also slowed a bit. Power of Winterhalter as an artist should help make this a potent entry." The Victor Young Orchestra was "an outstanding version.... It's performed in lush, warm style ... with the fiddles stressing the lovely melody. Side is a mighty potent one, and should easily share some of the loot on the tune, which is already breaking for a big, big hit via [Chacksfield's] London version."[15]

The trade journal reported Wally Stott's rendition was "another tasteful version that lets the music sing for itself. If the tune builds as expected, there should be enough action left for this entry."[16] Jackie Gleason's orchestra gave "a smooth and warm instrumental performance. There are so many good versions of the tune now available, that this one will run into heavy competition. It should get a share of the loot, however."[17] "It's a tossup [*sic*] as to which version of this beautiful tune will come out on top," said *Daily Variety*.[18] The tune charted for a total of thirteen weeks before falling off the list of top twenty. Chacksfield's recording was number twenty-seven overall for the year in retail sales.

A comparison of Chacksfield and Hayman's recordings points up the different styles, plus the similarities that appealed to the early-1950s record-buying public. Chacksfield's arrangement follows closely the structure of Bourne's official piano solo that Arthur Kelly had sent to London, staying in the key of F major. Hayman's version provides more interesting harmonic progressions and modulations to break up the monotony of the single key structure. Hayman also gives the solo instruments more to do than Chacksfield's block sectional voicings, providing soaring countermelodies for the French horns in the theme's final statement. Both arrangements feature sweeping piano solos in the middle, a staple of 1950s easy listening instrumentation, and both arrangers take full advantage of the *rubati* (musical freedom) that Chaplin built into the tune.

Noro Morales had a gentle mambo version on RCA Victor, and there were waxings by Guy Lombardo (Decca), Ron Goodwin (Coral), and Melachrino (HMV). There were four recordings in Sweden, nine in France, and an astonishing twenty in Italy. United Artists' agent in Australia thought recordings of the music would not be profitable "for the simple reason the picture has already played its main accounts." Arthur Kelly shot off a terse note to Louis Lober at UA—"I would like your manager to explain to them that the picture has played throughout the principal key cities in the United States under severe adverse conditions and we have only just released the records of LIMELIGHT in America and it has taken the country by storm. As you know, there is an indefinite life in a Charlie Chaplin picture. Therefore I would like your manager to press this agent of Bourne, Inc. to get going on the records and the sale of the sheet music."[19] Bourne's sheet music for the tune charted at number fourteen for the week ending June 20, 1953, remaining on the charts the rest of the summer and peaking at number eight. For the week ending July 4, the tune topped the charts in England, where it stayed for nine weeks.

Frank Chacksfield also recorded the film's "Incidental Music," a medley consisting of the ballet intro, the Columbine waltz, and, oddly enough, the "Shack Waltz" from *Modern Times* that Chaplin inserted into the score. *The Billboard* raved, "Again a good Chacksfield arrangement."[20] Wally Stott's is the only other contemporary recording of the medley, perhaps because *The Billboard* accurately predicted, "Background music from the same pic could be programmed effectively, altho [*sic*] ["The Theme from *Limelight*"] has the bigger potential."[21]

With its melodramatic sweep, "The Terry Theme" is perfectly suited to instrumental arrangements. Over the years various Chet Atkins, Darius Brubeck, and easy listening artists such as André Kostelanetz, Stanley Black, LeRoy Holmes, the Living Strings, and Liberace have also recorded the tune. Mantovani released a record in Germany as did Acker Bilk, which became "one of the top instrumental hits" of 1963.[22] The music was even used illegally to accompany a play in Russia. "We were not aware that the Russians were using 'LIMELIGHT' music to accompany a play," Bonnie Bourne wrote Rachel Ford. "This, of course, is not with our permission and has been a major problem to cope with since they use all music without permission. This will be brought to the attention of our Legal Department so that the necessary action can be taken."[23]

"The Terry Theme," like most film music, was not written with radio play in mind.

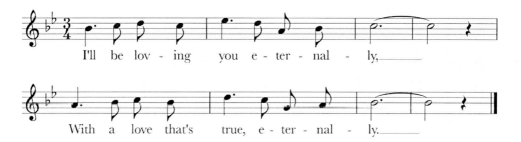

Limelight's "Terry's Theme" provides the opening notes of the chorus for "Eternally," 1953, music by Charles Chaplin, lyrics by Geoffrey Parsons.

There are few instances of film music themes cracking *Billboard*'s Top 20 up to that point. Anton Karas's "*The Third Man* Theme" had spent eleven weeks on the *Billboard* charts, peaking at number one in recordings by Karas and bandleader Guy Lombardo. In 1953, Mantovani had a number one hit with Georges Auric's *Moulin Rouge* theme, often beating Chaplin's tune on the charts. But most of the successful film music entries were conversions of themes into songs, such as Max Steiner's love theme from his Oscar-winning score for *Now, Voyager* ("It Can't Be Wrong"), or pre-existing songs like Herman Hupfeld's "As Time Goes By," which was written for the 1931 Broadway musical *Everybody's Welcome* and gained newfound life a decade later when Steiner featured it in his score for *Casablanca*. Chaplin's vocal version of "The Terry Theme"—"Eternally"—was also popular among vocal artists, though not to the extent of the instrumental version.

There are numerous poems and discarded lyrics penned by Chaplin among his papers, but he did not write the lyrics to "Eternally," perhaps due to the stress of being in exile. That exile also meant he was forced to utilize artists in the UK and "Eternally" featured lyrics by Brit Geoffrey Parsons, who would also co-write the words to Chaplin's "Smile" a year later. Parsons (1910–1987) worked at the London-based Peter Maurice Music Company, which managed Bourne's London arm and specialized in adapting foreign language songs into English. James Phillips, who wrote under the pseudonym John Turner (and would co-pen the lyrics to "Smile" with Parsons), was head of the company. Phillips would usually assign a song to Parsons and later suggest changes, thereby sharing credit for the lyrics.

Though it relies on standard ballad imagery, the lyric for "Eternally" uses a subtle internal rhyming scheme, especially when viewed in context of the music.

VERSE
Time will pass, I know,
Tides will ebb and will flow
Tho' the seas run dry,
Yet my love cannot die,
If there's one thing real
It's this love that I feel for you.

CHORUS
I'll be loving you eternally,
With a love that's true, eternally
From the start,
Within my heart,
It seems I've always known,
The sun would shine,
When you were mine
And mine alone.
I'll be loving you eternally,
There'll be no one new, my dear, for me.
Tho' the sky should fall,
Remember I shall always be
Forever true and loving you eternally.[24]

The quadruple time signature of the original theme is transposed to a more vocal-friendly 3/4 meter, a change that elongates the melodic structure, giving it a languid quality that is more properly suited for the human voice. Copies of the "Eternally" sheet music printed at the time also contained an introductory verse based on the "Awakening" theme from the *Limelight* score. Set in the somber key of B-flat minor, it is not surprising that vocalists decided to not perform the verse, and it was deleted from later printings of the sheet music. In the chorus, the word *eternally* is placed almost as an afterthought at the end of phrases, with the problematic *ee* sound bearing the weight of most of the held notes, and words such as *you, true, new* and *AL-ways* receive the ever-important top notes. Not until the final statement is *eternally* allowed the prominence that the title suggests. "Charlie said he would write a better lyric," Jerry Epstein told Arthur Kelly, who then questioned Saul Bourne about the commercial possibilities of such a proposal. "If you think there is a chance … I can get to the matter right away, and tell him to get working on a lyric."[25] If Chaplin took a stab at writing one, there is no evidence in the archive.

Many popular singers of the period recorded "Eternally." Dinah Shore relegated it to the B-side of "Blue Canary" on RCA Victor. Vic Damone on Mercury "belts it for all he's worth," said *The Billboard*.[26] "[He] turns in a tremendous performance … singing the sweeping ditty with all the stops pulled out. He is backed by the multi stringed Dick Hayman Ork in the grand style. With the tune now riding high via the instrumental versions, this is a potent hunk of wax that could bust thru [sic] as a big one."[27] The trade journal said of Jean Campbell's rendition on the Coral label, "A new English thrush impresses with her vocal ability on this fine reading…. Gal has some of the Vera Lynn quality which should make for wide appeal. She should get some of the action on the tune."[28] Over the years, Steve Lawrence, Engelbert Humperdinck, Jerry Vale, Petula Clark, and Plácido Domingo recorded the song. One of the finest renditions is Sarah Vaughan's 1960 recording. Released on the B-side of "You're My Baby," *The Billboard* claimed Vaughan "score[d]" with "a beautifully handled waxing."[29]

"Eternally" has not weathered the years to the same extent as other Chaplin songs, but the theme's success at the time—both instrumentally and vocally—set the stage for Chaplin's most lasting musical success, one based on a melody nearly twenty years old.

*   *   *

In 1954, there were plans to reissue *Limelight* in New York and other key cities. The film's music was a success, but Los Angeles was still missing from the list of cities, thanks to the objections of Charles P. Scours, the president of National Theatres, and its subsidiary, Fox West Coast Theatres. *Variety* reported that Arthur Kelly "believes the film's value has been considerably enhanced by the wide play given by the pic's music (especially 'Terry's Theme') and that much of this extra plus hadn't been a factor at the time of the initial release."[30] *Backstage* noted, "From *Limelight* the public walked away humming a musical theme and created the demand that made 'Eternally' one of the biggest hits of modern times. The Peter Maurice Music Company, inspired by this to explore to the full the potentialities of Charlie Chaplin as a popular composer, examined earlier Chaplin scores. And in his *Modern Times* soundtrack they discovered the simple theme that became another winner, 'Smile.'"[31]

Limelight conductor Keith Williams claimed he persuaded Chaplin to let him extract the "Smile" theme from *Modern Times* and got paid $85, though there is no record of this in the Chaplin Archive. Documentation does exist of a *Modern Times* screening in February 1954 for Saul Bourne and members of his staff. Chaplin planned on reissuing the film later in the year, and the Bourne group watched "with the idea of our trying to find a Theme Melody for a song, a possible song like 'ETERNALLY' or a possible instrumental composition like 'THE TERRY THEME.' We think there is a musical strain which might be desirable—there may be one or two other possibilities in that musical score."[32] "Bourne and his associates have picked out of MODERN TIMES score a theme which they believe could be made quite popular and could be called 'The MODERN TIMES Theme,'" Kelly wrote Chaplin.

> They think this theme lends itself to a lyric and after you have heard the record, if you wish to contribute a lyric, Bourne would greatly appreciate it…
>
> Bourne seems quite enthusiastic about it but I still don't think it would be as popular as the Terry Theme, but I could be completely wrong. However, as long as they are willing to go to the expense of launching the theme in published sheet music and records, I think we should not discourage them. As a matter of fact, the Paris office of United Artists has been asking whether we could dig out a theme from MODERN TIMES as they believe it would help the success of the picture considerably.[33]

Bourne recorded a piano version of the theme and once again began discussions with Decca London and the London Gramophone Company to record an instrumental version. But, as Chaplin wrote to Arthur Kelly, he had no intention of doing anything with the music from *Modern Times* because "the royalties, so far, on LIMELIGHT music are not satisfactory, to my mind."[34] Bourne drew up a contract regardless, giving Chaplin "the same royalty rates as received by the top composers of the country, which is 4¢ royalty per copy and 50% of mechanical revenue for the lyrics and the music—there are no lyrics at the present time. If the composition is published and mechanically reproduced as an instrumental composition, Chaplin is to receive the full 4¢ and 50%—if a lyric is written by any other than Chaplin, then the 4¢ and 50% is to be divided equally. Of course, Chaplin will receive his writers' performing fees through his membership in the English performing rights society."[35] But Kelly thought it was "premature to have our lawyers draw up a contract for MODERN TIMES until we can satisfy Mr. Chaplin about the delay in receiving statements and payments from the European countries where he hears the LIMELIGHT music and song more often than any other music or song."[36]

Over the next two months, Kelly ironed out the difficulties with the *Limelight* royalties and Bourne once again contracted Geoffrey Parsons to write a lyric, this time co-authored by John Turner. In May, Bourne and his wife traveled to Vevey to play for Chaplin the *Modern Times* theme with lyrics, now named "Smile," and to finalize the terms and conditions of the publishing rights. "As you probably know," Kelly wrote Chaplin, "we got a favorable [rate] with [Bourne] on the contract, the usual charges being 50%. I negotiated the contract and made him pay us 57% on *Limelight*. As I have told you before, he was trying to effect an adjustment which we have not granted. Therefore it's up to you to decide whether or not the conditions on *Modern Times* music will be the same as *Limelight*. I see no reason why they should be. There is approximately $14,000 due us from this firm which he has authorised the payment of and since he is in Paris he has collected a sizable sum on the background music royalties from the French Society."[37]

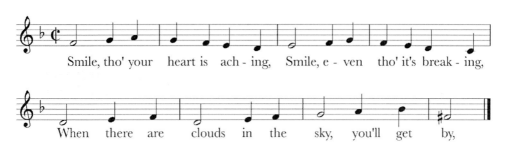

The *Modern Times* love theme was pulled out of obscurity for the classic "Smile" (1954), music by Charles Chaplin, lyrics by Geoffrey Parsons and John Turner.

It is hard not to equate the imagery evoked by the Parsons and Turner's lyric with screen images from Chaplin's films and events from his life. Since the song entered its status as a pop standard, "Smile" has become the equivalent of Chaplin's philosophy set to music.

> *Smile, tho' your heart is aching,*
> *Smile, even tho' it's breaking,*
> *When there are clouds in the sky, you'll get by,*
> *If you smile through your fear and sorrow,*
> *Smile and maybe tomorrow,*
> *You'll see the sun come shining thru for you.*
> *Light up your face with gladness,*
> *Hide ev'ry trace of sadness.*
> *Altho' a tear may be ever so near,*
> *That's the time you must keep on trying,*
> *Smile, what's the use of crying,*
> *You'll find that life is still worthwhile,*
> *If you'll just smile.*[38]

The melody for "Smile" is so ingrained in popular culture that its scarcity within the *Modern Times* score may come as a shock to first-time viewers expecting a more prominent theme. So how does a song written in the key of F major sound so poignant? Only two notes in the entire melody are chromaticized. Everything else falls within the F-major diatonic scale, leaving it up to the chord progressions to tug at the heartstrings. A series of minor, diminished, seventh, and ninth chords create harmonic instability, making the final resolution of "You'll find that life is still worthwhile, / If you'll just smile" that much more touching.

By September there were a number of recordings of both "Smile" and the instrumental version. Frank Chacksfield, Ron Goodwin, and the Melachrino Orchestra returned to Chaplin territory and Joe Henderson recorded a piano rendition. "Here is the lovely theme from the old Chaplin flick, 'Modern Times,' beautifully played by the sweet-stringed Chacksfield crew," *Billboard* said earlier that summer. "The tune's closeness to 'Limelight' could help it grab scores of jock spins and juke plays. Watch this one; it could go."[39] Duke Ellington's "pretty version of the Chaplin tune [is] starting to make noise," said the trade journal, "with Duke featured on piano and other soloists getting a chance, too. The ork plays it with sparkle and this disk could grab spins and some of the coins."[40] There were eight additional recordings in France, including one by Raymond Siozade, "a young and very good accordionist."[41] Unlike *Limelight*, the vocal version was more popular this time, with Nat "King" Cole's version leading the way.

Cole's rendition on Capitol Records became an immediate hit in 1954, peaking at #10 in September, while Sunny Gale's version on RCA topped out at #19 the following month. *Billboard*'s review of Cole's single said, "Dulcet-toned is this lovely reading of the pretty tune."[42] The trade journal said Gale's record "should kick up quite a fuss. The tune is ultra-lovely and Miss Gale does a nice job which should get her a share of the action which seems to be accruing for the tune. Good wax here."[43] The arrangements for the two singles have set the tone for other renditions of the song for sixty years.

Master orchestrator Nelson Riddle arranged Cole's version and established the standard for every recording to come after it. Cole's distinctive vocals float above a pillowy bed of string chords, while flute glissandi, a tinkling piano solo, and somber trombone tones fill the void during the vocal rests. Even during the instrumental break, Riddle keeps the orchestra in check, never allowing the tune to slip into bathos. His typically refined orchestration brings a note of class to the song without swamping it in syrupy strings, an unfortunate hallmark of many later arrangements. Sunny Gale's rendition is slightly faster than Cole's and the bright, clear timbre of her voice hides any "trace of sadness" in the melodic line. The inclusion of a chorus in the arrangement gives heft to the song, though most artists prefer Cole's more intimate solo voicing. British tenor David Whitfield's record was decidedly odd. His crisp diction and rolled R's focus the attention more on his quasi-operatic vocal inflections than the poignancy of the song. Later versions also charted, including renditions by Tony Bennett (#73) in 1959, Timi Yuro (#42) in 1961, dual pianists Ferrante and Teicher (#73) in 1962, and Betty Everett and Jerry Butler (#42) in 1965. In the UK, Lita Rozs and Petula Clark released rival versions of the song, and Clark later re-recorded it for her 1968 album *The Other Man's Grass Is Always Greener*, by which time she had become friends with Chaplin. Natalie Cole also included the song on her 1991 GRAMMY Award-winning tribute album to her father, *Unforgettable...with Love*.

In 1963, Bourne also arranged the Gershwinesque "Allegro" theme from *Modern Times* (first heard when the Tramp works for the ship builder) and created a new recording called "In the City." Chaplin, however, was not impressed. "Charlie listened to your recording 'In the City,'" Rachel Ford wrote to Bonnie Bourne. "He only just recognised his melody—the rest of us not at all—and I consider myself familiar with the MODERN TIMES music. Charlie does not want you to use it, though I pointed out to him that the more dreadful it sounded to our elderly ears, the better it would sound to the younger generation."[44] Bourne had wanted to include the melody on an album of Chaplin's music. "I am sorry that Charlie does not want this used and that he felt it sounded dreadful to his ears," Bourne replied to Ford. "Of course, if Charlie would like to improve upon the melody as submitted to him, that would be fine. It is important for me to know as soon as possible, if Charlie would like us to edit any of the themes from the scores and submit to him for his approval so as to have the necessary material available for the L.P. if we are to go ahead with this project."[45] As with most album projects related to Chaplin, compilation or otherwise, this too fell through.

In the summer of 1958, the Chaplin office discovered a song titled "The Secret of Happiness," written by Hoyt Curtin and recorded by Dinah Shore that "appeared to have a melody substantially the same as your melody 'Smile.'"[46] The song was published in New York by Manchester Music, Inc. and Essex Music Ltd. in London. Chaplin's attorneys in both cities took immediate steps to stop the exploitation of the song, which certainly bears more than a passing resemblance to Chaplin's classic tune. The publishers verbally agreed and the process took over six months of negotiating before they wisely ceded their copyrights.

"Smile" has become a bona fide standard, recorded by nearly every major recording artist of the 20th century and many beyond. ASCAP's repertory listing includes over 150 artists, everyone from Judy Garland, Barbra Streisand, and Donna Summer to Michael Bublé, Johnny Mathis, and Perry Como. Jerry Lewis also opened and closed his ABC variety show with the song. Renditions of the song were recorded by artists in nearly every genre—pop (Céline Dion, Trini Lopez), rock (Eric Clapton), R&B (Stevie Wonder, Diana Ross), jazz (Sun Ra, Chick Corea), Latin (Luis Miguel), folk (Rickie Lee Jones, Lyle Lovett), gospel (Clara Ward), and opera (Plácido Domingo, Julia Migenes). Robert Downey, Jr., who earned an Academy Award nomination for his starring role in Richard Attenborough's 1991 Chaplin biopic, recorded a contemporary rendition of the song for the soundtrack and later included an acoustic version on his 2004 album, *The Futurist*.

On July 7, 2009, the song took center stage before a worldwide audience. Set against banks of flowers and a stadium full of grieving family and friends at the Staples Center in Los Angeles, Jermaine Jackson performed a moving musical tribute to the "King of Pop" at Michael Jackson's memorial service. Backed by a symphony orchestra and sporting Michael's signature sequined glove, Jermaine's plaintive, quavering voice gave a poignant rendering of "Smile," Michael's favorite song. Michael had released it on his 1995 double album *HIStory: Past, Present and Future, Book I*, and perhaps no song in Jackson's catalog better captured the singer's inexhaustible sense of optimism through fear and sorrow. The enduring popularity of "Smile," with its simple, heartbreaking melody and unassuming lyrics, continues to inspire artists and touch generations of music lovers to this day.

Parsons and Turner would add lyrics to one more Chaplin tune. But except for one occasion in the final years of his life, Chaplin would never again allow someone else to write English lyrics to his music while he was still alive. While he reaped great financial rewards from his *Limelight* and *Modern Times* music, his biggest musical hit was still over a decade away. In the meantime, Chaplin's next musical outing did not fare as well.

CHAPTER 11

Now That It's Ended

CHAPLIN WROTE JAMES AGEE in December 1956: "I am so glad to be out of that stink-pot country of yours. To be over here, away from that torrid atmosphere, is like stepping out of the death house into the dree sunlight.... But seriously, we are very comfortable and happy living in Switzerland.... Strangely enough, I am not the lest [*sic*] bit bitter, neither is Oona and she is most sincere in her liking for Switzerland. As for my work, naturally I have had many distractions. It took me about a year to rearrange my life and we are just about getting it into shape. Nevertheless, I have written about 80 pages of the new script and made lots of notes. It is a story about an exiled King and will give me an opportunity to comment on current events."[1] The new film, called *The Ex-King*, was announced in 1954. Living in Switzerland, there were plenty of displaced monarchs to provide inspiration, but no doubt Chaplin himself proved to be his greatest muse. Chaplin wrote Sydney, "It will afford me lots of opportunities for satire and comedy etc. It will also have a great deal of music in it and perhaps I might go in for a little colour."[2] The retitled *A King in New York* was Chaplin's most divisive film yet.

When Chaplin chose not to return to the U.S., everything about his filmmaking changed. No longer could he call on the repertory group of actors and technicians that he relied on in Hollywood. Gone was the security of friends and contacts he made in nearly forty years of working in the industry. David Robinson rightly points out Chaplin "needed courage to undertake such a film at a time when most men would already have retired, in conditions which were quite new to him and far less favorable than the working situation he had known for the past forty years."

> He was no longer master of his own studio with familiar craftsmen, who knew his whims, on call. The only official member of the unit who had known the Hollywood studio was [Jerry] Epstein. There were no longer the relaxed script conferences with the opportunities they provided to test ideas on trusted colleagues. Certainly, there was no longer the luxury of time to stop and reflect, and try scenes over again, some different way. High studio rents, production costs and union crewing requirements necessitated a tight schedule.[3]

"The spring and summer of 1956 were very cold (it actually snowed one day in July)," Epstein remembered, "and Shepperton Studios seemed even colder. *Limelight* had been such a happy experience; with *A King in New York*, the atmosphere was frosty and strained. There seemed to be no heart at Shepperton. We felt we were *all* in exile."[4] Without the pool of Hollywood musicians, even the *sound* of his films changed. Working with primarily British musicians, and the occasional Russian émigré added to the mix, a new style of music emerged, more international in flavor with performance practices and a timbre that sometimes sounded far removed from the smooth polish of American studio musicians. "I had to get used to a new crew, different methods of work, but there were advantages," Chaplin said, "not the least that it cost 25 percent less." The British technicians are "slower, but more thorough."[5] Chaplin spent three months from August through October in Paris recording, editing, and dubbing the film.

A King in New York, while ostensibly a comedy, takes pointed jabs at the American way of life, skewering fame, plastic surgery, advertising, television, and rock and roll. Chaplin plays King Shahdov, a monarch who flees to the U.S. from his fictional European country after revolution breaks out. His financial advisor absconds with the royal funds, and Shahdov is forced to peddle whiskey on television to make money before he is brought before Congress to answer charges of being a communist. The film's most controversial aspect was the scenes involving Chaplin's son Michael as a schoolboy attacking McCarthyism and spouting Marxist diatribes.

A King in New York premiered September 12, 1957, at the Leicester Square Theatre in London in a charity benefit for The National Fund for Poliomyelitis Research and the Three Roses Society for Mentally Handicapped Children. Many reviewers referred to Chaplin's "outsize chip on his shoulder."[6] The *Daily Mail* called it "a lumpish mixture of subtle slapstick and clumsy political satire…. In comic dumb show Chaplin still has no equal, but serious words render him so inarticulate that I came away yesterday cursing the invention of the talkies."[7] *The Manchester Guardian* said the film "seems to be the rather confused protest of a man who is not bitter or angry, but hurt. There are enough dazzling flashes of the old genius to make it worth two hours of any cinema-goer's time, but there are also longish patches which are quite embarrassing."[8] *The Daily Telegraph* agreed, saying the film was "tendentious, wordy and (by his own standards) very funny only in patches."[9] "[Chaplin's] spleen against America since he left it five years ago," said Donald Gomery of the *London Daily Express*, "now overstays him into losing his sense of fun as he scurries around with a sledge hammer to crush a nut of 'persecution.' But most important of all is his handling of that small boy. Chaplin attacks the Americans for (allegedly) using a child for political purposes. Yet in the film he is using his own child—to attack America. No, Mr. Chaplin, this is not fair. It is easy to comment, 'I fully endorse everything I have said in this film.' But is it right to spit through the mouth of a child?"[10] The young actor took it all in stride. "It was wonderful," Michael said about the experience of shouting at his father on screen. "Ordinarily I can never be rude to father. If I am, he stops my four Swiss frances [*sic*] allowance."[11]

Other critics provided a more balanced viewpoint. "Chaplin's new film is not more political-looking than a plant grown in clay or sand or fibre looks clayey or sandy or fibrous, or reflects (except to a determinedly horticultural eye) the sort of manuring it has had," said *The Spectator*. "It is a highly personal film, with the intensity and the limitations that involves…. *A King in New York* is not, to my mind, a success. But the failures of a great artist are worth a hundred mediocre successes: you do not measure them with the same yardstick at all."[12] John Osborne in the *Evening Standard* called it "a calculated, passionate rage clenched uncomfortably into the kindness of an astonishing comic personality. Like the king in his film, [Chaplin] has shaken the dust of the United States from his feet, and now he has turned round to kick it carefully and deliberately in their faces. Some of it is well aimed—some is not."[13] Kenneth Tynan, who disliked the film overall, said, "The curious thing about the new Chaplin film is that it is never boring. It is seldom funny, sometimes hysterical and almost always predictable: but it is never boring…. The result, in the fullest sense of the phrase, is 'free cinema,' in which anything, within the limits of censorship, can happen. In every shot Chaplin speaks his mind. It is not a very subtle mind; but its naked outspokenness is something rare, if not unique, in the English-speaking cinema. A crude free film is preferable, any day, to a smooth fettered one."

"I am not a politician," Chaplin said in the *Daily Mail*. "I am an entertainer…. I can't understand why everybody should get excited because I'm now poking fun at a way of life and big business. They are not sacred."[14] In his interview at a Foreign Press Association luncheon prior to the regular Paris premiere, Chaplin said, "I love America even now. I disagree with reviews which said it was anti–American. I made it for laughter. I am not Russian. I am not pro–Communist. I'm no Communist, no Socialist. I never read Marx in my life. I am a citizen of the world."[15] He reaffirmed his love for his former adopted country but dodged questions about his return to the U.S. "I do resent the way I've been treated. I don't like being kicked around."[16]

Chaplin told the London *Daily Sketch*, "I'm not interested in the U.S. anymore. I don't know and I don't care whether my latest film will be shown there. But I don't want the Americans to see it."[17] He received a couple of offers from independent distributors but he knew the U.S. box office "could only equal peanuts."[18] (The film did not get a U.S. screening until 1974.) Many American reviewers not only made sure they found a way to see it, they took it as a personal affront to their way of life. *Variety* said Chaplin "is obviously more interested in hammering home his message, which is a straightforward, unsubtle tirade against some obvious aspects of the American way of life."[19] "Here is a film," said *The Atlanta Constitution*, "whose message [is] carved with a meat ax, a message that America is today the land of the mean and the home of the hysteria. Ironically, he has ended up doing an unintended service to America…. He has set off the most warm-hearted chain of pro–American press comment since the United States went to the defense of Korea seven years ago."[20] "Those who expected a vitriolic attack on America will be disappointed," countered *Picturegoer*. "Only Chaplin could tilt at the absurdities in TV advertising, high-paced American living so devastatingly—but it's satire without malice."[21] *The Christian Science Monitor*, however, said, "Behind this film of Mr. Chaplin's, I could sense only an excited dislike of a country which has, after all, made both his fame and his fortune. I shall forget it as soon as possible."[22]

The version shown in Jerusalem underwent "an operation that is even more thorough than the king's facelifting [in the film]," said *The Jerusalem Post*. "Objectionable political material has been deleted to such an extent that … what finally remained is far more a satire about television than about 'commie' witch-hunting which, as everyone agreed in the end, is just 'a passing fad' in the States."[23] Hedda Hopper was her typically snide self— "The picture won't be seen here [in the U.S.]—and, as Chaplin has shown his true colors, England feels as we do about him. But Russia will love it. I wonder if he's learned to speak Russian so he can do it in their language."[24]

*   *   *

Except for *Limelight*, music plays a more obvious role in *A King in New York* than in earlier Chaplin dialogue films. He said he planned the film as "more or less a musical."[25] But there is no indication in Chaplin documents that the songs were ever meant to function like in a traditional musical to illuminate characters or advance the plot. Instead, the songs offer pointed commentary on the American popular music scene and are primarily played as source cues in nightclubs. And, as with *Limelight*, many of the songs had to be recorded prior to filming. "Weeping Willows," the song that occupies the most screen time, went through many changes—and many singers—before Chaplin made up his mind about what he wanted.

> *I've got the weeping willows*
> *And I'm stepping through plate windows*
> *On account of you*
> *Oh my love what shall I do*
> *What shall I do?*
> *I love you so and yet I know*
> *You can't be true*
> *If I only had the will to get away*
> *But you have me in a spell*
> *Both night and day*
> *You have me in your power*
> *Every moment, every hour*
> *Leave me now or let me go*
> *Why, oh why torment me so—*
> *I despise you, idolize you*
> *Adore you, implore you*
> *Let me be free from your tyranny of love*
> *I'm stepping through plate windows*
> *Over you.*[26]

Chaplin hired British crooner Michael Holliday to sing the gentle loping blues number for £50. According to news reports, at the recording sessions on July 17 and 18, 1956, Holliday sang the song "slow and relaxed," but an executive told him, "I'm afraid Mr. Chaplin won't like that. He visualizes something more in the style of Johnnie Ray." Holliday protested, "Afraid I can't sing it that way. Not my style." "Sing it your way, then," said the executive. "But he won't like it." When Chaplin came to the set and heard Holliday singing, he exclaimed, "Wonderful!" "The way he carried on," Holliday said, "made me feel I was the greatest singer alive and I was quite embarrassed." Chaplin told him he felt like he had discovered him. "I reckon he'd never heard of me before," Holliday said.[27] Chaplin wanted the singer to appear on screen but Holliday's ten-week Variety contract prevented it.[28]

American-born Eddie Constantine was also brought on board to record the song. Édith Piaf had discovered Constantine singing in a Paris cabaret and cast him alongside her in the 1951 musical *La Petite Lili*, and he, in turn, helped her with the English lyrics for her 1956 album *La Vie en Rose—Édith Piaf Sings In English*. There is little information on Constantine's work on the film, other than a note from Rachel Ford to Saul Bourne ("Can his recording be used for a record?"), indicating there was interest in the recording. In the meantime, Jimmy Phillips, managing director of Peter Maurice Music Co., tried to convince Chaplin to sing the song. But, Ford said, he initially did not want to do it "as he was afraid that future buyers of the record would expect to see him singing in the film."[29] Chaplin sang his version, like Holliday's, "slow and relaxed."[30]

Written in the odd key of B-flat minor, there are two separate orchestrations for the song in the Chaplin Archive—one for four saxophones, four trombones, piano, guitar, bass, and percussion; and another featuring a more typical orchestral complement of strings, woodwinds, a pair of French horns, and guitar. Neither of these appears in the film. What is missing is the onscreen orchestration—a clarinet mimicking the vocal line, simple piano chords, and light percussion to keep the rhythm. This brief vocal bit is part of the musical voiceover during the New York montage as Shahdov and Jaume (Oliver Johnston) try to navigate the crushing throng of the clogged Manhattan sidewalks. Originally, the clip was longer but was edited out in 1973 for the U.S. release. Also missing from that release was more of the same vocal cue in a scene with Shahdov and Jaume coming out of the movie theater. In a neat bit of cinematic synchronicity, the film on the marquee is *The Baby and the Battleship*, directed by, of all people, Richard Attenborough. As the two men leave the theater, "Weeping Willows" restarts mid-phrase abruptly, as if the music was part of the city's cacophony and could only be heard outside on the street.

The song instead becomes Rupert's sad instrumental theme when Shahdov discovers the boy roaming the snow-swept streets. But the theme gains further poignancy underscoring a tearful Rupert watching his parents exposed as Communists on television and in the scene when Shahdov says goodbye to the boy after he has named names to save his family, an action that makes him a "hero and a true patriot"—so say the adults. "Weeping Willows" is the only song melody that appears as part of the instrumental score. But nearly every song in the film is truncated from its original length.

For instance, the first song, "Million Dollars," is only heard in one brief snippet on the city streets, just prior to "Weeping Willows":

> *When I think of a million dollars*
> *Tears come to my eyes*
> *I think of all the blue birds*
> *And a thousand rainbow skies*
> *Some folks cry for the heart of a rose*
> *Some for the morning dew*
> *But to think of a million dollars*
> *Makes me sigh and cry for you.*[31]

The song, scored for a simple ensemble of strings and harp, stops short of the end of the third line on the word "blue." In the cut scene of Shahdov and Jaume exiting the movie theater, the official cue sheet indicates another reprise of the song, one assumes in a continuation from where the vocal left off, much as Chaplin did with the substitution of "Weeping Willows."

A King in New York (1957)—**The chorus of "Weeping Willows," which was severely edited for the 1973 US release of the film.**

When Shahdov and Jaume walk into the movie theater, a big band blares from the stage what Chaplin simply named "Rock & Roll."

I got shoes, I got shoes
Shoes to step on all yer blues
When you do that rock and roll with me tonight.

Hold me tight. Baby you're right
If you hold me tight
When you do that rock and roll with me tonight.

I got pep. You got pep
Dynamite when two get pep
Two can do that rock and roll all night through

You're not well. Take a pill
Don't take one that will make you ill
If you do you'll rock and roll the whole night through

EXTRA VERSE
Hold me tight.
Let me go
Not too fast and not too slow
When you do that rock and roll tonight.[32]

British singer and actor Gary Miller was hired to sing the song at a fee of £25 at each of two recording sessions on January 29 and 30. The song is scored for a quartet each of saxophones, trumpets, and trombones, plus piano, guitar, bass, and drum set. There is no onscreen singer, and the microphone stands empty, even though there are scores of screaming teeny boppers dancing and fainting in the aisles. What is Chaplin trying to say with that visual? That rock and roll vocalists are interchangeable, nameless, faceless? That they are dispensable when the sound blaring from the stage sets the girls in the audience spinning? Chaplin makes no indication in the script and it hardly seems an oversight.

"I'd Sell My Soul for Love" first appears as an instrumental when Queen Irene (Maxine Audley) visits Shahdov in his hotel room. The lush strings of the melody give every indication of a love theme. But Chaplin uses the lyrics ironically.

I'd sell my soul for love
If I could find true love
There's nothing in the world
I wouldn't do
I'd commit every sin
If I could win
Someone that's tender and true

Like Faust I'd sign away my soul
If I could say
I'd found the one
The only one
To love, to love
I'd sell my soul for love.[33]

The *a capella* vocal track reappears three cues later as Shahdov hears Ann (Dawn Addams) warbling on the other side of his bathroom door and sees her singing naked in her bathtub through the keyhole. Shirley Norman, a singer with the Eric Winstone Orchestra, provided the vocals. In the first scene with Irene, Chaplin provides subtle musical hints that Shahdov indeed sold his soul for love, though the audience cannot know that without the

A King in New York (1957)—Ann sings an *a cappella* version of "I'd Sell My Soul for Love" in the bathtub.

lyrics. Ann's version, again, describes her Faustian bargain to lure Shahdov onto her live television show at the dinner party, though this too is foreshadowing.

Many of the cuts for the U.S. release affected bits and pieces of Chaplin's music. Perhaps the most egregious cut was the elimination of the entire "Juke Box" number. After Shahdov discovers he embarrassed himself in front of millions of viewers on live television, he and Jaume go to a nightclub. In the edited version of the film, the opening stinger note of "Juke Box" is still there to transition to the club, but the scene cuts abruptly to the number's instrumental break with the club patrons heading to the dance floor. Chaplin approved the deletion of the number for the U.S. print because the number sounded dated for audiences in the 1970s. But Shani Wallis's energetic screen performance went with it, though you can see her head bobbing briefly on the far right of the screen at the cut. Chaplin saw the 22-year-old Wallis, who would become best known for her performance of Nancy in the 1968 film version of *Oliver!*, playing Aladdin at the Golders Green Hippodrome. Before she began filming, Wallis told him she wanted to have plastic surgery on her nose. Chaplin quickly talked her out of his, saying "it would spoil her appealing face."[34]

I've gotta [sic] Juke Box	*With a hey, hey, hey*
A swell looking juke	*And have folks say*
Where the music goes round and around	*There's the kind of chicken*
Pa owns a drug store where you can dance	*That's going my way*
Where the customers jive and dig a hole in the ground	*Oh don't let that music go down*
And to hear that music playing	*If you do this hot babe*
You'll hear this daughter saying	*Will leave town*
	Mister won't you hurry
Mister won't you hurry	*And get out your money*
And get out your money	*Put a nickel in the slot*
Put nickel in the slot	*I'm getting hot*
I'm getting hot	*And when I get hot it means a lot*
I want to cut a rug	*So honey where's your money*
Right down Broadway	*And don't let that music go down.*[35]

A nightclub arrangement written in C major and scored for clarinet, tenor saxophone, trumpet, trombone, piano, bass, and drums was written, but Chaplin preferred an "orchestra" version beginning in the key of F minor and modulating to A-flat major. The conductor's score has a notation to lower "all down" a half-step to E minor and G major, no doubt to accommodate Wallis. Scored for two flutes, oboe, four clarinets (including bass), three trumpets and trombones, strings, piano, harp, guitar, and percussion, the song swings along, like "Weeping Willows," with a series of dotted rhythms, albeit in a far more robust tempo. There were reports that Chaplin wrote two "jive songs" for Wallis. "And Chaplin tunes in a Chaplin film have a habit of becoming hits. So Shani may be lucky," said *The Age*.[36] Alas, that was not to be.

"Spring's the Time for Making Love" accompanies the scene of Ann taking photos of Shahdov for his whiskey ad campaign.

A King in New York (1957)—Like many other songs in the film, Chaplin uses "Spring's the Time for Making Love" ironically as Ann pursues Shahdov during their photo shoot.

> *Spring's the time for making love*
> *When the skies are blue above*
> *Spring, oh Spring, eternal Spring,*
> *Of thee I sing—for I'm in love.*
> *Oh don't lose time but fall in love*
> *While the skies are blue above*
> *Time flies by—don't live to sigh,*
> *But fall in love—in love.*[37]

Like the other vocalists, Bobby Britton earned £25 per day (£50 total) to record the song at the January 25 and 29, 1957, recording sessions.[38] Titled "Ciel Etoile" ("Starry Sky") on the actual manuscript, the song, orchestrated for oboe, a pair of clarinets and bassoons, strings, and harp, vocally ends after the fourth line and the orchestra takes over in the lush arrangement under the rest of Shahdov and Ann's dialogue. Though Ann is obviously flirting with him, the lyrics, with Chaplin once again harping on the well-worn seasonal aspect of falling in love, serve as ironic counterpoint to Shahdov's feelings about her—"You're nothing but a delusion and a snare." A full-blown orchestral rendition of the melody accompanies the final scene as Shahdov flies over New York. Here, Chaplin offers the tune almost as a poignant goodbye to his once-adopted country and perhaps an apology for many of the potshots he took at it throughout the film.

The final song is the only occasion in which one of the vocalists appears on screen, at least in the standard cut version. "Now That It's Ended" serves as the nightclub performance when Ann takes Shahdov out on the town following his disastrous plastic surgery. Australian-born Joy Nichols was starring in *The Pajama Game* in London when Chaplin hired her to sing the song, at the standard rate of £50. "Here I am looking all over the world for the girl I want," Chaplin said, "and a casual visit to the theatre produces her for me."[39] *The Age* called the song "the bluest of blue numbers."[40] And blue it is.

> *Now that it's ended*
> *The romance is over*
> *The passions gone*
> *Like the wind and the rain*
> *Gone are the joys of our madness*
> *But the sadness goes on and on*
> *Goes on and on*
> *Goes on and on*
> *Gone are the joys of our madness*
> *But the sadness goes on*
> *Like an old fashioned song*
> *When I dream*
> *When I think of you.*[41]

As Shahdov struggles to drink through a straw, the camera pans to Nichols decked out in full nightclub garb, including long white gloves and an elegant off-the-shoulder sequined number. Scored only for strings and harp, the song exists in two different keys—

A King in New York (1957)—The beginning of the chorus from "Now That It's Ended," one of the few songs in the film performed in its entirety, sung by Joy Nichols during the nightclub scene.

D-flat major and B-flat major—as Chaplin also considered Shani Wallis to sing the song. The lush, yet transparent, voicing of an all-string arrangement provides another ironic backdrop to the trite lyric that "goes on and on." Robert Goulet recorded the song in 1964.

Another song, "A Thousand Windows," got shut out entirely and went through a number of instrumental permutations. The lyrics are typically benign:

> *When the setting sun glows on Manhattan Isle*
> *A hundred thousand windows all begin to smile*
> *They all seem to say as they look from above*
> *There's a guy down below and he's so much in love.*[42]

The song was originally slotted for the entrance of Queen Irene, which Chaplin replaced with the orchestral version of "I'd Sell My Soul for Love." But he did not want to give up the melody. In the first cabaret scene following their disastrous night at the movies, Shahdov and Jaume enter to the sounds of a lone pianist onstage, as the script says, "quietly rambling over the keys."[43] Next to it handwritten in red ink is the direction "Ziganne 30 secs." The music for "Ziganne" (or "Gypsy") no longer exists. Instead, Chaplin took the melody for "A Thousand Windows" and rescored it for piano solo, retitled "Serenade." The offscreen soloist—Eric James—would become a central figure in Chaplin's music from that point forward.

Eric James (1913–2006) played for silent films while in his teens and later became a song plugger. He accompanied Ray Bolger, Vera Lynn, Elsie Carlisle, Ann Blythe, and virtuoso harmonica player Larry Adler, and later wrote songs under the pseudonym of Jack Howard, including the hit "Blue Eyes." James caught diphtheria while serving with the Royal Air Force during World War II and spent five and a half months in the hospital. The paralysis caused by the disease was so severe that he had to relearn his piano technique all over again. James joined the Charles Shadwell Orchestra and later formed a piano duet with George Myddleton. In 1956, James and his friend organist Robinson

A King in New York (1957)—**Chaplin took the melody from the unused song "A Thousand Windows" and rescored it for piano solo, renaming it "Serenade" and featuring the offscreen performance of Chaplin's later musical associate, Eric James.**

Cleaver founded the Sound Music Publishing Co. to "set ourselves up in Tin Pan Alley." Without a sufficient catalogue of songs, the company struggled for two years before being bought out by Peter Maurice Music Co. for a few hundred pounds. "It was a pity," said James, "but I never regret doing it. I learned a very great deal and enjoyed the experience of once again being part of that great mecca of music."[44]

One day at Peter Maurice, Jimmy Phillips called James from his office next door with an offer of work. "As it is always policy never to say 'yes' to something immediately, but to 'hum and ha' a bit as if one is trying to work it in to a packed engagement book," James said, "I just crackled some papers and 'tumpty tummed' a bit, when Jimmy casually added that the job was for Charlie Chaplin and involved post synchronization. I blinked, gulped, and then as nonchalantly as I could, agreed to go down to the studios the following morning." James was to "provide the missing sound, matching it to the movements and positioning of the actor's hands," who was "playing" on a dummy keyboard. It was also "essential that I should prepare a pleasing, though not too flowery arrangement."

> Ever since I had wrecked my neck playing the piano as a background for his silent films, Chaplin had to me seemed an almost godlike figure whose immense shadow on the silver screen was the only contact that ordinary mortals such as I could ever have hoped to have had with him. That I was now to actually meet him in the flesh and, what was more, that I might even be granted the incomparable honor of having the sound of my playing incorporated into one of his masterpieces, was a situation almost beyond comprehension. I began to wonder if the proper thing would be for me to pay him for the privilege![45]

James had prepared two different arrangements. At the studio, Chaplin ran the scene and suggested James rehearse one of his transcriptions. "After the sound of my playing had died away," James said, "Mr. Chaplin called out, 'I'll buy that. That's exactly what I want.' He followed it with some very nice compliments about my interpretation. I thanked him and said, 'Well, when you are ready I'll do it again for real.' I was astonished when they all laughed and explained that the microphones had been live and my playing was an actual 'take.' What an ego-trip that was—straight in the studio, no rehearsal, play the piece once and that was that. I could hardly believe it."[46]

Chaplin also requested that James condense part of the full orchestral score for piano. "Musicians will readily appreciate that in order to give a passable performance of an orchestral score on the piano it is necesary for one to be able to rapidly condense the vast number of separate staves into a basic melody and harmonic form that can be played with two hands. In the first instance, the melody has to be found and immediate transposition made of some of the music written for the various orchestral instruments." When James finished playing, Chaplin applauded and Boris Sarbek, the latest arranger on the film, said in his French accent, "Formidable."[47]

"I was very pleased," said James, "especially as I felt that I had in fact been undergoing a sort of audition. The time came to depart and Chaplin thanked and complimented me again. I felt that he really did appreciate my work although in the back of my mind was the sneaking fear that it might be just 'show biz sweet talk' agreeable to the ears but nothing more. Perhaps it was this that prompted me to say as we shook hands, 'Mr. Chaplin the nicest compliment that you can pay me is to ask me to work for you again.' He smiled and said, 'I will certainly do that,' and as I turned and walked from the studio I felt that he really did mean it."[48] James was paid £9 per minute for his brief work on *A King in New York*, more than any musician on the film except the leader in the orchestra. Not only was it good pay for something that lasted only thirty seconds of screen time, the experience also resulted in a continuing collaboration and friendship that lasted for the next twenty years until Chaplin's death in 1977.

*   *   *

The score for *A King in New York*, while it contains a wide variety of styles, is not as consistent in tone as in some other Chaplin films. Part of that has to do with the revolving door of musicians. The first was British arranger Peter Knight, a Jimmy Phillips recommendation. In the 1950s, Knight (1917–1985) formed his own orchestra and singing group, and later accompanied Marlene Dietrich's cabaret show at the Café de Paris and became the first musical director for Granada Television. *The New Musical Express* said Knight's arrangements were used "by nearly every name band in Britain at one time or another."[49]

Knight was hired to orchestrate "Juke Box," "Now That It's Ended" in two different keys (D-flat and B-flat) for Joy Nichols and Shani Wallis, a piece called "Melee Opera" (now unfortunately lost), the instrumental version of "Plate Windows" (later renamed "Weeping Willows"), and "Million Dollars." He was paid £11.11.0 per minute for the complete arrangements and another £10 to conduct the recording session on March 14, 1956, at Elstree Studios in Borehamwood, Hertfordshire. Soprano Louise Trail was also hired to sing some of the songs for £60, but there is no mention in her contract or in Knight's paperwork which one(s). But Chaplin was unhappy with the results and put Knight back to work. For a new recording session on May 1, this time at Shepperton Studios, Knight resubmitted new orchestrations "in accordance with Mr. Chaplin's instructions" for "Juke Box," "Now That It's Ended," and the "Plate Windows" instrumental, plus a new vocal version of "Weeping Willows" for Nichols to sing.[50] Chaplin still had problems with "Juke Box." Knight went back to Shepperton on May 18 for conferences, plus rehearsing and recording the number with Wallis and the nightclub band (which included Eric James on piano) one last time on May 23. Knight received a total of £345.8.0, though, Rachel Ford later reported, "I think that very little of this music was finally used in the picture."[51]

*   *   *

Chaplin's unhappiness with Knight's work may be why "a friend" recommended noted British composer Philip Sainton.[52] After serving as a chemist in the Middle East during World War I, Sainton (1891–1967) became principal violist of the Queen's Hall Orchestra and later with the BBC Symphony, where he remained until 1944. As a composer, Sainton gained notoriety with *Sea Pictures* (1923) and his 1939 tone poem, *The Island*. He also orchestrated numerous works for South African composer Jack Gerber, who was also a conducting professor at Guildhall School of Music and Drama.

In April 1956, Gerber sent an odd letter to Jerry Epstein stating "that both you and Mr. Chaplin have my friend Philip Sainton's interests at heart, and secondly because you also made it clear that you did not object to my helping him over his financial arrangements." Humbly portraying himself as a steel manufacturer that had "no real knowledge of show business and therefore I do not feel competent to give a worthwhile opinion on agreements in your line of country," he proceeded to lay out the verbal arrangements. Sainton would receive a minimum of £300, which included being hired to "take down, harmonize and orchestrate two songs" for the fee of £50 each, £12 a minute "for any further music played," and £3 for visits to London and elsewhere.[53]

Rachel Ford sent an agreement letter to Sainton on May 1, which included the standard verbiage whereby the copyright of his work would belong "absolutely" to Chaplin and his new production company, Attica Film Co. Ltd.[54] This prompted a quick reply from Sainton's lawyers the next day that set the tone for the unhappy collaboration:

> As you are no doubt aware, Composers generally are most unbusinesslike people and often hard up, and Mr. Sainton is no exception. In this connection we gather that he has no Contract or Agreement either with Mr. Chaplin or with Attica Film Co. Ltd, setting out the terms of his employment, but that within the last few days a form of Agreement was submitted to him by Miss Ford for signature, which both our Client and ourselves regard as quite unsuitable. We believe you are aware that Mr. Sainton is a member of the Performing Right Society Ltd., and as such would normally be entitled to a share of any fees collected by that Society in respect of the performance of his Work, whether in conjunction with the exhibition of a film or otherwise. He now understands however, that Mr. Chaplin will not agree to any Composers employed by him receiving any such fees or any other royalties in connection with Work done for him, and in these circumstances, whilst our Client does not seek to vary the existing verbal arrangement for payment of £50 in respect of the two songs which he has now completed and delivered to Mr. Chaplin, he is not prepared to carry out the arrangement orchestration or composition of any further music at that fee, and if therefore his further services are required, we shall be glad to hear that on behalf of your principals you are prepared to pay our Client at the rate of £20 per minute of completed music, which is the normal charge for this type of Work.[55]

Sainton was paid a total of £142.15, though there is no record which songs he orchestrated or what number he conducted at the May 1 recording session. Sainton's daughter, Barbara Sainton Clark, later said the collaboration "fell apart when my father kept pointing out to Chaplin where Chaplin's music had originated."[56] A letter Sainton sent to Rachel Ford two weeks after the recording session sealed his fate. "In the event of Mr. Chaplin wanting me to help him with his music later on, I hope notice of this will be given to me in plenty of time before the recording date. It is quite a long process taking down another's music, and then producing a piano score followed by an orchestral one."[57] Sainton's services were not required again.

*   *   *

Chaplin had already run through two musicians and "neither were considered to have been very satisfactory," Rachel Ford wrote to Saul Bourne at the end of November. "I believe however that Mr. Chaplin did think of reconsulting Mr. Knight as no French or Swiss arranger had been procured."[58] Perhaps the search for a French or Swiss arranger was because Chaplin could spend only a specified number of days in the UK per year or pay taxes as a UK national.[59] Still, most of the suggested names, not surprisingly, were British, including John Addison (a future Oscar winner for his score to *Tom Jones* and nominee for *Sleuth*, alongside Chaplin for *Limelight*) and Kenneth Jones, the arranger for Norrie Paramor's orchestra. When Chaplin was in Paris in December, he interviewed composer Allan Gray, best known for his scores for *The African Queen*, and *The Life and Death of Colonel Blimp* and *A Canterbury Tale* for Michael Powell and Emeric Pressburger, but decided not to hire him. While he was there, however, he discovered his next arranger in a French cabaret.

Following the war, Jacques Lasry (1918–2014) accompanied singers like Michèle Arnaud and Serge Gainsbourg at the Milord l'Arsouille, the famous so-called *cabaret littéraire* in Paris where poets and avant-garde artists had the opportunity to present their work to a progressively minded audience. Chaplin heard Lasry one night and was so impressed with the pianist's ability to improvise that he invited him to work on *A King in New York*. Many biographies mistakenly report that Lasry refused Chaplin's offer but a letter in the Chaplin Archive indicates that Lasry was paid 60 francs for his time with Chaplin. There is no indication exactly what Lasry did on the film but the letter states the work was of a purely technical nature.[60] There were no recording sessions during that period so it can only be assumed he transcribed some of Chaplin's melodies or worked on new arrangements. No doubt Lasry found the work with Chaplin to be as demanding and stressful as the other arrangers and he left Chaplin's employ in short order.

In mid–December, Saul Bourne sent a telegram:

HAS CHARLEY [*sic*] FINALLY DECIDED MUSIC ARRANGER STOP BEFORE LEAVING LONDON LOCATED TWO GOOD MEN STOP HERE NEW YORK MITCH MILLER HAS EXCELLENT EXPERIENCED ARRANGER BUT THAT INVOLVES TRIP AND TIME AND CHARLEY [*sic*] MAY HAVE DEADLINE STOP ADVISE IF CAN DO ANYTHING[61]

But Chaplin had already found a new arranger. Boris Sarbek (Boris Saarbecoff, 1897–1966) "made his fortune" as a violinist and society bandleader on the Riviera and radio circuit.[62] Sarbek spelled his name in a number of ways—Sarbekoff, Sarbeck—and when he played Latin American music, he used the pseudonym "Oswaldo Berkas," the last name being an anagram of Sarbek.[63] According to the post-production schedule, Sarbek was due to begin working with Chaplin in Switzerland on December 18, 1956. Originally, the schedule only allowed three weeks to work on the score, with recording sessions due to take place January 7–11, 1957. But, as always, Chaplin took longer than expected. Sarbek earned 500 francs plus another 250 francs to his team, which included an assistant and copyist.

Chaplin brought on board a conductor skilled in film music. Leighton Lucas (1903–1982) got his start as a boy dancing with Diaghilev and later with Anton Dolin (who possibly recommended him to Chaplin) and Alicia Markova. He wrote ballets and operas, and eventually became an arranger and orchestrator for Jack Hylton's band. Lucas got his start in films in the early 1930s, doing mostly uncredited work. His first official credit was musical director for the 1935 British farce *Hyde Park Corner*, with his most notable score in 1950 for Alfred Hitchcock's *Stage Fright*.

For the first recording session on January 25, Lucas assembled a 53-piece orchestra, which included Eric James on piano. The afternoon session slimmed down to a 46-piece ensemble plus two mandolins, no doubt to record the "Mandolin Serenade" cues. At that session Bobby Britton recorded "Spring's the Time for Making Love, " and Shirley Norman sang "I'd Sell My Soul for Love." The January 29 session employed a 17-piece dance band orchestra—five saxophones, four trumpets, four trombones, piano, guitar, bass, and percussion—with Gary Miller recording the "Rock & Roll" number, which was added months after Chaplin had finished shooting. As for the musicians, the fees worked out to £9 for the leader, while principals received £6.15 and everyone else £6. "Everybody concerned seemed highly pleased with the results," Rachel Ford told Saul Bourne.[64]

Lucas was originally supposed to be paid £150 for two days conducting and one day of preliminary discussion with Chaplin. Due to confusion with Sarbek, Lucas came to the studio on several occasions before the recording dates and the sessions went into a third day. He wrote to Mickey Delamar, the film's production controller, that he wanted to discuss reimbursement for "time and services spent on the 22nd of January and for copyright of Song Copy, etc. These little tasks are hard to assess, but I feel a charge should be made for these services. Do you agree? The film has been such a panic and my mind has been so full of worries that it has been impossible to get down to a full discussion on these grounds. Let me say how much I have enjoyed working with you and Charlie Chaplin."[65] Chaplin suggested to Delamar that he pay Lucas an additional £200 "for his sterling work."[66] The original music budget was £4000. But with the numerous extra work with Peter Knight's orchestrations and added recording sessions, the total ballooned to £4343.

∗   ∗   ∗

The main title begins with a confident fanfare that foreshadows later newspaper headlines of "King Shahdov Subpoenaed" and "King Cleared of Communism." The bright D-major key comes across as a subtle middle finger of innocence thumbed at the U.S., which had so often accused Chaplin of Red ties. The cue proceeds into the orchestral background for the "Rock & Roll" number before transitioning into the first six notes of "The Star-Spangled Banner," ending on a striking Eb7 chord (voiced Eb-G-Bb-C#) punctuated by machine gun triplets clustered on the flatted second. Boris Sarbek's French ties, like Jacques Lasry's, meant that the conductor's score and instrumental parts for *A King in New York* are in French. So the main title closes out with the lively "Generique" cue for Shahdov's early scenes as he descends the stairs of the plane to the tarmac and later fingerprinted by Immigration, an ironic backdrop to Chaplin's dialogue—"I am deeply moved by your warm friendship and hospitality. This big-hearted nation has already demonstrated its noble generosity to those who come to seek a refuge from tyranny."

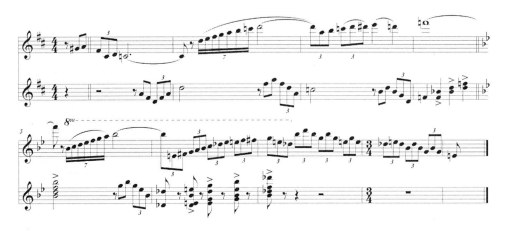

A King in New York (1957)—**Chaplin uses the opening fanfare's major key to ironically thumb his nose at the US.**

A King in New York (1957)—"Generique" is yet another carefree Chaplin promenade theme, this time capturing Shahdov's excitement at escaping the mobs and arriving in New York safely in exile.

The cue for the revolution in Shahdov's country flies through a series of unstable harmonic progressions and short accented motifs ascending and descending chromatically. Chaplin's feelings about New York are indicated in the pounding "Jungle Music" as the camera pans across shots of the Empire State Building and the United Nations. The original cut of the film included marquees for films like *Three Little Words* and *Pretty Baby*. When Chaplin cut the scenes for the 1973 cut version, it not only nixed much of the "Jungle Music," it also edited out the transition to Chaplin singing "Million Dollars," making the musical cut that much more abrupt. A series of CinemaScope Fanfares accompany the trailers for the innocuously titled *A Killer with a Soul, Man or Woman?*, and *Terror Rides Again*. With each title deliberately more insipid, uninspired, and dismissible,

Chaplin makes his point about Hollywood's "dying civilization" by using the same dull fanfare for each film.

In addition to the songs, Chaplin composed a series of instrumental source cues in the various restaurants and nightclubs. Following Eric James's "Serenade" piano instrumental, the stage revolves and Chaplin none too subtly supplies his views on the current music scene as a jazz band starts smashing drums and cymbals behind Shahdov's head, titled variously "Cymbal Sequence" and "Restaurant Jazz." After the brutal cut that eliminated Shani Wallis's "Juke Box" number, Chaplin composed one of his most delightful cues—"Martini"—though the dialogue and sound effects drown it out. The staccato chromatic melody line proceeds through a number of modulations underscoring the silly scene of Shahdov giving autographs to drunken patrons. Rachel Ford wrote to Saul Bourne she thought the tune "could become [a] big number."[67]

Chaplin underscores the comedy with a number of swinging and elegant cues. The "Comedy Gavotte" (also titled "Bathroom Gavotte") accompanies a series of slapstick scenes, including Shahdov and Jaume fighting to get a look at Ann through the bathroom peephole, and the scenes at the Queens County progressive school with students throwing spitballs and Shahdov's introduction to Rupert reading Karl Marx. The cue begins with dainty pizzicato in the strings and staccato in the winds, a nod to the classical dance of the title, before transitioning, like so many cues in the score, into jazzy dotted rhythms and syncopation. Between the two segments, Chaplin pokes fun at two old men leering at a young woman (shades of the bad press he had received over the years for his marriages to women years younger than him). He also takes on the pretentiousness of that type of schooling, making light of the Marxist views spewing from the mouth of a ten-year-old child. Like the "Comedy Gavotte," "Paperhangers" begins with a series of staccato notes transitioning to a jazz section that accompanies, as the name suggests, the slapstick Paperhangers comedy routine in the nightclub. The scene, as originally filmed, is a lengthy one and the music plays on repeat until the audience laughter drowns out the music.

The "Chess Music" for the game between Shahdov and Rupert plays off the sadness that "Weeping Willows" had engendered in the previous scene with Rupert wandering the cold, snowy streets. Originally, an Irish tune was originally slated for the scene and later omitted, though nothing in the Chaplin Archive indicates exactly which tune. Chaplin's theme, voiced in a plaintive English horn and cello duet, conveys Rupert's loneliness and his bitterness towards a life without any friends. The brief "Salle de Bain" ("Bathroom"), delicately orchestrated for two flutes, clarinet, strings, harp, and triangle, is a series of staccato notes, trills, and glissandi accompanying Shahdov's Pan-like dance before jumping into the tub. Chaplin used an image from this scene on the poster, and in marketing and press materials.

A King in New York (1957)—Though it is barely audible in the film, the "Martini" theme underscores Shahdov signing autographs in the nightclub.

A King in New York (1957)—"Bathroom Gavotte" (also called "Comedy Gavotte") underscores a series of slapstick scenes with Shahdov and Jaume trying to peep at Ann through the bathroom keyhole.

A King in New York (1957)—The brief, 13-second "Salle de Bain" cue accompanies Shahdov dancing around the bathroom.

Elegance also earmarks the "Park Avenue Waltz" that accompanies the dinner party. The waltz glides smoothly along, the perfect seen-but-not-heard backdrop to the gathering. Lyricist Irving Gordon added words to the tune in 1992. That year Gordon made headlines when his classic song "Unforgettable" won a controversial GRAMMY Award for Song of the Year thanks to Natalie Cole's recording, forty years after the song was a hit for her father. There is no record in the archive how or why Gordon wrote lyrics for Chaplin's melody, now titled "Without You." Whatever the reason, the words add little to the tune.

> CHORUS
> *All alone on streets of gold*
> *As the morning light unfolds.*
> *WITHOUT YOU,*
> *I walk around like an aimless vagabond.*
> *WITHOUT YOU,*
> *The streets are cold.*
> *WITHOUT YOU*
> *It's just fool's gold.*
> *An empty dream that can't come true,*
> *No, darling, not WITHOUT YOU.*
>
> INTERLUDE
> *Life without you is a cloud that will never clear.*
> *Moments without you all seem like years,*
> *And the laughter of children turns into tears without your love.*
> *Without your love there's no reason to be living.*
> *I just drift like a lost Gypsy song,*
> *My world is a world gone all wrong.*
> *Without your love,*
> *There's no Christmas or Thanksgiving.*
> *So come back, darling, come back to me.*
> *Till you come back to me I'll be...*
>
> REPEAT CHORUS[68]

The brief eight-measure "Whisky Montage," using the British spelling for the liquor, accompanies quick images of billboards in Times Square showing Shahdov choking on the liquid. Originally, the music also served as a transition to the doctor removing Shahdov's bandages following his plastic surgery and in the next scene as the front desk runs to get Shahdov's key after not recognizing him. Without those other scenes, which were cut from the U.S. print of the film, the cue mistakenly seems innocuous and hardly worth the effort of composing something new for the sequence.

The "Mysterioso" cue contains two distinct, opposed sections that accompany the ridiculous political scenes. The first is an *Allegro (leggero)* chase, ruled by triplets, chromatic alterations, and octave leaps that underscore Shahdov fleeing a subpoena in the hotel lobby chase and later as Shahdov and his lawyer run to the Committee meeting. A bumbling comedic march duet for piccolo and bassoon announces the arrival of the members of the Atomic Commission. It also chases Shahdov through the hotel lobby to avoid being served and serves as musical comedy when he gets his finger stuck in the nozzle of the fire hose.

By far the most prominent melody in the score is "Mandolin Serenade." The memorable theme, often titled "Mandoline Number" (or simply "Mandoline"), serves as a love theme for Shahdov and the Queen, conveying an affection that is missing from their cool interplay on screen. Sarbek judiciously orchestrates the theme for strings, harp, flute, and a pair of clarinets, bassoons, and mandolins. Chaplin obviously felt the theme could be a hit, both instrumentally and vocally. Lyrics were added in the spring, once again by Geoffrey Parsons and John Turner, in the hopes of another "Eternally" or "Smile." "New lyrics has [*sic*] made alterations which are being sent presumably to Mr. Philipps [*sic*]," Ford wrote to Saul Bourne. "I am to enquire what percentage of profits writer of new lyrics will take. If percentage is too high, [Chaplin] will use his own lyrics."[69] For "Eternally," Parsons and Turner received two cents per copy of the sheet music. But since *A King in New York* had no U.S. distribution, "Mandolin Serenade" had limited appeal stateside and Bourne was able to negotiate the lyricists' cut down to one-and-a-half cents. In addition, the pair received sixteen-and-two-thirds percent for any new recordings, down from the twenty-five percent they were paid for "Eternally."[70]

King Shahdov (Chaplin) dances in the bathroom in this publicity photograph from *A King in New York,* c. 1957 (© Roy Export SAS).

A King in New York (1957)—The lush "Park Avenue Waltz" glides along innocuously in the background of the society dinner party.

With-out you, the streets are cold. ___ With-out you it's just fool's gold.

"Without You," 1992, music by Charles Chaplin, lyrics by Irving Gordon)—The beginning of the chorus, based on the "Park Avenue Waltz" melody from *A King in New York*.

A King in New York (1957)—Frenetic triplets mark the beginning section of the "Mysterioso" cue as Shahdov is chased around the hotel lobby.

> *Ev'ry time you're near, music starts, and I hear mandolins,*
> *Playing on the strings of my heart, when you're near, mandolins*
> *Bringing me a mem'ry of the joy when first I found you,*
> *Like a serenade so gently played it's all around you.*
> *Ev'ry time we meet I repeat, I can hear mandolins,*
> *Singing love's refrain soft and wet, once again, it begins,*
> *If I never hear a songbird, never hear the charms of a thousand violins,*
> *I shall always hear the music when you're in my arms, of those lovely mandolins.*[71]

The lyric, while making the obvious reference to "strings of my heart" and the precious outdated "ev'ry"/"mem'ry" contractions, at least has one elegant internal rhyme with "Like a serenade so gently played." Chaplin's original lyric (titled "Mandoline"), however, not only rhymes in the most obvious ways, it simply rhymes too much:

A King in New York (1957)—The second section of "Mysterioso" is a loping march for piccolo and bassoon, Chaplin's musical statement on American congressional committees.

Magic's in the air,
I declare, everywhere,
When you're there.
Mandoline, guitars,
Shooting stars, in the blue, everywhere.

You are so disarming,
Your sense of humour charming
That I love you.
You are so adorable
That life would be deplorable
Without you.

Something in your style
In your smile
Makes me think life worthwhile.
Something in your glance
When you dance
Is the height of romance.

You may think I'm crazy
To say these foolish things
And to feel the way I do.
Maybe I'm too romantic
Maybe I'm a fool
To be so much in love with you.[72]

Chaplin wanted to record "Mandolin Serenade" and "The Spring Song" ("Spring's the Time for Making Love"), and HMV in Britain was definitely interested. He also wanted to conduct the recording, but he did not know how. It was agreed that Chaplin would conduct, but the orchestra would be well rehearsed beforehand. In addition, the session would be filmed with Chaplin making comments. "He has thought up a lot of good ones," Ford wrote to Saul Bourne.[73] The session was set for Friday, June 22, at the Studio de la Mutualité in Paris.

Chaplin would receive a royalty of 1–1/2d. (penny half-penny) for each record sold.[74] But there were other versions pairing the two songs—Mantovani's recording on Decca and Norrie Paramor on Columbia, as well as Kenneth McKellar (Decca) and Murray

Ev-'ry time you're near, mus - ic starts, and I hear man - do - lins,

Play - ing on the strings of my heart, when you're near, man - do - lins.

The opening of the chorus from "Mandolin Serenade" (1957), music by Charles Chaplin, lyrics by Geoffrey Parsons and John Turner.

Campbell (Philips). Walter J. Ridley, head of A&R for HMV, said Chaplin's version had a "very good reaction throughout the world."[75] The BBC wanted Chaplin to conduct the theme on a September 9 television show but given his lack of conducting skills he said no. Instead, the station used Norrie Paramor's version on the show, the arrangement of which Chaplin "found parts of it excellent, but some of it 'very choppy,'" Bourne wrote to Jimmy Phillips. "'Spring's the Time' he found excellent."[76] "'The Spring Song' makes pleasant listening," said *Melody Maker* of Paramor's recording, "but whether it will prove to be another 'Limelight Theme' remains to be seen. The reverse ('Mandolin Serenade') is an evocative piece."[77] "I like the music," said Keith Fordyce in *The New Musical Express*, "but don't find it very inspiring. Definitely must be heard several times before you make your mind up about it. Oddly enough, the Chaplin recording for HMV is the least impressive I have heard." Fordyce, however, praised Norrie Paramor's rendition and "the triumphant entry of sweeping strings half way through. This gives the music more variation and emphasis, cuts out the soporific effect that is otherwise a definite possibility." Wally Stott's "different interpretation" featured Murray Campbell on trumpet. "This Philips platter is more commercial than the other two mentioned, and could quietly snag a comfortable slice of the sales. Whatever happens, hit paradewise [*sic*], you're certain to hear plenty of broadcasts of 'Mandolin Serenade.'"[78]

    Chaplin's recording was not released in the U.S. until October 1958. Ford wanted to wait but "due to the picture having been released in Canada," Bonnie Bourne said, "it was impossible for the release of these songs to be held back any longer."[79] Chaplin also recorded "Weeping Willows" and "Paperhangers," though neither was released. The main draw of the Chaplin recording session, other than his name value on the record, was the chance to film Chaplin in action on the podium for a short film as an advance trailer for *A King in New York*. The music—and of course Chaplin—were the focus, with voiceover narration kept to a minimum:

> This is no ordinary orchestral rehearsal—and the man on the rostrum is no ordinary man. He is that clown, genius and superb master of all trades—Charles Chaplin, here conducting the music composed by him for his latest film A KING IN NEW YORK.
>   (Music swells and orchestra plays theme)
>   Charles Chaplin—actor—clown, storyteller, scriptwriter and NOW conductor—(Sir Malcolm Sargent and Igor Stravinsky had better look to their laurels) here takes his place on the rostrum for the first time to add yet another accomplishment to his credit.
>   This fabulous figure, known affectionately throughout the world as CHARLIE—who has made us laugh and cry through three generations, now returns once more triumphant to delight us anew with the latest evidence of his genius … in The Mandoline Serenade [*sic*] … from A KING IN NEW YORK. Composed and Directed by Charles Chaplin.[80]

Chaplin on the podium during the filming of the "Mandolin Serenade" short film that was to be shown in theaters prior to screenings of *A King in New York,* **c. June 22, 1957 (© Roy Export Co. Ltd.).**

"What a man! And what a day!" Ridley said about the recording session. Though Paris was engulfed in a heatwave, the day of recording was a busy one for Chaplin—four appointments before the eleven o'clock start and then another two hours of rehearsals, lunch, recording until four o'clock, followed by a private filming session of him conducting until nine o'clock. "And that at [age] sixty-eight!" said Ridley. "I was exhausted by teatime. Mr. Chaplin was working wonderfully hard all day, wringing with perspiration.... He knows just what he wants. And I've never seen an orchestra cooperate better and work harder for anyone."[81] "Personally," said A. M. G. Gelardi, managing director of Archway Film Exhibitors, the company distributing *A King in New York,* "I was very impressed with [how everything was] handled ... under rather difficult circumstances on the day the shooting took place. The organization was really first class."[82]

Chaplin thought the short was "a bit long." Gelardi agreed, but "this view was not shared by other people to whom I showed the picture and I think that now with the commentary and the title cards it does not seem quite as long. Moreover it was very difficult to find the proper place to cut this little film adequately and I feel it is best to leave it as it is."[83] The Chaplin office received letters from Emelka Film A.G. in Germany and Switzerland, neither of which found any use for the short. The film cost 2,088,236 francs and, as Gelardi told Ford, "this little film has, of course, come out very expensive but it was unfortunately done mainly on overtime. I am afraid that we will only get very little back from the U.K. distribution, as being only a few minutes long the exhibitors regard it more or less as advertising material."[84] Unseen for many years, the short was included as a bonus on the Image Laserdisc and later for the film's MK2 DVD in 2003.

*   *   *

Long before the film was even finished shooting, music publishers threw their hats into the ring to publish the first Chaplin tunes composed outside of the U.S. Mills Music in the UK sent their pitch in September 1956. Mills was relatively new but already had a stellar roster of artists, including Leroy Anderson, Duke Ellington, and Morton Gould. "In view of the importance of Mr. Charlie Chaplin and his music," said the letter, "I would not mind paying you higher royalties."[85]

As always, there was interest in producing a soundtrack album of *A King in New York*. Chaplin envisioned a concept album, with his running commentary introducing the various recorded tracks. Chaplin worked on the commentary diligently, with eight versions existing in the archive. Had an album been made, this is what Chaplin had in mind:

> How do you do, ladies and gentlemen, this is Charlie Chaplin talking. To listen to incidental music of a motion picture without knowing what's going on in the background is like listening to a beautiful girl singing in a bathtub—the visual effect is lacking. Thus my reason for explaining a little of the background music.
>
> First you will hear a fanfare accounting the main title "A King in New York," with all the credits, written by—directed by—who did it ... who helped to do it—and who saw them do it. So here it is!! A KING IN NEW YORK!!!
>
> (Title music)
>
> After the credit title, the picture now really begins.
>
> The scene is a revolution. Thousands are outside the palace gates, shouting: "We want the head of King Shahdov!" (Incidentally, that's me.) They smash in the palace gates, Rush up the palace stairs and break into the King's room, and there!—However, this is revolution music.
>
> (Revolution music)
>
> The palace is stripped bare—not a carpet left ... to the treasury!!
>
> (Music)
>
> Gone!—He's taken everything!
>
> And now, from an aeroplane, we see the approaching skyline of New York and the King, safe at last in the arms of democracy!
>
> (Music—King's arrival)
>
> And now Broadway at night with its towering temples of industry and commerce, and the surging mass below.
>
> (Jungle Music)
>
> After many adventures, the Kind [*sic*] and his Ambassador visit a night club. This is a dance number called "A Double Dry Martini." It seems that this piece has difficulty in getting started—perhaps it's the double dry martini.
>
> (Music—Double Dry Martini)
>
> Then there is sentimental music played while the King and Queen are having lunch together for the last time. They are devoted, but not in love. Over lunch, they discuss the prospects of a friendly divorce. This piece is called "Mandoline Serenade." [*sic*]
>
> (Music Mandoline Serenade [*sic*], whole thing)
>
> (Music—Bathtub Nonsense)
>
> As the story progresses, the King becomes the social center of New York. He is wined, dined and fated. [*sic*] This number is called "Park Avenue Waltz."
>
> (Music—Park Avenue Waltz)
>
> Of course, in every film there is a romance. This number is called "Spring's the Time to Fall in Love." [*sic*]

(Music—Spring's the Time)

And no city is without the blues. When a prize fighter is punched drunk, they say: "Poor devil, he's stepping through plate Windows." This number is called "I'm Stepping Through Plate Windows Over You."

(Music—Stepping Through Plate Windows)

And no city is without mystery. This is Mysterioso music, which provides the background for comedy, intrigue and excitement. (You will notice that the oboe and the bassoon provide the comedy.)

(Mysterioso Music)

Another comedy theme called "The Paperhangers" which takes place in another nightclub.

(Music Paperhangers)

And so after many exciting adventures, the King bids farewell to New York and returns to Europe.[86]

Ridley said he now had "a very interesting and listenable EP of the music of the film with Mr. Chaplin's speech interwoven between the items. I propose to send this direct to Mr. Chaplin for him to listen to and hope he will be as enthusiastic about it as we are, as I would like to have this ready for the opening of the film in London."[87] Unfortunately, the EP was never released and copies have yet to surface.

On August 19, 1957, Columbia Records drew up a contract for a soundtrack album. "This exceptionally important Columbia album, with world distribution would be particularly good for Charlie and for us," said Saul Bourne, "because the Montavani [*sic*] and the Norrie Paramour [*sic*] records may not be released here [in the US]."[88] Less than a month after the film opened to its poor reception, Columbia decided once again "not to make the album at this time."[89] Throwing the music plans into turmoil was the death of Saul Bourne on October 13. In addition to Chaplin, over the years Bourne had been associated with Irving Berlin, Al Jolson, and Walt Disney, acquiring "one of the most extensive and richest music catalogues in the world," said *New Musical Express*.[90] Bonnie Bourne assumed control from her husband.

Talk of a soundtrack was reinstated in 1958, focusing on an album recorded in Italy for release in the U.S. "It will indeed be a feather in my cap if we are successful," Bonnie wrote to Rachel Ford.[91] Chaplin's suggested it was not "advisable to arrange for the marketing of the Italian long playing record in the United States at this time. If and when the picture is released here, it might be in order to reconsider the matter both as to the economics of the situation and the other consideration involved."[92] Knowing the precarious state the company was in with a new head, Bonnie wrote, "I do hope, Rachel, that you will let Charlie know that we are very interested in continuing to publish any music that he may write."[93]

While no soundtrack album was ever produced, Boris Sarbek recorded a 7-inch 45 rpm EP of four selections from the film—"Park Avenue Waltz," "A Spring Song" [*sic*], "Weeping Willows," and "Mandolin Serenade"—on the Philips label in the UK and on Fontana in France. Norrie Paramor also released an EP on Columbia of six numbers from the film—"The Spring Song," "Weeping Willows/Bathtub Nonsense," "Mandolin Serenade," and "Park Avenue Waltz/The Paperhangers."

Ford rightly predicted, "Disappointment will be expressed at the revenue so far received from the music of *A King in New York*."[94] By 1958, Bourne had reported only $9,489.46 amassed from the film's various recordings and sheet music, compared to *Limelight*'s $83,759.81 over a five-year period and $11,886.19 for *Modern Times* from 1954–1958.

* * *

In 1971, Mo Rothman, the former European representative for United Artists, made a deal with Roy Export to issue a group of nine Chaplin films, which included *A King in New York*. The deal paid Chaplin $6 million plus fifty-percent of the royalties. The film finally premiered as the closing entry of a Chaplin festival in Chicago in June 1972, though it had screened earlier in the year to a hundred college students in New York and also with students in the drama department at UCLA. Oliver Unger, the independent producer who organized the festival, said the film went to Chicago instead of New York because "we were forced to honor a contractual commitment to the Carnegie Theater. Chaplin didn't want to have the picture released at this time." Chaplin edited the film at the request of the festival, including "the removal of a couple of scenes which, in our opinion, either date the picture or break its flow."[95] The scenes involved two sequences with Shahdov and the estranged Queen, and Shani Wallis's "Juke Box" number. "For the record," said critic Roger Ebert, "the audience enjoyed it immensely. Chaplin's political satire no longer seems as daring as it must have been in the 1950s, but his social commentary is, if anything, more timely now. It's a relief, somehow, to learn at last that Chaplin didn't bow out in bitterness, and that the last film he starred in was as gentle, optimistic and funny as the first."[96]

By the time the film opened for its regular U.S. run, in the midst of the Watergate scandal, reviewers critiqued the film with a bit more political objectivity than their colleagues in 1957. "Despite Chaplin's denials, this is a very bitter film—and why should it be otherwise?" questioned *The New York Times*.

> We can applaud his anger, and it's easier than ever to sympathize with characters grown cautious about what they say over the phone, who worry that their rooms are bugged or sense that they're about to be subpoenaed. However, the great man botched his own political arguments, and this movie sags below the rest of his work.
>
> Yet, it's important to see *A King in New York*: it brings back the bad old days. And the fact that even Chaplin couldn't make guilt by association funny is crucial to our past and present history.[97]

Vincent Canby in the *Times* wrote, "*A King in New York* is like a letter written but unsent—until now—from a far-off time and place of great bitterness."

> It is quarrelsome, hard-headed, egomaniacal.... It is a living work. It is one of a kind, a movie that cannot be compared to movies made today, or even to movies made in 1957.... The film is so personal that to criticize it in any degree has a way of turning into a critique of the man.... As the king of comedy, actually the king of Hollywood, for so many years, he grew so powerful that he could explore a type of self-centeredness that less successful filmmakers must disguise. Chaplin didn't have to. This independence is so rare in films that I find the results fascinating even when they are not completely successful. I also suspect that this independence, backed by Chaplin's ability to survive, must nettle a lot of people."[98]

One of those was Pauline Kael of *The New Yorker*, who called it "maybe the saddest (and worst) film ever made by a celebrated film artist."[99] In response, Oona, a staunch fan of the magazine for years, canceled her subscription.

A King in New York, even with the Chicago cuts, was still too long to fit comfortably in a two-hour television slot with commercials. Bert Schneider, Mo Rothman's junior partner on the distribution deal, was supervising the re-release and asked Chaplin if he could cut several more minutes from the film. Chaplin told Schneider to make the edits himself; he was not interested in seeing the result. The cuts were made in May 1973, many of which impacted the flow of the score. At the society party, twenty-two seconds of dialogue with a drunken partygoer were cut, eliminating the introduction and opening strains of the "Park Avenue Waltz," as well as the waltz's accompaniment to a later cut scene with the hotel manager in the lobby. Snippets of the Paperhangers comedy routine were cut and the accompanying music was relaid over the newly edited scene. Schneider tried to eliminate all the scenes with the Queen, but Chaplin would not allow it.

The original complete version of *A King in New York* occasionally appeared in theaters and on television, and David Shepard restored the deleted sequences for his home video releases in 1993 without consulting Roy Export. The MK2 edition went with the cut version of the film (as will all future editions as of this writing), though the cut scenes were included as extras. The current home video version does not conform to Chaplin's original vision and, as such, is not the best way to see it, especially when it comes to his musical efforts. For his next film, he returned to his old silent shorts where he could once again exert total control over the film—and the music.

CHAPTER 12

Flat Feet

OR YEARS CHAPLIN HAD BEEN adamant about not bringing back the Tramp. But after the vicious reception accorded *A King in New York*, he recanted. "I am bringing back the little man exactly as he was," he said. "Of course he will be a little older…. I was wrong to kill him. There is room for the Little Man in the atomic age."[1] But the filmmaker was too old to portray the spry iconoclast, and at age seventy he could not physically perform the stunts that were such a part of the iconic character. Chaplin was also embroiled in a legal dispute in England over pirated copies of *The Kid* and several shorts. "The pirated versions are in lousy condition and are mutilated," Rachel Ford wrote Bonnie Bourne. "Our negatives are in wonderful state, and I am very much hoping that Charlie will re-edit them, and add music. If he does, we should be able to knock the bottom out of the pirates' business."[2] Chaplin packaged three of his First National "Million Dollar Comedies," the first films for which he owned the copyright, adding introductory commentary, and, like the 1942 reissue of *The Gold Rush*, re-editing the films, and composing new scores.

Originally titled *The Big Parade of Charlie Chaplin*, the three films—*A Dog's Life* and *Shoulder Arms* (both 1918), and *The Pilgrim* (1923)—spanned the width of Chaplin's six-year First National contract, including his first and last films with the distributor and the first of his wartime comedies. As an introduction, Chaplin included clips from *How to Make Movies*, a never-seen 1918 comedy-documentary showing the behind-the-scenes construction and personnel of the Chaplin Studios. The retitled *The Chaplin Revue* also marks the first film with "music associate" Eric James, following his brief stint as a pianist on *A King in New York*.

The lengthiest discussion of Chaplin's musical working methods comes from James's 2000 biography, *Making Music with Charlie Chaplin*. When James arrived in Switzerland, he was beginning to unpack at his hotel when the receptionist rang to say that Chaplin and Oona were in the lounge. "Feeling extremely flattered that the mountain had come to Mohammed," James said, "I sped off to join them. They greeted me most warmly, more like old friends than employers. This ability to treat people from all walks of life with the same respect and consideration was and still is a positive plus when I come to assessing the realities of the Chaplin legend."[3]

James had played piano for silent films in his teens, including many Chaplin shorts. When the two began working together, Chaplin asked him, "What did you really think of my early pictures?" James looked at him "with a straight face" and said, "To tell you the truth, Charlie, they gave me a pain in the neck!" Taken aback, Chaplin exclaimed, "Well, I'll say this much for you Eric, you're nothing if not honest." "If you had been sitting playing an Orgapian with your head held back, looking up at a screen," James explained, "you too would have found your own films a pain in the neck." Always one to appreciate a good joke, Chaplin said, "That's a good one, Eric. I shall have to tell Oona."[4]

James had answered Chaplin's call without even knowing what the job was. Chaplin told him when he arrived in Switzerland, "I still own quite a number of films and I'm fed up with the Mickey Mouse–type of accompaniment that they've been given by so many musicians all over the world. With your help I hope that we'll be able to write music which will be played by a fifty to sixty-piece orchestra as a background to some of the films I still own."[5] While James was "enthusiastic about the experience of working with this fine artist and also the work they are accomplishing," he learned early on that his continued employment was not guaranteed.[6] On the fourth day, James asked Eileen Burnier, Chaplin's secretary, why his hotel reservation was only for three days. "The other musicians that he's had here to work with him, they haven't lasted more than a couple of days," said Burnier. "They've just walked away. They can't stand it." James told himself, "That's not going to happen to me. I'll stick it out."[7]

Because of the continuous nature of the scores, "it was an extremely formidable challenge and I often felt that I wouldn't be able to stay the course," James said.

> To help me mentally and physically I kept up a daily routine. I would rise each morning at 7:30 a.m., take a shower and then enjoy a leisurely breakfast, after which I would have a brisk walk along the promenade of [Lake Geneva], returning to the hotel by the main street of the little town. Thus by 9:30 I was fully awake and alert and ready to face the exhausting demands and mental acrobatics that Charlie would inevitably expect of me.
>
> Charlie usually declared that he had done enough work for the day at about 5:30 and he would then take the lift upstairs, where he would have a bath or sauna and then reemerge at about 6:00 p.m. dressed in what he called his siren suit. As soon as he rejoined me, Gino would enter the salon to serve us drinks. Charlie always downed his gin and tonic at great speed and then was served a second, which he dealt with more slowly and usually made it last until dinner was served promptly at 6:45.[8]

James said Chaplin used only the first three fingers of his right hand at the piano "to play sufficient notes to indicate the type of tune that was in his mind and that was usually enough for me to understand, providing he didn't try to bring in his left hand, when the resultant discords made it necessary for me to ask him to repeat the exercise one handed." Chaplin's "dexterity with his three fingers on the keyboard of the piano did not match that of the creative side of his brain. Wrong notes would resound unceasingly while he played. Nevertheless, I always endeavored to write everything down since he would rarely follow a melodic thought through to its logical conclusion. It was extremely difficult to transcribe his compositions onto paper, particularly in the early stages of our association, before I appreciated the full importance of the part I needed to play in order that his ideas might be interpreted and made into an acceptable music score."

> My job, after listening to the notes he had played on the piano as a basic melody line, was to formulate them into an acceptable musical composition, which I would then play back to him complete with chords and harmony. Hopefully, he would accept it. If not, he would ask me to try again or to emphasize this or that aspect of the melody and harmony or to change the mood and so on.
>
> This was a tremendous challenge because his first thoughts were virtually random jottings of his melodic ideas, and bore very little or no resemblance to the finished product. An hour or more would frequently be spent on perhaps one or two bars of the music until eventually his face would light up with a smile and he would say, "I'll buy that" (the only "Americanism" I ever heard him use during my long association with him).[9]

James said he and Chaplin "must have presented a comic sight while at work because we would constantly be changing places at the piano. He would try to indicate with his limited playing ability what he was after and I would immediately change places and try to create the melody line that I felt he was searching for. It was like a game of musical chairs!"[10] An even bigger challenge was transcribing Chaplin's singing, which was "as out of tune as his playing and I used to dread this form of composition," James said. "He also was inclined to sing his melodies far more quickly than it was possible for me to transcribe them on paper. Patience was not one of Chaplin's virtue[s] and he would frequently shout, 'Haven't you got it down yet?' My reply was always the same: 'I am a musician not a magician. I can only write music at a speed which is anatomically possible.' I usually then added, 'If you will sing a little slower I'll be able to keep up with you.' He would then apologize and we would continue on and make good progress for a while at least."[11]

Chaplin "considered himself a perfectionist in everything," even when it came to music. Days of work often produced only two or three minutes of original composition a day. "The music would be rewritten over and over again until finally we had reached a point when the entire composition was finished," James said. "When I played it back to him ostensibly for the last time, he would yet again start to make alterations. He would alter a couple of bars from one stave, then perhaps three from the stave below and one from the stave above and so on. Quite often I would cry 'Stop' just in order to rest my mind for a few minutes and to give me the opportunity to rewrite the music yet again!"

I think it was this aspect of working with Chaplin that caused many of my predecessors to walk out of the salon. When he told me of these occasions he added (perhaps as a warning) that as they made to leave he told them, "When you leave this room you will never, and I mean never, set foot in it again!" It was the memory of this that made me grit my teeth on many occasions and suffer the arguments and bullying that happened so frequently.[12]

Chaplin and James worked every day from ten o'clock in the morning until lunchtime at twelve-thirty when Oona would enter the salon and Chaplin would say, "Mummy, listen to the music that Eric and I have done this morning." "The inclusion of my name in the composition," James said, "made me smile inwardly."

James discovered early on that Chaplin was "a glutton for work." Apart from lunch and a brief tea break, the duo worked continuously "from the moment I arrived at the Manoir until at least 5:30 p.m."[13] Chaplin "never seemed to understand" that even though James was younger, he was "was utterly

Publicity photograph of Eric James, date unknown (courtesy of Julia Hitchcock).

exhausted not the least by the frequent illustrations of his fiery temperament. When we did reach this moment he would go upstairs to his suite to rest and change for dinner while I continued the enormous amount of revision and rewriting." Chaplin, who was not a fan of tea, begrudged James his traditional British afternoon respite. "Every afternoon at four o'clock there'd be a knock at the drawing room door and the butler would walk in solemnly with a tray of tea and a wedge of chocolate cake. And Charlie would sit in his favorite arm chair biting his fingernails, defying me to take off about three minutes to eat the cake and drink the tea. And then we would go on again."[14]

And "woe betide me," said James, "if there was the slightest deviation from the melodic or harmonic pattern that he claimed had been agreed upon."

> As it began to dawn on me what a very hard and demanding task master he was, I realized that my ability as a musician had to be balanced by my ability to suffer all silently, to maintain the patience of Job, and to be a super diplomat. He resented having to accept my advice at any time and when at the beginning I simply told him what was right he would shout, "Don't tell me what to do!" and I would have to wait until he reproduced my suggestions later and we could then get on.
>
> I ultimately decided to simply play the correct thing and say, "However clever of you to think of that." It saved time and face! At times he could be quite difficult and I began to wonder if I were equal to the task. Certainly I now really understood why other musicians had left the salon forever, after only a few days.
>
> Likewise my adoring attitude to the great Charlie Chaplin, which had remained with me from my boyhood days, disappeared rather rapidly and although I continued to admire him for his work, I realized that in other directions he was no better than any other man and probably a good deal worse than some.
>
> His one redeeming feature was his ability to acknowledge his shortcomings. After I had been there about a week he turned to me after we had finished work one evening and said, "Eric, you must try not to be too upset by the things I say to you whilst we are working. I find that whenever I am doing creative work I am drawing on my nervous energy and seem unable to prevent myself from making these emotional outbursts." It was this self-effacing statement plus many other apologies thereafter that gave me the strength to endure the daily sessions, and it indeed gave me a deeper understanding of my employer and preserved my otherwise wilting respect for him. Perhaps it was this extra something within me that I was able to draw upon, that enabled me first to stay when others had left and then to go on for twenty years, during which time a genuine friendship existed between us.[15]

London's *News of the World* also gave readers a detailed glimpse into Chaplin's working methods:

> At the risk of being on the receiving end of a custard pie, I'm going to reveal Charlie Chaplin's greatest secret. Not his formula for being funny. But how this man, who can't write a musical note, composed two hours 20 minutes of melodies for his latest film, *The Chaplin Revue*.
>
> This is the timetable of A Day in the Life of the World's Most Curious Composer. It begins at 10:30 a.m. on the shores of Lake Geneva. A Chaplin car duly deposits British pianist Eric James at the comedian's front door.
>
> Butler, wearing white coat and big smile, leads him into 40 ft. lounge. Chaplin enters briskly, gives James a warm handshake.
>
> "Nice to meet to meet you again," he says. "I haven't forgotten the time we worked together at Shepperton in *A King in New York*. Now—what about some music?"
>
> He starts humming a melody.
>
> "Let's try this—will you take it down?" And James, not quite at home in this kingdom of comedy as he is in his London flat, feverishly scribbles down note for note, trying to keep pace with the mass of melody.
>
> "We want a ponderous rhythm—like this," says the composer. It's possible background music for a shot in *Shoulder Arms*, part of *The Chaplin Revue*.

"Ta-da-da-da. Dah-dum-di-da-da." He moves across the lounge. Never still.

James jots down the score, caresses the keyboard, and makes a tentative correction.

"No, that isn't what I'm looking for," says the composer. "I don't want that." He wants perfection.

In walks his lovely wife, Oona. *She* wants lunch. And a few minutes later Joseph, the butler, intones: "Luncheon is served, madam."

Afterwards it's back to the piano. So it goes on until 6 p.m. Sweating out the sequences, hour by hour, six days a week; for two months altogether.

"Sometimes I thought I would go mad," says James, "but I learned more from Chaplin than in the rest of my life."

At the end of each day's work the composer becomes the host. At 6:30 p.m. a chauffeur returns from Lausanne with a bundle of the world's papers. Dinner. Conversation. Wit and wisdom.[16]

James said Chaplin insisted he "write down his wishes and carry them out to the letter.... He did not wish to waste valuable time in the recording studios correcting errors because I had failed to make proper notes. He would always end this dissertation with, 'Studio time is expensive and so I warn you—be accurate.' There was little doubt that it was just the expense that worried him."[17]

There was never a day "without arguments or disagreements over this or that passage of music," James said. "I soon found that it was virtually impossible for me ever to win, even when I could show the truth by demonstrating the musical correctness on the piano."[18] One of the warning signs of storms ahead was when Chaplin would arrive wearing white cotton gloves to hide his mild eczema. "Alas," said James, "the sight of him wearing them inevitably indicated that he would be bad tempered and difficult to work with. It was on just such an occasion that he greeted me affably enough but suggested quite sharply that we should get right on with the work, indicating, or so it seemed to me, that I needed pushing."[19]

Occasionally Chaplin would greet James in the morning "with a happy smile and, switching on his little tape recorder, eagerly study my face as he played over the outline of a melody. Often at the end he would glower and say, 'I can see by your face that you don't think much of it.' I would reply, 'On the contrary Charlie, I think it's absolutely wonderful but what a pity that Tchaikovsky thought of it before you did.' His face would fall and he'd say, 'I've been working on that melody for more than two hours and you've destroyed it in two seconds.' I always replied the same: 'Two seconds disappointment now is better than years of embarrassment later.'"[20]

Once when James suggested to Chaplin that he should have taken time off to study harmony and counterpoint, Chaplin replied that he "preferred to think freely, like a gypsy, and not be hemmed in by all the music rules and inhibitions by which most musicians are governed. As I swallowed hard and sought desperately for a reply, he added, quite apart from all else, 'If I had been as knowledgeable as a musician, I would not have had the pleasure of working with Eric James.' ... Perhaps if he had understood a bit more about the technicalities he would not have dictated countless ideas and melodies to me with the speed of a machine gun, which were almost impossible to cope with and resulted in considerable tidying-up work for me each day."[21]

When James felt Chaplin was ignoring his suggestions, he employed his own methods of getting his point across. "First of all, let me make it quite clear that it was Charlie's ideas. I only helped to develop them. But it would be true to say that I endeavored to get my ideas across to him. And he would never accept them unless I put it in a different way. I would say, for instance, 'You know that thought you had about a certain melody,

I was thinking about it last evening when I got home to the hotel, and I think your idea was so right.' And I would play what I knew was the best answer to the phrase that we had written, and he would thus agree and not lose face, and I would get my own way. I found that worked quite successfully on numerous occasions."[22]

James said working with Chaplin was "a very great strain at times because he wanted a concert performance any time I ever played any of his music back to him. So I devised a system which made it a little easier by writing the melody that he suggested on the first stave, leaving the next one blank, the next one would be written on. So as we would go through, I could zigzag up and down on the various staves to play the piece in its entirety." Sometimes at the end of the hour, James told his boss, "Stop! You'll have to give me some time to do repair work." Chaplin would then go into his study "and he would stay there until I would come to a knotty problem where perhaps I wasn't sure of the harmony. So I would deliberately play a wrong note. The door of his study would open and he would come into the salon like an express train and say, 'I never said that!' I said, 'I know that but I did that so I knew I could get your attention immediately.'"[23] On Chaplin's more abusive days, James would look out at the Alps through the window by the piano "and count to ten and not say the things that I had in my mind. The trouble was he was very impatient. He had a brain like a dynamo and expected everyone to think just as quickly as he did, which wasn't easy. He said, 'Haven't you got it down yet, Eric?' I said, 'Look, I am a musician not a magician.'" And yet James was "always very happy" when he was at the Manoir. "It was a very nice, homely atmosphere at all times."[24]

After six and a half weeks, Chaplin wanted to hear a run-through of the piano scores one evening after dinner.

> Charlie settled himself in his favorite armchair and Oona carried out her usual task of being the projectionist, while I began to give a concert performance. I had to punctuate the music by loudly exclaiming the various orchestral annotations while at the same time watching the film very closely so that I might change the various pieces of music at the prearranged cues.
>
> It gave me a tremendous sense of satisfaction to observe how perfectly the music fitted the various scenes in the film. As the notes died away, Charlie, positively beaming with pleasure, got to his feet, put his hand on my shoulder and said, "Eric, you've done a good job. You may write your own screen credit." I hesitated and then cheekily suggested, "Music written and composed by Eric James in spite of Charlie Chaplin." Fortunately, he laughed heartily and I subsequently suggested, "Eric James—Music Associate." Charlie accepted this immediately and said, "It shall be a half plate credit and it shall follow my own full plate credit." The length and timing of the film footage for the credit were quite considerable, usually around 15 seconds, and they have remained unaltered for all the films on which I have worked with Charlie.[25]

*   *   *

After *A King in New York*, it is no surprise that from this point forward, Chaplin was no longer commenting on contemporary culture. He was looking back; a decision also represented in his musical choices. *A Dog's Life* was the first of eight films in Chaplin's "Million Dollar Comedy Series" for First National Exhibitor's Circuit and the first filmed at the new Chaplin Studios. Originally titled *I Should Worry*, *A Dog's Life* represented a new direction in Chaplin's filmmaking. "I was beginning to think of comedy in a structural sense, and to become conscious of its architectural form," he said. "Each sequence implied the next sequence, all of them relating to the whole."[26] *A Dog's Life* bowed at the Strand Theatre in New York on April 14, 1918. *Variety* called it "a corking good comedy film for Chaplin to inaugurate his latest contract with."[27] The Tramp is once again among the unemployed, sleeping on the streets and stealing food like his canine friend, Scraps, whom he saves from a pack of dogs. Inside the Green Lantern dance hall, Charlie meets the beautiful and shy Edna Purviance, looking lost in the sleazy atmosphere of women selling themselves for a dance. When he later finds money a pair of robbers has stolen off a drunken millionaire, he helps capture the thugs and settles in the country with his beloved. Forty years later, it also made a charming opener to *The Chaplin Revue*.

Chaplin and Eric James began work on the music to *Shoulder Arms* first but *A Dog's Life* was the first completed score. James started working at Vevey originally with a verbal contract, not uncommon with Chaplin's musicians. And if James found it challenging to work with him, the feeling was mutual. "Mr. Chaplin is very tired and is resting today after a very exhausting time with the music," Eileen Burnier wrote at the end of November 1958.[28] A couple of weeks later, Rachel Ford was instructed not to sign any contract or agreement or to deposit money in James's bank account before Chaplin received and approved of a duplicate copy of the final piano score for all three films. Chaplin also would only make a contract for one film, *A Dog's Life*, at £9 per minute of recorded music. "If the *Dog's Life* turns out satisfactorily," Burnier told Ford, "then we will continue with the rest."[29] Ford was still unclear as to the financial arrangements for the work James was doing compiling the piano scores for the three films, "in the event of Mr. Chaplin not liking [them]. Am I right in presuming that I am supposed to stall him regarding the contract, or am I to frankly state the true facts?"

Ford could not "help being worried" about the James situation. "I deduct that Mr. Chaplin is not altogether happy with the work that Mr. James is doing and very naturally wishes to wait until he is certain that he has got hold of the right arranger. We have a precedence with Mr. Sainton whose services [on *A King in New York*] were not utilized as much as he had hoped but, in his case, the contract foresaw this eventuality and the matter was easily disposed of. I am wondering whether a verbal arrangement has been made with Mr. James as to what will be his in the event of Mr. Chaplin not wishing to continue to use his services."[30]

James broke protocol and wrote directly to Chaplin, hounding him for payment, a process Chaplin always left to others to handle. "I shall be most grateful if you would ask Miss Ford to send me the necessary contract and authorise the interim payments that I have requested," James wrote. "(I am sure that you won't have forgotten that Christmas—always a very expensive time—is nearly here and of course I have to take nourishment fairly regularly in order to keep up my health and strength.)"[31] This was the first of many often petulant letters from James over the next twenty years asking for remuneration, which unfortunately set the tone for his financial dealings with the Chaplin office for the rest of Chaplin's life.

Chaplin hired a second Eric to help with the arrangements and serve as conductor. Eric Spear (1908–1966) entered show business as an actor and toured with The Old Vic during the 1920s, becoming a stage director at the Arts Theatre in 1929. Spear started writing music for cabaret and working in films as a composer and conductor in 1934. His first chance at writing film music came at the Stoll Studios at Cricklewood, writing the music for six shorts with only a three-piece orchestra. He later became the musical director for the City Film Corporation before joining the BBC as a variety producer in 1936, staying with the company for twenty years, except during the war, producing an average of 150 shows a year. In 1952, Spear wrote the popular theme for the detective drama *Meet Mr. Callaghan*.

The two Erics spent "many, many hours" discussing "the most effective way of orchestrating the enormous amount of music" James had brought back to England. "We also had to decide what would be the ideal combination of instruments to bring out the vast musical sound," James said, "taking into account Charlie's marked preference for the strings. We finally came up with eight woodwind, eight brass, two percussion, harp and piano, and thirty-one strings—a total of fifty-one musicians with the option to augment in the case of special arrangements. Charlie approved this setup without hesitation and we were able to begin engaging the finest available players."[32]

The five recording sessions were spread out over three days, January 12–14, 1959, at Shepperton Studios. Instead of fifty-one musicians (probably a mistake of memory on James's part), Spear cut back on the strings to come up with a 37-piece ensemble that was hired to record all three films, a move that saved money but unfortunately thinned out the sound, though it did bring it closer to the timbre of an old movie palace pit orchestra during the silent era, which may have been the idea in the first place. "One policy we adopted to cope with Charlie's inevitable interventions," James said, "was to deliberately cue in the melody lines for alternative instruments when scoring; this was a tremendous saving of time when we were called upon to make last minute changes. This system of arranging the music in a more or less foolproof way, applied throughout my long association with Charlie, was adopted by every arranger I engaged to make the orchestral score."[33] Chaplin paid Spear £25 per session, totaling £125 over the five sessions. James received his agreed upon £9 per minute of recorded music, which totaled £387 for the forty-three minutes of music. The total music costs for *A Dog's Life*, including various expenses like £30 for an accountant to attend the sessions to pay the musicians, came to £2,128.72.

One of the biggest changes Chaplin made in editing the films affected the music. During the silent era, depending on the studio, frame rates were variable, usually anywhere between 16 and 23 frames per second (fps), sometimes as high as 40 fps. Between 1926 and 1930, theaters worldwide equipped themselves to a new standard projection frame rate of 24 fps. To accommodate the films in *The Chaplin Revue* to the standard 24 fps, Chaplin employed "stretch-printing," a process in which film frames are repeated at regular intervals to slow down the action. Blurring was noticeable in action sequences and, as author Hooman Mehran points out, the process "caused a noticeable 'drag' in Chaplin's movements, effectively ruining his exquisitely timed comic sequences."[34] In the 1990s, producer David Shepard used modern technology to help correct this for the video reissues but the original solution effectively altered how Chaplin approached the music.

"I have composed two hours of music which I hope will be more agreeable than the sound of steps on the gravel paths, as it were, or a lot of yakkety-yak talking as I'm doing now," Chaplin said in *The Chaplin Revue*'s voiceover introduction. "It will be music and action, a sort of a comic ballet. And now I shall retire behind my curtain of silence." Because Chaplin did not reimagine these films, as he did with *The Gold Rush* 1942 sound version, the scores for these shorts come closest to what he probably would have composed during the late teens and early '20s if he had had an orchestra at his disposal. These scores also set the stage for the music he would write for his other First National shorts during the last decade of his life, as well as *A Countess from Hong Kong*. Musical moods

A Dog's Life (1959 reissue as part of *The Chaplin Revue*)—The mixed subdivisions of the beat in the first section of the "Dog's Life Theme" is a prime example of Chaplin's use of *rubato* in his compositions.

sometimes change abruptly with cues dialed out equally unexpectedly. But for the first time since *Modern Times*, audiences were able to experience Chaplin's music, for the most part, without dialogue or sound effects.

A Dog's Life begins with, appropriately enough, the "Dog's Life Theme." An F-minor section full of mixed subdivisions of the beat—eighth notes, eighth note triplets, sixteenth notes—bookends the theme and underscores the languid, *rubato* feeling of the melody line, which is missing a particularly strong beat. The melodramatic nature of the theme conveys the sad state of Charlie's unemployment, sleeping on the ground and stealing hot dogs for food. This section also underscores the Tramp saving Scraps from the dog-fight and the two of them sleeping on the wallet the dog found and buried. As is often the case, Chaplin stops the music mid-phrase if it is time to move on to something else. This is particularly noticeable in the final scene with the Tramp and Edna surrounding the baby crib with Scrap and her pups, where the music ends on a dominant chord, leaving the ear waiting for a tonic chord resolution that never materializes. Chaplin transforms the last few bars of the first section into triplet rhythms to transition into a much more uptempo B section. When Charlie tangles with the police, the key switches to its relative major, a bright A-flat, with a lively melody in clarinet duet, marked by Chaplin's trademark use of triplet pickup notes and carefree dotted rhythms.

"Coffee and Cakes," the other primary theme, underscores the scene with Chaplin and his brother Syd as the food cart vendor. As Charlie sneakily steals the cakes from the cart, Syd keeps turning around trying to catch him in the act. The pair perform their comic *pas de deux*, basically moving only from the waist up, accompanied by a tender theme for violin solo that bears the *rubato* style of many of Chaplin's melodies. The theme has a yearning quality that takes on a greater poignancy in later scenes when Charlie tries to cheer up Edna, he and Scraps get thrown out of the Green Lantern dance hall,

A Dog's Life (**1959 reissue as part of** *The Chaplin Revue*)—**The second section of the "Dog's Life Theme," a lively melody for clarinet duet as Charlie tangles with the police.**

and in the finale "when dreams come true" as Charlie becomes a farmer and sets up home with Edna.

Chaplin composed a number of jazz pieces for the Green Lantern dance hall. With its thinly veiled hints at prostitution, this "tender spot in the Tenderloin" is the greatest source of diegetic source music in the score, including the frenetic "Green Lantern Rag" and the banjo-strumming (though confusingly titled) "Green Lantern Snag," most memorable in the scene with Charlie and Edna dancing and dragging Scraps around. The banjo frantically strums its way through the brief "Shimmy" for one of the dance hall performers and a musical saw substitutes for Edna's voice as she sings a "Song Triste" ("Sad Song"), with Henry Bergman dressed in drag crying buckets and squirting "tears" by leaning on a seltzer bottle.

Furious sixteenth notes (and a humorous quote from Wagner's "Ride of the Valkyries") accompany the dog chase and the "Galop" for the robbers chasing Charlie through the streets. Other extended musical cues include the staccato march of the unemployed at the "Labour Exchange," and the chirping winds and drunken muted brass carrying on a "Tete a Tete" over the hollow sound of the wood blocks after Charlie knocks out one of the robbers and becomes his limbs. And never one to miss the chance to insert a waltz, Chaplin's latest in three-quarter time underscores Charlie's tender dance with Edna as the two robbers look on overhead and see that Charlie has found the money they stole from the millionaire.

"I am pleased to say that everything went off extremely well down at the recording studios," James wrote to Rachel Ford, "and Mr. Chaplin seemed very pleased with my work."[35] Ford, in turn, wrote to Bonnie Bourne, "I heard that Charlie was pleased with the recording of the music for *A Dog's Life* which took place this week and that he has given the green light for the orchestration of *The Pilgrim* and *Shoulder Arms*."[36] James finally signed a contract in February and, like all the other arrangers before him, he waived any legal rights to the music. As Chaplin told him, "Where there's a hit, there's a writ, so it is best to confirm once and for all in writing to whom all compositions *must* be attributed!"[37]

*   *   *

Shoulder Arms was the first film Eric James began scoring with Chaplin. For its inclusion in *The Chaplin Revue*, Chaplin inserted an introduction to the short accompanied by archival footage of the war from the Imperial War Museum. "Fighting was different in those days," Chaplin said in his voiceover. "They lived in trenches

Chaplin and Scraps on the set of *A Dog's Life*, c. 1918 (© Roy Export SAS).

A Dog's Life (1959 reissue as part of *The Chaplin Revue*)—The appropriately named "Coffee and Cakes" underscores the onscreen pairing of Chaplin and his brother Syd at the food cart.

A Dog's Life (1959 reissue as part of *The Chaplin Revue*)—The frenetic "Green Lantern Rag," one of two source dance cues for the notorious Green Lantern dance hall.

A Dog's Life (1959 reissue as part of *The Chaplin Revue*)—Charlie, with Scraps in tow, drags Edna around the dance floor to the tune of the "Green Lantern Snag."

for months, languishing in dugouts and mud. There were no atomic bombs or guided missiles. Then, it was only cannons, bayonets, and poisoned gas. [*laughs*] Those were the good ol' days." Charlie is the Army's most inept soldier, unable to distinguish his right foot from his left, until he miraculously picks off the enemy one by one from the trenches, foils the remaining troops, saves Edna from marauding Germans, and captures the Kaiser—only to find out it has all been a dream. As with *The Great Dictator*, only a star of Chaplin's caliber had the chutzpah to turn such a devastating event like the First World War into a comedy.

When the war broke out on July 28, 1914, it could not have come at a worse time for

Chaplin. He was in the middle of his Keystone contract with his star on the rise. And as his popularity grew, Chaplin felt pressure to join the war effort. A 1915 English soldier's song, "When the Moon Shines Bright on Charlie Chaplin," took the comedian to task— "When the Moon Shines Bright on Charlie Chaplin / His boots are cracking / For want of blacking / And his little baggy trousers they want mending / Before we send him / To the Dardanelles."[38] The song was "all the rage," said *Pictures and The Picturegoer*. "Everybody who is anybody in the juvenile world is singing [it.]"[39] "I went home and read about the Dardanelles after that," Chaplin told Alistair Cooke, "and for a time I was certain they were out to get me."[40]

Chaplin received white feathers, the symbol of cowardice during the war. There were calls on him to enlist, both at home and in Great Britain, a movement that escalated once the U.S. entered the war on April 6, 1917. Chaplin was forced to issue a press statement—"I am ready and willing to answer the call of my country to serve in any branch of the military service at whatever post I might do the most good. But, like thousands of other Britishers, I am awaiting word from the British embassy in Washington. Meanwhile I have invested a quarter of a million dollars in the war activities of America and England.... I registered for the draft here, and asked no exemptions or favors. Had I been drawn, I would have gone to the front like any other patriotic citizen. As it is, I shall wait for orders from the British government through its embassy at Washington."[41]

In April 1918, Chaplin joined Douglas Fairbanks and Mary Pickford on the third and final Liberty Bonds Tour. Over the course of the month, the trio lent their star power to raise money for the troops "so that we can drive that old devil, the Kaiser, out of

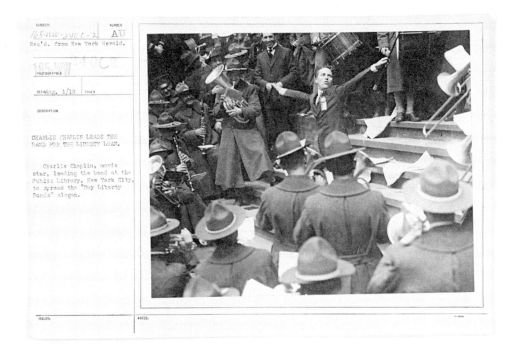

Chaplin leading the band outside the Public Library in New York to promote the "Buy Liberty Bonds" campaign. Original photograph from the *New York Herald*, c. August 1, 1918 (National Archives, no. 165-WW-240C-2).

France."[42] The trio was mobbed at their two stops in New York and Washington, D.C. At the corner of Broad and Wall Streets in New York, Fairbanks hoisted Chaplin on his shoulders and the crowd went wild. In Washington, Chaplin fell off the platform and landed on Assistant Secretary of the Navy Franklin D. Roosevelt. *Shoulder Arms* premiered on October 20, 1918, only a couple of weeks before the Armistice was signed, so, as author Charles Maland points out, it is unlikely the film had much direct effect on soldier morale. "Nevertheless, Chaplin's contribution to the war effort was significant: not only did he lend his celebrity status and his energies toward raising large amounts of money (and indeed contributing sizable sums of his own), but he also through this and earlier films provided pleasure and reminders of home for soldiers abroad who saw them."[43]

"The name of Chaplin spells money if we are to take the long line of ticket chasers at the Strand as a criterion of popularity," said *The Billboard*. "For the crowds came early and late, while loud guffaws and peals of laughter spread an epidemic across the auditorium. There was just provocation for all this hilarity, for Chaplin has never done anything better or has appeared funnier.... The public owes Chaplin a vote of thanks for enlivening the gloomy hours caused by anxiety for the loved ones 'over there' and for presenting the funny side of life in his irresistible manner."[44] One audience member at the Strand Theatre in New York simply stated, "The fool's funny."[45]

"It moves like a drumroll," Jean Cocteau said of the film.[46] *Shoulder Arms* became Chaplin's most popular comedy yet, and the film was shown in 49 countries in 1918 and 1919.[47] Mae Tinée from the *Chicago Daily Tribune* poignantly described her emotional viewing of the film on Armistice Day:

> With the whistles blowing, the bells ringing, the crowds shouting, and PEACE ON EARTH, it's pretty hard to get down to writing a review of even a Charlie Chaplin picture. *Shoulder Arms* was, however, one of the features of yesterday, the greatest day in history, and so mustn't be neglected.
>
> I thought everybody was on the streets celebrating, but when I got inside McVicker's theater I discovered differently. The Chaplin fans were true and right on the job to see his latest picture.
>
> They streamed in waving flags, throwing confetti, and wearing strong patriotic headgear, rakishly awry. When the favorite name was flashed upon the screen, greeted it with a rousing cheer.
>
> "Hey, Charlie!" "To Hell with the kaiser, Charlie." "Don't stand no nonsense from Bill, Chas!" "When it's sauerkraut time in Holland we'll be marching t'ro Berlin, Charlie!" And so on. They talked to his celluloid self, joyously and spontaneously confidential. It was sure some gathering![48]

Like *A Dog's Life*, it was still too early in film music development for a cue sheet for *Shoulder Arms*. Silent film musicians no doubt heaped on the patriotic tunes much to the delight of audiences. For the 1927 reissue, Eugene Conte compiled a cue sheet for Cameo Music Service using the usual assortment of library cues plus popular World War I tunes like Irving Berlin's "Oh, How I Hate to Get Up in the Morning" and George M. Cohan's "Over There." Chaplin would later interpolate Cohan's famous melody into his own score, but he had something far more ironic in mind as his primary musical theme.

On Eric James's first day, while they were waiting for new copies of the film to arrive, Chaplin told him the story of *Shoulder Arms* using the furniture as props, the settee substituting for a dugout and a walking stick as a rifle. "From thence on," James said, "he dodged imaginary shells, stumbled and crawled about the floor on his stomach and virtually reenacted the entire film. It was unforgettable and I was completely exhausted with laughing.... At the end of this crazy session he threw himself onto the piano stool, hit a sequence of notes and said, 'That's the sort of melody with which I want to open this film.'"[49]

Shoulder Arms (1959 reissue as part of *The Chaplin Revue*)—"Flat Feet," the main theme from the film and the first piece written on Eric James's first day of employment as Chaplin's musical associate.

That sequence of notes turned into "Flat Feet," a gently loping theme in 6/8 first heard down in the trenches. Slide whistle and booming timpani give voice to the bombs exploding nearby and the theme trots along as the oblivious Charlie goes about his business. "I wondered what a mess it would be when it came to fitting it to the particular 'trench' sequence," James said. When James finally saw the film projected onto the screen, "the music fitted the mood and movement of Chaplin to perfection. Needless to say we were both very pleased."[50] The lackadaisical theme also underscores the absurdity of allowing enemy fire to open a bottle of wine or light a cigarette when Charlie sticks them up above the trench line. Chaplin also incorporated the theme in the main titles of *The Chaplin Revue* and even in a scene in *A Dog's Life*, where Charlie enters the Green Lantern with Scraps stuffed in his trousers and his wagging tail sticking out of a hole in the back. "Shell Happy," a drunken jazz melody for saxophone and trombone duet, serves as a charming mealtime ditty for Charlie and Syd's "quiet lunch" with timpani and cymbal bombs exploding overhead, and as Charlie stands guard in the rain, dreaming of cocktails and a dry life back home. The theme returns a few scenes later as Charlie wakens in his flooded sleeping quarters.

A number of Army bugle calls signal lights out and morning, and Chaplin composed a series of marches and march-like tunes for the score. The stodgy "Sauerkraut March" thumbs its nose at the invaders, accompanying the arrival of a package of old Limburger cheese delivered from home and as the Germans' marching music when Charlie takes them prisoner. The theme in its parallel minor becomes a stealthy "Mysterioso March" that underscores Charlie (in his priceless tree disguise) knocking out the enemy, and later as the background for the leering Germans and Syd's dual role as the Kaiser, while Charlie hides in the closet. The "Inner March" is the Tramp's musical statement—bright, almost heroic music that perhaps Chaplin wished he had for himself during that tense period of pressure to join the war effort. The theme originates with "a call for volunteers" and becomes the Tramp's music of heroism as he surprises the Germans and makes them hand over their guns, and later dons a German uniform to help the Kaiser "escape." The theme also ends the film on a bright note as it rolls over the end credits.

Even in a wartime comedy, Chaplin still finds a place to insert a couple of waltzes. "The Post" is a yearning melody full of memory as the soldiers receive packages from back home, while the "D Minor Waltz" is a holdover from *A Dog's Life*. In the earlier

Shoulder Arms (1959 reissue as part of *The Chaplin Revue*)—The drunken "Shell Happy" duet for saxophone and trombone.

film, the theme represented Charlie consoling Edna. In *Shoulder Arms*, the roles are reversed as Edna helps Charlie after he gets trapped in the hollow, bombed ruins of a house.

The opening march from the main titles also closes the film as "Bringing Home the Bacon," accompanying Charlie as he drives the unsuspecting captured Kaiser to the Allies. But the most ingenious cue is the music that scores the soldiers heeding the call to go "Over the Top" to meet the enemy in battle. Bookended by the *agitato* music used in later tree scenes and trumpet fanfares, the cue's centerpiece is an Ivesian mélange of wartime tunes—"Over There," "Keep the Home Fires Burning," and "It's a Long Way to Tipperary"—followed by jazz clarinet underscoring Charlie's realization that his dog tag number (13) is anything but lucky.

If there is a throughline to the three films in *The Chaplin Revue*, it is the Tramp—and by extension Chaplin—thumbing his nose at life's insanities. For *A Dog's Life*, it was poverty, and war was the obvious culprit in *Shoulder Arms*. The third film in the triptych showcased Chaplin's disdain for that most entrenched institution—religion.

*   *   *

The Pilgrim, Chaplin's final film under his First National contract, is one of his best. It is the first film for which a written scenario and gag notes survive. Chaplin began work

In *Shoulder Arms,* three doughboys—Park Jones, Chaplin, and Syd Chaplin-pass the time in their barracks, appropriately named the Vermin Club, c. 1918 (© Roy Export SAS).

Shoulder Arms (1959 reissue as part of *The Chaplin Revue*)—Chaplin pokes fun at the Germans with the stodgy "Sauerkraut March."

on February 23, 1922, one day before *Pay Day* was released, and shooting began on April 10. Monta Bell, who had helped Chaplin with *My Trip Abroad*, assisted him in writing the scenario. The first working title was simple marked "Western" followed by *The Tail End*, a sly reference to the end of Chaplin's contract.

Chaplin's role as an escaped convict who poses as a chaplain for a small Texas town pokes pungent fun at the trappings of religion, a controversial stance that caused some theater owners to refuse to show the film. "Perhaps the most hilariously humorous aspect of *The Pilgrim* was provided by the Pennsylvania censors, who barred the picture from that sacrosanct State because, said they, it made the ministry look ridiculous," said future Oscar and four-time Pulitzer Prize winner Robert Sherwood. "A number of interested

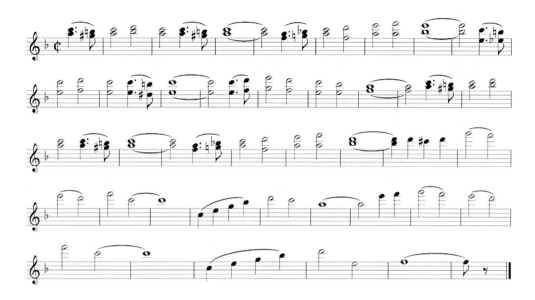

Shoulder Arms **(1959 reissue as part of** ***The Chaplin Revue*****)—Charle's theme, the rousing "Inner March."**

observers have been waiting, since then, to hear that the Pennsylvania censors have suppressed several thousand clergymen on the same charge."[51] The Atlanta Ministers' Association also demanded the film withdrawn from a local theater because "the comedian ridicules the ministry."[52] In South Carolina, even the Daniel Morgan Chapter of the Ku Klux Klan objected to the film holding the clergy up to ridicule. The Palace Theater in Mason City, Iowa, deleted the scene of Charlie making sport of saying grace and censored almost one-fourth of the film after a visit by the delegation from the Protestant Preachers' Association and a representative of the Ku Klux Klan.[53]

Critics, however, focused on the comedy. The *Boston Daily Globe* said, "While *The Pilgrim* is not as pretentious as many other of Chaplin's photoplays, it is a very amusing and extremely well-acted satire on 'Main Street' life."[54] *The American* admitted, "You'll feel ashamed of yourself for laughing at the incredibly grotesque adventures of Chaplin in this new picture and yet you can't help it."[55]

When it came to the musical accompaniment in 1922, musical directors in the UK and the U.S. finally had cue sheets for a Chaplin film. A comparison between the cue sheet from the British and American versions demonstrates the differences in suggestions submitted by two different publishers. They also show how important these melodic quotes were and why they proved to be such a big hit with music directors and orchestra leaders.

The U.S. cue sheet, compiled by Broadway Theatre music director and former *Moving Picture World* columnist James C. Bradford, focuses more on Tin Pan Alley songs, one-steps, and ragtime numbers from the period. For instance, Bradford suggested George Little, Jack Stanley, and Henry Dellon's 1919 one-step "Somebody" as Charlie's theme. The verse, obviously unheard in the theater, is particularly appropriate to Chaplin's character—"I have been lost in dreams, / That won't come true, it seems, / Still I am dreaming, / Keep right on scheming."[56] The inclusion of Jerome Kern's 1916 classic "They Didn't Believe Me" to underscore Charlie's sermon points up the disbelieving looks on the faces

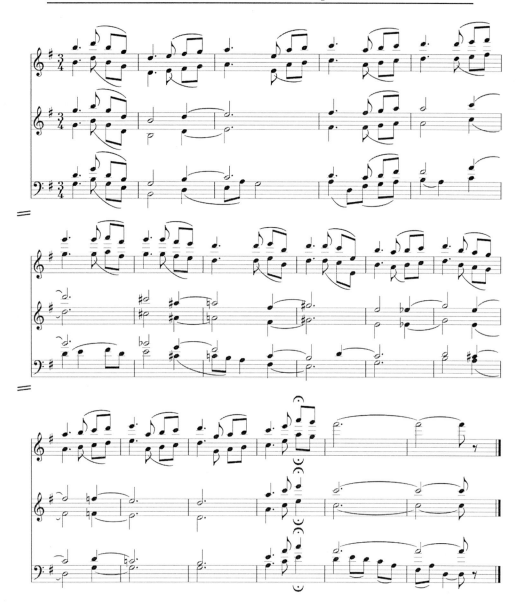

Shoulder Arms (1959 reissue as part of *The Chaplin Revue*)—Chaplin wrote the yearning "The Post" waltz to underscore the scene of soldiers receiving letters from home.

The "D Minor Waltz" appears in the scores for both *A Dog's Life* and *Shoulder Arms*.

of the congregation. Howard Whitney's *A Lucky Duck* (1913) escorts Charlie and the Deacon out of the church afterward. Irving Berlin's "Lady of the Evening" (1922) slyly winks at the uptight Mrs. Brown (Kitty Bradbury) as does James Thornton's "She May Have Seen Better Days" (1896).

Edward Van Praag of the London Opera House compiled the British cue sheet, so it naturally leans more heavily towards the classical. Gilbert and Sullivan's "The Vicar's Song" from *The Sorcerer* (1877) represents the parson, Giacomo Meyerbeer's *Les Huguenots* (1836) for the convict, and Charles Gounod's *The Queen of Sheba* (1862) underscores Charlie's sermon. Schubert's *Six moments musicaux* (1828) was proper parlor music for the sitting room while Tchaikovsky's *Chanson Triste* from *Twelve Pieces* (1828) underscored the gambling den. Van Praag also suggested Kern's "They Didn't Believe Me," this time for the morning after the hold-up. But it is the use of Gounod's *Funeral March of the Marionette* as Charlie's theme that is particularly intriguing. Chaplin and Arthur Kay used the theme in the 1928 compilation score to *The Circus* for the brief scene of the Ring Master yelling at the clowns. The use of this minor key piece in the context of *The Pilgrim* seems almost judgmental towards Chaplin, as if Van Praag is finger wagging at Chaplin's outlook on the clergy. While the familiar loping melody certainly captures the Tramp's distinctive waddle, today it is difficult to disassociate it from the figure of Alfred Hitchcock, with whom the tune is now forever linked.

When it came time for Chaplin to compose a new score for *The Chaplin Revue* thirty-five years later, he obviously had the cantering rhythms of traditional cowboy tunes in mind. Chaplin wrote two versions of lyrics for the song that opens the film—"Texas Vocal," also known as "Bound for Texas"—which provide a window into how he revised his written work.

Matt Munro, who later scored a worldwide hit with John Barry and Hal David's theme song to *Born Free* (and whose name is misspelled "Monroe" in the *Pilgrim* credits), sang the song. Munro "did a great job and was warmly congratulated by Charlie," said Eric James.[59] The vocal version is used most prominently, except for an amusing instrumental rendition, orchestrated for a wheezing accordion and fiddle obbligato, when Charlie spies his old cell mate Picking Pete (Charles Reisner) on the street and later when the Sheriff (Allan Garcia) shows Edna his "Wanted" poster.

The second primary theme, "Texas Border," was originally slotted for *The Pilgrim*'s main titles. Instead, this gentle tango accompanies Charlie disembarking from the train, and meeting the Sheriff and members of the congregation welcome committee. The theme later underscores Charlie and Edna's conversation over the white picket fence and, most memorably, in the final scene (which would have provided a nice musical bookend had Chaplin left the theme in the main title sequence) as Charlie walks off into the sunset, straddling the border between the U.S. and Mexico. By the time *The Chaplin Revue* was released in 1959, the shot of the Sheriff kicking Charlie out of the country must have hit home with audiences who remembered Chaplin's trials at the hands of the U.S. Attorney General in 1952.

Even with a comedy that was nearly forty years old by that point, Chaplin still made a stinging political point on his contemporary situation. Bonnie Bourne later sent a lead sheet of the "Texas Border" theme with a lyric written "by one of our outstanding young lyricists."[60] The lead sheet unfortunately no longer survives and apparently the lyric went no further. It seems an unmarketable tune to turn into a song and smacks of a desperate attempt on the part of the publisher to keep themselves relevant in Chaplin's eyes while legal hassles over their public auction played out in the news.

I'm tired of the town
Of the smoke stack and steel
The grip and the grind of the factory wheel
I've got my wings
And I'm ready to fly
To the blue of the wide Texas sky.

REFRAIN
I'm bound for Texas
Dear old Texas
Bound for Texas way
To hear the moo and rattle
Of snake and cattle
Down in Texas way.

I'll get me a horse
And I'll get me a wife
A home and wife I'll be set for life

I'll buy her a home
And she'll never roam
And we'll sit on the lawn in the shade.

REFRAIN

I'll sing her a song
At the end of the day
A song that will drive all her cares away
I'll sing of the desert,
The blue starry skies
And the stars shinning [sic] bright in her eyes.[57]

I'm tired of the city
Of smoke, stack, and steel
I'm tired of the grind of the factory wheel
I'm spreading my wings
And I'm ready to fly
To the land of the wide open sky.

REFRAIN
I'm bound for Texas
Bound for Texas
Bound for Texas land
To hear the moo and rattle
Of snakes and cattle
I'm bound for Texas land.

I'll work on a ranch
Where there's plenty of sun
With my horse and my saddle, my rope and gun.
I'll ride on the prairie
My face to the sky
And the rest of the world can go by.

REFRAIN

I'll save up my money
And look for a wife
A wife who'll be true and a pal for life.
I'll build her a home
And a room for a child
With the roses around growing wild.

REFRAIN

I'll sing her a song
At the end of the day
A song that will drive all our cares away
I'll sing of the prairie,
The blue starry skies
And the stars shining bright in her eyes.

REFRAIN[58]

The Pilgrim (1959 reissue as part of *The Chaplin Revue*)—Chaplin's original and revised lyric, and the opening of the "Texas Vocal" chorus, also known as "Bound for Texas."

The Pilgrim (1959 reissue as part of *The Chaplin Revue*)—The gentle "Texas Border" tango accompanies Charlie straddling the line between the US and Mexico.

The Pilgrim's prophetic final scene with Charlie astride the border between the US and Mexico while the Sheriff (Allan Garcia) tries to keep him from re-entering the country, c. 1918 (© Roy Export SAS).

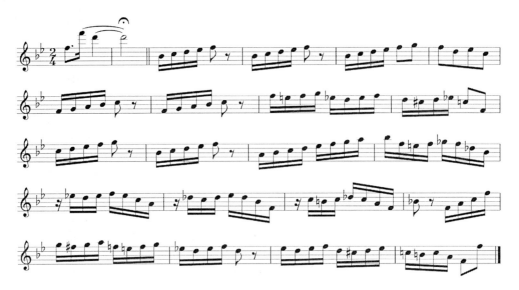

The Pilgrim (1959 reissue as part of *The Chaplin Revue*)—**Charlie as The Pilgrim gets chased around the train platform to the strains of Chaplin's delightful "Jitters" cue.**

For *Shoulder Arms,* Chaplin wrote a three-note motif for those rare occasions when Charlie is at peace. In *The Pilgrim,* he reuses that motif as the calm introduction before his delightful "Jitters" tune, which first accompanied the *How to Make Movies* lead-in to *A Dog's Life.* In *The Pilgrim,* the jittery theme underscores the eloping groom chasing Charlie on the train platform. It later shows up when Charlie once more poses as the priest to steal the money back from Picking Pete. Chaplin once again mixes triplet and dotted rhythms in the "The Old Ladies March," an uptight theme for the straight-backed, straight-laced women of the congregation. That same mixture of triplets and dotted notes is associated with the music for the "Prison Companions," aurally relating the stuffy busybodies of the congregation with the criminals.

"The Deacon Presents" consists of two separate sections. The first is a comical duet for oboe and bassoon as Charlie takes the podium and later compares the weight of the two collection boxes, which reprises during the tea party and Charlie's comic business with the "cake." The second section of the theme has the religious overtones of a four-part chorale. For the classic "David and Goliath" sermon, Chaplin ties all three scores from *The Chaplin Revue* together. Underneath the mocking oboe melody, he quotes the wood blocks and *oom-pah-pah* accompaniment found in the "Tete a Tete" cue from *A Dog's Life* and the main theme from *Shoulder Arms.* The wartime comedy also underscores Charlie's bows following the sermon with the "Bringing Home the Bacon" theme.

For the tea party, Chaplin composed a warm F-major theme to represent Charlie's feelings towards Edna. But the highlight of the scene is the lively string melody accompanying the destruction caused by the disruptive child ("Dinky" Dean Reisner, whose father plays Picking Pete). While filming in 1922, Reisner later remembered, a musician named Earl Taylor was hired to play harmonium and "give background music to the scene."[61] For the cake scene, Chaplin composed an elegant gavotte to point out the absurdity of mistaking a hat for food. And of course there is a waltz—"Waltz Despair"—as Char-

The Pilgrim (1959 reissue as part of *The Chaplin Revue*)—"The Old Ladies March" perfectly captures the town's local band of uptight busybodies.

The Pilgrim (1959 reissue as part of *The Chaplin Revue*)—The first section of "The Deacon Presents" cue is a comical duet for oboe and bassoon.

Chaplin's classic pantomime rendition of David and Goliath is one of the comedic highlights of *The Pilgrim,* c. 1923 (© Roy Export SAS).

The Pilgrim (1959 reissue as part of *The Chaplin Revue*)—Dainty staccato eighth notes give a frenzied elegance to the "Tea Party."

lie "dances" around the sitting room in a *pas de deux* to keep Picking Pete from stealing the old lady's money.

Since Chaplin had approved of what Eric James had done with *A Dog's Life,* the recording of *Shoulder Arms* and *The Pilgrim* could now proceed. James received £50 a week while working in Vevey and was paid £300 each for *A Dog's Life* and *Shoulder Arms,* and £400 for *The Pilgrim,* plus an extra £9 per minute of recorded music of the three films, which totaled another £882. The rank and file musicians were paid £6 for every twenty minutes of film music, while the Principals received £6.10, and £8.0 for the Leader.

The recording sessions for *Shoulder Arms* and *The Pilgrim* were scheduled for February 18–20 and 23–25, a total of eleven sessions. Eric Spear received £275 total (£25 per session) to conduct. Chaplin also hired another arranger and orchestrator, Jack Moss, whether because there was so much music or he did not trust Eric James to get it all done is unclear. Moss, who had arranged Spear's popular *Meet Mr. Callaghan* theme for dance band, was paid out of the copyist fees and made £34.14.6 for his work on the two scores. The recording costs for *Shoulder Arms* and *The Pilgrim*, including the £65 paid to the accountant who issued the musician vouchers, totaled £4,587.9.9.

*   *   *

"*The Chaplin Revue* was a haven of refuge and delight," said London's *Daily Express*, "not only because it consists of three great films from the greatest comic of them all but because all of them were made in the good old days—and are therefore silent. True, Chaplin has given them a sound-track consisting of some of his own music, but this will be bearable once they turn the amplifier down."[62] *The Spectator* said the film was "not to be missed by man, woman, child or (I almost said) dog, since dogs have as human a place there as the average person."[63] Though Toronto's *The Globe and Mail* said all three films contained "a great deal of the pantomimic genius of Chaplin," *Shoulder Arms* "was a rather artless bit of war propaganda…. It is *A Dog's Life* that shines as an almost unflawed work of silent art."[64] *The Jewish Chronicle* said it was "convincing proof of the lasting greatness of the world's most famous, most lovable comic mime…. Quite often one could not hear the music (composed, by the way, by Chaplin himself) because of the gusts of laughter that rang through the theatre. The best parts of *A Dog's Life*, *Shoulder Arms*, and *The Pilgrim* are coupled together in two hours of irresistible mirth alternating with poignant tearfulness. This wonderful show is an absolute *must*."[65] *The Spectator* "could have done without the jazzing-up of the sound track, but nothing really much matters when you have Chaplin in action."[66]

In November 1959, Bourne started the process of negotiating a soundtrack album. UA had recently released a soundtrack for *Modern Times*, but none of Chaplin's films had ever had a soundtrack during their initial release. While there was always interest, and more often than not a contract, the deal always fell through. With *The Chaplin Revue*, Chaplin finally got a new soundtrack album, but the process was nerve-racking and expensive.

At the end of the first set of recording sessions in January, Bourne sent over contracts for "Coffee and Cakes," "Green Lantern Rag," "Green Lantern Snag," "Texas Border," and two cues that have been lost—"Charlot's Romance" and "Waltz Consolation." But in March, *Variety* reported that the company was "going under the block." The firm was to be sold at public auction on April 21 by order of the New York Surrogate Court. "The court stated that the public auction would be 'an ideal way' to settle the estate of the late Saul N. Bourne." Differences between Bonnie and her daughter Beebee, both vice presidents in the company, were "cueing the sale since one of the two is likely to emerge as sole owner…. It's expected that the starting point in the public auction will be at the $2,000,000 mark."[67]

"I was very upset to read the article which appeared in last week's *Variety*," Rachel Ford wrote to Bonnie. "I can but hope that all this unpleasantness will soon be a thing of the past. I am afraid, however, that it is going to greatly hamper, if not prevent our present negotiations … from being finalized. I had intended to ask you to make some amendments to the proposed contract in our favour, for example, that an album of the music should come out immediately. Now I am afraid that it will no longer be possible for the music of the *Big Parade* to be handled by Bourne Inc., if the news contained in *Variety* should be true."[68]

"Believe me," Bonnie wrote back, "I was more upset than anyone to read the article in *Variety*, and it was as much a surprise to me as to everyone, but then young people sometimes forget to use their heads. I think I can say with confidence that everything will be worked out satisfactorily and harmoniously. With you I can share the problem that happens to be truly one between mother and daughter, and that is all, and sometimes it takes time for such relationships to be smoothed out. I sincerely hope that our long and mutually successful business relationship will not be hampered by foolish articles in trade papers since we have both shared such adverse publicity together."[69]

Even though Bonnie firmly stated in a telegram, "FIRM NOT BEING SOLD," Ford was still uneasy.[70] Roy Export could not enter into any contract regarding the *Chaplin Revue* music without Bonnie signing a letter from Roy's lawyers, "stating that Messrs. Bourne are not involved in any litigation whatsoever concerning the ownership of their firm, and that it will remain under your management during our proposed licence period," said Ford. "Some sort of bond will be required, and as I have previously intimated we will also want certain amendments to the proposed contract."[71]

Bonnie tried to put her fears at ease. "The difficulty which does exist is purely a family matter which, unfortunately, found its way into the trade papers. Should you feel more secure by having your lawyers draft a statement, by all means do so, and as long as it does not ask that I live longer than the time the good Lord has designated for me, I can see no reason at this time why I should not sign it."

> I do not understand what you mean by bond required. Our firm is, no doubt, one of the few firms with a very substantial amount of liquid assets in this business. Our credit is the finest; why would you require a bond? You have always received your statements and checks on time. Perhaps I misunderstood your thinking…
>
> Rachel, you know from past experience that it is the desire of Bourne, Inc. to give Charlie Chaplin the maximum amount of exploitation and cooperation. This has always been our policy and will continue to be.
>
> I trust this clears up a few of the matters you feel have hampered you which was not our intention at all.[72]

By July the issue was still not settled. "I told Charlie that you would agree to our terms," Rachel wrote to Bonnie.

> There is no doubt in my mind that he would very much like you to handle the music. He knows you and thinks you have his interests at heart. But he is most alarmed at the possibility of your firm being put up for auction. If the management and/or ownership changed hands, this might entail a change of policy.
>
> The idea that this could occur greatly perturbs him and he would like you to guarantee that your firm will not change hands. He thinks that this guarantee should take the form of a bond in escrow, to be paid over to Roy Export in the event of your firm being sold during the period that it will be publishing this music.
>
> Do you think that an equitable way of working this out could be found?[73]

In a letter to Chaplin, Ford stated, "Mrs. Bourne is still taking evasive action and has avoided answering my precise questions. Time is getting short as the music ought to be out here before the premiere on September 25th. I think there are now only two alternatives: to let United Artists handle the music or to let Bourne do so and not press for this bond in escrow, the amount of which has not even been discussed." Chaplin decided to forgo the bond, let Bourne have the music, and "take the risk of the [public] sale."[74]

Decca Records could now proceed with plans for the soundtrack album. "The score is very exciting and I feel Mr. Chaplin has done a remarkable job," Decca's Milt Gabler wrote to Ford. "The music has great charm and nostalgia. I find myself enjoying it immensely even without the visual assistance of the film itself."[75] Ford made sure that the liner notes reflected what Chaplin wanted:

> Only Chaplin can create such an atmosphere to complement his stories, interweaving theme after theme into a well-formed mosaic. Today, Chaplin music has become almost as identifiable as his baggy pants and bowler hat. A famous Hollywood director has been heard telling his composer "I want Chaplin-type music here."
>
> In THE CHAPLIN REVUE, Chaplin has drawn upon the mood of the twenties for his themes, the period in which the films were made. [He has scored them for a full orchestra without losing an iota of the character familiar to those who can remember the old pit pianos which pounded these delightful sounds.] Not only does the music so aptly suit the pictures, but on hearing it we can actually see the tramp being chased by cops, evading thieves, drilling in the army and giving a sermon in Church as the Pilgrim.[76]

"I am very pleased that you sincerely enjoyed the CHAPLIN REVUE recording," Gabler wrote to Ford.

> The task was a tremendous one as there were many repeated segments in the original sound track, and the whole had to be segued in the form of a musical suite. I tried to retain as many of the important Chaplin melodies as possible, and also keep the flavor of the original scores. All this had to be done within the time limitation of a single 12" LP disc. The task was accomplished after transferring the entire sound track to acetate records and memorizing the performance by repeated playings. The editing time which followed encompassed over fifty hours of studio time. I was a tired man but very proud of the final product. I only hope that Mr. Chaplin likes the record as much as yourself.[77]

Decca wanted to postpone the album since no release date for the film had been set for the U.S. "We have no plans for releasing THE CHAPLIN REVUE in the States whatsoever," Ford wrote to Herbert Jacoby, Chaplin's lawyer. "On the other hand, it is being released in a great many countries just now and it is particularly desirable that the Decca record should come out as soon as possible. For your private information, I am at my wits end as Messrs. Bourne have produced no records at all as yet and we are daily receiving requests for same."[78]

The album was released in the UK on the Brunswick label in August 1960. The *New Musical Express* claimed that "divorced from the visual side they sound rather quaint and unimpressive."[79] But *Melody Maker* said, "The Chaplin music brings just that modern touch to these celluloid masterpieces."[80] *Billboard* called it "a remarkable package.... [It] is full of nostalgia and entertainment value."[81] The *North Western Evening News* in Britain said the record was of "unusual interest.... Mr. Chaplin's own melodies, which fit the varying moods of the films so successfully, have been arranged for full orchestra and are splendidly played under the direction of Eric Spears [*sic*]. This is a record for all, but those who remember the original films will get the greatest pleasure from it."[82]

But the British musicians that had recorded the material had only been paid for the film usage and not for any records, which necessitated paying them a second fee equal to what they received for the first recording, no matter the length of the album. In November, the issue was still unresolved. "I am afraid that the time has come when it will have to be decided one way or the other whether the musicians involved are legally entitled to receive anything," Ford wrote to Jacoby.

> When this matter was first brought up, I thought Decca would obviously know every facet of the question—and I remember being surprised that they were not sure whether payment had to be made or not. No doubt this was because they did not know whether Roy [Export] had paid a double fee at the time the recordings were made and what were the commitments, if any, we had with the British Musicians Union. My endeavours to ascertain the position were not entirely successful.
>
> I continue to think that this must be a routine affair for Decca and that they should know the answer. At the time of writing, I do not know whether the Brunswick record was made in England or not and whether this affects the re-recording fee or not.
>
> Furthermore, I do not know how the fee is computed in the event of it having to be paid as Mr. James said that there was a fee of £6 to every musician (slightly more for the leader and principals) for every twenty minutes of sound track used on records???
>
> I would be very grateful if you would take this matter up with Decca as there is no doubt that all the musicians are applying to Mr. James, who in turn raises the questions with me.[83]

Eric James tried to extract a re-use fee for the recording as "arranger" of the music "for every 20 minutes of sound track music used on records," but his contract negated that possibility.[84] "As I understand it," Ford wrote him in December, "the payment we made you was in full consideration of all your services and for the copyright in the orchestrations."[85] Perhaps that explains James's exasperation in his letter to Ford the following month. "It is nearly three months since I spoke to you on the telephone about the fees due to the musicians involved in the above recording and still nothing has been done," he wrote. "Surely you are not denying your liability to them in this matter? I find this all very embarrassing and would appreciate some prompt action."[86]

A letter from Decca's London branch to the New York office stated that "due to the problem we always have with the Musicians Union, and because it was felt that the potential sale of this album would be somewhat restricted (as is the case with most albums of film back-ground music) it was decided that, after we were informed that the amount of £286.10s.0d was to be paid by us ... the release of the album was not a feasible proposition."

> The publishers owning the musical rights were informed of this decision and were understandably somewhat disappointed, though they appreciated the reasons behind the decision. On June 15th, however, they informed by letter that ... "as Chaplin's secretary, Miss Ford, has paid the necessary money to the musicians, and that was the only thing that was holding up the release" ... it was agreed that the release of the album was now possible. Production accordingly commenced on 20th June, and the record was in the stores the early part of August.
>
> In view of the above, [we were] somewhat puzzled by your letter of December 27th asking if the Musicians Union had been paid, as it had been assumed that you would have previously been informed that this had, in fact, been done...
>
> In view of all the foregoing [we feel that] we are in no way responsible for payment to the Musicians Union, especially in view of the fact that negotiations were between Miss Ford, Bourne Music New York, and yourselves. As originators of the soundtrack re-recording are you not yourselves normally responsible for payment to the musicians? I understand the British Musicians Union do not have a clause in any contract regarding the re-recording of a film sound-track for release on record, and that each and every request by a record company for the re-recording of any music-

track is subject to individual negotiation, and that the payment of a re-recording fee does not automatically entitle a record company to release a sound-track recording. They do, however, verbally intimate that such requests would not normally be refused.[87]

Ford told her lawyers that Decca London was under the impression that re-recording fees had been paid; if not, "they were not going to pay it." "I am deeply shocked," Jacoby wrote Decca, "by the attitude of your London office on this subject. Our contract dated December 18, 1959 is clear and unequivocal. Paragraph 4 of that contract expressly states that you agree to pay the re-recording fee to the British musicians 'amounting to no more than £286.'"

> Neither Miss Ford nor I know anything about the correspondence or discussions which your London office claims to have had with Bourne, Inc., and certainly no one at the company is authorized to make representations on our behalf or to modify the terms and provisions of the agreement.... For my part I do not propose to take this matter up with third parties and to be subjected to further months of delay.
>
> Under the existing contract the matter of the re-recording fees is the responsibility of your company. It is our position that it is up to you to see that appropriate steps are taken to pay the same promptly.[88]

As the months went by, Ford wrote to Jacoby that relations were "somewhat strained" with Eric James.[89] By the end of March, Decca informed Jacoby that instruction had been given to the London office to finally pay the re-recording fees. "Though I have no written confirmation ... that these instructions have been issued, or that that they have been complied with," he wrote to Ford, "I trust that ... the matter has now been taken care of."[90] Jacoby also suggested Ford send extracts of the Decca contract and letters to James. "It should serve to help take some of the pressure off you and to show that Decca is the party to blame for the musicians not having received their fees before now."[91] After twelve tense months, the issue was finally settled.

* * *

"With the music attached," Jerry Epstein said of *The Chaplin Revue*, "these films took on a new life."[92] And in the 1970s, with the Chaplin renaissance in full swing, Chaplin made further changes to the compilation. At the time, Mo Rothman was packaging Chaplin's films in pairs—*The Kid* and *The Idle Class*, *The Circus* and *A Day's Pleasure*, *The Gold Rush* and *Pay Day*, and *A Woman of Paris* with *Sunnyside*. But in December 1971, Rothman and his associate Bert Schneider felt *The Chaplin Revue* was too long and removed *A Dog's Life*. A year later Oona wanted to rename the film as *The Pilgrim/Shoulder Arms*, in the manner of the other pairings, and to have a new title that read "CHARLES CHAPLIN IN TWO COMEDIES WITHOUT WORDS."[93] At one point there was a U.S. version of the film and an international one. *Pay Day* was substituted into the U.S. version for either *The Pilgrim* or *Shoulder Arms*, though no record exists giving details. *The Chaplin Revue* was never permanently released in any format other than Chaplin's original, stretch-printing and all.[94]

In May 1976, James began combing through seventy cans of the music tracks from *The Chaplin Revue* to compile a complete music track, labeling the cues for each film included in the compilation, even though the original cue sheets still existed in Chaplin's papers somewhere deep in the Manoir basement. James said he also would check the tracks against his original piano scores for any compositions that were recorded and not used. This way, any duplicate recording takes could be eliminated. He found only two unused pieces—a waltz and a German march. Rachel Ford decided the tunes were of little value and unfortunately trashed all seventy cans of music tracks.

*   *   *

"It was a great experience," James said of his time working on *The Chaplin Revue*, "and when it was ended I had no guarantee that it would all be repeated."

> It is true that we got on well and [Charlie] liked me, but my greatest hopes were for, perhaps, a spasmodic engagement. I certainly never for one moment imagined that our association was to last twenty years, and that I should make the journey to Vevey some forty times. The six and a half weeks we had spent together, locked in musical battle, had been enough for both of us to learn a great deal about the other. Working with him was something like walking on a tightrope that was constantly being shaken and made me all the more determined not to fall off. Charlie, oddly enough, seemed to respect me because of this.
>
> The fact that I had also reached a point where I refused to be kicked around and did not hesitate to criticize or answer him back also seemed to earn me a grudging admiration, in spite of the fact that it was doubtless a new experience for him. All this, plus the knowledge that I now understood the true dimensions of the work I had to do, made the next visit and all those thereafter so much easier in every way. As time went by I really did feel like one of the family and was treated by all as such.[95]

In the years following *The Chaplin Revue*, the hopes of a new Chaplin film seemed remote at best. Bourne wanted to do a collector's album of Chaplin music. But, Rachel Ford wrote to Chaplin, "my understanding of the position is that music recorded to-day as originally arranged has apparently no appeal for teen-agers. This applies especially to waltzes and tangos."

> Composers are faced with two choices: to let the best recording companies make records of their compositions at a tempo that goes with modern dancing. A company like Decca spends about $12,000 to do such a record using good orchestras, etc.
>
> If composers refuse to do this, they are nevertheless unable to prevent any Tom, Dick or Harry recording the melodies in any tempo, in any fashion, however bad, provided that royalties are paid. Bonnie Bourne naturally argues that the better the record the more substantial the royalties.[96]

Ford made a note on the letter that Chaplin was "not at all keen—unless kept recognizable," but he was too busy working on his autobiography to focus on anything else.[97] Chaplin began working on his memoirs after he finished *A King in New York*. His daily routine while writing was to rise at seven, take a swim, eat breakfast, then kiss Oona goodbye, as if he was going to the office, and work until lunch. He took a nap and worked again until five, had tea, played tennis, dinner at seven, and then more work until ten. The writing apparently helped him purge some ghosts as well. "I have no bitter feeling about America now," Chaplin told *The New York Times*. "It is not a thing one can carry on. Some of my best friends are Americans. I like them. They come off very well in the book. Writing the book is like developing a photograph, and they come out very well. What happened to me—I can't condemn or criticize the country for that. There are many admirable things about America and about their system too. I have no ill feeling. I carry no hate."[98]

My Autobiography was published in September 1964. Chaplin reportedly received a

$500,000 advance for the British and American rights. Reviewers were effusive in their praise for the first eleven chapters, which included Chaplin's vivid reconstruction of his Dickensian childhood up through his days with the Mutual films. From that point on, Chaplin rarely mentions his films, perhaps a reference to his feeling that "if people know how it's done, all the magic goes."[99] Still, the omissions of longtime collaborators such as cinematographer Rollie Totheroh, and members of his stock company like Henry Bergman, Mack Swain, and Eric Campbell, are glaring. And though he vividly describes the moment "music first entered my soul," there is no mention of his compositions or any of the musicians he worked with. Such questionable decisions on Chaplin's part, especially when it comes to the music, are even more frustrating when he was on the cusp of his most popular musical success.

CHAPTER 13

This Is My Song

IN 1936, FOLLOWING THE RELEASE OF *Modern Times*, Chaplin and Paulette Goddard went on a tour of the Far East. One night in Shanghai, with friend Jean Cocteau in tow, the trio visited a nightclub and watched American sailors dancing with "taxi-girls," Russian women who had escaped their country during the revolution and now made a living as prostitutes. By the time Chaplin returned home, he had written a 10,000-word scenario for Paulette and Gary Cooper called *Stowaway* about a Russian countess who stows away in the cabin of an American diplomat. But the world was heading towards war and Chaplin could not focus on the story. "How could I throw myself into feminine whimsy or think of romance or the problems of love," he said in his autobiography, "when madness was being stirred up by a hideous grotesque—Adolf Hitler?"[1] Chaplin picked the script back up again after *A King in New York*. Five years later, he said it was almost finished. "It's something I've had in my mind for many years," he told *The New York Times*. "It has been half-written for the last ten years. It's real slapstick burlesque. I have some very funny business which I've been keeping and cooking up."[2]

Shooting on the newly titled *A Countess from Hong Kong* finally began on January 25, 1966, and wrapped May 11, fifty-two years and three months after Chaplin's debut with Keystone. It was his first film in color and the first in the anamorphic process he had ridiculed in *A King in New York*. Chaplin described the film as "a romantic comedy that I am treating realistically." Chaplin cast Sophia Loren as Natascha, a White Russian countess now earning her living as a Shanghai taxi-girl who stows away in the room of a wealthy American diplomat. Much of the character of Natascha was based on May Reeves, Chaplin's companion for eleven months in 1931 during his world tour. Chaplin had interviewed Gary Cooper years earlier for the diplomat role, but Cooper had died in 1961. Loren accepted the part immediately at a dinner with Chaplin and suggested Marlon Brando as her co-star. "I'd work for [Chaplin] even if he wanted to direct me in the telephone book," Brando said. "How many times is it given to an actor to work for a man who is a living legend?"[3]

Journalists were allowed on the set, and there was plenty to write about. Chaplin celebrated his 77th birthday during the shoot and Loren secretly married Carlo Ponti. But there were reports of friction between her and her co-star, and certainly between Brando and his director. Chaplin broke his ankle and Brando was admitted to the hospital for severe abdominal pains. Then there was nineteen-year-old Michael Chaplin, who had been estranged from his father due to a series of rifts in 1965. He had married 25-year-old Patrice Johns, disclosed he had been living on government relief, and was involved in a high-profile court case regarding his ghost-written autobiography, *I Couldn't Smoke the Grass on My Father's Lawn*. Michael gave up "his Beatnik life and his beard, " and Jerry Epstein helped him get work on the film as an assistant producer using the name Michael James. "I guess Michael used the assumed name because he did not want any publicity," said a spokesman for the film. "It is a responsible job and an ideal way to learn the film business."[4]

Whatever the problems reported in the press, Chaplin was always happiest when he was at work. "I am the servant of the Muses," he said. "When they say 'Get back to work, you lazy bum,' I get back. I don't mind. Work is my salvation."[5]

> It's so exciting, so stimulating, I don't even begin to get tired until the day's work is over. And then I'm pooped.... The exciting thing is seeing it all come to life—all this that only existed on paper and in one's head for so long. This act of creation is unique to films. The theater and writing don't have it.... Nobody in this film is "being funny"—I mean coming on with the obvious intention of getting laughs. Who would ask stars like Sophia and Marlon to clown? This is romantic comedy—high, delicate comedy, I hope, about real people; humane, happy, touching, funny. In other words, entertainment.[6]

"If the picture doesn't come off," Chaplin said, "it's all my fault."[7] In his naiveté, Chaplin found the film "such fun to do, I thought the whole world was going to go mad for it."[8] But for all his boasts in interviews, Chaplin prophetically quipped, "I feel like I'm waiting for the guillotine."[9] The morning after the London premiere on January 5, 1967, the blade dropped.

The London *Times* said that the film, "for all the care lavished on it, ends up so dull, so unfunny, and when all is said and done, so terrible, unforgivably ordinary." The *Sun* said it was a "bad, sad frolic of a movie. The heart of the film lies pickled in the formaldehyde of the thirties. Perhaps Chaplin should rest on his well-earned laurels." The *Daily Express* called it "a third-rate farce performed by an uninspired repertory company. It croaks and creaks and lumbers like an aged mechanical toy. A sort of cuckoo clock that was stopped dead around 1925 and just can't be restored to running order." The *Daily Mirror* hit on the true issue behind the critical drubbing—"Without the celebrated name on it, this picture would pass as being pleasantly undemanding, genially entertaining."[10] It did not help that Chaplin only appeared in a trio of quick cameos, each lasting only a couple of seconds. "Every time I saw that face disappear," said James Kennedy in *The Guardian*, "I wanted to cry out in anguish."[11] "I would like to believe that the whole thing was a gigantic spoof—Chaplin laughing at modern screen styles," said Felix Baker in the *London Evening News*, "but I am forced to a sadder conclusion. This is the work of a genius of the cinema who has not kept pace with his medium."[12]

"If they don't like it, they're bloody idiots," Chaplin responded. "A millionaire falling in love with a beautiful prostitute—what better story can they have than that?"[13] He admitted that the reviews of his film had always been "mixed."

> The one *everybody* praised was The Kid—and then they went too far, talked about Shakespeare. Well, it wasn't *That*! But what shocked me about the English reviews of the *Countess* was the fact that they were unanimous. And they seemed so personal, an attack on *me*. All they were interested in was "Chaplin has a flop." In the old days, critics could slaughter quite a good play with just one quip. But there was nothing like that—these were so dull! Why couldn't they poke fun at it? Where's *their* humour, for God's sake? They picked on such puerile things to say. "Brando is wooden"—but that's just the whole point! I think it's the best thing I've done.[14]

"Hope to goodness the U.S.A. audiences will like it," Rachel Ford wrote to Bonnie Bourne. "So far in Europe it's appreciated in spite of having been absolutely murdered by the English press. I have not yet understood why, for they did not criticize the picture, but just damned it."[15] Unfortunately, even though this was the first new Chaplin film released in the U.S. since *Limelight* fifteen years earlier, the stateside critiques were equally brutal. "The saddest thing about this wan romantic comedy," said *Monthly Film Bulletin*, "is that there is absolutely nothing to say about it."[16] Even longtime Chaplin champions like Bosley Crowther in *The New York Times* were disappointed, calling it a "painfully antique bedroom farce."

> And if an old fan of Mr. Chaplin's movies could have his charitable way, he would draw the curtain fast on this embarrassment and pretend it never occurred…. So the dismal truth is it is awful. It is so bad that I wonder, at one point, whether Mr. Chaplin, who wrote and directed it, might not be trying to put us on—trying to travesty the kind of hiding-in-the-closet comedies, where people banged on doors and those in the room dived for cover, that were popular as two-reel silent films.[17]

Other critics took a more equitable view. "Not that this romance does not have moments of naive charm and a few good laughs," said *Boxoffice BookinGuide*, "but the film … will appeal mostly to the older filmgoers of today."[18] "You should catch Charlie Chaplin's *A Countess from Hong Kong* if only for old times' sake," said the *Los Angeles Times*. "And if you are too young to remember the old times, this will throw some illumination—sometimes funny, sometimes tender—on a bygone age of innocence…. There is a certain old-fashioned gentility, even gallantry, about it and there are also, equally characteristically, the vulgarities of the music-hall milieu from which Chaplin sprang…. I was reminded of the tongue-in-cheek boudoir affairs of the late Ernst Lubitsch; there certainly haven't been as many doors opened and slammed shut in one movie since then."[19]

While the movie did not fare well with critics, Chaplin received some of the best reviews of his life for, of all things, his music.

*   *   *

A Countess from Hong Kong required "an enormous amount of music," said Eric James. "Charlie was bubbling over with enthusiasm and full of ideas."[20] But long before James began working on the score in August 1966, Chaplin hired Boris Sarbek, his arranger for *A King in New York*. Why Chaplin chose Sarbek rather than James is a matter of debate. In 1959, Chaplin wrote to Darryl Zanuck, ostensibly for a film project that never materialized, "I consider Mr. Sarbeck [*sic*] to be an excellent musician and a very good arranger."[21] Also, since Sarbek had been born in Odessa, perhaps Chaplin felt he was more appropriate for a continental story with Russian countesses and an opening Hong Kong atmosphere. Or maybe after the trials of working with James on *The Chaplin Revue*, he wanted to work again with someone he trusted more. A number of the cues that ended up with different titles in James's handwriting exist in earlier drafts in Sarbek's distinctly different musical engraving style, complete with French directions and French cue names. According to his contract, Sarbek received 1,800 francs, and the work was to be delivered to Chaplin no later than December 15, 1965, the date of the first recording session at Société Phonographique Philips in Paris. There is no record of the cues that were recorded that day nor does all of Sarbek's original work survive in the Chaplin Archive. Sarbek died sometime in 1966 so it is possible that he became too ill to continue work on the score, which necessitated Chaplin finding another arranger.

In February 1966, Philip G. Jones of Film Orchestral Management & Music Services

Ltd. supplied a list of musicians to The Rank Organisation of potential orchestrators and conductors for the film. Jones "very highly" recommended Gerry Hughes, who had orchestrated high-profile films like *Becket, The Cardinal,* and portions of *The Fall of the Roman Empire,* where Dimitri Tiomkin said he was "very pleased with his work." Pianist Robert Docker, who orchestrated Larry Adler's *High Wind In Jamaica,* was "a very imaginative orchestrator," as evidenced by his unique, Oscar-nominated harmonica-piano score for *Genevieve* (1953). Other names on the list included Lawrence Leonard and Joseph Horowitz, "an outstanding young composer" who had written ten ballets and the scores for numerous documentaries, "but I'm afraid only one feature film TARZAN'S THREE CHALLENGES—he would I'm sure also do a fine job of orchestration, as he is quick to grasp situations, and is a most congenial person to work with."[22]

Horowitz and Leonard, who had conducted the London production of *West Side Story,* were also listed as potential conductors, as well as Marcus Dods, a prolific conductor over the previous twenty years on films such as *Quo Vadis, The Horse's Mouth,* and *Young Cassidy,* and *Doctor Who* in television. Then there was Romanian-born Francis Chagrin, who was at the end of his film career but had composed and conducted the scores for films like *The Colditz Story, Greyfriars Bobby,* and *An Inspector Calls.* "I'm sure that he would conduct another composer's music for the screen," Jones said, "and of course he has had a very wide experience of this medium."[23]

At the end of April, Bonnie Bourne also sent a list "of top quality experts in their respective music fields" for consideration. On the list of Latin American arrangers were Johnny Gregory, Geoff Love, Gordon Franks, and Stanley Black, whose name was crossed out. Larry Ashmore and Peter Jeffries were listed as musicologists, as was Eric James, who should have not needed an introduction. There were plenty of suggestions for musical directors, including Johnny Douglas, Frank Barber, Johnny Gregory, Geoff Love, Harry Robinson, and Eric Rogers, who would later orchestrate and conduct the remaining new scores for Chaplin's shorts and silent features beginning with *The Kid* in 1971. Len Stevens and Tony Hatch were penciled in, Frank Cordell had a box around his name, and Stanley Black again was crossed out as was Peter Knight, no doubt because Chaplin had been so unhappy with his work on *A King in New York.*[24] With time running out, Chaplin turned once again to Eric James, who received £100 per week for a five-day week. Any weekend work paid an additional £20 per day.[25] "Charlie's score is as sentimental as a series of Strauss waltzes," said the *Los Angeles Times.*[26] Chaplin composed seventeen themes for the film, including a quintet of waltzes, but, he said, "I don't know whether there will be a hit in it."[27] He was wrong.

Chaplin's favorite theme was the "Countess from Hong Kong" waltz. Handwritten notes in the archive indicate that Chaplin wrote a number of versions of lyrics for the tune, the first of which in the first person:

> *Now I'm the countess from nowhere*
> *I used to reside in a mansion grand.*
> *I am the countess of nowhere.*
> *I once was the toast of May Fair.*
> *My friend was the Tsar*
> *We ate caviar* [word unintelligible] *at the opera.*
> *I've been husselled and busselled* [sic]
> *Wherever I rome* [sic].
> *I'm a penniless countess without any a home.*

> *I am the countess of nowhere*
> *Nowhere to go.*
> *I hear those slay [sic] bells ringing*
> *As we go riding through the snow.*
> *Then I had an unlucky spell*
> *I fell for a dance hall girl.*[28]

A later version switched to third person:

> *She is the Countess of Hong Kong*
> *Far, far from home*
> *She is a Countess from Hong Kong*
> *Gay, wistful, and alone.*
> *Polite and refined*
> *She'll dance for a dime.*
> *Although a Countess*
> *She has no dress*
> *She is the Countess of Hong Kong,*
> *Far, far from home.*[29]

A still later version expanded on that theme:

> *She is a Countess from Hong Kong,*
> *Far, far from home.*
> *She is a Countess from Hong Kong,*
> *Gay, wistful, alone.*
> *Although a Countess,*
> *She has no address,*
> *She sleeps anywhere,*
> *In the park,*
> *Or in a chair.*
> *She is a Countess from Hong Kong,*
> *Far, far from home.*[30]

Written in Chaplin's favorite key of F major, the melody has a lilting 1930s nostalgia to it and is certainly hummable. "Year's later," said Jerry Epstein, "when we talked about 'The Countess from Hong Kong Waltz' … he'd wink at me and say, 'That's the *Merry Widow* waltz transposed!'"[31] To Chaplin's "marked irritation," Eric James thought the theme was not particularly radio-friendly. James's partner and future wife, Phyllis O'Reilly, "felt quite confident" that "Neapolitan Love Song" would be the big hit. Like the love theme from *Modern Times* that became "Smile," "Neapolitan Love Song" is not accorded a lot of screen time but Phyllis had a good nose for smelling a hit. "I will always be proud of this particular piece," James said, "as Phyllis was convinced that it was an absolute winner and how right she was."

The cue is written in the uncommon meter (at least for Chaplin) of 6/8. The lilting three-quarter subdivisions capture the flirtatious *pas de deux*—literally and figuratively— that Ogden and Natascha perform throughout the film. The rhythmically repetitive accompaniment, common in the music's barcarolle form, suggests the gentle stroke of Venetian gondoliers. Chaplin, whose lyrics sit comfortably within the melodic line, told James that "he was not very good at lyric writing and usually placed that chore elsewhere." In a letter to Jerry Epstein in September, Chaplin said he was working on the lyrics, which went through multiple drafts. Early versions show the seeds of the hit to be, and Eric James confirmed that Chaplin "spent an enormous amount of time and effort before finally completing [them]."[32]

Flowers are smiling bright,
Smiling for my delight,
Smiling so tenderly for the world and for me.
Alone I sing in moonlight,
With you in my heart supreme,
To hear you say I love you,
That is my hope my dream.

CHORUS
Love here is my song,
Here is my song,
My serenade to you.
The world can't be wrong,
If ever my dream comes true,
I care not what the world may say,
Without romance the world is grey,
Love here is my song.[33]

Cyril Simons of Leeds Music sent back suggestions for changes:

Flowers are smiling bright
Here in the fading light
Sweet perfume everywhere
Fills the air everywhere.
Here all alone I sing
Sing of the love I bring
I'd sing the whole night through
If you'd say "I love you."
Three simple words I long for
Lovers know what they mean.
You are the one I long for.
You are my hope, my dream.

CHORUS
Love here is my song
Love's serenade
My song for you
My world then would belong
If all the dreams I dream came true
I care not what the world may say
Without romance my/the world is lonely
So—
Love here is my song
Here is my song
Of love I'm singing for you.[34]

Chaplin was not pleased and Simons sent another revision three days later. But Chaplin would not accept having his song altered by anyone. He eventually deleted the "Alone I sing in moonlight" section of the verse and went back to his original handwritten version of the chorus—"Love this is my song, / Here is a song, / A serenade to you. / The world can't be wrong, / If in this world there's you. / I care not what the world may say, / Without you there would be no day."[35] By April 1967, that chorus had spread around the world. *Billboard* called "This Is My Song" a "runaway" hit that was "proving to be one of the most lucrative copyrights of 1967." Petula Clark's now-iconic rendition topped the charts in Britain, France, Belgium, Holland, and Ireland. But her initial impression was "This is not my song."[36]

Early in 1966, Clark was in London for a taping of *Show of the Week* on the BBC, when her publicist/husband Claude Wolff received a call from Simons, who had suggested to Louis Benjamin, the head of Pye Records, that he wanted Clark to record "This Is My Song." Though Wolff agreed it was a good idea, it took until October before he finally called Simons asking what had happened to the song. Simons was unhappy with the "lousy" demo. "I wouldn't insult Pet by asking her to do it. We've been touting it around and the only person who makes any sense of it at all is Harry Secombe [who also released a chart-topping version shortly after Clark's]. I don't think it's really the sort of song Petula wants to sing."[37]

Clark, who was working practically full time in the U.S., agreed. "I was right in the middle of doing other things and 'This Is My Song' was so different to anything I had been recording up until then—'Downtown,' 'Don't Sleep in the Subway,' 'I Know a Place,' all that kind of thing. And I thought, 'I don't know. I'm not sure about this.' And I just didn't take much notice of it."[38] Though the song had the cachet of Chaplin's notoriety, Petula had had a remarkable run of luck with songwriter Tony Hatch, the author of her hits "Downtown" and "Don't Sleep In the Subway" (co-written with his wife, Jackie Trent). Petula and Jackie had had their differences, but Clark "was worried about breaking what she felt was an unwritten contract between them" by recording Chaplin's song.[39] Union laws also prohibited Hatch, who also was unimpressed by the song, from doing a backing track.

Petula was performing in Reno, Nevada, and Simons sent her a reel-to-reel tape of the song with an orchestral backing track that was in Paris. But the size of the tape meant that one of the few places she could hear it was at a local radio station. After hearing it, "I didn't think it sounded all that great," she says. "So I shrugged it off again. Actually it was my husband who seemed to think it was better than I did. I hadn't honestly listened to the song properly." Wolff eventually contacted Warner Bros., which was releasing the single, and said, "I think this song is good. Petula could sing it very well and it would be charming."[40] Since Wolff was unhappy with the French arrangement, Ernie Freeman, Frank Sinatra's arranger on "Strangers in the Night," flew to Reno to create a new one.

"This Is My Song" "didn't seem to be [Ernie's] cup of tea," Clark says. Freeman, "bless his heart, arrived in Reno, somewhat the worse for drink. [He]was just terrified of flying, which was why he had been drinking. I had two little girls at the time, and they had never seen anybody tiddly before. They thought it was quite amusing." Clark and Freeman spent a day working together on the song, plus Billy Strange and Lee Hazle-wood's "High," which was slated for the B side of the U.S. release. Clark had brought along the children's Dutch nurse on the trip. "She heard us going through this song for the record and afterwards she couldn't stop singing it. She was the one who somehow seemed to think it was great." When Freeman flew back from Reno the same day, liquidly fortified for the flight, Clark thought, "'Well, this should be interesting.' I turned up in Los Angeles a week later and walked into the studio and of course Ernie had done this absolutely wonderful orchestration."[41]

With his eye instead on the French market, Wolff contacted songwriter Pierre Delanoë ("What Now My Love") in Paris. Delanoë also thought Clark was making a mistake but started work on the French lyrics regardless. "The lyric was absolutely perfect," Clark says. "And I actually found it prettier in French than in English."[42] Wolff had earlier contacted Petula's longtime songwriter, Jack Fishman, in London to help change Chaplin's original lyrics. "We can't use sentences like: 'I care not what the world may say,'" Wolff told Fishman. "Petula thinks they've come out of the ark. But be subtle. Chaplin would hate to think anyone else had altered a word."[43]

Clark went into a Reno studio in late January 1967 to record the song. Sonny Burke, a regular producer for Sinatra, produced the record. Clark recorded Delanoë's French version ("C'est Ma Chanson"), a German translation ("Love, So Heißt Mein Song," lyrics by Joachim Relin), and one in Italian ("Cara Felicità," lyrics by Ciro Bertini). "I was still somehow reluctant about recording it in English," she says. "I thought this was not the right time to put out this kind of song. I found the English lyrics a bit quaint, mixed with my feelings about doing a romantic, slightly old-fashioned song coming on the heels of some of the other hits that I had. Sonny said, 'Just do it. Don't think about it, just do it.' After recording in three other languages, it was so easy to sing in English."[44]

When both the French and English rewrites were completed, Chaplin unexpectedly asked to hear the English version with the music. Jack Warner, head of Warner Bros. Records, played Chaplin the disc, convinced he would not notice the difference. "If a single word of the English version is changed, then you don't get the song," Chaplin said, "I wrote it and it will be sung as I wrote, word for word. No song—no film."[45] Warner had no choice but to agree.

Clark first performed "This Is My Song" live on *The Hollywood Palace* variety show. "I was unsure of myself singing it," she says. "But it got a standing ovation immediately. They just went wild about it. So I thought, 'Okay, I get the message.' The same thing happened when I performed it on television in the UK. So it was really a runaway hit. I wasn't surprised at it being a hit in French, but it was a hit immediately in German, Italian, and, of course, in English too. It was quite a surprise for me."[46]

The *New Musical Express* said, "Beautifully handled, partly in dual-track, it features cascading strings and mandolin effect, giving it a Continental flavor. Good to hear Pet with a ballad again—and it's a gorgeous one, too."[47] "In the U.S., chances are the lush Chaplin score and the theme song, 'This Is My Song,' will be as strong a promotional factor as any," said *Boxoffice BookinGuide*.[48] The song shot to number one within days of its release. It topped the charts in the U.S. and the UK, France, Italy, Germany, Spain, the Scandinavian countries, Dubai, and Japan. It also charted in Singapore, South Africa, Argentina, and Malaysia. Harry Secombe's version, which was recorded before Clark's, topped out at number two. Frank Sinatra, Ray Charles, Jim Nabors, Bobby Vinton (whose version charted in the Philippines) also recorded English versions. When Andy Williams recorded the song for his 1968 album *Honey*, publicity blurbs for the album already called the song a "pop standard."

By April 1967, world sales of Clark's version were fast approaching the two million mark and further sparked a series of recordings for the French and Belgian markets. "C'est Ma Chanson" became the biggest hit of the year in France, with four other vocal recordings by Les Compagnons de la chanson, John William, Tino Rossi, and Mireille Mathieu. Instrumental versions included the orchestra of Franck Pourcel, Caravelli, Raymond Lefevre, Roger Nores, Georges Jouvin, and Claude Ciari. There were even five accordion interpretations, including by André Verchuren, Bruno Lorenzoni, Yvette Horner, and Jo Privat.[49] Over fifteen Italian artists covered the song and there were more than a dozen recordings in Scandinavia and Holland.

In July 1968, French singer-composer Charles Trenet sued Chaplin for one million francs and interest for allegedly plagiarizing his "La Romance de Paris," which he had written in 1941. After listening to a recording and piano versions of both songs, the judge ruled the first four notes were the same, but Chaplin's lawyers contended that the rhythms were different.[50] The court asked film composer and musicologist George van Parys to study the four notes and "determine whether the resemblance appeared to be fortuitous, and whether the tune appeared in other songs written before 1941."[51] No reports exist detailing the court's final judgment.

By the time "This Is My Song" took the radio airwaves by storm, Chaplin's earlier political troubles had been forgotten and, to some degree, so had he. Though the reviews and box office receipts for *A Countess from Hong Kong* were dismal for his first and only color film, Chaplin was once again on top of the world, at least musically. When Eric James returned to Switzerland to work with him on a new score for the rerelease of *The Circus*, Chaplin said, "Eric, I'm sure that you'll be delighted to know that we're off the hook." When James asked him what he meant, Chaplin explained that he had recouped all of the money he had invested in the film. "I congratulated him," James said, "and said I was convinced that this situation had been brought about to a great extent by the song I had said would be a hit. To my surprise he admitted his error of judgement and gave Phyllis and me full credit for accurately forecasting the potential commercial success of that particular number, but his generosity stopped there!"[52]

Thrilled by the song's success, Chaplin began work on another song for Petula immediately. Clark and Wolff went to see Chaplin in Geneva just before he died and he played them a tape of the song. "It's for Petula," Charlie told Claude, "But you can't have it yet. It isn't finished. As soon as I've completed it, I'll send it to you." But Chaplin died soon after that, and the song was lost. "Nobody knows what happened to it," said Wolff, "not even Chaplin's wife, Oona. After his death, I spoke to her about it and she searched for it but it had gone."[53]

*   *   *

In addition to the lyrics for the "Countess from Hong Kong Waltz" and "Neapolitan Love Song," the copyrighted script from 1965 contains handwritten lyrics inserted for certain scenes, indicating that Chaplin perhaps envisioned this as a musical at some point. The first lyric is inserted around the scene when Mr. Clark (Oliver Johnston) has his brief cameo. The character, who has no need for botanical gardens or museums, convinces Ogden (Brando) and Harvey (Chaplin's son, Sydney) to go out on the town. These lyrics, though not expressly indicated for Clark's character, seem to belong to the swinging octogenarian—"I've come from London Town / Where they're swinging high and low / No matter where you go / The pace is anything but slow."[54]

Another proposed song was an anachronistic lyric bashing pop music. With its references to beatniks, the words seem more appropriate for *A King in New York* than *A Countess from Hong Kong*—"Pop singing all the rage / Among the old and the teen age / Where do we go from here / Now you're in it / Now you're with it / Man, get an awful kick / When dancing with a beat nick [*sic*]."[55]

A couple of handwritten lyrics appear to be centered around Natascha, written perhaps as a way for Chaplin to solidify the character in his mind. Both sets of lyrics give a little more backstory for the character. The first is inserted on the back of the script page for Natascha's first conversation with Ogden ("I like quiet people"), but seems more appropriate for her later conversation with Harvey.

I don't want to fall in love
As I did many times before
I don't want the thrill
Or the ecstasy
That's just a snare,
A delusion to me.

I don't want a broken heart
I've had all that by the score
I once was in love with a leading man
And for his autograph given my life
Until one day he sent me a postcard
Signed by himself and his wife.[56]

Another lengthy lyric went through at least one revision, though it is unlikely Chaplin ever meant for it to be performed in the film. Instead, it seems to be a poetic way of working out a character's backstory. Early references to a friendship with the Tsar point to Natascha's Russian heritage, though she was born in Hong Kong and never knew the Motherland. The friendship in the lyric indicates wealth, as do lines telling of gifting estates as presents, which suggest the lyric was meant for Ogden since he is the son of the richest oil baron in the world. While it is hard to imagine Brando singing the song (or any song for that matter after his off-key performance in the film version of *Guys and Dolls*), the song would have fleshed out the character, giving even Brando's half-hearted performance more humanity.

Don't look at me now
I'm not what I was,
In society I was once popular
My friend was the Czar
We'd eat caviar
Jar after jar at the opera.
But I ruined my name
With a lot of ill fame
Got involved with a ballerina
She wasn't tall,
She wasn't small
In fact she could have been leaner.

She was a ballerina
She took me to the cleaner
I bought her diamonds and beautiful clothes
But I could never her get off her toes.
What a dance, what a dancer,
But oh what a wreck she was.

Although she could dance
She wouldn't romance.
My devotion was unrequited.
She wouldn't concur
To a pas de deux
For years my life was blighted.
But this pretty young miss
Drank like a fish
Was the center of every scandal.
At two in a bar,
She'd go quite far,
But she never once dropped a spangle.

(CHORUS)

I followed her here,
I followed her there,
From Moscow to Prague,
New York and Mayfair.

But I didn't mind,
What gave me a pain,
Was the three other men
Who were doing the same.
I gave her estates
But she made other dates,
Flirted with Tom, Bill and Dick.
When I reproached her
All she could say
I can only be true to my public.

(CHORUS)

Then came the day
The first of May,
I was thrown into confusion.
To my dismay
I awoke that day
In the midst of a revolution.
Those commies were tough,
Cruel and mean
Each day I was made
To eat strawberries and cream.
I didn't mind
But my evil star
Deserted me flat
For a commissar.

(CHORUS)

We danced through life,
Laughed at fate.
I gambled away my estate.
Though I had no remorse,
But many regrets,
For I'm sorry to say,
That my poor father
The Duke of Palaver,
Chops down the trees in our park
To pay off my debts.[57]

The lively "Bonjour," or "Bonjour Madame" in a proposed vocal version, is primarily heard as instrumental source music played by the dance band.

I seem to see you everywhere,	*CHORUS*
I smile but you only stare,	*Bonjour Madame, Bonjour,*
Your manner is like frigid air.	*That is all I dare to say,*
We both stay at the same Hotel,	*I'd like to say much more…*
And I know friends that you know well.	*But your coldness keeps me away.*
Why can't we get acquainted,	*I'd love to say J'tame* [sic],
And perhaps related.	*And to say—J'Vous* [sic] *adore,*
At last we meet upon the street,	*But all that I can say is*
My nerves must be firmer	*Bonjour Madame, Bonjour.*[58]
But I can only murmur.	

In the vocal lead sheet for "Bonjour," Eric James wrote a note to orchestrator Lambert Williamson explaining why the manuscript contained only the melody line, text, chord symbols, and minimal rhythmic markings in the accompaniment—"Have not included figures—You'll prefer your own." By the time the recording sessions had arrived, however, Chaplin apparently decided against recording it with vocals.

The lyrics Chaplin wrote, whether attached to the music manuscript or as standalone lyric sheets, indicate he had grander music plans for *A Countess from Hong Kong* or at least more vocal selections. The only song heard in the finished film is a short chorus of "They Believe in Love," as source music on the radio, sung by Tommy Scott, who was paid £25 to record the number. By the time Chaplin began scoring, he had a more elegant, purely orchestral musical accompaniment in mind.

✳   ✳   ✳

The many waltzes Chaplin wrote for the score are a clear reflection of that elegance. In every score, Chaplin included at least one piece in three-quarter time—*A Countess from Hong Kong* has nine. The lazy saxophone lead in the "Dance Hall Waltz" perfectly captures the slightly seedy milieu of the taxi-girls, former royalty who are forced to sell themselves to strangers at "ten cents a dance." The theme is later converted into a quick-step in cut time to accompany Natascha playing cards. The G-minor "Crossing the Floor" waltz underscores the mystery of the countesses' pasts and their boredom with their current situation. A note from Jerry Epstein said, "This music to be slower (even if out of sync with dancers)…. Music must be very romantic."[59] "The Big Waltz" is the flip side of that equation, a joyous Straussian "change your partners" sister confection in G major that swirls and twirls aboard the ship and serves as Natascha's entrance into shipboard society after days in seclusion. The languid "Ambassador Takes a Bath," voiced in the cellos, flows over the body like the promise of Ogden's problems soon melting away in the steam heat. The theme's later use for Martha's (Tippi Hedren) entrance is a questionable choice. As Eric James cautioned in a note on the piano score, "On recording be prepared for an abrupt finish." The equally gentle "To Sleep" uses Chaplin's favorite key, F major, to ironically underscore the comic business between Ogden and Natascha as she announces she will be sleeping in his room and later as Ogden kicks his butler Hudson (Patrick Cargill) out of his makeshift bridal suite. Unfortunately, the waltzes often sound alike and using the same key for many of them makes them indistinguishable from one another. But other themes also provide the score with a lightness and elegance.

"Natascha's First Night" is a pair of cues full of harp glissandi, sustained strings chords, and chirping woodwind figures. Lighthearted hiccupping flute and bass intervals, and staccato strings cannot keep the "Incidental Business" from being nothing more than background accompaniment for Natascha's comic business trying on Ogden's pajamas and later attempting to fit into ridiculously oversized clothes (titled "An Ill-Fitting Dress"). "Incidental Business" shares the same outline as "Comic Business" (originally titled "Rough Sea"), a trio of cues that mimic the ship rising and falling on the sea. The combination of triplets, both quarter note and otherwise, in the 4/4 time signature (marked "Tempo rubato 'a la Drunken Reel'" on the manuscript) gives a heaving hemiola effect, while the brass belch and the piccolo screams like the blustery winds. The music also accompanies the absurdity of Hudson's marriage of convenience to Natascha and the morning after the wedding. Hudson also gets his own lighthearted "bedroom music" as he makes a fool of himself in front of his new bride. The lush "Chamber Music," another piece that exists in Boris Sarbek's handwriting, serves as a radio source cue in Ogden's bedroom and later, strangely enough, inside the Waikiki Hotel.

Though much of the score is carefree, Chaplin does not shrink from the underlying drama of the story. The film begins with the "Resolve" theme, a motif of four repeated notes that descends stepwise sequentially. The theme, later retitled "My Star," neatly bookends the film, as a dramatic beginning to underscore the Universal Pictures logo and at the end as Ogden returns to the Waikiki Hotel having abandoned his marriage to be with Natascha. Chaplin also interpolated the theme for a possible vocal version—"Love is a star / A star that I must follow / Through paradise and sorrow / Love is my guiding star / Love is my destiny / I'll follow thee."[60] He apparently abandoned the idea quickly as only the first three measures of the melodic line were written out.

The "Chinese Music" that opens the film sets the stage of the story following two world wars, when "Hong Kong was overcrowded with refugees." The piano score for the cue, entitled "Chine" ("Chinese"), is written in French, yet another cue arranged by Boris Sarbek. Sarbek also outlined a number of Chaplin's other themes that were later incorporated into James's piano scores or discarded altogether.

The gypsy-like quality of the violin solo for the Countesses' entrance ("Girls' Entrance Music") leads directly into the "Gypsy Violin Caprice." Another piece, "Gypsy Czardas," was written "in deference to gypsy blood that [Charlie] claimed ran through the veins of some of his ancestors," Eric James said. "I was able to produce, with his guidance, an ambitious composition, very difficult to play."[61] "Gypsy Czardas" was replaced with a cue simply titled "Natascha," again with French musical terms on the manuscript paper, another Sarbek cue. The solo violin is also the voice of Natascha's "Defeat" (listed in French as "Perdu," or "Lost," on Sarbek's manuscript), a somber theme underscoring her realization that her plans to stow away are falling apart.

Chaplin made changes to the score while editing the film. Certain cues that were marked on the cue sheet and recorded never made it into the film. For instance, a brief reprise of the "Resolve" theme was supposed to underscore Ogden preparing for his bath. But the music is far too dramatic for the scene and Chaplin wisely cut it. For Natascha's declaration of falling in love to Harvey, "Bonjour" was listed as an alternative to accompany part of the scene. Chaplin smartly kept the scene anchored all the way through with the "Neapolitan Love Song." Later, Hudson's drunken exit from his wedding table seems to be calling for music (and was marked on the cue sheet to be scored, though which theme is unclear), but Chaplin apparently felt the fifty-three seconds of comedy played fine without underscore. "Awakening" was supposed to accompany Ogden and Hudson's fumbling the morning after the wedding but Chaplin decided to also leave this scene *sans* music. "Incidental Business" would have helped lift Natascha out of the water, onto the quayside, and hitch a ride on the lorry. But when Chaplin split the sequence with scenes on the ship, the music no longer worked as originally conceived. The "Gypsy Music" seems an odd choice to underscore Ogden and Martha's first scene alone as does "Crossing the Floor" for Natascha's entrance into the Waikiki Hotel. Smartly, Chaplin left both cues out. "Tango" is an interesting way to end the film, with the end credits rolling over Ogden and Natascha, and the hotel restaurant guests dancing around the floor. Once the camera fades away from the dancers, the cue sheet indicates a reprise of the main themes from the score. Using the tango theme gives the film a much more ambiguous ending.

⋆　　⋆　　⋆

Eric James said it was "a joy" working with Eric Spear on *The Chaplin Revue*, but Spear was ill and his death in November 1966 "was quite a shock." Taking his place was Lambert Williamson. Williamson (1907–1975) began working in the film industry as an arranger and conductor. As a composer, he wrote music for a string of little known British films in the late 1940s and '50s. He found more success conducting the music of other composers, such as Georges Auric (*Moulin Rouge, Heaven Knows, Mr. Allison,* and *Bonjour Tristesse*), Roman Vlad's stunning score for the 1954 Laurence Harvey *Romeo and Juliet*, and Mario Nascimbene's *Room At the Top*.

According to James, he "invited" Williamson to work with him, praising the arranger as "most cooperative and efficient in his writing."[62] However, Williamson had met with Denis Johnson, production manager for *A Countess from Hong Kong*, back in February, long before James was hired. At the time Williamson told Johnson that "apart from any capabilities as Music Director/Conductor, Composer, Orchestrator, Composing, etc. I am [an] expert amanuensis, taking down onto paper from either voice or single note piano very quickly and accurately."[63] Whether Williamson tried his hand at transcribing with Chaplin before James came on board is unknown. Williamson was paid £400 to conduct the score for the film and another £400 for the soundtrack album's separate stereo recording. He also received eight shillings per bar for arranging and orchestrating the 1,942 bars of music (total £776.16.0). In total, he received £1712.6.0 for his work on the film.

The score was recorded in mono September 19–23, 1966, at Anvil Recording Studios, using a 45-piece orchestra augmented by a mandolin and an accordion player. The session on September 21 consisted of a 10-piece ensemble—flute, bass clarinet, trumpet, percussion, piano, bass, two electric guitars, and two percussion. The first cue recorded for that session was the brief Hawaiian-flavored "We'll Meet Again" for the electric guitars. Tommy Scott recorded his vocals for "They Believe In Love," and the session ended with the "French Samba," the shimmy number for the Society Girl (Angela Scoular) also known as "The Deb Shakes," which originally began life as a Boris Sarbek arrangement titled "Beguine." Next to "French Samba" on the cue sheet is the notation "already recorded." The piece was not re-recorded in stereo for the soundtrack album so it is likely that the version heard in the film and on the LP is Sarbek's. The rest of the orchestral cues were recorded over the other four days.

With Universal Pictures as distributor of the film, Universal Music Company became an extra layer of red tape when it came to the rights. RCA Victor made a firm proposal for a soundtrack album, guaranteeing a $50,000 promotional campaign with the release of the film and then a continuation of five percent of ninety percent of album sales.[64] But since Chaplin was unwilling to travel to London, the orchestra would have to come to Geneva to record and the deal fell through. Decca was "all out to do the album," Rachel Ford wrote to Bonnie Bourne. But "Universal have offered a substantial advance, and I must admit, I do understand their very legitimate desire to obtain the music, so that they can control the entire thing. I now find it difficult to realize that this time everything is so different, owing to the fact that we have parted with the film rights."[65]

Two separate dates—September 27 and 28—were set aside to record selections from the score in stereo for the soundtrack album. A handwritten note also suggested to theater owners—"Play music in Lobby in Theatre."[66] Certain cues were renamed for the album—"The Big Waltz" became the more appropriate "Change Partners," "Occidental and Oriental" was renamed "Chinese Music," "Resolve" was rebranded as the more sheet music-friendly "My Star," and "Neapolitan Love Song" not surprisingly was changed to "This Is My Song." But Chaplin was having issues putting together the album. "I have listened to some of the music on the small tape, and there are one or two important corrections to be made on the melody line," he wrote to Jerry Epstein. "This is why I do not want to go on with the Sterophonic. [*sic*] Sometimes there is a beat too much, and sometimes a bar is missing. It is important that these corrections are made before I can OK the music."[67]

Few film critics mentioned the score in their reviews—they were too busy trashing Chaplin and "This Is My Song" was not released yet. The *New Statesman* said the music "remorsely floods the echoing emptiness of the film, somehow emphasising its shortcomings."[68] *Newsday* called the score "undistinguished."[69] But divorced from the film, Chaplin received far better reviews for the soundtrack album. "Charles Chaplin gained wide recognition as a composer with his compelling themes for *Limelight* and once again he is sure to reap awards with this film score that's throbbing with beauty and depth," said *Billboard*. "The current hit 'This Is My Song' is featured and adds to the sales appeal."[70] "Chaplin's score is spotlighted as a liltingly melodic stanza with themes reminiscent of Chaplin's music for such films as *Limelight* and *City Lights*. A couple of themes, notably 'My Star' and 'This Is My Song,' should step out. This LP soundtrack has been attractively packaged with a folio of old Chaplin stills."[71] "Music is lyrical and beautiful, and catching on with people of all ages," said the reviewer for *The Hartford Courant*. "Biggest hit will be 'This Is My Song.' Remaining melodies, while lyrical, do not have the ability to sail upward on the charts. Hats off to Chaplin."[72]

Bourne, Inc., of course, wanted the publishing rights. But, again because of the advance, "Universal had to have the music," Ford said. "I need not add how sorry I am, especially now that I have heard the music."[73] "Naturally, I was very disappointed," Bonnie replied, "as it would have meant a great deal of prestige to me and our firm that Charlie regarded us important enough, that above all opposition, he would again assign his music to Bourne. Of course, I wish Charlie the greatest success and hope that the music comes up to all of his expectations."[74]

*   *   *

Petula Clark says her initial reluctance to sing "This Is My Song" "is totally gone. There are a couple of songs that I've recorded in the past that I didn't want to do. 'My Love' is absolutely one which I didn't want to do. When I sing it now, I sing it in a totally different way because I still can't quite come to grips with it."

> But "This Is My Song" I do in exactly the same way because that's the way it's supposed to be. Some things are just meant to be that way. I can't imagine trying to do anything else with it. Some things just click and you don't know why. And the more you try and figure out why, the less you know. Every song to me is a bit like a mini-film going on in my head. I don't just stand there and sing a song. "This Is My Song," there's almost a moment of peace and knowing things are as they should be. There are songs that grow on you and I think "This Is My Song" has grown on me. And so I have a different feeling about it to the other songs that I fell in love with immediately. It took time for me to grow to love "This Is My Song." It's a bit like a love affair. When you fall madly in love, it's a different thing to gradually falling in love with someone.[75]

Clark continues to sing the song in every show "and it has the same wonderful reaction to it. People absolutely adore it. It has that 'something.' Is it the music? Is it the lyric? I think it must be the music, which of course is Charlie. I think it's just a song that people connect with. It's not rock and roll, I can't see anybody rapping it or anything like that. It doesn't need it. It's just there. Like 'Smile' is just there. I think 'Smile' and 'This Is My Song' are here to stay. Some things just are."[76]

At age 78, Chaplin's days as a filmmaker were at an end. But he was unable to sit still for the last decade of his life. His project for his daughter Victoria, *The Freak*, never got off the ground but he still had work to do—revisiting and re-editing the remainder of his earlier silent feature films and shorts, and composing new music for them.

CHAPTER 14

The Sound of Silents Reprise

CHAPLIN SAID IN 1962, "My only enemy is time."[1] That feeling must have grown with each passing year. In 1965, Chaplin's beloved older brother Sydney died on April 16—Chaplin's birthday. The summer of 1967 saw the loss of his principal cameraman for many years, Rollie Totheroh. The following year, his oldest child, Charles Chaplin, Jr., suffered a pulmonary embolism. With the clock ticking louder and louder, Chaplin rushed to complete a project he had started in 1941—composing original scores for the remainder of films he still owned that were still missing music.

A distinct musical shift happens in Chaplin's final scores. Chaplin was a mature artist revisiting the world of his youth, so it is perhaps forgivable if the new music leaned toward sentimentality more than usual. Chaplin composed seven film scores after the age of eighty and, as Timothy Brock points out, "one must assume that a composer has the right to reflect upon his life in any way he chooses, in either a more reflective sentimental fashion or otherwise."[2] With this last batch of scores, Chaplin completed his musical vision—one of the most personal contributions to film music by any artist.

*   *   *

Chaplin had wanted to compose a score for *The Circus* for decades. In 1942, with the "music and words" reissue of *The Gold Rush* proving an unexpected hit, *The New York Times* reported he would continue the same process with a new musical score "and a commentary" for *The Circus*. But it would take nearly thirty years before he got around to composing music for it.[3] The first attempt to permanently attach music came in 1947 when Chaplin contacted his friend Hanns Eisler to compose a new score for a proposed reissue of the Oscar-winning film.

Eisler wrote to Lois Runser, Chaplin's secretary, quoting a fee of $7,500. "This includes all orchestral arrangements," he said. "Of course *The Circus* needs more music than any other film I composed. But it is up to Mr. Chaplin to decide what salary he wants to pay me. I also like to mention the fact that my scoring of the picture will be done with the greatest economy. I am using mostly 10 to 12 instruments. I don't think that a special contract is necessary between us. Please let me know by letter, what Mr. Chaplin has decided [sic]."[4] Chaplin certainly would have known Eisler's arch, atonal style. A composer that had written the Communist Party's "Comintern March" and scored *Hangmen Also Die*, Fritz Lang's noirish take on the assassination of Nazi leader Reinhard Heydrich, was an odd choice to compose music for such an ebullient silent comedy.

Eisler had always been a polarizing figure. And in the fall of 1946, his political troubles escalated after his sister Ruth Fischer attacked him in the press, and his brother Gerhardt was denounced as a communist. "I was dragged before this 'Unamerican Committee,' was also arrested, and that put an end to it," Eisler said in a later interview. "That was a difficult fight and I couldn't do any more film music."[5] By asking Eisler to help transcribe the score for *Monsieur Verdoux* and offering him the chance to score *The Circus*, Chaplin's motive in both cases may have been purely financial to help his friend during his political troubles with HUAC. Eisler even admitted, "[Chaplin] was immensely generous and decent in these matters."[6]

Eisler's music for *The Circus* is a far cry from the hummable tunes and Victorian waltzes that Chaplin was so fond of. Eisler composed six cues, indicating with notes in the manuscript exactly where in the film each cue was located. He eventually arranged these into the six movements of his *Septet No. 2*, scored for flute, clarinet, bassoon, and string quartet. And since he no longer had to follow the film order, he reordered the cues to make more sense as a concert work.

"Mealtime after the show" (Mvt. I) features chirping woodwinds and pizzicato strings, plus mixed meters and rubato tempos, features of Chaplin's own music. Warring woodwind voices capture some of the tension between Merna and the Ring Master, who refuses to allow her to eat. When the camera cuts to Charlie asleep in the chariot, tremolo strings, a sustained flute tone, and a crowing clarinet suggest his peaceful dreams. "Early the next morning" (Mvt. II), pizzicato strings and staccato winds (taken from the end section of the first movement) imitate Charlie chasing the prancing chicken running in search of an egg. Charlie cautions Merna against eating too quickly accompanied by a lovely section for the string quartet. The clowns' William Tell act (Mvt. VI) features flutter-tongued flute and a demented clarinet solo. Seesawing melodic lines in the two instruments mimic Merna swinging on the trapeze ("The Circus Prospers," Mvt. V), while staccato strings underscore manic clarinet and bassoon solos as Charlie tries to discreetly throw the food up to her. When Charlie accidentally swallows the horse pill (Mvt. IV), the music imitates the mule chase, with staccato strings adding tension to Charlie's predicament in the lion cage. The andante of the third movement underscores the scene by the fire after Charlie and Merna have run away from the circus.

On February 28, 1948, Leonard Bernstein, Aaron Copland, David Diamond, Roy Harris, Walter Piston, Roger Sessions, and Randall Thompson organized a benefit concert of Eisler's music in defense of their colleague, who had been branded "The Karl Marx of Music." The program consisted of the 1932–33 *Seven Piano Pieces for Children*, the 1937 Violin Sonata, the 1938 String Quartet, the 1940 Septet (titled *Fourteen Ways to Describe Rain*) based on music Eisler had written for the 1929 film *Regen*, the 1942 *Hollywood Elegies* song cycle, and excerpts from *The Circus*. Chaplin appealed to Pablo Picasso to put together a committee of French artists whose public letter to the U.S. embassy in Paris was published in *Les lettres françaises*. Signed by Picasso, Henri Matisse, Jean Cocteau, Georges Auric, and many others, the letter stated that Eisler's extradition to the "American zone" in Germany meant he would be incarcerated as a Nazi together with other Nazis. The letter had no effect on the government wheels that were already in motion. On March 26, Eisler bid a bitter, final farewell to the U.S. from the tarmac at LaGuardia Airport in New York—the first victim of the Hollywood blacklist. A performance of the Septet cues with *The Circus* was planned for the 1982 Berlin Film Festival and that year's Holland Festival already had a performance in their program. An application for the rights through the Chaplin Estate was denied, though over the years a few authorized public perform-ances of Eisler's music with the scenes from the film have occurred.[7] Even with the musical risks heard in the *Monsieur Verdoux* score (which undoubtedly was influenced by Eisler's style), it is hard to imagine Chaplin allowing Eisler to complete his idiomatic musical vision for *The Circus* had he remained in the country. But the music has its own charms and provides a fascinating window into another musician's interpretation of Chaplin's film work.

Twenty years later, Chaplin was ready to revisit *The Circus* and had left behind the bitterness and drama surrounding the filming. He had removed the film from distribution in 1936. Decades later, critics greeted the 1969 reissue with rapturous reviews, especially after the poor showing of *A Countess from Hong Kong*. "This version of *The Circus* com-municates a sense of simultaneous 'pastness' and 'presentness' that is unique," said Vincent Canby in *The New York Times*. "No other filmmaker has remained active and in full con-trol of his talents for so long…. By enduring time, Chaplin has presented us with a price-less gift—his extraordinary perspective, a sense of continuity, a promise of survival."[8]

Eric James was back to assist Chaplin with the score, a position he occupied on sub-sequent films for the next decade until Chaplin's death. James started work on the score on October 30, 1967, for nine weeks at the rate of £100 per week, and an additional £20 for any Saturdays or Sundays. Including the recording sessions, James received a total of $2,800.17. Lambert Williamson was once again on board as arranger and conductor, but there was a misunderstanding with his fee. "I very much hope that Mr. Williamson will see his way to suggesting reasonable terms," Rachel Ford wrote James, "as Mr. Chaplin cannot treat the re-release of this old silent picture on the same footing as 'COUNTESS FROM HONG KONG,' which was, as you know, financed through Universal."[9] Though his contract no longer survives, final studio figures show that Williamson received £1200 ($2,889.10) for conducting and orchestrating for a small orchestra of twenty-five musi-cians.[10] Recording sessions took place at Anvil Recording Studios on April 18 and 20, 1968, plus a third day on the 22nd, thanks to Richard Attenborough, who kindly gave up his reservation at Anvil for the day.[11]

Chaplin was always a fan of circuses, taking his family to Cirque Knie's annual visit in Vevey. An early idea for an opening song demonstrates that Chaplin left behind the humor emphasized in the 1928 compilation score for a more sentimental tone—"When the circus comes to town / With the lions, the tigers and the clowns / As they putting [*sic*] up the ring / Boys and girls begin to sing / And gayly columned flags are all around / All the animals and clowns / They begin to play around / They'll [*sic*] be lots of smiles / And not a frown."[12] The lyric was never set to music and eventually discarded.

The new main title for the reissue inserts into the credits shots from later in the film of Merna swinging on the trapeze bar high above the tent floor, accompanied by a new song—"Swing High, Little Girl." Chaplin's lyrics include a verse that is not sung in the film—"She worked in a circus. / She rode a white horse. / She worked on a flying trapeze, / But the audience she could not please. / When business was bad / And the clowns looked sad / She would smile / But tears were not far away / As she heard an old clown say"—while the chorus implores Merna to follow what reads like Chaplin's philosophy of life—"Swing little girl, swing high to the sky, / And don't ever look at the ground. / If you're searching for rain-bows / Look up to the sky—/ You'll never find rainbows / If you're looking down."[13]

Chaplin asked Eric James to find "someone who specialized in singing the current

Chaplin and Merna Kennedy in *The Circus* right before Charlie climbs the rope for his memorable tightrope act, c. 1927 (© Roy Export SAS).

The Circus **(1968 reissue)—The beginning of "Swing High, Little Girl," music and lyrics by Charles Chaplin.**

pop songs of the day" to record the song. James contacted John McCarthy, the conductor and arranger of The McCarthy Singers, who sent three male vocalists to Star Sound Studios in London to make a demo record of the song. Chaplin chose vocalist Ken Barrie, but he would "invariably burst into song whenever I played the introduction to it," James said. "His voice … was anything but good, and yet it sounded quite effective when he sang this particular song. Maybe it was because he gave a performance that resembled the way a music hall or vaudeville artist would sing it, so I decided that it might be a good idea to have a set of music parts written in his key just in case the contract vocalist didn't give the kind of treatment that was required for this number."[14]

On the day of the recording session, James, who did not care for Barrie's interpretation, said to Chaplin, "Wouldn't it be a nice idea if you were to make a recording so that Oona and all the family could enjoy hearing you sing 'Swing High Little Girl' with the backing of this lovely orchestra?" Chaplin agreed and laid down a vocal track. Everyone agreed his performance was the better of the two, and Chaplin told James, "Eric, you 'conned' me into doing that, didn't you?" James replied that had he suggested it at home in Vevey, Chaplin would have "refused on principle … and so in order to get my way I had to resort to a little subterfuge."[15] The few critics that remarked on the song in their reviews were less than complimentary. "In best kindness, let us say that the song is an echo of a bygone age," said Stanley Kauffmann in *The New Republic*.[16] Director Peter Bogdanovich later called the song "terribly corny."[17] Today, Chaplin's vocals lend the song a sweetness and poignancy. "Swing High, Little Girl," though given prominent placement in that main title sequence, is heard only one other time, during the actual scene in the film of Merna on the trapeze, this time in an instrumental version. It is merely one of the sixteen themes Chaplin composed for the score.

Chaplin replaces the *Pagliacci* melodrama of the 1928 compilation score with the newly composed "Incidental Music," the rousing main theme that accompanies the circus acts in the ring. With its joyful energy, the theme becomes the background source music for the circus itself, as if there is a band playing somewhere in the tent. Usually, the theme plays as straight accompaniment to the acrobats, Prof. Bosco Magician's act, Merna and the fortuneteller, and Charlie on the tightrope. But occasionally the F-major key can be interpreted ironically as when the theme, probably part of the music heard out in the tent, plays against the Ring Master's cruelty to Merna backstage.

The *hurry*s and *agitato*s of the compilation score are replaced with Chaplin's own "Chase Music." As in the earlier stock pieces, chromatic swirls of sixteenth notes propel Charlie as he runs aways from the cop into the funhouse. The music dissolves into half-step clusters as Charlie and the pickpocket imitate the jerky animatronic figures in the side show. Further uses of the chase include Charlie running into the tent and away from the magician's act he destroyed. Chaplin's "Galop" is the flip side of the "Incidental Music," with staccato eighth notes and a descending, rather than ascending, melody line. The staccato eighth notes and rests of "Breathless" are the musical equivalent of Charlie panting in fright inside the lion's cage, while the interpolation of the opening brass fanfare from Rimsky-Korsakov's *Scheherazade* portends doom.

Chaplin once again uses an Irish-flavored melody for the character of the Tramp. "An Irish Echo" consists of two sections—one in 9/8, the other in 6/8. The melody starts out as Charlie's theme and later evolves into a love theme for Charlie and Merna. When Rex comes on the scene, the melody becomes *their* love theme. The same music also accompanies Charlie's tightrope practice in the hopes of impressing Merna and their final night together huddled over the fire after the two have left the circus. "His Try-Out" is the latest in a string of Chaplin promenade themes. The dotted rhythms of this carefree melody elegantly underscore the William Tell routine.

The Circus (1968 reissue)—The "Horse Music" fanfare that, like the music of *Pagliacci* in the original 1928 compilation score, invites the audience into Chaplin's circus.

A two-note pickup motif helps unite the score, giving the various themes a lift. For instance, the motif is used in the "Horse Music" theme at the beginning to convey the animal's canter around the ring. In "Around the Side-shows," the figure changes from a duplet to a triplet, which bleeds into the "Recitative" pizzicato strings and again in the sneaky G-minor pizzicatos of the funhouse's "Mirror Music." The figure finally evolves into the "Vanishing Lady" waltz, which provides a quiet musical alternative to fast-moving scenes such as Charlie running behind the cop on the circular platform or doing acrobatics at the top of the tent pole.

The delicate "Tight-Rope Waltz" for Rex underscores his graceful agility atop the high wire. A raw *oom-pah-pah* rendition of the "Incidental Music" in three-quarter time accompanies Charlie's excursion on the wire. The poignant mandolin waltz of the "Dreaming" theme accompanies Charlie's dream sequence of him kicking Rex in the pants (scored with *Pagliacci*'s "Vesti la giubba" melody in the compilation score), though Chaplin felt the mandolin solos "swell too much."[18] Merna and Rex's wedding owes more

The Circus (1968 reissue)—Chaplin's rousing "Incidental Music" captures the chaotic world energy under the big top.

The Circus (1968 reissue)—Furious sixteenth notes battle against this joyous fanfare in the "Chase Music" and propel Charlie through the comedic mayhem.

The Circus (1968 reissue)—"Galop" is the energetic musical cousin to the score's "Incidental Music."

than a little to Wagner's overture to *Tannhäuser* (and perhaps a bit of Elgar's *Pomp and Circumstance* in the melodic line).

In 1928, the circus leaves the Tramp behind accompanied by Irving Berlin's "Blue Skies." For the reissue, Chaplin composed a "Sadness" theme for this one place in the score, in which the circus fanfare is now seen as something diabolical, with minor-key brass triplets. Low strings sigh while the winds and violins, saxophones, and finally the full orchestra tugs at the heartstrings. Chaplin thought the end had "a shade too much trumpet."[19]

The New York Times' Vincent Canby praised the film but dismissed Chaplin's music as a "circusy, sentimental score."[20] His colleague Roger Greenspun was a bit more forgiving, calling it "a model of rectitude and willingness to let well enough alone."[21] "Anybody who has seen recent Chaplin movies, especially the miracle *A Countess from Hong Kong*," said Greenspun, "knows that he writes the loveliest kitsch background music since the Oskar Straus [*sic*] waltzes that graced the great Max Ophuls films of the early 1950's."[22]

Chaplin's opinion of *The Circus* as a film had changed in the intervening four decades. Where Arthur Kay's 1928 compilation score played up the comedy, Chaplin's compositional style, particularly in the string of Victorian-style waltzes he composed, attempts to give dignity to the character of the Tramp even in the most ridiculous of situations. And though "Swing High, Little Girl" does not play a significant role in the score, its use over the main titles musically sets the tone for the rest of the film and gives some indication as to Chaplin's mindset at this stage in his life. "It *is* good, isn't it?" Chaplin asked *The New York Times* about the film. "Good shape to it. Very cleanly done."[23]

*   *   *

Mo Rothman's lucrative deal to distribute Chaplin's film catalog helped him persuade Chaplin to end his twenty-year, self-imposed exile and return to the U.S. in 1972 to pro-

The Circus (1968 reissue)—"Breathless" mimics Charlie's fear inside the lion's cage.

mote it. The trip included receiving an Honorary Oscar in Los Angeles and a tribute by the Film Society of Lincoln Center, featuring a double bill screening of *The Kid* and *The Idle Class* with newly composed Chaplin scores. But Chaplin felt parts of *The Kid* "seem too sentimental now; fifty years makes a difference."[24] With that in mind, he removed scenes from the film that he thought might be too maudlin, most of them revolving around the Mother.

When it came time to work on the score, Eric James had to find a new orchestrator since Lambert Williamson was retiring due to ill health. James highly recommended Eric Rogers, "who has a long list of films to his credit and who is a both agreeable and likeable person who does not believe in time wasting in a Recording Studio."[25] James told Rachel Ford that Rogers "could cope with everything if Williamson [is] not available."[26]

Rogers (1921–1981), born Eric Gauk-Roger, began his film career in 1946 after serving in the Royal Air Force and as a Spitfire pilot in Burma during the war. He worked as an orchestrator and largely uncredited composer of additional music on a number of films,

The Circus (1968 reissue)—"An Irish Echo" is Chaplin's sentimental love theme for Charlie
and Merna.

The Circus (1968 reissue)—"His Try-Out" is yet another Chaplin "promenade" theme to
accompany Charlie's William Tell audition with the clowns.

The Circus (1968 reissue)—The second section of the "Horse Music" is a sequence of prancing
leaps.

including *Night and the City* (1950) and *Genevieve* (1953). Rogers composed the signature
tune for the successful *Sunday Night at the London Palladium* television show in the
1950s and '60s and conducted the score for James Bond's debut in *Dr. No* (1962). In a
foreshadowing of his work with Chaplin, he also transcribed Lionel Bart's singing
and orchestrated the score for the musical *Oliver!*, later serving as a member of the
team of orchestrators and the associate music supervisor on the 1968 Oscar-winning
film. But Rogers is best known as the composer for twenty-two of the popular *Carry On*
films.

Because of the Lincoln Center tribute, Chaplin composed the scores for *The Kid*
and *The Idle Class* at the same time. Eric James's letter of agreement stated he would be
paid £150 per week plus £30 for any Sundays.[27] Rogers originally quoted a total music
budget of £3500, which included his fee as well as costs for copying, booking, and the

The Circus (1968 reissue)—The "Horse Music" two-note duplets become two-note triplets in the "Around the Side-shows" cue.

The Circus (1968 reissue)—Now the two-note triplets of "Around the Side-shows" flip into half-step descending intervals in the "Recitative" cue's pizzicato strings.

musicians. But in a letter to Rachel Ford four days before the first session, Rogers said that on his visit to Vevey,

> I discovered that there is some 85 minutes of music (I didn't even know they were silent pictures!!), which necessitates, according to Musicians' Union Rules, at least 5 sessions of 3-hours duration, as one is not allowed to record more than 20 minutes of music per session. This, therefore, invalidates my original quotation of £3500 for the music costs.
>
> Subsequently, I have given to Jerry [Epstein] my personal quotation for my own involvement, which is £1000 for orchestrating the music, plus £50 per 3-hour recording session—giving a total of £1250–£1300.
>
> Added to this fee will be the musicians' fees, which, with an orchestra of 41 will be approximately £550 per session, plus a 10% booking fee for the contractor and a music copying fee of approximately £500. This gives a total of somewhere between £5000 & £6000, depending on how much time we need to record this rather enormous amount of music, bearing in mind that Mr. Chaplin does not (probably) work at my rather fast pace.[28]

Between his work on *The Kid* and *The Idle Class*, plus recording sessions, traveling expenses, and "relevelling [*sic*] music," James received £1,827 and Rogers £1,355. The music budget, including studio fees, eventually totaled £14,637.45, a far cry from Rogers's original estimate.[29]

The combined recording sessions for *The Kid* and *The Idle Class* were scheduled for three days—October 25, 27, and 29, 1971. On the last day, a crew arrived to film Chaplin conducting the orchestra for a documentary Mo Rothman was planning. In the grainy, faded video that survives, the setting is cramped and nondescript. Spidery directional microphones point and hover over the heads of the bored group of gentlemen crammed into the ordered chaos of a typical recording studio. A dapper, white-haired, 82-year-old Chaplin enters the room to a smattering of polite applause. With an "off you go, sir," Rogers cedes the podium. Chaplin cracks a joke about being left-handed, even though he isn't using a baton (most conductors hold it in their right hand) and begins to conduct the main theme from *The Kid*. Chaplin looks at the score (probably for the sake of the camera), his waving arms properly laying down the rubato 4/4 beats. Yet Rogers, who *Carry On* producer Peter Rogers (no relation) called "a round, jolly fellow," steps in from the side to point to the spot in the score where Chaplin should be looking, knowing full well he cannot read the music.[30] Was Rogers being helpful or merely pointing out for the cameras that Chaplin could not understand what he saw on the page? Either way, the gesture was unnecessary and borders on rude.

Between camera and sound crews, film, equipment, editing, and other "sundries," the project cost a total of £292.33.[31] But a problem quickly arose when it was discovered that the cameras had also filmed the orchestra. Rothman did not get authorization from the musicians union and had to make a donation of £205 to the Musicians' Union Benevolent Fund, which cleared the footage for use in the 1975 documentary *The Gentleman Tramp*.[32]

"The hardest work for all concerned," said James, "was when the moment came for carrying out the music balance at the recording studios."

> This task was made no easier because Charlie insisted on sitting in the control room with the engineers and myself and virtually directing the sensitivity of the various mikes in use. He would demand that this mike or that should predominate on this or that passage and in general he tried to carry out the whole technical process, which the engineer and I could have managed quite satisfactorily on our own. Charlie would justify himself by saying that he was a perfectionist, implying that the balance engineer and particularly myself were not. I found these sessions so irritating that I would remain silent and let him chatter on, knowing that in the end we would have to try to do what was unquestionably correct.[33]

After the tracks were laid to Chaplin's satisfaction, "there would follow a nail-biting period" while Chaplin watched the complete film. "With bated breath we would await Charlie's acceptance or otherwise of the 'married' print and finished article."

> As [Charlie] began to get older it became apparent that he was beginning to lose his confidence because he would, just now and then, take the unprecedented step of asking my advice on some of the problems that would arise. If only he had been prepared to take a back seat all the time and allow the technicians and myself to do the job, which we were after all being paid to do, the embarrassing situation over *The Kid* would not have happened.
>   When the reels were run through and he confirmed his approval, I was anything but happy and knew that all was not well. However, as he had stamped his seal of approval on it, I was in no position to voice my criticism…
>   A private run through of *The Kid* was set up, at which, thankfully, Charlie was not present. As a result, there was strong criticism from all sides in regard to the music balance and it was realized that the film could not be presented to the public without damaging Charlie's reputation…. A conference was called, the outcome of which was an unanimous agreement that under no circum-

stances whatsoever could Charlie be made aware that his work on the balancing was unacceptable; nevertheless, complete rebalancing had to be carried out.[34]

Rothman told James to go ahead. "I was sworn to absolute secrecy," James said. "I used to break out in a cold sweat when I thought of the consequences should Charlie ever find out. The shock would have been frightening and could well have destroyed him. To him, his personal satisfaction was everything and no one but no one could ever make decisions concerning his films but him!"[35] Even with all the problems, "I can honestly say that *The Kid* was my favorite of all the Chaplin's films on which we worked. The music was quite operatic in parts and complemented the contrasting scenes perfectly. There was a truly delightful theme, which was effectively scored mainly featuring the string section of the orchestra."[36]

The genesis of that theme began in June 1969 at the wedding of Chaplin's daughter Josephine. When James, who had flown to Switzerland for the wedding, approached the head of the receiving line, Chaplin left his place next to Oona, ran across the room, and, "without even a formal word of greeting, said, 'Eric, I have a most marvelous idea for the theme music of our next film, *The Freak*,' and he at once began to go into rapturous details." James was appalled at Chaplin's behavior. "Stop Charlie, for goodness sake!" he said. "Of course the music is important to you but this is your daughter's wedding day! It's her day, a day for eating, drinking, and celebration, not for talking about music, and films. For once, this must take second place."[37] The day after the wedding, James returned to the Manoir, where he transcribed the idea for the melody Chaplin had described the day before. "I put in quite a lot of effort on the piece and was pleased with the result," James said.[38] When work on *The Freak* was shelved, Chaplin used the melody as the theme for *The Kid*.

The theme is a prime example of a Chaplin melody—a four-note motif (three eighth pickup notes and a tied half note) that moves stepwise, boxed within the close interval of a fourth. Filling the holds in the half notes are arpeggiated eighth notes and sobbing two-note motifs in the woodwinds, a musical reference to the film's first title card—"A picture with a smile—and perhaps, a tear." The theme, which represents the Mother's

The Kid (1972 reissue)—Chaplin's moving main theme.

love for her child, also served as the intermission music in between screenings of *The Kid* and *The Idle Class*.

A typewritten document in the Chaplin Archive contains lyrics Chaplin wrote and considered adding to the theme, as he had done with "Swing High, Little Girl" in *The Circus*—"I walk the streets—the avenue / But all the time I think of you. / No more those eyes light up the room / Eyes that dissipate the gloom. / I've searched and searched but all in vain / For I don't even know your name."[39] James and his wife Phyllis O'Reilly later incorporated the song as part of a musical tribute to Chaplin they performed for over a decade.

A sneaky theme in 6/8 embodies the thieves who accidentally get more than they bargained for when they steal the car containing the baby in the back seat. Strings and guitar provide a steady rhythm, the tritone (or the *diabolus in musica* ["the Devil in music"]) in the French horns lends tension, and a steady sequence involving a three-note motif in the woodwinds and muted trumpets propel the burglars to their just desserts. The jaunty "Morning Promenade" serves as Charlie's entrance through the back alleys of the slum. Sets of four sixteenth notes rush into an *oom-pah* accompaniment underneath dotted rhythms in the flutes, oboe, xylophone, and piano, while *nyah-nyah* glissandi in the strings give the cue some bite. A bridge of singing strings and French horns, and bell-tone stacked chords in the trombones and trumpets lead into further restatements of the original theme in various orchestrations. When Charlie finds the baby with a note—"Please love and care for this orphan child"—the strings take center stage, with the note rendered in the key of F minor before morphing into the parallel F major as he smiles at the little tyke and brings him home. The music later returns as Edna comes back to retrieve her baby only to find the car missing.

As always, Chaplin composed a couple of waltzes, the most prominent of which is the "Garret Waltz." "A set means so much to me," Chaplin later said. "I think myself into a thing and whatever comes out has been influenced a great deal by environment. This room was based to a large extent on the places in Lambeth and Kennington where Sydney and I had lived with our mother when we were children. Perhaps that's why the film had some truth."[40] The elegant waltz flows along in gentle contrast to the Tramp's obvious poverty, as well as underscoring ingenious solutions to quell the baby's crying, including a rubber-nippled teapot for the bottle, a sling for a crib, and cutting a hole in a wicker

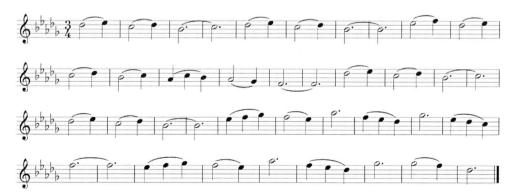

The Kid (1972 reissue)—The elegant "Garret Waltz," the first of three waltzes in the score, provides musical counterpoint to the Tramp's poverty.

The Kid (1972 reissue)—The "Blue Eyes" waltz serves as ironic counterpoint to the Kid's tough guy stance.

The Kid (1972 reissue)—Dance band orchestrations give the "Organ Waltz" a 1920s period feel to underscore the scene in the Mother's dressing room.

chair to serve as a toilet. The theme later accompanies the tender bonding scenes with Charlie and the Kid cooking and in Dreamland when the Kid enters in a pair of wings, hardly the perfect little angel.

Another waltz, labeled "Blue Eyes," underscores the Kid "five years later" filing his nails on the curb, leading back into the "Garret Waltz" once the scene moves inside. The minor key waltz also accompanies the scene in which the Doctor (Jules Haft) attends to the boy's illness and finds out Charlie is not the real father. In the Mother's dressing room, cup-muted trumpets and a jazzy alto saxophone lend a period big band feel to the "Organ Waltz," which gives her a musical air of sophistication as "a star of great prominence" that matches the wardrobe and chic set pieces.

The rollicking "Breaking Windows" cue underscores some of the film's most delicious interplay between the Tramp and the Kid as they scam their neighbors through their smash-and-repair business. The theme, which begins once again in the key of F major and goes through a number of modulations, can be broken up into a number of sub-themes. A call-and-answer session between the woodwinds and strings leads into a fanfare-like melody in the brass punctuated by octave chirps in the flute, piccolo, and violins that summon the cop (Tom Wilson) to the scene, while his music is a plodding, accented melody in the clarinets, bassoon, and strings. "The Kid's Fight" employs some of the same techniques as a combination of triplets and dotted rhythms lure the ear into hearing 6/8 in the cue's cut time, while the xylophone and wood blocks provide the wooden sounds of punching little fists.

The flowing string melody that represents the "Country Doctor" gives no clue to the man who rats out Charlie to the social worker. A theme simply called "Menace" is exactly that. Borrowing the two-note chirping motif from "Breaking Windows," the cop returns with the Welfare Officer (Frank Campeau) to pick up Charlie's charge. A steady heartbeat pulses under a three-note cry in the English horn and French horns while tremolo strings furiously saw away dramatically. The music turns operatic in its use of rubato as sixteenth notes and quarter note triplets fight for dominance, while timpani rolls and cymbal crashes clash as the Tramp fights to keep the Kid.

The famous scene of the Kid crying from the back of the orphanage truck brings forth Chaplin's most passionate music. The elongated melody of the "Sick Kid" theme appeared briefly as the Mother carries the sick child into the garret. When Charlie escapes onto the roof to rescue him, anyone with a passing knowledge of Chaplin's history of being separated from his mother on numerous occasions can see the Dickensian parallels

The Kid (1972 reissue)—The loping "Breaking Windows" cue provides melodic accompaniment to the Tramp and the Kid's scam to make money.

The Kid (1972 reissue)—"The Kid's Fight" is a rollicking mixture of triplets and dotted rhythms underscoring the David-and-Goliath meeting between the Kid and a neighborhood bully.

The Kid (1972 reissue)—The passionate "Sick Kid" theme underscores the film's most emotional scene of the Kid getting hauled away in the back of the orphanage truck.

in the scene. But the sobbing music for strings and winds, which goes over the top for some critics, conveys something more primal and universal—a child's worst nightmare of abandonment.

After the rescue, Charlie smuggles the Kid into a doss-house to sleep for the night. James said Chaplin called the cue his "Tchaikovsky music, because it's rather sad," a mournful waltz for violas and cellos that uses chromatic accidentals and a wave-like motion to convey unrest and weariness.[41] The staccato eighth notes in the woodwinds and strings impart stealth, whether it is Charlie trying to sneak the Kid into his bed or the doss-house keeper (Henry Bergman) kidnapping the boy for the ransom money. The waltz occurs later during the final "flight-y" segment of the dream sequence as the neighborhood bully (Charles Reisner) enters the scene, a fight ensues and feathers fly. Chaplin composed two gavottes for the scene—the Tramp's shopping spree for his wings (in F major) and a variation in F minor when the Devil shows up, played by Jack Coogan, Sr.

Chaplin once admitted he hated it "more than anything when they call me sentimental."[42] And his score for *The Kid* has more than its share of unabashed sentimentality. Author Mervyn Cooke was not impressed with what he called Chaplin's "sentimental lyricism, mock-sinister music

Chaplin and Jackie Coogan wring tears in *The Kid*'s emotional reunion, c. 1921 (© Roy Export SAS).

The Kid (1972 reissue)—Chaplin called his melancholy cello waltz for "The Doss-House" his "Tchaikovsky music."

for villains, circus slapstick for comic capers, a light operetta style enlivened by occasional ragtime syncopations, folksy jauntiness, stentorian pomposity and banal Edwardian waltzes."[43] Eric Rogers's orchestrations are light on wit and bear the mark of a pit orchestra economy. Yet Chaplin had always been averse to "too many notes" in his scores and the music most likely reflects exactly what he wanted. Perhaps a younger Chaplin would have had the energy to find ways to alleviate the sense of boxiness when Rogers simply moves melodic and harmonic figures from one group of voices to another or repeats sections over and over again with little relief except modulating to a new key signature. But these traits would plague all of Rogers's orchestrations and Chaplin's scores for the rest of his life. Still, Chaplin's "sentimental lyricism" rarely fails to wring tears from an audience. "I always said that music was a fundamental factor of dreams, tenderness, irony," Chaplin remarked. "I'm therefore going to place a kind of mirror behind the images and they will be reflected ad infinitum. To tell the truth, *The Kid* will therefore only really be finished in 1972, and until now we will only have seen outlines of it."[44]

*   *   *

In April 1971, even before work began on the music for *The Kid*, Eric James wrote to Rachel Ford inquiring about Chaplin's plans to record a new score for *The Idle Class*. "Possibly Mr. Chaplin may have lost some of his enthusiasm for composing," James said, "because it takes so much out of him when he works."

> I hesitate to suggest this but I feel that if he decides to work on any music in the future, he should limit his working day to 3 or 4 hours. I recall that we used to slog away until 5.0 or even 5.30 pm most days and although I consider myself to be fairly strong, I must say that the sustained effort of concentration of the kind demanded by Mr. Chaplin was absolutely exhausting for both of us. Do let me know (in confidence) if there is any likelihood of my receiving the "royal command" to proceed to the Manoir de Ban in the next few months?[45]

Ford replied that when she saw Oona in London, "she mentioned that she did so hope that Mr. Chaplin would do the music. So do I, and if and when the time comes I will find a way to relay your comments to Mr. Chaplin."[46]

With so little in common, the pairing of *The Kid* and *The Idle Class* seems strange on the surface. But in 1921, the latter film followed on the heels of the former in a quick burst of creativity that must have brought relief to First National executives who did not look forward to another extended period waiting for a new Chaplin film. Originally titled *Home Again* and *Vanity Fair*, Chaplin worked on *The Idle Class* over a five-month period from January to June 1921. During that time, he finally brought Hannah over to live out her days in the U.S. No doubt that strain kept him from concentrating on anything more than a quick two-reel short, though it probably also served as a balm to take his mind off having his mother nearby. *The Idle Class* is one of the few films that gave audiences two Charlies for the price of one, with the Tramp mistaken for Edna Purviance's look-alike wealthy husband.

"Like most of the Chaplin comedies," said *The New York Times*, "*The Idle Class* doesn't concern itself much with a story. Its main purpose is to give Chaplin a chance to contrast two characters—a wealthy fop and a foppish tramp.... It's hard to see how you can help enjoying both, even if they are exaggerated and the story they are in doesn't mean anything."[47] The *Los Angeles Times* said, "*The Idle Class* is as freshly original, as full of brilliant touches, as adroitly put over as only a man who has worked as long and as faithfully and as cleverly as Charlie Chaplin could make it."[48] "Chaplin plays both roles with subtle shadings and appreciation of class distinction," said *The Globe*. "It is not as funny as many Chaplin pictures we have seen, but it is funnier than any film comedy that is not Chaplin."[49]

But *The Idle Class* available to today's audiences, at least on video, is not the film audiences saw in 1921. Before he started working on the music in 1971, Chaplin had to decide what speed he was going to use. As he had done in 1959 on the three films compiled for *The Chaplin Revue*, Chaplin employed "stretch-printing" on *The Idle Class*, a process in which frames are repeated at regular intervals to slow down the action. A film that began as a two-reeler of 1,910 feet in 1921 became a three-reeler of 2,975 feet fifty years later. The longer running time affected the music Chaplin wrote and not always in a positive light.

The film opens with a theme ("Suspense") conveying the hustle and bustle of the arriving train. Harmonically, the theme ascends chromatically until Edna alights from her compartment with the nine shimmering chords of the "Box Theme" in the strings,

The Idle Class (1972 reissue)—**The chromatic sequence of five-note motifs in the "Suspense" cue is nothing more suspenseful than the embarrassing sight of the husband's gartered legs.**

celeste, vibraphone, and glockenspiel, which continue the chromatic movement. A mournful rubato in the violins and English horn represents Charlie's down-and-out existence as a hobo riding the rails. The "Suspense" music also underscores the entrance of Chaplin's dual role as Edna's wealthy husband, running late to pick her up at the station. Only in a later scene does it become apparent that the suspense comes from a number of visual gags covering the sight of the husband's embarrassingly exposed gartered legs. Charlie's theme plays in "unison," not only to underscore the "lonely husband" but also foreshadowing the dual roles that will be mistaken later in the film.

Chaplin's use of his "Golf Links Waltz" is a prime example of him incorporating music that would not interfere with his comedy. The delicate theme trips lightly over the golf course but the stretch-printing wears out the scene's welcome, and a never-ending succession of modulations and minor changes in orchestration cover the elongated running time, with the endless repetitions numbing the ears. Belching brass renditions of the theme give voice to Charlie's arguments before returning to the delicate woodwinds

The Idle Class (1972 reissue)—**The nine chords of the "Box Theme," more a motif than a theme.**

The Idle Class (1972 reissue)—**The F-minor key signature and the lonely English horn of "Charlie's Theme" provide a mournful accompaniment to his life as a hobo riding the rails.**

The Idle Class (1972 reissue)—**The joyful "Golf Links Waltz" runs through a series of seemingly never-ending modulations that quickly wears out the theme's welcome.**

Charlie uses Henry Bergman as a golf tee in *The Idle Class*, c. 1921 (© Roy Export SAS).

and violins as he scampers off with chaos in his wake. Saxophone and muted trumpet play the "Optimism" waltz as Charlie sees Edna ride by on her horse and dreams of a married life with her. Back on the golf course, the "Golf Links Waltz" continues its series of monotonous modulations.

A delightful "Carefree" dance band theme accompanies the costume ball. A saxophone plays the "Optimism" waltz as Charlie is mistaken for the husband who has become stuck in his armor costume. When Charlie realizes Edna is the woman he saw on the horse, lush strings take over the theme. A "South American" conga-type number underscores scenes where Charlie is continually mistaken for Edna's husband. Bonnie Bourne thought the theme "might prove interesting for promotion," a recommendation that was wisely ignored.[50] A saxophone "Fox-trot" irons out the mistaken identities. The dance band "Carefree" theme, which for some reason James did not list as such on the cue sheet, wraps up the film's closing moments as Edna's father throws Charlie out and he delivers one last swift kick before fleeing the scene.

Chaplin must have been particularly pleased following the recording of *The Kid* and *The Idle Class*. "I can't read a note," he told *The New York Times*, "but I like all the music I've ever written."[51]

*　*　*

The Idle Class (1972 reissue)—"Carefree" provides a lighthearted accompaniment to the costume ball.

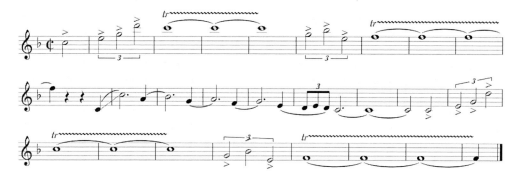

The Idle Class (1972 reissue)—The Latin conga rhythms of the "South American" cue underscore the final showdown between the two Charlies.

Chaplin and the Academy Awards have always had a combative relationship. For the first awards ceremony in 1929, the Academy removed Chaplin's name from the competitive categories and awarded him a special Oscar for *The Circus* instead. Chaplin thought "the whole institution of Academy awards was foolish." He did not think it was "much of an honor when a small group of people decides I have the best picture. I want my acclaim from the public. If they like my work that's reward enough for me." He did not attend the banquet in 1929 and the Academy had to send his Oscar to him. Originally, Chaplin valued his Oscar so little that he used it as a doorstop. "But ever since I can remember," his son later said, "he has kept it on a high shelf with a bust of himself and his treasured Dresden and Staffordshire figurines. Even in Vevey.... I saw it still occupying this place of honor. So perhaps his opinion of the Academy awards has improved with the years."[52]

The Academy overlooked *City Lights* and *Modern Times* altogether and Chaplin lost every subsequent nomination for *The Great Dictator* and *Monsieur Verdoux*. But after his two decades of self-imposed exile in Switzerland, Chaplin's political troubles were mostly a thing of the past. Now the Academy wanted to make amends to the legendary filmmaker by honoring him with a lifetime achievement award at the 1972 ceremony. For months it was unclear if Chaplin would be able—or even *want*—to attend the awards ceremony in April. But the Oscar plus the Film Society of Lincoln Center tribute were enough to bring Chaplin to the U.S. for the first time in twenty years.

Mo Rothman's business partner Bert Schneider was the driving force behind the

Oscar, and Chaplin's appearance on the telecast was the zenith of a public relations campaign Rothman had set in motion the previous year with the re-release of Chaplin's catalogue. Author Jeffrey Vance called it "one of the greatest P.R. coups, and personal rehabilitations" in the history of the film industry. "Rothman is the guy who re-made Chaplin."[53] But having Chaplin accept the award posed problems for producer Howard Koch. "Charlie Chaplin should be very emotional," he said in the Academy's newsletter. "We don't know how to rehearse that. Will he get an ovation, or won't he? We've been trying to figure out, maybe five minutes, maybe six. Could be twenty. We thought we should rehearse the ovation on the days we rehearse at the Music Center. But then we thought, maybe not, maybe it ought to be completely spontaneous. These decisions have to be made right up to air time."[54]

The night of the awards, Academy President Daniel Taradash introduced Chaplin with a moving tribute.

> The inscription reads: "To Charles Chaplin for the incalculable effect he has had in making motion pictures the art form of this century." Chaplin has become more than a name. It is a word in the vocabulary of films. And anyone who has ever seen a movie is in his debt. A few years ago, Mr. Chaplin said, "My only enemy is time." We regretfully disagree. For wherever and whenever there is communication—a screen and an audience—whether here on Earth and now or in some unfathomable future on some faraway star, time is Charlie Chaplin's dearest and eternal friend."[55]

Chaplin did indeed get a well-deserved standing ovation. Visibly moved, he at first seemed unsure if the applause and shouts of "Bravo!" were meant for him. But basking in the sincere affection from the audience, he waved and blew kisses to those on their feet in the auditorium as well as the group behind him onstage. Chaplin offered a short, heartfelt acceptance speech—"Oh, thank you so much. An emotional moment for me. And words seem so futile, so feeble. I can only say thank you for the honor of inviting me here. And you're wonderful, sweet people. Thank you."[56]

In addition to the other accolades, Chaplin finally received a star on the Hollywood Walk of Fame. E. M. Stuart, the volunteer president of the Hollywood Chamber of Commerce, initiated the idea of the Walk of Fame in 1953 to "maintain the glory of a community whose name means glamour and excitement in the four corners of the world."[57] Between the spring of 1956 and the fall of 1957, committees representing the four major branches of the entertainment industry selected 1,558 honorees. Chaplin was initially among the 500 names proposed in 1956 but the filmmaker was still *persona non grata* in Hollywood and the selection committee ruled him out. In October 1959, Charles Chaplin, Jr., filed a lawsuit seeking damages but the case was dismissed. When the Chamber of Commerce finally awarded Chaplin his star in 1972, the office still received angry letters from across the country disputing the decision, calling Chaplin "traitor to this country," a Revolutionary Zionist, and "Comrade Charlie."[58] To many, he still was not welcome. Chaplin returned to his home in Switzerland and never set foot on American soil again.

*   *   *

Chaplin wasted no time getting back to work on his music. Except for *The Circus*, which he had been planning on scoring for years, and the pairing of *The Kid* and *The Idle Class* for the Film Society accolade, there is no apparent rhyme or reason to the order in which Chaplin scored his last films. Perhaps Mo Rothman dictated the order based on an internal schedule for the reissues. If there were reasons, there is no written evidence. By August 1972, Chaplin and Eric James were hard at work on the music for *Pay Day*.

Chaplin began filming *Pay Day* in August 1921. He was in the "last mile" of his contract with First National and "looking forward to its termination." He described the studio as "inconsiderate, unsympathetic and shortsighted, and I wanted to be rid of them." But even with light at the end of the tunnel, completing the last two pictures left on the contract—*Pay Day* and *The Pilgrim*—"seemed an insuperable task."[59] Chaplin filmed *Pay Day* over thirty working days and, for the first time, departed from his normal practice of shooting in narrative continuity, filming the second part first. This time, the Tramp is a henpecked construction worker in love with the foreman's daughter (Edna Purviance).

The *Exhibitors Herald* review said, "The musical accompaniment must not be overlooked in putting the picture over."[60] But research has not unearthed a cue sheet that most likely would have been supplied by Cameo Music Publishing, and there is no indication in any other review what music was used. However, when the film played on a vaudeville bill at the Palace Theatre (with such luminaries as Paul Whiteman and his Palais Royal Band, and Ona Munson), a notice in *The Music Trade Review* noted that the song "Angel Child," which had topped the charts in a recording by Al Jolson earlier that year, was played. Given the lyrics of the chorus—"Angel child, I'm just wild about you / Angel child, hey that you love me too"—it most likely accompanied a scene with Charlie and Edna. Hopefully, some musicians with a dark sense of humor chose it as an ironic commentary on Charlie's relationship with his unloving wife.[61]

When it came time to revisit the film fifty years later, Eric James worked on the score with Chaplin at Vevey for four weeks in August and September 1972, though his letter of agreement was not signed until November 27. James was paid £150 per week, with his total fees amounting to £1,200, as well as another £300 for a couple weeks' work to write new cue sheets for *Limelight* and *The Gold Rush*. Eric Rogers put together a 33-piece orchestra, ten less than the ensemble assembled for *The Kid* and *The Idle Class*, and received £650 for orchestrating and conducting each of the two three-hour recording sessions on November 22 and 24. The music budget totaled £5,661.43.[62]

The martial snare drums and alternating ascending and descending arpeggios of

Pay Day (1973 reissue)—The "Opening Music" fanfare.

Pay Day (1973 reissue)—The endlessly repeating "Digging the Trench Music" is as monotonous as Charlie's onscreen job.

Pay Day (1973 reissue)—Chaplin's "Debussy Music" tips its hat to the French composer's celebrated *Prélude à l'après-midi d'un faune.*

the opening music serves as a clarion call for the workers. A set of six accented notes signals the "hard shirking men" to work, while a few bars of "Digging the Trench Music" conveys the monotony of performing the same task over and over again. Chaplin tips his hat to Debussy's *Prélude à l'apès-midi d'un faune* with sinuous chromatic parallel thirds as Charlie appears through the opening in the wooden fence, lily in hand as an apology to the foreman (Mack Swain) for being late. The use of the music in this brief cue mirrors the seductiveness of Chaplin's gestures, much as Nijinsky's original choreography had, and the theme later conveys Charlie's love for Edna. The ascending and descending motion of the music mimics the up-and-down motion of the elevator as Charlie pines for her.

The brick-laying scene is one of the film's most enjoyable sequences, both visually

Charlie pines for the foreman's daughter (Edna Purviance) in *Pay Day*, c. 1922 (© Roy Export SAS).

Pay Day (1973 reissue)—The lively "Brick Music" for Chaplin's reverse camera shots of Charlie catching bricks in the air.

and musically. Thanks to a clever reversal of film, workers on the ground throw bricks "up" to Charlie on the scaffold, where he catches them two-handed, in the crook of his knee, under his arm, and under his chin. *Nyah-nyah* sixteenth-note figures at the beginning taunt him, repeated accents hammer the notes, and a brief quote of the "Digging the Trench Music" underscores the monotony of the job. Charlie walks the proverbial tightrope while the music conveys a circus-like tone through the seesaw movement of the melody, the *oom-pah* afterbeats, and the cue's frenetic pace. The three-quarter strains of the "Lunch Waltz" accompany Charlie's clever *pas de deux* with his barrel seat on the elevator and later when he receives his money and tries to hide it from his wife under his hat. Dotted half notes give the theme a lugubrious quality that ironically underscores the peril if he happens to miss his seat. Unfortunately, later modulations of the theme are hampered by wide, flat timbres in the oboe, clarinet, and bassoon.

The "Last Bus Music" accompanies two scenes of struggle. In the first, Charlie tries to fight the foreman for higher pay, while his wife (Phyllis Allen)—with an amusing title card, "first national bank"—paces on the other side of the fence, to make sure he actually brings home his pay. Later, Charlie struggles to literally catch the "last bus" home, continually being kicked off by the overcrowded passengers. In his drunken state he hangs on to a roll of sausage in a food cart, mistaking it for a strap on a cable car. The theme

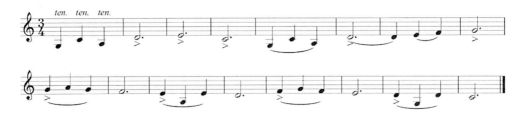

Pay Day (1973 reissue)—The "Lunch Waltz" is a *pas de deux* in three-quarter time between Charlie and his barrel seat.

Pay Day (1973 reissue)—The sluggish "Last Bus Music" carries weight, whether underscoring Charlie's big-boned wife or a cable car bulging at the seams.

employs Chaplin's trademark triplet pickups and a heavy melody that conveys the girth of Charlie's wife's and the weight of the foreman's authority in the first scene, and Charlie's drunken stumbling in the second. The most traditional use of "drunken" music occurs outside the Bachelors Club as intoxicated barflies stumble onto the sidewalk. Grace notes, muted trombones, and slides in the strings give the music a boozy feel, while the bent notes match Charlie's dexterous use of his cane on a sewer grate.

Chaplin ran into problems when it came time to score the barbershop quartet of inebriates "singing" outside of the Bachelors Club. In February 1973, Rachel Ford wrote to Eric James asking him to "unearth" the piano score to the old barbershop standard, "Sweet Adeline." "You may think I'm drunk," she quipped, "but I ain't."[63] The tune was the obvious choice to match the title card that announces it, and theater musicians surely played it in 1922. Ford enlisted Joe Murrells of London's Music Research Bureau concerning the song, "which is a tune [Chaplin's] mother used to sing when he was very young. Must ensure that it is in *Pay Day*." However, what Chaplin remembered as "Sweet Adeline" was instead a variation on the traditional 19th-century Irish folk song, "The Gentle Maiden." A clip from *The Gentleman Tramp* (1976) shows Chaplin listening to a reel-to-reel playback of the "Sweet Adeline Waltz" in his living room at the Manoir, along

Pay Day (1973 reissue)—Though Chaplin named the music for the barbershop drunkards outside the bar the "Sweet Adeline Waltz," what he remembered as "Sweet Adeline" was actually a variation on the traditional 19th-century Irish folk song, "The Gentle Maiden," a melody his mother Hannah used to sing to him as a child.

with Oona, and friends Walter and Carol Matthau. "Quite beautiful," he comments. "My mother used to sing this to me."[64] Murrells remarked that "Sweet Adeline" had a "marked similarity … here and there" to the Irish tune.[65] The question then became one of copyright, which in Great Britain lasted fifty years after the author's death. Unfortunately, "Sweet Adeline," which was written by composer Harry Armstrong (1879–1951), with lyrics by Richard H. Gerard (1876–1948), was based on a tune Armstrong had written in 1896 at age eighteen that had been published in 1903 and was still under copyright. Ford halted the research and paid Murrells £116.20 for the work.

Ford next sent Stanley Rubinstein, head of the venerated law firm Rubinstein, Nash & Co., Chaplin's "Sweet Adeline" music and a copy of Murrell's findings. The firm had made a name for itself defending Radclyffe Hall's infamous lesbian novel *The Well of Loneliness* and later, acting for Penguin Books, prosecuting D. H. Lawrence's *Lady Chatterley's Lover* for obscenity. Ford reassured Rubinstein that all the music in *Pay Day* was original except for "Sweet Adeline." Rubinstein said if the song is a traditional melody, Chaplin was "in the clear." There were questions as to Eric Rogers's arrangement resembling other published arrangements, which, Ford said, "would be unintentional as [Charlie] had no knowledge that such an arrangement existed." Rubinstein gave the "All Clear," and Rogers filled in the "Notification of Works" form for the Performing Right Society with a bar of the music.[66]

As Charlie stumbles home at five o'clock in the morning, all is not well. His wife is sleeping with a rolling pin in her arms and his attempts to remain quiet are foiled by pesky cats and a squeaky toy on the floor. The latest of Chaplin's minor-key "Misterioso" themes incorporates trademark sixteenth-note triplet grace notes and a great deal of musical space. Except for the grace notes, all movement happens on the beat, with the music timed to Chaplin's hiccups and sips of water. From his earliest attempts at film composing, Chaplin always sought to pare down the music to its essentials. A look at the original orchestrations for this cue shows busy sixteenth-note sextuplets in the strings that Chaplin eliminated from the recording. He incorporates a new easygoing major-key theme full of dotted rhythms when Charlie crawls into bed, but the alarm goes off and he put his clothes back on. Instead of going to work, he looks for a place to catch some shuteye and ends up in a bathtub of cold water, reminiscent of scenes from his earlier films *A Night Out* and *One A.M.*

The New York Times review in 1922 said *Pay Day* was "not to be classed with *Shoulder Arms* and *The Kid*, but touched with the genius of Chaplin, nevertheless. It makes you laugh, but it may also reveal something of life to you, and if it does, the heartiness of your laughter depends upon the freedom of your spirit."[67] *Photoplay* noted, "*Pay Day* made even the ushers laugh in the theater where we saw it. Ushers see a picture more times than anybody else, excepting the policemen. It had been running almost all week when we saw the ushers laugh. We can never hope to offer a critique as poignant as this. And Charles Spencer's epitaph could not be more glorious than, 'He made even ushers chuckle.'"[68]

* * *

A Day's Pleasure, the next film in Chaplin's scoring project, must have triggered painful memories. The simple story of Charlie and his family, including wife Edna Pur-

viance and two sons (one of whom was Jackie Coogan), out for "a day's pleasure" of summer fun should have been a pleasure-filled experience to film back in 1919. But the death
of Chaplin's first son, Norman Spencer Chaplin, on July 11, after only living three days,
caused Chaplin to go into a "terrible depression."[69] Eleven days later, he set aside the
6,570 feet of film he had already shot for what he called *Charlie's Picnic* and began auditioning children roles for what would eventually become *The Kid*. But realizing that that
film would be bigger than anything he had attempted so far, and with First National
breathing down his neck for a new picture, Chaplin stitched together the film he had
already shot with the children and the car for *Charlie's Picnic* and rechristened it *The
Ford Story*. The film was completed over the next two months, retitled *A Day's Pleasure*,
and released on December 8, 1919.

Though *The New York Times* proclaimed Chaplin "screamingly funny,"[70] *The Billboard* said, "Seems as if Chaplin was loafing on the job."[71] In its report from Montreal,
Variety claimed, "The new Charlie Chaplin film was a failure, so far as public enthusiasm
was concerned. The same may be said of the Chaplin film so far as its presentation at
three other houses in the city simultaneously is concerned."[72] *Picture-Play Magazine*
expected "something more original, more startling and, indeed, more humorous from
the man who made *Shoulder Arms* and *A Dog's Life*."[73]

In May 1973, Chaplin made quick progress on the score, which was completed and
recorded in short order by the end of the summer. Eric James signed his letter of agreement on May 4 for £150 per week and began working at Vevey three days later, eventually
earning £930 for his contribution.[74] Eric Rogers signed his letter of agreement on August
24, receiving £600 for orchestrating and conducting.[75] When Rogers filled out the cue
sheet for the Performing Right Society, he claimed he was the arranger (as he had done
with the *Pay Day* PRS cue sheet), not Eric James. The score for *A Day's Pleasure* was
recorded in two afternoon sessions at Anvil Recording Studios on August 28 and 30 at
a total cost of £6293.34.

Over the opening credits, trumpet and string arpeggiated fanfares sound a bugle
call to awaken the day. A weaving, carefree violin theme, perfect for a day's pleasure, is
underscored by an ostinato in the low strings and xylophone. Staccato woodwinds chirp

A Day's Pleasure (1973 reissue)—The brass fanfares of the "Opening Music" announce the
beginning of what should have been "a day's pleasure" for Charlie and family.

A Day's Pleasure (1973 reissue)—The lazy melody of the "Car Music" gives false hope that
Charlie's old jalopy will ever start.

in laughter as Charlie fails to get his bouncing jalopy started. The syncopated main theme is sped up as he and his family attempt to board the boat.

During filming, Chaplin hired comedienne Babe London, fifteen extras, and four black musicians, and bussed them all to San Pedro to film the scenes aboard the pleasure boat, the *Ace*. Seasickness (a throwback to similar scenes in *The Immigrant*), the frustration of collapsing deck chairs, and jealous husbands on the storm-tossed boat gave Chaplin inspiration. The black jazz band provides music on the cruise, though Chaplin does not bother to match the movements of the musicians in his music, except for the boozy trombone that mimics the wave-like motion in the "Sea Music" waltz following. The four black members of the band (John Williams, E. Sorral, J. A. Irvin, C. Allen) were listed by name on the Daily Work Sheet, but merely as "4 × Colored" on the Daily Production Report. They were, however, paid $7.50 each per day, the same rate as Babe London, and higher than the $5.00 fee paid to the fifteen women and men day players on the film.

The primary jazz number is a Charleston that almost ran into legal difficulties. Rachel Ford notified Eric James that Bonnie Bourne felt the first three bars of the "Jazz" cue sounded suspiciously like the famous *12th Street Rag*. "I am enclosing a comparison chart," said Bourne, "so that Mr. James can give you his recommendation. After reviewing this situation, perhaps Mr. James might recommend a modification in the music as it now stands so as to avoid any possible conflict." Bourne suggested substituting "Green Lantern Rag" from *A Dog's Life* if Chaplin did not want to re-edit the film.[76] Though James inexplicably did not think there would be any copyright infringement, he repeated the cue's intro to replace any possible "offending" material.[77]

The Tramp dances his own fumbling *pas de deux* with a deck chair accompanied by a hummable waltz, yet another example of Chaplin scoring a comedic scene with ironic elegant music. The "Sea Song" waltz serves as a duet with a pugilistic seasick passenger who thinks Charlie has been flirting with his wife. A brief quote of "For He's a Jolly Good

A Day's Pleasure (1973 reissue)—The lively "Jazz" music for the boat ride, bearing more than a slight resemblance to the famous *12th Street Rag*.

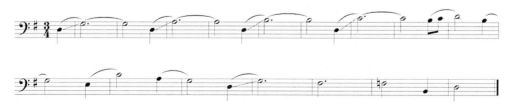

A Day's Pleasure (1973 reissue)—A rocking "Sea Music" waltz mimics the waves and sends the riders heaving their meals over the side.

Aboard the rocking boat, Charlie and a seasick jazz trombonist find their excursion is anything but *A Day's Pleasure,* c. 1918 (© Roy Export SAS).

A Day's Pleasure (1973 reissue)—Charlie uses the "Deck Chair Waltz" as a comic *pas de deux* with the flimsy piece of furniture.

Fellow" accompanies the disembarking passengers and sets up the first five notes of the "Crossroads" cue as the car gets stuck at an intersection on the way home. The scene was originally slated to precede the boat scenes but instead provides a nice "auto" bookend to the film. Bass clarinet and timpani give a low drunken accompaniment to the "Tar" music. When Charlie gets stuck in the ooze, his seesawing movements back and forth mimic dancing with the cop, accompanied by yet another waltz. The film ends with Chaplin's jalopy billowing smokes as it drives off—"The end of a perfect day."

    A Day's Pleasure is minor Chaplin, and the film certainly feels like the filler it is, but it is all silly fun made more enjoyable by Chaplin's charming tunes. But the music is marred by Eric Rogers's lackluster orchestrations and the flabby and piercing sounds emanating from the orchestra. Eric James definitely wanted to take credit for the recording sessions by this point, so perhaps the fault is his. Or maybe this is exactly the sound Chaplin wanted. While neither Chaplin, his audience, nor his critics considered *A Day's*

A Day's Pleasure (1973 reissue)—"Sea Song" accompanies the woozy fight with a pugilistic passenger.

A Day's Pleasure (1973 reissue)—Chaplin ironically interpolates "For He's a Jolly Good Fellow" in the "Crossroads" cue as his car gets stuck in the road.

A Day's Pleasure (1973 reissue)—Stuck in tar, Charlie argues with the cop, swaying to and fro to this bottom-heavy waltz.

Pleasure to be "perfect," it still provides twenty-two minutes of pleasure, especially when coupled with Chaplin's score.

* * *

Rachel Ford informed Eric James in early February 1974 that Chaplin was considering composing music for *Sunnyside*. Originally titled *Jack of All Trades* (indicated by the "etc. etc. etc." in the title cards), the film follows the Tramp as a farmhand who also works at the rundown Hotel Evergreen. When not at the hands (or feet) of his cruel boss (Tom Wilson), Charlie's only bright spot is his love for the daughter of a neighboring farmer, played as usual by Edna Purviance. But Edna forgets her affection for the adorable drudge when a city slicker crashes into town and begins to show interest.

Sunnyside was shot over six months between November 1918 and April 1919, but critics primarily did not find the film to be "very sunny nor very funny."[78] "*Sunnyside* assuredly does not portray Charlie Chaplin's 'funnyside,'" said *Variety*'s "Among the Women" column. "Except for firm idolators of Chaplin, many of whom laugh as soon as his face is flashed, the new release holds few legitimate snickers even."[79] The central *Variety* review stated that the film "suggests to many casual and inexperienced observers that the said talent is running dry." Though the anonymous reviewer said the film "moves too slowly and is rough without humor," he admitted, "as pictures go, this one is worth the money."[80]

A caption in Chaplin's 1922 *My Trip Abroad* under a photo for *Sunnyside* states the film was "one of my favorite photo plays," a quote that may not be accurately attributed to Chaplin.[81] But in his autobiography forty years later, Chaplin admitted the experience was "like pulling teeth."[82] At a party to celebrate the publication of his *My Life in Pictures* in 1974, Chaplin went even further, saying, "I loathe it."[83] Even with little passion for the film, discussions with Eric James to help with the score proceeded hastily. He signed his letter of agreement on February 15, 1974, and quickly traveled to Vevey to begin work two days later, wrapping up on the 27th. James received £200 per week and £40 per day after that, totaling £1175.[84] Eric Rogers signed his letter of agreement on April 8, agreeing to a fee of £800 for orchestrating the score and conducting at two four-hour recording sessions.[85] The rest of the £9391.82 music tab consisted of the recording sessions at Anvil Recording Studios on April 30 and May 2, payments to Denlabs, and expenses for the Chaplins and Rachel Ford.

In the mid–1950s, René Micha of *Sight and Sound* called *Sunnyside* an *opera-bouffe*, "its movement is that of music."[86] And Chaplin's score for *Sunnyside* twenty years later does indeed move, swirling around a string of sunny, major-key waltzes. Following a *grandioso* version of the "Sunnyside Waltz" in the main titles, the theme begins the picture proper on a quiet Sunday morning in the early morning hours of the rural village of Sunnyside. Harp glissandi portend the rising sun at four o'clock, while woodwind figures imitate chirping birds. Charlie's farmhand cannot get out of bed, no matter the number of swift kicks administered by his boss. Staccato accompaniment in the muted trumpets and the wide vibrato of the clarinet in the modulation section convey the feeling of a dance band.

Sunnyside (1974 reissue)—The "Sunnyside Waltz," the sunny main theme.

Sunnyside (1974 reissue)—The "Evergreen Waltz" for Charlie's humble duties inside the Hotel Evergreen.

Sunnyside (1974 reissue)—**Churchgoers make their way to "Morning Service" with Chaplin's latest promenade theme.**

In addition to his duties at the farm, Charlie serves as a clerk in the ironically named, rundown Hotel Evergreen and general store. The "Evergreen Waltz" accompanies his duties mowing the weeds sticking up through the lobby's brick floor. Like most of the waltzes in the score, this one follows a basic I–V7-I chord progression. Back at the farm, the "Sunnyside Waltz" reappears as Charlie puts a chicken on the stove to lay an egg directly into the skillet and he milks a cow directly into the coffee cups.

Chimes signal the village churchgoers to "Morning Service," a promenade theme that combines quarter notes, triplet upbeats, and a series of dotted rhythms, the latter of which will be closely associated with villagers later in the score. Meanwhile, "the unwilling sinner" Charlie is forced to bring the cows home. Accompanied by spare orchestrations of the "Sunnyside Waltz," the block chorale movement of the "Emotional" theme is appropriate to the Sunday morning church setting. As the theme modulates, Charlie loses the cows and staccato woodwinds punctuate the accompaniment until a grand statement of the theme, much like the bovine on screen, crashes through, with Charlie riding and leading the way.

In the most iconic scene from the film, the steer bucks Charlie off a bridge, knocking him unconscious. What follows is a brief dream ballet with four lovely nymphs, a clear homage to Nijinsky. Chaplin had first met the famous dancer in 1917 during the filming of *Easy Street* when he came to town with the Ballets Russes. Nijinsky visited the set for three days, at the end of each day complimenting Chaplin: "Your comedy is *balletique*, you are a dancer."[87] When Chaplin went to a matinee later that week, Diaghilev changed the program to include Nijinsky's famous *Prélude à l'après-midi d'un faune*. In his autobiography, Chaplin said "no one has ever equaled Nijinsky in *L'Après-midi d'un Faune* [*sic*]. The mystic

Sunnyside (1974 reissue)—**"Ballet Music" is yet another musical homage to Debussy's *Prélude à l'après-midi d'un faune*,** underscoring Charlie's dream sequence with the nymphs.

world he created, the tragic unseen lurking in the shadows of pastoral loveliness as he moved through its mystery, a god of passionate sadness—all this he conveyed in a few simple gestures without apparent effort."[88] The same applies to Chaplin's pantomime. A sinuous waltz underscores Charlie's balletic moves, saluting Debussy's iconic ballet music with chromatic parallel thirds.

The scene switches gears visually and musically as Charlie and the nymphs gallop and cavort through the fields. An eight-bar oom-pah-pah vamp rides along under a steady stream of the first five notes of the "Sunnyside Waltz" beginning with E major and modulating chromatically fourteen times for over an octave, with various solo instruments participating in a Ravel-like orchestration exercise. The addition of tambourine, snare drum, and guitar gives the cue a rustic country and western feel until his rescuers shake Charlie awake and haul him up on the bridge, only to have the farmer kick him down the road for laying around on the job.

Chaplin breaks the film into two acts with the title card "And now, the 'romance.'" The appropriately titled "Romance Waltz" underscores Charlie's visit to Edna's house to woo her, with a melody that moves innocuously step-wise in seconds and thirds. The second half of the waltz, equally unmemorable, serves as nothing more than musical backdrop to Charlie's blindfolding Edna's brother Willie and putting him in the middle of the road to fend off oncoming traffic. This half also accompanies some funny bits with

Chaplin channels his inner Nijinsky in this classic scene from *Sunnyside*, c. 1919 (© Roy Export SAS).

Sunnyside (1974 reissue)—Charlie woos Edna with the appropriately named "Romance Waltz."

Charlie and Edna at the organ, with chord cluster sound effects, flies on the music, and goats hidden in the back of the instrument. The bright key of (not surprisingly) F major suggests that the cruelty towards Willie is all in loving fun, while the romance is emotionless, much like the melody. The score receives a welcome break from three-quarter time as jaunty dotted rhythms introduce the villagers to the lobby of the Hotel Evergreen. The dotted rhythms make fun of the country bumpkins, as does Charlie's visual antics with the mop. Chaplin gives us the first musical indication of Charlie's affection for Edna with her arrival at the hotel. When the city slicker follows Edna outside, Charlie realizes he has missed his chance. So it is perhaps no coincidence that the first five notes of the lovely "Forgotten" string theme bear a strong resemblance to the song "Now That It's Ended" from *A King in New York*.

Chaplin forgoes his own music for the final heartbreaking scenes. On February 26, Eric James called Rachel Ford, who made notes of the discussion—"CC very keen on 'When Other Lips' public domain dirge 70 years old."[89] The melody, which later became known as the ballad "Then You'll Remember Me," comes from Irish composer Michael William Balfe's (1808–1870) now-forgotten opera *The Bohemian Girl* (1843). The opera tells the tale of Count Arnheim's daughter Arline, who was kidnapped as a child and raised by gypsies. Though reunited with her father, she has fond memories of the man she loved, Thaddeus. Thaddeus sings the serenade at her window—"When other lips and other hearts / Their tales of love shall tell, / In language whose excess imparts / The power they feel so well: / There may, perhaps, in such a scene, / Some recollection be / Of days that have as happy been, / And you'll remember me!"[90]

Its placement at the end of the film shows that Chaplin was indeed "keen" on using

Sunnyside (1974 reissue)—The first five notes of the heartbreaking "Forgotten" theme bear a strong resemblance to "Now That It's Ended" from *A King in New York*.

Sunnyside (1974 reissue)—Chaplin was "very keen" on ending the film using the melody from "When Other Lips," an aria from Michael William Balfe's long-forgotten 1843 opera *The Bohemian Girl.*

the melody. With a title card of "Oh, cruel fate," Edna eventually spurns Charlie's advances. In a finale that still sparks debate, Charlie steps out in front of a rushing car. The scene abruptly cuts to a denouement in which he fights the city slicker and wins the hand of Edna. Is the real ending the suicide and the finale a glimpse of what audiences wished to happen? Is it the dream he sees before he is killed? Or is it truly a happy ending? The music provides a clue. Balfe's languid tune is traded among the lonely solo instruments of the orchestra. The strings soar in the final bars of the melody and Chaplin adds a final fanfare of the first five notes of the "Sunnyside Waltz," answering the question of his intentions for the closing of the film. Thanks to Eric James, the opening credits for *Sunnyside* contain a rare acknowledgment of the use of this pre-existing tune. Though he considered it "unnecessary," James suggested acknowledging the tune in the credits, perhaps to fend off any possible litigation. So underneath Chaplin's "Music Composed by" credit and the Roy Export copyright notice sits a credit for the Balfe/Rogers melody.[91]

Unfortunately, Chaplin's over-reliance on waltzes casts a musical pallor over *Sunnyside*, which does nothing to change the public's perception of the film as one of his lesser efforts. Even Eric James admits that Chaplin "was beginning to run out of original ideas for the music."[92] Once again, Eric Rogers's arrangements modulate from key to key with only slight changes in the orchestration, rarely creating aural interest. Still, the various uses of the "Sunnyside Waltz," the melodic richness of "When Other Lips," and the emotional heft of the "Forgotten" cue all indicate that even with the monotony that occasionally overtakes the score, Chaplin was still in charge of what he wanted to say musically. But the focus on simplicity in his compositions was clearly taking a toll.

*   *   *

As the years went by, Eric James said, "Charlie found it more and more difficult to think of ideas for the music and he would leave a great deal of it to me. I would suggest what I thought he would like, and then play it over to him for his approval, which was usually forthcoming."[93] At the end of 1974, James wrote to Rachel Ford saying he had "hopes" that Chaplin would compose a new score for *A Woman of Paris*, the only film

Chaplin owned that was still missing his music. Chaplin locked it away after its poor box office run in 1923 and audiences had not seen it since. But before he had a chance to begin work on the score, on March 4, 1975, Chaplin became Sir Charles, finally a proper recognition from his home country. He had suffered a series of strokes and was wheelchair-bound. When Chaplin was wheeled into the hall in Buckingham Palace for the decoration ceremony, the band struck up the theme to *Limelight*. Queen Elizabeth tapped a sword on each shoulder and stooped to hang the KBE insignia around his neck. A few weeks later, Rachel Ford wrote to James that "CC hasn't yet made up his mind" about *A Woman of Paris*,[94] but by mid–April James had signed his contract for his fee of £200 per week and £40 per Sunday to work on the new score.[95]

When James arrived at the Manoir, Chaplin "looked quite weak and ill," he said. "His very first words to me were 'Eric, I haven't got an idea in my head for the music of this film.' I was very distressed to find him in such a state and I could see that he found even talking quite an effort. I therefore told him not to worry but that when I had finished each piece and played it over to him, he need only nod or shake his head to indicate his judgment of it."[96]

But even with that simple way of working, the score proceeded "at [a] snail's pace."[97] It was evident that Chaplin was not going to be up to the task of composing. Rachel Ford made notes that certain pieces of music on various cassette tapes could be used for the new score, including one from *A Day's Pleasure*, though there is no indication which one. No paperwork survives in the Chaplin Archive that definitively states which themes were pulled from old sources (if any) and which ones were new.

In November 1975, James wrote to Ford:

> I am sure that you will be pleased to know that all continues well with *A Woman of Paris* to date. I marked up the music cues with [editor] John Guthridge a couple of weeks ago and Eric Rogers and myself now have the essential footages and timings for the music for the first 4 Reels…. Eric is proceeding with the orchestrating of this music whilst I am preparing the Piano Scores for the final four Reels. Doubtless you know that even with the few minor cuts and trims, the film will run 1 hour 30 minutes and Eric and I are going to do our damndest [*sic*] to get this music recorded in FOUR sessions—officially one isn't allowed to record more than 20 minutes in any one session but I have worked out a way in which we utilise certain recordings several times and thus save the cost of an extra session.[98]

And there lies the problem with much of the score for *A Woman of Paris*. The same melodies were slotted into the film over and over again—sometimes as many as seven or eight times—with little or no variation in orchestration, key, or tempo, all with an eye to saving money. In fact, both James's piano sketches and Rogers's full orchestrations make it abundantly clear that the numbers were to be recorded once and then plugged into their respective scenes. Sometimes it worked, sometimes it did not.

When Rogers asked to see the film to get "atmosphere," Oona had no objection but told him he had to use a "special machine" and warned him "that he can only use it once."[99] The recording sessions were scheduled for February 17, 19, 21, and 23, 1976, at Anvil Recording Studios. Given the length of the film, Chaplin increased Rogers's fee to £2,300 for orchestrating the music and conducting the recording sessions.[100] In her notes, Rachel Ford pointed out that Rogers was "rather embarrassed about size of fee" when he sent back his contract. Whether it was too much or too little is unclear, though considering that much of the full conductor score contains repeat markings, Rogers seemed to have spent as little effort as possible when it came to the orchestrations. He assembled a small 25-piece orchestra, the same size as *The Circus*, a decision that also harms the score—the size of the drama deserved a fuller sound. The musicians' fees, budgeted at £3,000 but which actually totaled £2482.03, were deemed "more than necessary … unless decided to pay a fee for use on TV. AWOP is a collector's item, unlikely to be extensively shown. But if it is advantageous to pay them now let's do so." Eric James received £3290 and Eric Rogers £2484. The total music budget ran to £19,691.69.[101]

Because Chaplin's ability to communicate had "regrettably deteriorated tremendously," James wrote to Ford, and "knowing his style of composition as intimately as I do after so many years, I was able to suggest melodies and ideas that were agreeable to him. As a result I can truthfully say that the majority of the music stemmed from my brain. It also enabled the music for the film to be completed in Switzerland in three weeks instead of three months which might easily have been the time taken if Charlie had had to compose every bar of music required for a film lasting more than one hour twenty mins." James stated Ford never replied to the letter and he was "disappointed to find that no additional screen credit was given when *A Woman of Paris* was shown. I was equally disappointed that no ex gratis payment was forthcoming in appreciation of the efforts I had made."[102]

"Rumour has it that you let it be thought that you are the composer or co-composer of the Chaplin music," Ford wrote to James a few weeks after Chaplin's death. "I am therefore obliged to ask you to be kind enough to write me a formal denial, which will enable me to refute any further rumour."[103] In his response, James told Ford her letter "distressed me very much indeed. However, I am replying immediately to confirm that in my capacity of Music Associate to the late Sir Charles Chaplin I took down his melodies and melodic ideas and then helped him in the subsequent development and composition of his music to the very best of my ability as a trained and experienced musician. I deny most vehemently that I have ever claimed to be composer or co-composer of his music."[104] Vehement or not, James's backpedaling seemed to be playing both sides of the fence when it came to his remuneration and credit.

The newly edited *A Woman of Paris* screened at the Museum of Modern Art in New York in 1976, the first time the film had been shown in over fifty years, as part of a salute to silent film comedy hosted by Leonard Maltin. Chaplin edited the film down to eighty-three minutes and presented the last missing musical piece to complete his film canon. When the film was finally re-released in April 1978, four months after Chaplin's death, critics took notice. "When *A Woman of Paris* was originally released in 1923," said Vincent Canby of *The New York Times*, "the fans of Charlie Chaplin reacted as if they'd been the target of some kind of gigantic swindle. Here was a Chaplin film without Charlie, which seemed as obvious a contradiction-in-terms as an egg salad sandwich without egg."

> The film is not only a treasure in itself—witty, sophisticated and often beautifully funny, though it means to be "serious," as Chaplin says—it's also a rare opportunity to see what Chaplin is like as a filmmaker when he is not contemplating his own image. *A Woman of Paris* is immensely entertaining, but, more important, it's an inside report on the essential Chaplin talent that, in the films in which he is also a star, seems so closely bound to the performer's personality we can't easily tell where one starts and the other leaves off…. *A Woman of Paris* is the world of that talent at the peak of its vigor…
>
> One does not truly know the work of Chaplin until one has had the good fortune to see this rediscovered masterpiece.[105]

Janet Maslin, also in the *Times*, called the film "radiantly beautiful…. The wisdom of *A Woman of Paris*, which was first released in 1923 but often feels as if it were made yesterday, really does seem boundless; so do the affection and generosity with which Mr. Chaplin presents his characters."[106]

"Like all Chaplin's film scores," David Robinson wrote, "this one recreates the method and style of Victorian theatre music—an idiom which seems wholly appropriate to this fine melodrama, outside time, but at least as closely linked to the nineteenth century as to the twentieth." Robinson attended one of the recording sessions and asked Chaplin if preparing the score had been a lengthy job. "Not long," Chaplin replied, "inspiration mostly."[107]

The score consists of twenty-three themes, most of which are slotted in more than once. Approximately three-quarters of them are in a major key, an odd choice for such a dramatic, tragic story. Like most of Chaplin's late scores, *A Woman of Paris* suffers from a lack of variety in orchestrations, which is hindered further by the small orchestra and the one-size-fits-all balance in the recording level, for which Eric James wanted credit. "I sometimes think that although the secret about *The Kid* was kept from [Charlie]," James said, "he was perhaps, deep in his subconscious mind, beginning to doubt his own ability to work on the music, because he began to delegate more and more of the work at the studios to me. I completed the balancing on *Pay Day*, *A Day's Pleasure*, *Sunnyside*, and *A Woman of Paris*, and during the whole time taken for this he seldom turned up at the studios at all. Happily for me he always seemed satisfied with my work and was generous with his compliments, but nothing else."[108] The result comes across as repetitive and monotonous due to Rogers's lazy orchestrations and the cutting of corners to save money in the recording studio. But the score does show that thought often went into the placement of the various themes.

The "A Woman of Paris" theme bookends the score in the main title and final scene

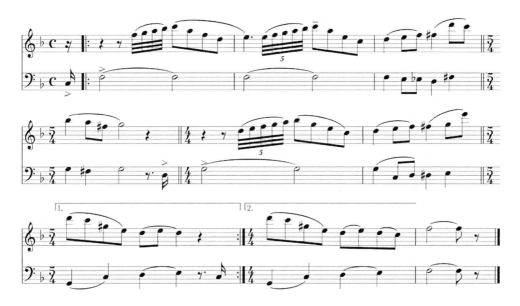

A Woman of Paris (1976 reissue)—**The main theme bookends the film only and is used nowhere else in the score.**

only. James took the melody from the scene in *Monsieur Verdoux* when Verdoux plays the piano preceding Lydia's murder. The F major key may go against a film that publicizes itself as "a drama of fate," but the theme has more to do with the ending than setting up the story. On a country back road, Pierre's car drives by Marie, who has caught a lift on a passing wagon. The two lives, once so intertwined, no longer intersect as Pierre leaves Marie—once "a woman of Paris"—in his dust.

The "Nocturne" key of E-flat major, which occurs six times in the score, seems an oddity in its first placement underscoring Marie's appearance as the "victim of an unhappy home." But it does foreshadow the love between Marie and Jean and the ghost of Jean in the final sequence as his mother and Marie run a daycare together. Marie's stepfather is given his own "Suspense" motif, a three-note, half-step tango figure over a bed of tremolo whole notes. The "Shock" theme is the flip side of "Nocturne." The somber, melodramatic theme occurs seven times, at moments of high drama—when Jean's father orders Marie to leave, Jean tells Marie they will have to postpone their elopement following his father's heart attack, Marie overhears Jean telling his mother he will not marry her, Jean loads the gun and the aftermath of his suicide, and his mother seeks revenge on Marie for her son's death.

The "Restaurant Waltz" underscores the glitzy scenes among the wealthy, including one odd placement at the end of the film when the priest shows up at the daycare and asks when Marie will marry and have children of her own. Chaplin obviously meant for this theme to provide nothing more than a pleasant source cue, but the endlessly repeating eight-bar phrase and the unsurprising harmonic progressions quickly grow tiresome from overuse.

"Revel's Music," with its snare drum riffs, trumpet fanfares, and unimaginative I–V7 chord progression, seems more appropriate down in the trenches of *Shoulder Arms* than embodying "a gentleman of leisure, whose whims have made and ruined many a woman's career." The E-flat major waltz that underscores the scenes in "Marie's Apartment" convey her nonchalant existence as a kept woman, while the theme for "Revel's Business Office" is equally carefree. The flabby tone of the English horn player mars the easygoing tune, but it still gives the impression of a man unconcerned by what he reads on the ticker tape as he lounges on a chaise or later when he finds Jean hidden in Marie's bedroom.

The English horn player (most likely the same musician) also blemishes the poignant "Bad News" theme. Whether it is Marie depressed by Pierre's engagement news, her finding out it was the death of Jean's father that kept him from joining her at the train station, her breaking it off with Pierre, or a dejected Jean going home, the theme is nearly ruined by the poor balance in the orchestra.

A Woman of Paris (1976 reissue)—"Nocturne" serves as the love theme for Marie and Jean.

A Woman of Paris (1976 reissue)—The "Shock" cue is used at moments of high drama.

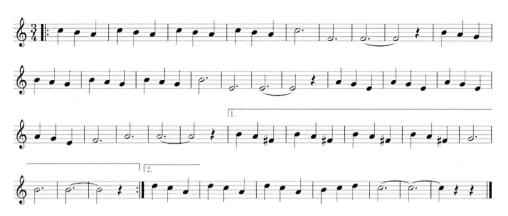

A Woman of Paris (1976 reissue)—The endlessly repeating "Restaurant Waltz" usually accompanies scenes among the wealthy.

The dance band swing of the "Latin Quarter" cue has not the faintest Parisian whiff about it. But the saxophone's theme in an "Easy 2" (as marked in the score) makes for a pleasant aural diversion and does not interfere with the decadence of the dancer twirling and unraveling on the pedestal at the party. The "Necklace Waltz" underscores Marie's dilemma—"marriage or luxury." Disgusted by Pierre's gift, she throws a pearl necklace out the window. In Frederick Stahlberg's printed version of the compilation score back in 1923, the brief sequence of Revel playing the saxophone was written for a morose bassoon solo that seemed completely out of place, while the original and revised compilation scores ignored the saxophone visuals on screen altogether. In Chaplin's score, Pierre's schtick with the saxophone is finally mirrored in the music.

"The characteristic care that Chaplin lavished on the film's production," said John Pym of *Monthly Film Bulletin*, "does not, unhappily extend to the dreary score."[109] David Robinson said the small critical notice of the score was "unappreciative. Like all Chaplin's film scores, this one recreates the method and style of Victorian theatre music—an idiom which seems wholly appropriate to this fine melodrama, outside time, but at least as closely linked to the nineteenth century as to the twentieth." The score was the last completed work of that "phenomenal creation, a working life that had spanned three quarters of a century. After this he did not often leave his home."[110]

✴   ✴   ✴

In *A Woman of Paris*, all eyes at the restaurant are on the unhappy couple—Pierre Revel (Adolph Menjou) and Marie St. Clair (Edna Purviance), c. 1923 (© Roy Export SAS).

A Woman of Paris (1976 reissue)—"Revel's Music" sounds more appropriate for the trenches of *Shoulder Arms* than a well-dressed man about time.

Eric James called his time with Chaplin "a labor of love because the financial reward was out of all proportion to my value to him.... I foolishly adopted the attitude that working for and being with him was such an honor that it was a reward in itself. I thus asked and received a very nominal figure."

In view of the fact that the various films that I worked on with him have netted some millions, a more generous increase in my salary would hardly have put him on the road to bankruptcy. The legal document I had signed disclaimed any rights to the compositions. It also prohibited me from receiving any royalties from the music or any precuniary advantage whatsoever over and above my salary. I would be less than honest if I did not say that I feel disappointed about this. Quite apart

A Woman of Paris (1976 reissue)—"Marie's Apartment" (above) and "Revel's Business Office" (below) are two carefree melodies entirely appropriate for a kept woman and "a gentleman of leisure."

from the undoubted legality of my position, I think that I should have received some solid recognition as a purely voluntary gesture.

It may well be that Charlie never knew at any time what I was being paid, but over a period of twenty years that does seem unlikely.... I started working for him for £60 ($120) a week, that being the sum I myself had asked. Thereafter my remuneration was raised from time to time by Rachel Ford without recourse to me until after twenty years of service I was receiving £200 ($400). It must also be remembered that I was not working with Charlie every week of the year but unlike many other persons on his payroll, I was never paid a retainer.[111]

After work on *A Woman of Paris* was complete, James broached the subject of an album of Chaplin's music. James was in the midst of a bitter divorce, with his ex-wife "insist[ing] that I have large sums of money stashed away in Switzerland, which of course, is absolute nonsense, I only wish I had."[112] Rachel Ford sent a letter to Oona in July, saying, "I believe Eric's divorce is proving costly, also his failing eye-sight may prevent him doing certain work, etc. and that he may imagine that a new record containing choice morsels [*sic*] from Charlie's music might be profitable for him."[113] When it was agreed that James would go to Vevey in August, Ford told him, "Wish I was going to be there to enjoy it. I hope the outcome of this musical séance will produce such a delectable selection that our music publishers will be prompted to use it and get a record out."[114]

James listened to all of the taped tracks of Chaplin's films and recorded about fifty separate items on cassette tapes. He suggested to Ford a double LP set with the title *Sir Charles Chaplin Conducts His Music from the Movies*. "Obviously it wouldn't be necessary for him to do any conducting," James wrote, "but at least the idea might appeal to a record

A Woman of Paris (1976 reissue)—"Bad News" accompanies every appearance of this theme.

company, which brings me to the next question. Do you have any suggestion as to who I might contact at one of the larger companies who would be interested in listening to my tape of Charlie's music (when I've completed it) in a week or so's time? I know two or three recording markets here but obviously you will know higher placed executives than I would and I could follow up any suggestion that you may have re[garding] this."[115]

Ford was "alarmed" that James did "not appear to have understood that the music publishers … hold the rights for most of Charlie's music for records. The exceptions are THE CIRCUS, CITY LIGHTS and MONSIEUR VERDOUX, each of which has a different publisher. I would therefore have to know whether anything has been selected from these three pictures. In view of our contractual obligations, there can be no questions of any-body being able to approach a record company, except Messrs. Bourne, who, if necessary, would contact our other three publishers…. I would advise your not incurring any additional time or expense until I hear Mrs. Bourne's reaction."[116]

Rachel wrote to Bonnie of James's proposal. "I had the utmost difficulty to prevent his approaching a record company and still have not convinced him that you have the records rights to most of Charlie's music. Needless to say, should you approve of the selection, it would be lovely for it to become a record."[117] Bourne, however, could not recommend the recording. "With the standard market at such a low ebb," she said, "it would have been unwise at this time to invest all that money to properly record the music as selected on the cassette. It would not be a safe investment. Our professional department are securing good standard recordings by conductors who are under contract to record companies. These recordings will have a guaranteed income. If Eric James had in mind a recording with Sir Charles Chaplin conducting for the purpose of a library collectors item, then this is entirely another story and it has merit if for that purpose only."[118] As usual with these types of Chaplin compilation albums over the years, nothing came of it.

*   *   *

One of the great question marks in the Chaplin canon is *The Freak*, which he began working on in 1968. The film was to star Chaplin's daughter Victoria as a young South American girl who sprouts a pair of wings, and is kidnapped and paraded before London society as an angel. Chaplin made copious notes and developed a treatment of the story, but Victoria eloped with her fiancé, French actor Jean-Baptiste Thierrée. Photos and amateur footage were later taken on the Manoir lawn of her in her wings, and Chaplin reportedly wrote a musical theme for the film, but he shelved the project.

Following the success of "This Is My Song," Chaplin invited Petula Clark, who lived on the other side of Lake Geneva, to the Manoir for tea. "I thought, 'That might be nice. Might be a decent cup of tea too!'"

> We go over to Vevey, to his lovely house. We ring the bell and there's Charlie, who opens the door. It was kind of stunning to just see him standing there. A sweet, rather small person and absolutely delightful smile. Perhaps he was pleased to meet me, I don't know. But he was certainly very pleased about the success of the song. I was amazed to be greeted at the door by a legend. We had tea and it was a very good cup of tea. We talked and laughed. He was in a wonderful mood. He was thrilled with the whole experience of the success of ["This Is My Song"] and meeting me, part of the success of the song. He got me to play the piano because he felt like dancing. Don't ask me what I played. I was in a bit of a daze through the whole thing. He danced around his living room and right in the middle of that there was a knock on the door and in came his children and Oona and it turned into a sort of party. It was a most extraordinary afternoon.[119]

Clark and Chaplin talked about his songs and his songwriting. "He told us he had written several other things. His music has always had this sweetness, this wistfulness built in. I remember him playing two or three things, including this song that was later used in a documentary."[120] That documentary was *The Gentleman Tramp* and the melody, which had no lyrics at the time of Chaplin and Clark's meeting, was eventually known as "You Are the Song." Written in the bright primary key of C major, the song is a straight-forward ballad, without a single chromatic alteration in the tune, which is rare for Chaplin and indicates the theme may have only existed in a rough draft. According to Eric James, Chaplin wrote it as a love song to Oona. But the song would go through a tortuous series of lyrics before finally being recorded for the 1976 documentary.

Roy Export contracted lyricist Tim Rose Price to write the first lyric, entitled "Secrets In Your Eyes." Price knew Rachel Ford, "a most wonderful woman in every way," from her visits to his parents' house during the making of *A Countess from Hong Kong*. Price used to "assist" her and "visited the set quite often." Price's mother, who became close friends with Ford, later painted Chaplin's portrait, which hung at the Manoir. Price also assisted Ford on her annual visits to London to check the nearby film vaults at Denham. "I'd pick her up at The Savoy with my mini," Price remembers, "and we'd go through every tin, meticulously checking for rust because of the danger of the explosive nitrate stock. Occasionally we felt it necessary to view some of the material and occasionally we had to blow some of it up—I mean explode!"[121]

Price was writing and painting, and "Rachel, being Rachel, was always trying to help

The opening chorus of "You Are the Song," with a melody originally written for *The Freak* (1974/1978, music by Charles Chaplin, lyrics by Glen Anthony).

with my attempts. On one occasion she left some of my writing out and Oona noticed it
and liked it very much. I think this encouraged Rachel and there was a time when, worried
about a [musical] that they didn't want to happen ... she got me to write an outline called
'Chaplin, Citizen of the World' as a smokescreen to put them off." Price went to the re-
release of *Modern Times* in Paris, where he met Chaplin and Oona and escorted Victoria
to the premiere and supper afterward.[122]

In the summer of 1975, Ford approached Price to try his hand at writing lyrics to
Chaplin's music. Price had been writing lyrics for years, as well as treatments and scripts
for radio, stage, and film. With composer Paul Patterson, he wrote *Time Piece* for the
King's Singers, as well as "a carol or two" for Herbert Chappell and some unpublished
work with Richard Rodney Bennett. "'Secrets In Your Eyes' was my title," says Price, "and
all the seasonal ideas and bird images."[123]

> *You came to me in Spring*
> *With secrets in your eyes*
> *That taught a freedom to me*
> *In blowing winds*
> *And sea-bird cries.*
>
> *All through the Summer nights*
> *You danced upon the sand*
> *And I was waiting for you*
> *To touch your cheek*
> *And take your hand*
>
> *When Autumn shed her leaves*
> *I caught you in my arms*
> *And tried to hold you by me*
> *To break your spell*
> *And own your charms*
>
> *But never pinion wings*
> *A caged bird cannot fly*
> *You vanished softly from me*
> *Just like a breeze*
> *Across the sky*
>
> *And now I dream of Spring:*
> *Those secrets in your eyes*
> *That taught a freedom to me*
> *In blowing winds*
> *And sea-bird cries.*[124]

Price felt the song had a sentimentality that "would appeal to Charlie, especially as
I was told it was to be the theme song for *The Freak*, the film he was planning to make
with his daughter. And 'the caged bird cannot fly' all seemed to fit with that theme."[125]
Today, he feels the lyric is "a bit old fashioned and probably more poem than lyric," and
he freely admits it "would have needed some massaging to fit the music better" had the
song gone any further.[126] "I was told by Rachel that my lyrics were the ones that Charlie
liked best and were chosen by him."[127]

In July 1976, Bonnie Bourne sent over a different lyric—"My Love," written by Glen
Anthony"—which the publisher felt "would be more commercial in this country."[128] Since
Rachel Ford had been instrumental in putting Price's lyric before Chaplin, it is not surprising she wrote back that Anthony's lyric was "accepted but not appreciated [on] this
end!!"[129] Ford did not listen to the tape, "but gather the Love Song lyric is ghastly and

the same can be said of the singing."[130] Eric James also wrote a lyric—"unasked"—"which is un-likely to ever see the light of day."[131] "My Love," which Chaplin eventually approved, was changed to "You Are the Song," said Bonnie Bourne, "so as to make a clearer distinction between the lyric version and the instrumental version." Tony Bennett was reportedly working on an arrangement, but the recording never surfaced. There were also Japanese and South American recordings of "Secrets In Your Eyes," and Andre Kostelanetz recorded an instrumental version ("Love Song") on an album devoted to Duke Ellington and Chaplin, which also included "Smile," "Terry's Theme," "Green Lantern Rag" from *A Dog's Life*, and *The Kid*'s "Morning Promenade." "I feel," Bourne wrote to Ford, "that too many lyric versions to LOVE SONG will not do the song any good. Let us work with the two already contracted for. Although poetic lyrics are not always acceptable in the U.S., they are highly accepted in many other countries of the world."[132]

> *My love you are the song*
> *That sings inside of me.*
> *The song is always the same;*
> *It starts with love and ends with your name.*
> *The more that I love you*
> *There's more in you to love;*
> *And yet I just don't know how*
> *I could love you more than I do right now.*
> *They say that love grows old,*
> *But our love turned to gold.*
> *You kiss my sorrows away;*
> *You warm my heart;*
> *What more can I say?*
> *Each day my life is new,*
> *For God blessed me with you;*
> *And when my life is all through*
> *Without a word*
> *You always knew*
> *That all of my life,*
> *My life was you.*[133]

Anthony's lyrics continue in the sentimental tradition of earlier Chaplin songs, while Chaplin's plaintive melody is, as always, simple and unassuming. But Anthony's lyrics do not sit as well on the melody as they could have. Odd, closed-consonant word choices such as *yet*, *sing* and *God* receiving the weight of the long notes, while other simple phrases such as "What more can I say?" are awkwardly placed in the melodic line. For all its pitfalls from the viewpoint of lyric craft, the heartfelt emotion behind Chaplin's melody still shines through.

Jerry Epstein felt the melody for "You Are the Song" was "the best music [Charlie] ever wrote." "This," Chaplin used to say, "is real Puccini!"[134] But few artists have seemed interested in recording it. The Fureys included it as a selection on their 2001 tribute album, *Charlie Chaplin & The Fureys*, produced by Josephine Chaplin, and folk legend Arlo Guthrie sang the song on his 2007 album, *In Times Like These*, accompanied by the University of Kentucky Symphony Orchestra. Though it is one of Chaplin's lesser-known works, Bourne's initial involvement meant that Glen Anthony's lyrics, not Price's, would be the version included in the sheet music collection, *The Songs of Charlie Chaplin*.

* * *

"I tried to compose elegant and romantic music to frame my comedies in contrast to the tramp character," Chaplin said, "for elegant music gave my comedies an emotional dimension. Musical arrangers rarely understood this. They wanted the music to be funny."

> But I would explain that I wanted no competition, I wanted the music to be a counterpoint of grace and charm, to express sentiment, without which, as Hazlitt says, a work of art is incomplete. Sometimes a musician would get pompous with me and talk of the restricted intervals of the chromatic and the diatonic scale, and I would cut him short with a layman's remark: "Whatever the melody is, the rest is just a vamp." After putting music to one or two pictures I began to look at a conductor's score with a professional eye and to know whether a composition was over-orchestrated or not. If I saw a lot of notes in the brass and woodwind section, I would say: "That's too black in the brass," or "too busy in the woodwinds." Nothing is more adventurous and exciting than to hear the tunes one has composed played for the first time by a fifty piece orchestra.[135]

"The truth of the matter is that I don't know a note," Chaplin later admitted. "I can't read music, and what I have learnt," he said, pointing to a phonograph in the corner of the room, "I owe to this teacher."[136]

Epilogue: Time Is the Great Author

"Wow!" Dyan Cannon exclaimed at the 45th annual Academy Awards. "The winners are Charles Chaplin, Raymond Rasch, and Larry Russell for *Limelight!*"[1] With "Terry's Theme" playing from the orchestra pit, Candice Bergen quickly explained the controversy of a twenty-year-old film winning an Oscar and accepted the award for Chaplin, "one of the warmest, most wonderful men I have met," who was at home in Switzerland. Linda Russell Morgan thanked the Academy on behalf of her late father, who died in 1954. And a visibly emotional Paul Rasch, whose father passed away in 1964, said, "On behalf of my dad, I would like to thank the Academy. He always wanted to write something that would be remembered after he was gone, and he did it. Thank you very much."[2] Chaplin was "delighted" with the Oscar, but there were concerns about Rasch's comments indicating that his father had co-composed the score.[3] In fact, the entire Oscar process had been a mess from the beginning and was about to get a lot worse.

Academy rules state that a film has to run in a Los Angeles theater for at least a week to qualify for the Academy Awards. So in 1972, with Chaplin's renaissance in full swing thanks to Mo Rothman's re-packaging of Chaplin's classic films and the Honorary Oscar in April, Columbia Pictures booked *Limelight* into the UA Cinema Center in Westwood for a qualifying run. Kevin Thomas in the *Los Angeles Times* said it was "a gesture that should be taken seriously by the Academy membership. Most movies would be destroyed by being withheld from release for two decades, but in the instance of *Limelight* the passing of the years serves only to underline the timelessness of this masterpiece."[4]

It was common knowledge that Chaplin could not read or write music and had always used other musicians to transcribe and arrange his music. When the eligibility of *Limelight* had been decided, the Academy contacted Chaplin directly through Bert Schneider to ask if he would include his arranger(s) on the ballot. "ONLY CHARLIE COMPOSED LIMELIGHT," said Oona's telegram to Schneider, "HOWEVER HE SAYS HE DOESN'T CARE IF ARRANGERS SHARE CREDIT FOR PRIZE LOVE OONA."[5] Whether or not it was a typo, the plural *arrangers* caused headaches for months. Chaplin named Ray Rasch and "Russell," but without further clarification, or approval from Chaplin, the Academy named Larry Russell as the "Russell" on the ballot.

Russell (1913–1954) began his arranging career in the late 1930s with jazz trumpeter Henry Busse, and his arrangements made a regular appearance in the 1940s, in particular on the "Design for Happiness" radio program. He arranged for harmonica legend Larry Adler and was staff arranger for radio station WBBM in Chicago before leaving in September 1941 to join Ted Fio Rito's band in California. Russell began his film career in

1943 as an orchestrator for *Crazy House*. He arranged for bandleader Bob Mohr and made a number of recordings with Dinah Shore and Sons of the Pioneers.

After Bernard Katz left *Limelight* following the first recording sessions for the ballet music, Russell wrote to Chaplin. "As per our conversation, I understand that Mr. Katz may not be available as conductor on the next recording," he wrote. "I would appreciate an interview and at that time will state my background, etc."[6] The timing of the letter— September 12, 1951—is critical. By that time, Rasch had already been working on the score for ten months. The ballet music was scheduled to be re-recorded with Keith Williams conducting a week later, and Chaplin would record the vocals of his songs with Rasch at the piano in October. So the musical cast of characters was set in stone. "Everybody I could talk to," Paul Rasch remembered, "nobody had ever heard of Larry Russell having any connection with *Limelight*. I had no doubt that knowing how close my dad and Larry were, kind of like I would do with you if you were a friend of mine and we were both still musicians, or you might do with me, I would run something by you and say, 'What do you think of this?' [hums melody] And then you might give me a tip to make it a little bit better. That, I'm sure, was his involvement."[7] If Rasch ever employed Russell to help him with the orchestrations, there is no evidence in photographs or in paperwork in the Chaplin Archive.

In January 1973, Inez James Russell, Larry's widow, contacted the American Society of Composers, Authors and Publishers (ASCAP) "to advise you that Larry Russell is in fact co-composer of the music written for the motion picture entitled 'Limelight,' published by Bourne Music Inc., along with Ray Rasch (Rausch) and Charles Chaplin. Therefore Mr. Russell is rightfully entitled to 33⅓% of all performance monies received by ASCAP.... Would you please take the necessary steps to adjust Larry Russell's ASCAP account and advise me as soon as possible."[8] ASCAP contacted Adele Sandler in the copyright department at Bourne, who replied, "LIMELIGHT has been in our Catalog since 1953 and none of the papers by which we acquired this music show any name other than Charles Chaplin."[9]

When the Oscar nominations were announced on February 13, Mo Rothman cabled Oona: "LIMELIGHT HAS BEEN NOMINATED FOR OSCAR FOR BEST ORIGINAL DRAMATIC SCORE STOP AS YOU KNOW WE WERE ONE OF TEN LAST WEEK AND WE ARE NOW ONE OF FIVE STOP KEEP YOUR FINGERS CROSSED LOVE TO YOU BOTH MO."[10] Two days later, Sandler, who was apparently unaware of the nominations, contacted Rachel Ford. "ASCAP has just called because they have had several urgent calls from the American Academy of Motion Pictures about this matter. I gather from my conversation that before they nominate Charles Chaplin and LIMELIGHT for an Academy Award, they want to be sure that Inez James Russell will not give them any trouble. Mrs. Russell is claiming one-third interest in LIMELIGHT and, of course, what ASCAP and the Motion Pictures Academy require is a statement from Mr. Chaplin denying her claim."[11]

That same day, with an Oscar nomination in hand for her deceased husband, Inez contacted ASCAP:

> While I wrote my previous letter with the best of intent and in good faith, I had been misinformed. I am now fully informed and I now fully understand all of the previously misinterpreted and misunderstood circumstances.
>
> I now understand that the request made of Charles Chaplin by the Academy of Motion Picture Arts and Sciences for his consent to include the name of Larry Russell as his collaborator [*sic*] in

the creation of the score of the film, "LIMELIGHT," was for the sole purpose of honoring all those who, in the purview of the Academy's rules, participated in the creation of the achievement. I now fully understand that such recognition by the Academy has no bearing whatsoever on participation in the copyright.

It is with this understanding that I ask you to disregard my original letter. I also ask that you notify all concerned parties.[12]

"After wasting <u>hours</u> on this topic," Ford wrote Sandler, "Russell's widow has withdrawn her claim—why I don't know—and still less on what grounds she even made it. I think the next time a query goes to Vevey, it will be referred to me."[13] Ford later talked to Bert Schneider and was under the impression he had talked to Inez. "Very many thanks for telephoning and for procuring Mrs. Russell's abdication," Ford wrote. "Whilst I am relieved to have it—its wording as such unfortunately does not exclude the possibility of her making further claims later on and I am wondering whether we should not try and iron out this matter for good and all."[14]

Ford contacted Herbert Jacoby, explaining the situation with Inez.

Fortunately, she wrote again later, retracting her statements completely, stating that she had made her claim due to a misunderstanding. Unfortunately nothing indicates that she may not start again at a later date.

Also, there might well be a possibility of other claims occurring and it would be of immsense help if we could find copies of the employment contracts presumably made between Celebrated and the arranger of the music Ray Rasch, and Celebrated and Keith R. Williams, the conductor. Oddly enough, though we find a letter from Larry Russell asking to be considered for the job of conductor, there is no trace of him ever having been employed. Mr. Chaplin has always been sole composer of the original musical compositions in his films, and the arranger and conductor have been employees. Furthermore, we have no copies of any of the artists contracts.[15]

Bourne was still getting panicked telegrams from the Academy, looking for the Rasch/Russell incident to be cleared up. "I don't know what else we can do," Schneider wrote to Ford. "Leaving the *Limelight* score eligible for an award does not in any way affect the legal status of the situation. Anyone can always sue you if they so choose. I really think we should let things go as is but if your people feel differently, we will be guided accordingly."[16] Ford replied, "Not knowing why on earth Mrs. Russell ever made her claim and still less why she withdrew same, I regretfully agree that I must let the matter drop."[17]

Paul Rasch contacted Ford, protesting Russell's inclusion on the Oscar ballot. "Unfortunately," she told Schneider, "I cannot answer him, or anybody else for that matter, as I have never been able to understand what actually happened for it has never been fully explained to me. I think that while the matter is fresh it would simplify things if I were told exactly what did occur. My guess is that when Mrs. Russell made herself known, you put the question to Oona, who cabled you quite clearly that though Charlie was the sole composer, the arrangers could share credit. Actually there was only one arranger—Ray Rasch. Am I right in assuming that without further ado both Russell and Rasch figured as arrangers?"[18] But there was indeed further ado.

According to Paul Rasch, "Chaplin told [Inez] that if she didn't drop the lawsuit, he was going to tell the Academy he was going to renege and he would take their names off. So she dropped the lawsuit…. From everything I could determine from what my mother told me and friends told me about Larry, I think Larry would have rolled over in his grave if he'd known that Inez had gotten his name on [the ballot]."[19] Complicating matters even further, Inez Russell was a member of the Music Branch.[20] "And that's how [Larry's] name appeared there," says Paul, "because Inez Russell was on the board to set up the nominations."[21]

"Linda [Russell Morgan] was very upset with me," Paul remembered. "I would never stand up for the fact that [Larry] was really connected with it." But Paul had his own legal issues. "I was going to sue Chaplin," he says. "As it turns out I would have had to sue and include Larry. I probably would have had to get Linda involved and sue [Chaplin] for royalties and admission that my dad was actually the writer or certainly to acknowledge enough that he would, in fact, have to start including royalties and probably pay something for past royalties." Paul found "a very good, high-powered attorney but he wanted a ten-thousand-dollar retainer. I didn't have ten thousand dollars. That was a hell of a lot of money back in 1973. I just had to let it die. Chaplin had the sort of resources to keep you in court for a lifetime. Otherwise I would have proceeded." In addition, Paul had "a couple of meetings" with John Green, the head of the Academy's Music Branch nominating subcommittee, who finally told him, "Look, if you don't agree to have Larry's name on there, we're just going to throw the whole thing out and take it off. That's all there is to it." "And so I said, 'Okay, we'll go with that.'"[22]

Burt Reynolds, Linda Russell Morgan, Dyan Cannon, Paul Rasch, and *Cabaret* **arranger Ralph Burns in the Academy Awards press room, March 27, 1973 (copyright © Academy of Motion Picture Arts and Sciences).**

"*Limelight*'s romantic theme is as familiar as the film itself is unknown," said the *Los Angeles Times*.[23] No doubt the familiarity of that theme, further affection for Chaplin, and the disqualification of *The Godfather* from contention all led to the victory for Chaplin, Rasch, and Russell. *Variety* said Chaplin's win was "obviously a sentimental choice."[24] "HAD WE LISTENED TO YOU AND ALL YOUR OBJECTIONS IN SUBMITTING LIMELIGHT," Mo Rothman cabled Ford, "WE WOULD NEVER HAVE WON THE OSCAR THAT WE HAVE WON TONIGHT STOP YOUR UNSTINTING COOPERATION IN REMOVING ALL OBSTICLES [*SIC*] IS ALWAYS DEEPLY APPRECIATED LOVE MO."[25] Ford replied, "I would be very interested to know what objections I made regarding the submitting of this picture. I knew nothing about it until I was made aware that the widow of an unknown man [*sic*] had written to ASCAP claiming a commission on the music royalties paid to Charlie." "Rachel my Darling," Mo shot back, "You have a bad memory—you even wanted to pull the Picture out of the running for an Oscar." "True," she said, "<u>WHEN</u> I heard this."[26]

When *Variety* recapped the Oscar winners, under the Original Dramatic Score category it read "For Which Only the Composer Is Eligible," listing Chaplin, Rasch, and Russell, giving the further impression that all three were co-composers. "The very pleasant news about the Oscar award was dissipated by the account of the actual proceeding," Ford wrote to Schneider. "Oona and Charlie are <u>NOT</u> amused. Charlie wants to know as soon as possible all the details about the Russells and how it comes about that he was named together with Ray Rasch…. The lawyers may advise us to do something but I hope not as I do not think there is much one can do bar a formal dementi."[27]

Ford wrote to Herbert Jacoby to ask his advice "as to what extent harm was done to Mr. Chaplin's reputation as a composer by the unexpected speech made at the Academy award [*sic*] last week by Mr. Rasch, the arranger's son…. Nobody could possibly foretell what young Rasch would say, but the presence of the Russell family remains a mystery. We just cannot discover how they entered into the picture…. There has been such a to-do about this that it has dissipated the pleasure of having the Oscar. I hope we can let matters rest as they are—nothing will dispel the audience's deducting that Mr. Chaplin got considerable help."[28]

Bonnie Bourne thought *Variety* should post a retraction. "Needless to say," Ford wrote to her, "Oona is most annoyed about it all and agrees with you that something should be done."[29] Ford wrote to Jacoby, "I personally think that all the viewers of the 1973 Academy Awards think that Mr. Chaplin is a co-composer. An insertion in *Variety* will only be seen by a fraction of those that viewed the proceedings."[30] Jacoby agreed:

> In the first place, you are quite correct in stating that such an insertion will be seen by only a fraction of those who viewed the proceedings. In the second place, I do not see any basis for demanding a retraction in that whatever appeared in the press was a true and correct report of what actually took place and, under these cirumstances, no newspaper would give even serious consideration to publishing a retraction.
>
> At first blush, it would appear that whatever harm has been done has already occurred and that no useful purpose can be served by resurrecting a matter which, presumably, has been forgotten by the great majority of those who viewed the program. Such an appraisal of the situation, however, overlooks the very genuine possibility that claims may be asserted at some future date by either the Rasch or Russell estates which might cause problems with performing rights societies and could prove embarrassing to Bonnie Bourne as your publisher. Therefore, I do not think that we could afford to let the matter rest in its present posture.
>
> It does seem to me that the proper place to seek redress is with the Academy itself. From your correspondence, it would appear that the dealings with the Academy on Mr. Chaplin's behalf were

handled by and through Bert Schneider and, of course, I am not aware of just what he may have told the Academy in respect of this particular award. Certainly, the cable which Mrs. Chaplin sent to Bert ... contributed to whatever misunderstandings may have taken place.

Since, however, as I am assured by Mrs. Bourne's office, only the composer is eligible for this award, the only person entitled to the same was Mr. Chaplin himself. Rasch and Russell (to the extent that the latter may have been involved at all) merely acted as arrangers and, as such, should not have been permitted to share in the award at all. Accordingly, I would recommend that the true situation be called to the attention of the Academy and that it be requested to issue some statement to the effect that the award took the form that it did through mistake and inadvertent misinformation.

I would be happy, if you so desire, to write a letter to the Academy setting forth the fact and requesting that some action be taken to rectify the mistake. On the other hand, it might be far more practical to endeavor to handle the matter through Bert Schneider rather than through an attorney. After all, he is in Los Angeles where the Academy has its office and is a prestigious member of the industry. Moreover, he is the person who presumably dealt with the Academy in the first place and can best explain how the mistake occurred.[31]

Reporting that the Oscar win might trigger lawsuits, *Daily Variety* said Paul Rasch and Linda Russell Morgan were "investigating the legal situation respect to copyright, publishing, etc." "There are complications," Rasch said. "Chaplin is out of the country. It's a Federal copyright case." John Green said Chaplin "readily and courteously agreed" to share the credit with Ray Rasch and Larry Russell. Keith Williams, who knew of no work by Larry Russell on the film, said in *Variety* he and "the orchestral contractor for the picture (arranger Russ Garcia)" did some on-the-spot "fixing up" of Rasch's scores before recording. Bonnie Bourne stayed out of the fray and offered "no comment."[32]

Rasch also felt that Bourne's post–Oscar ad "was in poor taste. It only mentioned Chaplin—no other composers." Rasch said at the time that he possessed the entire score of *Limelight*, including all the instrumental parts and several drafts of the theme. "The whole thing is very unprofessional," Williams told the trade paper. "Larry Russell may have helped Ray Rasch, as I did. I have ghosted on many things in my time. You have to if you want to get ahead in this business.... Chaplin won this film scoring award and he wasn't a member of the (musicians) union. It's against the collective bargaining agreement. But though Chaplin can't write music, you play a wrong note and he knows it."[33]

Admitting that "all this is now past history," Ford wrote to John Green and Arthur Hamilton, the co-chairs of the Academy's nominating subcommittee, to state once and for all what had transpired behind the scenes.

(1) The *Limelight* production files and accounts do not mention Mr. Larry Russell, except for a letter of application for the job of conductor written before the production started. Perhaps Mr. Ray Rasch engaged Mr. Russell to orchestrate the score. Mr. Keith Williams was the conductor.

(2) The query should of course have been addressed to this office and not directly to Mr. Chaplin who assumed, I think, it was a request that the arranger should be given credit—as an arranger, not as co-composer. Their cable to Mr. Schneider especially stressed the fact that Mr. Chaplin was sole composer.

(3) People who worked on the production do not know Mr. Russell's name and Mr. Rasch's son recently protested to the former Chaplin Studio manager that Mr. Russell's name had been linked to that of his father.

(4) The Performing Right Society reassured me that in their opinion Mr. Chaplin was sole composer. Mr. Rasch was employed as an arranger.[34]

Adding to the confusion was the location of Chaplin's Oscar statue. The mess began on the telecast. When Marlon Brando was named Best Actor for his role as Don Corleone in *The Godfather*, he refused the award. In one of the most famous acceptance speeches in Oscar history, "Sacheen Littlefeather" (who was actually actress Maria Cruz) went to the stage and informed the audience at the Dorothy Chandler Pavilion that Brando was refusing the award because of the U.S. treatment of Native Americans. In the melee backstage, Roger Moore, who presented the award, took home statue #1616 for safekeeping and returned it to the Academy two weeks later. Chaplin returned his Oscar to the Academy since it was damaged in shipment overseas. That Oscar was destroyed, and #1616 was fitted with the plate for Best Score and sent to Chaplin. So Chaplin received Brando's Oscar, which now resides in the Chaplin's World museum on the grounds of the Manoir de Ban.

The issues that arose from Chaplin's Oscar required the Music Branch to change its rules the next year:

> If the composer in question has not, by himself, composed the dramatic score of a motion picture … those who collaborate with him in extending his thematic or motival ideas into a score-as-such must, for Academy Award consideration, be given co-composing credit. We all understand that in today's film music ambience, it is possible for an unschooled musician to have ideas, concepts and performing abilities that can be developed into a full score. It is the position of the Music Branch that those who collaborate in a substantial way in so developing song themes, ideas, themes or motifs into an extended score are not merely arrangers and/or orchestrators, they are indeed and in fact co-composers.
>
> The wording of Revised Paragraph 4 refers to the composition of a dramatic score as differentiated from songwriting. Where songwriting is concerned, it is possible and proper for a purely intuitive musical talent to compose a song, even though he may not be able himself to commit it to paper or professionally perform it personally. Conversely, the Music Branch takes the firm and unalterable position that this is not possible in the case of what we all know to be a dramatic score.
>
> 3. An Original Dramatic Score is defined as one in which all of the principal thematic material and the development thereof are original with the composer(s) and were specifically composed for or first professionally used in the picture in which eligibility is claimed.
>
> 4. In the case of a solo composing credit for the score of a dramatic film (meaning composer other than songwriting), the Music Branch has established the following criteria:
>
> (a) The scoring of a dramatic film embraces a large number of sophisticated and precise techniques, a knowledge of and proficiency in which are inherent in the ability to score a dramatic film.
>
> (b) A film composer of a dramatic score is one who composes music and commits it to paper in the form of a properly timed, cued and otherwise detailed sketch (or a so-called "short score") on at least three staves, ready for orchestration as such.
>
> (c) In the case of a dramatic score not conventionally committed to paper, a film composer is one who performs his or her compositions on an instrument, or who directs other instrumentalists (and/or vocalists) in the performance thereof in the precise form in which it is heard on the sound track of the release print of the film in which eligibility is claimed.
>
> The Executive Committee of the Music Branch may, at its discretion, require proof of the abilities set forth in Item (a) and in Item (b) and/or (c) above.… In the absence of established knowledge of a composer's abilities as above set forth, or in the event of the failure of a composer to supply proof as above set forth, it will be assumed that such a composer had co-composing collaboration. In such cases, a solo composing screen credit will not be accepted by the Music Branch as a qualification for eligibility for Academy Award consideration in the Dramatic Score category. If this occurs, the composer will be given the opportunity of adding the name(s) of his co-composing collaborator(s) to the Academy credit … and thus achieve eligibility.[35]

Chaplin's Oscar also prompted a change in the general rules, which prevented films more than two years old from competing for awards. The change was unpublicized, but starting with the 1979 calendar year, "pictures publicly exhibited elsewhere prior to their exhibition in the Los Angeles area shall not be eligible unless exhibition has occurred after Jan. 1, 1979 in a commercial motion picture theatre." Previews and film festivals were excluded so that a film would be eligible once it started its commercial run in Los Angeles.[36]

One positive outcome from the Oscar brouhaha was that Chaplin agreed to add an extra credit card to *Limelight,* properly crediting Raymond Rasch as music arranger and Keith Williams as conductor. If Schneider ever explained the exact chain of events that led to the confusion over Larry Russell, no record exists of the conversation. Even though "people who worked on the production do not know Mr. Russell's name," the exhausting matter of Larry Russell's involvement died a quiet, if frustrating, death.[37]

Enter Russell Garcia.

*   *   *

"I also worked on Charlie Chaplin's film, LIMELIGHT," Garcia said in a 1985 interview in *Soundtrack* magazine. "That was a big rhubarb later. Charlie Chaplin wrote the themes, the melodies. He was a real talent…. Ray Rasch was the pianist—and he said, 'Ray, why don't you score this film? I've written all the melodies, why don't you score it?' Ray said 'okay.' But he didn't know how to orchestrate, so he got me to work with him and I orchestrated the whole film. Of course we had to do a lot of composing with Charlie's themes, but they were all Chaplin's themes."[38]

Russell Garcia (1916–2011) was one of the founding fathers of the West Coast big band sound and an early pioneer of atonal arranging. During World War II, he was a staff arranger at NBC Radio before serving in the Army infantry. As a trumpet player after the war, he toured with the bands of Al Donahue, Horace Heidt, and Bob Crosby, and later recorded with Harry James's bands. In Hollywood, Garcia studied composition and arranging with Ernst Toch, Edmund Ross, and Mario Castelnuovo-Tedesco, and conducting with Sir Albert Coates. While teaching at Westlake College of Music in Los Angeles, he developed his classic workbook *The Professional Arranger-Composer.*

Keith Williams was a student of Garcia's[39] and Ray Rasch was "a friend of mine," Garcia said later in an interview with Marc Myers on the JazzWax website. "Ray must have told Charlie about me. At the time, I was already known for being able to write for large-size orchestras and do so fairly quickly. Chaplin had already worked through the theme with Ray when I was first called over to his house." Chaplin played the movie's theme "with one finger on the piano. Then I scored the theme and composed and arranged the film's incidental music. I also was in the engineer's booth when it was recorded."[40]

Garcia "had to do a lot of composing based on Chaplin's single theme…. There was no written music…. Charlie clearly had thought it out in advance. From there I had to build music for an entire movie, and time the music so it was in sync with what was up on the screen." But on *Limelight,* like all of his other films, Chaplin was going to get sole composer credit. "It was his film," Garcia said. "I worked anonymously on hundreds of movies that I never got credit for…. That's how it worked. And probably still does…. While he composed the film's theme, he obviously didn't know how to arrange for a symphony-sized orchestra. Neither did Ray Rasch."[41] When it came to the Oscar nomination, Garcia said, "I'm not that comfortable talking about this because I don't want to make trouble for anyone or spoil anyone's fond thoughts or memories." Garcia praised Larry Russell as "a composer and movie arranger, and a good one. He also was a nice guy.... [But] he had nothing to do with the picture."[42]

The day after the Oscars, Garcia's phone in New Zealand "rang off the hook. Keith Williams ... called to apologize. So did Larry Russell's son. I'm not sure why everyone was sorry after the award was given. Maybe they didn't realize my role until those who were actually there started talking. I don't know. I'm sure it didn't help that I lived so far away." Garcia was matter of fact when it came to his role in the film. "I know that I arranged the score for the film. And so do those who were there and those who have spoken to those who know." As to why he rarely had spoken of the incident over the years, Garcia explained, "I'm a Baha'i. It's part of my faith never to be the source of grief to anyone. I didn't want Larry's widow or family or anyone to feel bad. I still don't. I've won plenty of awards. I just forgot about it."[43] "Besides," as he wrote in his autobiography, "I think awards are for kids to post on the refrigerator."[44] Garcia's widow Gina says he often quipped, "You could see through him he did so much ghost-writing. And he never worried much about whether he got credit or not. So long as he knew he did it, that's what mattered to him."[45]

Russell Garcia and Chaplin at the *Limelight* recording sessions, c. June 1952 (courtesy Gina Garcia).

In the comments section of the JazzWax blog post with Garcia's interview, Linda Russell Morgan, who had accepted the Oscar on her father's behalf, vehemently disputed Garcia's statements:

> Over the years, I have run across Mr. Garcia's claims regarding his alleged work on *Limelight* and his claim that my father had nothing to do with it and I am, frankly, appalled. My father worked very closely with Ray Rasch every day for months at our house in Laurel Canyon. Ray would meet each morning with Chaplin, then come directly to my father, since Ray had never scored anything in his life. I have no idea who Mr. Garcia is, but I can tell you, that I have personal knowledge of my father's work on *Limelight*—I was there when Ray came to our house every day. You may or may not know, that my father composed the standard "Vaya Con Dios" (which incidentally was recorded by Anita O'Day, another person who Mr. Garcia claims to know). Perhaps you should ask Mr. Garcia if he also wrote "Vaya Con Dios"? As for his claim that one of my three brothers called him to apologize about our father being awarded the Oscar, this is unadulterated hogwash[46]—I just find it so interesting that Mr. Garcia continues to lay claim to my father's work—perhaps because he knows that my father passed away at the age of 41 (in 1954), that his widow, Inez James (another author of "Vaya Con Dios"), has now passed away, that Ray Rasch is gone, that Charlie Chaplin has died—(and oh yes, Anita O'Day is gone too)—so convenient that there is no living person to refute his allegations. But, rest assured, I am still here and so are two of my brothers, Gordon and George, and we will continue to urge all of you to check your facts a little more.[47]

The comment comes across as incredibly antagonistic, especially since Garcia had nothing but praise for Larry Russell as a musician. His only claim was that Russell had nothing to do with *Limelight*, as Paul Rasch had also maintained. A simple online search would have yielded pages of proof that Garcia had worked with Anita O'Day. And since Morgan did not provide any documents or photos to substantiate her claims, the comments that followed turned into, as they often do, nothing more than "he said/she said."[48]

The true story of *Limelight* and its musical collaborators may never be known in full. Garcia was under contract to Universal Pictures at the time and that may explain why he was not listed in the credits (though neither were Rasch nor Williams) or in the studio paperwork. All the musicians involved are dead and what descendants have discussed the matter, the information is still second hand.[49] It is unfortunate that so much of the studio documents for the film, including much of the score itself, have not survived over the years. What little manuscript still exists bears Ray Rasch's AFM stamp, when it is credited at all. But a photo of Russell Garcia and Chaplin, who wears the same jacket he wore for the *Look* magazine photo shoot at the recording sessions, proves that Garcia indeed was part of the *Limelight* team and, as he stated, he was most likely in the engineering booth during the recording. Larry Russell's involvement, if there was any, remains a mystery.[50]

*   *   *

The careers of Chaplin's music associates—whether as amanuenses, arrangers, orchestrators, or conductors—did not start with Chaplin, nor did they end with him. With the advent of sound in 1927, Carl Edouarde and Louis F. Gottschalk were nearing the ends of their lives and the transition to the new technology provided fewer opportunities.[51] Other names from the silent era like Frederick Stahlberg and Carli Elinor, and later Max Terr and Gerard Carbonara found themselves lost in the factory of the studio system.[52] Some collaborators like Arthur Johnston branched off into successful songwriting careers,[53] while Rudy Schrager continued to work in radio,[54] and Arthur Kay and Meredith Willson made names for themselves on Broadway.[55] No doubt the revolving door of musicians who got fired from *A King in New York* were happy to move on.[56] Alfred Newman, Edward Powell, and David Raksin carved out lengthy—and legendary—careers in Hollywood,[57] but unless your name *is* Alfred Newman, few people in or out of the film music community recognize film music conductors, so it is no surprise, yet unfortunate, that only die-hard film music fans know the names Leighton Lucas, Eric Spear, Lambert Williamson, and Eric Rogers.[58]

And then there was Eric James, Chaplin's music associate for nearly twenty years.[59] "We became very, very close," James said. "I was treated more like a son. He once said to me, 'You know, of all the musicians I've ever known, you're the one that I've got on best with in the last forty years.'"[60] Perched on top of his living room piano, James kept a signed photograph of him with Chaplin that was inscribed, "To Eric, with many thanks for your patience and understanding."

*   *   *

"Patience and understanding." These two qualities were certainly a prerequisite for working with Chaplin. But most musical collaborators found both virtues tested to the limit to last beyond one film. Or perhaps the choice was Chaplin's. Letters from Arthur

Johnston and others indicate that some musicians were willing to work for the taskmaster again. If Chaplin had not continued scoring his earlier silent films in the last years of his life, Eric James's steady gig would have been cut short. But it is telling that no matter who worked on a certain film, Chaplin's music sounds like Chaplin, further proving his deep involvement in the music making process and making a strong case for the strength of Chaplin's musical voice.

With his death on December 25, 1977, Chaplin the composer had said all he wanted to say musically. He had fulfilled his mission of scoring all the films he still owned—all his First National films beginning with *A Dog's Life* in 1918 through his final feature *A Countess from Hong Kong* in 1967—a total of eighteen scores. After his death, Petula Clark went back to the Manoir "and we did a special tribute to him where I played the piano again and sang 'This Is My Song.' It was strange going back with him not being there. But every time I sing the song I talk about him and I find myself back in that room where we had this rather lovely meeting."[61]

Film music is a collaborative art in which a composer must at times tamper down his musical voice to serve the needs of a film. But the same Chaplin who had written the story, directed the actors to mimic exactly what he demonstrated, and created an iconic character in the Tramp also became his films' musical voice. The list of director-composers is short—Clint Eastwood, Mike Figgis, Robert Rodriguez, a few others. Perhaps only John Carpenter comes closest in seamlessly melding his musical voice with his cinematic vision. But even Carpenter is missing Chaplin's complete auteur vision and the unique creation of the Tramp, whose essence is still visible in Chaplin's performances long after the character's final screen appearance. So Chaplin's music becomes yet another character in the stories he wanted to tell, whether created alongside the film or decades later.

Ever since Chaplin first self-deprecatingly described his compositional skills as merely "la-la'ing," the press and certainly the film music community have been critical of his music. And to some extent the criticism is understandable. For musicians who have spent years studying and perfecting their craft, amateur musicians like Chaplin who cannot read or write music and who rely on others to complete their musical vision can seem simplistic in the extreme. But Irving Berlin's inability to read or write music has not hurt his reputation as one of the world's great songwriters. Nor is Chaplin the only film composer missing one or both of those capabilities. At the beginning of his career, Danny Elfman, who received his musical training as part of the rock band The Mystical Knights of Oingo Boingo, could write music but not read it. Hans Zimmer has admitted he cannot read standard music notation very well. In addition, both composers, like most film composers, have relied on one or more arrangers and/or orchestrators to get the job done. Film music is composed on an often incredibly short timeline. Some composers hand off detailed short scores or lead sheets to their orchestrators, others pass along far less. And with the advent of computers and other electronic instruments, the ability to read and write music is less necessary than it once was. Now anyone with a keyboard, a music notation program, and a decent sample library can create something close to the musical vision they have in their head. Had this setup been around during Chaplin's doodling sessions on the piano, his musical career might have taken a decidedly different turn.

Shortly after Chaplin's death, Mike Gould, Bourne's West Coast manager, said Chaplin's talents as a musician "were hardly known even in the music business."[62] But, as Calvero says in *Limelight*, "Time is the great author. It always writes the perfect ending."

The pendulum has begun to swing regarding Chaplin's musical gifts. Concerts of Chaplin's music shown live to picture are becoming increasingly more popular. The practice began with the centennial of Chaplin's birth in 1989 when Carl Davis arranged the music to *City Lights* for live presentation. Davis's arrangement took into consideration the full symphonic forces at his disposal, a far cry from the dance band orchestrations Chaplin had commanded in 1931. Gillian Anderson reconstructed the compilation scores for *The Gold Rush* and *The Circus*, performing them both live in the mid–1990s.

But Chaplin's greatest musical champion has been Timothy Brock. In January 1998, Brock was asked by the Los Angeles Chamber Orchestra and Association Chaplin to begin the exhaustive (and exhausting) task of reconstructing Chaplin's *Modern Times* for live performance based on the conductor's score and the instrumental parts. Since then, Brock's reconstructions of *City Lights* and a new one of *The Kid* from 2016, as well as every Chaplin silent feature and his First National shorts, have now become the standard rentals to orchestras around the world. He even went back to the twenty hours of Chaplin noodling at the piano in the 1950s to compose a "new" Chaplin score, using Chaplin's own melodies, to replace the problematic music for *A Woman of Paris*.

For the period October 2016 through July 2017, seventy-five concerts of Chaplin's films with orchestras performing the music live to picture were scheduled around the world, nearly twenty different conductors conducting over a dozen orchestras in over a dozen countries. These concerts feature Chaplin's scores lovingly restored by Brock to their original orchestrations. They bring Chaplin's music to the forefront, allowing audiences to experience the music with first-class musicians without the technological sound limitations resulting from the initial recording sessions.

Charlie Chaplin—the man and his films—will always take center stage over the music, as it should be. But to ignore the music is like dismissing Rollie Totheroh's slow fade at the end of *Modern Times*, Mack Swain's comic histrionics in *The Gold Rush*, or Edna Purviance's awkward wink in *A Dog's Life*. They are all part of one singular, unique vision—Chaplin's vision. Chaplin ignored advances in film and film music his entire life. That is part of their charm and part of their frustration.

Jerry Epstein claimed, "Charlie was cheeky about his music and never took it seriously." Perhaps Chaplin *was* "cheeky" with his inner circle. But his hands-on involvement in every score says otherwise. Chaplin was "deeply flattered" when he heard that John Huston had told a composer, "I want the same kind of music that Chaplin composes for his pictures."[63] The statement alone speaks volumes. That Chaplinesque quality is not something to be dismissed lightly when contemplating Chaplin's musical vision as well as the stories of the men who worked under sometimes less than ideal conditions to help him realize it.

And so the story circles back to Gilbert Seldes's summation of Chaplin's musical abilities—"As a writer and as composer of music for his films, Chaplin remains an amateur. He gains because his movies (and his alone) are the product of a single individual, as a novel is or a poem."[64] As Eric James wrote in his autobiography, Chaplin "always wanted music that was tuneful even if a little old-fashioned. He once commented that if the public didn't like his picture they should be able to close their eyes and enjoy the music!"[65]

That was Chaplin's gift.

That was his song.

THE END

APPENDIX A

Timeline

*With great appreciation to David Robinson for the
inspiration and many of the dates.*

1863	March 18	Charles Chaplin, Sr. (CC's father) born in Marylebone, London
1864	October 7	Louis F. Gottschalk born in St. Louis, Missouri
1865	August 6	Hannah Harriett Pedlingham Hill (CC's mother) born in Walworth, London
1870	January 18	Kate Hill (CC's aunt) born in Walworth, London
1875	October 31	Carl Edouarde born in Cleveland, Ohio
	November 2	Adolf Tandler born in Vienna, Austria
1877	May 7	Frederick Stahlberg born in Ketzin, Germany
1881	January 16	Arthur Kay born in Berlin, Germany
1885	March 16	Sidney John Hill (Sydney Chaplin, CC's brother) born in London
	June 22	Charles Chaplin, Sr., marries Hannah Hill
1886	November 6	Gus Kahn born in Koblenz, Germany
	December 8	Gerard Carbonara born in New York City
1887	April 6	Alois Reiser born in Prague, Czechoslovakia
1889	April 16	BIRTH OF CHARLIE CHAPLIN
1890		Publication of Charles Chaplin Senior's songs "Eh, Boys?" and "Every-Day Life"
	September 21	Carli Elinor born in Bucharest, Romania
	November 16	Max Terr born in Odessa (present-day Ukraine)
1891		Publication of Charles Chaplin Senior's song "As the Church Bells Chime"
	August 10	Romo Falk born
	November 10	Philip Sainton born in Arques-la-Bataille, Seine-Maritime, France
1892	August 31	Wheeler Dryden (CC's half-brother) born in London
1895	October 21	Edna Purviance born in Paradise Valley, Nevada
1897		Boris Sarbek (Boris Saarbecoff) born in Russia (exact date unknown)
	August 4	Abe Lyman born in Chicago, Illinois
	September 4	Gus Arnheim born in Philadelphia
1898	January 10	Arthur Johnston born in New York City
	July 6	Hanns Eisler born in Leipzig, Germany
1900	August 28	Rudy Schrager born in Czernowitz, Bukovina, Austria-Hungary
1901	March 17	Alfred Newman born in New Haven, Connecticut
	May 9	Charles Chaplin, Sr., dies in St. Thomas's Hospital, London, age 37
1902	May 18	Meredith Willson born in Mason City, Iowa
1903	January 5	Leighton Lucas born in London
1904	January 15	Eddie DeLange born in Long Island, New York
	July 24	Leo Arnaud born in Lyon, France
1907	April 28	Lambert Williamson born in Cleothorpes, Lincolnshire, England
	August 28	Roy Chamberlain born in New York City
1908	February 21	Chaplin signs first contract with Fred Karno
	April 8	Eric Spear born in Croydon, Surrey, England

1909	December 5	Edward Powell born in Carroll County, Illinois
1910	January 7	Geoffrey Parsons born
1912	August 4	David Raksin born in Philadelphia, Pennsylvania
1913	August 11	Eric James (Eric James Barker) born in London
	September 25	Chaplin signs contract with Kessel and Baumann to join Keystone Film Company at $150 per week for one year
	October 14	Larry Russell born in Indiana
1914	July 28	Carmen Dragon born in Antioch, California
		At the end of 1914, Chaplin signs contract with Essanay for $1,250 per week to make 15 films
1916		Chaplin forms the Charlie Chaplin Music Publishing Co. with Sydney Chaplin and Bert Clark; publishes Chaplin's "Oh! That Cello," *The Peace Patrol,* and "There's Always One You Can't Forget"
	January 22	Kate Mowbray (Kate Hill, CC's aunt) dies in London, age 46
	February 20	Chaplin conducts John Philip Sousa's band at New York's Hippodrome in performances of the *Poet and Peasant Overture* and his own *The Peace Patrol*
	February 26	Chaplin signs with Mutual Film Corporation for $10,000 per week plus a $150,000 signing bonus
	April 12	Russell Garcia born in Oakland, California
	July 10	*The Vagabond* released, first appearance of Chaplin onscreen with his left-handed violin
1917	March 1	Raymond Rasch born in Toledo, Ohio
	June 17	Chaplin signs with First National Exhibitor's Circuit for an unprecedented $1 million plus $75,000 signing bonus
	June 23	Peter Knight born Exmouth, Devon, England
	October	Chaplin breaks ground on his own studio at the southeast corner of La Brea and Sunset Boulevard in Los Angeles
1918	January	Chaplin moves into new studio
	January 28	Jacques Lasry born in French Algeria
	April 1	Chaplin leaves Hollywood to join Douglas Fairbanks and Mary Pickford on Liberty Bonds Tour
	April 14	*A Dog's Life* released
	October 20	*Shoulder Arms* released
1919	February 5	Chaplin signs contracts of incorporation for United Artists with D. W. Griffith, Douglas Fairbanks, and Mary Pickford
	June 15	*Sunnyside* released
	December 15	*A Day's Pleasure* released
1921	January 21	*The Kid* premieres at Carnegie Hall in benefit for the National Board of Review's Children's Fund
	February 6	*The Kid* begins theatrical release at the Strand Theatre, New York; score compiled and conducted by Strand music director Carl Edouarde
	March 29	Hannah Chaplin arrives in America
	September 25	*The Idle Class* released
	September 25	Eric Rogers (Eric Gauk-Roger) born in Halifax, England
1922	April 2	*Pay Day* released
1923	February 26	*The Pilgrim* released
	September 26	*A Woman of Paris* premieres at the Criterion Theatre, Los Angeles; score compiled by Louis F. Gottschalk, conducted by Adolf Tandler
	October 1	*A Woman of Paris* New York premieres at the Lyric Theatre, most likely with a completely different score than the Los Angeles premiere five days earlier
1924	July 24	Keith Williams born in Garfield, Utah
1925	June 26	*The Gold Rush* premieres at Grauman's Egyptian Theatre, Los Angeles; score compiled by Carli D. Elinor, conducted by Gino Severi
	July 3	"New musical score" begun for *The Gold Rush's* New York premiere; how much was changed or if it was used is unclear

1928	January 6	*The Circus* premieres at the Strand Theatre, New York; score compiled by Arthur Kay; conducted by Alois Reiser
	January 27	Arthur Kay conducts the West Coast premiere of *The Circus* at Grauman's Chinese Theatre
	August 28	Hannah Chaplin dies in Glendale, California, age 63
1930	November 14	Arthur Johnston begins work on *City Lights*
	December 29	First orchestra rehearsal for *City Lights*
	December 31	*City Lights* recording sessions begin; sessions end January 6, 1931
1931	January 30	*City Lights* premiere
1932	December 8	Carl Edouarde dies in Locust, New Jersey, age 57
1934	July 15	Louis F. Gottschalk dies in Los Angeles of a stroke, age 69
1935	November 18	*Modern Times* recording sessions begin; sessions end four weeks later on December 17
	December 4	Chaplin has disagreement with conductor Alfred Newman on the *Modern Times* sound stage; Newman storms off and quits; Edward Powell takes over the few remaining conducting duties
1936	February 5	*Modern Times* premieres at Rivoli Theatre, New York
1937	July 23	Frederick Stahlberg dies in Los Angeles, age 60
1940	July 3	Meredith Willson begins working with Chaplin on the score for *The Great Dictator*
	August 15	*The Great Dictator* recording sessions begin at RCA Studios, conducted by Meredith Willson; sessions end August 23
	August 27	Premiere of "Prelude to *The Great Dictator*" with the San Francisco Symphony, conducted by Meredith Willson
	October 15	*The Great Dictator* premieres at the Capitol and Astor Theatres, New York
1941	August 23	Max Terr begins working with Chaplin on score for *The Gold Rush* reissue
	October 8	Gus Kahn dies of a heart attack in Beverly Hills, age 54
	October 27	*The Gold Rush* recording sessions begin at RCA Studios, Max Terr conducting; sessions end November 3
1942	May 19	*The Gold Rush* "with music and words" released
1946	November 18	Rudy Schrager begins working with Chaplin on the score for *Monsieur Verdoux*
1947	January 9	*Monsieur Verdoux* recording sessions begin at RCA Studios, conducted by Rudy Schrager; sessions end January 17
	April 11	*Monsieur Verdoux* premieres at Broadway Theatre, New York
1948	February 28	Benefit concert of Hanns Eisler's music at Town Hall in New York City, organized by Leonard Bernstein, Aaron Copland, David Diamond, Roy Harris, Walter Piston, Roger Sessions, and Randall Thompson
	March 26	Hanns Eisler deported and flies to Prague
1949	July 15	Eddie DeLange dies, age 45
1950	November 28	Bernard Katz leaves *Limelight* weeks after being hired to take a job as general musical director of NBC in Chicago
	December 15	Ray Rasch begins working with Chaplin on the score to *Limelight*
1951	August 2	Max Terr dies in Los Angeles, age 60
	August 3	Bernard Katz, rehired, conducts pre-recording of *Limelight* ballet music at Glen Glenn Sound Studio
	September 12	Larry Russell writes to Chaplin requesting work as a conductor
	September 19	Keith Williams conducts re-recording of *Limelight* ballet music at Glen Glenn; sessions end September 20
	October 18	Chaplin records vocals for three *Limelight* songs at Glen Glenn; Ray Rasch accompanies on piano and records two piano "concertos"
	November 6	Recording background for Chaplin's three *Limelight* songs at Glen Glenn
	November 19	Shooting on *Limelight* begins
1952	May 28	Recording *Limelight* street musicians' music at RCA Studios
	June 10	*Limelight* recording sessions begin at RCA Studios, Keith Williams conducting; sessions end June 17

	August 13	Half-hour recording session of *Limelight* barrel organ music; Ray Rasch on piano
	September 17	Chaplin sails from New York to London on the *Queen Elizabeth* for premiere of *Limelight*
	September 19	U.S. Attorney General James McGranery rescinds Chaplin's re-entry permit
	October 16	*Limelight* premieres at Odeon Theatre, Leicester Square, London, in a benefit for the Royal London Society for Teaching and Training the Blind
	October 23	*Limelight* opens in the U.S. at the Astor and Trans Lux Theatres in New York
1953	May 23	Frank Chacksfield's popular recording of "Terry's Theme" from *Limelight* enters the *Billboard* charts at #19, eventually reaching #6
	September 30	Adolf Tandler and his 50-year-old daughter, Hedwig, die in Los Angeles of asphyxiation inside a parked car, an apparent suicide
1954	February 14	Larry Russell dies in Los Angeles, age 40
	May 1	Arthur Johnston dies in Corona del Mar, California, age 56
	July 27	"Smile" released by Nat "King" Cole
1955	January 19	Gus Arnheim dies of a heart attack in Beverly Hills, age 67
1956	March 14	Peter Knight begins recording songs for *A King in New York* at Elstree Studios
	May 1	Peter Knight records new *King in New York* arrangements (with some Philip Sainton orchestrations and Sainton conducting one number) at Shepperton Studios; two follow-up dates (May 18 and 23), once again with new Knight arrangements
	December 7	Jacques Lasry letter stating he had been paid 60 francs for work on *A King in New York*
	December 18	Boris Sarbek begins working with Chaplin on the score to *A King in New York*
1957	January 25	Recording sessions for the score to *A King in New York* begin at Shepperton Studios, Leighton Lucas conducting; sessions end January 29
	June 22	"Mandolin Serenade" short filmed at Studio de la Mutualité in Paris
	September 12	*A King in New York* released, but not in the U.S.
	September 30	Wheeler Dryden (CC's half-brother) dies in Los Angeles, age 65
	October 23	Abe Lyman dies in Los Angeles of cancer, age 59
1958	January 13	Edna Purviance dies in Los Angeles of throat cancer, age 62
	October 20	Carli Elinor dies of a heart attack in Los Angeles, age 68
1959	January 11	Gerard Carbonara dies in Los Angeles, age 72
	January 12	Recording sessions for *A Dog's Life* begin at Shepperton Studios, Eric Spear conducting; sessions end January 14
	February 18	Recording sessions for *Shoulder Arms* and *The Pilgrim* begin at Shepperton Studios, Eric Spear conducting; sessions end February 25
	September 25	*The Chaplin Revue* released, but not in the U.S.
1961	November 24	Romo Falk dies, age 70
1962	September 6	Hanns Eisler dies in East Berlin, East Germany, of a heart attack, age 64
1964	December 23	Raymond Rasch dies of a heart attack, sitting at his piano, in Los Angeles, age 47
1965	April 16	Sydney Chaplin (CC's half-brother) dies in Nice, France, age 80
1966		Boris Sarbek dies (exact date unknown)
	September 19	Recording sessions for *A Countess from Hong Kong* begin at Anvil Recording Studios, Lambert Williamson conducting; sessions end September 23
	September 27	Recording sessions for *A Countess from Hong Kong* soundtrack album (in stereo) begin at Anvil Recording Studios, Lambert Williamson conducting; sessions end September 28
	November 3	Eric Spear dies of a stroke in Southampton, Hampshire, England, age 58
1967	January 5	*A Countess from Hong Kong* released
	February 16	Petula Clark's recording of "This Is My Song" reaches #1 in the UK

	August 2	Philip Sainton dies in Petersfield, Hampshire, England, age 75
	October 30	Eric James begins working with Chaplin on the score to *The Circus*
1968	April 18	*The Circus* recording sessions begin at Anvil Recording Studios, Lambert Williamson conducting; sessions end April 22
1969	December 19	Arthur Kay dies in Los Angeles, age 88
1970	February 17	Alfred Newman dies in Los Angeles of emphysema, age 68
1971	October 25	Recording sessions for *The Kid* and *The Idle Class* begin at Anvil Recording Studios, conduced by Eric Rogers; sessions end October 29, during which a camera crew filmed Chaplin conducting the orchestra for *The Gentleman Tramp* documentary
1972	April 10	Chaplin receives Honorary Oscar
	November 22	*Pay Day* recording sessions begin at Anvil Recording Studios; Eric Rogers conducting; sessions end November 24
1973	March 27	Chaplin, Raymond Rasch, and Larry Russell win Best Dramatic Score Academy Award for *Limelight*
	August 28	*A Day's Pleasure* recording sessions begin at Anvil Recording Studios, Eric Rogers conducting; sessions end August 30
1974	April 30	*Sunnyside* recording sessions begin at Anvil Recording Studios, Eric Rogers conducting; sessions end May 2
1975	March 4	Chaplin knighted by HM Queen Elizabeth II
	November 13	Lambert Williamson dies in Chiltern & Beaconsfield, Buckinghamshire, England, age 68
1976	February 17	*A Woman of Paris* recording sessions begin at Anvil Recording Studios, Eric Rogers conducting; sessions end February 23
1977	April 4	Alois Reiser dies in Los Angeles, age 89
	December 25	CHARLIE CHAPLIN DIES, age 88
1981	April 8	Eric Rogers dies in Chalfont St. Peter, Buckinghamshire, England, age 60
	May 14	Roy Chamberlain dies in Monterey, California, age 73
1982	November 1	Leighton Lucas dies in London, age 79
1983	August 24	Rudy Schrager dies in Santa Monica, California, age 82
1984	February 28	Edward Powell dies in Los Angeles, age 74
	March 28	Carmen Dragon dies Los Angeles, age 69
	June 15	Meredith Willson dies in Santa Monica, California, of heart failure, age 82
1985	July 30	Peter Knight dies of lung cancer, age 68
1987	December 22	Geoffrey Parsons dies in Eastbourne, East Sussex, England, age 77
1991	April 26	Leo Arnaud dies in Los Angeles, age 86
2004	August 9	David Raksin dies in Van Nuys, California, of heart failure, age 92
2006	March 28	Eric James dies in Whitby, Ontario, Canada, age 92
2008	December 27	Keith Williams dies, age 84
2011	November 20	Russell Garcia dies of cancer in Kerikeri, New Zealand, age 95
2014	March 26	Jacques Lasry dies in Jerusalem, age 96

Cue Sheets

The Kid (1921 Compilation Score)

"Selected by Charles Chaplin"
As listed in the order found in the March 5, 1921,
playbill for the Kinema Theatre, Los Angeles

Ave Maria (Charles Gounod–J. S. Bach)
"Oh, Don't You Remember Sweet Alice, Ben
   Bolt" (Nelson Kneass)
Dramatic Andante (Irénée Bergé)
Agitato No. 3 (Otto Langey)
Misterioso No. 1 (Otto Langey)
Pizzicato-Bluette (Théodore Lack)
Intermezzo (Anton Arensky)
"Rock-a-Bye Baby"
Dramatic Tension No. 44 (Gaston Borch)
"Florindo" from *Carnival Venetian* (Jules
   Burgmein)
Tarantella (Carl Bohm)
Impish Elves (Gaston Borch)
Menuetto All'antico (Génari Karganoff)
Perpetual Motion (Gaston Borch)
"Tell Me Pretty Maiden" from *Floradora*
   (Leslie Stuart)
Le Secret (Léonard Gautier)
The Wooing Hour (J. S. Zamecnik)
Serenade (Henry Ern)
Elegie (Jules Massenet)
Atonement (J. S. Zamecnik)
Cupid's Frolic (Walter E. Miles)
Chaconne (Auguste Durand)
"Les Romani" from *Gitanilla Suite* (Paul
   Lacombe)
Little Serenade (Alfred Grünfeld)
Melodie (Rudolf Friml)
Flirty-Flirts (Sol P. Levy)

A Woman of Paris
(1923 Original Compilation Score)

Compiled by Louis F. Gottschalk

Prelude—*Tout Paris* (Émile Waldteufel)
1—Symphony No. 6 in B Minor

("Pathétique"), Op. 74: *Adagio Lamentoso*
   (Fourth Movement Finale) (Pyotr
   Tchaikovsky)
2—*Andante Appassionato* (Lloyd G. del
   Castillo)
3—*Elegie* (Maurice Baron)
4—"The Girl I Loved" (Louis F. Gottschalk)
5—*Resignation* (Gaston Borch)
6—*Lamentoso* (Gaston Borch)
7—*Vision of Salome* (Archibald Joyce)
8—*Land of Delight* (Christopher O'Hare)
9—*Thousand and One Nights*, Op. 346
   (Johann Strauss)
10—*Badinage* (Victor Herbert)
11—*Frivolette* (Maurice Baron)
11a.—*The Vampire* (Al B. Coney)
12—"Adagietto" from *Symphonette* (Irénée
   Bergé)
13—*La Bella Cubanera* (M. L. Lake)
14—*Song Without Words* (Vladimir Rebikov)
15—*Élégie* (G. Lubomirsky)
16—*Valse Lente*, Op. 34, No. 2 (Frédéric
   Chopin)
16a—*When the Leaves Begin to Fall* (Maurice
   Baron)
17—*Lamento* (Jean Gabriel-Marie)
18—*A Pathetic Story* (Gaston Borch)
19—*Pizzicato Polka* (Johann Strauss)
20—*Pathetic Melody* (Gaston Borch)
21—*Dramatic Lamento* (Irénée Bergé)
22—*Les sirènes* (Émile Waldteufel)
23—"A Song of India" from *Sadko* (Nicolai
   Rimsky-Korsakov)
24—*Valse triste* (Jean Sibelius)
25—*Pirouette* (Herman Finck)
26—*Solemn Scenes from Nature* (Christopher
   O'Hare)
27—*Je t'aime* ("I Love Thee") (Émile
   Waldteufel)
28—*Lamento* (Maurice Baron)
29—*Sorrow Theme* (Edouard Roberts)
30—*Pathetic Andante No. 1* (Paul Vely)
31—*Child's Dreams* (Gaston Borch)

32—"Auprès de ma blonde" (17th century French folk song, handwritten in the instrumental parts)

A Woman of Paris (1923 Revised Compilation Score Cue Sheet)

Compiled by Louis F. Gottschalk
This list retains the cue sheet misspelling of "John" for "Jean."
(T)itle or (D)escription

1—At screening—"Prélude de la grotte aux Aigles" from *Jocelyn* (Benjamin Godard)

2—(T) In a small village—*Le roi d'Ys* Overture (Édouard Lalo)

3—(D) Marie walks to window—*Mysterioso No. 18* (Herbert E. Haines)

4—(T) Midnight—Theme: *Chanson bohémienne* (J.B. Boldi)

5—(T) He's locked the window—*My Abode* (Franz Schubert)

6—(D) Marie weeping—Theme

7—(D) Marie and John enter—*Mélodie* (Charles Huerter)

8—(T) I want to see you alone—*My Abode*

9—(D) John and Marie at the station—Theme

10—(D) John enters house—*Lamento* (Jean Gabriel-Marie)

11—(D) John cries out "Mother"—*Turbulence* (Gaston Borch)

12—(D) Mother weeping—*Phèdre* Overture (Jules Massenet)

13—(T) A year later—*Vision of Salome* (Archibald Joyce)

14—(T) Pierre Revel made a study of eating—*L'Esprit français* (Émile Waldteufel)

15—(D) Pierre sits at table—"Fascination" (Fermo Dante Marchetti)

16—(T) Marie St. Clair's apartment—*La lettre de Manon* (Ernest Gillet)

17—(T) The business office of Pierre Revel—*Babillage* (Ernest Gillet)

18—(T) Paulette, a new friend—"Im chambre séparée" from *Der Opernball* (Richard Heuberger)

19—(T) In the evening—*Soirée d'été* (Émile Waldteufel)

20—(D) Marie at mantle—*Andante Appassionato* (Lloyd del Castillo)

21—(T) That evening—*Crazy Love* (Licco Liggy)

22—(D) Following announcement—"My Spanish Rose" (José Padilla)

23—(D) John goes to open door—*Disperazione* (Jean Gabriel-Marie)

24—(D) Immediate after John reaches door—Theme

25—(D) Cabaret scene—*Ninette* (Henri Christiné)

26—(D) Flash back John's studio—*Ronde Lointaine* (Ernest Gillet)

27—(D) John and Marie leave—Theme

28—(T) The following morning—*Song Without Words* (Vladimir Rebikov)

29—(D) Pierre enters apartment—Sees white collar—*Valse Lente* (Frédéric Chopin)

30—(D) John and Marie—Theme

31—(T) And the passing days—*Adoration* (Edmond Filippucci)

32—(D) Marie looks at painting—Theme

33—(T) In the mind of Marie—*Tragic Andante* (Domenico Savino)

34—(D) Marie runs away from window—*Furioso No. 2* (Otto Langey)

35—(D) Pierre enters Marie's room—*Pathetic Melody* (Gaston Borch)

36—(T) An eternal problem—*Dramatic Lamento* (Irénée Bergé)

37—(D) John and Marie face each other—Theme (3 bars only)

38—Segue—*Dramatic Lamento*

39—(D) That night—"Coralito Tango" ("Red Rose of Spain") (D. Caputo)

40—(T) And that night—"Clair de lune," from *Werther* (Jules Massenet)

41—(D) Butler sleeping—*Before the Footlights* (Charles Manney)

42—(D) Mother waiting—*Valse triste* (Jean Sibelius)

43—(T) The following morning—*Plume au vent* (Joseph Farigoul)

44—(D) Paulette and other friends go into next room—"Coralito Tango"

45—(D) Marie at dressing table—*La lettre de Manon*

46—(T) And as evening—"Lento 116" from *Symphonette* (Irénée Bergé)

47—(D) Pierre and Marie—*La lettre de Manon*

48—(D) Marie and Pierre leave—"Lento 116"

49—(D) Fade in cafe—*Poor Jeanne Marie* (Maurice Yvain)

50—(D) John arrives—*Les vêpres siciliennes* Overture (Giuseppe Verdi)

51—(D) John attacks Pierre—*Agitato* (Hugo Riesenfeld)

52—(D) John is led out of dance room—*Ninette*

53—(D) John shoots himself—*Lamento* (Maurice Baron)

54—(D) Doctor enters Mother's apartment—*Pique Dame* (Pyotr Ilyich Tchaikovsky)

55—(D) Marie at bier of John—Theme
56—(D) Time is a great healer—*Mireille* Overture (Charles Gounod)
57—(D) Marie and boy jump on wagon— "Auprès de ma blonde"

The Gold Rush
(1925 Compilation Score)

Score compiled by Carli D. Elinor
Premiere at Grauman's Egyptian Theatre, Los Angeles, on June 26, 1925
Conducted by Gino Severi
As is the case with most compilation scores of the silent era, the piano/conductor score for *The Gold Rush*, located in the Chaplin Archive in Montreux, Switzerland, does not list every piece of music that was used. Even with years of detective work and the help of numerous silent film music experts, the identification of certain cues still remains. Below is a list of musical works heard in the original compilation score that have been identified to date.

However, James C. Bradford took many of these cues for his own cue sheet that was sent around to theaters and left them in the same order as the compilation score. So until the rest of the compilation score cues are identified, for pieces of music that match between the two lists, the cue sheet (which appears in the appendix following) provides a good idea of the order for the compilation score.

Agitato (Irénée Bergé)
Agitato No. 1 (William Axt)
Agitato No. 2 (Ernö Rapeé-William Axt)
The Alaskan (Harry Girard)
American Festival March (Hugo Riesenfeld)
"Andromeda and the Storm King," from symphonic poem *Andromèda* (Augusta Mary Holmes)
"Auld Lang Syne" (Trad.)
Babette, "There Once Was An Owl" (Victor Herbert)
"The Bowery," from *A Trip to Chinatown* (Percy Gaunt)
"Chicken Reel" (Joseph M. Daly)
The Christmas Tree (Vladimir Rebikov)
"Fascination" (Fermo Dante Marchetti)
From the South Suite, "In the Tavern" (J. L. Nicode)
Grotesque Elephantine (Lester Brockton)
"The Keel Row" (Trad.)
"Loch Lomond" (Trad.)
Lovey-Dovey (Robert A. Hellard)

"The Man Who Broke the Bank at Monte Carlo" (Fred Gilbert)
The Mikado, "A Wand'ring Minstrel I" (Arthur Sullivan)
Misterioso Dramatico (Paul Fauchey)
Misterioso Dramatique No. 54 (Gaston Borch)
Misterioso Infernale (Gaston Borch)
Moonlight Dance (Herman Fink)
"My Wild Irish Rose" (Chauncey Olcott)
Mysterioso (Leo Kempinski)
Natoma, "Natoma's Love Theme" and "Oh, Child of Love" (Victor Herbert)
L'Onde tragique (Jean Gabriel-Marie)
Der Opernball, "Im chambre séparée" (Richard Heuberger)
Orfée aux enfers Overture (Jacques Offenbach)
Peer Gynt, "In the Hall of the Mountain King" and "Morning Mood" (Edvard Grieg)
Piano Sonata No. 8 in C minor, Op. 13 ("Pathétique"), Mvt. I (Ludwig van Beethoven)
Pomp and Circumstance No. 1 (Edward Elgar)
Rigoletto, "Quel vecchio maledivami" and Act III storm music (Giueseppe Verdi)
Rose-Mousse (Auguste Bosc)
"Sailing, Sailing" (James Frederick Swift)
Le Secret (Léonard Gautier)
Shadowed (J. S. Zamecnik)
Shadows in the Night (Gaston Borch)
Sigurd Jorsalfar, "Intermezzo" ("Borghild's Dream") (Edvard Grieg)
"The Teddy Bear's Picnic" (John Walter Bratton)
"Terence's Farewell to Kathleen" (Lady Durrin)
A Thousand Kisses (Archibald Joyce)
"Turkey in the Straw" (Trad.)
"When You Look in the Heart of a Rose" (Florence Methven)
Zampa (Louis Joseph Ferdinand Hérold)

The Gold Rush (1925 Cue Sheet)

Compiled by James C. Bradford
Published by Cameo Thematic Music Co.
The cue sheet included many of the major themes of the compilation score such as "The Bowery" for Charlie's theme, Georgia's themes, the love theme, and the use of Victor Herbert's *Natoma*, Hugo Riesenfeld's *American Festival March*, and more.

1—At screening—*Natoma* Selection (Victor Herbert) (2 min.)
2—(T) During the…—*American Festival March* (Hugo Riesenfeld) (1¼ min.)

3—(T) Three days from…—CHAPLIN THEME: "The Bowery" from *Old Timers Waltz* (arr. M. L. Lake) (1 min.)

4—(T) Another…—Repeat No. 2 *American Festival March* (2 min.)

5—(T) Then came a storm—"Storm in the Desert" from *Le désert* (Felicién David) (1½ min.)

6—(A) Charlie enters cabin—*Misterioso No. 1* (Ernö Rapeé-William Axt) (1¼ min.)

7—(T) Get out of here—*Il Guarany* (Antônio Carlos Gomez) (1 min.)

8—(A) Charlie shuts door—Repeat No. 6 *Misterioso No. 1* (1½ min.)

9—(T) Get out, the pair of you—*Agitato No. 1* (Ernö Rapeé-William Axt) (2 min.)

10—(T) I'll stay right here—Repeat Chaplin Theme No. 3 (½ min.)

11—(T) Three hungry men—*Misterioso No. 82* (Irénée Bergé) (3 min.)

12—(A) Door opens—Repeat No. 7 *Il Guarany* (¾ min.)

13—(T) The hand of the law—*A Frivolous Patrol* (Gustave Goublier) (1 min.)

14—(T) Black Larsen—*Allegro Agitato* (Carl Kiefert) (½ min.)

15—(T) Thanksgiving—*Entr-acte Gavotte* (Ernest Gillet) (3½ min.)

16—(T) Still waiting—*Humpty Dumpty's Funeral March* (Frederick Brandeis) (2¼ min.)

17—(A) Exterior—Chicken transforms–*Humpty Dumpty's Funeral March* (¼ min.)

18—(A) Charlie enters cabin—*Agitation poignante* (Jean Gabriel-Marie) (1 min.)

19—(A) Charlie struck on head with bar—"Intermezzo" from *Sigurd Jorsalfar* (Edvard Grieg) (2nd move.) (1 min.)

20—(A) Jim opens eyes—*L'Onde tragique* (Jean Gabriel-Marie) (1¼ min.)

21—(T) Then came the…—*Êlêgie* (G. Lubomirsky) (1 min.)

22—(T) Back to the…—*Agitato No. 3* (Otto Langey) (1¼ min.)

23—(T) The North—"Andromeda and the Storm King" (Augusta Mary Holmes) (1¼ min.)

24—(T) One of the many cities—*Alaskan March* (Harry Girard) (1¼ min.)

25—(T) Georgia—"My Wild Irish Rose" (Chauncey Olcott) (¾ min.)

26—(T) A disappointed prospect—Repeat Chaplin Theme–No. 3 (¾ min.)

27—(T) That night—Repeat No. 25 "My Wild Irish Rose" (1¼ min.)

28—(A) Charlie appears outside—SAD THEME: "The Pretty Girl Milking Her Cow" (Katherine DeWitt) (¾ min.)

29—(A) Fiddler starts to play—*Over the Waves* (Juventino Rosas) (¾ min.)

30—(A) Girl at bar—GIRL THEME: *Valse Fascination* (Frank H. Grey) (¾ min.)

31—(T) What's wrong with you tonight—"Im chambre séparée" (Richard Heuberger) (1 min.)

32—(A) Picks up photograph—Repeat Girl Theme No. 30 (¾ min.)

33—(A) Girls at table—*Rose-Mousse* (Auguste Bosc) (1½ min.)

34—(T) Hey you, come here—*A Thousand Kisses* (Archibald Joyce) (2¼ min.)

35—(A) Charlie falls—Repeat Girl Theme No. 30 (1½ min.)

36—(A) Man pushes Charlie's hat—*Danse of the Serpents* (Heinrich Arends) (½ min.)

37—(A) Charlie fixes suit—Repeat Chaplin Theme No. 3 (1 min.)

38—(T) The following morning—*Natoma Selection* (Victor Herbert) (1 min.)

39—(A) Man opens door—*Intermezzo* (Anton Arensky) (1¾ min.)

40—(T) Big Jim McKay—*Humoresque* (Herman Finck) (1½ min.)

41—(T) Away from the dance hall—*Moonlight Dance* (Herman Finck) (3 min.)

42—(A) Close-up of Georgia—Charlie opens door—Repeat Girl Theme No. 30 (1¼ min.)

43—(A) Close-up of photograph—LOVE THEME: "When You Look in the Heart of a Rose" (Florence Methven) (2 min.)

44—(T) Will you really come to dinner—*Rendez-vous* (William Aletter) (1 min.)

45—(A) Charlie bows—Repeat Chaplin Theme No. 3 (1¼ min.)

46—(T) To make possible—*Lovey-Dovey* (Robert A. Hellard) (1¾ min.)

47—(T) New Year's Eve—"In the Tavern" from *From the South* Suite (J. L. Nicode) (1 min.)

48—(A) Second flash-back to Charlie in cabin—Repeat Sad Theme No. 28 (1½ min.)

49—(A) Charlie sits at table—Repeat No. 31 "Im chambre séparée" (2 min.)

50—(A) After title: "I'll dance the Oceana Roll"—Chord in "G" (¼ min.)

51—(A) Charles start roll dance—"Highland Fling" from *Bonnie Scotland Overture* (E. N. Catlin) (¾ min.)

NOTE: Orchestra burlesque; sustained chord for end.

52—(A) Fade-out—Repeat Sad Theme No. 28 (½ min.)

53—(A) Fade of clock—Dance Hall—Repeat No. 47 "In the Tavern" (1¼ min.)

54—(A) Scotty starts to sing—"Auld Lang Syne" (arr. Emil Ascher) (2 min.)

55—(A) Dance starts—"Chicken Reel" (Joseph M. Daly) (1¼ min.)

56—(A) Charlie appears at window—Repeat Sad Theme No. 28 (¾ min.)

57—(A) Georgia enters cabin—*From the South* Suite (J. L. Nicode) (1¾ min.)

58—(T) The Recorder's office—Repeat No. 2 *American Festival March* (1¾ min.)

59—(T) In the dance hall that night—Repeat Girl Theme No. 30 (3 min.)

60—(A) Charlie opens letter—*Rustic Allegro* (Domenico Savino) (1 min.)

61—(T) The cabin—*Agitation No. 9* (Gaston Borch) (2¼ min.)

62—(T) After a long tedious journey—*The Philanderer* (Bertram Srawley) (2½ min.)

63—(T) Man proposes but storm disposes—*Storm and Strife* (Reginald Somerville) (1 min.)

NOTE: Storm effects ad lib.

64—(T) And as our slumbering heroes—"Morning Mood" from *Peer Gynt No. 1* (Edvard Grieg) (1¼ min.)

65—(T) Preparing for breakfast—"Teddy Bear's Picnic" (John Walter Bratton) (2½ min.)

66—(A) Both fall to floor—*Mystery Hurry* (Irénée Bergé) (1¼ min.)

67—(A) Charlie lands safely after jump—"Sailing, Sailing" (Godfrey Marks, arr. Luz) (¼ min.)

68—(T) Make way for…—"Big Boy" (Milton Ager) (1 min.)

69—(A) Charlie takes off hat—*Babette* Selection (Victor Herbert) (1 min.)

70—(A) Close-up of Georgia's photograph—Repeat Love Theme No. 43 (½ min.)

71—(A) Curtains in rear open—Charlie enters—Repeat Chaplin Theme No. 3 (1¼ min.)

72—(A) Charlie and Georgia look at each other—Repeat Love Theme No. 43 (1½ min.)

73—(T) James, make arrangements—Repeat No. 54 "Auld Lang Syne" (1¼ min.)

74—(T) Gee, this will make—Repeat Love Theme No. 43 (½ min.)

The Circus
(1928 Compilation Score)

Score compiled by Charlie Chaplin and Arthur Kay

Conducted by Alois Reiser (NY) and Arthur Kay (LA)

Premiere at the Strand Theatre, New York, on January 6, 1928

Like *The Gold Rush* compilation score, the listing for the cues for *The Circus* is unfortunately incomplete. Gillian Anderson's groundbreaking reconstruction of the score in 1993 identified many of the pieces involved. But even after years of detective work during the research for this book and, again, even with the generous help of numerous silent film music experts, many of the cues are still unidentified. Below is a list of musical works heard in the original compilation score that have been identified to date.

The Accuser (Arthur Kay)

Agitation (Gaston Borch)

Agitato (Will L. Becker)

Allegro Agitato (Carl Kicfert)

Allegro Vivace No. 1 (Otto Langey)

"L'amour, Toujours, L'amour" (Rudolf Friml)

"Blue Skies" (Irving Berlin)

Bon Vivant (J. S. Zamecnik)

Carmen, "Toreador Song" (Georges Bizet)

"The Charleston" (James P. Johnson, Cecil Mack)

"Down in Honky Tonk Town" (Chris Smith, Chas. R. McCarron)

Excitement and Hurry (Maurice Hoffman)

The Flatterer (Cécile Chaminade)

Funeral March of the Marionette (Charles Gounod)

A Funny Story (Arthur Kay)

Gossip (Arthur Kay)

Her Regiment, "Someday" (Victor Herbert)

Humoresque, Op. 10, No. 2 (Pyotr Ilyich Tchaikovsky)

Hurry (Adolf Minot)

Hurry No. 1 (Otto Langey)

Jolly Fellows Waltz (R. Vollstedt)

"Just a Memory" (Buddy De Sylva, Lew Brown, Ray Henderson)

Lohengrin, Prelude to Act III (Richard Wagner)

"Lucky Day" (Buddy DeSylva, Lew Brown, Ray Henderson)

Lyric Pieces, Book II, Op. 38, No.6 ("Elegie") (Edvard Grieg)

Maple Leaf Rag (Scott Joplin)

Marceline (George J. Trinkaus)

Mysterious Stranger (Arthur Kay)

Naughty Marietta, "For I'm Falling In Love With Someone" (Victor Herbert)

"Oh! You Circus Days" (James V. Monaco, Edith Maida Lessing)

Pagliacci, Prelude, Act I Chorus, Tonio's theme, and "Vesti la giubba" (Ruggiero Leoncavallo)

Peer Gynt, "Morning Mood" (Edvard Grieg)
Pirouette (Herman Finck)
"Please Let Me Sleep" (James T. Brymn, R. C. McPherson)
Punchinello (Victor Herbert)
"The Sneak" (Nacio Herb Brown)
Speed (Paul Biese)
Symphonette, "Finale" (Irénée Bergé)
Thunder and Blazes (Julius Fučik)
"When Day Is Done" (Robert Katcher, Buddy De Sylva)

The Circus (1928 Cue Sheet)

Compiled by Ernst Luz
Published by Cameo Thematic Music Co.
In addition to the common information found in cue sheets at this stage of film music development, compiler Ernst Luz included color-coded suggestions (RED, BROWN, etc.) from his *Motion Picture Synchrony* to help theater musicians easily substitute other pieces in the same music style.
(T)=Title, (A)=Action

1—At Screening—*Thunder and Blazes* March (Julius Fučik) (1 min.)
2—(T) A world of sawdust—*Skaters Galop* (P. Fahrbach) (1 min.)
3—(T) So you missed—*Suspicions* (Maurice Baron) (RED) (½ min.)
4—(T) For that—*Jocoso* (Herman Finck) (½ min.)
5—(T) And you're supposed to be funny—*Psyche* (Gustave D'Aquin) (¾ min.)
6—(T) Around the side shows—*Down South* (W. H. Myddleton) (½ min.)
7—(A) Charlie Chaplin shows his face—*Here Is Charley* (Henri Casadesus) (BROWN) (1 min.)
8—(A) Crook tries to take purse out of Chaplin's pocket—*Cynical Scherzando* (William Axt) (¾ min.)
9—(A) Street scene—Policeman leading—*Restless Bows* (Bertram Srawley) (DK. BLUE) (½ min.)
10—(A) Chaplin runs from stand—*Whip and Spur* (Thomas S. Allen) (½ min.)
11—(A) Chaplin in side show—Repeat No. 9 (DK. BLUE) (2 ¼ min.)
12—(A) Crook falls down—Repeat No. 10 (¼ min.)
13—(A) Chaplin arrested by policeman—Repeat No. 9 (DK. BLUE) (¾ min.)
14—(A) Chaplin escapes from policeman—Repeat No. 10 (1 min.)
15—(A) Men moving cabinet into circus ring—*The Joker* (Bertram Srawley) (1 min.)
16—(A) Chaplin shows in cabinet—*The Get-Away* (Hugo Frey) (¾ min.)
17—(A) Chaplin hands purse to policeman—*The Town Clown* (M. L. Lake) (1 min.)
18—(T) Meal time after show—*Desolation* (Giovanni E. Conterno) (¾ min.)
19—(T) Early the next morning—*Here Is Charley* (BROWN) (1 min.)
20—(A) Girl opens wagon door—*The Enchantress* (William Frederick Peters) (2 min.)
21—(T) Run along home—"I'm Falling In Love With Someone" (Victor Herbert) (WHITE) (½ min.)
22—(A) Circus owner shows—Repeat No. 3 (RED) (¼ min.)
23—(A) Circus owner off screen—Repeat No. 21 (WHITE) (¼ min.)
24—(T) The tryout—Repeat No. 19 (BROWN) (1¼ min.)
25—(A) Chaplin sits down second time—*Pirouette* (Herman Finck) (2 min.)
26—(T) Put on the barber shop act—*A Game of Tag* (George J. Trinkaus) (2¾ min.)
27—(T) Now hit me—*Restless Bows* (Bertram Srawley) (DK. BLUE) (1¼ min.)
28—(T) Get out and stay out—*Turf Classic* (Paul Marquardt) (½ min.)
29—(A) Pony chased off—Girl shows—Repeat No. 19 (BROWN) (1 ¼ min.)
30—(T) Show's starting—Repeat No. 21 (WHITE) (1 min.)
31—(T) The show on—*Farcical Allegro* (Morris Aborn) (1 ¾ min.)
32—(A) Chaplin has plates—Repeat No. 28 (1 ½ min.)
33—(A) Chaplin bows to audience—*Here Is Charley* (BROWN) (1 min.)
34—(T) The circus prospered—*Sunshine and Flowers* (William C. Schoenfeld) (1¼ min.)
35—(A) Pie hits man in face—Repeat No. 22 (RED) (½ min.)
36—(T) Keep him busy—Repeat No. 33 (BROWN) (¾ min.)
37—(T) A sick horse—Repeat No. 27 (DK. BLUE) (¼ min.)
38—(A) Chaplin blows pill—Repeat No. 28 (½ min.)
39—(A) Chaplin in lion's cage—*The Clown* (Dudley Peele) (2 min.)
40—(A) Girl on ground recovers from faint—Repeat No. 33 (BROWN) (1 min.)
41—(A) Chaplin slides down tent pole—"I'm

Falling In Love With Someone" (WHITE) (½ min.)

42—(A) Chaplin disturbed by big boss—*Restless Bows* (DK. BLUE) (¾ min.)

43—(A) Big boss off screen—Repeat No. 41 (WHITE) (½ min.)

44—(A) Circus owner shows—*Suspicions* (RED) (¾ min.)

45—(T) If you strike that girl—Repeat No. 33 (BROWN) (½ min.)

46—(T) The next show—*Thunder and Blazes* (2¼ min.)

47—(T) A new added attraction—*Gloaming* (Leo Kempinski) (2 ¼ min.)

48—(A) Chaplin has plates—*20th Century* (Frank Bub) (¼ min.)

49—(T) The act over—*A Remembered Kiss* (Kate Vannah) (1 ¼ min.)

50—(A) Tight rope walker puts on cloak and enters circus ring—*Valse Nanette* (Rudolf Friml) (2 ½ min.)

51—(T) Time brought—*Here Is Charley* (BROWN) (1 min.)

52—(T) The next performance—Repeat No. 44 (RED) (¾ min.)

53—(A) Chaplin walks off from circus manager—Repeat No. 42 (DK. BLUE) (1 ¾ min.)

54—(T) He'll kill himself—Repeat No. 51 (BROWN) (¾ min.)

55—(A) Chaplin meets girl—Repeat No. 41 (WHITE) (¾ min.)

56—(A) Bag hits Chaplin—*The Clown* (1 ¼ min.)

57—(A) Chaplin walks into circus ring—*Valse Nanette* (2 ½ min.)

58—(A) Safety rope breaks from Chaplin's waist—Repeat No. 42 (DK. BLUE) (2 ½ min.)

59—(A) Bicycle runs into grocery store—*The Seething Mob* (Edmond Varnier) (¾ min.)

60—(T) You're through—"My Blue Heaven" (Walter Donaldson) (1 ½ min.)

61—(A) Circus scene after title: "You stay here"—Repeat No. 56 (1 ¼ min.)

62—(T) The next morning—"I'm Falling In Love With Someone" (WHITE) (¾ min.)

63—(T) The Circus ready to leave—*Suspicions* (Baron) (RED) (½ min.)

64—(A) Circus owner reads paper—Repeat No. 62 (WHITE) (1 ½ min.)

65—(A) Chaplin stands up after circus moves off—Repeat No. 51 (BROWN) (¾ min.)

Notes printed at the end of the cue sheet: Proper rest period is Nos. 31 to 45 inclusive.

IMPORTANT NOTE: The Chaplin number— "Here Is Charley," used for No. 7 and thereafter, should always begin at the 11th bar. The repetition of numbers in this cue sheet is simplified by the use of the "LUZ" SYMPHONIC COLOR GUIDE…. The color suggested for repetition of numbers designates the Mood or Emotion, and is used as a code for such repetitions.

City Lights (Original Cue Sheet, 1931)

Music by Charles Chaplin
Arranged and orchestrated by Arthur Johnston
Conducted by Alfred Newman
Recorded at United Artists, December 31, 1930, and January 2–3, 5–6, 23–24, 1931

1—Original Opening Music
2—Original
3—Fanfare
4—Original
5—Fanfare
6—Original
7—Fox-Trot
8—"The Star-Spangled Banner"
9—Original
10—"Hail, Hail the Gang's All Here"
11—Original Theme
12—"Dixie"
13—Original
14—"I Hear You Calling Me"
15—Original
16—"Home, Sweet Home"
17—Promenade Theme
18—Valse Theme
19—"Who'll Buy My Violets?"
20—Original
21—Original
22—Original
23—Original
24—Original
25—Clarinet Effects
26—Dramatic Music
27—Original
28—Original
29—Original
30—Original
31—Original
32—"Swanee River"
33—Original
34—"How Dry I Am"
35—Original
36—Original
37—"Who'll Buy My Violets?"
38—Original Valse
39—Original Valse

40—Original
41—Original
42—Original
43—Piano Crash
44—Original
45—Fox-Trot
46—Piano Extemporaneous
47—Original
48—Original
49—Valse
50—Valse
51—Fox-Trot
52—Valse
53—Original
54—Original
55—Chimes
56—Original
57—Original
58—"How Dry I Am" (Paraphrase)
59—Original
60—"Who'll Buy My Violets?"
61—Original
62—Original
63—Original
64—Original
65—Chimes
66—Original
67—Original
68—Original
69—Original
70—Original
71—Original
72—"St. Louis Blues"
73—Original
74—Extemporaneous
75—"I Hear You Calling Me"
76—Whistling
77—"I Hear You Calling Me"
78—Chimes
79—Original
80—Original
81—Valse
82—Original
83—"Who'll Buy My Violets?"
84—Original
85—Original
86—Original
87—Original
88—Original
89—Bassoon Solo
90—Horn Solo
91—Violin Pizzicato
92—Original
93—Original
94—Original
95—Original

96—Oboe Solo
97—Horn Solo
98—Horn Solo
99—2 Trumpets
100—Original
101—Original
102—Original
103—Original
104—Original
105—Original
106—Original
107—Original
108—Original
109—Original
110—Original
111—Original
112—Original
113—Original
114—Original
115—Original
116—Original
117—Original
118—Original
119—Bass Pizzicato
120—Original
121—Original
122—Original
123—Original
124—Chimes
125—Original
126—Original
127—Original
128—Original
129—"Who'll Buy My Violets?"
130—Original
131—"Who'll Buy My Violets?"
132—Original

City Lights
(Revised Cue Sheet, July 1972)

Compiled by Eric James

1—Original Opening Music
2—Cast Credits
3—Fade in to Crowd (fanfare)
4—Title: "To the people of this city, etc."
5—Speaker beckons (fanfare)
6—Statue unveiled
7—Cut back from C.C. on statue
8—"The Star-Spangled Banner"
9—Policeman beckons C.C. (lively fox-trot)
10—S.T. "Afternoon"
11—As C.C. walks towards shop window
   (Valse "Promenade")
12—Fade in to flowers ("Who'll Buy My Violets?")

13—S.T. "Evening"
14—Virginia Cherrill waters flowers (Violin melody)
15—S.T. "Night" (Misterioso)
16—Man picks up heavy stone (Fast dramatic)
17—Clarinet effects
18—C.C. hops on one leg
19—S.T. "No, I'll end it all"
20—Man puts out his arm
21—C.C. climbs out of the water (minor music)
22—"Swanee River" (2-bar interpolation)
23—Minor music continues
24—"How Dry I Am" (4-bar interpolation)
25—Man falls into the water
26—Man helps C.C. out of water
27—C.C. walking down steps ("Who'll Buy My Violets?")
28—Fade in to drawing room (Valse in Apr)
29—Man approaches C.C. (Valse in C)
30—C.C. pours drink over his chest (includes piano crash)
31—Man throws drink on floor
32—C.C. holds man's arm
33—Piano crash (long reverb.)
34—C.C. gets up from couch
35—S.T. "No, I'll live" (Fast Fox-trot)
36—Piano extemporization
37—Waitress takes ticket from C.C.
38—Cigarette girl at table
39—Woman sits on chair (Valse)
40—Waiter takes plates from table (Bright Fox-trot)
41—Apache dancers enter (Valse)
42—Shot of band (Fast Fox-trot)
43—S.T. "Early morning, homeward bound" (Chimes)
44—C.C. & man enter car
45—Car drives off quickly (Fade out)
46—Car stops outside house
47—S.T. "I like your Car" ("How Dry I Am")
48—C.C. goes to closed door
49—C.C. sits on steps ("Who'll Buy My Violets?")
50—C.C. runs into house
51—C.C. runs out of house
52—C.C. talks to girl (Virginia Cherrill)
53—C.C. kisses girl's hand
54—Shot of man with milk bottle
55—S.T. "The sober-dawn wakens a different man" (Chimes)
56—Man asleep on couch
57—C.C. arrives in car
58—C.C. pushed away from door
59—Back shot of C.C.'s legs
60—Man approaches C.C.

61—Elderly lady cuts bread (Valse)
62—S.T. "That afternoon"
63—"St. Louis Blues"
64—S.T. "The Party"
65—Cut to crowd (Chimes)
66—Vocalist prepares to sing (but never does) ("I Hear You Calling Me")
67—Taxi stops outside building
68—S.T. "The morning after" (Chimes)
69—C.C. in bed
70—C.C. scratches
71—C.C. snatches food from tray (Galop)
72—Cut to man pouring coffee (Valse)
73—F.I. to street
74—Girl (V.C.) in bed ("Who'll Buy My Violets?")
75—S.T. "Determined to help the girl he found work"
76—Letter insert
77—S.T. "Lunchtime"
78—C.C. hangs up towel
79—Boss calls C.C.
80—S.T. "To play the part of a gentleman, etc."
81—C.C. walks toward V.C.
82—C.C. returns with album
83—S.T. "Late"
84—C.C. walks toward man in doorway
85—S.T. "That night"
86—Man softening boxing gloves
87—Man throws cigar on floor
88—C.C. passes matches to boxer
89—C.C. returns lucky mascot (rabbit's foot) to boxer
90—Seconds bring boxer into dressing room
91—C.C. scratches his head
92—C.C. puts down smelling salts
93—As C.C. comes out of corner of boxing ring
94—C.C.'s second massages his knee
95—C.C. commences final round
96—C.C. is counted out
97—C.C.'s opponent exits from ring
98—C.C. lying on table
99—S.T. "Still hoping to get money, etc."
100—S.T. "Back from Europe"
101—F.I. to burglars in bedroom
102—C.C. enters
103—C.C. leans against back of settee
104—Burglars appear from behind curtain
105—C.C. talks to man on settee
106—Man leans back on settee
107—C.C. gets up from settee
108—The police arrive
109—Music commences under sound of police siren

110—F.I. beginning of reel
111—C.C. kisses girl's (V.C.) hand
112—C.C. walks toward girl
113—C.C. held by cops
114—S.T. "Autumn" ("Who'll Buy My Violets?")
115—Pan to C.C. walking across street
116—C.C. picks up rose from gutter
117—C.C. looks at girl (V.C.) through shop window
118—Girl holds C.C.'s hand—Music to "The End" title

Modern Times

Music by Charles Chaplin
Arranged and orchestrated by Edward Powell and David Raksin
Conducted by Alfred Newman
Recorded at United Artists, November 18–22, 29–30, December 2–4, 16–17, 1935

1—Main Title—"Modern Times"
2—Sheep
3—Shot of Factory Machine
4—Bolt Stops
5—Factory Set
6—Valse
7—After President's image says "Hey"
8—Fanfare
9—Chords
10—"Lunch time."
11—Charlie's exit bars
12—Dance
13—Machine starts to turn
14—Inventor comes
15—Feeding machine
16—Charlie at belt
17—Charlie in machine
18—Ballet
19—Fat woman
20—Presto
21—Charlie & Sammy at switchboard
22—Interior
23—Coda
24—"Cured of a nervous breakdown…"
25—Visions
26—"Hallelujah, I'm a Bum"
27—Calls "Hey"
28—Paraphrase on "Hallelujah, I'm a Bum"
29—The gamin
30—Slow
31—Interior of shack
32—The father
33—Girl sneaks thru
34—"Prisoners Song"
35—Charlie marches to new cell
36—Charlie sits
37—Prisoners mark time
38—Warden exits
39—Searching
40—C. starts eating
41—After first whistle
42—Group seen
43—After first shot
44—"Hallelujah, I'm a Bum"
45—Trouble
46—Warden turns
47—The minister
48—Charlie smiles
49—Charlie and warden
50—Allegro
51—"Hallelujah, I'm a Bum"
52—Alone and hungry
53—He grabs her arm
54—It was the girl
55—C. puts hands to hips
56—Valse
57—Black Maria
58—Girl gets in wagon
59—C.U. girl
60—Points cane
61—Dream house
62—As Charlie lifts
63—Fast
64—Toy Department
65—Valse
66—Fifth floor
67—Basement
68—Charlie is parallel
69—Man in basement
70—Girl sleeping
71—Clock at 9:30
72—"How Dry I Am" paraphrase
73—"Hallelujah, I'm a Bum"
74—Ten days
75—Girl moves
76—"She picks up—"
77—Fade in
78—Girl points to table
79—C.U. Newspaper
80—Work at last
81—Agitato
82—Fanfare
83—The mechanic…
84—Machinery still
85—At picture
86—Charlie pushes lever
87—"Hallelujah, I'm a Bum"
88—Mysterioso
89—Coda
90—Hurdy gurdy
91—One week later

92—Chatter
93—Fade in
94—That night
95—C. pushes door
96—Presto
97—After C. points
98—Football player
99—Fanfare
100—College song
101—Fanfare
102—Singing waiters
103—"In the Evening by the Moonlight"
104—"Come Along, Sister Mary"
105—Fanfare
106—"Titine"
107—Charlie throws kiss
108—After Henry exits
109—Dawn
110—Love theme and end title

The Great Dictator

All cues by Charles Chaplin and Meredith
Willson unless otherwise indicated
Arranged and orchestrated by Leo Arnaud,
Roy Chamberlain, Carmen Dragon, Romo Falk,
John Hicks, and Meredith Willson
Conducted by Meredith Willson
Recorded at RCA Studios, August 15, 16, 21,
and 23, 1940
Cues used in the film are numbered
Unused cues are not numbered
Arrangers are listed in parentheses

1—Main Title (Romo Falk)
Trench Sequence (Falk)
Grease Her Up (Falk)
The Dud (Roy Chamberlain)
Check the Fuse (Chamberlain)
Grenade Humoresque (Carmen Dragon)
Lost in a Fog (Falk)
Every Man to the Front (Falk)
Schultz's Entrance (Chamberlain)
The Escape (Chamberlain)
Soliloquy (Chamberlain)
Unreadable cue title (Chamberlain)
2—Schultz's Dream (Chamberlain)
3—Montage #1 (The Old Order Changeth)
(Falk)
Dispatches to Schmeloffel (Dragon)
4—Horse's A--manship March (Hicks)
5—Ghetto Sign (Chamberlain)
6—Entrance of Hannah (Chamberlain)
7—Aryan Song (in F) (Falk)
Trench Sequence #1 (Falk)
8—Hannah at the Doorstep (Chamberlain)

9—Barber Shop Opening (Dragon)
10—Barber Shop Fight (Dragon)
11—Stagger Dance (Dragon)
12—They've Gone (Chamberlain)
13—Charlie's Last Capture (Chamberlain)
Dissolve to Palace (Chamberlain)
14—Horse's A--manship March (Hicks)
15—Piano Improvisation (Charles Chaplin)
16—Bugle Call (Falk)
17—Rape of Leeda (Falk)
Fade Into Ghetto (Leo Arnaud)
18—Zigeuner (Arnaud)
19—Hannah's Soliloquy (Arnaud)
Transformation Scene (Chamberlain)
20—Hope Springs Eternal (Chamberlain)
21—Hope Springs Eternal (Chamberlain)
22—Scene De Ballet (Falk)
23—Vorspeil *Lohengrin* (Richard Wagner,
arranged by Willson)
24—*Hungarian Dance #5* (Johannes Brahms,
arranged by Willson)
Jaeckel's Exit (Falk)
Quaintness of Hannah (Chamberlain)
25—Zigeuner (Arnaud)
26—Ze Boulevardier (Dragon)
27—Aryan Song (in E) (Falk)
Roof Top Scene (Chamberlain)
28—Hope Springs Eternal (Chamberlain)
29—Minuet (Ignacy Jan Paderewski) (Chaplin)
Empty Street Montage (Chamberlain)
30—Zigeuner (Arnaud)
31—Pudding Mysterioso (Dragon-Falk)
Roof Top Hurry (Falk)
32—The Escape (Falk)
33—Concentration Camp (no orchestrator
listed)
34—Osterlich Bridge (Dragon-Chamberlain)
35—Pretzelberger March (Willson)
36—Napoli March (Arnaud)
Schwein Knocken March (Hicks)
Spaghetti March (Willson)
37—Bugle
38—Napoli March (Arnaud)
39—Valse Triste (Chamberlain-Dragon)
40—Ball Room Appassionato #1 (Arnaud)
41—Ball Room Appassionato #2
(Chamberlain)
42—Bugle (Arnaud)
At the Border (Falk)
43—Invasion of Osterlich (Falk)
Our Only Hope (Falk)
44—Drum Beats
45—Hope Springs Eternal (Chamberlain)
46—Vorspeil *Lohengrin* (Wagner, arranged by
Willson)
End Title (no orchestrator listed)

The Gold Rush (1942 Score)

All cues composed by Charlie Chaplin and Max Terr unless otherwise indicated
Conducted by Max Terr
Recorded at RCA Studios, October 27–November 3, 1941
Cue titles from the 1972 cue sheet compiled by Eric James and John Guthridge that differ from the original 1942 cue sheet are marked in parentheses and quotes

1—Opening Reel #1
2—Snowbound (Max Terr-Gerard Carbonara)
3—Love Theme in D-flat (Brahms-Chaplin-Terr)
4—On the Trail
5—Chaplin Medley ("The Bluebells of Scotland"/"Coming Thru the Rye"/On the Trail/"Loch Lomond")
6—Coming Thru the Rye/On the Trail
7—Blizzard (Carbonarra)
8—Charlie's Entrance
9—*The Flight of the Bumblebee* (Rimsky-Korsakov-Terr)
10—The Bone
11—The Fight (Carbonara-Terr)
12—Charlie & Jim
13—On the Trail
14—Hunger Theme ("Evening Star") (Wagner-Chaplin-Terr)
15—The Candle
16—On the Trail
17—Snowbound (Terr-Carbonara)
18—Larsen & the Law (Terr-Carbonara)
19—Hunger Theme ("Evening Star") (Wagner-Chaplin-Terr)
20—Valse Mange
21—Hunger Theme ("Evening Star") (Wagner-Chaplin-Terr)
22—Chicken Sequence (Terr-Carbonara)
23—Leaps & Creeps (Chaplin)
24—Next Morning & Chicken Chase
25—Leaps (Chaplin)
26—Triumph
27—Larsen's Escape (Carbonara)
28—Farewell
29—Larsen's Escape (Carbonara)
30—The Waste
31—Snowbound (Terr-Carbonara)
32—*A Thousand Kisses* (Archibald Joyce)
33—Pagliapin
34—*A Thousand Kisses* (Joyce)
35—Love Theme (Brahms-Chaplin-Terr)
36—Valse Elegant
37—Love Theme (Brahms-Chaplin-Terr)
38—Valse Charmante
39—Valse Introduction
40—Valse Specialty ("Sleeping Beauty") (Tchaikovsky-Terr)
41—Valse Charmante
42—Charlie & Jack
43—The Winnah
44—Farewell
45—Papillons (Terr)
46—Work Theme (Terr)
47—Farewell
48—Snow Scene (Brahms-Chaplin-Terr)
49—Love Theme ("Georgia at Door") (Brahms-Chaplin-Terr)
50—Pagliapin
51—Love Theme (Brahms-Chaplin-Terr)
52—Valse Elegante (Chaplin)/Valse Elegant Part #2 (Terr)
53—Love Theme (Brahms-Chaplin-Terr)
54—Snow Scene (Brahms-Chaplin-Terr)
55—Love Theme ("Georgia's Glove") (Brahms-Chaplin-Terr)
56—Work Theme (Terr)
57—Carnival (Terr)
58—Valse Elegant
59—Snow Scene ("Charlie's Surprise") (Brahms-Chaplin-Terr)
60—Donkey Serenade (Terr-Carbonara)
61—Love Theme (Brahms-Chaplin-Terr)
62—Valse Charmante
63—Mother's Dance
64—Love Theme ("Before Transformation") (Brahms-Chaplin-Terr)
65—"Happy New Year" ("Doxology") (Louis Bourgeois-Terr)
66—"Auld Lang Syne"
67—Country Dances ("Speed the Plow" & "Liverpool Hornpipe")
68—"Pretty Girl Milking Her Cow"
69—Snow Scene (Brahms-Chaplin-Terr)
70—Pagliapin ("Georgia Sees Table")
71—Jim at Recorder's
72—Valse Mange
73—Love Theme (Brahms-Chaplin-Terr)
74—Leaps Around
75—Snowbound (Terr-Carbonara)
76—Love Theme (Brahms-Chaplin-Terr)
77—On the Trail ("Back to Cabin")
78—Work Theme (Terr)
79—"Good Night, Ladies"
80—Work Theme (Chaplin-Terr)
81—Blizzard (Carbonara)
82—*William Tell* ("After the Storm") (Gioachino Rossini)
83—Hands on Head
84—See Saw
85—Jim Excited

86—Leaps to Safety
87—*The Flight of the Bumblebee* (Rimsky-
   Korsakov-Terr)
88—On the Trail ("Eureka")
89—*The Flight of the Bumblebee*
90—On the Trail
91—Jolly ("For He's a Jolly Good Fellow")
92—Valse Mange
93—Easy
94—Pagliapin
95—Easy
96—Work Theme (Chaplin-Terr)
97—Love Theme (Brahms-Chaplin-Terr)
98—Valse Elegante
99—Finale ("Love Theme") (Brahms-Chaplin-
   Terr)

Monsieur Verdoux

Music by Charles Chaplin
Arranged and conducted by Rudy Schrager
Recorded at RCA Studios, January 9, 14–17, 1947
Parentheses indicate different title names on
the music manuscripts

1—Main Title
2—The Garden
3—Prefect of Police ("Connection Motif")
4—House for Sale ("For Sale Sign")
5—Train
6—A Paris Boulevard ("Can Can")
7—A Cat
8—Train
9—Prelude to Murder
10—Stairway Mysterioso
11—Dawn
12—A Kitchen
13—Train
14—Mona
15—Mona ("Wheels Mona Into House")
16—Train
17—A Paris Boulevard
18—That Night
19—Train
20—A Paris Boulevard
21—Train
22—An Experiment
23—A Girl in the Rain
24—Scrambled Eggs
25—A Kindness (Mona Theme)
26—Train
27—A Paris Boulevard
28—Train
29—A Paris Boulevard
30—Train
31—A Mixup

32—An Aftermath
33—The Lake
34—A Paris Apartment
35—A Paris Apartment
36—A Paris Apartment
37—Insert
38—The Crash
39—Montage
40—A Paris Boulevard
41—Tango Bitterness
42—Rhumba Hysteria
43—Train
44—Train
45—Train
46—Finale

Limelight (Handwritten Cue Sheet)

Music by Charles Chaplin
Arranged by Raymond Rasch, Larry Russell
(?), and Russell Garcia
Ballet Music recorded on August 3, 1951, at Glen
Glenn Sound Studio, Bernard Katz conducting
Ballet Music re-recorded September 19–20,
1951, at Glen Glenn Sound Studio, Keith Williams
conducting
Song vocals recorded October 18, 1951, at Glen
Glenn Sound Studio, Ray Rasch accompanied
on piano
Song background recorded November 6, 1951,
at Glen Glenn Sound Studio, Keith Williams
conducting
Street musicians recorded May 28, 1952, at
RCA Studios
Score recorded June 10 & 17, 1952, at RCA
Studios, Keith Williams conducting
Barrel organ re-recorded August 13, 1952, at
RCA Studios, Ray Rasch at the piano

1—Main Title
2—Terry's Theme in G
3—Pas de Deux
4—Hurdy Gurdy
5—Awakening (Long)
6—Awakening
7—Awakening
8—Derelicts—Big Ben
9—"Animal Trainer"
10—Criterion Waltz
11—Hurdy Gurdy
12—Derelicts—Big Ben
13—"Spring Song"
14—"Spring Song" Vamp
15—Satire Waltz
16—Hurdy Gurdy
17—Awakening

18—I Can Walk (Piano)
19—Twilight
20—Child's Theme
21—"Sardine Song" (Middlesex)
22—Awakening
23—I Can Walk (Orch)
24—Empire Intro
25—Empire Promenade
26—Nocturne
27—Nocturne Sweetener
28—Piano—Terry's Tryout (Ballet Music)
29—Awakening
30—Love Waltz
31—Ballet Intro
32—Terry's Theme in F
33—Comic Motion (Perpetual Slow Motion)
34—Anxiety
35—Dance Columbine
36—Transition
37—Moon Dance
38—Emotion
39—Corps de Ballet
40—Regrets
41—Terry's Theme
42—Button Bridge
43—Pas de Deux
44—End Dance
45—Criterion Waltz
46—Love Waltz
47—Hurdy Gurdy
48—Awakening
49—Child's Theme
50—Banjo Track ("It's Love")
51—Nocturne
52—Derelicts—Big Ben
53—Empire Intro
54—Empire Promenade
55—Criterion Waltz
56—Shack Waltz (from *Modern Times*)
57—"Animal Trainer"
58—"Animal Trainer" Background
59—"Sardine Song"
60—"Sardine Song" Splits
61—Violin Concerto
62—Death Scene
63—Finale
64—Terry's Theme
65—Criterion Waltz

Limelight (1972 Cue Sheet)

Prepared by Eric James & John Guthridge

1—Ballet Intro
2—Terry's Theme
3—Hurdy Gurdy Waltz

4—Awakening
5—Awakening
6—Awakening
7—Derelicts—Big Ben
8—Trumpet Fanfare
9—"Animal Trainer" Song (Vocal)
10—"Animal Trainer" Song (Vocal)
11—Derelicts—Big Ben
12—"Spring Song" Vocal
13—Satire Waltz
14—Awakening
15—I Can Walk (Solo Piano)
16—Twilight (Solo Piano)
17—Child's Theme
18—"Sardine Song" (Vocal)
19—Awakening
20—I Can Walk
21—Empire Intro & Promenade
22—Nocturne
23—Terry's Try-Out (Solo Piano)
24—Terry's Theme ("Eternally") (Solo Piano)
25—Ballet Music (Solo Piano)
26—Awakening
27—Love Waltz
28—Love Waltz (2nd part)
29—Ballet Intro
30—Terry's Theme ("Eternally")
31—Comic Notion
32—Anxiety
33—Dance Columbine
34—Transition
35—Moon Dance
36—Emotion
37—Corps de Ballet (Waltz)
38—Regrets
39—Terry's Theme
40—Button Bridge
41—Terry's Theme
42—Pas de Deux
43—End Dance
44—Criterion Waltz
45—Love Waltz
46—Awakening
47—Child's Theme
48—"It's Love" Song (Vocal with banjo accomp.)
49—Nocturne
50—Derelicts—Big Ben
51—Empire Intro
52—Empire Promenade
53—Love Waltz
54—"Animal Trainer" Song (Vocal)
55—"Sardine Song"
56—"Sardine Song" Splits
57—Bright Orchestral Background
58—Bright Orchestral Background
59—Bright Orchestral Background

60—Violin Concerto
61—Violin Concerto
62—Violin Concerto
63—Death Scene
64—Terry's Theme ("Eternally")
65—Criterion Waltz

A King in New York
(Handwritten Cue Sheet)

Music by Charles Chaplin
Arranged by Boris Sarbek, Peter Knight, Philip Sainton
Conducted by Leighton Lucas
Songs recorded on March 14, 1956, at Elstree Studios, Peter Knight conducting
Songs re-recorded May 1, 1956 (Philip Sainton conducting one number), plus May 18 & 23 at Shepperton Studios
Score and songs recorded January 25–29, 1957, at Shepperton Studios, Leighton Lucas conducting

M1–4—Main Titles Music–Fanfare
M2–3—Main Titles Music–Generique
M4–2—Revolution
M4–2—Revolution
M2–3—Generique
M1–1—Jungle Music
M3–9—"Million Dollars"
M25–6—"Weeping Willows"
M23–2—"Rock & Roll" (Gary Miller)
M5–3—CinemaScope Fanfare
M6–3—CinemaScope Fanfare
M7–1—CinemaScope Fanfare
M8–1—CinemaScope Fanfare
M9–1—CinemaScope Fanfare
M3–9—"Million Dollars"
M30–1—(Piano) For Restaurant
M24–2—Jazz for Restaurant
M1A–1—Jazz for Restaurant
M16–2—Mandoline (Queen's music)
M16–3—Mandoline (Varied Version)
M16–1—Mandoline (Varied Version)
M16–2—Mandoline (Same as Reel 2)
M1X–T2—"I'd Sell My Soul for Love"
M20–3—Gavotte (Comedy Music)
M21–1—Comedy for Bathroom (Salle de Bain)
M14–3—Park Avenue Waltz
M14–4—Park Avenue Waltz (Varied Version)
M7–1—"Juke Box"
M12–2—Martini
M14–4—Park Avenue Waltz
M20–3—Gavotte (Comedy Music)
M20–3—Gavotte (Comedy Music)

Boys Hum (Ad lib) "Black Eyes" (distorted version)
M15–5—"Spring's the Time for Making Love"
M15–6—Ditto (Orchestra Section Only)
M11–1—Crown Whiskey Montage
M11–1—Ditto
M11–1—Ditto
M3–1—"Now That It's Ended" (Joy Nichols)
M11–1—Crown Whiskey Montage
M25–5—"Weeping Willows"
M25–5—"Weeping Willows"
M10–2—Mysterioso
M22–2—Chess Piece
M10–2—Mysterioso
M25–5—"Weeping Willows
M10–2—Mysterioso
M10–2—Ditto
M4–1—Fanfare (Press Montage)
M10–2—Mysterioso
M4–1—Fanfare (Press Montage)
M16–2—Mandoline (Queen's)
M25–5—"Weeping Willows"
M3–2—End Titles Music

A King in New York
(Official Cue Sheet)

1—Main Titles (Fanfare & Generique)
2—Revolution
3—Generique
4—Jungle Rhythm
5—"Million Dollars"
6—"Weeping Willows"
7—"I Got Shoes (Rock & Roll)"
8—'Scope Fanfares
9—"Million Dollars"
10—Serenade
11—Restaurant Jazz
12—Mandoline Number
13—Mandoline Number
14—"I'd Sell My Soul for Love"
15—Bathroom Gavotte
16—Salle de Bain
17—Park Avenue Waltz
18—Park Avenue Waltz
19—"Juke Box"
20—Martini
21—Park Avenue Waltz
22—Comedy Gavotte
23—Black Eyes
24—"Spring's the Time for Making Love"
25—Whisky Montage
26—"Now That It's Ended"
   ["Paperhangers," accidentally left off original cue sheet]
27—Whisky Montage

28—"Weeping Willows"
29—"Weeping Willows"
30—Mysterioso
31—Chess Music
32—Mysterioso
33—"Weeping Willows"
34—Mysterioso
35—Fanfare
36—Mysterioso
37—Fanfare
38—Mandoline
39—"Weeping Willows"
40—End Titles Music

The Chaplin Revue

Music by Charles Chaplin
Arranged by Eric James, with the assistance of Jack Moss on *Shoulder Arms* and *The Pilgrim*
Orchestrated and conducted by Eric Spear
A Dog's Life recorded at Shepperton Studios, January 12–14, 1959
Shoulder Arms and *The Pilgrim* recorded at Shepperton Studios, February 18–20, 23–35, 1959

A Dog's Life
1—Dog's Life Theme
2—Labour Exchange
3—Dog's Life Theme
4—Dog Chase
5—Dog's Life Theme
6—Green Lantern Rag
7—Coffee and Cakes
8—Green Lantern Snag
9—Flat Feet
10—The Shimmy
11—Song Triste
12—Coda
13—3 Rags
14—Coffee and Cakes
15—Jazz
16—Coffee and Cakes
17—Robbers
18—Robber Buries Money
19—Jazz
20—Dog Digging
21—Charley [*sic*] Finds Money
22—Rag
23—Coda
24—Romance
25—March
26—D–Minor Theme
27—Robbers
28—Tete a Tete
29—Bar (Robbers)
30—Galop

31—Coffee and Cakes
32—Dog's Life Theme

Shoulder Arms
1—Main Titles
2—Flat Feet
3—Sauerkraut March
4—Shell Happy
5—Changing Guard
6—Peace
7—The Post
8—Sauerkraut March
9—Bugle Call
10—Flat Feet
11—Bugle Call
12—Shell Happy
13—Over the Top
14—Sauerkraut March
15—Peace
16—Flat Feet
17—Inner March
18—Tree Cam
19—Suspense Cam
20—Agitato
21—Agitato
22—Mysterioso March
23—The Enemy
24—Agitato
25—D–Minor Waltz
26—Inner March
27—The Enemy
28—Inner March
29—Mysterioso March
30—Bugle Call
31—Sauerkraut March
32—Mysterioso March
33—Mysterioso March
34—Inner March
35—Eerie
36—Inner March
37—Trombone Sweetener
38—Eerie
39—Bringing Home the Bacon
40—Trumpet Call
41—End Title
42—The Post

The Pilgrim
1—Texas Vocal
2—Jitters
3—Hope and Faith
4—Texas Vocal
5—Texas Border
6—Old Ladies March
7—The Service
8—The Deacon Presents

9—Opening Hymn
10—The Deacon Presents
11—The Collection Hymn
12—The Deacon Presents
13—David and Goliath
14—Bringing Back the Bacon
15—Kitchen and Curate
16—The Collection Box
17—Texas
18—Prison Companions
19—Family Album
20—Tea Party
21—Family Album
22—Kitchen and Curate
23—The Deacon Presents
24—Cake
25—Texas Border
26—Prison Companions
27—Conjuring Thieves
28—Conjuror No. 2
29—Waltz Despair
30—Door Opening
31—Waltz despair
32—Door Opening (2)
33—Peace
34—Texas
35—Prison Companions
36—Jitters
37—But You Don't Care
38—Texas Border
39—Texas Vocal

The Pilgrim (1922 Cue Sheet)

Compiled by James C. Bradford
* Published by Cameo Thematic Music Co.

1—At Screening—*Peter Piper* (S. R. Henry) (1¼ min.)
2—(Action) Pilgrim At R.R. Station—THEME: "Somebody" (George Little) (1¾ min.)
3—(Action) Pilgrim Enters R.R. Station—*Spangles* (John W. Bratton) (1½ min.)
4—(Action) Deacons At Bulletin—*The Hay Ride* (Theodore Bendix) (1¾ min.)
5—(Title) Sunday Morning—"Somebody" (2¾ min.)
6—(Action) Insert—Telegram—"I'm Always Stuttering" (Maceo Pinkard) (1¼ min.)
7—(Action) Deacon Tears Telegram—*Mosquito Parade* (Howard Whitney) (1 min.)
8—(Title) The Choir—"On a Sunday Afternoon" (Harry Von Tilzer) (1¼ min.)
9—(Title) Page Hymn 23—"Rejoice and Be Glad" (J. J. Husband) (Hymn) (¾ min.)

10—(Action) Choir Stops—Resume Singing—"Sweet Hour of Prayer" (William B. Bradbury) (1 min.)
11—(Title) The Sermon—"They Didn't Believe Me" (Jerome Kern) (2½ min.)
12—(Action) Pilgrim & Deacon Leave Church—*A Lucky Duck* (Howard Whitney) (2 min.)
13—(Title) Mrs. Brown—"Lady of the Evening" (Irving Berlin) (1¼ min.)
14—(Action) Vision of Jail—*Comrades* (Felix McGlennon, arr. M. L. Lake) (½ min.)
15—(Action) Pilgrim & Mrs. Brown Enter Room—"She May Have Seen Better Days" (James Thornton) (1¾ min.)
16—(Title) Visitors—*Razz Berries* (Frank Banta) (2¾ min.)
17—(Action) Pilgrim Enters Kitchen—"This Is the Life" (Irving Berlin) (2½ min.)
18—(Title) Won't You Stay for Tea?—*Nights of Gladness* (Charles Ancliffe) (1¾ min.)
19—(Action) Pilgrim Starts to Carve—"Where Did You Get That Hat?" (Joseph J. Sullivan) (1 min.)
20—(Title) In the Evening—"How Many Times" (J. Russel Robinson) (2¼ min.)
21—(Action) Enter House—Repeat Theme No. 2 (1¾ min.)
22—(Title) Then You Must Stay—*Marceline* (George J. Trinkaus) (2¾ min.)
23—(Title) Don't Worry, I'll Get It—*Crazy Love* (Licco Liggy) (2¼ min.)
24—(Title) Next Morning—"Just a Little Love Song" (Joe Cooper) (1 min.)
25—(Title) I'm Sorry, Miss—"I Ain't Nobody's Darling" (Robert King) (¾ min.)
26—(Action) Stop At the Border—"Nobody Knows Where Tosti Goes" (George W. Meyer) (1½ min.)
27—(Title) Mexico A New Life—Repeat Theme No. 2 (1 min.)

The Pilgrim (UK Cue Sheet)

Compiled by Edward Van Praag, London Opera House, Kingsway
(T) = Title, (D) = Description

1—(D) View of prison—*Creepy Creeps* (9th bar without repeat) (Billee Taylor)
2—(D) Parson appears—"The Vicar's Song" (*The Sorcerer*) (Arthur Sullivan)
3—(D) Eloping couple—*Humoresque* (Herman Finck)
4—(D) Booking office—*Romany Love* (J. S. Zamecnik)
5—(T) In chapel—"Uncle Remus" from *Woodland Sketches* (Edward MacDowell)

6—(D) Scene in railway carriage—*Greenwich Witch* (Zez Confrey)

7—(D) When out of train—Repeat No. 2

8—(T) You are just in time—*Funeral March of the Marionette* (from 22nd bar) (Charles Gounod)

9—(D) When lacing boots—Pause

10—(D) When resuming walk—Repeat No. 8

11—(D) When given telegram—"Violets" (Ellen Wright)

12—(D) When resume walk—Repeat No. 8

13—(D) When falling—Pause

14—(D)When resume walk—Repeat No. 8

15—(T) Service—Organ Solo (light religious) (Obvious)

16—(T) Hymn 23—*Iphigénie en Tauride* (Letter F to G) (Christoph Willibald Gluck, arr. Tavan)

17—(T) Collection—Repeat No. 16

18—(D) When parson receives boxes—Repeat No. 2

19—(T) Sermon—*The Queen of Sheba* (Mod. Maesto 15 bars repeated) (Charles Gounod)

20—(D) Finish of sermon—Chord off

21—(D) Congregation leave—"Moonlight In Versailles" (George Gershwin)

22—(D) After picking flower—Repeat No. 8

23—(T) Introducing—*Misterioso No. 1* (Otto Langey)

24—(T) In the good old days—Repeat No. 8

25—(D) In the room—*Fairy Tiptoe* (Julian Fredericks)

26—(D) Boy annoys company—*Baby's Sweetheart* (William Corri)

27—(D) When fly-paper on face—"My Mammy Knows" (Harry DeCosta)

28—(D) When Chaplin in kitchen—"Eleanor" (Jessie L. Deppen)

29—(D) In sitting room—*Moments musicaux* (Franz Schubert)

30—(T) Please go on with tea—"Swanee Smiles" (Frederick W. Hager)

31—(D) Sitting at table—Short organ solo

32—(D) Dipping nose in cream—"Away Down East In Maine" (Walter Donaldson)

33—(D) When hat discovered—Pause

34—(No direction)—"Who Tied the Can on the Old Dog's Tail?" (chorus) (Mike Fitzpatrick)

35—(T) In the evening—"In the Gloaming" (Annie Fortescue Harrison)

36—(D) Convict appears—*Les Huguenots* (Letter E) (Giacomo Meyerbeer)

37—(T) Won't you come inside—*Piazza del Popolo* (from *Allegretto*) (Emil Juel-Fredericksen)

38—(D) Trick with handkerchief—*Mysterioso No. 2* (Adolf Minot)

39—(T) I have the money—*Burlesca* (Louise Talma)

40—(T) I'll get lights—*Hurry No. 1* (Otto Langey)

41—(D) Woman returns—Soft tympani roll

42—(D) Woman turns her back—Repeat No. 40

43—(D) Going upstairs—"In the Night" (Joseph G. Gilbert)

44—(D) When fight— *Misterioso No. 3* (J. E. Andino)

45—(D) Chaplin knocked out—Same mysterious beginning

46—(D) Gambling den—*Chanson Triste* (last 28 bars) (Pytor Ilyich Tchaikovsky)

47—(T) A hold-up—*Agitato No. 2* (J. E. Andino)

48—(T) Next morning—"They Didn't Believe Me" (Jerome Kern)

49—(T) I'm sorry—"We'll Have a Jubilee in My Old Kentucky Home" (slow and soft) (Walter Donaldson)

50—(T) Pick some flowers—"He Picked a Rose" (Joseph G. Gilbert)

51—(D) When Sheriff leaves—"The End of a Perfect Day" (Carrie Jacobs-Bond)

52—(D) Shooting—Pause

53—(D) After shots—Repeat No. 8 *vivace*

Shoulder Arms (1927 Reissue Cue Sheet)

Compiled by Eugene Conte
Published by Cameo Thematic Music Co.
(T) = Title, (A) = Action

1—At screening—*The Wooden Soldier* (John W. Bratton) (2 min.)

2—(T) Over there—"Over There" (George M. Cohan) (2¼ min.)

Note: Play one chorus and segue.
SEGUE—*Ouch* (Mel B. Kaufman)

3—(T) The enemy—*Deutscher Walzer* (J. T. Kaine) (½ min.)

4—(T) A quiet lunch—*Ouch* (1¾ min.)

5—(A) Chaplin alone after mail is distributed—"All Alone" (Irving Berlin) (½ min.)

6—(T) This must be yours—*The Hustler* (Bertram Srawley) (3 min.)

7—(T) To the day—*Carnival Grotesque* (Domenico Savino) (1½ min.)

8—(T) Morning—*Happy Go Lucky* (Mel B. Kaufman) (1½ min.)

9—(A) Officer runs into trench—*Hurry No. 1* (J. S. Zamecnik) (2 min.)

10—(T) The captured trench—*Bohemiana* (Lee Orean Smith) (1 min.)

11—(T) Poor France—"Madelon" (Camille Robert) (¾ min.)

12—(T) Two of a kind—*Keep Going* (Auguste Kleinecke) (1¼ min.)

13—(T) Within the enemy's—Repeat No. 7 *Carnival Grotesque* (1½ min.)

14—(T) More heroic work—*Misterioso No. 5* (J. S. Zamecnik) (¾ min.)

15—(A) Fade-back to Chaplin—Repeat No. 7 *Carnival Grotesque* (¾ min.)

16—(A) Chase starts—*Comedy* (Albert W. Ketelbey) (2 min.)

17—(A) Girl sees Chaplin—"Un peu d'amour" (Lao Silesu) (2 min.)

18—(A) Germans enter—Repeat No. 14 *Misterioso No. 5* (1¼ min.)

19—(A) Chaplin grabs gun—Repeat No. 16 *Comedy* (1 min.)

20—(T) Arrested for aiding—*La Forêt Perfide* (Jean Gabriel-Marie) (1 min.)

21—(A) Soldiers lined up—Repeat No. 1 *The Wooden Soldier* (1¾ min.)

22—(T) His pal captured—*Mignonette* (Domenico Savino) (2 min.)

23—(T) The capture—Repeat No. 8 *Happy Go Lucky* (2 min.)

24—(T) Peace on Earth—"Oh, How I Hate to Get Up in the Morning" (Irving Berlin) (¾ min.)

A Countess from Hong Kong

Music by Charles Chaplin
Arranged by Eric James
Orchestrated and conducted by Lambert Williamson
Recorded at Anvil Recording Studios, September 19–23, 1966
Stereophonic soundtrack album tracks recorded September 27–28

1—Resolve Theme / Chinese Music
2—Dance Hall Waltz / Countess from Hong Kong
3—Girls' Entrance Music / Radio Music
4—Gypsy Violin Caprice
5—Crossing the Floor
6—Ambassador Takes a Bath
7—Defeat
8—(nothing listed on the cue sheet)
9—Resolve
10—Natascha's First Night / Countess from Hong Kong
11—To Sleep / Incidental Business
12—To Sleep / Awakening
13—Chamber Music
14—Incidental Business (Pizzicato Version)
15—Comic Music

16—Comic Music
17—Comic Music
18—Bonjour
19—French Samba
20—Dance Hall Waltz (as quickstep) / Bonjour
21—The Big Waltz / Countess from Hong Kong
22—Countess from Hong Kong
23—Neapolitan Love Song / Bonjour
24—"They Believe in Love"
25—Incidental Business
26—(nothing listed on the cue sheet)
27—Hudson's Bedroom Music / Incidental Business
28—To Sleep / Awakening
29—Incidental Business
30—The Ambassador Takes a Bath
31—Gypsy Music
32—Chamber Music / Crossing the Floor
33—Bonjour
34—We'll Meet Again / Resolve
35—The Tango / Music Reprise of Main Themes

The Circus (1968 Score)

Music Associate Eric James
Orchestrated and conducted by Lambert Williamson
Recorded at Anvil Recording Studios, April 18, 20, 22, 1968

1—"Swing High, Little Girl"
2—Horse Music & Incidental Music
3—Around the Side-shows
4—Recit & Chase
5—Recit & Chase
6—Recit & Chase
7—Mirror Music
8—Chase Music, Mechanical Figures, Chase Music
9—Mirror Music
10—Vanishing Lady
11—Fanfare & Chase
12—Fanfare & Chase
13—Fanfare & Chase
14—His Try-out
15—An Irish Echo
16—His Try-out
17—Barber Shop Music
18—Mule Music
19—An Irish Echo
20—Incidental Music
21—"Swing High, Little Girl"
22—Vanishing Lady
23—Breathless
24—Breathless
25—Vanishing Lady

26—Incidental Music
27—An Irish Echo
28—Incidental Music
29—Fanfare & Galop
30—Dreaming
31—Tight Rope Waltz
32—Tight Rope Waltz
33—Vanishing Lady
34—Vanishing Lady
35—Incidental Music
36—Circus Waltz, Galop & Incidental Music
37—Tight Rope Waltz
38—Rex Missing
39—An Irish Echo
40—Final Wedding
41—Sadness

The Kid (1972 Score)

Arranged by Eric James
Orchestrated and conducted by Eric Rogers
Recorded at Anvil Recording Studios, October
25–29, 1971

1—Opening Music (The Kid)
2—Thieves Music
3—Morning Promenade
4—Letter Music
5—Letter Music
6—Garret Waltz
7—Letter Music
8—Garret Waltz
9—Blue Eyes
10—Breaking Windows
11—Breaking Windows
12—Garret Waltz
13—Organ Waltz
14—The Kid
15—Garret Waltz
16—The Kid's Fight
17—The Kid's Fight
18—Sick Kid
19—Blue Eyes
20—Country Doctor
21—Menace Part 1
22—Menace Part 2
23—Sick Kid
24—Sick Kid
25—The Doss-House
26—The Kid
27—Heavenly Music
28—Jig
29—Garret Waltz
30—Gavotte
31—Minor Gavotte
32—The Doss-House
33—The Kid

The Idle Class

Arranged by Eric James
Orchestrated and conducted by Eric Rogers
Recorded at Anvil Recording Studios, October
25–29, 1971

1—Opening Music
2—Box Theme
3—Charlie's Theme
4—Suspense
5—Charlie's Theme
6—Suspense
7—Charlie's Theme
8—Suspense
9—Unison Theme
10—Suspense
11—Golf Links Waltz
12—Optimism
13—Golf Links Waltz
14—Golf Links Waltz
15—Carefree
16—Optimism
17—South American
18—Fox-trot
19—3M 6 (no cue title given)

Pay Day

Arranged by Eric James
Orchestrated and conducted by Eric Rogers
Recorded at Anvil Recording Studios, November 22 and 24, 1972

1—Opening Music
2—Debussy Music
3—Digging the Trench Music
4—Debussy Music
5—Brick Music
6—Lunch Waltz
7—Brick Music
8—Lunch Waltz
9—Last Bus Music
10—Lunch Waltz
11—Singing Outside the Club Music
12—Sweet Adeline Waltz
13—Last Bus Music
14—Misterioso
15—Finale Music

A Day's Pleasure

Arranged by Eric James
Orchestrated and conducted by Eric Rogers
Recorded at Anvil Recording Studios, August 28 and 30, 1973

1—Opening Music
2—Car Music

3—Boat Ride
4—Jazz
5—Sea Music (featuring Trombone)
6—Deck Chair Waltz
7—Sea Song
8—"Oh, We Won't Get Home 'Till the Morning"
9—Crossroads
10—Tar

Sunnyside

Arranged by Eric James
Orchestrated and conducted by Eric Rogers
Recorded at Anvil Recording Studios, April 30 and May 2, 1974

1—Opening Music
2—Sunnyside Waltz
3—Evergreen Waltz
4—Morning Service
5—Emotional
6—Ballet Music
7—Vamp Number
8—Romance Waltz
9—Bandolero
10—Country Vamp
11—Lounge Lizards
12—Forgotten
13—"When Other Lips" (from *The Bohemian Girl*) (Balfe)
14—"When Other Lips" (from *The Bohemian Girl*) (Balfe)

A Woman of Paris (1976 Score)

Arranged by Eric James
Orchestrated and conducted by Eric Rogers
Recorded at Anvil Recording Studios, February 17, 19, 21, 23, 1976

1—A Woman of Paris
2—Melody in F
3—Nocturne
4—Suspense
5—Nocturne
6—Suspense
7—Nocturne
8—Minor Melody

9—Shock
10—At the Station
11—Shock
12—Restaurant Waltz
13—Revel's Music
14—Restaurant Waltz
15—Revel's Music
16—Restaurant Waltz
17—Marie's Apartment
18—Revel's Business Office
19—Marie's Apartment
20—Champagne
21—Bad News
22—Latin Quarter
23—Latin Quarter
24—Homespun
25—Nocturne
26—Latin Quarter
27—Nocturne
28—Cassette Waltz
29—Bad News
30—Revel's Business Office
31—Bad News
32—Painting Music (Fox-trot)
33—The Necklace (Waltz)
34—The Necklace (Waltz)
35—Bad News
36—The Argument
37—Agitato
38—Shock
39—Revel's Music & Champagne
40—Marie's Apartment & Restaurant Waltz
41—Bad News
42—Massage Scene
43—Shock
44—Revel Waltz
45—Dramatique
46—Restaurant Waltz
47—Shock & Agitato
48—Shock (Theme)
49—At the Station
50—Minor Waltz Melody
51—Shock Theme
52—The Argument
53—Nocturne
54—Restaurant Waltz
55—A Woman of Paris

Chapter Notes

Introduction

1. Howard Lucraft, "Stricter Check on Music Oscars for 'Integrity' & 'Authenticity': Cite Credits to 'Wrong' Parties," *Variety*, January 24, 1973, 5.
2. *Ibid.*, 25.
3. "Tag *Godfather* As Rota Retread In Oscar Hassle," *Variety*, March 7, 1973, 59.
4. "*Limelight* and *Cabaret* Win Music Awards: 1973 Oscars," YouTube video, 4:21, from a performance televised by NBC on March 27, 1973, posted by "Oscars," https://www.youtube.com/watch?v=fmQJqxdLnMo.
5. Rachel Ford to David Raksin, 10 July 1973, ECCI00023494, Charlie Chaplin Archive, Cineteca di Bologna, Bologna, Italy (hereafter cited as CCA).
6. David Robinson, *Chaplin, His Life and Art* (New York: McGraw-Hill, 1985; London: Penguin Books, 2001), xv. Citations refer to the Penguin edition.
7. Henry Gris, "Hollywood Chaplin," ECCI00030190, CCA, 16.
8. *Ibid.*
9. Timothy Brock, "*The Gold Rush*," http://www.timothybrock.com/joomla/articles/18-articles/31-the-gold-rush.
10. Gilbert Seldes, "I Am Here To-day," in *The Essential Chaplin: Perspectives on the Life and Art of the Great Comedian*, ed. Richard Schickel (Chicago: Ivan R. Dee, 2006), 116.

Chapter 1

1. Charlie Chaplin, *My Trip Abroad* (New York: Harper and Brothers, 1922), 62.
2. Charles Chaplin, *My Autobiography* (New York: Simon and Schuster, 1964), 38.
3. Charles Chaplin, *My Life In Pictures* (1974; repr. London: Peerage Books, 1985), 40.
4. Barry Anthony, *Chaplin's Music Hall: The Chaplins and Their Circle in the Limelight* (London: I. B. Tauris & Co. Ltd., 2012), 6.
5. Robinson, *Chaplin*, 7.
6. Chaplin, *My Autobiography*, 18.
7. *Ibid.*
8. Cecilia H. Porter, *Charles Chaplin Senior: Victorian Music Hall Songs* (London: Porter House of Publishing, 2013), 23.
9. Chaplin, *My Autobiography*, 14.
10. Anthony, *Chaplin's Music Hall*, 32.
11. *The Stage*, July 18, 1886, quoted in Anthony, *Chaplin's Music Hall*, 54.
12. *The Era*, January 9, 1886, quoted in Anthony, *Chaplin's Music Hall*, 54.
13. *The Era*, May 8, 1886, quoted in Anthony, *Chaplin's Music Hall*, 54.
14. *The Stage*, March 8, 1894, quoted in Anthony, *Chaplin's Music Hall*, 63.
15. *The North Echo*, quoted in Anthony, *Chaplin's Music Hall*, 62.
16. *Coventry Evening Telegraph*, March 14, 1899, quoted in Anthony, *Chaplin's Music Hall*, 64.
17. *Pearson's Weekly*, September 24, 1921, quoted in Anthony, *Chaplin's Music Hall*, 65.
18. Chaplin, *My Autobiography*, 19.
19. *Ibid.*
20. *Ibid.*, 18.
21. *Evening News*, quoted in Anthony, *Chaplin's Music Hall*, 126.
22. Robinson, *Chaplin*, 41.
23. *Film Weekly*, April 4, 1931, quoted in Anthony, *Chaplin's Music Hall*, 43.
24. Chaplin, *My Autobiography*, 20.
25. *Ibid.*, 21.
26. *Ibid.*, 22.
27. Peter Haining, *The Legend of Charlie Chaplin* (Secaucus, NJ: Castle, 1982), 18.
28. Chaplin, *My Life In Pictures*, 40.
29. Chaplin, *My Autobiography*, 33.
30. *Ibid.*, 20.
31. Anthony, *Chaplin's Music Hall*, 71.
32. Chaplin, *My Autobiography*, 19.
33. Robinson, *Chaplin*, 32.
34. Chaplin, *My Autobiography*, 16.
35. Chaplin, *My Life In Pictures*, 43.
36. Chaplin, *My Autobiography*, 18.
37. Chaplin, *My Autobiography*, 96.
38. Robinson, *Chaplin*, 80.
39. Konrad Bercovici, "Making a Picture with Charlie Chaplin," *The Royal Magazine* (1925), ECCI00029647, CCA, 490.
40. David Robinson, "Charlie & Music" in *The Songs of Charlie Chaplin* (New York: Bourne, 1992), 18.
41. Charles Chaplin and David Robinson, *Footlights with The World of Limelight* (Bologna, Italy: Edizioni Cineteca di Bologna, 2014), 202.
42. John McCabe, *Charlie Chaplin* (1978; repr. London: Robson Books, 1992), 41.
43. A. J. Marriot, *Chaplin Stage by Stage* (A. J. Marriott, 2005), 190.
44. McCabe, *Charlie Chaplin*, 87.
45. Robinson, *Chaplin*, 215.
46. "Roderick White, Right-Handed; Chaplin Still the Sole Left-Handed, Violinist," *Musical America*, March 5, 1921, 34.
47. Robinson, *Chaplin*, 246.

48. Mordaunt Hall, "Shy Charlie Chaplin Opens His Heart," *The New York Times*, August 9, 1925, SM5.

49. "Charlie Chaplin Reciprocates," *The Music Trade Review*, December 21, 1918, 43.

50. Bercovi, "Making a Picture," 490.

51. McCabe, *Charlie Chaplin*, 41.

52. "Music and Musicians: Music Notes and Comment," *The Boston Globe*, February 22, 1925, A44.

53. Chaplin, *My Life in Pictures*, 116.

54. Bercovi, "Making a Picture," 490.

55. "Charley [*sic*] Chaplin Buys Brambach Player," *The Music Trade Review*, January 26, 1918, 38.

56. "Charlie Chaplin Buys Organ," *The Music Trade Review*, July 15, 1922, 18.

57. "Charlie Chaplin's Organ," *PRESTO*, February 3, 1923, 21.

58. "Chaplin Buys Robert-Morton," *The Music Trade Review*, February 7, 1923, 41.

59. "Screen News," *Screenland*, March 1931, 94.

60. "Chaplin Buys An Ampico," *The Music Trade Review*, January 26, 1926, 16.

61. "Through German Eyes," *The New York Times*, August 18, 1929, X4.

62. Jacob Deschin, "Screen Reflections," *The Hartford Courant*, May 9, 1929, 20.

63. *City Lights* Press Book, ECCI00004693, CCA.

64. Charles Chaplin, Jr., N. and M. Rau, *My Father, Charlie Chaplin* (New York: Random House, 1960), 27.

65. *Ibid.*, 71.

66. Anthony, *Chaplin's Music Hall*, 65.

67. Eric James, *Making Music with Charlie Chaplin: An Autobiography* (Lanham, MD: The Scarecrow Press, Inc., 2000), 101.

68. James, *Making Music with Charlie Chaplin*, 93.

69. Robinson, *Chaplin*, 171.

70. *Ibid.*, 106.

71. *Ibid.*, 107.

72. McCabe, *Charlie Chaplin*, 27.

Chapter 2

1. Robinson, *Chaplin*, 112.

2. Chaplin, *My Autobiography*, 141.

3. Robinson, *Chaplin*, 114.

4. Chaplin, *My Autobiography*, 144.

5. *Ibid.*

6. Robinson, *Chaplin*, 123.

7. Chaplin, *My Autobiography*, 153.

8. *Ibid.*, 159.

9. *Ibid.*, 210.

10. Charles J. McQuirk, "Chaplinitis," *Motion Picture Magazine*, July 1915, 121.

11. Chaplin, *My Autobiography*, 114.

12. Chaplin Jr., Rau, Rau, *My Father, Charlie Chaplin*, 19.

13. Georgia Hale, Heather Kieran, ed., *Charlie Chaplin: Intimate Close-Ups* (Lanham, UK: The Scarecrow Press, Inc., 1999), 164.

14. Chaplin, *My Autobiography*, 397.

15. Chaplin Jr., Rau, Rau, *My Father, Charlie Chaplin*, 199.

16. Benjamin De Casseres, "The Hamlet-Like Nature of Charlie Chaplin," in *Charlie Chaplin: Interviews*, ed. Kevin J. Hayes (Jackson, MS: University Press of Mississippi, 2005), 11.

17. "Charlie Chaplin Organizes Music Company for Own Songs," *Motion Picture News*, March 25, 1916, 1728.

18. "Blanchard Hall Is To Be Enlarged," *Los Angeles Sunday Herald*, June 12, 1904, Part Two, 1.

19. Chaplin, *My Autobiography*, 226.

20. Charles Chaplin, "Oh! That Cello" (Los Angeles: Charlie Chaplin Music Publishing Co., 1916), ECCI 00029804, CCA.

21. Charles Chaplin, "There's Always One You Can't Forget," ©Copyright 1974 (Renewed). Published Worldwide by Bourne Co., New York, NY. All Rights Reserved. International Copyright Secured. (ASCAP)

22. "Q R S Co.," *The Music Trade Review*, August 26, 1916, 15.

23. "Western Comment," *The Music Trade Review*, September 9, 1916, 34.

24. Chaplin, *My Autobiography*, 226.

25. *Ibid.*, 227.

26. Frank Vreeland, "Charlie Chaplin, Philosopher, Has Serious Side" in *Charlie Chaplin: Interviews*, ed. Kevin H. Hayes (Jackson, MS: University Press of Mississippi, 2005), 54.

27. "Chaplin at the 'Hip,'" *The Bronxville Review*, February 25, 1916, 4.

28. Cheque to Charles Chaplin/New York Hippodrome, 1916, ECCI00028364, CCA.

29. John Philip Sousa, *Marching Along: Recollections of Men, Women and Music* (1928; repr. Boston: Hales, Cushman & Flint, 1941), 347.

30. "See Chaplin in the Flesh," *The New York Times*, February 21, 1916, 9.

31. "Minus His Cane Chaplin Is Shy," *New York Tribune*, February 21, 1916, 9.

32. Sousa, *Marching Along*, 347.

33. "See Chaplin in the Flesh," *The New York Times*, February 21, 1916, 9.

34. "6,500 Persons See Charlie Chaplin Lead Sousa Band," *St. Louis Post-Dispatch*, February 21, 1916, 1.

35. Pat Padua, "Pic of the Week: Passing the Baton Edition," *In the Muse* (blog), Library of Congress, May 20, 2011, http://blogs.loc.gov/music/2011/05/pic-of-the-week-passing-the-baton-edition/.

36. Vreeland, "Charlie Chaplin," 54,

37. Jeffrey Vance, *Chaplin: Genius of the Cinema* (New York: Harry N. Abrams, 2003), 56.

38. Chaplin Jr., Rau, Rau, *My Father, Charlie Chaplin*, 24

39. Robinson, *Chaplin*, 232.

40. Chaplin, *My Autobiography*, 204.

41. "Charlie Chaplin Will Build Own Film Plant," *Los Angeles Times*, October 16, 1917, I11.

42. Alistair Cooke, *Six Men* (London: The Bodley Head, 1977), 28.

Chapter 3

1. "Need for Intelligent Film Players," *Music Trade Review*, September 25, 1915, 19.

2. Carli D. Elinor, "From Nickelodeon to Super-Colossal: The Evolution of Music to Pictures," *The Cue Sheet*, October 1995, 5.

3. *Ibid.*, 10.

4. Horace Johnson, "Frederick Stahlberg, Conductor of the Rivoli Theatre Lauds Men of Motion Picture Orchestras," *The Metronome*, February 1921, 76.

5. J. Bodewalt Lampe, *Remick Folio of Moving Picture Music, Vol. 1* (New York: Jerome H. Remick & Co., 1914), cover.

6. Ernö Rapée, *Encyclopedia of Music for Moving Pictures* (1925; rep. New York: Arno Press, Inc., 1970), 24.

7. *Ibid.*, 18.

8. *Ibid.*, 20.

9. *Ibid.*, 21.

10. "New Type Music Cue Sheet Is Published," *Exhibitors Herald*, July 8, 1922, 66.

11. "Offer Music Score For Every Feature," *Exhibitors Herald*, November 20, 1920, 38.

12. Synchronized Scenario Music Company, Advertisement, *Motion Picture News*, November 1920, 3508.

13. Synchronized Scenario Music Company, Advertisement, *Exhibitors Herald*, December 25, 1920, 195.

14. Elinor, "From Nickelodeon to Super-Colossal," 12.

15. "Synchronized Music Service To Be Available by April 1," *Exhibitors Herald*, February 26, 1921, 41.

16. Robert Van Gelder, "Chaplin Draws a Keen Weapon." *The New York Times*, September 8, 1940, 22.

17. Chaplin, *My Autobiography*, 228.

18. *Ibid.*, 230.

19. Charles Beardsley, *Hollywood's Master Showman: The Legendary Sid Grauman* (Cornwall Books: Cranbury, NJ, 1983), 33.

20. *Ibid.*, 34.

21. Chaplin, *My Autobiography*, 223.

22. Ackroyd, *Charlie Chaplin*, 134.

23. Chaplin, *My Autobiography*, 239.

24. *Ibid.*, 238.

25. *Ibid.*, 224.

26. "National Board Show To Include Chaplin Comedy," *Moving Picture World*, January 22, 1921, 405.

27. "Million-Dollar Theatre Opens," *The Motion Picture News*, April 18, 1914, 23.

28. "Moving Pictures: Strand," *Variety*, February 6, 1920, 54.

29. "Moving Pictures: The Strand," *Variety*, April 18, 1919, 53.

30. "Carl Edouarde of the Films Dies," *The New York Times*, December 9, 1932, 28.

31. "Instructional Films and Where to Get Them," *Moving Picture Age*, May 1921, 26.

32. "What the Big Houses Say With First Run Theatres," *Motion Picture News*, February 19, 1921, 1450.

33. "The Screen: *The Kid*," *The New York Times*, February 7, 1921, 16.

34. "*The Kid*," *Exceptional Photoplays*, January–February 1921, 2/7.

35. Robert Nichols, "Future of the Cinema: Mr. Charles Chaplin," in Kevin J. Hayes, *Charlie Chaplin Interviews* (Jackson, MS: The University Press of Mississippi, 2005), 80.

36. "Musical Progress in Cinema: Overlooking 'the Masses'—Cheap 'Broadmindedness,'" *Musical News and Herald*, October 3, 1925.

37. Playbill, Kinema Theater, March 5, 1921, ECCI 00004518, CCA.

38. Chaplin, *My Life In Pictures*, 188.

39. Robinson, *Chaplin*, 278.

40. "Chaplin Breaks All Records of Picture History," n.d., unidentified newspaper clipping, CCA.

41. Chaplin, *My Autobiography*, 297.

42. *Ibid.*

43. *Ibid.*, 298.

44. "Chaplin Discusses His New Picture," *Motion Picture News*, October 6, 1923, 1634.

45. "Does Public Want Truth in Motion Pictures?: Answer Will Be Comedian's Guide," *Exhibitors Trade Review*, August 11, 1923, 467.

46. *A Woman of Paris* Premiere Program, private collection.

47. Harry Carr, "Will Charlie Kick Off His Old Shoes?," *Motion Picture Magazine*, December 1923, 28.

48. Edwin Schallert, "Chaplin Opens New Epoch," *Los Angeles Times*, September 27, 1923, II9.

49. "Chaplin Feature Is Highly Praised," *Motion Picture News*, September 8, 1923, 1231.

50. Laurence Reid, "*A Woman of Paris*," *Motion Picture News*, October 13, 1923, 1783.

51. "The Screen: *A Woman of Paris*," *The New York Times*, October 2, 1923, 7.

52. Carr, "Will Charlie Kick Off His Old Shoes?," 28.

53. Adolphe Menjou and M. M. Musselman, *It Took Nine Tailors* (New York: McGraw-Hill, 1948), 114.

54. Burton Rascoe, "A Bookman's Day Book," *New York Tribune*, October 14, 1923, SM32.

55. "Chas. Chaplin's *Woman of Paris* Wins High Praise At Its Premiere," *The Winnipeg Evening Tribune*, December 15, 1923, 3.

56. "Chaplin Smashes Sacred Film Conventions: *A Woman of Paris*," *Los Angeles Times*, August 15, 1923, WF2.

57. *A Woman of Paris* Premiere Program, private collection.

58. *Ibid.*

59. *Ibid.*

60. "The Big Little Feature," *Exhibitors Trade Review*, November 17, 1923, 1164.

61. Chaplin, *My Autobiography*, 256.

62. "*Woman of Paris* Closes Next Week," *Los Angeles Times*, November 5, 1923, II7.

63. "Strand and Capitol Almost Neck and Neck Last Week," *Variety*, October 4, 1923, 20.

64. "What Chaplin Thinks," *The New York Times*, October 7, 1923, X4.

65. "Screen Music," *The New York Times*, October 14, 1923, X5.

66. "*Woman of Paris*, by Chaplin, Is Unbeatable," *Evening Telegram*, undated newspaper clipping, CCA.

67. Rascoe, "A Bookman's Day Book," SM32.

68. Carr, "Will Charlie Kick Off His Old Shoes?," 28.

69. "Entire Score Is Memorized by Conductor," *Los Angeles Times*, October 5, 1923, III1.

70. "Sixth Week for Chaplin Picture," *Los Angeles Times*, October 30, 1923, III1.

71. Edwin Schallert, "Chaplin Opens New Epoch," *Los Angeles Times*, September 27, 1923, II9.

72. "What Chaplin Thinks," *The New York Times*, October 7, 1923, X4.

73. Mordaunt Hall, "The Changeable Chaplin," *Motion Picture Classic*, August 1926, 17.

74. Winfield Scott Downs, Ed., "Frederick Stahlberg," *Encyclopedia of American Biography* (New York: The American Historical Society, Inc., 1938), 312.

75. "Music of the Movies," *The New York Times*, November 4, 1923, X5.

76. "Ohio Censor Chief Puts Ban on *Woman of Paris*," *Motion Picture News*, November 17, 1923, 2348.

77. Chaplin, *My Autobiography*, 300.

78. Jack Lait, "*A Woman of Paris*," *Variety*, September 27, 1923, 25.

79. "*Woman of Paris* Off," *Variety*, November 8, 1923, 22.

80. Tino Balio, *United Artists: The Company That Changed the Film Industry* (Madison, WI: The University of Wisconsin Press, 1976), 45.

81. Beardsley, *Hollywood's Master Showman*, 32.

82. Jack Jungmeyer, "Charlie Chaplin Picks Unknown For Coveted Lead in Picture," *Battle Creek Enquirer* (Michigan), April 30, 1934, 10.

83. "Chaplin's Violin Disk," *Variety*, June 24, 1925, 1.

84. "Chaplin-Lyman Song: Comedian and Band Leader Using 'Plug' to Get Title," *Variety*, April 8, 1925, 43.

85. Charles Chaplin, Abe Lyman, Gus Kahn, "I Like That Little One," ©Copyright 1925 (Renewed). Unpublished.

86. Charles Chaplin, Abe Lyman, Gus Arnheim, "Sing a Song," ©Copyright 1925 (Renewed). Published Worldwide by Bourne Co., New York, NY and Bienstock Publishing Company o/b/o Redwood Music Ltd. All Rights Reserved. International Copyright Secured. (ASCAP)

87. "Inside Stuff: On Music—Chaplin's Own Songs and Disk," *Variety*, July 1, 1925, 35.

88. M. Witmark & Sons and Charles Chaplin, "With You, Dear, In Bombay," Contract, June 4, 1925, ECCI 00022541, CCA.

89. Charlie Chaplin, "With You, Dear, In Bombay," M. Witmark & Sons, 1925, ECCI00030086, CCA.

90. "Melody Mart," *The Billboard*, August 15, 1925, 31.

91. "Chaplin's Violin Disk," 1.

92. "Charlie Chaplin—Composer," *Gravesend Report*, October 10, 1925, ECCI00316500, CCA.

93. "Charlie Chaplin Shines as Musician and Composer," *Music Trade Review*, July 18, 1925, 45.

94. "Inside Stuff: On Music," *Variety*, August 12, 1925, 35.

95. "Milwaukee Music Merchants Report a Slight Advance With Opening of July," *The Music Trade Review*, July 25, 1925, 13.

96. "Cincinnati Demand Experiences Rapid Recovery From the Summer Lull in Trade," *The Music Trade Review*, October 17, 1925, 21.

97. Kelcey Allen, "Amusements," *Women's Wear*, June 16, 1925, 11.

98. B. Feldman & Co., advertisement, *The Stage*, September 17, 1925, 5.

99. Abel, "Disk Reviews—'Sing a Song' (Fox-Trot)—Charlie Chaplin and Lyman's California Orchestra; 'With You, Dear, In Bombay'—Same—Brunswick No. 2912," *Variety*, September 2, 1925, 40.

100. "Charlie Chaplin On the Records," advertisement, *Picturegoer and The Theatre*, October 1, 1925, 4.

101. "Charlie Chaplin—Composer," *Gravesend Report*, October 10, 1925, ECCI00316500, CCA.

102. "New York's 'First Nighters' Pay Homage to Charlie Chaplin and *The Gold Rush*," *Moving Picture World*, August 29, 1925, 926.

103. Allen, "Amusements," 11.

104. "New Score Arranged for Film," *Los Angeles Times*, June 24, 1925, A11.

105. "Egyptian Theater Mecca," *Los Angeles Times*, June 26, 1925, A9.

106. Rosalind Shaffer, "All the Old Guard of Movieland Sees Chaplin Premiere," *Chicago Daily Tribune*, July 5, 1925, C3.

107. "Premiere Plan Continued at *The Gold Rush*," *Los Angeles Times*, July 7, 1925, A11.

108. "Gino Severi to Lead Orchestra at Loew's State," *Los Angeles Times*, August 31, 1925, A9.

109. "House Reviews: Grauman's Egyptian, Los Angeles, June 26," *Variety*, July 1, 1925, 27.

110. "Novel Prologue Arranged for Chaplin Picture," *Los Angeles Times*, September 17, 1925, A11.

111. "House Reviews: Grauman's Egyptian, Los Angeles, June 26," *Variety*, July 1, 1925, 27.

112. "Chaplin Laughter Broadcasted," *Dunfermline Journal* (Scotland), October 3, 1925, CCA.

113. Allen, "Amusements," 11.

114. "New Score Arranged for Film," A11.

115. Linda Danly, Ed., *Hugo Friedhofer: The Best Years of His Life: A Hollywood Master of Music for the Movies* (Lanham, MD: The Scarecrow Press, Inc., 2002), 34.

116. "Victor Herbert's First Serious Opera," *The New York Times*, October 10, 1910, 9.

117. Vance, *Chaplin*, 162.

118. Kevin Brownlow, *The Search for Charlie Chaplin* (2005; repr. London: UKA Press, 2010), 149.

119. Kevin Brownlow, email to the author, September 20, 2014.

120. Sue McConachy, Interview with Mischa Terr, n.d., provided to the author by Kevin Brownlow.

121. For the prints of *The Gold Rush* used in live performance, Association Chaplin eliminated the "Oceana Roll" reference in the title cards, said Kate Guyonvarch, "because it seemed so silly."

122. Florence Methven and Marian Gillespie, "When You Look In The Heart Of A Rose" (1918). Vocal Popular Sheet Music Collection. Score 1699. http://digitalcommons.library.umaine.edu/mmb-vp/1699.

123. Konrad Bercovici, "Charlie Chaplin," *Collier's*, August 15, 1925, 5.

124. Matthew Sweet, "Was Charlie Chaplin a Gypsy?" *The Guardian*, February 7, 2011, https://www.theguardian.com/film/2011/feb/17/charlie-chaplin-gypsy-heritage.

125. Dufferin and Clandeboye, Helen Selina Blackwood, and Henry Le Patourel, "Terence's farewell to Kathleen" (London: Chappell & Co, 188-?), http://nla.gov.au/nla.obj-181798765.

126. Chaplin, *My Autobiography*, 210.

127. James C. Bradford compiled the cue sheet for M. J. Mintz's Cameo Thematic Music Company, using many of the same primary themes, including "The Bowery" for Charlie's theme, Georgia's themes ("My Wild Irish Rose" and "When You Look in the Heart of Rose"), "Fascination" for the love theme, "Pretty Girl Milking Her Cow," Victor Herbert's *Natoma*, Hugo Riesenfeld's *American Festival March*, and more.

128. *The Gold Rush* Daily Production Report, ECCI00313697, CCA, 17.

129. Mordaunt Hall, "Shy Charlie Chaplin Opens His Heart," *The New York Times*, August 9, 1925, SM5.

130. James Thornton, "She May Have Seen Better Days" (New York: T. B. Harms & Co., 1894), The Lester S. Levy Sheet Music Collection, Johns Hopkins University, http://levysheetmusic.mse.jhu.edu/catalog/levy:143.140.

131. Hall, "Shy Charlie Chaplin Opens His Heart," SM5.

132. Robinson, *Chaplin*, 390.

133. "Joe Plunkett's Rest," *Variety*, January 18, 1928, 5.

134. "Plunkett Spikes Rumor He Is Quitting Strand," *The Billboard*, January 7, 1928, 36.

135. "Chaplin's New Picture Premiere Stirs Distinguished N.Y. Crowd," *The Billboard*, January 14, 1928, 8.

136. Jack Harrower, "Presentations: Prologue Flash on Strand Stage; Simple, but Highly Effective," *The Film Daily*, January 15, 1928, 4.

137. Mordaunt Hall, "The Screen: Chaplin of Hollywood: *The Circus*," *The New York Times*, January 9, 1928, 29.

138. Gillian B. Anderson, "The Music of *The Circus*," *LC Information Bulletin*, September 20, 1993, 347.

139. Ray Murray, "*The Circus* Opens at Grauman's Chinese with One Ring Circus," *Exhibitors Herald and Moving Picture World*, February 4, 1928, 36.

140. "Clown to Come Here for Show," *Los Angeles Times*, January 19, 1928, A9.

141. *The Circus* Program, Grauman's Chinese Theatre, University of Washington Libraries, Special Collections, UW 37427.

142. Murray, "*The Circus* Opens at Grauman's Chinese with One Ring Circus," 36.

143. Balio, *United Artists*, 72.

144. Bruno David Ussher, "Arthur Key [*sic*] Resigns from Grauman's in Los Angeles," *Pacific Coast Musical Review*, September 25, 1920, 5.

145. "Kay Is Far From Being a 'Yes' Man," *Los Angeles Times*, November 25, 1923, III46.

146. Anderson, "The Music of *The Circus*," 347.

147. *The Circus* Special Award, The Official Academy Awards' Database, http://awardsdatabase.oscars.org/.

148. Bob Waters, "Performing Arts: National Symphony Orchestra," *The Washington Post*, August 9, 1993, B4.

149. Edward Rothstein, "The Little Tramp to a Different Tune," *The New York Times*, February 28, 1994, C11.

Chapter 4

1. Gladys Hall, "Charlie Chaplin Attacks the Talkies," *Motion Picture*, May 1929, 29.

2. Rob Wagner, "Charlie Chaplin," *Screenland*, December 1929, 27.

3. Charles Lapworth, "Chaplin Talks!" *The Film Weekly*, December 6, 1930, 9.

4. Wagner, "Charlie Chaplin," 110.

5. Hall, "Charlie Chaplin Attacks the Talkies," 29.

6. *Year Book of Motion Pictures 1930*, The Film Daily, 3.

7. Cooke, *Six Men*, 40.

8. Vance, *Chaplin*, 195.

9. Alfred Reeves to Sydney Chaplin, 21 January 1929, ECCI00008427, CCA.

10. Cal York, "Girl Wanted—No Experience Required," *Photoplay*, January 1929, 34.

11. "Projection Jottings," *The New York Times,* October 21, 1928.

12. "Virginia Cherrill," *Variety*, April 1, 1931, 14.

13. York, "Girl Wanted."

14. Brownlow, *The Search for Charlie Chaplin*, 58.

15. Richard Meryman, "Ageless Master's Anatomy of Comedy: Chaplin, An Interview," in *Charlie Chaplin: Interviews*, ed. Kevin Hayes (Jackson, MS: University of Mississippi Press, 2005), 140.

16. *Ibid.*

17. Brownlow, *The Search for Charlie Chaplin*, 59, 61.

18. *Ibid.*, 61.

19. Mordaunt Hall, "Chaplin's Film Nearing Completion," *The New York Times*, July 6, 1930, 91.

20. "Sound Aids the Screen," *The New York Times*, September 7, 1930, X4.

21. Charles Chaplin, "Pantomime and Comedy," *The New York Times*, January 25, 1931, X6.

22. Balio, *United Artists*, 91.

23. John S. Cohen, Jr., "Chaplin Triumphs Anew in *City Lights*," *New York Sun*, February 7, 1931, 6.

24. Mordaunt Hall, "Chaplin Hilarious In His *City Lights*," *The New York Times*, February 7, 1931, 17.

25. "Voice Wins In Films," *The New York Times*, February 8, 1931, 111.

26. Wagner, "Charlie Chaplin," 27.

27. Robinson, *Chaplin*, 419.

28. "Chaplin To Sing Own Songs," *Motion Picture News*, June 28, 1930, 46.

29. *City Lights* Press Book, ECCI00004693, CCA.

30. Wagner, "Charlie Chaplin," 110.

31. Charles Chaplin, "Beautiful, Wonderful Eyes," ©Copyright 1929 (Renewed). Published Worldwide by Bourne Co., New York, NY. All Rights Reserved. International Copyright Secured. (ASCAP)

32. *City Lights* Press Book, ECCI00004693, CCA.

33. Rachel Ford to Saul Bourne, 3 July 1957, ECCI00023076, CCA.

34. Charlie Chaplin, *A Comedian Sees the World*, ed. Lisa Stein Haven (Columbia, MO: University of Missouri Press, 2014), 28.

35. Balio, *United Artists*, 91.

36. Charlotte Higgins, "The Great Composer," *The Guardian*, November 27, 2000, 54.

37. Richard Meryman, Charlie Chaplin Interview Transcript, circa 1967, Collection 815 (33.f-302), Special Collections, Margaret Herrick Library, Academy of Motion Picture Arts and Sciences, Beverly Hills, California.

38. Jack Burton, "The Honor Roll of Songwriters: No. 105—Arthur Johnston," *Billboard*, August 25, 1951, 34.

39. "Marks and Berlin," *Variety*, May 12, 1926, 48.

40. Sam Coslow, "Up and Down the Alley," *Exhibitors Herald and Moving Picture World*, January 21, 1928, 58.

41. James, *Making Music with Charlie Chaplin*, 71.

42. Meryman, Charlie Chaplin Interview Transcript.

43. James, *Making Music with Charlie Chaplin*, 71.

44. Epstein, *Remembering Charlie*, 152.

45. "In Chaplin's Studio," *The New York Times*, January 12, 1930, 113.

46. *City Lights* Press Book, ECCI00004693, CCA.

47. Nathan, *Passing Judgments*, 212.

48. Chaplin, *My Life In Pictures*, 34.

49. "Glimpses of Chaplin's Comedy," *The New York Times*, August 11, 1929, X3.

50. Mr. Chaplin's Copy, cues complete music, reels 1 to 9 *City Lights*, 1930, ECCI00004701, CCA.

51. Chaplin, *A Comedian Sees the World*, 193.

52. Chaplin Jr., Rau, Rau, *My Father, Charlie* Chaplin, 99.

53. Meryman, Charlie Chaplin Interview Transcript.

54. Fred Johnson, "Action & Reaction," *San Francisco Call-Bulletin*, June 5, 1931, CCA.

55. Robinson, *Chaplin*, 444.

56. "To Pay on Chaplin Movie Song," *The New York Times*, June 13, 1934, 27.

57. Robinson, *Chaplin*, 438.

58. David Robinson, "Chaplin & Music," *The Songs of Charlie Chaplin* (1989; repr. New York: Bourne Co., 1992), 18–19.

59. John S. Cohen, Jr., "Chaplin Triumphs Anew in *City Lights*," *New York Sun*, February 7, 1931, 6.

60. Mordaunt Hall, "Chaplin Hilarious In His *City Lights*," *The New York Times*, February 7, 1931, 17.

61. Robinson, *Chaplin*, 438.

62. Nathan, *Passing Judgements*, 211.

63. "Mr. Chaplin's Copy: complete music cues: reels 1 to 9 *City Lights*," ECCI00004701, CCA.

64. Timothy Brock, "The Intimate Score of the Tramp-Composer: Restoring Music for *City Lights*," 2004, http://

www.timothybrock.com/joomla/articles/18-articles/27-the-intimate-score-of-the-tramp-composer-restoring-music-for-city-lights.

65. Chaplin, *A Comedian Sees the World*, 192.

66. Chaplin, *My Autobiography*, 395.

67. Mayme Peak, "The Man Who Knows Charlie Chaplin Best," *Daily Boston Globe*, February 22, 1931, B3.

68. Copy of agreement with Editions Campbell Connelly King re *City Lights* music, July 24, 1931, ECCI 00004905, CCA.

69. Library of Congress Copyright Division, *Catalogue of Copyright Entries: Part 3, Musical Compositions, New Series, Volume 27 for the Year 1932* (Washington: United States Government Printing Office, 1933), 401.

70. Epstein, *Remembering Charlie*, 152.

Chapter 5

1. Chaplin, *My Autobiography*, 366.

2. Chaplin Jr., Rau, Rau, *My Father, Charlie* Chaplin, 111.

3. Chaplin, *My Autobiography*, 366.

4. Chaplin, *A Comedian Sees the World*, 15.

5. Chaplin, *A Comedian Sees the World*, 21.

6. "Enter Charles Chaplin, Tardily," *The New York Times*, February 2, 1936.

7. Chaplin, *My Autobiography*, 344.

8. Terry Ramsaye, "Chaplin Ridicules Reds' Claim Film Aids 'Cause,'" *Motion Picture Herald*, December 7, 1935, 13.

9. *Ibid.*

10. "2,000 Curious in Near-Riot at Chaplin Picture," *New York Herald Tribune*, February 6, 1936, 12.

11. Frank S. Nugent, "Heralding the Return, After an Undue Absence, of Charlie Chaplin in *Modern Times*," *The New York Times*, February 6, 1936, 23.

12. Abel Green, "Film Reviews: *Modern Times*," *Variety*, February 11, 1936, 16.

13. Charles J. Maland, *Chaplin and American Culture: The Evolution of a Star Image* (Princeton, NJ: Princeton University Press, 1989), 157.

14. Brooks Atkinson, "Beloved Vagabond: Charlie Chaplin Canonized Out of a Sentimental Memory Book," *The New York Times*, February 16, 1936, X1.

15. David Raksin, "Life with Charlie," *The Quarterly Journal of the Library of Congress*, Summer 1983, 234.

16. *Ibid.*, 237.

17. Alfred Newman to Alfred Reeves, 20 February 1936, ECCI00315188, CCA.

18. Raksin, "Life with Charlie," 237.

19. *Ibid.*, 238.

20. David Raksin, "Interview," *Modern Times*, Blu-ray. Criterion Collection, 2010.

21. Raksin, "Life with Charlie," 240.

22. Raksin, "Interview."

23. *Ibid.*

24. Brownlow, *The Search for Charlie Chaplin*, 115.

25. Raksin, "Interview."

26. Raksin, "Life with Charlie," 240.

27. *Ibid.*

28. Raksin, "Interview."

29. C. Sharpless Hickman, "Music News," *Music Journal*, February 1955, 38.

30. Raksin, "Life with Charlie," 241.

31. *Ibid.*

32. *Modern Times* Daily Production Report, ECCI 00313388, CCA.

33. Raksin, "Interview."

34. Raksin, "Life with Charlie," 241.

35. Raksin, "Interview."

36. Brownlow, *The Search for Charlie Chaplin*, 116.

37. Raksin, "Interview."

38. Raksin, "Life with Charlie," 243.

39. *Ibid.*, 246.

40. Chaplin Jr., Rau, Rau, *My Father, Charlie Chaplin*, 126.

41. Timothy Brock, "*Modern Times*," http://www.timothybrock.com/joomla/articles/18-articles/18-modern-times-2004.

42. Sidney Skolsky, "Chaplin's *Modern Times*," *The Washington Post*, November 27, 1935, 18.

43. Louis Kaufman, with Annette Kaufman, *A Fiddler's Tale: How Hollywood and Vivaldi Discovered Me* (Madison, WI: The University of Wisconsin Press, 2003), 121.

44. David Raksin, *The Bad and the Beautiful: My Life in a Golden Age of Film Music*, ed. Alex Raksin, 2012, Kindle edition, loc. 2921.

45. Raksin, "Interview."

46. Raksin, "Life with Charlie," 250.

47. *Ibid.*

48. Chaplin Jr., Rau, Rau, *My Father, Charlie Chaplin*, 127.

49. D.W.C., "The Curious Mr. Chaplin," *The New York Times*, February 16, 1936, X4.

50. Raksin, "Life with Charlie," 251.

51. *Ibid.*, 253.

52. Raksin, *The Bad and the Beautiful*, loc. 3192.

53. Meryman, Charles Chaplin Interview Transcript.

54. Alfred Newman to Alfred Reeves, 20 February 1936, ECCI00315188, CCA.

55. Alfred Reeves to Loyd Wright, 20 February 1936, ECCI00315189, CCA.

56. Raksin, *The Bad and the Beautiful*, loc. 3260.

57. *Ibid.*, loc. 3076.

58. Raksin, "Interview."

59. Robinson, *Chaplin*, 496.

60. Brock, "*Modern Times*."

61. Raksin, "Interview."

62. John J. Husband and William P. Mackay, "Revive Us Again" (1863), Hymnary.org, http://www.hymnary.org/text/we_praise_thee_o_god_for_the_son_of.

63. Edith Fowke, Joe Glazer, *Songs of Work and Protest* (Mineola, NY: Dover Publications, 1973), 127.

64. *Ibid.*

65. "Vienna Won't Let Chaplin Wave Red Flag in Picture," *The New York Times*, April 3, 1936.

66. Raksin, "Interview."

67. *Ibid.*

68. "Coming Attractions In the Theaters: Columbia," *East Liverpool Review*, March 24, 1936, 6.

69. Dialogue Continuity, *Modern Times*, ECCI 00313408, CCA.

70. Alfred Reeves to Sydney Chaplin, 31 December 1935, ECCI00315267, CCA.

71. Criterion Collection edition of *Modern Times* includes the original, unedited version of "Titine" as a bonus supplement.

72. "*Modern Times*: 'Titine,'" memorandum, ECCI 00315204, CCA.

73. *Ibid.*

74. Irving Berlin, Inc. and Charles Chaplin Film Co., contract, 30 June 1936, ECCI00315231, CCA.

75. Arthur Kelly to Charles Chaplin, 11 June 1954, ECCI00023224, CCA.

76. Arthur Kelly to Saul Bourne, 14 June 1954, ECCI 00023225, CCA.

77. Saul Bourne to Arthur Kelly, 2 July 1954, ECCI 00023221, CCA.

78. H. Walter, Chappell & Co. Ltd to The Performing Right Society, 17 August 1936, ECCI00023263, CCA.

79. Clifford McCarty, *Film Composers In America: A Filmography, 1911–1970*, Second ed. (New York: Oxford University Press, 2000), 364.

80. Otis Ferguson, "Hallelujah, Bum Again," *The New Republic*, February 19, 1936, 48.

81. Mollie Merrick, "Musical Score Often Responsible for Film Being a Hit: Fans Approve Movie Melody," *The Detroit Free Press*, March 1, 1936, 14.

82. Raksin, *The Bad and the Beautiful*, loc. 3221.

83. "Chaplin: *Modern Times*," *The Guardian*, July 14, 1936.

Chapter 6

1. Chaplin Jr., Rau, Rau, *My Father, Charlie* Chaplin, 179.

2. *Ibid.*, 180.

3. Van Gelder, "Chaplin Draws a Keen Weapon," 9.

4. Robinson, *Chaplin*, 528.

5. *Ibid.*

6. *Ibid.*, 530.

7. Dixie Willson, "Chaplin Talks," *Photoplay*, December 1940, 82.

8. *Ibid.*, 20.

9. Frank Scheide, "*The Great Dictator* and Chaplin's Tramp as an Awakened 'Rip Van Winkle,'" in *Chaplin: The Dictator and the Tramp*, eds. Hooman Mehran and Frank Scheide (London: British Film Institute, 2004), 24.

10. Bosley Crowther, "The Screen in Review: *The Great Dictator*," *The New York Times*, October 16, 1940, 33.

11. Douglas W. Churchill, "Screen News Here and In Hollywood," *The New York Times*, October 28, 1940, 21.

12. Douglas W. Churchill, "Hollywood Gets a Peek at *Fantasia*," *The New York Times*, October 20, 1940, 139.

13. Bosley Crowther, "Still Supreme," *The New York Times*, October 20, 1940, 139.

14. Charles Chaplin, "Mr. Chaplin Answers His Critics," *The New York Times*, October 27, 1940, 133.

15. Balio, *United Artists*, 164.

16. "Chaplin Declines Award by Critics," *The New York Times*, January 5, 1941, 3.

17. "Man Named Squiz Said He Was Good So Willson Plays the Flute," *The Austin Statesman*, October 20, 1940, 11.

18. Robert Lewis, *Slings and Arrows: Theater In My Life* (New York: Applause, 1984), 160.

19. Nicolas Slonimsky, *Music Since 1900*, 5th Edition (New York: Schirmer Books, 1994), 452.

20. Royal S. Brown, *Overtones and Undertones: Reading Film Music* (Berkley, CA: University of California Press, 1994), 285.

21. Meredith Willson, *And There I Stood With My Piccolo* (1948; repr. Minneapolis: University of Minnesota Press, 2009), 129.

22. Bill Oates, *Meredith Willson: America's Music Man* (Bloomington, IN: AuthorHouse, 2010), 68.

23. Meredith Willson and Alfred Reeves, Charles Chaplin Film Corporation, Agreement, 24 July 1940, ECCI0029770, CCA.

24. Chaplin Jr., Rau, Rau, *My Father, Charlie Chaplin*, 228.

25. Meredith Willson, "Music Maker to Charlie Chaplin," *New York Herald Tribune*, October 27, 1940, E3.

26. "Reminiscences of Meredith Willson," June 1959, Columbia Oral History Archives, Rare Book & Manuscript Library, Columbia University in the City of New York, 36.

27. Daily production report 1939–1940, Production No. 6, Charles Chaplin Film Corporation, ECCI 00312471, CCA.

28. Raksin, "Life with Charlie," 242.

29. "Man Named Squiz," 11.

30. "Al Pearce Group on Radio Tonight," *The Daily Republican* (Belvidere, IL), August 23, 1940, 5.

31. Bruno David Ussher, "Music in the Films," *Los Angeles Daily News*, August 26, 1940.

32. Dixie Willson, "Chaplin Talks," 20.

33. Meredith Willson, "Music Maker to Charlie Chaplin," E3.

34. Production No. 6, Script No. 8, Mr. Wilson, 29 November 1939, ECCI00312587, CCA.

35. Van Gelder, "Chaplin Draws a Keen Weapon," 9.

36. Victor and Marina A. Ledin, Liner Notes, *Meredith Willson: Symphony No. 1 in F minor ("A Symphony of San Francisco"), Symphony No. 2 in E minor ("The Missions of California")*, Moscow Symphony Orchestra, William T. Stromberg, Naxos 8.559006, 1999, compact disc.

37. Daily production report 1939–1940, ECCI 00312471, CCA.

38. Meredith Willson, "Music Maker to Charlie Chaplin," E3.

39. Van Gelder, "Chaplin Draws a Keen Weapon," 9.

40. John C. Skipper, *Meredith Willson: The Unsinkable Music Man* (El Dorado Hills, CA: Savas Publishing Company, 1999), 54.

41. Robinson, *Chaplin*, 535.

42. Chaplin Jr., Rau, Rau, *My Father, Charlie* Chaplin, 200.

43. Chaplin, *My Life In Pictures*, 34.

44. Production No. 6, Script No. 5, Wheeler Dryden, ECCI00312425, CCA.

45. Meredith Willson, "Music Maker to Charlie Chaplin," E3.

46. Music Recording Schedule—*The Great Dictator*, 15 August 1940, Archives de Montreux, PP 75—Fonds Charles Chaplin, Clarens, Switzerland.

47. *Ibid.*

48. Louella O. Parsons, "Louella O. Parsons," *The Washington Post*, September 1, 1940, A1.

49. Charles Chaplin, Meredith Willson, Eddie DeLange, "Falling Star," ©Copyright 1941 (Renewed). Published Worldwide by Bourne Co., New York, NY and Shapiro Bernstein & Co. All Rights Reserved. International Copyright Secured. (ASCAP)

50. "Reminiscences of Meredith Willson," 36.

51. Irving Berlin, Inc., Meredith Willson, and Charles Chaplin, "Falling Star" Contract, 11 December 1940, ECCI00029769, CCA.

52. *Ibid.*

53. Meredith Willson, "Music Maker to Charlie Chaplin," E3.

54. Daily production report 1939–1940, Production No. 6, Charles Chaplin Film Corporation, ECCI 00312471, CCA.

55. "Reminiscences of Meredith Willson," 38.

56. Music Recording Schedule—*The Great Dictator*, 21 August 1940, Archives de Montreux, PP 75—Fonds Charles Chaplin, Clarens, Switzerland.

57. Music Recording Schedule—*The Great Dictator*, 23 August 1940, Archives de Montreux, PP 75—Fonds Charles Chaplin, Clarens, Switzerland.

58. Ussher, "Music in the Films."

59. Dixie Willson, "Chaplin Talks," 82.

60. Meredith Willson, "Music Maker to Charlie Chaplin," E3.

61. "Music: Composer Chaplin," *Time*, September 9, 1940.

62. Hedda Hopper, "Hedda Hopper's Hollywood," *Los Angeles Times*, October 16, 1940, 17.

63. "Making Fun of Something That's Serious," *New York Herald Tribune*, October 13, 1940, E1.

64. Bruno David Ussher, "Music in the Films," *Los Angeles Illustrated Daily News*, October 21, 1940.

65. Robinson, *Chaplin*, 543.

66. Virgil Thomson, "Chaplin Scores (1940)," in *Virgil Thomson: A Reader: Selected Writings, 1924–1984*, ed. Richard Kostelanetz (New York, Routledge, 2002), 153.

67. *The Great Dictator*, Instructions concerning film music for theatrical release, ECCI00023253, CCA.

68. "Music: Composer Chaplin," *Time*, September 9, 1940.

69. Donald Martin, "Two Outstanding Films With Music," *The Etude*, December 1940, 805.

70. Meredith Willson, *And There I Stood*, 166.

71. *Ibid.*, 168.

72. Chaplin Jr., Rau, Rau, *My Father, Charlie Chaplin*, 186.

73. Chaplin, *My Autobiography*, 456.

74. Chaplin Jr., Rau, Rau, *My Father, Charlie Chaplin*, 187.

75. Chaplin, *My Autobiography*, 392.

76. "Chaplin Refutes Report On Withdrawal of Film," *The Christian Science Monitor*, May 23, 1940, 15.

Chapter 7

1. Alfred Reeves to Sydney Chaplin, 10 February 1934, ECCI00005594, CCA.

2. Thomas M. Pryor, "Noting the Week's Screen Events," *The New York Times*, October 20, 1940, 139.

3. "Of Local Origin," *The New York Times*, April 8, 1942, 23.

4. "Late Reviews: *The Gold Rush*," *Motion Picture Herald*, March 7, 1942, 42.

5. "The Box Office Slant: *The Gold Rush*," *Showmen's Trade Review*, March 7, 1942, 12.

6. "Reviews of the New Films: *The Gold Rush*," *The Film Daily*, March 5, 1942, 8.

7. Hale, *Charlie Chaplin*, 158.

8. *Ibid.*, 160.

9. *Ibid.*

10. *Ibid.*, 162.

11. Alfred Reeves to Loyd Wright, 11 December 1941, ECCI00313878, CCA.

12. Loyd Wright to Alfred Reeves, 15 December 1941, ECCI00313897, CCA.

13. Alfred Reeves to Loyd Wright, 11 December 1941, ECCI00313878, CCA.

14. Daily Production Report, *The Gold Rush*, 21 June 1941–7 March 1942, ECCI00313439, CCA.

15. *The Gold Rush* Playbill, ECCI00313700, CCA.

16. "Chaplin Promises New Surprises in *Gold Rush*; Sound Track for *Circus*," *Variety*, November 26, 1941, 9.

17. "*Sleeping Beauty* Waltz" Agreement, 19 September 1941, ECCI00024877, CCA.

18. "Motion Picture Music and Musicians: *The Gold Rush*," *Pacific Coast Musician*, March 7, 1942, 9.

19. Chaplin, *My Autobiography*, 44.

20. "Motion Picture Music and Musicians: *The Gold Rush*," 9.

Chapter 8

1. Chaplin Jr., Rau, Rau, *My Father, Charlie Chaplin*, 71.

2. Lisa Stein Haven, "Planting the Seeds for *Monsieur Verdoux*," http://charliechaplin.com/en/articles/215-Planting-the-Seeds-for-Verdoux, May 2006.

3. Philip K. Schemer, "Drama and the Arts: New Chaplin Will Greet Public in Latest Picture," *Los Angeles Times*, January 26, 1947, B1.

4. *Ibid.*

5. *Ibid.*

6. Chaplin, *My Autobiography*, 407.

7. *Ibid.*

8. *Ibid.*, 411.

9. Robinson, *Chaplin*, 551.

10. *Ibid.*, 562.

11. *Ibid.*, 563.

12. *Ibid.*, 569.

13. *Ibid.*, 570.

14. *Ibid.*, 571.

15. *Ibid.*, 572.

16. Nathan Notowicz. *Wir reden hier nicht von Napoleon. Wir reden von Ihnen!*, edited by Jürgen Elsner. (Berlin: Verlag Neue Musik Berlin, 1971), 197.

17. Schemer, "Drama and the Arts," B1.

18. "Charles Chaplin Talks About His New Comedy," *The New York Times*, January 26, 1947, X5.

19. Schemer, "Drama and the Arts," B1.

20. J. E. Luebering, "Till Eulenspiegel," *Encyclopedia Britannica*, https://www.britannica.com/topic/Till-Eulenspiegel-German-literature.

21. "Charles Chaplin Talks About His New Comedy," *The New York Times*, January 26, 1947, X5.

22. *Ibid.*

23. C. Sharpless Hickman, "Music News," *Music Journal*, February 1955, 38.

24. Maland, *Chaplin and American Culture*, 259.

25. "Legion of Decency Reviews Seven New Productions," *Motion Picture Herald*, April 19, 1947, 23.

26. "Can't Scare Me," *Motion Picture Herald*, September 20, 1947, 9.

27. Lewis, *Slings and Arrows*, 163.

28. *Ibid.*

29. *Ibid.*, 164.

30. "Chaplin Pic Stirs Storm," advertisement, *Daily Variety*, June 27, 1947, 45.

31. "Film Reviews: *Monsieur Verdoux*," *Variety*, April 16, 1947, 8.

32. "Monsieur Chaplin Comes To Town with a Film—And Meets the Press," *Motion Picture Herald*, April 16, 1947, 15.

33. Ed Sullivan, "Little Old New York," *The Hartford Courant* (CT), April 6, 1952, A6.

34. "'Little Man' Meets Press in Big Interview; No Communist, He Says," *Showmen's Trade Review*, April 19, 1947, 8.

35. "Chaplin Calls Himself 'Paying Guest' of U.S.," *Los Angeles Times*, April 11, 1947, 1.

36. Live Comment WNEW, "I Had the Good Fortune of Helping," ECCI00019415, CCA.

37. Mo Wax, "Why Boycott Chaplin?," *Film Bulletin*, May 12, 1947, 3.

38. *Ibid.*

39. "Memphis Bans *Verdoux*," *The New York Times*, June 11, 1947, 33.

40. Senator Rankin, speaking on the Deportation of Charlie Chaplin, June 12, 1947, 80th Cong., 1st sess., *Congressional Record* 93, pt. 5: 6895.

41. "To the Point," *Harrison's Reports*, August 2, 1947, 124.

42. Senator Rankin, speaking on the Deportation of Charlie Chaplin, June 12, 1947, 80th Cong., 1st sess., *Congressional Record* 93, pt. 5: 6895.

43. "Holifield to Answer Pix Smear in House," *The Film Daily*, June 13, 1947, 5.

44. "UA to Withdraw *Verdoux* for Sock Ad Drive," *Variety*, May 14, 1947, 3.

45. "United Artists Production at Standstill," *Independent Exhibitors Film Bulletin*, September 15, 1947, 13.

46. *Exhibitors' Manual for The United Artists Production of Charles Chaplin in* Monsieur Verdoux, William K. Everson Archive, New York University, https://www.nyu.edu/projects/wke/press/monsieurverdoux/monsieurverdoux.pdf, 2.

47. "Chaplin Accepts House 'Invitation,'" *The New York Times*, July 21, 1947, 12.

48. Mo Wax, "Booby Prize for U.A.," *Film Bulletin*, September 29, 1947, 5.

49. "Can't Scare Me," 9.

50. Wax, "Booby Prize for U.A.," 5.

51. "Chaplin Pic Stirs Storm," 45.

52. "Product Digest: *Monsieur Verdoux*," *Motion Picture Herald*, April 19, 1947, 3585.

53. "Film Reviews: *Monsieur Verdoux*," 8.

54. Chappell & Co. and The Chaplin Studios, contract, 19 June 1947, ECCI00312947, CCA.

55. Rudy Schrager to Charles Chaplin, 26 April 1951, ECCI00022854, CCA.

Chapter 9

1. Chaplin, *My Autobiography*, 458.

2. *Ibid.*, 261

3. Richard Lauterbach, "The Whys of Chaplin's Appeal," *The New York Times Magazine*, May 12, 1950, 33.

4. "Chaplin Musical?," *Yorkshire Evening News*, February 9, 1949.

5. Brenda Watkinson, "Jerome Epstein," in *Chaplin's* Limelight *and the Music Hall Tradition*, Frank Scheide and Hooman Mehran, eds. (Jefferson, NC: McFarland & Co., Inc., 2006), 93.

6. Thomas Pryor, "How Mr. Chaplin Makes a Movie," *The New York Times*, February 17, 1952, 22.

7. Thomas F. Brady, "Video Union Acts In Movie Dispute," *The New York Times*, April 4, 1951.

8. A. H. Weiler, "By Way of Report: Charlie Chaplin Tests New Leading Lady Here—Score by Dietz and Schwartz," *The New York Times*, April 29, 1951, X5.

9. Gris, "Hollywood Chaplin," 18.

10. Arthur Johnston to Charles Chaplin, 10 May 1950, ECCI00022857, CCA.

11. K.P. to Arthur Johnston, 24 May 1950, ECCI00022856, CCA.

12. Claude Lapham to Charles Chaplin, 1 September 1951, ECCI00022853, CCA.

13. Harry Tobias to Charlie Chaplin, 2 January 1952, ECCI00022851, CCA.

14. Bernard Katz to Lee Cobin, 28 November 1950, ECCI00022858, CCA.

15. Gris, "Hollywood Chaplin," 16.

16. Mae Findlay, email to author, August 6, 2016.

17. Paul Rasch, in discussion with the author, March 20, 2017.

18. *Ibid.*

19. Gris, "Hollywood Chaplin," 16.

20. Pryor, "How Mr. Chaplin Makes a Movie," 22.

21. "*Limelight*…with Tunes by a Man who Can't Write Music…!," *Bristol* (UK) *Evening World*, February 3, 1953.

22. Pryor, "How Mr. Chaplin Makes a Movie," 22.

23. Gris, "Hollywood Chaplin," 13.

24. *Ibid.*, 6.

25. *Ibid.*, 20.

26. Pryor, "How Mr. Chaplin Makes a Movie," 22.

27. Notes on *Limelight* Music, December 1973, ECCI00022698, CCA.

28. Gris, "Hollywood Chaplin," 17.

29. Pryor, "How Mr. Chaplin Makes a Movie," 22.

30. Chaplin, *My Autobiography*, 458.

31. Anton Dolin, "*Limelight* Fails to Solve Problem of Film Ballet," *Dance and Dancers*, March 1953.

32. "Chaplin Ballet Set for Markova-Dolin," *Variety*, March 1, 1950, 1.

33. Anton Dolin, "*Limelight* Fails to Solve Problem of Film Ballet," *Dance and Dancers*, March 1953.

34. Celebrated Films Corporation and André Eglevsky, agreement, 13 September 1951, ECCI00312514, CCA.

35. Gris, "Hollywood Chaplin," 16.

36. Chaplin, *My Autobiography*, 458.

37. Scott Eyman and Hooman Mehran, "Melissa Hayden," in *Chaplin's* Limelight *and the Music Hall Tradition*, Frank Scheide and Hooman Mehran, eds. (Jefferson, NC: McFarland & Co., Inc., 2006), 80.

38. *Ibid.*, 76.

39. *Ibid.*, 79.

40. *Ibid.*, 77.

41. Anton Dolin, "*Limelight* Fails to Solve Problem of Film Ballet," *Dance and Dancers*, March 1953.

42. Chaplin and Robinson, *Footlights*, 111.

43. Charles Chaplin, "Animal Trainer," ©Copyright 1953 (Renewed). Published Worldwide by Bourne Co., New York, NY. All Rights Reserved. International Copyright Secured. (ASCAP)

44. Charles Chaplin, "Spring Song," ©Copyright 1953 (Renewed). Published Worldwide by Bourne Co., New York, NY. All Rights Reserved. International Copyright Secured. (ASCAP)

45. *Limelight* incomplete script, 1951, ECCI00312557, CCA, 13.

46. Charles Chaplin, "Sardine Song," ©Copyright 1953 (Renewed). Published Worldwide by Bourne Co., New York, NY. All Rights Reserved. International Copyright Secured. (ASCAP)

47. Charles Chaplin, "Sardine Song," Charlie Chaplin Official Website, http://www.charliechaplin.com/en/films/9-Limelight/articles/241-Sardine-Song.

48. Robinson, *Chaplin*, 619.

49. "Radio Followups," *Variety*, October 15, 1952, 24.

50. Arthur W. Kelly to Lois C. Runser, 13 August 1952, ECCI00022832, CCA.

51. William Starr to Arthur W. Kelly, 9 September 1952, ECCI00023208, CCA.

52. Saul H. Bourne to Arthur W. Kelly, 27 August 1952, ECCI00022825, CCA.

53. Arthur W. Kelly to Lois C. Runser, 3 November 1952, ECCI00022795, CCA.

54. Eric James to Hooman Mehran, 8 June 2004, private collection.

55. Chaplin and Robinson, *Footlights*, 42.

56. Wheeler Dryden to Arthur W. Kelly, telegram, 6 February 1952, ECCI00022845, CCA.

57. Gris, "Hollywood Chaplin," 17.

58. Bonnie McCourt, "Julian Ludwig," in *Chaplin's Limelight and the Music Hall Tradition*, Frank Scheide and Hooman Mehran, eds. (Jefferson, NC: McFarland & Co., Inc., 2006), 87.

59. *Ibid.*, 89.

60. Epstein, *Remembering Charlie*, 94.

61. *Limelight* cutting, sound, and music notes, First post-score, 28 May 1952, ECCI00312463, CCA.

62. Bacon, "Chaplin on *Limelight* Set," 1D.

63. Kevin Brownlow, "Eugène Lourié," in *Chaplin's Limelight and the Music Hall Tradition*, Frank Scheide and Hooman Mehran, eds. (Jefferson, NC: McFarland & Co., Inc., 2006), 68.

64. C. Sharpless Hickman, "Movies and Music," *Music Journal*, November 1952, 28.

65. C. Sharpless Hickman, "Music News," *Music Journal*, February 1955, 38.

66. Ivy Wilson Cable, "Charlie Chaplin Gives A Music-Hall Turn," *The Star*, January 9, 1952, 8.

67. Frank Leyendecker, "Chaplin Wizardry Proven By Serio-Comic *Limelight*," *Boxoffice*, October 11, 1952, 20.

68. Mae Tinée, "Chaplin's New Film Superior Despite Flaws," *Chicago Daily Tribune*, January 14, 1953, A3.

69. Virginia Graham, "Cinema: *Limelight*," *The Spectator*, October 17, 1952, 501.

70. "*Limelight* with Charles Chaplin," *Harrison's Reports*, October 11, 1952, 163.

71. Otis L. Guernsey Jr., "On the Screen: *Limelight*," *New York Herald Tribune*, October 24, 1952, 14.

72. Alex Barris, "On the Screen," *The Globe and Mail*, November 14, 1952, 10.

73. Thomas R. Dash, "Theatres: *Limelight*," *Women's Wear Daily*, October 24, 1952, 42.

74. C. Sharpless Hickman, "Movies and Music," *Music Journal*, November 1952, 28.

75. Chaplin Jr., Rau, Rau, *My Father, Charlie* Chaplin, 353.

76. Kenneth Schuyler Lynn, *Charlie Chaplin and His Times* (New York: Simon & Schuster, 1997), 488.

77. "U.S. Attorney-General Criticises Chaplin," *The Irish Times*, October 3, 1952, 3.

78. *Ibid.*

79. Raymond T. Blair, "Charles Chaplin Barred Pending Hearing by U.S.," *New York Herald Tribune*, September 20, 1952, 1.

80. Bosley Crowther, "The Modern—Mellower—Times of Mr. Chaplin," *The New York Times*, November 6, 1960, SM52.

81. Francis O'Neill, *David Raksin*. 1952, Black and white photographic print, 2192 × 2947 px. Available from: Photofest, https://photofest.wamnet.com.

82. Guernsey Jr., "On the Screen: *Limelight*," 14.

83. Tinée, "Chaplin's New Film Superior," A3.

84. Bosley Crowther, "Mr. Chaplin's *Limelight*," *The New York Times*, November 2, 1952, X1.

85. Hedda Hopper, "Looking at Hollywood: Screen Folk, Big and Little, Hail Action Against Chaplin," *Chicago Tribune*, September 20, 1952, A2.

86. John Cameron Swayze, "New York: Tamales and Buttermilk," *Daily Boston Globe*, January 2, 1953, 11.

87. Maland, *Chaplin and American Culture*, 308.

88. "Hughes Asks R.K.O. To Ban *Limelight*," *The New York Times*, January 28, 1953, 23.

89. D.M. Marshman, Jr., "'Censor' Fears," *Los Angeles Times*, January 20, 1953, A4.

90. "Legion Rejected On Film," *The New York Times*, March 4, 1953, 22.

91. "Rowdies Score Big Hit Against Charlie Chaplin," *Chicago Daily Tribune*, December 23, 1952, 12.

92. Robinson, *Chaplin*, 639.

93. *Ibid.*, 640.

94. Charles Chaplin to Sydney Chaplin and Gypsy, August 26, 1953, ECCI00006301, CCA.

95. Sydney Chaplin to Charlie Chaplin, October 1953, quoted in Lisa Stein Haven, *Syd Chaplin* (Jefferson, NC: McFarland & Company, Inc., 2011), 218.

96. Cooke, *Six Men*, 48.

97. Wes D. Gehring, *Chaplin's War Trilogy: An Evolving Lens in Three Dark Comedies, 1918–1947* (Jefferson, NC: McFarland & Company, Inc., 2014), 162.

Chapter 10

1. Laurie Henshaw," Soundtrack—Music from the Movies," *Melody Maker*, October 25, 1952, 9.

2. Arthur W. Kelly to Charles Chaplin, 24 October 1952, ECCI00022804, CCA.

3. DURIUM to George H. Ornstein, 3 March 1953, ECCI00022762, CCA.

4. Arthur W. Kelly to Charles Chaplin, 16 March 1953, ECCI00022958, CCA.

5. Louis Lober to Arthur Kelly, 19 March 1953, ECCI00022760, CCA.

6. Arthur W. Kelly to Louis Lober, 20 March 1953, ECCI00022759, CCA.

7. David J. Oppenheim to Arthur Kelly, 9 March 1953, ECCI00022767, CCA.

8. Arthur W. Kelly to Sol Bourne, 27 February 1953, ECCI00022967, CCA.

9. Arthur W. Kelly to Charles Chaplin, 10 March 1953, ECCI00022962, CCA.

10. Arthur W. Kelly to Louis Lober, 4 March 1953, ECCI00022768, CCA.

11. Arthur W. Kelly to W. J. Smith, 15 April 1953, ECCI00022754, CCA.

12. "Reviews of This Week's New Records: Popular," *The Billboard*, May 23, 1953, 136.

13. "Reviews of This Week's New Records: Popular," *The Billboard*, May 30, 1953, 32.

14. R. M. Ford to Mrs. S. H. Bourne, 30 November 1962, ECCI00023277, CCA.

15. "Reviews of This Week's New Records: Popular," *The Billboard*, June 6, 1953, 24.

16. "Reviews of This Week's New Records: Popular," *The Billboard*, May 30, 1953, 32.

17. "Reviews of This Week's New Records," *The Billboard*, June 13, 1953, 22.

18. Herb Schoenfeld, "Jocks, Jukes and Disks," *Variety*, June 3, 1953, 42.

19. Arthur W. Kelly to Louis Lober, 4 June 1953, ECCI00022748, CCA.

20. "Reviews of This Week's New Records: Popular," *The Billboard*, May 23, 1953, 136.

21. "Reviews of This Week's New Records: Popular," *The Billboard*, May 30, 1953, 32.

22. Jimmy Jungermann, "German Artists Still Cover Hits," *Billboard*, February 9, 1963, 20.

23. Rachel M. Ford to Bonnie Bourne, 31 January 1963, ECCI00023320, CCA.

24. Charles Chaplin and Geoffrey Parsons, "Eternally," ©Copyright 1953 (Renewed). Published Worldwide by Bourne Co., New York, NY. All Rights Reserved. International Copyright Secured. (ASCAP)

25. Arthur W. Kelly to Saul Bourne, 21 July 1953, ECCI00022934, CCA.

26. "New Records to Watch: Popular,'" *The Billboard*, July 4, 1953, 32.

27. "Reviews of This Week's New Records," *Billboard*, July 18, 1953, 24.

28. "Reviews of This Week's New Records," *Billboard*, August 1, 1953, 24.

29. "Reviews of This Week's Singles: Spotlight Winners of the Week," *The Billboard*, January 4, 1960, 45.

30. "'54 Reissue of *Limelight* In N.Y., Other Keys, Though Still Blacked Out in L.A.," *Variety*, August 19, 1953, 3.

31. "Film Notes," *Backstage*, December 18, 1954, iv.

32. S. H. Bourne to Herbert P. Jacoby, 18 March 1954, ECCI00023235, CCA.

33. Arthur W. Kelly to Charles Chaplin, 11 February 1954, ECCI00023237, CCA.

34. Charlie Chaplin to Arthur Kelly, 10 March 1954, ECCI00023236, CCA.

35. S. H. Bourne to Herbert P. Jacoby, 18 March 1954, ECCI00023235, CCA.

36. Arthur W. Kelly to Saul Bourne, 19 March 1954, ECCI00023232, CCA.

37. Arthur W. Kelly to Charles Chaplin, 12 May 1954, ECCI00023230, CCA.

38. Charles Chaplin, John Turner, and Geoffrey Parsons, "Smile," ©Copyright 1954 (Renewed). Published Worldwide by Bourne Co., New York, NY. All Rights Reserved. International Copyright Secured. (ASCAP)

39. "Reviews of New Pop Records," *Billboard*, July 24, 1954, 27.

40. "Reviews of New Pop Records," *Billboard*, October 2, 1954, 38.

41. R. de Bailleux to Arthur W. Kelly, 25 October 1954, ECCI00023212, CCA.

42. "Review Spotlight on...Records," *Billboard*, August 21, 1954, 40.

43. "Reviews of New Pop Records," *Billboard*, August 21, 1954, 40.

44. R. M. Ford to Mrs. S. H. Bourne, 29 January 1963, ECCI00023321, CCA.

45. Mrs. S. H. Bourne to Rachel M. Ford, 31 January 1963, ECCI00023320, CCA.

46. Bonnie Bourne to Charles Chaplin, 24 March 1959, ECCI00020445, CCA.

Chapter 11

1. Charles Chaplin to James Agee, 16 December 1953, ECCI00008462, CCA.

2. Charles Chaplin to Sydney Chaplin and Gypsy, August 26, 1953, ECCI00006301, CCA.

3. Robinson, *Chaplin*, 644.

4. Epstein, *Remembering Charlie*, 137.

5. Ella Winter, "But It's Sad, Says Chaplin, It's Me," in Kevin J. Hayes, *Charlie Chaplin Interviews* (Jackson, MS: The University Press of Mississippi, 2005), 119.

6. "Calm Down, Charlie Boy, Says Candidus," *Daily Sketch* (London), September 11, 1957, 8.

7. Cecil Wilson, "A Comic Genius Turns to Politics...Charlie the Pompous Defeats the Clown," *Daily Mail* (London), September 11, 1957, CCA.

8. W. L. W., "Flashes of Old Chaplin Genius: *A King in New York*," *The Manchester Guardian*, September 17, 1957, 5.

9. Campbell Dixon, "Chaplin *King* Funny Only In Patches," *The Daily Telegraph*, September 11, 1957.

10. Donald Gomery, *London Daily Express*, quoted in Art Buchwald, "Charlot's Revenge?" *Los Angeles Times*, September 17, 1957, B5.

11. Leonard Lyons, "Lyons Den," *Chicago Daily Defender*, September 3, 1957, 8.

12. Isabel Quigly, "Contemporary Arts: Bitterness Creeps In," *The Spectator*, September 20, 1957, 368–369.

13. John Osborne, "Chaplin Aims a Kick At America," *Evening Standard*, September 12, 1957, ECCI 00011059, CCA.

14. Wilson, "A Comic Genius Turns to Politics."

15. "Chaplin Not Anti-U.S., No Communist, He Says," *The New York Times*, September 12, 1957, 38.

16. "Chaplin Says He Loves U.S.," *The Baltimore Sun*, September 12, 1957, 12.

17. "Angry Charlie," *Daily Sketch* (London), September 10, 1957, ECCI00011025, CCA.

18. Harold Myers, "'I Have Done a Positive Service In Making *A King in N.Y.*': Chaplin," *Variety*, September 18, 1957, 1.

19. "*A King in New York*," *Variety*, September 18, 1957, 6.

20. Roscoe Drummond, "Chaplin Produces Un-American Flop," *The Atlanta Constitution* September 28, 1957, 4.

21. "He's Still the Screen's Genius: *A King in New York*," *Picturegoer*, September 14, 1957, 16.

22. Harold Hobson, "Chaplin Premiere in London: New Films," *The Christian Science Monitor*, September 24, 1957, 5.

23. S. W. "At the Cinema," *The Jerusalem Post*, December 23, 1957, 2.

24. Hedda Hopper, "Looking at Hollywood: Chaplin Film Satirizes U.S.; Won't Be Shown Here," *Chicago Daily Tribune*, May 9, 1956, B8.

25. Robinson, *Chaplin*, 641.

26. Charles Chaplin, "Weeping Willows," ©Copyright 1957 (Renewed). Published Worldwide by Bourne Co., New York, NY. All Rights Reserved. International Copyright Secured. (ASCAP)

27. "Wonderful, Said Chaplin," *Picturegoer*, October 20, 1956, 9.

28. "Holliday Too Busy for Chaplin Part," *Melody Maker*, August 25, 1956, 4.

29. R. M. Ford to Saul Bourne, 21 May 1957, ECCI 00023093, CCA.

30. "Wonderful, Said Chaplin," 9.

31. Charles Chaplin, "Million Dollars" Lyrics, ECCI 00009506, CCA.

32. Charles Chaplin, "Rock and Roll" Lyrics, ECCI 00009505, CCA.

33. Charles Chaplin, "I'd Sell My Soul" Lyrics, ECCI00009542, CCA.

34. "*A King in New York*—Shani Wallis," ECCI 00010329, CCA.

35. Charles Chaplin, "Juke Box" Lyrics, ECCI 00009507, CCA.

36. L. R. Swainson, "Little King with Bowler and Cane," *The Age*, March 13, 1956, 9.

37. Charles Chaplin, "Spring's the Time for Making Love," ©Copyright 1957 (Renewed). Published Worldwide by Bourne Co., New York, NY. All Rights Reserved. International Copyright Secured. (ASCAP)

38. Bobby Britton to Attica Film Company Ltd., 1 February 1957, ECCI00010018, CCA.

39. "Joy Nichols to Sing in New Chaplin Film," *The Age*, March 15, 1956, 4.

40. L. R. Swainson, "Chaplin's Film Vow," *The Age*, May 7, 1957, 10.

41. Charles Chaplin, "Now That It's Ended," ©Copyright 1957 (Renewed). Published Worldwide by Bourne Co., New York, NY. All Rights Reserved. International Copyright Secured. (ASCAP)

42. Charles Chaplin, "A Thousand Windows (Serenade)" Lyrics, ECCI00009503, CCA.

43. Charles Chaplin, *A King in New York* Script, ECCI00009550, CCA.

44. James, *Making Music with Charlie Chaplin*, 55.

45. *Ibid.*, 56.

46. *Ibid.*, 57.

47. *Ibid.*

48. *Ibid.*

49. "Geraldo and Brother Sid (pianist with the band for 20 years) Part Company," *New Musical Express*, June 19, 1957, 7.

50. Peter Knight to Attica Film Co., bill, 1 May 1956, ECCI00022908, CCA.

51. Rachel M. Ford to Charles Chaplin, 2 December 1958, ECCI00020525, CCA.

52. R. M. Ford to Sol Bourne, 26 November 1956, ECCI00022994, CCA.

53. Jack Gerber to Jerry Epstein, 14 April 1956, ECCI00022900, CCA.

54. Rachel Ford to Philip Sainton, 1 May 1956, ECCI00022617, CCA.

55. Syrett & Sons to Mickey Delamar, 2 May 1956, ECCI00022900, CCA.

56. Barbara Clark, "Philip Sainton (1891–1967): A Personal Memoir," *British Music Society Journal*, Vol. 20 (1998), 7.

57. Philip Sainton to Rachel Ford, 17 May 1956, ECCI00022896, CCA.

58. R. M. Ford to Sol Bourne, 26 November 1956, ECCI00022994, CCA.

59. Kate Guyonvrach, email with the author, December 31, 2016.

60. Jacques Lasry to R. M. Ford, 7 December 1956, ECCI00022881, CCA.

61. Bourne Music to Rachel Ford, telegram, 14 December 1956, ECCI00022995, CCA.

62. Richard J. Doyle, "It's Recorded: Hear Naples and Cry Via Globe-Trot Discs," *The Globe and Mail* (Toronto), June 1, 1957, 27.

63. David Ades, Liner Notes, *Melodies for Romantics*, Guild Light Music, GLCD5155, 2009, compact disc.

64. R. M. Ford to S. H. Bourne, 4 February 1957, ECCI00023130, CCA.

65. Leighton Lucas to Mickey Delamar, 28 January 1957, ECCI00022903, CCA.

66. Mickey Delamar to A. Richards, 1 February 1957, ECCI00022902, CCA.

67. R. M. Ford to Saul Bourne, 13 May 1957, ECCI00023102, CCA.

68. Charles Chaplin and Irving Gordon, "Without You," ©Copyright 1992. Published Worldwide by Bourne Co., New York, NY. All Rights Reserved. International Copyright Secured. (ASCAP)

69. R. M. Ford to Saul Bourne, 13 May 1957, ECCI00023102, CCA.

70. Adele Z. Sandler to R. M. Ford, 29 November 1957, ECCI00023025, CCA.

71. Charles Chaplin, Geoffrey Parsons, and John Turner, "Mandolin Serenade," ©Copyright 1957 (Renewed). Published Worldwide by Bourne Co., New York, NY. All Rights Reserved. International Copyright Secured. (ASCAP)

72. Charles Chaplin, "Mandoline" Lyrics, ECCI00009500, CCA.

73. R. M. Ford to Saul Bourne, 31 May 1957, Association Chaplin/Roy Export SAS, Paris, France.

74. Walter J. Ridley to Charles Chaplin, 8 July 1957, ECCI00022868, CCA.

75. Walter J. Ridley to R. M. Ford, 12 August 1957, ECCI00022866, CCA.

76. Bourne Inc. to J. J. Phillips, 23 August 1957, ECCI00023047, CCA.

77. Laurie Henshaw, "Pop Discs: Art Lund Is Back Again," *Melody Maker*, July 27, 1957, 11.

78. Keith Fordyce, "Chaplin's 'Mandolin,'" *The New Musical Express*, August 2, 1957, 4.

79. Bonnie Bourne to R. M. Ford, 12 October 1958, ECCI00023137, CCA.

80. Tease for *A King in New York*, 1957, ECCI00009495, CCA.

81. "Chaplin—What a Man," *Picturegoer*, August 10, 1957, 17.

82. A. M. G. Gelardi to R. M. Ford, 23 July 1957, ECCI00009471, CCA.

83. A. M. G. Gelardi to R. M. Ford, 2 September 1957, ECCI00009497, CCA.

84. A. M. G. Gelardi to R. M. Ford, memorandum, 16 December 1957, ECCI00009460, CCA.

85. Cyril Gee to R. M. Ford, 13 September 1956, ECCI00022891, CCA.

86. *A King in New York* Musical Commentary, 8th version, 4 July 1957, ECCI00009549, CCA.

87. Walter J. Ridley to R. M. Ford, 12 August 1957, ECCI00022866, CCA.

88. Bourne Inc. to J. J. Phillips, 23 August 1957, ECCI00023043, CCA.

89. K. G. Allison to Rachel Ford, 7 October 1957, ECCI00022876, CCA.

90. "Saul Bourne Dies," *New Musical Express*, October 18, 1957, 11.

91. Bonnie Bourne to Rachel Ford, 18 June 1958, Association Chaplin/Roy Export SAS, Paris, France.

92. Herbert P. Jacoby to R. M. Ford, 16 July 1958, Association Chaplin/Roy Export SAS, Paris, France.

93. Bonnie Bourne to Rachel Ford, 18 June 1958, Association Chaplin/Roy Export SAS, Paris, France.

94. R. M. Ford to Mrs. S. H. Bourne, 5 December 1958, ECCI00023142, CCA.

95. Gene Siskel, "Carnegie Contract Commitment Gets Us the First Look," *Chicago Tribune*, June 4, 1972, K11.

96. Roger Ebert, "*A King in New York*," http://www.rogerebert.com/reviews/a-king-in-new-york-1957.

97. Nora Sayre, "Film: *A King in New York* At Last," *The New York Times*, December 22, 1973.

98. Vincent Canby. "Chaplin—Once a King, Always a King." *The New York Times*, January 20, 1974, 101.

99. Pauline Kael, *5001 Nights at the Movies* (1982; repr. New York: Picador, 1991), 395.

Chapter 12

1. "Chaplin Returns to the Beginning," *Los Angeles Times*, April 22, 1959, B4.

2. Rachel M. Ford to Mrs. Saul Bourne, 10 October 1958, ECCI00023138, CCA.

3. James, *Making Music with Charlie Chaplin*, 58.

4. *Ibid.*, 10.

5. Eric James, *Silent Music: The Story of Eric James*, directed by Christopher Lane (2002; Ontario).

6. Mrs. S. H. Bourne to Rachel Ford, 2 December 1958, ECCI00023136, CCA.

7. James, *Silent Music: The Story of Eric James*.

8. James, *Making Music with Charlie Chaplin*, 76.

9. *Ibid.*, 64.

10. *Ibid.*, 65.

11. *Ibid.*

12. *Ibid.*

13. *Ibid.*, 67.

14. James, *Silent Music: The Story of Eric James*.

15. James, *Making Music with Charlie Chaplin*, 67.

16. Weston Taylor, "Chaplin Hits a New Note," *News of the World* (London), June 12, 1960, CCA.

17. James, *Making Music with Charlie Chaplin*, 79.

18. *Ibid.*, 69.

19. *Ibid.*

20. *Ibid.*, 72.

21. *Ibid.*

22. James, *Silent Music: The Story of Eric James*.

23. *Ibid.*

24. *Ibid.*

25. James, *Making Music with Charlie Chaplin*, 77.

26. Chaplin, *My Life In Pictures*, 161.

27. Sime., "Moving Pictures: *A Dog's Life*," *Variety*, April 19, 1918, 45.

28. Eileen Burnier to Rachel Ford, 28 November 1958, ECCI00020528, CCA.

29. Eileen Burnier to Rachel Ford, 9 December 1958, ECCI00020522, CCA.

30. R. M. Ford to Madame Burnier, 10 December 1958, ECCI00020515, CCA.

31. Eric James to Charles Chaplin, 11 December 1958, ECCI00020513, CCA.

32. James, *Making Music with Charlie Chaplin*, 80.

33. *Ibid.*

34. Hooman Mehran, "New DVD Releases of Chaplin Films," in *Chaplin's* Limelight *and the Music Hall Tradition*, Frank Scheide and Hooman Mehran, eds. (Jefferson, NC: McFarland & Co., Inc., 2006), 201.

35. Eric James to R. M. Ford, 15 January 1959, ECCI 00020504, CCA.

36. R. M. Ford to Mrs. S. H. Bourne, 16 January 1959, ECCI00023202, CCA.

37. James, *Making Music with Charlie Chaplin*, 66.

38. B. Feldman & Co., advertisement, *The Stage*, December 9, 1915, 19.

39. "Picture News and Notes," *Pictures and The Picturegoer*, November 13, 1915, 126.

40. Cooke, *Six Men*, 35.

41. "Chaplin Angry Over Criticism In London Paper," *Chicago Daily Tribune*, July 29, 1917, 12.

42. "20,000 Throng Wall St. to Hear Movie Stars Tell How to Win War," *New York Tribune*, April 9, 1918, 8.

43. Maland, *Chaplin and American Culture*, 40.

44. "Films Reviewed: *Shoulder Arms*," *The Billboard*, November 2, 1918, 52.

45. "Chaplin As Soldier Drops Old Disguise," *The New York Times*, October 21, 1918, 15.

46. Theodore Huff, *Charlie Chaplin* (1951; repr. New York: Arno Press & *The New York Times*, 1972), 102.

47. Christian Delage, *Chaplin Facing History* (Paris: Jean-Michel Place, 2005), 24.

48. Mae Tinée, "A Great Picture with a Great Man on a Great Day: *Shoulder Arms* with Charlie Chaplin," *Chicago Daily Tribune*, November 12, 1918, 18.

49. James, *Making Music with Charlie Chaplin*, 63.

50. *Ibid.*, 65.

51. Robert E. Sherwood, ed., "*The Pilgrim*" From *The Best Moving Pictures of 1922–23* by Robert E. Sherwood (Boston: Small, Maynard & Company, 1923), 62.

52. "News of Dailies," *Variety*, April 5, 1923, 50.

53. "Chaplin Film Is Censored by Iowa Ku Klux," *Los Angeles Times*, April 4, 1923, I16.

54. "Movie Facts and Fancies," *Boston Daily Globe*, February 28, 1923, 14.

55. *The American*, quoted in "*Pilgrim* Makes Critics Laugh: New York Reviewers Admit Falling Under Chaplin Spell In His Latest," *Motion Picture News*, March 10, 1923, 1198.

56. George Little, Jack Stanley, and Henry Dellon, "Somebody : Song One-Step" (1919). The University of Maine, *Vocal Popular Sheet Music Collection*. Book 1478. http://digitalcommons.library.umaine.edu/mmb-vp/1478.

57. Charles Chaplin, "Bound for Texas" Lyrics, Archives de Montreux, PP 75—Fonds Charles Chaplin, Clarens, Switzerland.

58. *The Chaplin Revue*, 1960 Decca Records, DL 4040, LP.

59. James, *Making Music with Charlie Chaplin*, 75.

60. Mrs. S. H. Bourne to R. M. Ford, 12 October 1960, ECCI00023273, CCA.

61. Brownlow, *The Search for Charlie Chaplin* 56.

62. "Superb," *Daily Express* (London), May 27, 1960.

63. Isabel Quigly, "The Chaplin Revue," *The Spectator*, June 3, 1960.

64. Frank Morriss, "*Chaplin Revue*: Best of Trio Almost Flawless," *The Globe and Mail* (Toronto), April 19, 1960, 28.

65. Untitled, *Jewish Chronicle* (London), May 27, 1960.

66. Quigly, "The Chaplin Revue."

67. "Bourne Music Going Under Hammer; Managerial Dispute Cues Sale," *Variety*, March 11, 1959, 57.

68. R. M. Ford to Mrs. S. H. Bourne, 25 March 1959, ECCI00023198, CCA.

69. Bonnie Bourne to R. M. Ford, 1 April 1959, ECCI00023195, CCA.

70. Bonnie Bourne to R. M. Ford, telegram, 7 April 1959, ECCI00023192, CCA.

71. R. M. Ford to Mrs. S. Bourne, 16 April 1959, ECCI 00023191, CCA.

72. Bonnie Bourne to R. M. Ford, 24 April 1959, ECCI00023189, CCA.

73. R. M. Ford to Mrs. Saul Bourne, 16 July 1959, ECCI00023169, CCA.

74. R. M. Ford to Charles Chaplin, 3 August 1959, ECCI00023164, CCA.

75. Milt Gabler to R. M. Ford, 4 March 1960, ECCI 00020420, CCA.

76. R. M. Ford to Murray Lorber, 17 May 1960, ECCI 00020402, CCA.

77. Milt Gabler to R. M. Ford, 20 June 1960, ECCI 00020399, CCA.

78. R. M. Ford to H. Jacoby, 29 April 1960, ECCI 00020374, CCA.

79. Allen Evans, "LPs: *The Chaplin Revue*," *New Musical Express*, August 26, 1960, 4.

80. "Stage and Film Music: *The Chaplin Revue*," *Melody Maker*, September 10, 1960, 14.

81. "*The Billboard*'s Music Popularity Charts...Packaged Records: Very Strong Sales Potential: *The Chaplin Revue*," *The Billboard*, June 20, 1960, 58.

82. "Tuneful Trifles as the Composer Intended," *North Western Evening News* (UK), September 17, 1960, CCA.

83. R. M. Ford to H. Jacoby, 28 November 1960, ECCI0020359, CCA.

84. W. P. Robinson to R. M. Ford, 7 April 1960, ECCI 00020421, CCA.

85. R. M. Ford to E. James, 13 December 1960, ECCI 00020470, CCA.

86. Eric James to R. M. Ford, 3 January 1961, ECCI 00020468, CCA.

87. Decca Record Company to Hubert J. Stone, 23 February 1961, ECCI00020347, CCA.

88. Herbert P. Jacoby to Isabelle Marks, 2 March 1961, ECCI00020346, CCA.

89. R. M. Ford to H. Jacoby, 24 March 1961, ECCI 00020336, CCA.

90. Herbert P. Jacoby to R. M. Ford, 27 March 1961, ECCI0020335, CCA.

91. Herbert P. Jacoby to R. M. Ford, 28 March 1961, ECCI00020334, CCA.

92. Epstein, *Remembering Charlie*, 152.

93. R. M. Ford to Jack Berner, 14 December 1972, ECCI003135380, CCA.

94. Kate Guyonvarch, email with the author, December 2, 2016.

95. James, *Making Music with Charlie Chaplin*, 81.

96. R. M. Ford to Charles Chaplin, 31 May 1963, ECCI00023307, CCA.

97. *Ibid.*

98. "Chaplin Plans 2 New Comedies; Denies Bitterness Toward U.S.," *The New York Times*, June 29, 1962, 12.

99. Robinson, *Chaplin*, xv.

Chapter 13

1. Chaplin, *My Autobiography*, 391.

2. "Chaplin Plans 2 New Comedies; Denies Bitterness Toward U.S.," *The New York Times*, June 29, 1962, 12.

3. Harold Mendelssohn, "Chaplin Back In Film Harness," *Los Angeles Times*, February 27, 1966, B10.

4. "Chaplin's Son Forsakes Beard, Gets Movie Job," *The Globe and Mail*, January 5, 1966, 12.

5. Mendelssohn, "Chaplin Back In Film Harness."

6. Stephen Watts, "Chaplin Directs, But the Spotlight Is On Sophia," *The New York Times*, March 20, 1966, 123.

7. Gene Sherman, "Chaplin Breaks Silence to Announce Return to Films," *Los Angeles Times*, November 3, 1965, C11.

8. Robinson, *Chaplin*, 673.

9. Raymond E. Palmer, "Chaplin Waited, Got Guillotine," *The Austin Statesman*, January 6, 1967, 40.

10. *Ibid.*

11. Sally K. Marks, "Charles Chaplin: Man Who Cares: Chaplin Story," *Los Angeles Times*, March 19, 1967, C14.

12. "Chaplin Film Is Panned," *The Washington Post*, January 6, 1967, C9.

13. "An Irked Chaplin Calls Critics 'Bloody Idiots,'" *The New York Times*, January 7, 1967, 20.

14. Francis Wyndham, "Chaplin on the Critics, the Beatles, the Mood of London," *South China Sunday Post-Herald*, April 16, 1967, 17.

15. R. M. Ford to Mrs. S. H. Bourne, 28 February 1967, ECCI00023441, CCA.

16. "Entertainment Films: Longer Notices: *Countess From Hong Kong, A*," *Monthly Film Bulletin*, January 1, 1967, 23.

17. Bosley Crowther, "Screen: *A Countess From Hong Kong*," *The New York Times*, March 17, 1967, 35.

18. "Feature Reviews," *Boxoffice BookinGuide*, April 3, 1967, 4010.

19. Philip K. Schemer, "*A Countess From Hong Kong* Premieres at the Pantages," *Los Angeles Times*, March 20, 1967, D24.

20. James, *Making Music with Charlie Chaplin*, 100.

21. Charles Chaplin to Darryl Zanuck, 29 September 1959, ECCI00022880, CCA.

22. Philip G. Jones to M. Woodward, 28 February 1966, ECCI00010706, CCA.

23. *Ibid.*

24. Bonnie Bourne to Charles Chapin, 29 April 1966, ECCI00010710, CCA.

25. Jerome Epstein to Eric James, 9 April 1966, ECCI00022620, CCA.

26. Schemer, "*A Countess From Hong Kong* Premieres," D24.

27. "A Film of 'Real, Happy Humanity,'" *The Irish Times*, November 2, 1965, 1.

28. Charles Chaplin, *Stowaway: Hong Kong 1946*, 1965, ECCI00010270, CCA.

29. *Ibid.*

30. Charles Chaplin, "A Countess from Hong Kong" Waltz, Lyrics, ECCI00010697, CCA.

31. Epstein, *Remembering Charlie*, 152.

32. James, *Making Music with Charlie Chaplin*, 101.

33. Charles Chaplin, "Neopolitan Love Song," Lyrics, ECCI00010699, CCA.

34. Rachel Ford to Charles Chaplin, 7 November 1966, ECCI00010671, CCA.

35. Charles Chaplin, "This Is My Song," Lyrics, ECCI00011070, CCA.

36. Mike Hennessey, "Chaplin's 'Song' Catches Fire In Europe," *Billboard*, April 24, 1967, 60.

37. Andrea Kon, *This Is My Song: A Biography of Petula Clark* (London: W.H. Allen, 1983), 181.

38. Petula Clark, in discussion with the author, October 9, 2014.

39. Kon, *This Is My Song*, 183.

40. Petula Clark, in discussion with the author, October 9, 2014.

41. *Ibid.*

42. Petula Clark, in discussion with the author, October 9, 2014.

43. Kon, *This Is My Song*, 182.

44. Petula Clark, in discussion with the author, October 9, 2014.

45. Kon, *This Is My Song*, 182.

46. Petula Clark, in discussion with the author, October 9, 2014.

47. "Beautiful Pet Clark," *New Musical Express*, January 28, 1967, 6.

48. "Feature Reviews," *Boxoffice BookinGuide*, April 3, 1967, 4010.

49. "'Song' Wave Is Hitting France," *Billboard*, March 11, 1967, 66.

50. "Trenet's Suite Charges Chaplin a Tune Thief," *Variety*, July 3, 1968, 45.

51. "Expert Asked to Study Song," *The Washington Post*, July 9, 1968, A12.

52. James, *Making Music with Charlie Chaplin*, 101.

53. Kon, *This Is My Song*, 185.

54. Chaplin, *Stowaway: Hong Kong 1946*.

55. *Ibid.*

56. *Ibid.*

57. *Ibid.*

58. Charles Chaplin, "Bonjour Madame" Lyrics, ECCI00010698, CCA.

59. Jerome Epstein, "On music and sound effects," ECCI00010678, CCA.

60. Charles Chaplin, "Love Is a Star" Lyric, Archives de Montreux, PP 75—Fonds Charles Chaplin, Clarens, Switzerland.

61. James, *Making Music with Charlie Chaplin*, 100.

62. *Ibid.*, 80.

63. Bill Williamson to Denis Johnson, 15 February 1966, ECCI00010663, CCA.

64. Bourne Music to Rachel Ford, telegram, 6 July 1966, ECCI00023455, CCA.

65. R. M. Ford to Mrs. S. H. Bourne, 24 August 1966, ECCI00023450, CCA.

66. "*A Countess from Hong Kong*: Stereophonic Music Recording," 27–28 September 1966, ECCI 00010690, CCA.

67. Charles Chaplin memos on *A Countess from Hong Kong*, 27 September 1966, 42.f-385, Margaret Herrick Library, Academy of Motion Picture Arts and Sciences.

68. John Coleman, "Films: Without the Prince," *New Statesman*, January 13, 1967, 57.

69. Joseph Gelmis, "Chaplin's *Countess* No Laughing Matter," *Newsday*, March 17, 1967, 2A.

70. "Soundtrack Spotlight: *The* [*sic*] *Countess From Hong Kong*," *Billboard*, March 25, 1967, 76.

71. "Record Reviews: *A Countess From Hong Kong*," *Variety*, March 15, 1967, 52.

72. Edward C. Kosicki, "A Look At the Records: Charles Chaplin's *A Countess From Hong Kong*," *The Hartford Courant*, August 27, 1967, 2G.

73. R. M. Ford to Mrs. S. H. Bourne, 4 November 1966, ECCI00023445, CCA.

74. Bonnie Bourne to Rachel Ford, 9 November 1966, ECCI00023444, CCA.

75. Petula Clark, in discussion with the author, October 9, 2014.

76. *Ibid.*

Chapter 14

1. "Chaplin Plans 2 New Comedies; Denies Bitterness Toward U.S.," *The New York Times*, June 29, 1962, 12.

2. Brock, "*Modern Times*."

3. "Screen News Here and In Hollywood: Chaplin Plans to Make Score and Commentary For His 1927 Picture, *The Circus*," *The New York Times*, March 17, 1942, 25.

4. Hanns Eisler to Lois Runser, 16 September 1947, University of Southern California Library, Hanns Eisler Papers, Collection no. 0207 (Box 2, Folder 3), Feuchtwanger Memorial Library, Special Collections, USC Libraries, University of Southern California.

5. Berndt Heller, "The Reconstruction of Eisler's Film Music: *Opus III, Regen* and *The Circus*," *Historical Journal of Film, Radio and Television*, Vol. 18, No. 4, 1998, 551.

6. Notowicz, *Wir reden hier nicht von Napoleon. Wir reden von Ihnen!*, 197.

7. Heller, "The Reconstruction of Eisler's Film Music: *Opus III, Regen* total and *The Circus*," 553.

8. Vincent Canby, "If You Haven't Laughed Lately," *The New York Times*, December 7, 1969, D5.

9. Rachel Ford to Eric James, December 21, 1967, Association Chaplin/Roy Export SAS, Paris, France.

10. "Mr. Williamson—*The Circus*," Association Chaplin/Roy Export SAS, Paris, France.

11. R. M. Ford to The Rank Organisation, 3 April 1968, Association Chaplin/Roy Export SAS, Paris, France.

12. Charles Chaplin, "Swing little girl," ECCI 00015641, CCA.

13. Charles Chaplin, "She worked in a circus," ECCI00015614, CCA.

14. James, *Making Music with Charlie Chaplin*, 86.

15. *Ibid.*, 87.

16. Stanley Kauffmann, "*The Circus*" from Richard Schickel, Ed., *The Essential Chaplin: Perspectives on the Life and Art of the Great Comedian* (Ivan R. Dee: Chicago, 2006), 191.

17. Peter Bogdanovich, *Who the Hell's In It: Conversations with Hollywood's Legendary Actors* (New York: Ballantine Books, 2004), 356.

18. *Ibid.*

19. *Ibid.*

20. Canby, "If You Haven't Laughed Lately," D5.

21. Roger Greenspun, "Screen: *The Funniest Man in the World*," *The New York Times*, December 18, 1969.

22. Roger Greenspun, "Little Tramp: *Circus*, '28 Film with Chaplin, Is Revived," *The New York Times*, December 16, 1969, 52.

23. Mark Shivas, "Remembrance of Tramps Past," *The New York Times*, December 12, 1971.

24. Chaplin, *My Life In Pictures*, 188.

25. Eric James to Rachel Ford, 21 September 1971, Association Chaplin/Roy Export SAS, Paris, France.

26. "*Kid/The Idle Class* Music Track: Correspondence with Eric James," Association Chaplin/Roy Export SAS, Paris, France.

27. Rachel Ford to Eric James, 1 July 1971, ECCI 00022621, CCA.

28. Eric Rogers to Rachel Ford, 14 October 1971, ECCI00022635, CCA.

29. J. Foster to R. M. Ford, 21 December 1972, ECCI 00022678, CCA.

30. Morris Bright and Robert Ross, *Mr. Carry On: The Life and Work of Peter Rogers* (London: BBC Worldwide Ltd, 2000), 109.

31. Mo Rothman to Steven Mellor, 14 December 1971, ECCI00004805, CCA.

32. John Jenkins to Eric Rogers, 19 February 1975, ECCI00004797, CCA.

33. James, *Making Music with Charlie Chaplin*, 108.

34. *Ibid.*, 109.

35. *Ibid.*, 10.

36. *Ibid.*, 81.

37. *Ibid.*, 102.

38. *Ibid.*, 103.

39. Charles Chaplin, "I walk the streets," ECCI 00022637, CCA.

40. Chaplin, *My Life In Pictures*, 188.

41. Elizabeth Renzetti, "Side by Side with Charlie Chaplin," *The Globe and Mail* (Toronto), January 19, 1995, E1

42. Ray W. Frohman, "Charlie Chaplin," in *Charlie Chaplin: Interviews*, ed. Kevin Hayes (Jackson, MS: University of Mississippi Press, 2005), 44.

43. Mervyn Cooke, *A History of Film Music* (New York: Cambridge University Press, 2008), 27.

44. Claude Bergnières, "Le retour de Chaplin," *Le Figaro*, October 29, 1971, CCA.

45. Eric James to R. M. Ford, 28 April 1971, ECCI 00023380, CCA.

46. R. M. Ford to Eric James, 30 April 1971, ECCI 00023379, CCA.

47. "The Screen," *The New York Times*, September 26, 1921.

48. Grace Kingsley, "Flashes: *Idle Class* Zippy," *Los Angeles Times*, October 31, 1921, III2.

49. *The Globe*, quoted in "First Runs On Broadway: Their Presentation and Press Comments," *Exhibitors Trade Review*, October 8, 1921, 1328.

50. Mrs. S. H. Bourne to R. M. Ford, 12 November 1976, ECCI00023392, CCA.

51. Shivas, "Remembrance of Tramps Past."

52. Chaplin Jr., Rau, Rau, *My Father, Charlie* Chaplin, 41.

53. Paul Vitello, "Mo Rothman Dies at 92; Revived Interest in Charlie Chaplin," *The New York Times*, September 26, 2011.

54. "Interview with Howard Koch," *Academy Leader*, April 1972, 4.

55. "Charlie Chaplin's Honorary Award: 1972 Oscars," YouTube video, from a performance televised by NBC on April 10, 1972, posted by "Oscars," https://www.youtube.com/watch?v=J3Pl-qvA1X8.

56. Charles Chaplin's Honorary Academy Award acceptance speech, Academy Awards Acceptance Speech Database, http://aaspeechesdb.oscars.org/link/044-23/.

57. "History of the Walk of Fame," http://www.walkoffame.com/pages/history.

58. Doug Shuit, "Bitterness Survives 20 Years: They Haven't Given Up—Letter Writers Assail Chaplin," *Los Angeles Times*, April 9, 1972, B.

59. Chaplin, *My Autobiography*, 295.

60. "*Pay Day*," Reviews, *Exhibitors Herald*, April 1, 1922, 55.

61. "Witmark Songs In Evidence," *The Music Trade Review*, April 29, 1922, 56.

62. R. M. Ford to Jack Foster, 28 May 1974, ECCI 00315320, CCA.

63. "*Pay Day* Music Track, 1972–1973, Sweet Adeline To-Do," Association Chaplin/Roy Export SAS, Paris, France.

64. *The Gentleman Tramp*, directed by Richard Patterson (Paris: Roy Export Company Ltd., 1976), DVD.

65. "*Pay Day* Music Track, 1972–1973, Sweet Adeline To-Do."

66. "*Pay Day* Music Track."

67. "Screen Pictures of 1922," *The New York Times*, July 2, 1922, 3.

68. "The Shadow Stage," *Photoplay*, June 1922, 58.

69. Lita Grey Chaplin and Morton Cooper, *My Life with Chaplin: An Intimate Memoir* (New York: Grove Press, 1966), 170.

70. "The Screen," *The New York Times*, December 8, 1919, 20.

71. "*A Day's Pleasure*," *The Billboard*, December 13, 1919.

72. S. Morgan Powell, "Montreal," *Variety*, January 1920, 46.

73. Peter Milne, "A Tabloid Review," *Picture-Play Magazine*, March 1920, 68.

74. Roy Export Company to Eric James, 4 May 1973, ECCI00022623, CCA.

75. Roy Export Company to Eric Rogers, 24 August 1974, ECCI00022614, CCA.

76. Mrs. S. H. Bourne to Rachel Ford, 27 November 1973, CCA.

77. "*A Day's Pleasure* Music Track," Association Chaplin/Roy Export SAS, Paris, France.

78. Linda A. Griffith, "Comments and Criticisms of a Free-Lance: Chaplin's 'Sunny' Not So Funny," *Film Fun*, September 1919, 9.

79. Patsy Smith, "Among the Women," *Variety*, June 1919, 18.

80. "Moving Pictures: *Sunnyside*," *Variety*, June 1919, 53.

81. Chaplin, *My Trip Abroad*, 149.

82. Chaplin, *My Autobiography*, 231.

83. "Little Tramp Plans Movie on *The Freak*," uncited newspaper, CCA.

84. Roy Export Company to Eric James, 15 February 1974, ECCI00022624, CCA.

85. Roy Export Company to Eric Rogers, 8 April 1974, ECCI00023135, CCA.

86. René Micha, "Chaplin As Don Juan," *Sight and Sound*, January 1, 1954, 134.

87. Chaplin, *My Autobiography*, 192.

88. *Ibid.*, 193.

89. "*Sunnyside*—Adding Music Track," Association Chaplin/Roy Export SAS, Paris, France.

90. M. W. Balfe, "Then You'll Remember Me" from *The Bohemian Girl* (Baltimore, MD: Charles A. Vogeler Co.), Bloomington, IN: The Lilly Library, Indiana University, http://webapp1.dlib.indiana.edu/inharmony/detail.do?action=detail&fullItemID=/lilly/devincent/LL-SDV-187010.

91. "*Sunnyside*—Adding Music Track," Association Chaplin/Roy Export SAS, Paris, France.

92. James, *Making Music with Charlie Chaplin*, 81.

93. *Ibid.*, 111.

94. "*A Woman of Paris*—Music Track," ECCI 00030163, CCA.

95. R. M. Ford to Eric James, 18 April 1975, ECCI 00022625, CCA.

96. James, *Making Music with Charlie Chaplin*, 111.

97. "*A Woman of Paris*—Music Track."

98. Eric James to Rachel Ford, 24 November 1975, Association Chaplin/Roy Export SAS, Paris, France.

99. "*A Woman of Paris*—Music Track."

100. Roy Export Company to Eric Rogers, 2 February 1976, ECCI00022612, CCA.

101. "*A Woman of Paris*—Music Track."

102. James, *Making Music with Charlie Chaplin*, 112.

103. R. M. Ford to Eric James, 17 January 1978, ECCI00023353, CCA.

104. Eric James to Rachel Ford, 22 January 1978, ECCI00023352, CCA.

105. Vincent Canby, "Film View: A 'Lost' Chaplin Masterpiece," *The New York Times*, April 23, 1978, D1.

106. Janet Maslin, "Rare Chaplin, *A Woman of Paris*," *The New York Times*, April 14, 1978, C13.

107. Robinson, *Chaplin*, 688.

108. James, *Making Music with Charlie Chaplin*, 110.

109. John Pym, "*A Woman of Paris*," *Monthly Film Bulletin*, January 1, 1978, 34.

110. Robinson, *Chaplin*, 688.

111. James, *Making Music with Charlie Chaplin*, 73.

112. Eric James to Rachel Ford, 24 November 1975, Association Chaplin/Roy Export SAS, Paris, France.

113. R. M. Ford to Lady Chaplin, 20 July 1976, ECCI00023407, CCA.

114. R. M. Ford to Eric James, 20 July 1976, ECCI 00023357, CCA.

115. Eric James to Rachel Ford, 8 August 1976, ECCI 00023406, CCA.

116. R. M. Ford to Eric James, 18 August 1976, ECCI 00020455, CCA.

117. R. M. Ford to Mrs. S. H. Bourne, 29 September 1976, ECCI00023400, CCA.

118. Mrs. S. H. Bourne to Rachel Ford, 29 November 1976, ECCI000233391, CCA.

119. Petula Clark, in discussion with the author, October 9, 2014.

120. *Ibid.*

121. Tim Rose Price, email with the author, October 11, 2016.

122. *Ibid.*

123. *Ibid.*

124. Tim Rose Price, "Secrets In Your Eyes," unpublished, provided to the author, November 23, 2016.

125. Tim Rose Price, email with author, October 11, 2016.

126. Tim Rose Price, email with author, November 23, 2016.

127. Tim Rose Price, email with author, October 11, 2016.

128. Bonnie Bourne to R. M. Ford, 21 October 1976, ECCI00023394, CCA.

129. R. M. Ford to Mrs. H. S. [*sic*] Bourne, 12 October 1976, ECCI000233398, CCA.

130. R. M. Ford to Mrs. S. H. Bourne, 29 September 1976, ECCI00023400, CCA.

131. R. M. Ford to Mrs. H. S. [*sic*] Bourne, 12 October 1976, ECCI000233398, CCA.

132. " Mrs. S. H. Bourne to Rachel M. Ford, 12 October 1976, ECCI00023399, CCA.

133. Charles Chaplin and Glen Anthony, "You Are the Song," ©Copyright 1974 & 1978 (Renewed). Published Worldwide by Bourne Co., New York, NY. All Rights Reserved. International Copyright Secured. (ASCAP)

134. Epstein, *Remembering Charlie*, 152.

135. Chaplin, *My Autobiography*, 328.

136. Bercovici, "Making a Picture," 490.

Epilogue

1. "*Limelight* and *Cabaret* Win Music Awards: 1973 Oscars," YouTube.

2. Academy Awards Acceptance Speech Database, http://aaspeechesdb.oscars.org/link/045–13/.

3. R. M. Ford to Savoy Hotel London, telegram, 28 March 1973, ECCI00022723, CCA.

4. Kevin Thomas, "*Limelight* in L.A.—At Last," *Los Angeles Times,* December 13, 1972, C28.

5. Oona Chaplin to Bert Schneider, telegram, 16 December 1972, ECCI00022740, CCA.

6. Larry Russell to Charlie Chaplin, 12 September 1951, ECCI00022852, CCA.

7. Paul Rasch, in discussion with the author, March 20, 2017.

8. Inez James Russell to Lenore Terry, 24 January 1973, ECCI00022741, CCA.

9. Adele Z. Sandler to Dorothy A. Jetter, 31 January 1973, ECCI00022743, CCA.

10. Mo Rothman to Oona Chaplin, telegram, 15 February 1973, ECCI00022742, CCA.

11. Adele Z. Sandler to Rachel M. Ford, 15 February 1973, ECCI00022735, CCA.

12. Inez James Russell to Lenore Terry, 15 February 1973, ECCI00022736, CCA.

13. R. M. Ford to Adele Z. Sandler, 20 February, 1973, ECCI00022734, CCA.

14. R. M. Ford to Bert Schneider, 20 February 1973, ECCI00022733, CCA.

15. R. M. Ford to Herbert P. Jacoby, 21 February 1973, ECCI00022732, CCA.

16. Bert Schneider to Rachel Ford, 5 March 1973, ECCI00022730, CCA.

17. Rachel Ford to Bert Schneider, 5 March 1973, ECCI00022729, CCA.

18. R. M. Ford to Bert Schneider, 27 March 1973, ECCI00022726, CCA.

19. Paul Rasch, in discussion with the author, March 20, 2017.

20. Robert Reneau, email with the author, March 22, 2017.

21. Paul Rasch, in discussion with the author, March 20, 2017.

22. *Ibid.*

23. Thomas, "*Limelight* in L.A.—At Last," C28.

24. Addison Verrill, "N.Y. View On Oscar: Scant Wit, Gaffs, Amateur Timing, Cue Cards, Agit-Prop," *Variety*, April 4, 1973.

25. Mo Rothman to Rachel Ford, telegram, 27 March 1973, ECCI00022725, CCA.

26. R. M. Ford to Mo Rothman, 29 March 1973, ECCI00022719, CCA.

27. R. M. Ford to Bert Schneider, 3 April 1973, ECCI00022717, CCA.

28. R. M. Ford to Herbert P. Jacoby, 3 April 1973, ECCI00022716, CCA.

29. R. M. Ford to Mrs. Bourne, 10 April 1973, ECCI00022713, CCA.

30. R. M. Ford to Herbert P. Jacoby, 9 April 1973, ECCI00022714, CCA.

31. Herbert P. Jacoby to R. M. Ford, 13 April 1973, ECCI00022709, CCA.

32. Howard Lucraft, "*Limelight* Oscar for Music Score Likely to Trigger Unique Lawsuits," *Variety*, April 12, 1973.

33. *Ibid.*

34. R. M. Ford to John Green and Arthur Hamilton, 29 May 1973, ECCI00022701, CCA.

35. John Green and Arthur Hamilton to Studio Music Department Heads, et al, "46th Annual Academy Awards: Special Rules for the Music Awards (Covering Films Released in 1973)," ECCI00022699, CCA.

36. "After 1973 *Limelight* Academy Win, Oldies Quietly Ruled Out," *Variety*, January 28, 1981, 20.

37. R. M. Ford to John Green and Arthur Hamilton, 29 May 1973, ECCI00022701, CCA.

38. Randall Larson, "Past, Present, and Future: The Film Music of Russell Garcia," *Soundtrack*, http://www.colemanzone.com/Time_Machine_Project/garcia_interview.htm.

39. Gina Garcia, in discussion with the author, December 28, 2014.

40. Marc Meyers, "The Case of the Misplaced Oscar," September 19, 2008, http://www.jazzwax.com/2008/09/the-case-of-the.html.

41. *Ibid.*

42. Meyers, "The Case of the Misplaced Oscar."

43. *Ibid.*

44. Russell Garcia, *I Have Hundreds of Stories, Some of Them True* (Albany, GA: BearManor Media, 2013), 12.

45. Gina Garcia, in discussion with the author.

46. Garcia probably meant Rasch's son, Paul.

47. Meyers, "The Case of the Misplaced Oscar."

48. Numerous attempts by the author to reach Morgan or anyone in her family through various online and offline channels were unsuccessful.

49. During the research and writing of this book, numerous attempts were made to reach Linda Russell Morgan without success.

50. If there is still a question about Larry Russell's participation in *Limelight*, there is no doubt about his lasting impression on popular music. The 1952 song "Vaya Con Dios" ("Go with God"), written with wife Inez James and Buddy Pepper, was first recorded by Anita O'Day in December. The following year, Les Paul and Mary Ford's rendition topped *The Billboard*'s charts, where it remained for eleven weeks. Thirty weeks later, the tune was still in the Top Ten. "Vaya Con Dios" was *Billboard*'s number one tune for 1953, while Chaplin's "Terry's Theme" from *Limelight* came in at a distant thirty-four. In 2005 the Les Paul and Mary Ford recording of Russell's song was inducted into the Grammy Hall of Fame and, in 2010, the Western Writers of America chose it as one of the Top 100 Western songs of all time. Larry Russell died at the age of forty on February 14, 1954.

Russell Garcia continued his work in jazz, arranging strings for Buddy DeFranco and Oscar Peterson's 1954 album of George Gershwin standards. His 1955 *Wigville* album was one of the first jazz albums to utilize Schoenberg's tone-row method, while *Four Horns and a Lush Life* featured Garcia's original four-trombone concept. The list of artists he worked with reads like a *Who's Who* of popular and jazz music—Judy Garland, Stan Kenton, Julie London, Mel Tormé, and Margaret Whiting, as well as arranging and conducting Louis Armstrong and Ella Fitzgerald's classic 1957 recording of *Porgy and Bess*. Garcia's work in television and film began in the late 1940s and he later scored a number of episodes of popular television shows like *Playhouse 90*, *Perry Mason*, *Rawhide*, *The Untouchables*, and *The Fugitive*. Producer and director George Pal was a fan of Garcia's 1959 exotica album *Fantastica*, which led him to hire the composer to compose two classic scores—*The Time Machine* (1960) and *Atlantis, The Lost Continent* (1961). In 1966, Garcia sold his possessions and left behind his career in Hollywood to sail the Pacific with his wife in a trimaran spreading the word of the Bahá'í faith before settling in New Zealand in 1971. Russell continued to compose and arrange, and he and Gina spent much of their time volunteering to teach primary school children. In 2002, the couple wrote the opera *The Unquenchable Flame*, and, in 2009, were awarded The New Zealand Order of Merit from HM Queen Elizabeth II for their Service to Music. Garcia was still touring and playing jazz until a few weeks prior to his death on November 19, 2011, at age ninety-five.

As for the other *Limelight* music collaborators, not much is known about Bernard Katz's career in the forty years following his time with Chaplin beyond his death in 1982 in San Francisco at the age of eighty-two. Keith Williams, on the other hand, organized a new 17-piece band labeled "The Dazzling Sound," recording for Liberty Records. A 1957 Disc Jockey Poll listed the group as one of the country's top ten "Most Promising Orchestras." Williams toured with Johnny Mathis and the Hi-Lo's and later became President of the Musician's Union Local-47 in Los Angeles. Williams eventually earned his Master's degree in music from California State University, Northridge, and taught in the Los Angeles School District, retiring in 1988. Williams died on December 27, 2008, at the age of eighty-four.

After *Limelight*, Raymond Rasch continued his nightclub work, accompanying artists such as Marie Wilson and Jane Morgan. In December 1958, he released a concept album of Columbus's discovery of America in song form from the vantage point of the three ships—*The Nina, The Pinta and The Santa Maria*—co-composed and lyrics written by Ray Gilbert. The album had narration by Eddie Albert, who also voiced the sea monster, with Joanne Gilbert, Lee Millar, and Thurl Ravenscroft as the three ships. Rasch's biggest hit was the 1960 concept album *Wild Is Love*, written with lyricist Dotty Wayne, for Nat "King" Cole. In September of that year, Rasch released his own album *Let's Do the Town* and two years later *Flutes Front and Center* with the Pipers 10. Rasch died of a heart attack on December 23, 1964, at the age of forty-seven, sitting at his piano. "I shall always remember Ray as a kind, loving, considerate person," said his sister Mae in our interview, "and our time together, unfortunately, was too short."

51. *The Kid* was just one of hundreds of films Carl Edouarde worked on during his long tenure as musical director of the Strand Theatre in New York. He resigned in 1927 at the dawn of the talkies to enter film sound production. Along the way, he composed the scores to *The Hunchback of Notre Dame* (1924) and *The Private Life of Helen of Troy* (1927), and conducted the music for *Steamboat Willie* (1928), Walt Disney's first animated short to feature synchronized sound. On December 10, 1929, the Pathé Studio in New York caught fire, killing several people. Edouarde, who was working on a musical short, survived by leaping from a second-story window which broke his ankle and effectively ended his career as a musician. He died at his home in Locust, New Jersey, on December 8, 1932, at the age of fifty-seven. On October 20, 1924, Daniel Frogman, B. A. Rolfe, John Philip Sousa, and Adolph Zukor presented Edouarde with a silver loving cup to commemorate the conducting of his 15,000th overture. A hand-carved walnut stand bearing a gold plate containing a record of his accomplishments was installed in the Strand's orchestra pit, a fitting tribute to Edouarde's distinguished career in silent films.

Louis F. Gottschalk scored only two more films after *A Woman of Paris*—*Romola* (1924), starring Lillian and Dorothy Gish, and William Powell, and uncredited work on *Rainbow Man* in 1929. He became a consultant on the scoring and syncing of films, but the last three years of his life he spent in virtual retirement due to ill health. Gottschalk died on July 16, 1934, at age sixty-nine from a paralytic stroke. At his funeral, a quartet from the Uplifters' Club, of which he was an honorary member, sang "He Is Just Away," which Gottschalk had written in remembrance of his son who had died eight years earlier.

52. Frederick Stahlberg, who revised and adapted Gottschalk's *A Woman of Paris* score for publication, continued working with Hugo Riesenfeld at the Rivoli Theatre in New York. When the new Roxy Theatre opened in 1926, Stahlberg was named as one of the

music staff along with H. Maurice Jacquet, Ernö Rapée, and Charles Previn, but he walked out on opening night after a clash with his associates. In 1929, he moved to Los Angeles and became a conductor at M-G-M. Stahlberg died on July 23, 1937, at age sixty, leaving behind a string of compositions that have long been forgotten, including a concerto for violin and string quartet, the symphonic sketch *Across the Sea of the Worlds*, a *Symphony to the Memory of Abraham Lincoln*, a *Capriccio* for nineteen solo instruments, the ballet pantomime *The Bridal Choice*, and an opera, *The Witch's Trial*.

Carli Elinor's obituary in *Variety* stated he scored more than one thousand films and was one of the first to introduce sound effects in films. Following his work on *The Gold Rush*, Elinor became general music director for Fox Film studio in 1930, and counted among his staff arrangers Erich Wolfgang Korngold and the young Hugo Friedhofer. Elinor built Santa Monica's Elmiro Theatre in 1933 but later sold it to move back to Rumania. He returned to Hollywood in the late 1930s but had to take work as a character actor, especially in onscreen conducting roles. His last appearance was a cameo in the star-studded *Around the World in 80 Days* in 1956. Elinor died of a heart attack on October 20, 1958, at age sixty-eight.

In between serving as Meredith Willson's assistant on *The Great Dictator* and working again with Chaplin on the 1942 version of *The Gold Rush*, Max Terr helped orchestrate Willson's score for *The Little Foxes*. After completing work on *The Gold Rush*, Terr signed a contract with Metro-Goldwyn-Mayer in 1942 and got stuck scoring primarily shorts (sometimes up to twenty a year) over the next five years. After Terr's death on August 2, 1951, at age sixty, Willson went on Edward R. Murrow's *This I Believe* radio program to reminiscence about his longtime friend. "Since Max has gone not a day passes that isn't a pleasanter day because of the things he left behind him," Willson said. "In every room of our apartment there are memories of Max Terr.... I believe pretty firmly that you don't have to be a Beethoven or a Rembrandt, or even a father to leave a heritage to the mortal world.... I think if I leave behind me any part of the kind of things that keep Max Terr alive in the hearts of his fellows, I will have justified my brief hour of strutting and fretting upon the stage."

Terr's Paramount colleague Gerard Carbonara continued to plug away behind the scenes, composing stock music for dozens of feature films, for which he rarely received credit. In 1943, thanks to an AMPAS rule at the time that allowed every studio to nominate a film in all the technical categories, of which Music Score of a Dramatic or Comedy Picture was one, Carbonara finally received an Oscar nomination for *The Kansan*, a B-western released by United Artists starring Richard Dix, Jane Wyatt, and Albert Dekker. Like so many film composers, Carbonara's concert works which include a number of pieces for piano, the *Concerto Orientale* for violin and orchestra, the symphonic poem *Ode to Nature*, numerous songs, and the 1925 opera *Armand* have been ignored. Carbonara died January 11, 1959, at the age of seventy-three.

53. Chaplin gave Arthur Johnston credit in interviews for his work on *City Lights*, but Johnston's days as an amanuensis were coming to a close. He teamed up with lyricist Sam Coslow, writing a number of hit songs, including "Just One More Chance" and "Cocktails for Two." When Bing Crosby first heard Johnston's title song for *Pennies from Heaven* (1936), written with lyricist

Johnny Burke, he insisted that the studio delay the picture until Johnston could recover from an illness and write the entire score, a move that helped the hit song snag an Academy Award nomination. Following the war, Johnston's songwriting pursuits dried up. After a lengthy illness, Johnston died May 1, 1954, at age fifty-six.

54. Chaplin may have suffered at the hands of the critics and the public over the controversial *Monsieur Verdoux*, but not his arranger. As a freelancer not tied to any studio, Rudy Schrager continued to find work, though usually scoring "B" pictures. With the new threat of television wreaking havoc on the film industry, the musicians union was not allowing its members to work in the new medium. As a result, Schrager became involved with David Chudnow, a music director and producer who, with a nod to music practices during the silent days, specialized in assembling scores for films. Schrager joined a team of composers who would write new music or adapt music they had previously written and used. Chudnow recorded the music in Europe where the labor was cheaper than in Hollywood and provided pseudonyms for his composers to protect them from the wrath of the musicians union. Schrager took over as musical director on the *Lux Radio Theatre* from Louis Silvers in 1949 and continued in that position for four years with the *Lux Video Theatre*. In addition to numerous film scores, Schrager composed for television, including such popular Westerns as *Rawhide*, *Gunsmoke*, and *The Big Valley* before dying on August 24, 1983, just days shy of his 83rd birthday.

55. After his work on *The Circus*, Arthur Kay became one of the first music directors at the newly formed Fox Film studio in 1929, where he conducted the 100-piece Fox orchestra. He later performed on Broadway in Harold Arlen and E.Y. "Yip" Harburg's 1937 musical *Hooray for What!* While his name mainly went uncredited when it came to his film music, from 1938 to 1955 Kay supplied the voice of Gandy Goose in a series of 48 animated shorts. He became the musical director of the Los Angeles Civic Light Opera on its formation in 1938 and remained in the position for twenty years, except for a two-year stint on Broadway. There, he provided additional lyrics as well as orchestrations, choral arrangements, and served as musical director for *Song of Norway*, Robert Wright and George Forrest's 1944 operetta of Edvard Grieg. He later served as musical director for Heitor Villa-Lobos' 1948 musical *Magdalena*, and orchestrated and wrote the choral arrangements for Wright and Forrest's Tony Award-winning musical *Kismet*, based on the music of Alexander Borodin. Kay died on December 19, 1969, at the age of eighty-eight.

Following his work on *The Great Dictator*, Meredith Willson scored one more film, William Wyler's pungent adaptation of Lillian Hellman's *The Little Foxes* starring Bette Davis, receiving his second Oscar nomination. During the war, Willson worked for the Armed Forces Radio Service and played a regular character on the George Burns and Gracie Allen radio program. He also wrote hit songs like "You and I," a number one hit for Glenn Miller, "Two in Love," and "May the Lord Bless You and Keep You." In 1957, he performed a Broadway hat trick as composer, lyricist, and librettist of the phenomenally successful *The Music Man*, which beat *West Side Story* for the Best Musical Tony Award. His follow-up, *The Unsinkable Molly Brown*, ran for two seasons, but *Here's Love*, his 1963 adaptation of *Miracle on 34th Street*, flopped, and his fourth musical, *1491*, about Columbus's attempts to finance his famous voyage, never made it to Broadway. Willson died of heart failure in 1984 at the age of eighty-two. In 1991, his third wife, Rosemary Willson, donated $5 million to The Juilliard School in memory of her late husband. The school's first residence hall bears his name to this day.

56. Most of the musicians working on *A King in New York* didn't last long under Chaplin's employ, but their careers did not seem to suffer from their uncredited association with the filmmaker. Peter Knight went on to a successful career with the likes of Dusty Springfield, Scott Walker, Peters and Lee, and the Moody Blues, arranging, conducting and co-composing the band's 1967 concept album *Days of Future Passed*, which included the classic "Nights In White Satin." In the late 1970s Knight worked with The Carpenters on their two Christmas specials, and scored and conducted the Los Angeles Philharmonic on the duo's 1977 album *Passage*, including the trippy classic "Calling Occupants of Interplanetary Craft." Knight's television work included shows by Morecambe and Wise, Bruce Forsyth, Harry Secombe, and the *Song by Song by...* series. In film, he orchestrated scores by Philippe Sarde (*Tess, Ghost Story, Quest for Fire*) and Trevor Jones (*The Dark Crystal*). Knight died on July 30, 1985, of lung cancer at age sixty-eight. Following his death, Yorkshire television launched the annual Peter Knight award to honor excellence in musical arranging. Knight's son, also named Peter, co-produced the original cast recording of *Hair* in 1968.

After his brief stint with Chaplin, Philip Sainton gained his greatest notoriety with his only film score, for John Huston's *Moby Dick* (1956). A certain number of Sainton's concert works have been recorded, though much of his output has fallen into oblivion. Sainton died on September 2, 1967, at age seventy-five.

In the 1950s, Jacques Lasry and his friend François Baschet invented the Cristal, a metal construction that produces sound from oscillating glass cylinders. With his wife Yvonne and Bernard Baschet, they formed the quartet Les Structures Sonores Lasry-Baschet, which toured in Europe, performed on *The Ed Sullivan Show*, and recorded several albums, including the avant-garde *Chronophagie (The Time Eaters)* (1969). From 1957–1958, Lasry composed and arranged the music for thirty-nine broadcasts of Francis Claude's radio program *Monsieur Flute s'en mêle*. He composed ballets and began scoring films, including *Le songe des chevaux sauvages* (1960), *Le roi du village* (1963), and *Elle est à tuer* (1964). In 1968, Lasry converted to Orthodox Judaism, abandoning all of his professional activities. A decade later, Lasry and his wife moved to Israel to settle down in Jerusalem, where he died March 26, 2014, at age ninety-six.

If there is little information on Boris Sarbek's life prior to working with Chaplin on *A King in New York*, there is even less for the decade after. Other than his work on *A Countess from Hong Kong*, Sarbek continued to record albums of light music with his orchestra, including *A Touch of Paris* and *Tangos in Hi-Fi* (both 1957), and *Dark Eyes* (1958). Sarbek died in 1966, though there is no record of the actual date or cause of death.

57. Alfred Newman made good on his promise to never work with Chaplin again. Instead, he became one of the giant figures in film music. As the musical director of United Artists, Newman, who had studied composition with Rubin Goldmark and Arnold Schoenberg, composed his first film score in 1931 with *Street Scene*, the theme of which became a popular instrumental hit.

The list of stellar Newman scores is long—from early successes like *The Prisoner of Zenda* and *Wuthering Heights* to classics from his twenty-year reign at the head of the 20th Century Fox music department (*How Green Was My Valley, The Song of Bernadette, Love Is a Many-Splendored Thing, Anastasia, The Diary of Anne Frank*) and later independents like *How the West Was Won, The Greatest Story Ever Told*, and his final score, *Airport*. On the podium at Fox, he was widely considered the finest conductor in Hollywood and "the Newman strings" were a distinctive feature of the Fox orchestra. Newman mentored a number of future legendary film composers during his tenure at the studio, including Bernard Herrmann, Alex North, Jerry Goldsmith, and John Williams. He received forty-four Oscar nominations over the course of his career (a tally that stood for decades until Williams topped it in 2012) and a record nine awards. A heavy smoker for most of his life, Alfred Newman died at his home in Hollywood on February 17, 1970, at age sixty-eight from complications of emphysema.

Edward Powell orchestrated nearly every Alfred Newman for thirty years, as well as classics by Franz Waxman and Alex North, and later became a member of the board of governors of the Academy of Motion Picture Arts and Sciences. He died at the Motion Picture & Television Hospital in Woodland, California, on February 28, 1984, at age seventy-four.

Like Newman, David Raksin, Powell's partner in crime on *Modern Times*, went on to a celebrated career in Hollywood. As a composer, Raksin worked without credit on forty-eight films before finally sharing screen credit on *The Adventures of Sherlock Holmes* in 1939. His big break came when Alfred Newman and Bernard Herrmann refused to score Otto Preminger's 1944 film noir, *Laura*. Newman assigned Raksin, one of his staff composers at Fox, to write the score and Raksin's haunting theme became an instrumental and jazz classic. He went on to score over 100 films, including *Forever Amber, The Bad and the Beautiful, Pat and Mike*, and *Separate Tables*. Raksin, a former member of the Communist Party briefly in the 1930s, was called before the House Un-American Activities Committee and reluctantly named names of eleven party members who were dead or who had already been named. "What I did was a major sin," he said in a 1997 interview with the *Los Angeles Times*, "but I think I did as well as most human beings would've done under torture.... But there I was, a guy with a family to support and a fairly decent career that was about to go down the drain." Raksin taught film composition at the University of Southern California beginning in 1956 and was an eight-term president of ASCAP from 1962 to 1970. He also served as an advisor on the 1991 Chaplin biopic directed by Richard Attenborough. In a devastating span of three weeks in 2004 that saw the deaths of film music greats Jerry Goldsmith (July 21) and Elmer Bernstein (August 18), David Raksin died at his home in Los Angeles from heart failure on August 11 at age ninety-two.

58. After *A King in New York*, Leighton Lucas's film career ended with the close of the 1950s and a slate of undistinguished films. Lucas returned to his roots in the world of ballet, premiering *Pavane for Mary* about Mary, Queen of Scots with the Edinburgh Ballet Theatre in 1963 and later arranging the music of Jules Massenet for Kenneth MacMillan's *Manon* in 1974. In 1967, he published *Mini Music*, a series of music clerihews that includes a prescient "If I had a computer / Instead of

tutor, / Who knows / What I mightn't compose?" Lucas later became a professor at the Royal Academy of Music and died November 7, 1982, in London at age seventy-nine.

Following his conducting on *The Chaplin Revue*, Eric Spear wrote *Kookaburra*, a musical about Australia, with lyricist Charles Hardy, which had a brief West End run in 1959. He composed the music for BBC serials like *Round the Bend* and *The Bouncing Bear*. But he is best known for theme for *Coronation Street* (1960), which, in its original form, accompanied the opening credits of the popular show for over thirty years. Spear died November 3, 1966, age fifty-six, after a stroke at his home in Guernsey, Channel Islands.

After arranging and conducting *A Countess from Hong Kong* and Chaplin's new score for *The Circus*, Lambert Williamson composed and conducted his final film score for Jerry Epstein's *The Adding Machine* (1969), based on Elmer Rice's 1923 play. Williamson died November 13, 1975, at the age of sixty-eight.

Eric Rogers, Chaplin's arranger and conductor the last years of his life, went back to composing the final *Carry On* films as well as a number of television shows, including *The Chiffy Kids* and *Spider-Woman*. In December 1980, he conducted the score for Disney's *A Dream Called Magic*, written by Buddy Baker, who had been nominated for the Oscar alongside Chaplin et al. in 1973. Rogers died April 8, 1981, at age sixty after a short illness.

59. In between his work with Chaplin, Eric James worked with Ron Moody on the 1968 film version of *Oliver!* and served as the vocal coach for the lead actors in the 1971 *Fiddler on the Roof* film. After Chaplin's death in 1977, James and his wife Phyllis O'Reilly created a stories-slides-and-songs *Tribute to Charlie Chaplin* that they performed for over a decade. Eric and Phyllis moved to Canada in 1988 and, in 2000, he published his autobiography *Making Music with Charlie Chaplin*. James passed away peacefully at Sunnycrest Nursing Home in Whitby on March 28, 2006, at age ninety-two.

60. James, *Silent Music: The Story of Eric James*.

61. Petula Clark, in discussion with the author, October 9, 2014.

62. Dave Dexter, Jr., "Charlie Chaplin: Hit Songwriter As Well As Comedian," *Billboard*, January 7, 1978, 14.

63. Epstein, *Remembering Charlie*, 152.

64. Seldes, "I Am Here To-day," 116.

65. James, *Making Music with Charlie Chaplin*, 71.

Bibliography

Abel. "Disk Reviews—'Sing a Song' (Fox-Trot)—Charlie Chaplin and Lyman's California Orchestra; 'With You, Dear, in Bombay'—Same—Brunswick No. 2912." *Variety,* September 2, 1925.

Academy Awards Acceptance Speech Database. http://aaspeechesdb.oscars.org/link/044–23/.

Ackroyd, Peter. *Charlie Chaplin: A Brief Life.* New York: Nan A. Talese/Doubleday, 2014.

Ades, David. *Melodies for Romantics* Liner Notes. Guild Light Music, GLCD5155, 2009, CD.

"After 1973 *Limelight* Academy Win, Oldies Quietly Ruled Out." *Variety,* January 28, 1981.

"Al Pearce Group on Radio Tonight." *The Daily Republican* (Belvidere, IL), August 23, 1940.

Allen, Kelcey. "Amusements." *Women's Wear,* June 16, 1925.

Anderson, Gillian B. "The Music of the *Circus.*" *LC Information Bulletin,* September 20, 1993.

Anthony, Barry. *Chaplin's Music Hall: The Chaplins and Their Circle in the Limelight.* London: I. B. Tauris & Co. Ltd., 2012.

Atkinson, Brooks. "Beloved Vagabond: Charlie Chaplin Canonized Out of a Sentimental Memory Book." *The New York Times,* February 16, 1936.

B. Feldman & Co. *The Stage,* September 17, 1925.

_____. *The Stage,* December 9, 1915.

Bacon, James. "Chaplin, on *Limelight* Set Is Captain and Crew." *The Atlanta Journal and the Atlanta Constitution,* February 17, 1952.

Balio, Tino. *United Artists: The Company That Changed the Film Industry.* Madison, WI: The University of Wisconsin Press, 1976.

Barris, Alex. "On the Screen." *The Globe and Mail,* November 14, 1952.

Beardsley, Charles. *Hollywood's Master Showman: The Legendary Sid Grauman.* Cornwall Books: Cranbury, NJ, 1983.

"Beautiful Pet Clark." *New Musical Express,* January 28, 1967.

Bercovici, Konrad. "Charlie Chaplin." *Collier's,* August 15, 1925.

_____. "Making a Picture with Charlie Chaplin." *The Royal Magazine,* 1925.

Bergnièries, Claude. "Le Retour de Chaplin." *Le Figaro,* October 29, 1971.

Bergreen, Laurence. *As Thousands Cheer: The Life of Irving Berlin.* Reprint, Boston: Da Capo Press, 1996.

"The Big Little Feature." *Exhibitors Trade Review,* November 17, 1923.

"*The Billboard*'s Music Popularity Charts...Packaged Records: Very Strong Sales Potential: The *Chaplin Revue.*" *The Billboard,* June 20, 1960.

Billy Rose Theatre Collection, The New York Public Library for the Performing Arts.

Blair, Raymond T. "Charles Chaplin Barred Pending Hearing by U.S." *New York Herald Tribune,* September 20, 1952.

"Blanchard Hall Is to Be Enlarged." *Los Angeles Sunday Herald,* June 12, 1904, Part Two.

Bogdanovich, Peter. *Who the Hell's in It: Conversations with Hollywood's Legendary Actors.* New York: Ballantine Books, 2004.

"Bourne Music Going Under Hammer; Managerial Dispute Cues Sale." *Variety,* March 11, 1959.

"The Box Office Slant: The *Gold Rush.*" *Showmen's Trade Review,* March 7, 1942.

Brady, Thomas F. "Video Union Acts in Movie Dispute." *The New York Times,* April 4, 1951.

Bright, Morris, and Robert Ross. *Mr. Carry On: The Life and Work of Peter Rogers.* London: BBC Worldwide Ltd, 2000.

Brock, Timothy. "*The Gold Rush.*" http://www.timothybrock.com/joomla/articles/18-articles/31-the-gold-rush.

_____. "The Intimate Score of the Tramp-Composer: Restoring Music for *City Lights.*" http://www.timothybrock.com/joomla/articles/18-articles/27-the-intimate-score-of-the-tramp-composer-restoring-music-for-city-lights.

_____. "*Modern Times.*" http://www.timothybrock.com/joomla/articles/18-articles/18-modern-times-2004.

Brown, Royal S. *Overtones and Undertones: Reading Film Music.* Berkley, CA: University of California Press, 1994.

Brownlow, Kevin. "Eugène Lourié." In *Chaplin's* Limelight *and the Music-Hall Tradition,* edited by Frank Scheide and Hooman Mehran, 65–71. Jefferson, NC: McFarland, 2006. London: British Film Institute, 2006.

_____. *The Search for Charlie Chaplin.* Reprint, London: UKA Press, 2010.

Buchwald, Art. "Charlot's Revenge?" *Los Angeles Times,* September 17, 1957.

Burton, Jack. "The Honor Roll of Songwriters: No. 105—Arthur Johnston." *Billboard,* August 25, 1951.

Burton, Nigel. *The Bohemian Girl.* In *The New Grove Dictionary of Opera* (Vol. 1), edited by Stanley Sadie, 521–522. New York: Oxford University Press, 1997.

Cable, Ivy Wilson. "Charlie Chaplin Gives a Music-Hall Turn." *The Star,* January 9, 1952.

"Calm Down, Charlie Boy, Says Candidus." *Daily Sketch,* September 11, 1957.

Canby, Vincent. "Chaplin—Once a King, Always a King." *The New York Times,* January 20, 1974.

420

_____. "Film View: A 'Lost' Chaplin Masterpiece." *The New York Times,* April 23, 1978.

_____. "If You Haven't Laughed Lately." *The New York Times,* December 7, 1969.

"Can't Scare Me." *Motion Picture Herald,* September 20, 1947.

"Carl Edouarde of the Films Dies." *The New York Times,* December 9, 1932.

Carnegie Hall Archives, New York.

Carr, Harry. "Will Charlie Kick Off His Old Shoes?" *Motion Picture Magazine,* December 1923.

Catalogue of Copyright Entries: Part 3, Musical Compositions, New Series, Volume 27 for the Year 1932. Washington: United States Government Printing Office, Library of Congress Copyright Division, 1933.

Chaplin, Charles. "Beautiful, Wonderful Eyes." New York: Bourne Co., 1929.

_____. "Mr. Chaplin Answers His Critics." *The New York Times,* October 27, 1940.

_____. *My Autobiography.* New York: Simon & Schuster, 1964.

_____. *My Life in Pictures.* Reprint, London: Peerage Books, 1985.

_____. "Oh! That Cello." Los Angeles: Charlie Chaplin Music Publishing Co., 1916.

_____. "Pantomime and Comedy." *The New York Times,* January 25, 1931.

_____. "There's Always One You Can't Forget." Los Angeles: Charlie Chaplin Music Publishing Co., 1916.

Chaplin, Charles, Abe Lyman, and Gus Arnheim. "Sing a Song." New York: Irving Berlin, Inc., 1925.

Chaplin, Charles, Abe Lyman, and Gus Kahn. "I Like That Little One." Unpublished, 1925.

Chaplin, Charles, and David Robinson. *Footlights with the World of Limelight.* Bologna, Italy: Edizioni Cineteca di Bologna, 2014.

Chaplin, Charles, and Geoffrey Parsons. "Eternally." New York: Bourne Co., 1953.

Chaplin, Charles, and Glen Anthony. "You Are the Song." New York: Bourne Co., 1974 & 1978.

Chaplin, Charles, and Irving Gordon. "Without You." New York: Bourne Co., 1992.

Chaplin, Charles, Geoffrey Parsons, and John Turner. "Mandolin Serenade." New York: Bourne Co., 1957.

Chaplin, Charles, John Turner, and Geoffrey Parsons. "Smile." New York: Bourne Co., 1954.

Chaplin, Charles, Meredith Willson, and Eddie De-Lange. "Falling Star." New York: Irving Berlin Inc., 1941.

Chaplin, Charles, Jr., and N. and M. Rau. *My Father, Charlie Chaplin.* New York: Random House, 1960.

Chaplin, Charlie. *A Comedian Sees the World.* Edited by Lisa Stein Haven. Columbia: University of Missouri Press, 2014.

_____. *My Trip Abroad.* New York: Harper and Brothers, 1922.

_____. "With You, Dear, in Bombay." M. Witmark & Sons, 1925.

Chaplin, Lita Grey, and Morton Cooper. *My Life with Chaplin: An Intimate Memoir.* New York: Grove Press, 1966.

"Chaplin: *Modern Times.*" *The Guardian,* July 14, 1936.

"Chaplin Accepts House 'Invitation.'" *The New York Times,* July 21, 1947.

"Chaplin Angry Over Criticism in London Paper." *Chicago Daily Tribune,* July 29, 1917.

"Chaplin as Soldier Drops Old Disguise." *The New York Times,* October 21, 1918.

"Chaplin at the 'Hip.'" *The Bronxville Review,* February 25, 1916.

"Chaplin Ballet Set for Markova-Dolin." *Variety,* March 1, 1950.

"Chaplin Buys an Ampico." *The Music Trade Review,* January 26, 1926.

"Chaplin Buys Robert-Morton." *The Music Trade Review,* February 7, 1923.

"Chaplin Calls Himself 'Paying Guest' of U.S." *Los Angeles Times,* April 11, 1947.

"Chaplin Declines Award by Critics." *The New York Times,* January 5, 1941.

"Chaplin Discusses His New Picture." *Motion Picture News,* October 6, 1923.

"Chaplin Feature Is Highly Praised." *Motion Picture News,* September 8, 1923.

"Chaplin Film Is Censored by Iowa Ku Klux." *Los Angeles Times,* April 4, 1923.

"Chaplin Film Is Panned." *The Washington Post,* January 6, 1967.

"Chaplin Laughter Broadcasted." *Dunfermline Journal* (Scotland), October 3, 1925.

"Chaplin-Lyman Song: Comedian and Band Leader Using 'Plug' to Get Title." *Variety,* April 8, 1925.

"Chaplin Musical?" *Yorkshire Evening News,* February 9, 1949.

"Chaplin Not Anti-U.S., No Communist, He Says." *The New York Times,* September 12, 1957.

"Chaplin Pic Stirs Storm." *Daily Variety,* June 27, 1947.

"Chaplin Plans 2 New Comedies; Denies Bitterness Toward U.S." *The New York Times,* June 29, 1962.

"Chaplin Promises New Surprises in *Gold Rush*; Sound Track for *Circus.*" *Variety,* November 26, 1941.

"Chaplin Refutes Report on Withdrawal of Film." *The Christian Science Monitor,* May 23, 1940.

"Chaplin Returns to the Beginning." *Los Angeles Times,* April 22, 1959.

The Chaplin Revue. Decca Records, 1960.

"Chaplin Says He Loves U.S." *The Baltimore Sun,* September 12, 1957.

"Chaplin Smashes Sacred Film Conventions: A *Woman of Paris.*" *Los Angeles Times,* August 15, 1923.

"Chaplin to Sing Own Songs." *Motion Picture News,* June 28, 1930.

"Chaplin—What a Man." *Picturegoer,* August 10, 1957.

"Chaplin's New Drama at Two Theaters." *San Francisco Chronicle,* November 25, 1923.

"Chaplin's New Picture Premiere Stirs Distinguished N.Y. Crowd." *The Billboard,* January 14, 1928.

"Chaplin's Son Forsakes Beard, Gets Movie Job." *The Globe and Mail,* January 5, 1966.

"Chaplin's Violin Disk." *Variety,* June 24, 1925.

"Charles Chaplin Talks About His New Comedy." *The New York Times,* January 26, 1947.

"Charley [*sic*] Chaplin Buys Brambach Player." *The Music Trade Review,* January 26, 1918.

Charlie Chaplin Archive. Archives de Montreux, PP 75—Fonds Charles Chaplin, Clarens, Switzerland.

_____. Association Chaplin/Roy Export SAS, Paris, France.

_____. Cineteca di Bologna, Bologna, Italy.

"Charlie Chaplin Buys Organ." *The Music Trade Review,* July 15, 1922.

"Charlie Chaplin—Composer." *Gravesend Report,* October 10, 1925.

"Charlie Chaplin on the Records." *Picturegoer and the Theatre,* October 1, 1925.

"Charlie Chaplin Organizes Music Company for Own Songs." *Motion Picture News,* March 25, 1916.

"Charlie Chaplin Reciprocates." *The Music Trade Review,* December 21, 1918.

"Charlie Chaplin Shines as Musician and Composer." *Music Trade Review,* July 18, 1925.

"Charlie Chaplin Will Build Own Film Plant." *Los Angeles Times,* October 16, 1917.

"Charlie Chaplin's Honorary Award: 1972 Oscars." YouTube, https://www.youtube.com/watch?v=J3Pl-qvA1X8.

"Charlie Chaplin's Organ." *PRESTO,* February 3, 1923.

"Chas. Chaplin's *Woman of Paris* Wins High Praise at Its Premiere." *The Winnipeg Evening Tribune,* December 15, 1923.

Churchill, Douglas W. "Hollywood Gets a Peek at *Fantasia.*" *The New York Times,* October 20, 1940.

_____. "Screen News Here and in Hollywood." *The New York Times,* October 28, 1940.

"Cincinnati Demand Experiences Rapid Recovery From the Summer Lull in Trade." *The Music Trade Review,* October 17, 1925.

Clark, Barbara. "Philip Sainton (1891–1967): A Personal Memoir." *British Music Society Journal,* Vol. 20 (1988).

Clifford McCarty Collection. Margaret Herrick Library, Academy of Motion Picture Arts & Sciences.

"Clown to Come Here for Show." *Los Angeles Times,* January 19, 1928.

Cohen, John S., Jr. "Chaplin Triumphs Anew in *City Lights.*" *New York Sun,* February 7, 1931.

Coleman, John. "Films: Without the Prince." *New Statesman,* January 13, 1967.

Columbia Oral History Archives. Rare Book & Manuscript Library, Columbia University.

"Coming Attractions in the Theaters: Columbia," *East Liverpool Review,* March 24, 1936, 6.

"Composer Dedicated Life to Building a Better World." http://news.bahai.org/story/869, November 28, 2011.

Cooke, Alistair. *Six Men.* London: The Bodley Head, 1977.

Cooke, Mervyn. *A History of Film Music.* New York: Cambridge University Press, 2008.

Coslow, Sam. "Up and Down the Alley." *Exhibitors Herald and Moving Picture World,* January 21, 1928.

Crowther, Bosley. "The Modern—Mellower—Times of Mr. Chaplin." *The New York Times,* November 6, 1960.

_____. "Mr. Chaplin's *Limelight.*" *The New York Times,* November 2, 1952.

_____. "Screen: A *Countess from Hong Kong.*" *The New York Times,* March 17, 1967.

_____. "The Screen in Review: The *Great Dictator.*" *The New York Times,* October 16, 1940.

_____. "Still Supreme." *The New York Times,* October 20, 1940.

Danly, Linda, Ed. *Hugo Friedhofer: The Best Years of His Life: A Hollywood Master of Music for the Movies.* Lanham, MD: The Scarecrow Press, Inc., 2002.

Dash, Thomas R. "Theatres: *Limelight.*" *Women's Wear Daily,* October 24, 1952.

David Raksin Papers, Library of Congress, Washington, D.C.

"*A Day's Pleasure.*" *The Billboard,* December 13, 1919.

Delage, Christian. *Chaplin Facing History.* Paris: Jean-Michel Place, 2005.

Deschin, Jacob. "Screen Reflections." *The Hartford Courant,* May 9, 1929.

Dexter, Dave, Jr. "Charlie Chaplin: Hit Songwriter as Well as Comedian." *Billboard,* January 7, 1978.

Dixon, Campbell. "Chaplin *King* Funny Only in Patches." *The Daily Telegraph,* September 11, 1957.

"Does Public Want Truth in Motion Pictures?: Answer Will Be Comedian's Guide." *Exhibitors Trade Review,* August 11, 1923.

Dolin, Anton. "*Limelight* Fails to Solve Problem of Film Ballet." *Dance and Dancers,* March 1953.

Doyle, Richard J. "It's Recorded: Hear Naples and Cry Via Globe-Trot Discs." *The Globe and Mail* (Toronto), June 1, 1957.

Drummond, Roscoe. "Chaplin Produces Un-American Flop." *The Atlanta Constitution* September 28, 1957.

Dufferin and Clandeboye, Helen Selina Blackwood, and Henry Le Patourel. "Terence's Farewell to Kathleen." London: Chappell & Co, 188-?.

D.W.C. "The Curious Mr. Chaplin." *The New York Times,* February 16, 1936.

Ebert, Roger "*A King in New York,*" http://www.roger ebert.com/reviews/a-king-in-new-york-1957.

"Egyptian Theater Mecca." *Los Angeles Times,* June 26, 1925.

Elinor, Carli D. "From Nickelodeon to Super-Colossal: The Evolution of Music to Pictures." *The Cue Sheet,* October 1995.

"Enter Charles Chaplin, Tardily." *The New York Times,* February 2, 1936.

"Entertainment Films: Longer Notices: *Countess from Hong Kong, A.*" *Monthly Film Bulletin,* January 1, 1967.

"Entire Score Is Memorized by Conductor." *Los Angeles Times,* October 5, 1923.

Epstein, Jerry. *Remembering Charlie.* New York: Doubleday, 1989.

Evans, Allen. "LPs: The *Chaplin Revue.*" *New Musical Express,* August 26, 1960.

"Expert Asked to Study Song." *The Washington Post,* July 9, 1968.

Eyman, Scott, and Hooman Mehran. "Melissa Hayden." In *Chaplin's* Limelight *and the Music-Hall Tradition,* edited by Frank Scheide and Hooman Mehran, 74–82. Jefferson, NC: McFarland, 2006. London: British Film Institute, 2006.

"Feature Reviews." *Boxoffice BookinGuide,* April 3, 1967.

Ferguson, Otis. "Hallelujah, Bum Again." *The New Republic,* February 19, 1936.

"'54 Reissue of *Limelight* in N.Y., Other Keys, Though Still Blacked Out in L.A." *Variety,* August 19, 1953.

"Film Notes." *Backstage,* December 18, 1954.

"A Film of 'Real, Happy Humanity.'" *The Irish Times,* November 2, 1965.

"Film Reviews: *Monsieur Verdoux.*" *Variety,* April 16, 1947.

"Films Reviewed: *Shoulder Arms.*" *The Billboard,* November 2, 1918.

"First Runs on Broadway: Their Presentation and Press Comments." *Exhibitors Trade Review,* October 8, 1921.

Flom, Eric L. *Chaplin in the Sound Era: An Analysis of the Seven Talkies.* Jefferson, NC: McFarland, 1997.

Fordyce, Keith. "Chaplin's 'Mandolin.'" *The New Musical Express,* August 2, 1957.

Fowke, Edith, and Joe Glazer. *Songs of Work and Protest.* Mineola, NY: Dover Publications, 1973.

Frohman, Ray W. "Charlie Chaplin." In *Charlie Chaplin: Interviews,* edited by Kevin Hayes, 38–45. Jackson, MS: University of Mississippi Press, 2005.

Garcia, Russell. *I Have Hundreds of Stories, Some of Them True.* Albany, GA: BearManor Media, 2013.

Gehring, Wes D. *Chaplin's War Trilogy: An Evolving Lens in Three Dark Comedies, 1918–1947.* Jefferson, NC: McFarland, 2014.

Gelmis, Joseph. "Chaplin's *Countess* No Laughing Matter." *Newsday,* March 17, 1967.

The Gentleman Tramp, directed by Richard Patterson. Paris: Roy Export Company Ltd., 1976.

"Geraldo and Brother Sid (Pianist with the Band for 20 Years) Part Company." *New Musical Express,* June 19, 1957.

"Gino Severi to Lead Orchestra at Loew's State." *Los Angeles Times,* August 31, 1925.

"Glimpses of Chaplin's Comedy." *The New York Times,* August 11, 1929.

Graham, Virginia. "Cinema: *Limelight.*" *The Spectator,* October 17, 1952.

Green, Abel. "Film Reviews: *Modern Times.*" *Variety,* February 11, 1936.

Greenspun, Roger. "Little Tramp: *Circus,* '28 Film with Chaplin, Is Revived." *The New York Times,* December 16, 1969.

_____. "Screen: The *Funniest Man in the World.*" *The New York Times,* December 18, 1969.

Griffith, Linda A. "Comments and Criticisms of a Free-Lance: Chaplin's 'Sunny' Not So Funny." *Film Fun,* September 1919.

Guernsey, Otis L., Jr. "On the Screen: *Limelight.*" *New York Herald Tribune,* October 24, 1952.

Haining, Peter. *The Legend of Charlie Chaplin.* Secaucus, NJ: Castle, 1982.

Hale, Georgia. *Charlie Chaplin: Intimate Close-Ups.* Edited by Heather Kieran. Lanham, UK: The Scarecrow Press, Inc., 1999.

Hall, Gladys. "Charlie Chaplin Attacks the Talkies." *Motion Picture,* May 1929.

Hall, Mordaunt. "The Changeable Chaplin." *Motion Picture Classic,* August 1926.

_____. "Chaplin Hilarious in His *City Lights.*" *The New York Times,* February 7, 1931.

_____. "Chaplin's Film Nearing Completion." *The New York Times,* July 6, 1930.

_____. "The Screen: Chaplin of Hollywood: The *Circus.*" *The New York Times,* January 9, 1928.

_____. "Shy Charlie Chaplin Opens His Heart." *The New York Times,* August 9, 1925.

Harrower, Jack. "Presentations: Prologue Flash on Strand Stage; Simple, but Highly Effective." *The Film Daily,* January 15, 1928.

Haven, Lisa Stein. "Planting the Seeds for *Monsieur Verdoux.*" http://charliechaplin.com/en/articles/215-Planting-the-Seeds-for-Verdoux, May 2006.

Hayes, Kevin J., ed. *Charlie Chaplin: Interviews.* Jackson, MS: University Press of Mississippi, 2005.

Heller, Berndt. "The Reconstruction of Eisler's Film Music: *Opus III, Regen* and the *Circus,*" *Historical Journal of Film, Radio and Television,* Vol. 18, No. 4, 1998.

Hennessey, Mike. "Chaplin's 'Song' Catches Fire in Europe." *Billboard,* April 24, 1967.

Henshaw, Laurie. "Pop Discs: Art Lund Is Back Again." *Melody Maker,* July 27, 1957.

_____. "Soundtrack—Music from the Movies." *Melody Maker,* October 25, 1952.

"He's Still the Screen's Genius: A *King in New York.*" *Picturegoer,* September 14, 1957.

Hickman, C. Sharpless. "Movies and Music." *Music Journal,* November 1952.

_____. "Music News." *Music Journal,* February 1955.

Higgins, Charlotte. "The Great Composer." *The Guardian,* November 27, 2000.

"History of the Walk of Fame." http://www.walkoffame.com/pages/history.

Hobson, Harold. "Chaplin Premiere in London: New Films." *The Christian Science Monitor,* September 24, 1957.

"Holifield to Answer Pix Smear in House." *The Film Daily,* June 13, 1947.

"Holliday Too Busy for Chaplin Part." *Melody Maker,* August 25, 1956.

Hopper, Hedda. "Hedda Hopper's Hollywood." *Los Angeles Times,* October 16, 1940.

_____. "Looking at Hollywood: Chaplin Film Satirizes U.S.; Won't Be Shown Here." *Chicago Daily Tribune,* May 9, 1956.

_____. "Looking at Hollywood: Screen Folk, Big and Little, Hail Action Against Chaplin." *Chicago Tribune,* September 20, 1952.

"House Reviews: Grauman's Egyptian, Los Angeles, June 26." *Variety,* July 1, 1925.

Huff, Theodore. *Charlie Chaplin.* Reprint, New York: Arno Press & *The New York Times,* 1972.

"Hughes Asks R.K.O. to Ban *Limelight.*" *The New York Times,* January 28, 1953.

Husband, John J., and William P. Mackay. "Revive Us Again." http://www.hymnary.org/text/we_praise_thee_o_god_for_the_son_of.

"In Chaplin's Studio." *The New York Times,* January 12, 1930.

IN Harmony: Sheet Music from Indiana. The Lilly Library, Indiana University.

"Inside Stuff: On Music." *Variety,* August 12, 1925.

"Inside Stuff: On Music—Chaplin's Own Songs and Disk." *Variety,* July 1, 1925.

"Instructional Films and Where to Get Them." *Moving Picture Age,* May 1921.

"Interview with Howard Koch." *Academy Leader,* April 1972.

"An Irked Chaplin Calls Critics 'Bloody Idiots.'" *The New York Times,* January 7, 1967.

James, Eric. *Making Music with Charlie Chaplin: An Autobiography.* Lanham, MD: The Scarecrow Press, Inc., 2000.

"Joe Plunkett's Rest." *Variety,* January 18, 1928.

Johnson, Fred. "Action & Reaction." *San Francisco Call-Bulletin,* June 5, 1931.

Johnson, Horace. "Frederick Stahlberg, Conductor of the Rivoli Theatre Lauds Men of Motion Picture Orchestras." *The Metronome,* February 1921.

Jones, Lorenzo, Jr. "Photoplay News: A *Woman of Paris* by Charles Chaplin." *The Atlanta Constitution,* December 30, 1923.

"Joy Nichols to Sing in New Chaplin Film." *The Age,* March 15, 1956.

Jungermann, Jimmy. "German Artists Still Cover Hits." *Billboard,* February 9, 1963.

Jungmeyer, Jack. "Charlie Chaplin Picks Unknown for Coveted Lead in Picture." *Battle Creek* (Michigan) *Enquirer,* April 30, 1934.

Kael, Pauline. *5001 Nights at the Movies.* Reprint, New York: Picador, 1991.

Kauffmann, Stanley. "*The Circus.*" In *The Essential Chaplin: Perspectives on the Life and Art of the Great Comedian,* edited by Richard Schickel, 188–191. Ivan R. Dee: Chicago, 2006.

Kaufman, Louis, with Annette Kaufman. *A Fiddler's Tale: How Hollywood and Vivaldi Discovered Me.* Madison, WI: The University of Wisconsin Press, 2003.

"Kay Is Far from Being a 'Yes' Man." *Los Angeles Times,* November 25, 1923.

"*The Kid.*" *Exceptional Photoplays* (National Board of Review), January–February 1921.

The Kid. The New York Times, January 16, 1921.

"*A King in New York.*" *Variety,* September 6, 1957.

"*A King in New York.*" *Variety,* September 18, 1957.

Kingsley, Grace. "Flashes: *Idle Class* Zippy." *Los Angeles Times,* October 31, 1921.

Kon, Andrea. *This Is My Song: A Biography of Petula Clark.* London: W.H. Allen, 1983.

Kosicki, Edward C. "A Look at the Records: Charles Chaplin's a *Countess from Hong Kong.*" *The Hartford Courant,* August 27, 1967.

Kubizek, August. *The Young Hitler I Knew.* Translated by Geoffrey Brooks. Reprint, London: Greenhill Books, 2006.

Lait, Jack. "*A Woman of Paris.*" *Variety,* September 27, 1923.

Lampe, J. Bodewalt. *Remick Folio of Moving Picture Music, Vol. 1.* New York: Jerome H. Remick & Co., 1914.

Lapworth, Charles. "Chaplin Talks!" *The Film Weekly,* December 6, 1930.

Larson, Randall. "Past, Present, and Future: The Film Music of Russell Garcia." *Soundtrack,* http://www.colemanzone.com/Time_Machine_Project/garcia_interview.htm.

"Late Reviews: The *Gold Rush.*" *Motion Picture Herald,* March 7, 1942.

Lauterbach, Richard. "The Whys of Chaplin's Appeal." *The New York Times Magazine,* May 12, 1950.

Ledin, Victor, and Marina A. Ledin. *Meredith Willson: Symphony No. 1 in F Minor ("A Symphony of San Francisco"), Symphony No. 2 in E Minor ("The Missions of California"),* Liner Notes, Moscow Symphony Orchestra, William T. Stromberg, Naxos 8.559006, 1999.

"Legion of Decency Reviews Seven New Productions." *Motion Picture Herald,* April 19, 1947.

"Legion Rejected on Film." *The New York Times,* March 4, 1953.

Lewis, Robert. *Slings and Arrows: Theater in My Life.* New York: Applause, 1984.

"*Limelight* and *Cabaret* Win Music Awards: 1973 Oscars." YouTube, https://www.youtube.com/watch?v=fmQJqxdLnMo.

"*Limelight* with Charles Chaplin." *Harrison's Reports,* October 11, 1952.

"*Limelight* …with Tunes by a Man Who Can't Write Music…!" *Bristol* (UK) *Evening World,* February 3, 1953.

"'Little Man' Meets Press in Big Interview; No Communist, He Says." *Showmen's Trade Review,* April 19, 1947.

LOOK Magazine Photograph Collection, Library of Congress, Prints & Photographs Division.

Lucraft, Howard. "*Limelight* Oscar for Music Score Likely to Trigger Unique Lawsuits." *Variety,* April 12, 1973.

_____. "Stricter Check on Music Oscars for 'Integrity' & 'Authenticity': Cite Credits to 'Wrong' Parties." *Variety,* January 24, 1973.

Luebering, J. E. "Till Eulenspiegel." *Encyclopedia Britannica,* https://www.britannica.com/topic/Till-Eulenspiegel-German-literature.

Luz, Ernst. *Motion Picture Synchrony.* New York: Music Buyers Corporation, 1925.

Lynn, Kenneth Schuyler. *Charlie Chaplin and His Times.* New York: Simon & Schuster, 1997.

Lyons, Leonard. "Lyons Den." *Chicago Daily Defender,* September 3, 1957.

"Making Fun of Something That's Serious." *New York Herald Tribune,* October 13, 1940.

Maland, Charles. *City Lights.* London: British Film Institute, 2007.

Maland, Charles J. *Chaplin and American Culture: The Evolution of a Star Image.* Princeton, NJ: Princeton University Press, 1989.

Mamorstein, Gary. *A Ship Without a Sail: The Life of Lorenz Hart.* New York: Simon & Schuster, 2012.

"Man Named Squiz Said He Was Good So Willson Plays the Flute." *The Austin Statesman,* October 20, 1940.

Margaret Herrick Library, Special Collections, Academy of Motion Picture Arts and Sciences.

"Marks and Berlin." *Variety,* May 12, 1926.

Marks, Sally K. "Charles Chaplin: Man Who Cares: Chaplin Story." *Los Angeles Times,* March 19, 1967.

Marriot, A. J. *Chaplin Stage by Stage.* A. J. Marriott, 2005.

Marshman, Jr., D.M. "'Censor' Fears." *Los Angeles Times,* January 20, 1953.

Martin, Donald. "Two Outstanding Films with Music." *The Etude,* December 1940.

Maslin, Janet. "Rare Chaplin, a *Woman of Paris.*" *The New York Times,* April 14, 1978.

McCabe, John. *Charlie Chaplin.* Reprint, London: Robson Books, 1992.

McCarty, Clifford. *Film Composers in America: A Filmography, 1911–1970,* Second ed. New York: Oxford University Press, 2000.

McConachy, Sue. Interview with Mischa Terr, n.d.

McCourt, Bonnie. "Julian Ludwig." In *Chaplin's Limelight and the Music-Hall Tradition,* edited by Frank Scheide and Hooman Mehran, 83–91. Jefferson, NC: McFarland, 2006.

McQuirk, Charles J. "Chaplinitis." *Motion Picture Magazine,* July 1915.

Mehran, Hooman. "New DVD Releases of Chaplin Films." In *Chaplin's* Limelight *and the Music Hall Tradition,* edited by Frank Scheide and Hooman Mehran, 198–206. Jefferson, NC: McFarland, 2006.

Mehran, Hooman, and Frank Scheide, eds. *Chaplin: The Dictator and the Tramp.* London: British Film Institute, 2004.

Mellen, Joan. *Modern Times.* London: British Film Institute, 2006.

"Melody Mart." *The Billboard,* August 15, 1925.

"Memphis Bans *Verdoux.*" *The New York Times,* June 11, 1947.

Mendelssohn, Harold. "Chaplin Back in Film Harness." *Los Angeles Times,* February 27, 1966.

Menjou, Adolphe, and M. M. Musselman. *It Took Nine Tailors.* New York: McGraw-Hill, 1948.

Meredith Willson Papers, Great American Songbook Foundation.

Merrick, Mollie. "Musical Score Often Responsible for Film Being a Hit: Fans Approve Movie Melody." *The Detroit Free Press,* March 1, 1936.

Methven, Florence, and Marian Gillespie. "When You Look in the Heart of a Rose." New York: Leo Feist, Inc., 1918.

Meyers, Marc. "The Case of the Misplaced Oscar." Jazzwax.com (blog), September 19, 2008, http://www.jazzwax.com/2008/09/the-case-of-the.html.

Micha, René. "Chaplin as Don Juan." *Sight and Sound,* January 1, 1954.

"Million-Dollar Theatre Opens." *The Motion Picture News,* April 18, 1914.

Milne, Peter. "A Tabloid Review." *Picture-Play Magazine,* March 1920.

"Milwaukee Music Merchants Report a Slight Advance with Opening of July." *The Music Trade Review,* July 25, 1925.

"Minus His Cane Chaplin Is Shy." *New York Tribune,* February 21, 1916.

"Monsieur Chaplin Comes to Town with a Film—And Meets the Press." *Motion Picture Herald,* April 16, 1947.

Morriss, Frank. "*Chaplin Revue*: Best of Trio Almost Flawless." *The Globe and Mail* (Toronto), April 19, 1960.

"Motion Picture Music and Musicians: The *Gold Rush.*" *Pacific Coast Musician,* March 7, 1942.

"Movie Facts and Fancies." *Boston Daily Globe,* February 28, 1923.

"Moving Pictures: *Sunnyside.*" *Variety,* June 1919.

"Moving Pictures: Strand." *Variety,* February 6, 1920.

"Moving Pictures: The Strand." *Variety,* April 18, 1919.

Murray, Ray. "*The Circus* Opens at Grumman's Chinese with One Ring Circus." *Exhibitors Herald and Moving Picture World,* February 4, 1928.

"Music and Musicians: Music Notes and Comment." *The Boston Globe,* February 22, 1925.

"Music: Composer Chaplin." *Time,* September 9, 1940.

"Music of the Movies." *The New York Times,* November 4, 1923.

"Musical Progress in Cinema: Overlooking 'The Masses'—Cheap 'Broadmindedness.'" *Musical News and Herald,* October 3, 1925.

Myers, Harold. "'I Have Done a Positive Service in Making a *King in N.Y.,*': Chaplin." *Variety,* September 18, 1957.

Nathan, George Jean. *Passing Judgments.* Reprint, Rutherford, NJ: Farleigh Dickinson University Press, 1970.

"National Board Show to Include Chaplin Comedy." *Moving Picture World,* January 22, 1921.

"Need for Intelligent Film Players." *Music Trade Review,* September 25, 1915.

"New Records to Watch: Popular.'" *The Billboard,* July 4, 1953.

"New Score Arranged for Film." *Los Angeles Times,* June 24, 1925.

"New Type Music Cue Sheet Is Published." *Exhibitors Herald,* July 8, 1922.

"New York's 'First Nighters' Pay Homage to Charlie Chaplin and the *Gold Rush.*" *Moving Picture World,* August 29, 1925.

"News of Dailies." *Variety,* April 5, 1923.

Notowicz, Nathan, Jürgen Elsner, ed. *Wir Reden Hier Nicht Von Napoleon. Wir Reden Von Ihnen!* Berlin: Verlag Neue Musik Berlin, 1971.

"Novel Prologue Arranged for Chaplin Picture." *Los Angeles Times,* September 17, 1925.

Nugent, Frank S. "Heralding the Return, After an Undue Absence, of Charlie Chaplin in *Modern Times.*" *The New York Times,* February 6, 1936.

Oates, Bill. *Meredith Willson: America's Music Man.* Bloomington, IN: AuthorHouse, 2010.

"Of Local Origin." *The New York Times,* April 8, 1942.

"Offer Music Score for Every Feature." *Exhibitors Herald,* November 20, 1920.

The Official Academy Awards® Database. http://awardsdatabase.oscars.org/.

"Ohio Censor Chief Puts Ban on *Woman of Paris.*" *Motion Picture News,* November 17, 1923.

"Ohio Indies Ask National Exhibs to Nix Chaplin." *Variety,* May 14, 1947.

Osborne, John. "Chaplin Aims a Kick at America." *Evening Standard,* September 12, 1957.

"Oscar Nominees Re-Tabulated." *Variety,* March 14, 1973.

"Oscars: Songs Nominated." *The Washington Post,* March 7, 1973.

Padua, Pat. "Pic of the Week: Passing the Baton Edition." *In the Muse* (blog), Library of Congress, May 20, 2011, http://blogs.loc.gov/music/2011/05/pic-of-the-week-passing-the-baton-edition/.

Palmer, Raymond E. "Chaplin Waited, Got Guillotine," *The Austin Statesman,* January 6, 1967.

Parsons, Louella O. "Louella O. Parsons." *The Washington Post,* September 1, 1940.

"*Pay Day.*" *Exhibitors Herald,* April 1, 1922.

Peak, Mayme. "The Man Who Knows Charlie Chaplin Best." *Daily Boston Globe,* February 22, 1931.

"Picture News and Notes." *Pictures and the Picturegoer,* November 13, 1915.

"*Pilgrim* Makes Critics Laugh: New York Reviewers Admit Falling Under Chaplin Spell in His Latest." *Motion Picture News,* March 10, 1923.

"Plunkett Spikes Rumor He Is Quitting Strand." *The Billboard,* January 7, 1928.

Porter, Cecilia H, ed. *Charles Chaplin Senior: Victorian Music Hall Songs.* London: Porter House of Publishing, 2013.

Powell, S. Morgan. "Montreal." *Variety,* January 1920.

"Premiere Plan Continued at the *Gold Rush.*" *Los Angeles Times,* July 7, 1925.

Price, Tim Rose. "Secrets in Your Eyes." Unpublished, private collection.

"Product Digest: *Monsieur Verdoux.*" *Motion Picture Herald,* April 19, 1947.

"Projection Jottings." *The New York Times,* October 21, 1928.

Pryor, Thomas. "How Mr. Chaplin Makes a Movie." *The New York Times,* February 17, 1952.

_____. "Noting the Week's Screen Events." *The New York Times,* October 20, 1940.

Pym, John. "*A Woman of Paris.*" *Monthly Film Bulletin,* January 1, 1978.

"Q R S Co." *The Music Trade Review,* August 26, 1916.

Quigly, Isabel. "*The Chaplin Revue.*" *The Spectator,* June 3, 1960.

_____. "Contemporary Arts: Bitterness Creeps In." *The Spectator,* September 20, 1957.

"Radio Followups." *Variety,* October 15, 1952.

Raksin, David. "Interview." *Modern Times,* Blu-ray, Criterion Collection, 2010.

_____. "Life with Charlie." *The Quarterly Journal of the Library of Congress,* Summer 1983.

Raksin, David, Alex Raksin, ed. *The Bad and the Beautiful: My Life in a Golden Age of Film Music.* Kindle edition, 2012.

Ramsaye, Terry. "Chaplin Ridicules Reds' Claim Film Aids 'Cause.'" *Motion Picture Herald,* December 7, 1935.

Rapée, Ernö. *Encyclopedia of Music for Moving Pictures.* Reprint, New York: Arno Press, Inc, 1970.

Rascoe, Burton. "A Bookman's Day Book." *New York Tribune,* October 14, 1923.

"Re-Takes." *Exhibitors Herald,* March 4, 1922.

"Record Reviews: A *Countess from Hong Kong.*" *Variety,* March 15, 1967.

Reid, Laurence. "*A Woman of Paris.*" *Motion Picture News,* October 13, 1923.

Renzetti, Elizabeth. "Side by Side with Charlie Chaplin." *The Globe and Mail* (Toronto), January 19, 1995.

"Review Spotlight On ... Records." *The Billboard,* August 21, 1954.

"Reviews of New Pop Records." *The Billboard,* July 24, 1954.

"Reviews of New Pop Records." *The Billboard,* August 21, 1954.

"Reviews of New Pop Records." *The Billboard,* October 2, 1954.

"Reviews of the New Films: The *Gold Rush.*" *The Film Daily,* March 5, 1942.

"Reviews of This Week's New Records." *The Billboard,* June 13, 1953.

"Reviews of This Week's New Records." *The Billboard,* July 18, 1953.

"Reviews of This Week's New Records." *The Billboard,* August 1, 1953.

"Reviews of This Week's New Records: Popular." *The Billboard,* May 23, 1953.

"Reviews of This Week's New Records: Popular." *The Billboard,* May 30, 1953.

"Reviews of This Week's New Records: Popular." *The Billboard,* June 6, 1953.

"Reviews of This Week's Singles: Spotlight Winners of the Week." *The Billboard,* January 4, 1960.

Robinson, David. *Chaplin, His Life and Art.* Reprint, London: Penguin Books, 2001.

_____. *Chaplin: The Mirror of Opinion.* London: Martin Secker & Warburg Limited, 1984.

_____. "Charlie & Music." In *The Songs of Charlie Chaplin.* New York: Bourne, 1992.

"Roderick White, Right-Handed; Chaplin Still the Sole Left-Handed, Violinist." *Musical America,* March 5, 1921.

Rothstein, Edward. "The Little Tramp to a Different Tune." *The New York Times,* February 28, 1994.

"Rowdies Score Big Hit Against Charlie Chaplin." *Chicago Daily Tribune,* December 23, 1952.

"Saul Bourne Dies." *New Musical Express,* October 18, 1957.

Sayre, Nora. "Film: A *King in New York* at Last." *The New York Times,* December 22, 1973.

Schallert, Edwin. "Chaplin Opens New Epoch." *Los Angeles Times,* September 27, 1923.

_____. "Chaplin Opens New Epoch." *Los Angeles Times,* September 27, 1923.

Scheide, Frank. "*The Great Dictator* and Chaplin's Tramp as an Awakened 'Rip Van Winkle.'" In *Chaplin: The Dictator and the Tramp,* edited by Hooman Mehran and Frank Scheide, 16–32. London: British Film Institute, 2004.

Scheide, Frank, and Hooman Mehran, eds. *Chaplin's Limelight and the Music Hall Tradition.* Jefferson, NC: McFarland, 2006.

Schemer, Philip K. "*A Countess from Hong Kong* Premieres at the Pantages." *Los Angeles Times,* March 20, 1967.

_____. "Drama and the Arts: New Chaplin Will Greet Public in Latest Picture." *Los Angeles Times,* January 26, 1947.

Schickel, Richard, ed. *The Essential Chaplin: Perspectives on the Life and Art of the Great Comedian.* Chicago: Ivan R. Dee, 2006.

Schoenfeld, Herb. "Jocks, Jukes and Disks." *Variety,* June 3, 1953.

"The Screen." *The New York Times,* December 8, 1919.

"The Screen." *The New York Times,* September 26, 1921.

"The Screen: A *Woman of Paris.*" *The New York Times,* October 2, 1923.

"Screen Music." *The New York Times,* October 14, 1923.

"Screen News." *Screenland,* March 1931.

"Screen News Here and in Hollywood: Chaplin Plans to Make Score and Commentary for His 1927 Picture, the *Circus.*" *The New York Times,* March 17, 1942.

"Screen Pictures of 1922." *The New York Times,* July 2, 1922.

"The Screen: The *Kid.*" *The New York Times,* February 7, 1921.

"See Chaplin in the Flesh." *The New York Times,* February 21, 1916.

Seldes, Gilbert. "I Am Here To-Day." In *The Essential Chaplin: Perspectives on the Life and Art of the Great Comedian,* edited by Richard Schickel, 103–119. Chicago: Ivan R. Dee, 2006.

Senator Rankin, speaking on the Deportation of Charlie Chaplin, June 12, 1947, 80th Cong., 1st sess., *Congressional Record* 93, pt. 5.

"The Shadow Stage." *Photoplay,* June 1922.

Shaffer, Rosalind. "All the Old Guard of Movieland Sees Chaplin Premiere." *Chicago Daily Tribune,* July 5, 1925.

Sherman, Gene. "Chaplin Breaks Silence to Announce Return to Films." *Los Angeles Times,* November 3, 1965.

Sherwood, Robert E., ed. *The Best Moving Pictures of 1922–23.* Boston: Small, Maynard & Company, 1923.

Shivas, Mark. "Remembrance of Tramps Past." *The New York Times,* December 12, 1971.

Shuit, Doug. "Bitterness Survives 20 Years: They Haven't Given Up—Letter Writers Assail Chaplin." *Los Angeles Times,* April 9, 1972.

Silent Music: The Story of Eric James, directed by Christopher Lane (Ontario, 2002).

Sime. "Moving Pictures: A *Dog's Life.*" *Variety,* April 19, 1918.

Siskel, Gene. "Carnegie Contract Commitment Gets Us the First Look." *Chicago Tribune,* June 4, 1972.

"6,500 Persons See Charlie Chaplin Lead Sousa Band." *St. Louis Post-Dispatch,* February 21, 1916.

"Sixth Week for Chaplin Picture." *Los Angeles Times,* October 30, 1923.

Skipper, John C. *Meredith Willson: The Unsinkable Music Man.* El Dorado Hills, CA: Savas Publishing Company, 1999.

Skolsky, Sidney. "Chaplin's *Modern Times.*" *The Washington Post,* November 27, 1935.

Slonimsky, Nicolas. *Music Since 1900,* 5th Edition. New York: Schirmer Books, 1994.

Smith, Patsy. "Among the Women." *Variety,* June 1919.

Solomon, Matthew. *The Gold Rush.* London: Palgrave, 2005.

"'Song' Wave Is Hitting France." *Billboard,* March 11, 1967.

The Songs of Charlie Chaplin. New York: Bourne Co., 1992.

"Sound Aids the Screen." *The New York Times,* September 7, 1930.

"Soundtrack Spotlight: The [*sic*] *Countess from Hong Kong.*" *Billboard,* March 25, 1967.

Sousa, John Philip. *Marching Along: Recollections of Men, Women and Music.* Reprint, Boston: Hales, Cushman & Flint, 1941.

"Stage and Film Music: The *Chaplin Revue.*" *Melody Maker,* September 10, 1960.

Stein, Lisa K. *Syd Chaplin.* Jefferson, NC: McFarland, 2011.

"Strand and Capitol Almost Neck and Neck Last Week." *Variety,* October 4, 1923.

Sullivan, Ed. "Little Old New York." *The Hartford Courant,* April 6, 1952.

"Superb." *Daily Express* (London), May 27, 1960.

S.W. "At the Cinema." *The Jerusalem Post,* December 23, 1957.

Swainson, L. R. "Chaplin's Film Vow." *The Age,* May 7, 1957.

_____. "Little King with Bowler and Cane." *The Age,* March 13, 1956.

Swayze, John Cameron. "New York: Tamales and Buttermilk." *Daily Boston Globe,* January 2, 1953.

Sweet, Matthew. "Was Charlie Chaplin a Gypsy?" *The Guardian,* February 7, 2011: https://www.theguardian.com/film/2011/feb/17/charlie-chaplin-gypsy-heritage.

"Synchronized Music Service to Be Available by April 1." *Exhibitors Herald,* February 26, 1921.

Synchronized Scenario Music Company. *Exhibitors Herald,* December 25, 1920.

Synchronized Scenario Music Company. *Motion Picture News,* November 1920.

"Tag *Godfather* as Rota Retread in Oscar Hassle." *Variety,* March 7, 1973.

Taylor, Weston. "Chaplin Hits a New Note." *News of the World* (London), June 12, 1960.

Theodore M. Finney Music Library, University of Pittsburgh.

Thomas, Kevin. "*Limelight* in L.A.—At Last." *Los Angeles Times,* December 13, 1972.

Thomson, Virgil. *Virgil Thomson: A Reader: Selected Writings, 1924–1984.* Edited by Richard Kostelanetz. New York, Routledge, 2002.

Thornton, James. "She May Have Seen Better Days." New York: T. B. Harms & Co., 1894.

"Through German Eyes." *The New York Times,* August 18, 1929.

Tinée, Mae. "Chaplin's New Film Superior Despite Flaws." *Chicago Daily Tribune,* January 14, 1953.

_____. "A Great Picture with a Great Man on a Great Day: *Shoulder Arms* with Charlie Chaplin." *Chicago Daily Tribune,* November 12, 1918.

"To Pay on Chaplin Movie Song." *The New York Times,* June 13, 1934.

"To the Point." *Harrison's Reports,* August 2, 1947.

"Trenet's Suite Charges Chaplin a Tune Thief." *Variety,* July 3, 1968.

"Tuneful Trifles as the Composer Intended." *North Western Evening News* (UK), September 17, 1960.

"20,000 Throng Wall St. to Hear Movie Stars Tell How to Win War." *New York Tribune,* April 9, 1918.

"2,000 Curious in Near-Riot at Chaplin Picture." *New York Herald Tribune,* February 6, 1936.

"UA to Withdraw *Verdoux* for Sock Ad Drive." *Variety,* May 14, 1947.

Underbid, Harriette. "On the Screen: Charles Chaplin at Strand in the *Pilgrim.*" *New York Tribune,* February 26, 1923.

Undersell, Harriette. "On the Screen." *New York Tribune,* November 7, 1923.

"United Artists Production at Standstill." *Independent Exhibitors Film Bulletin,* September 15, 1947.

The University of Maine, Vocal Popular Sheet Music Collection.

University of Southern California Library. Hanns Eisler Papers, Feuchtwanger Memorial Library, Special Collections.

University of Washington Libraries, Special Collections.

Untitled, *Jewish Chronicle* (London), May 27, 1960.

"U.S. Attorney-General Criticises Chaplin." *The Irish Times,* October 3, 1952.

Ussher, Bruno David. "Music in the Films." *Los Angeles Daily News,* August 26, 1940.

_____. "Music in the Films." *Los Angeles Illustrated Daily News,* October 21, 1940.

Vance, Jeffrey *Chaplin: Genius of the Cinema.* New York: Harry N. Abrams, 2003.

Van Gelder, Robert. "Chaplin Draws a Keen Weapon." *The New York Times,* September 8, 1940.

Verrill, Addison. "N.Y. View on Oscar: Scant Wit, Gaffs, Amateur Timing, Cue Cards, Agit-Prop." *Variety,* April 4, 1973.

"Victor Herbert's First Serious Opera." *The New York Times,* October 10, 1910.

"Vienna Won't Let Chaplin Wave Red Flag in Picture." *The New York Times,* April 3, 1936.

"Virginia Cherrill." *Variety,* April 1, 1931.

Vitello, Paul. "Mo Rothman Dies at 92; Revived Interest in Charlie Chaplin." *The New York Times,* September 26, 2011.

"Voice Wins in Films." *The New York Times,* February 8, 1931.

Wagner, Rob. "Charlie Chaplin." *Screenland,* December 1929, 27.

Walker, Don. *Men of Notes.* Pittsburgh: Dorrance Publishing, Inc., 2013.

Warga, Wayne. "*Cabaret* Second with 10: *Godfather* Receives 11 Oscar Nominations." *Los Angeles Times,* February 13, 1973.

Waters, Bob. "Performing Arts: National Symphony Orchestra." *The Washington Post,* August 9, 1993.

Watkinson, Brenda. "Jerome Epstein." In *Chaplin's Limelight And the Music Hall Tradition,* edited by Frank Scheide and Hooman Mehran, 92–97. Jefferson, NC: McFarland & Co., Inc., 2006.

Watts, Stephen. "On Britain's Varied Movie Fronts: Up to Date 'King.'" *The New York Times,* March 3, 1957.

Wax, Mo. "Booby Prize for U.A." *Film Bulletin,* September 29, 1947.

_____. "Why Boycott Chaplin?" *Film Bulletin,* May 12, 1947.

Weiler, A. H. "By Way of Report: Charlie Chaplin Tests New Leading Lady Here—Score by Dietz and Schwartz." *The New York Times,* April 29, 1951.

"Western Comment." *The Music Trade Review,* September 9, 1916.

"What Chaplin Thinks." *The New York Times,* October 7, 1923.

William K. Everson Archive, New York University.

Willson, Dixie. "Chaplin Talks." *Photoplay,* December 1940.

Willson, Meredith. *And There I Stood with My Piccolo.* Reprint, Minneapolis: University of Minnesota Press, 2009.

_____. "Music Maker to Charlie Chaplin." *New York Herald Tribune,* October 27, 1940.

Wilson, Cecil. "A Comic Genius Turns to Politics... Charlie the Pompous Defeats the Clown." *Daily Mail* (London), September 11, 1957.

Winter, Ella. "But It's Sad, Says Chaplin, It's Me." In *Charlie Chaplin Interviews,* edited by Kevin J. Hayes, 119–121. Jackson, MS: University Press of Mississippi, 2005.

"Witmark Songs in Evidence." *The Music Trade Review,* April 29, 1922.

W.L.W. "Flashes of Old Chaplin Genius: A *King in New York*." *The Manchester Guardian,* September 17, 1957.

"*Woman of Paris,* by Chaplin, Is Unbeatable," *Evening Telegram,* n.d.

"*Woman of Paris* Closes Next Week." *Los Angeles Times,* November 5, 1923.

"*A Woman of Paris* Feature at Strand." *The Brooklyn Daily Eagle,* November 18, 1923.

"*Woman of Paris* Off." *Variety,* November 8, 1923.

"Wonderful, Said Chaplin." *Picturegoer,* October 20, 1956.

Wranovics, John. *Chaplin and Agee: The Untold Story of the Tramp, the Writer, and the Lost Screenplay.* New York: Palgrave Macmillan, 2005.

Wyndham, Francis. "Chaplin on the Critics, the Beatles, the Mood of London." *South China Sunday Post-Herald,* April 16, 1967.

Year Book of Motion Pictures. The Film Daily, 1930.

York, Cal. "Girl Wanted—No Experience Required." *Photoplay,* January 1929.

Index

Numbers in **_bold italics_** indicate pages with illustrations

429